North Sea and Channel Connectivity during the Late Iron Age and Roman Period (175/150 BC – AD 409)

Francis M. Morris

BAR International Series 2157
2010

Published in 2016 by
BAR Publishing, Oxford

BAR International Series 2157

North Sea and Channel Connectivity during the Late Iron Age and Roman Period (175/150 BC-AD 409)

ISBN 978 1 4073 0699 5

BAR Publishing is the trading name of British Archaeological Reports (Oxford) Ltd. British Archaeological Reports was first incorporated in 1974 to publish the BAR Series, International and British. In 1992 Hadrian Books Ltd became part of the BAR group. This volume was originally published by Archaeopress in conjunction with British Archaeological Reports (Oxford) Ltd / Hadrian Books Ltd, the Series principal publisher, in 2010. This present volume is published by BAR Publishing, 2016.

Printed in England

BAR
PUBLISHING

BAR titles are available from:

BAR Publishing
122 Banbury Rd, Oxford, OX2 7BP, UK
EMAIL info@barpublishing.com
PHONE +44 (0)1865 310431
FAX +44 (0)1865 316916
www.barpublishing.com

Abstract

This book utilises archaeological evidence to establish that during the Late Iron Age and Roman periods there were three maritime exchange systems operating in the waters of the North Sea and Channel: the Atlantic system, encompassing the Western Channel and Europe's Atlantic seaboard; the Southern North Sea and Eastern Channel system, focusing on the Strait of Dover; and the Eastern North Sea system, which stretched from the mouth of the Rhine to the North Sea coast of Denmark. These three systems were all to some extent coherent, although the Atlantic and Southern North Sea and Eastern Channel systems displayed considerable overlap. Maritime connectivity in each of these systems was highly variable over time in terms of the mechanisms of exchange employed and particularly in terms of the scale and strength of exchange. This variability was principally a result of wider political and economic changes, which often had simultaneous effects upon all three systems, though the precise nature of these effects was often different in each of the systems.

The 'vulnerability' of connectivity in the North Sea and Channel contrasts with the picture of Mediterranean connectivity outlined by Horden and Purcell (2000); the Mediterranean saw much greater continuity with high levels of connectivity maintained over the *longue durée*. Two recent major surveys of maritime exchange have emphasised the importance of taking a long-term view and have, to some extent, downplayed short and medium-term changes (Cunliffe 2001; Horden and Purcell 2000). My findings suggest that short- and medium-term changes could be very significant; nevertheless, it appears probable that there was a structure, based ultimately on geography, which ensured that the three connective systems outlined in this survey endured across the *longue durée*. Hence, I argue that relating different scales of change to each another is crucial and should be a principal goal of future work in this field.

Contents

3. North Sea and Channel Connectivity 50 BC-AD 43

4. North Sea and Channel Connectivity AD 43-165

5. North Sea and Channel Connectivity AD 165-260

6. North Sea and Channel Connectivity AD 260-409

List of figures

List of tables

Preface and acknowledgements

This book is based on a D.Phil. thesis undertaken at Merton College, University of Oxford, between 2005 and 2009 (Morris 2009). Many people have helped and advised me during the course of the production of this work and I would like to thank as many as possible here. I would like to emphasise at the outset, however, that any faults in the details or interpretations presented in this book are my own.

Particular thanks are due to my long-suffering supervisors, Professor Andrew Wilson and Professor Helena Hamerow. Andrew Wilson's extensive knowledge of the Roman Empire's economy was a great influence. I am very grateful to the AHRC for funding my research and also to my examiners, Professor John Wilkes and Professor Michael Fulford, with whom I have had extremely fruitful discussions about my work. At Oxford assistance was also provided by Professor Barry Cunliffe, who supervised the early stages of my thesis and suggested the initial topic of investigation, John Sills (of the Celtic Coin Index), Martin Henig, Chris Gosden, Damian Robinson, Irene Lemos and Nigel James (of the Bodleian Map Room). David Davison and the staff at BAR have been most generous in agreeing to publish my work and for making the publication process as straightforward as possible.

Many thanks are also due to Paul Booth and Ed Biddulph of Oxford Archaeology for their assistance with my pottery analysis, as well as to the staff at numerous museums who were excellent hosts during my visits: Liz Royles, Gill Dunn and Alison Heke (Chester), Ian Rowlandson (Scunthorpe), Francis Grew and Dan Nesbitt (London), Paul Sealey (Colchester), Richard Halliwell (Oxfordshire Museums Service), Anne Taylor (Cambridge), the staff at Winchester Museum, Katherine Bearcock (York), Martin Veen (Noord Holland Depot), Arthur Oosterbaan (Ecomare, Texel), Evert Kramer (Fries Museum), Ernst Taayke (who also answered my many questions about archaeology in the northern Netherlands) and Tineke Volkers (NAD Nuis), Vincent Vilsteren (Drents Museum), Frank Both (Oldenburg), Hauke Jöns and the staff of the NIHK, Wilhelmshaven, Bodo Zehm (Osnabrück), Ulrike Weller and the staff at Landesmuseum Hannover, Dieter Bischop (Bremen), Wendowski-Schünemann (Cuxhaven), Matthias Schön and the staff at Burg Bederkesa, Michael Merkel (Museum Harburg, Hamburg) and the staff at Schloss Gottorf, Schleswig.

I offer my deep regards to the following individuals and institutions who have granted me permission to reproduce their copyrighted figures: Paul Tyers (Figs. 4.1, 4.8, 4.10, 4.12, 4.14, 4.16, 5.1, 6.2-4), Barry Cunliffe (Figs. 2.4, 2.7-9, 3.11-12), Michael Fulford (Fig. 4.40), David Mattingly (Fig. 3.1), Nico Roymans (Fig. 3.5), César Carreras Monfort (Fig. 4.28), Philip Kenrick and Habelt publishers (Fig. 3.3), National Museum of Denmark (Fig. 3.15), Tony Wilmott (Fig. 4.39), Academia Press (Fig. 4.41), Ulla Lund Hansen (Fig. 5.12) and the Institute of Archaeology, Oxford (cover image).

The following people have also provided crucial advice and help over the years, for which I am deeply grateful: Lindsay Allason Jones, Mike Athanson, Paul Belien, Paul Bidwell, Tony Brown, Stewart Bryant, Sarnia Butcher, César Carreras Monfort, Peter Carrington, Cheryl Clay, Hilary Cool, Nina Crummy (who provided me with access to the unpublished Hull Corpus of brooches), Simon Davies, Wim De Clercq, Mark Driessen, Michael Erdrich, Cate Frieman, Marjan Galestin, Dan Garner, Duncan Garrow, Chris Going, Thomas Grane, Karen Heslin, Catherine Hills, Fraser Hunter, Tatiana Ivleva, Vicky Jefferson, Matt Jenkinson, Georges Kazan, Malcolm Lyne, Hilary Major, Fritz Mangartz, Ingo Martell, Vincent Megaw, Jennifer Price, Professor Nico

Roymans, Ruth Shaffrey, Marie Louise Sørensen, Mansel Spratling, Ellen Swift, Louis Swinkels, Ester Van der Linden, Carol van Driel Murray, Sofie Vanhoutte, Tony Wilmott, Flip Woltering, the Heritage staff at Boulogne, and also my colleagues and the staff at the Institute of Archaeology in Oxford and at the Department of Archaeology in Cambridge, where I studied previously.

Finally, special thanks must go to my family and friends who offered great support throughout my studies, particularly my parents Mike and Myra to whom this book is dedicated.

Francis M. Morris
Oxford
June 2010

Email: francismorris@hotmail.com

1. Introduction

1.1. Background to the study

This book is a study of maritime connectivity in the North Sea and Channel regions over the course of the Late Iron Age and Roman periods (175/150 BC-AD 409). In simple terms I use "connectivity" to mean the transfer of materials and/or people from one place to another, such that a connection is established between those places and the people who occupy them. In essence this refers to exchange and the associated connections between places created through exchanges.

In recent years, the role of seas in exchange and in linking the communities surrounding them has been highlighted in two major studies. Horden and Purcell conducted a major survey of the pre-Industrial Mediterranean and introduced the term connectivity to archaeology.[1] Barry Cunliffe, meanwhile, has produced a synthesis of exchange along Europe's Atlantic façade from early prehistory to c. AD 1500.[2] My work examines a somewhat shorter time period than these authors, who focused explicitly on the *longue durée*. That said, six centuries is still a relatively lengthy period. By shortening the period of study somewhat, I am able to engage with the Late Iron Age and Roman Periods in more detail and achieve a better understanding of short- and medium-term change.

The emphasis of this book is first and foremost upon change. Indeed, my primary research questions are as follows:

1) How does North Sea and Channel connectivity change over time in terms of scale, direction and mechanism?

2) What factors lie behind these changes?

For reasons of clarity and ease I focus principally upon long-distance exchange, that is overseas exchange between Britain and the continent, and maritime exchange between the continental coastal regions which are separated by the river Rhine. I argue that during the Late Iron Age and Roman periods there were three distinguishable maritime systems in the waters of the North Sea and Channel, each of which was to some extent coherent, though the first two overlapped to a considerable degree (**Fig. 1.1**). These systems were: the Southern North Sea and Eastern Channel system, which focused on the narrow crossing of the Strait of Dover; the Atlantic system, encompassing the Atlantic façade of Britain and Western Europe and including the western half of the Channel; and finally, the Eastern North Sea system, which linked the communities living between the mouth of the Rhine and Southern Scandinavia. I propose that there were significant changes over time in the scale, direction and mechanisms of connectivity within each of these three systems. These changes were primarily the result of wider economic, political and demographic changes, which often had simultaneous impact upon all three systems. North Sea and Channel connectivity between 175/150 BC-AD 409 can be broken down into five main chronological periods, each of which will be discussed in their own chapter. My chronological division is based firmly upon changing patterns of long-distance exchange apparent in the archaeological record. Of necessity this privileges archaeologically visible material, principally coins, metalwork, pottery and amphorae, though attempts are made, where possible, to use proxy evidence to provide insights into exchanges of archaeologically invisible articles. Interpretation is placed onto this archaeological framework and does not form the basis for its construction.

Account is taken of the fact that different categories of archaeological material present different opportunities and challenges for an examination of exchange. Pottery and amphorae are eminently suitable in that they are typically common, fairly durable in the archaeological record, display typological changes over time that allow them to be dated with some degree of precision and, most importantly, the fabrics from which they were constructed can usually be petrologically provenanced to specific geographical sources. Scientific studies also allow stones to be assigned to particular geological sources with confidence.

Roman coins were usually marked with the mint at which they were produced, whilst their mint dates can also typically be closely determined, often to the exact year.

[1] Horden and Purcell 2000.
[2] Cunliffe 2001.

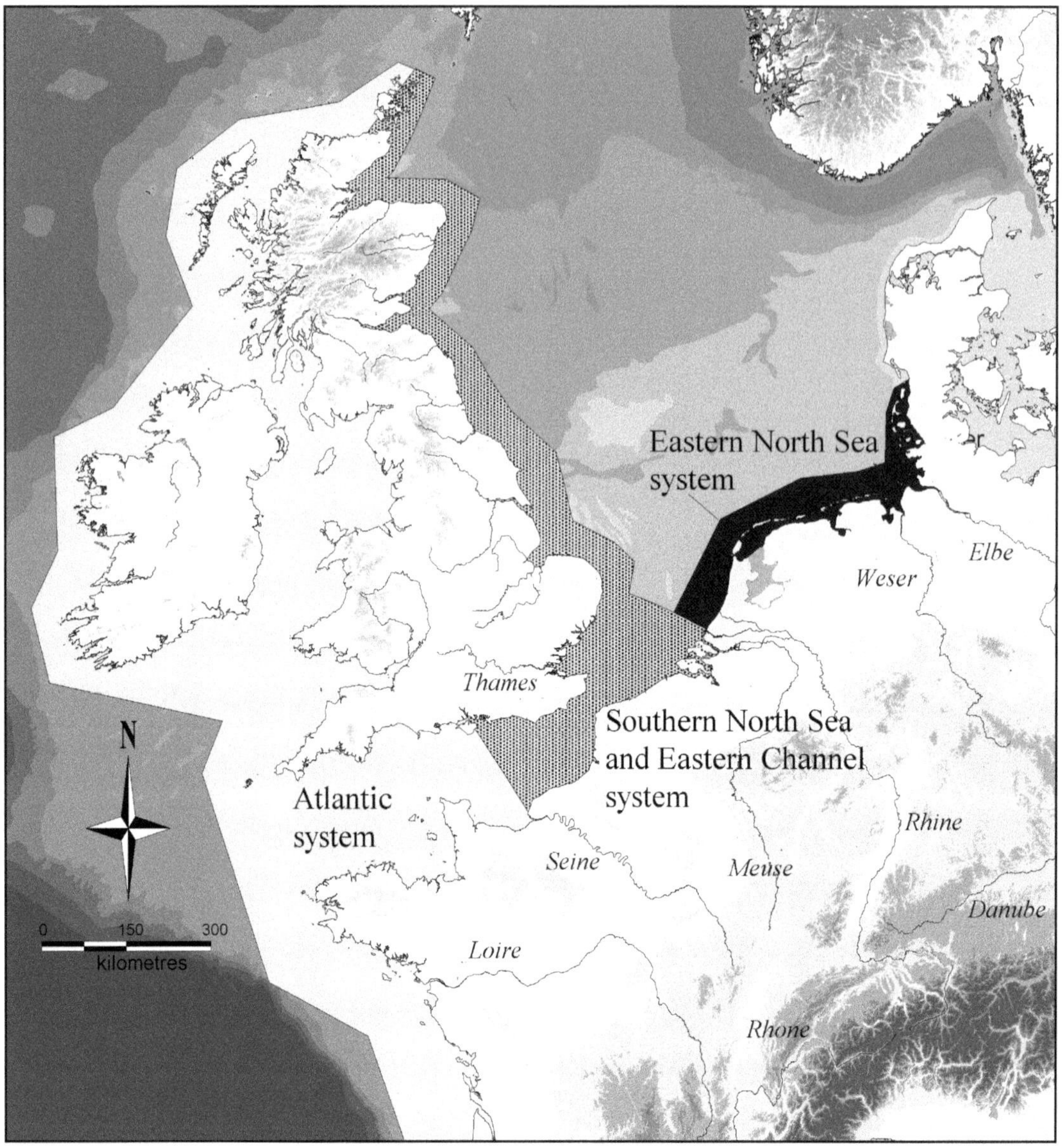

Fig. 1.1. Maritime systems in the North Sea and Channel.

Coins, however, are by no means a straightforward guide to the chronology and direction of exchange. Coin circulation is a complex issue and fuller treatment will be given to it in the main text. Other types of metalwork and also glass present further problems as a result of the regularity with which they were recycled in the past. Recycling meant materials from different sources could be mixed together, which makes assignation to specific sources difficult. Studies of typology and stamps on metal and glass objects can be used to inform us about exchange patterns, though in doing this we must be cautious and bear in mind that in certain contexts we may be dealing with the movement of craftsmen working in 'foreign' styles, rather than the movement of the objects themselves.

Proxy evidence can provide insights into the exchange of materials that would otherwise be difficult to prove through direct archaeological means, including metals, glass, agricultural products, as well as wine and salted fish products in barrels, though we must be cautious with its use. Where we can demonstrate, through archaeological and/or historical means, that high levels of production of a particular product took place in a particular area, and we can similarly demonstrate that high levels of consumption of this product took place in a different area that produced it on a much lower level, then the possibility that quantities of this product were transferred from the former region to the latter must be seriously considered.

Finally, it is important to note that this is principally an economic study. I am not dealing with the cultural aspects that one might expect to be associated with interaction and connectivity. Such cultural aspects would require a major survey in their own right. In any case, the cultural features associated with each of the connective systems outlined above would perhaps be most effectively explored in the context of a *longue durée* study.[3]

[3] C.f. Cunliffe 2001; Horden and Purcell 2000.

1.2. Previous work on North Sea and Channel exchange during the Late Iron Age and Roman period

Relations between Britain and the continent in the Late Iron Age

During the early to mid-twentieth century most scholars of later prehistory recognised that trade and exchange played some role in Britain's relations with the continent. In particular, during the century or so before Claudius's invasion of Britain in AD 43 the expansion of Roman control to Gaul was held to have led to a great increase in trade between Britain and Gaul. It was generally understood, however, that throughout later prehistory the most significant aspects of Britain's foreign relations were invasions and migrations of peoples from the continent.[4] Successive waves of incomers were seen as principally responsible for cultural and technological change in Britain, for structuring the island's external relations, and in some cases for bringing imported material with them. For example, the appearance of Gallo-Belgic coins in southern Britain during the later Iron Age was explained by Allen and Hawkes as representing the personal possessions of Gallo-Belgic immigrants.[5] This approach is well typified by Hawkes' influential division of the Iron Age material culture of southern Britain into three cultural groupings, A, B and C, which he argued corresponded with three chronologically distinct waves of migrants from the continent.[6]

As processualism, or the 'New Archaeology', developed during the 1960s British scholars of later prehistory began to move decisively away from an interpretative framework based on 'invasionist' perspectives and instead shifted their attention to concentrate on social processes.[7] In this vein, long-distance exchange began to receive increased attention from some quarters as it was recognised that this was an important process through which social and cultural change could be generated in the absence of large-scale population movements. By the 1980s scholars, such as Colin Haselgrove and Barry Cunliffe, had placed overseas exchange right at the top of the agenda of British Late Iron Age studies. These scholars sought to explain social change in Late Iron Age Britain principally through reference to trade, be it direct or indirect, with the Roman world. Drawing on Wallerstein's World systems theory, the expanding Roman state was visualised as a 'core', which drew on its 'peripheries', including Britain, for raw materials, such as metals and slaves.[8] In exchange for these basic commodities luxury goods, in particular wine, were traded with the periphery and were held to have had major socially transformative effects upon the periphery. These works that focused explicitly on 'core-periphery' relations have had staunch theoretical critics, though Barry Cunliffe has continued to apply a subtler version of this approach to south-central Britain during the Late Iron Age.[9]

In the aftermath of the rejection of the 'invasionist' theoretical framework, prehistorians have also placed increasing attention on social and political interchanges between Britain and the continent throughout prehistory.[10] Whilst rejecting large-scale migrations, these works have often emphasised the notion that small-scale movements of people did play a significant role in long-distance communications. For the Late Iron Age these ideas are best exemplified in the recent work of Barry Cunliffe, who has sought to explain Britain's overseas contacts during the Late Iron Age in terms of long-term, enduring exchange networks that are backed up by social and cultural links and low-level continuous population movement through mechanisms, such as intermarriage.[11] In an influential recent book, John Creighton has also argued that contacts between southeastern Britain and the continent between the invasions of Caesar and Claudius need to be understood in the context of direct political relations, extending to client kingship, between the Roman state and the rulers of the main tribes of southeast Britain.[12]

Relations between Britain and the continent in the Roman period

During the early to mid-twentieth century scholars working on Roman Britain gave some consideration to trade and exchange, but it would be fair to say that their main focus was to produce an event-driven narrative of Britain's political and military history as part of the Roman Empire.[13] The key works of this period provided a limited discussion of exchange, which was generally viewed in fairly modernist terms; certain goods, such as samian pottery and wine amphorae, were understood to have been traded over long-distances by traders who operated in an essentially free market economy.[14] The cash-laden military markets were seen as a particularly attractive draw to traders. Some consideration was also given to the role of the Roman state in organizing long-distance movements of materials through taxation, direct exploitation, as in the case of the extraction of mineral wealth from Britain, and in the provision of contracts to ensure the supply of Roman military garrisons.

From around the beginning of the 1970s onwards researchers working on Roman Britain began to focus increasingly upon economic issues. This was in part the result of a need to generate improved understanding of the ever increasing quantity of Roman finds that were being dug up at a time when the number of

[4] Fox 1932; Clark 1944; Piggott 1949, 56-67; Hawkes 1959; Frere 1978, 14-41; see discussion in Cunliffe 2005, 3-23.
[5] Allen 1960; Hawkes 1968.
[6] Hawkes 1931; 1959; Frere 1978.
[7] C.f. Renfrew 1973; Clark 1966.
[8] Haselgrove 1982; 1984a; Cunliffe 1988; Wallerstein 1974.
[9] Hill 2007; Woolf 1993a; Cunliffe 2005.
[10] C.f. Burgess and Shennan 1976; Megaw and Simpson 1979, 346; Clark 2004; 2009.
[11] Cunliffe 2001; 2005; 2009.
[12] Creighton 2000.
[13] Collingwood and Myres 1936, 226-246; Richmond 1963, 149-185; Liversidge 1973, 169-212; Frere 1978, 320-341.
[14] See also: Rostovtzeff 1926.

archaeological excavations was expanding dramatically. From this time, several studies appeared that examined Romano-British and continental pottery industries in great detail.[15] In addition, a number of works were produced that synthesised the detailed evidence and examined the nature of Britain's overseas exchanges.[16] Many of the economically focused works of the 1970s and 1980s were influenced by the views of Karl Polanyi and Moses Finley.[17] Polanyi argued that pre-modern economies needed to be viewed in culturally specific terms as 'embedded' and these ideas were applied to the Roman economy by Moses Finley, who argued that the Roman economy was essentially 'primitive' in nature, rather than modern. One impact of these approaches was for exchange between Roman Britain and the continental Empire to be increasingly interpreted in terms of the Roman state's demands; organised military supply, military contracts, taxation and exploitation were often afforded extremely significant roles.[18]

In recent decades there has been an ever increasing mass of data pertaining to exchange between Britain and the continent during the Roman period. The number of archaeological excavations undertaken in Britain has continued to increase dramatically, whilst high-quality site reports have been published for dozens of Roman sites. There have also been a growing number of excellent and detailed artefact specific studies, such as Paul Tyers' *Atlas of Roman Pottery*, Carreras Monfort and Funari's work on Dressel 20 amphorae and Ellen Swift's study of Late Roman bracelets, brooches and belt fittings.[19] Despite this, surprisingly few contemporary scholars have attempted to synthesise exchange between Roman Britain and the continental Empire. Much of the earlier work is of course still relevant, notably the series of papers by Michael Fulford.[20] Fulford has also produced a number of papers on this issue in the last few years, whilst David Mattingly's latest book on Roman Britain includes a brief consideration of the topic.[21] Nonetheless, I believe that my book fulfils a need to contribute to the debate on the contacts between Britain and the continent during the Roman period in the light of the increasingly large data sets and the detailed modern works that focus on specific artefact types. In addition, my work takes account of the last few years of work into the Roman economy in which, in contrast to Finley's 'primitivist' view, the Roman economy has been interpreted as a highly sophisticated and complex phenomenon that underwent considerable economic growth during the Late Republican period and the earlier phases of the Principate.[22]

Relations between the Roman world and the north European *Barbaricum*

During the early to mid-twentieth century a number of scholars, including Willers, Aubin, Bolin, Brogan, Ekholm, von Uslar and Wheeler, worked on the problem of exchange between the Roman Empire and the barbarian peoples living beyond the Empire's Rhine-Danube frontier.[23] In general these scholars interpreted the large number of 'Roman' products found beyond the Empire's European frontier in terms of a flourishing trade between Romans and barbarians. Other exchange mechanisms, such as political gift-giving, tribute, returning Germanic mercenaries and the taking of war booty, were typically recognised as making minor contributions as well. In works of this date the chronology of Roman-barbarian exchange contacts was poorly resolved, with trade seen as being fairly continuous over time, and perhaps even increasing as the frontier provinces developed economically. A North Sea route reaching to southern Jutland was seen as one of several important routes through which Roman goods entered the *Barbaricum*. The North Sea route was understood to have been either direct, involving Roman merchants sailing and trading up the North Sea coast as far as Jutland, or alternatively indirect, with border trade taking place between Roman merchants and the Frisian peoples of the northern Netherlands, with further onward maritime distribution in the hands of the Frisians.[24]

In 1951 Eggers published a landmark survey of imported Roman material from the whole of the European *Barbaricum* up to the pre-World War II Russian border, with a particular focus on the numerous copper-alloy and glass vessel finds. Eggers also set out a more precise chronological framework for dating the imported Roman material with reference to the associated Germanic context, though his main analyses and interpretations were in fact based on a very broad division of the material into an early and a late period.[25] Eggers stuck with the idea that the majority of the Roman artefacts entered the *Barbaricum* through trade and he confirmed von Uslar's earlier suggestion that there was a short-distance trade in 'everyday' Roman articles, such as pottery and brooches, which operated in the border regions of the *Barbaricum*, and a long-distance trade in 'luxury' Roman products, such as copper-alloy and glass vessels, which made their way deep into the *Barbaricum*

[15] C.f. Fulford 1975; Young 1977; Lyne and Jefferies 1979; Monaghan 1987; Peacock and Williams 1986. Various articles in: du Plat Taylor and Cleere (1978); Anderson and Anderson (1981) and Detsicas (1973).
[16] Fulford 1977; 1978; 1984; 1989a; 1991; Whittaker 1994; Middleton 1979; c.f. Hopkins 1980; Salway 1993, 443-486; Millett 1990.
[17] Polanyi 1944; 1957; Finley 1973.
[18] Whittaker 1994; Fulford 1984; 1989a; Middleton 1979; Peacock and Williams 1986.
[19] Tyers 1996a; 1996b; forthcoming; Carreras Monfort and Funari 1998; Swift 2000a.
[20] Fulford 1977; 1978; 1984; 1989a; 1991.
[21] Fulford 1996; 2004; 2007; Mattingly 2006, 491-528, 576-579.
[22] Scheidel *et al* 2007; Bowman and Wilson 2009; Scheidel 2009; Wilson 2002; 2009a; 2009b; 2009c; Harris 1993; Temin 2001; Mattingly and Salmon 2001.
[23] Willers 1901, 191-202; 1907; Aubin 1925; Bolin 1926; Brogan 1936; Ekholm 1937; von Uslar 1938; Wheeler 1954. A concise English summary of the work of these scholars is given by Hedeager (1978).
[24] C.f. Willers 1907; Aubin 1925; Brogan 1936; Ekholm 1937; Wheeler 1954.
[25] Eggers 1951; 1955.

as a result of their greater resilience to long-distance transport costs.[26]

Eggers' results provided the main platform for a number of scholars to examine cross-frontier contacts with 'processual' approaches during the 1970s, 1980s and 1990s.[27] For these scholars Roman-barbarian relations were typically seen in terms of mutual economic dependency with trade taking place on a considerable scale. The principal advances of the 1970s, 1980s and 1990s, however, came with a number of major surveys of Roman imports, such as those published by Wolagiewicz, Kunow, Lund Hansen and Berke.[28] In these surveys, Roman imports were dated with much greater precision. Whilst trade was still seen as the key exchange mechanism, the increased chronological specificity allowed the authors of these surveys to assess changes in the scale and nature of this trade in greater detail, and to be interpreted in the context of specific economic and political developments. North Sea contacts were still seen as important, with Lund Hansen notably arguing that an exceptionally strong concentration of imported Roman material, which was produced in the northwest provinces of the Empire, from east Danish graves of the early third century AD, reflected a direct trade route with the Empire's lower Rhine frontier that was maintained via the North Sea.[29]

In recent years there has been an increasing emphasis on explaining relations between the Roman Empire and the *Barbaricum* through mechanisms other than trade. Non-trade mechanisms have in fact long been recognised as being of importance. For example, Werner long ago explained the appearance of Roman products in late third-century AD graves in Thuringia in terms of political gifts and returning Germanic mercenaries who had served in the Roman army.[30] In the 1980s Rausing also suggested that the principal mechanism through which copper-alloy vessels entered the *Barbaricum* was as the personal possessions of returning Germanic auxiliaries; however, since the turn of the new millennium non-trade mechanisms have increasingly been invoked to explain the appearance of Roman material in the *Barbaricum*.[31] For example, Michael Erdrich conducted a comprehensive survey of the Roman material from northwest Germany and the northern Netherlands and argued that Roman products arrived in a series of intermittent 'waves', which coincided with political and military events along the lower Rhine frontier.[32] Rather than continuous trade, he believed that the Roman material arrived in his study region as either political gifts, or as the personal possessions of barbarian mercenaries who had served in the Roman army at times when the security of the lower Rhine frontier was threatened. Thomas Grane has also recently surveyed the Roman material from southern Scandinavia and has interpreted it in terms of direct diplomatic links, maintained via the North Sea, in the context of specific historical events.[33]

In the 1990s an ambitious program, the *Corpus der römischen Funde im europäischen Barbaricum* (CRFB), was initiated to identify, record and publish all the Roman objects that have been found in the European *Barbaricum*. The work for the CRFB has been divided amongst the various modern regions which lie within the area of the *Barbaricum*. Some of the regional volumes have already been published, but many others are still in progress.[34] When eventually complete, the CRFB will provide an immense resource for scholars to make new assessments of Roman-barbarian relations.

Review of previous work

The principal previous work on North Sea and Channel exchange during the Late Iron Age and Roman period has now been outlined and discussed. It is clear that work on this topic falls into three separate categories, each of which has had its own distinctive research history and theoretical trends.

This book presents the first synthetic study of North Sea and Channel exchange during the Late Iron Age and Roman period. The reasons why it has been necessary to produce a synthesis on this topic are to allow wider patterns in the changing nature of exchange to be identified for the first time, and for these patterns to be explained with reference to the broader context. Adopting a broader approach is particularly pertinent for the time period considered in this book because this was the period during which the Roman Empire's political and economic influence was at its most extensive. This book also takes account of the recent work on the Roman economy and seeks to examine its relevance to understanding maritime exchange in northwest Europe.[35]

Whilst reviewing the previous work we have seen a wide range of theoretical approaches being employed to investigate exchange. In this book I will employ a fairly new theoretical model, that of 'connectivity'. The precise details of this approach will be discussed in the following section. Suffice it to say here, I will be applying the broad tenants of this approach whilst also developing the model further by applying it to a new maritime environment. Despite employing a broad theoretical model I also seek to examine the evidence in contextually specific terms as far as it is possible. In particular, I seek to interpret the evidence according to an appropriate degree of chronological precision, as accurate as it is reliably secure to do so.

[26] Eggers 1951; von Uslar 1938. This idea was developed further by Hedeager (1978).
[27] C.f. Hedeager 1978; 1987; Bloemers 1983; 1989; Whittaker 1994; Wells 1996. See also: Fulford 1985.
[28] Wolagiewicz 1970; Kunow 1983; Lund Hansen 1987; Berke 1990.
[29] Lund Hansen 1987; 1995.
[30] Werner 1938; 1974.
[31] Rausing 1987; 1992.
[32] Erdrich 2001.
[33] Grane 2007. See also: Jørgensen *et al.* 2003.
[34] C.f. Voss 1998; Erdrich 2002; Erdrich and Carnap-Bornheim 2004.
[35] Scheidel *et al.* 2007; Bowman and Wilson 2009; Scheidel 2009; Wilson 2002; 2009a; 2009b; 2009c; Harris 1993; Temin 2001; Mattingly and Salmon 2001.

1.3. Previous works on connectivity

The term connectivity was introduced to archaeology from computing studies by Horden and Purcell.[36] In computing, connectivity is defined as one of several possible mathematical functions of the proportion of nodes to links and of the likely journey times. Horden and Purcell applied the term somewhat more loosely. They looked at the history of the Mediterranean with reference to the connectivity of geographical microregions, by which they meant the various ways in which microregions cohered, both internally and also with another, in aggregates that ranged from small clusters to something approaching the whole Mediterranean. They saw connectivity as being a series of networks along which goods, people and ideas moved. These networks could be long, but more commonly were short and involved small-scale movements of goods hopping along the coast, for which the metaphor of Brownian motion was invoked. The networks were envisioned as continuously shifting, but on a basic level they operated continuously throughout time, economically and culturally. Whilst Cunliffe did not use the term connectivity in his study of exchange and interaction along the Atlantic façade, his work had much in common with that of Horden and Purcell and utilised many of the same concepts.[37] Both these sets of authors were heavily influenced by the French historian Fernand Braudel's work on the Mediterranean Sea.[38]

Horden and Purcell outlined several key features of connectivity, most of which have to some extent been asserted by Cunliffe as well. First, the importance of geography: for Horden and Purcell it was the Mediterranean's division into distinctive geographical micro-regions, and differences in inter-annual rainfall between these micro-regions, that conditioned the requirement to engage in exchange with neighbouring communities so as to avoid risk.[39] When a region was affected by bad harvests it could obtain agricultural supplies from its neighbours. Horden and Purcell also asserted the role of the culturally experienced landscape, lines of sound and sight, perceptions and understanding of the landscape, in defining the routes and means of communication between different areas. For Cunliffe geography was also a key factor in the reason for strong networks of interaction emerging along the Atlantic coast. The peripheral location of these communities in relation to the rest of Europe and the rocky coastline and hinterlands facilitated an emphasis upon maritime exchange.

Horden and Purcell argued that the Mediterranean served to bind the communities around its shores culturally as well as economically. This they believed could tentatively be evidenced in apparently shared Mediterranean concepts of shame and honour. The Mediterranean facilitated the spread of Greek, Phoenician and Roman culture; during the first millennium AD, religious ideas, Christianity and, in the south, Islam, were propagated around its shores. Cunliffe also pointed out the role of the Atlantic in culturally binding the peoples who lived around it, both through direct interaction and shared experiences at the periphery of Europe.

The 'traditional' view of Mediterranean shipping is that the courses of ships were habitually determined and fixed into distinct shipping lanes.[40] Horden and Purcell argued that up until the Middle Ages the majority of voyages were in fact cabotage voyages, which involved regularly putting into small ports along the way, rather than necessarily requiring long uninterrupted sea journeys. Cabotage was seldom a pre-planned and fixed affair and the route often developed during the journey according to circumstances. As with journeys on land this resulted in a great multiplicity of actual routes. This reassessment is, however, clearly incorrect for the Roman period, when the Mediterranean was undoubtedly characterised by major shipping routes, focusing on the main urban centres, from which smaller scale redistribution took place.[41] Horden and Purcell also argued that the division of the year into a sailing season lasting from early April to late October was the chronological equivalent of shipping lanes. They pointed out that port records provided clear evidence for winter shipping, often to a degree not much reduced from the summer time.[42]

Finally, both Cunliffe and Horden and Purcell emphasise that connectivity and networks of interaction should be seen in terms of the *longue durée*. Horden and Purcell suggested that the networks of maritime interaction were essentially continuous over time, although their precise mechanisms and routes were subject to change. They took as a case study the so-called Early Medieval depression of the seventh to the early ninth centuries AD, characterised by Pirenne as witnessing the decline of Mediterranean exchange, particularly between east and west, which was brought about by the advances of Muslim pirates.[43] However, Horden and Purcell argued that even in this period connectivity was maintained. Amongst other things, they noted that the fact that Muslim piracy existed at all implies that there was shipping to prey upon. They also believed that piracy should not simply be dismissed, but should be reinterpreted as an important aspect of connectivity. As with trade, piracy also resulted in the redistribution of material and people around the Mediterranean basin. These ideas of continuous, long-term interaction are important, but, I believe greater account needs to be taken of short and medium term change, particularly in terms of scale. This will be heavily addressed in my work which will test the approach of Horden and Purcell in a different kind of maritime environment.

[36] Horden and Purcell 2000, 130.
[37] Cunliffe 2001.
[38] Braudel 1972; 2001.
[39] Horden and Purcell 2000; 2006.
[40] Pryor 1988.
[41] Nieto 1997; Arnaud 2005.
[42] C.f. Beresford 2005.
[43] Pirenne 1939.

1.4. The North Sea and Channel: geography and ancient conceptions

Geography plays an extremely important role in structuring exchange and connectivity. The North Sea and Channel coasts may be tentatively divided into three connective zones, which are principally determined by geography. These zones focus on short open-sea crossings, or suitable coastal routes. Large stretches of open sea appear to have obstructed connectivity and divided regions. The coastlines of the Western Channel and Atlantic seaways are typically jagged and rocky and possess distinctive coastlines and natural landmarks which are visible far out to sea. The Western Channel narrows to only 100 km in width between the Cotentin peninsula and Poole Bay. The Southern North Sea and Eastern Channel have gentler, less rocky coastlines.[44] Here Britain is extremely close to the continent at the narrow Strait of Dover. Major rivers, such as the Thames, Scheldt and Rhine discharge into the sea at this point and afford natural route ways into the inland regions of Britain and western continental Europe. North and east of the Rhine the continental coastline is low-lying and is marked by a long string of islands lying just off the coast. Between these islands and the mainland lies the Wadden Sea, which is tidal and its navigation has long proved a tricky feat.

Finally, we should consider a fourth geographical region, the northern part of the North Sea, or a north Atlantic zone, which is dominated by a rocky, hilly occasionally mountainous coastline. Here the shores of Norway and northern Britain are jagged and bear the remains of glacial action from the last Ice Age, steep cliffs and skerries are often to be found and in Norway deep fjords are carved into the coastal mountains. To some extent the seascape here approximates to that of the Mediterranean and the Atlantic façade- the coastlines are high and distinctive and as such are visible from far out at sea. According to the ideas of Horden and Purcell such strongly visible landscapes might have structured communication and promoted navigation; however, the distance across the northern North Sea is considerable and we lack evidence for its navigation during the Late Iron Age and Roman period.

To Roman writers, the North Sea and Channel were seen as part of the great Ocean which surrounded the mainland of Europe and within which Britain was situated. For example, the *Res gestae* proclaimed that Augustus had brought peace to the provinces of Spain and Gaul and Germania, the areas surrounded by the Ocean from Gades to the mouth of the Elbe.... his fleet had sailed across the Ocean from the mouth of the Rhine eastwards to the land of the Cimbri. Strabo recorded that Germanic coastal peoples such as the Cimbri lived along the shore of the Ocean, whilst Velleius Paterculus described how during the campaign led by Tiberius into Germania the fleet sailed through the bays of the Ocean on its way to the Elbe. Pomponius Mela also stated that the Ocean formed the northern border of Free Germany.[45]

[44] C.f. Cunliffe 2001; 2005, 70-73; Fox 1932.

However, on several occasions Classical authors did divide the Ocean into separate parts and we get hints that the Ocean was to some extent envisioned as comprising several distinct bodies of water, though there is a general lack of consistency in how this was done. For example, Pliny stated that the seas around the Gaulish coast comprised the Northern Ocean, flowing down to the mouth of the Rhine, the Britannic Ocean, between the Rhine and the Seine, and, between the Seine and the Pyrenees, the Gallic Ocean. Elsewhere he wrote of the German Sea and the amber obtained from the (Frisian) islands located within it.[46] In his *Geography* of the mid-second century AD Ptolemy differentiated the German Ocean, which formed the northern boundary of Germania and lay off the eastern side of Britain between Duncansby Head in the Highlands of Scotland and the southern foreland of Kent from the *Oceanus Duecaledonius*, which lay to the north of Britain, and the British Ocean to the south of Britain.[47] Eutropius, referred to the Belgic and Armorican sectors of the sea, whilst by the end of the late fourth century a long stretch of the southeast British and continental coastline was attested on the *Notitia Dignitatum* as the Saxon Shore (*litus Saxonicum*).[48] The Strait of Dover was explicitly recorded by several authors; Solinus named it the *freto Gallico*, (Strait of Gaul), Tacitus the *freto Oceani* (Strait of the Ocean), whilst Ammianus Marcellinus labeled it the *Oceanum fretalem* (Straits of the Ocean).[49]

1.5. Types of exchange

Different exchange systems, or mechanisms, play a major role in determining the nature of connectivity and need to be dealt with in detail. I argue that there are five main mechanisms by which objects are moved in human societies. It is important to stress that several, or even all, of these mechanisms can operate alongside each other. The distinctions between the different types of exchange are often not entirely clear. These categories must be considered a guide to exchange types rather than being regarded as mutually exclusive. We should also consider that during its lifecycle, between production and deposition in an archaeological context, an object may have moved through several different mechanisms. I will attempt to archaeologically identify these exchange types in the material utilized during the course of this study.

i. Personal possessions

This refers to objects on the body of, or possessed by, or simply carried and used by, an individual. The movement

[45] *Res gestae*. 26.2.4; Strabo. *Geog*. 7.2.1, 7.2.4; Velleius Paterculus *Historia Romana*. 2.105-109; Pomponius Mela. *De Chorographia* 3.25, 29.

[46] Pliny. *H.N.* 4.30, 4.33.

[47] Ptolemy. *Geography*. 2.2.1, 2.10.

[48] Eutropius. 9.21; *Notitia Dignitatum Occidentis*. 28, 37-38.

[49] Solinus (Mommsen 1895, 101.6-7); Tacitus. *Agricola*. 40.2; Ammianus Marcellinus. XXVIII. 2. 1.

of personal possessions is not true exchange, as they are not moved with the intention of being given to or exchanged with another individual. Nevertheless this represents a fundamentally important mechanism by which objects move.[50] The primary reasons for the long-distance movement of people in pre-modern societies were typically for the purposes of marriage, exchange, political visits, military activity, slavery and migration.

ii. Gift exchange

Gift exchange refers to the movement of objects between individuals or groups, where the primary intention is to establish a relationship, or friendship, between the giver and receiver.[51] The actual transfer of objects is of secondary importance to the establishment of these relationships. The relationship is rarely severed once an equivalent gift has been returned to the original giver. Rather, the links between the two parties often endure for a substantial period of time and facilitate a continuing flow of gifts between them.

Anthropologists argue that gift exchange is typically the dominant form of exchange in egalitarian clan-based societies. In such societies there is typically no conception of individual ownership of land, resources or possessions, which restricts the possibilities of engaging in market-type exchanges. Ownership is collective and an individual may have only a partial claim. In these societies participation in exchange relationships is restricted by obligations to other members of kin, age, gender and status-related groups.[52] Gifts exchanges are often linked to the movement of marriage partners and help maintain kinship links over the course of time. This was one of the prime mechanisms through which objects moved over long distances during much of European prehistory.[53]

In hierarchically organised societies gifts may also be exchanged between individuals or groups in order to gain the friendship or support of the other party.[54] The alliances and networks thus created can serve as an important source of prestige for the parties involved, as can the materials which pass between them, although this is rarely the main source of power in a society.[55] An example of this form of exchange would be the practice of gift-giving amongst the Roman elite in the Mediterranean regions at the centre of the Roman state, which is attested by substantial literary evidence.[56]

Certain forms of redistributive exchange also contain many elements of gift exchange but they will be dealt under the title of redistributive exchange.

iii. Redistributive exchange

Redistributive exchange may be defined as the systematic collection of goods from a wider populace by a central authority which may or may not reallocate those goods back to the wider populace, or parts of the populace.[57] Redistributive exchange may occur on a range of different levels, including at the household level and amongst co-residential groups on a community level.[58] What concerns us here, however, is redistribution on the intercommunity scale which is often a dominant form of exchange in hierarchical societies, particularly those defined as chiefdoms, and is usually present to some degree in most states.[59] The establishment of an intercommunity redistribution system will very probably lead to the movement of objects on an increased scale within the integrated regions than would be the case with a gift exchange system alone. Redistributive systems incorporate the vast majority of a population and typically involve the regular movement of goods. It is important to note, however, that redistributive systems are usually confined to the region over which the political and social authority of the central individual(s) extends. It is only when this authority extends over a wide area, as with the Roman Empire, that the possibility of long-distance redistributive exchange emerges.

Intercommunity redistribution can be split into two main forms. The first of these may be termed generalized redistribution.[60] Here, elites take in a surplus which they then redistribute to the rest of the population. Earle's levelling mechanisms would fall into this category.[61] Here wealth is collected and then redistributed on a lavish scale by a central person, or persons at an assembly, a feast, or another important social occasion. Redistribution in this form bears many similarities to gift-giving as relationships are established between the wider population and the central individual(s). The redistribution of wealth by the central person may eventually become socially expected or even an obligation of occupying their social position. It can often provide the basis for social competition as elites compete amongst themselves to collect and redistribute the most and thus gain the highest levels of support amongst the general population. A similar form of large scale gift redistribution is observable in the Roman elite practice of constructing monumental public buildings in urban areas (euergetism).[62]

The second main form of redistributive exchange can be termed mobilization.[63] Here elites take in a surplus from a primarily self-sufficient population, which they then keep for themselves or reallocate as they see fit. The surplus, or tribute, can be consumed entirely by the elite in order

---

50 Kristiansen and Larsson 2005; 35.
51 Bohannan 1996; Gregory 1982; 2000; Sharples 2007; Mauss 1954; Strathern 1988.
52 Sharples 2007, 175.
53 Vander Linden 2007; Bradley and Edmonds 1993.
54 Kristiansen and Larrson 2005, 35-37; Masson 2005, 1140; Frankenstein and Rowlands 1978.
55 *Ibid*; Gosden 1985; Earle 1997.
56 Peacock and Williams 1986, 56-57; Whittaker 1983.
57 Masson 2005, 1140; Tykot 2004; Earle 1977; Polanyi 1944; 1957; Layton 1997, 101.
58 Earle 1977.
59 Service 1971, 133-134; D'Altroy and Earle 1985.
60 Masson 2005, 1140.
61 Earle 1977; Peacock and Williams 1986, 55-59.
62 Blagg 1981; 1990; Walker 1981; Pobjoy 2000.
63 Masson 2005, 1140-1142; Earle 1977; Welch 1991; Peacock and Williams 1986, 55-59.

to support a lavish lifestyle of consumption. More commonly the elite redirect part of the tribute to certain sections of the wider society. This may include a dependent population, such as craft specialists or a military force, which is used by the elite to support their position of power and/or their lifestyle. In addition, the elite may redistribute tribute, or items obtained through long-distance exchange such as prestige goods, to a series of lesser individuals in order to obtain their friendship and support.

i. Market exchange

Market exchange involves the direct exchange of goods between individuals or groups, where, in contrast to gift exchange, the objects themselves are valued more than the relationships created between the participants.[64] An exchange of this sort requires no long-term relationship between the parties on either side. Market exchange is associated with a search for profit by its participants. It is also usually associated with regular or periodic meetings at some form of central place- a market place- where buyers and sellers are brought together. This type of exchange is particularly common in state societies, of which it is often a defining feature.[65]

In general, the development of a market exchange system facilitates an expansion in the scale on which objects move and are exchanged. One of the reasons for this is that in comparison to gift and redistributive exchanges, there are usually fewer restrictions placed on when, where, how much and with whom one can engage in exchange. Unlike gift exchange systems it is unnecessary to maintain continued relations with exchange partners, which means a wider range of exchange partners can be sought.[66] Market exchange systems can also become specialised, with the appearance of marketplaces and often a merchant class, who are entirely dependent upon exchange to make their living. It is important to note that markets are often heavily regulated by a political authority, which in many cases has the right to grant, or withhold, permission for markets to be held at particular times and places.[67]

There are two main forms of market exchange: those involving barter and those involving money. Barter refers to the direct exchange of goods and/or services. Money meanwhile, is a store of wealth and a unit of value, which serves to facilitate exchange.[68] The most common form of money is coin, which is issued by a central authority. The volume of coin in circulation can be expanded by issuing tokens, which have an exchange value greater than the inherent value of the metal upon which they are based. For this to occur, the tokens will have to be strongly backed both legally and politically by the issuing authority. Market exchange might be further facilitated by the development of credit money, which allows a claim against any physical or legal person that can be used for the purchase of goods or services.[69] This development is often associated with the appearance of banking.

ii. War booty

The final mechanism to be considered is war booty. This is not exchange as such, but is nonetheless an important mechanism through which objects can move over long distances. War booty refers to objects obtained through direct military action, or raiding. In many cases, such as in Early Medieval Europe, objects acquired in this manner were usually claimed by members of the elite and thus should be seen as part of redistributive mechanisms.[70] However, in some situations the spoils of war can be claimed by individual soldiers. The equipment of defeated enemies was often considered to belong to the gods of the victorious army, as in Iron Age temperate Europe, Iron Age and Roman-period Scandinavia and on occasion in Classical Greece and Rome.[71] As such it had to be dedicated to the gods at sacred places.

Bearing the previous work and the issues of exchange types and geography in mind I shall now proceed to the study proper and outline the changing nature of North Sea and Channel connectivity during the Late Iron Age and Roman period.

[64] Bohannan 1996; Gregory 1982; 2000; Sharples 2007; Layton 1997, 100.
[65] Masson 2005, 1142; Service 1971; Earle 1977.
[66] Layton 1997, 100.
[67] Britnell 2009; De Ligt 1993; Lo Cascio 2000.
[68] Greene 1986, 50-51; Mankiw 2007; Krugman and Wells 2006; Layton 1997, 100.
[69] Mises 1981, I.3, 25.
[70] Wickham 2005, 695.
[71] Worsaae 1865; Hagberg 1967, 65-69; Jørgensen 2003; Ilkjær 2003; Kaul 2003; Lund 2003; Caesar. *B.G.* VI.17; Paulus Orosius V.16.5; Tacitus. *Annales*. XIII.57.

2. North Sea and Channel connectivity 175/150-50 BC

2.1. The Southern North Sea and Channel systems

Introduction

From the mid- to late second century BC onwards there was an apparent increase in the scale of connectivity in both the Southern North Sea and Eastern Channel system and in the Atlantic system. This contrasts with the preceding Middle Iron Age for which evidence of long distance exchange is much more limited, although we should bear in mind that this may in part be due to the appearance of archaeologically visible exchange items, such as coins and amphorae during the course of the second century. The Southern North Sea and Eastern Channel system is particularly characterised by an influx of gold coins, minted in northern France, into southeast Britain. These are explained in terms of political and social payments made by groups or individuals in northern France to groups and individuals in southeast Britain. Helping to secure the aid of British groups in military conflicts on the near continent may have been one of their primary purposes. The factors determining the nature of these connections are population growth in parts of southeast Britain, military conflict in northern Gaul and increasing exploitation of gold resources in central Gaul. Violent conquest, and population movements directed from northern France to southeast Britain have been totally rejected as significant factors in recent years, but I do not believe they should be ruled out completely.

In the Atlantic system, Italian Dressel 1A wine amphorae and coins and pottery from Brittany were imported to south-central Britain via Brittany. Trade is the most plausible mechanism to account for their appearance, though the possibility that other mechanisms were involved cannot be excluded. British traded exports are largely undetectable archaeologically. They probably included tin, slaves and agricultural products. Change in the Atlantic system should be linked into contemporary political and economic expansion in the Roman world, which indirectly stimulated trade networks along the Atlantic coast of France, which extended up to south-central Britain. Improvements in ship technology may also have facilitated increasing connectivity in both the Southern North Sea and Eastern Channel and in the Atlantic system.

Continental imports

Coinage and metals

Gold objects seem to have been rare in Britain during the Early and Middle Iron Ages, from which time only a handful of ribbon torcs are known from northern and western Britain and Ireland.[72] Gold began to reappear in the archaeological record of southeast Britain in fairly large quantities from c. 175/150 BC onwards, principally in the form of Gallo-Belgic coins which were almost all produced in northern France.[73] The earliest imports were Gallo-Belgic A (broad-flan staters/ Scheers type 8) (**Fig. 2.1**). This type is difficult to date precisely, but its typological complexity suggests that it was fairly long-lived, and was most probably produced between c. 175-120 BC. Evidence in support of this starting date comes from the Tayac hoard from southwest France, which appears to date to the mid-second century BC and contains coins situated towards the middle of the Gallo-Belgic A typological sequence. Furthermore, there is evidence suggesting that the equivalent "secondary coinages" from other parts of northwest Europe, such as Germany and Switzerland, were first minted c. 175-150 BC.[74]

Gallo-Belgic B (staters and quarter-staters aux lignes entremêlés/ Scheers type 10) coins were also imported to southeast Britain in similarly large quantities (**Fig. 2.2**). These can be typologically connected to the dies used in the manufacture of Gallo-Belgic A, and can best be dated to the mid-second century BC down to c. 120 BC.[75] From c. 120-60 BC another type, known as Gallo-Belgic C (abstract biface staters/ Scheers 9) came into existence. Gallo-Belgic C coins are clearly derived from, and succeed, Gallo-Belgic A and B and were again produced in northern France.[76] They are present in Britain in roughly similar quantities to the earlier coinages, which

[72] Northover 1988; 1994; 1995.
[73] Sills 2003; Creighton 2000.
[74] Sills 2003; Haselgrove 1999; 2000; Burnett, 1996; Scheers 1977.
[75] Sills 2003, Fig. 68; Fitzpatrick 1992; Haselgrove 2000, 411-412.
[76] Sills 2003; Haselgrove 2000.

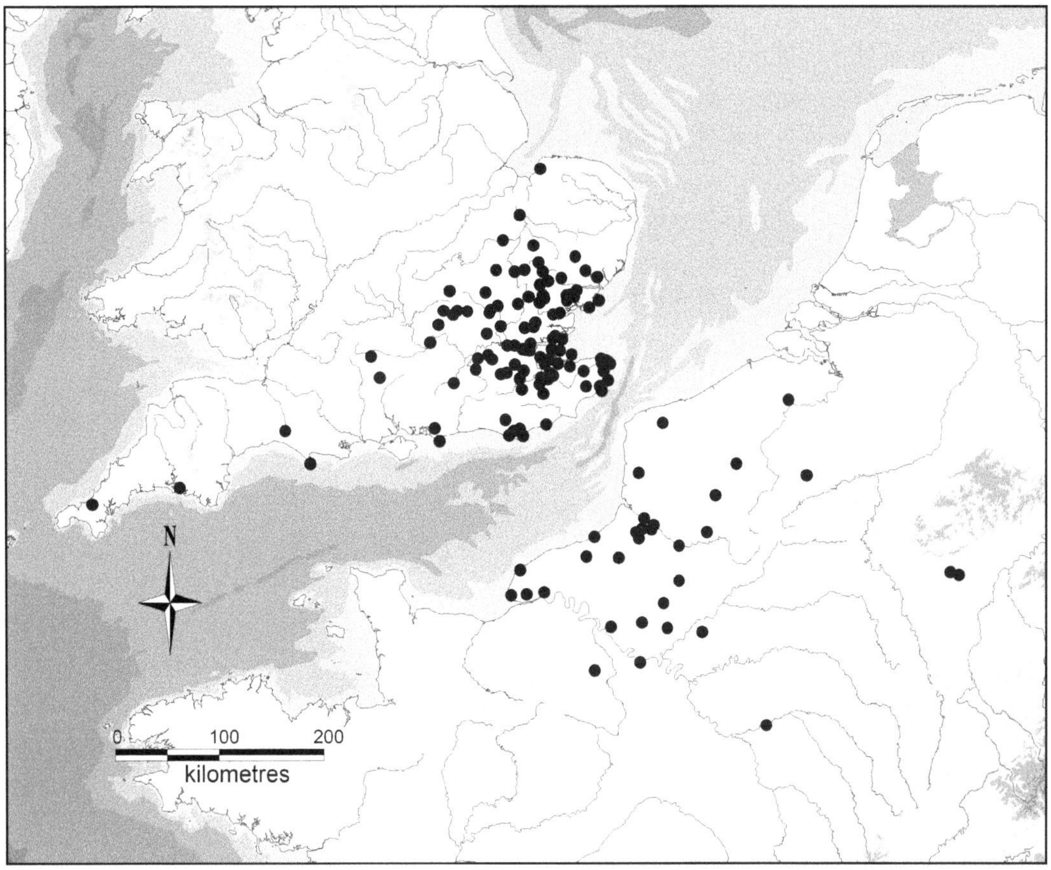

Fig. 2.1. Distribution of Gallo Belgic A gold coinage (after Sills 2003, Maps 16 and 19).[77]

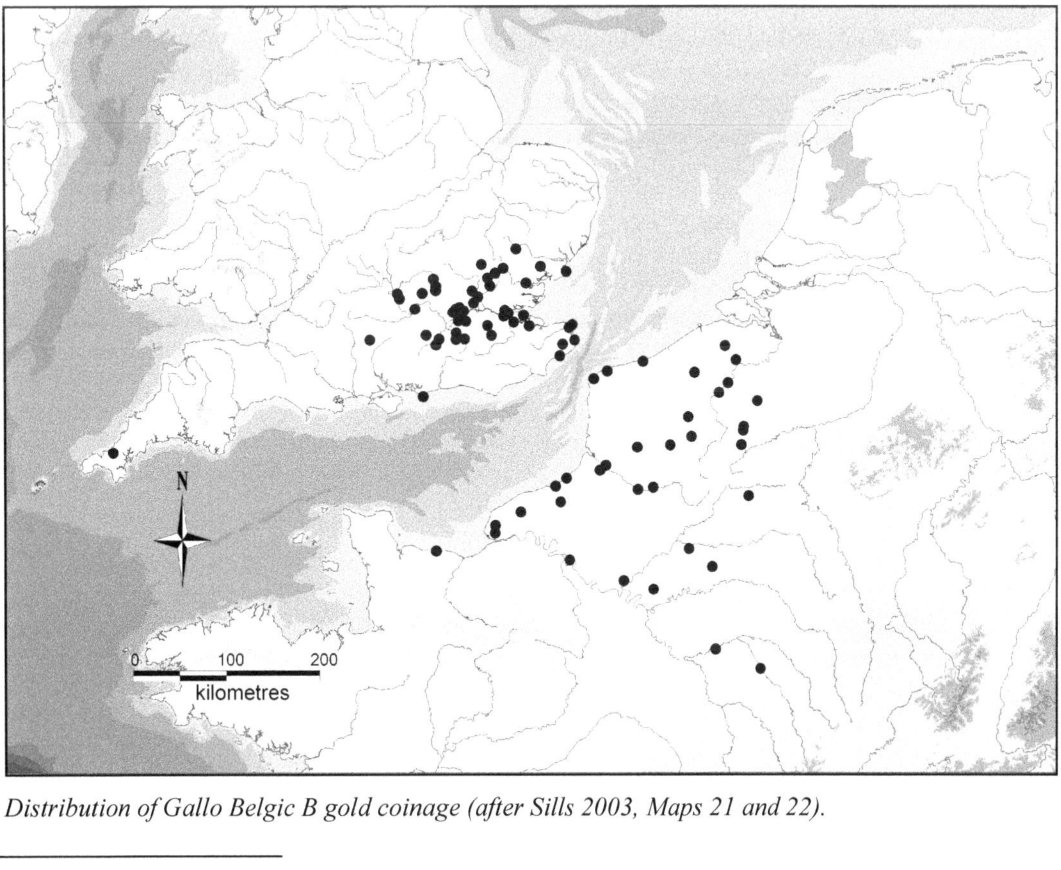

Fig. 2.2. Distribution of Gallo Belgic B gold coinage (after Sills 2003, Maps 21 and 22).

[77] N.B. Many types of Gallo-Belgic coins have been found in greater quantities in southeast Britain than in northern France, despite the fact that they were minted in the latter region. This disparity is in part due to the effectiveness of the Celtic Coin Index in recording Iron Age coins discovered in Britain, though this can only be part of the explanation and it is likely that the discrepancy does in fact reflect the real situation.

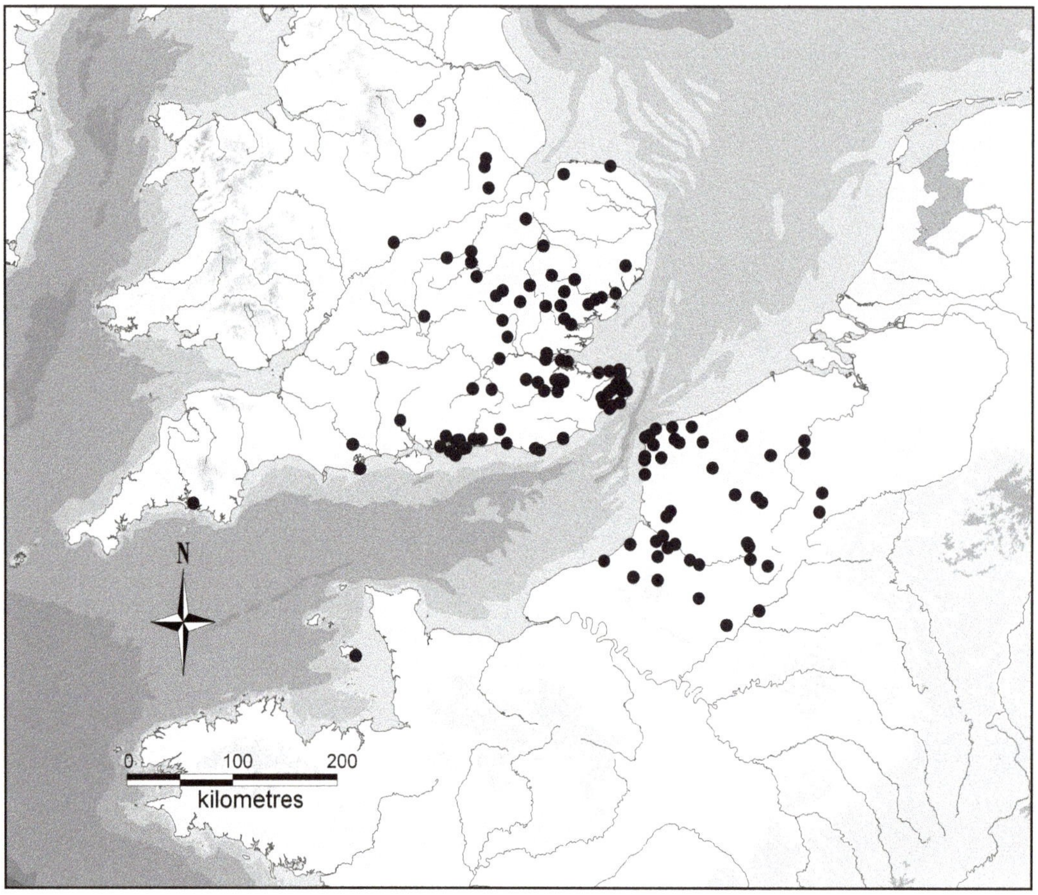

Fig. 2.3. Distribution of Gallo-Belgic D gold coinage (data from the Celtic Coin Index 2008).

hints at the continuation of import on a not too dissimilar scale. As with their predecessors, these coins are concentrated in northern France and southeast Britain, demonstrating strong links across the Southern North Sea and Eastern Channel (c.f. **Figs. 2.1-2**).[78]

Succeeding Gallo-Belgic C, and more debased than coins of this type, are Gallo-Belgic E staters (uniface series/ Scheers type 24) and their related quarter staters Gallo-Belgic D.[79] These were both struck in northern France, where they are found in quantity, and they also made their way to Britain in extremely large numbers. Gallo-Belgic E are the most common gold coins known from Iron Age Britain, with the Celtic Coin Index currently holding records for c. 2500 examples, principally from the southeast, although they are also found scattered throughout central England.[80] On the basis of die estimates, the total original issue of Gallo-Belgic E probably amounted to c. 5,000-6,000 kg of fine gold, far in excess of the estimated 300-400 kg required for the Gallo-Belgic A and C series.[81] Gallo-Belgic D are less common in Britain than Gallo-Belgic E, but around 600 are recorded, which is still a considerable number.[82] As with Gallo-Belgic E, Gallo-Belgic D are concentrated in northern France and southeast Britain, principally in West Sussex, East Kent and around the Lower Thames/Essex region, and hint at strong connections across the Southern North Sea and Eastern Channel focused on the Strait of Dover (**Fig. 2.3**). Both Gallo-Belgic E and D must have been issued prior to c. 50 BC because after this date tribes in continental northwest Europe only issued gold coin on a very small-scale, principally as a consequence of Caesar's Gallic campaigns leading to the removal of vast quantities of Gaulish bullion to Rome as war booty, or tribute.[83]

Aside from coins, gold torcs are attested in eastern Britain from the late second century onwards. The most notable finds derive from Snettisham, a hilltop site near the former coast of the Wash in Norfolk. About 175 complete torcs of gold, electrum, silver and bronze have been recovered from this site, as well as hundreds of torc fragments.[84] The sheer quantity suggests local manufacture rather than import, but the gold examples

[78] Sills 2003.

[79] N.B. Gallo-Belgic D, as originally defined by Allen (1960) has now been divided in two by John Sills (2003; 2006). Sills has re-assigned the earlier part of Allen's Gallo-Belgic D to Gallo-Belgic C, as Gallo-Belgic Ca2, which was a long series struck between c. 110 BC and the start of the Gallic wars. Gallo-Belgic D proper was clearly issued alongside Gallo-Belgic E during the Gallic wars and these two types are often found together in hoards.

[80] Sills 2005, 2; Haselgrove 1984b, Tab. 1; 2000. See Creighton (2000, Fig. 3.6a) for the overall distribution of Gallo-Belgic E (though this is out of date).

[81] Haselgrove 1984b, Tab. 1; Sills 2005.

[82] Sills 2006.

[83] Haselgrove 2000, 414.

[84] Hutcheson 2007; Hill 2007; Northover 1988; 1995.

were very probably derived from melted down Gallo-Belgic coins. Indeed, Gallo-Belgic A-C coins were found in association with the Snettisham torcs. The quantity of gold utilized at Snettisham was prodigious; the torcs from the 1990 finds alone had the same amount of gold as over 3000 Gallo-Belgic staters.[85]

Determining the precise mechanism by which Gallo-Belgic coins arrived in Britain is fraught with difficulty. Trade should not be ruled out, and it was probably an important secondary function of the coins; however, they should principally be understood in terms of gifts, or 'payments' made, in the first case, by individuals or tribal groups in northern France in order to create or maintain social and political relationships with individuals or groups in southeast Britain.[86] One piece of evidence in support of this is that whilst some of the Gallo-Belgic coin series occur regularly in Britain, others are almost entirely absent, despite being fairly common in northern France.[87] This implies that only certain issues were exported to Britain, rather than free circulation being the case.

These 'payments' may have intensified in response to particular events; Gallo-Belgic coins do not appear to have been minted on a continually low-level over a long period of time. Instead the die links and typologies imply batch production, often on a large scale in a relatively discrete time period.[88] John Sills has suggested that Gallo-Belgic A-C should be explained in terms of payments made to tribes in southeast Britain in return for mercenary service in inter-tribal warfare, or in resisting invading 'Germanic' groups.[89] That a violent situation prevailed in northern Gaul is supported by a few references from Classical authors.[90] However, whilst Sill's interpretations are plausible we simply cannot explain these coins in terms of the scant historical record with any degree of reliability.

Gallo-Belgic E and D coins were issued in prodigious quantities over a short period of time, c. 70/60-50 BC at the longest.[91] It is extremely tempting to interpret them as the war coinages of Belgic tribes at the time of Caesar's Gallic wars, although Haselgrove has argued that we should view them independently of historical events.[92] Sills has noted that Gallo-Belgic E has only seven relatively discrete die classes, with the first four better represented than the final three. This would fit an interpretation that they represent a series of annual issues struck in northern France from 58/7 down to 52/1 BC, when Belgic resistance to Caesar ended, with a disruption occurring after Caesar's second invasion of Britain in 54 BC.[93] Sills has also demonstrated that the start and end of the Gallo-Belgic D series are typologically related to the start and end of the Gallo-Belgic E series, and that, as with Gallo-Belgic E, Gallo-Belgic D can also possibly be divided into seven classes (with the latter two poorly represented) that were struck annually during the Gallic wars.[94] Both Gallo-Belgic E and D may have been sent to Britain to secure British support against the Romans; certainly Caesar records one of his main motives for an invasion of Britain as the fact that the Britons had aided the Gauls in almost all of his campaigns thus far.[95] Of course this is all very tentative and other explanations are possible. Large quantities of Gallo-Belgic E and D may have been transferred to Britain as a result of groups, or individuals, from northern France fleeing the Roman army, perhaps in an attempt to avoid the systematic looting of wealth that followed Roman conquest.

A small quantity of gold and silver billon coins (c. 150 in total) were imported from Brittany to south-central Britain across the Western Channel (**Fig. 2.4**).[96] Like the Gallo-Belgic coins some of these may also have travelled as a result of social and political payments; however, as I will discuss in greater detail below, there is evidence for a substantial trade between Brittany and south-central Britain and we might suspect that some of these coins arrived through trade.

Moving now to iron we can only point to a few examples of imports. Two double-pointed billets have been recovered from Portland in Dorset. These belong to a continental type most common north of the Alps, though the continental distribution suggests that these examples probably arrived across the Western Channel via Brittany.[97] Why they arrived is impossible to prove, although trade is a possibility; indeed Caesar wrote that in Britain iron bars functioned as currency alongside coins.[98] An iron sword, spear and shield boss of north French type, have also been found in a burial at Kelvedon in Essex, which is dated c. 75-25 BC.[99] If these really were produced on the continent, as opposed to being products of southeast Britain which had a very similar material culture to northern France at this time, then they were presumably personal possessions of an individual who had either seen military service on the continent or who had migrated to Britain.

Wine

Whilst Italian amphorae of Greco-Italic type, which were produced between the mid-fourth to mid-second centuries BC, have been identified in quantity in central France and are also occasionally found in northern and western France, they have not yet been noted in Britain, although there are possible Greco-Italic/Dressel 1A transitional

[85] Creighton 2000, 31.
[86] C.f. Hill 2007; Fitzpatrick 1992; Cunliffe 2004; 2005; 2009; Haselgrove 1996b; Van Arsdell 1989, 2-7, 31-32; Burnett 1996; Creighton 2000.
[87] Sills 2003, Maps 20, 27-29.
[88] Sills 2003, 3, 212-224, 325-341; 2005.
[89] Sills 2003.
[90] Caesar *B.G.* I.1, 28-54, II.3-4, 8, 15, 17, VI. 2, 24, VII.59, VIII.6; Strabo *Geog.* 4.4.3.
[91] Sills 2005; 2006; Scheers 1977; Haselgrove 1996b, 71.
[92] Haselgrove 1984b; 1987a, 80-1; 1993; 1999; 2000, 412, 414; 2006a; Burnett 1996.
[93] Sills 2005; see also: Scheers 1977; Haselgrove 1996b, 71.
[94] Sills 2006.
[95] *B.G.* IV.20.
[96] Cunliffe and de Jersey 1997; Cunliffe 2005, Fig. 21.7.
[97] Doswald 1994, Fig. 4.
[98] *B.G.* V.12.
[99] Sealey 2007, 39.

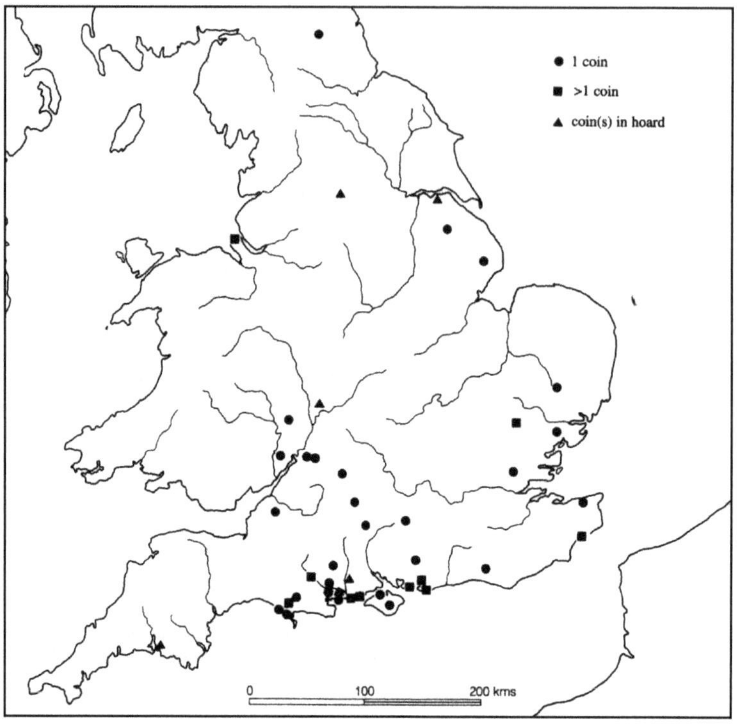

Fig. 2.4. Breton coins in Britain (Cunliffe and de Jersey 1997, Fig. 42).

types at Yarmouth Roads off the Isle of Wight.[100] The earliest evidence for the importation of wine into Britain comes from Dressel 1A (Dr.1A) amphorae. The Dr.1A type is a broad and by no means coherent grouping which masks a considerable degree of variation in forms. They were a predominantly Italian phenomenon, with the focus of production located in Etruria and Campania, although kilns producing Dressel 1 are known along the west coast of Italy, as far as Calabria and on a much smaller scale in southern France, North Africa and Spain.[101] Each amphora had a capacity of c. 25 litres and *tituli picti* (painted inscriptions) and residue analyses, demonstrate that Dr.1A principally transported wine, although other products such as *defrutum* may occasionally have been carried.[102] This wine was the product of the vast slave-powered Late Republican estates of central Italy.[103]

Dr.1A amphorae are known from at least 25 sites in southern Britain, principally around the coast of the Solent and central-southern Britain, although four finds have been made in the Essex-Hertfordshire region (**Fig. 2.5**). The quantities from each find-spot are typically small, although at Hengistbury Head in Dorset at least thirty separate examples of Dr.1A and nearly 1000 sherds of Dressel 1 species have been recovered.[104] At Bowcombe and Yarmouth Roads, both on the Isle of Wight, ten and at least twenty-one Dr.1A have respectively been found.[105] Nevertheless, the overall quantity of Dr.1A reaching Britain was fairly low.

This import probably occurred during the late second to mid-first century BC. The earliest known Dr.1A from the Roman world comes from the 146 BC destruction layers at Carthage in Tunisia, whilst an example with a consular date of 129 BC derives from Rodez in France.[106] They begin to appear on Mediterranean shipwrecks from the mid-second century BC onwards, peaking on shipwrecks c. 125-75 BC and declining rapidly thereafter; however, Dr.1A were probably still being manufactured down to c. 50 BC at a few sites. Contextually dated British examples are rare, although the amphorae from Hengistbury Head are principally found in contexts dated c. 100-50 BC, whilst the settlements with Dr.1A on the Isle of Wight appear to date to a roughly similar period.[107] In northern and western France Dr.1A occur at sites from the late second century BC onwards.[108]

Dr.1A are present at numerous sites along the Atlantic coast of France, particularly Brittany (**Fig. 2.5**). It is extremely probable that the examples from south-central Britain were imported from Brittany across the Western Channel. Trade is the most plausible mechanism to account for their movement; both Caesar and Strabo state that the Veneti of southern Brittany were trading with Britain prior to their revolt against Caesar in 56 BC (**Fig. 2.6**).[109] Hengistbury Head, which possesses the largest British Dr.1A amphorae assemblage, also has a range of contemporary imports, including glass and figs from the Mediterranean world and coins and pottery from Brittany, which suggests it was a trading site, although an

[100] Fitzpatrick 2003a; Loughton, 2003.
[101] Loughton 2003, 182-3; 2009, 80-81; Parker 1990, 330.
[102] Loughton 2003, 182; Sealey 1985, 25, 62-3; Fitzpatrick 2003a, 11.
[103] Brun 2004; Marzano 2007.
[104] Cunliffe 1987; Carver 2001, 24, 99.
[105] Carver 2001, 25.
[106] Hesnard 1990, 51; Gruat 1993.
[107] Cunliffe 1987; Carver 2001, 24-5.
[108] Haselgrove 1996a, 168; Fitzpatrick 1985, 315; Loughton 2009.
[109] *B.G.* III.8; Strabo *Geog.* IV.4.1.

175/150-50 BC

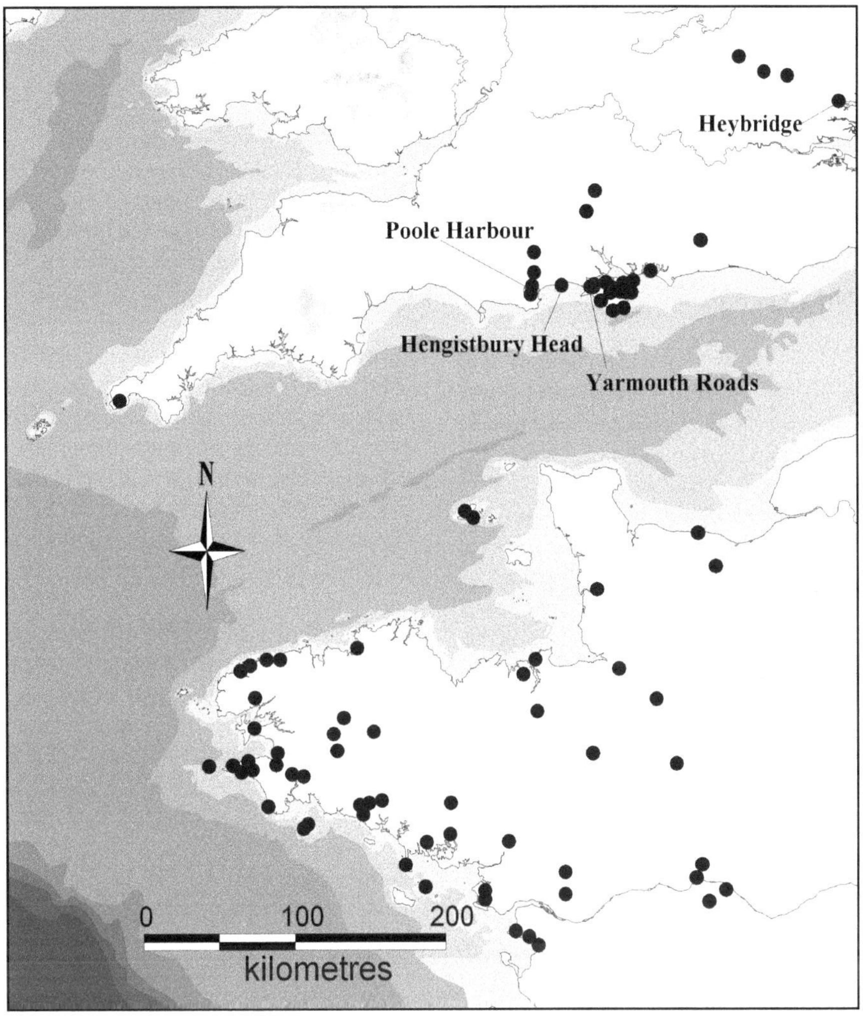

Fig. 2.5. Distribution of Dr.1A amphorae in northwest France and Britain (Sources: Cunliffe 2005, Fig. 17.28; Carver, 2001; Trott and Tomalin 2003. See also: Fitzpatrick 2003a, Fig. 2).

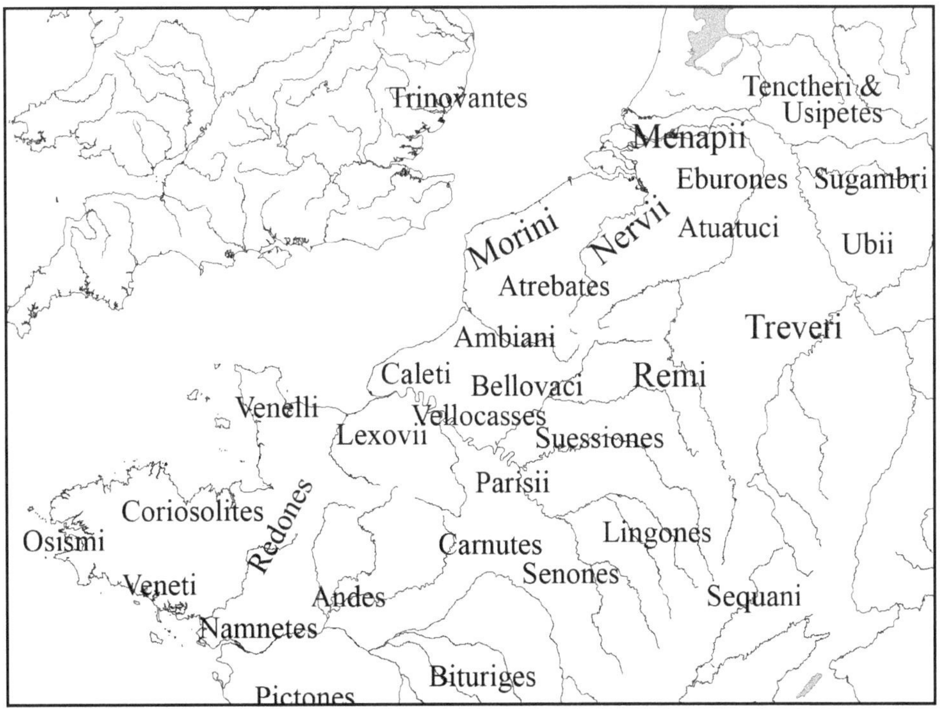

Fig. 2.6. Location of northwest European tribes at the time of Caesar's Gallic campaigns (58-51 BC).

alternative interpretation of the site as a redistributive feasting centre has also been proposed.[110]

The small group of Dr.1A from Essex-Hertfordshire may also have been traded via Brittany, but they might equally well have arrived via northern France as Dr.1A are occasionally found in this region as well.[111] In the latter case, trade or gift exchange could potentially account for their appearance.

Pottery

A wide range of pottery from northern Brittany arrived in south central Britain via the Western Channel between c. 120-50 BC (**Figs. 2.7-9**).[112] By far the largest assemblage derives from Hengistbury Head in Dorset, where an estimated 12-13,000 vessels have been identified.[113] Trade is probable, but we should not rule out the possibility that some of the pots moved with people as personal possessions. Late-Republican Italian Campanian ware vessels are also known from two British sites: Ower in Dorset and Silchester in Hampshire.[114] Campanian ware is extremely rare in northwestern and northern France, but we can suspect that it reached Britain across the Western Channel along with the Dr.1A amphorae and Breton pottery.[115]

British exports

In contrast to the considerable, though restricted, archaeological evidence we have for continental objects arriving in Britain, direct evidence for British products reaching the continent is extremely limited. Aside from the possibility that some Gallo-Belgic coins re-circulated from Britain back to northern France (which was never the primary direction of movement) through trade, or through the fulfilment of social and political obligations, there is some evidence for the earliest British-minted coinages moving to the continent (**Fig. 2.10**).

Potins (high tin bronze coins), were probably the first coins minted in Britain. These were manufactured in east Kent and, to a lesser extent, around the Thames estuary between the late second century BC and the middle of the first century BC.[116] British potins have been found at nine sites on the continent, primarily focused in northern France in the locality of the river Somme (**Fig. 2.10**).[117] The probable 'low value' of these coins relative to gold and silver makes trade a likely explanation for their function, though Haselgrove has argued that, as with the gold coinage, potins were used for social and political transactions.[118] Whether they were carried to the continent through trade is another matter and the relatively small numbers involved could well have arrived as personal possessions with individuals who had moved. Personal possessions is certainly the best explanation for the four potins found at the *oppidum* of Corent in south-central France.[119]

A small group of the earliest gold and silver coinage minted in southeast Britain c. 60-20 BC are also present in northern France, although two silver coins from the Netherlands hint at the possibility of contacts with the south Dutch coast (**Fig. 2.10**). Two mid- to late first-century BC hoards from the Channel Islands contain coins minted by the Durotriges, a tribe from Dorset, and a silver Durotrigan coin is also known from from Calvados (**Fig. 2.10** (Nos. 14, 19-20)). The British coins, though small in number, neatly illustrate the division of Britain's external contacts into a Southern North Sea and Eastern Channel zone and a Western Channel zone. How they reached the continent is hard to determine. Trade, movement of people, or payments for social and political purposes are all possible options.

Tin sources were relatively rare in Europe; sizeable deposits were present in the granites of the Iberian massif in northwest Spain and Portugal, although it is improbable that tin mining began here on any scale before the late first century BC.[120] The remaining major tin sources were situated in Brittany, along the northern edge of the Massif Central, in the Erzebirge Mountains along the German-Czech border and on the Devon-Cornwall peninsula in Britain, though there are also a handful of minor tin sources.[121]

The presence of tin in southwest Britain and its relative rarity elsewhere in Europe meant that it was an important commodity for long-distance trade with the Mediterranean world. There is no direct archaeological evidence pertaining to Iron Age tin mining in Britain, but tin ore was probably obtained from water-concentrated deposits on the beds of old streams – a technique which is very hard to detect archaeologically.[122] Classical authors, whose accounts probably derive from Pytheas's lost work on his visit to Britain in the late fourth century BC, state that tin from Devon and Cornwall (the Belerion peninsula) was extracted by the natives and conducted to a tidal island called Ictis (possibly Mount Batten). At Ictis it was obtained by traders who conveyed it across the Channel to Gaul and thence overland for thirty days to the mouth of the Rhône.[123] Although these accounts relate to the Middle Iron Age we can suspect that tin continued to be traded down to the Late Iron Age. It may well have been transported from Devon-Cornwall to south-central Britain and thence across the Western Channel to Brittany. We should not envision Mediterranean traders in southwest Britain, rather British tin would have reached the Mediterranean world indirectly via intermediate Gaulish groups.

---

110 Cunliffe 1987; Cunliffe and de Jersey 1997; Fitzpatrick 2001.
111 Fitzpatrick 1985; Roymans 1990, Tab. 7.1, Fig. 7.2.
112 Cunliffe and de Jersey 1997; Fitzpatrick and Timby 2002, 162-163.
113 Cunliffe and de Jersey 1997, 47.
114 Fitzpatrick and Timby 2002, 163.
115 Roymans 1990, 150, Tab. 7.2.
116 Gruel and Haselgrove 2007; Sills 2003; Haselgrove 2006b.
117 Gruel and Haselgrove 2007.
118 Haselgrove 2006b.
119 *Ibid.*
120 Merideth 1998; Domergue 1987.
121 Penhallurick 1986; Merideth 1998, 29-33, Fig. 5.1.
122 Tylecote 1986, 43.
123 Diodorus Siculus *Bibliotheca Historia.* V.22; Pliny *H.N.* IV.16; Cunliffe 2002, 73-79; 2005, 502; Hawkes 1984.

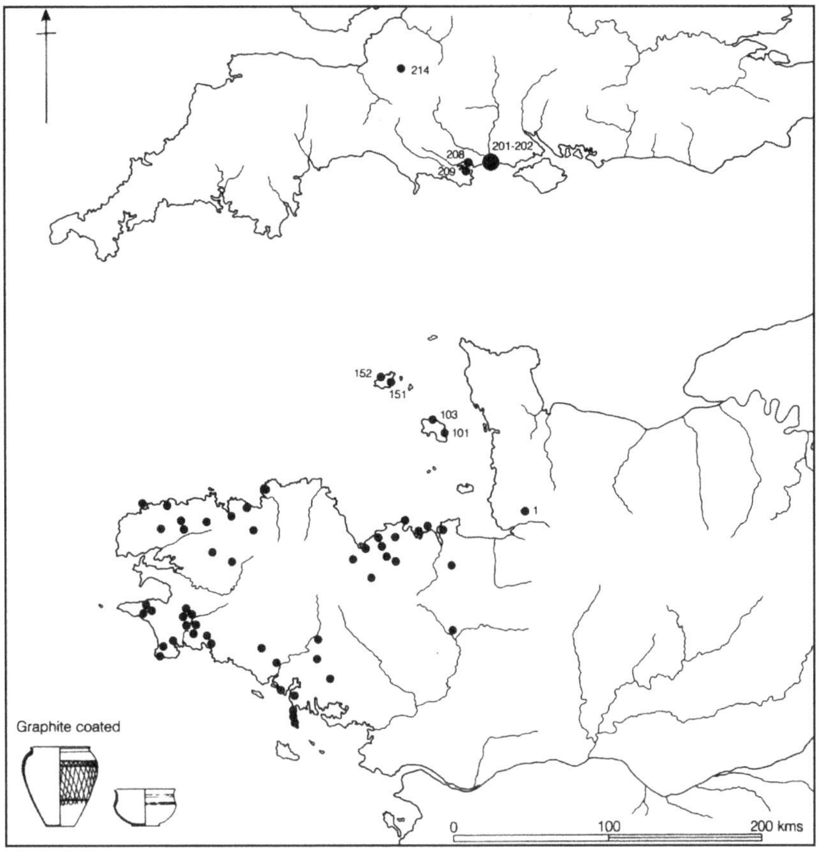

Fig. 2.7. Distribution of Graphite-coated ware (Cunliffe and de Jersey 1997, Fig. 30).

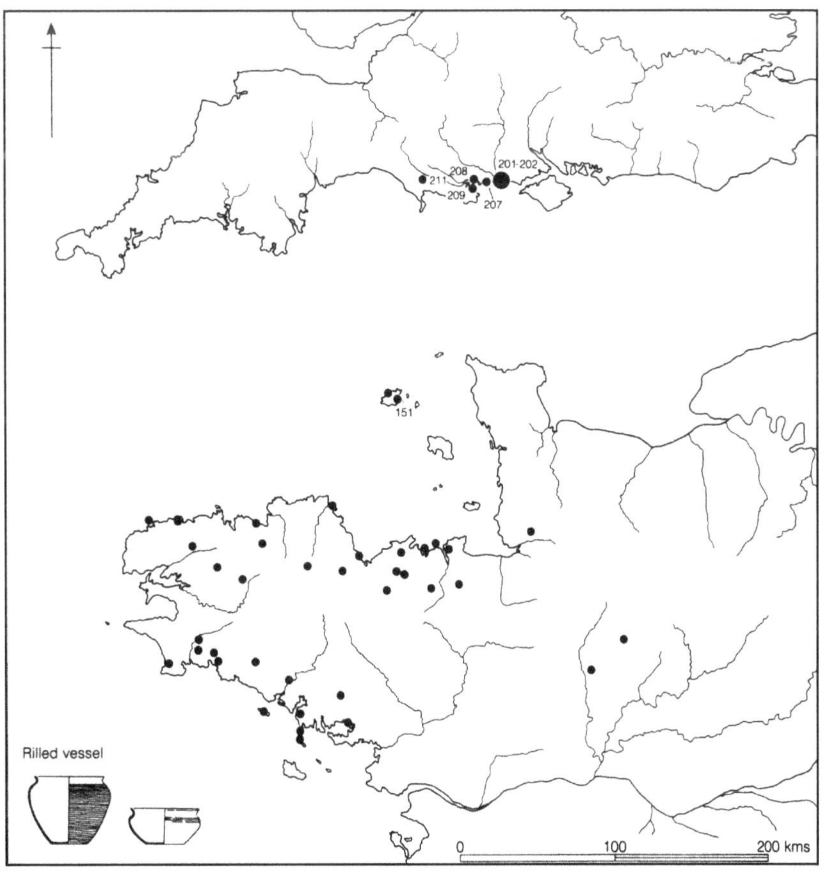

Fig. 2.8. Distribution of Rilled Micaceous ware (Cunliffe and de Jersey 1997, Fig. 31).

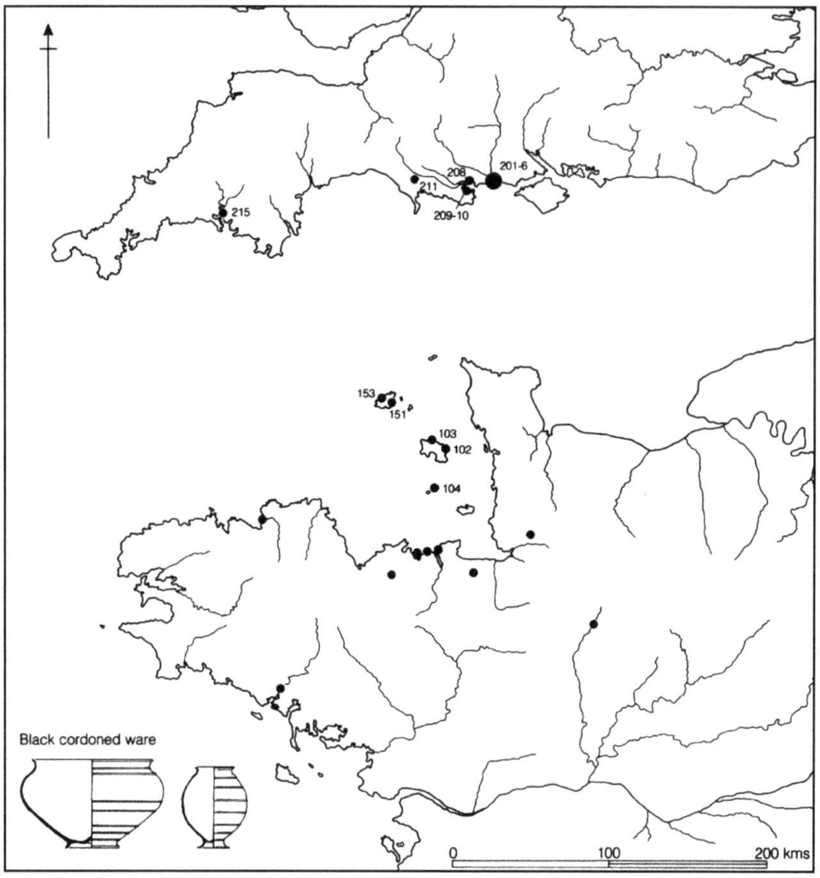

Fig. 2.9. Distribution of fine Black Cordoned ware (Cunliffe and de Jersey 1997, Fig. 32).

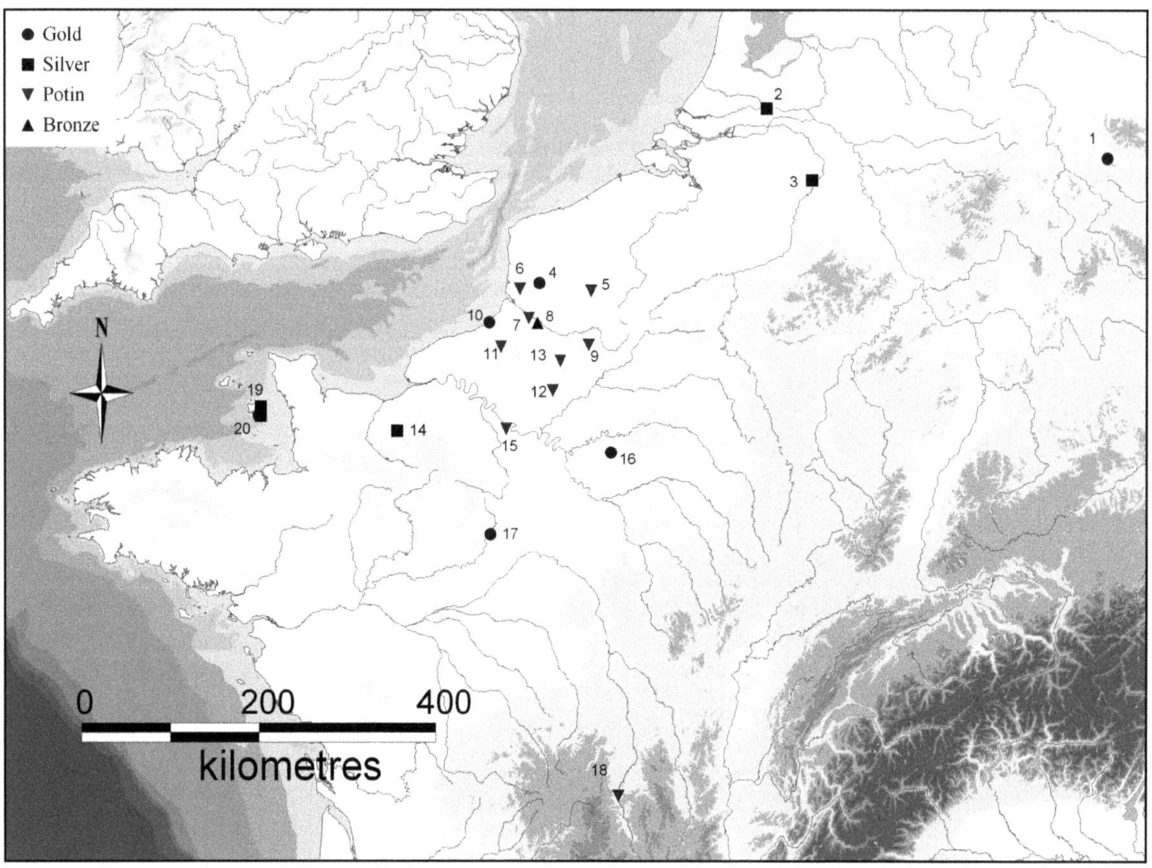

Fig. 2.10. Continental sites with British Celtic coins c. 120-20 BC (see Appendix 1).

Given the relatively abundant evidence for imports, many of which, in south-central England at least, arrived through trade, we must consider that a much wider range of exports actually left Britain for the continent, but that they are archaeologically undetectable. Insight into these may be gained from Strabo's list of British exports, written c. AD 18.[124] Alongside gold, silver and iron he lists grain, cattle, hides, slaves and hunting dogs, which are all archaeologically invisible.

Ports

There are a number of coastal settlements with evidence for long-distance exchange in south-central England around the Solent coast. Of greatest importance is Hengistbury Head which, as I have discussed, possesses a wide range of imported material which arrived via northern Brittany.[125] This appears to have been Britain's primary point of contact with the continent in the Atlantic system. Several other ports with smaller quantities of imported goods will probably have received them direct from Brittany as well, though we cannot rule out that they received them indirectly via Hengistbury Head.[126] Imported wine amphorae, pottery and coins have been found around Poole Harbour in Dorset.[127] There is also evidence for port infrastructure here, with two moles, of 160 m and 55 m long, constructed from tree trunk piles with layers of clay, sand, flint rubble and brushwood and a surface of stone slabs.[128] Radiocarbon dates from the piles support a construction date of c. 250-200 BC. Other coastal sites with somewhat limited evidence for long-distance exchange are Mount Batten in Devon, from which small quantities of Breton pottery and coins have been identified, and the Isle of Portland in Dorset, which has imported iron ingots and coins.[129]

In contrast, in southeast Britain there is no evidence for any specialist port infrastructure which might have encouraged or facilitated shipping. Indeed, as Stephen Willis has noted, there appears to have been a general avoidance of settlement in coastal regions in the Late Iron Age, although there is evidence, primarily in the form of Gallo-Belgic and native coin finds, for settlement on the Isle of Thanet in eastern Kent.[130] External contacts were probably mediated through sites all around Britain's southeast coast, though on present evidence we must assume that these would have been basic landing places, perhaps far up rivers, or on beaches.

Synthesis

In contrast to the Middle Iron Age there is substantial evidence for exchange between Britain and the continent from the mid- to late second century onwards. In all probability this does relate to a real upturn in the intensity of contacts, although, as Barry Cunliffe has pointed out, we should bear in mind that this picture may be distorted by the appearance of archaeologically detectable exchange items, such as coins and wine amphorae, which allow us to trace exchange networks that may already have existed, but hitherto were invisible.[131]

Two distinct maritime exchange systems are visible, one encompassing the waters of the Southern North Sea and Eastern Channel, the other the waters of the Western Channel and the Atlantic.[132] The first of these systems is principally evidenced by gold Gallo-Belgic coins, minted in northern France, which entered Britain in large quantities from c. 175/150 BC down to c. 50 BC, with a particularly sizeable influx around the time of the Gallic wars. These coins should be interpreted as payments made for political and social purposes, although they may have had a range of secondary functions including use in trade. One of the main political and social reasons lying behind the payments was probably attempts by individuals and groups from northern France to secure the support of individuals and groups from southeast Britain in military conflicts taking place on the near continent. Certainly, Gallo-Belgic E and D can very plausibly be explained as payments made in the context of the Gallic wars. A handful of coins minted in southeast Britain made their way to the near continent, particularly northern France. A range of possible explanations could lie behind their appearance, including trade or political or social payments, but their small quantity means that they could simply have moved with people as personal possessions. There is practically no archaeological evidence for ports along the southeast British coast and connections between southeast Britain and northern France will almost certainly have been effected via numerous small coastal landing places, or up rivers, such as the Thames.

The Atlantic system is characterised by a group of imports to the coastal regions of south-central Britain, and to a lesser extent the coast of southwest Britain. These imports included Italian Dr.1A wine amphorae, and pottery and gold and silver coins from Brittany, which came to Britain from the late second century BC down to c. 60/50 BC. They were all evidently transferred to Britain via Brittany and trade is the best explanation for their appearance, although political and social payments, or gift exchange cannot be ruled out entirely. The British exports traded in return are almost entirely archaeologically invisible, though tin, slaves and agricultural products are plausible suggestions. The clearest example of a coastal port in south-central Britain is Hengistbury Head in Dorset, which has a sizeable import assemblage. This site may have played the dominant role in articulating exchange between south-central Britain and Brittany in the Atlantic system, though several other coastal sites along the south-central British coast possess imported material and were probably in direct contact with Brittany as well.

124 *Geog.* IV.5.2.
125 Cunliffe 1987.
126 Cunliffe 2004, 3-4.
127 Cunliffe and de Jersey 1997.
128 Markey *et al.* 2002.
129 Cunliffe and de Jersey 1997; Cunliffe 1988b; Taylor 2001.
130 Willis 2007; Holman 2005; Hamilton 2007.
131 Cunliffe 2009.
132 Cunliffe 2009.

The determinants of connective change

In the past it has been argued that there was a migration of people from northern France into southeast England during the Late Iron Age.[133] If this event really did occur then it must have had an important role in underlying the fairly strong connections across the Southern North Sea and Eastern Channel from the second century BC onwards. Historical evidence has been used to support the notion of a Belgic migration; Caesar wrote that the coastal areas of Britain were inhabited by Belgic invaders, who had initially come to the island to make war and plunder, but later settled, whilst the tribes of the interior were, in contrast, indigenous.[134] Caesar also recorded that within living memory, Diviciacus, a ruler of the Suessiones from northern France, had held control over large parts of Belgica and Britain.[135] Cassius Dio stated, in reference to Caesar's campaigns, that the Belgae dwelt near the Rhine and extended across the Ocean to Britain.[136] There are also very strong links evident in the pottery styles and burial rites of northern France and southeast Britain from c. 100/75 BC onwards.[137]

In recent times, however, the idea of a Belgic migration has been rejected. The historical and archaeological evidence previously used to support it have been reinterpreted in terms of political and social inter-change which occurred in the absence of large-scale, violent population movements.[138] Whether we should completely rule out violence and warfare as important factors in later prehistory is perhaps somewhat questionable and we should bear in mind the possibility that the conquest of parts of southeast Britain by groups from northern France, or population movements from northern France to southeast Britain, may in fact have occurred.

A factor which probably did have an important role in determining the nature of contacts across the Southern North Sea and Eastern Channel during the Late Iron Age was population expansion in southeast Britain. Throughout much of southeast Britain, including Hertfordshire, Essex, Bedfordshire, southern Cambridgeshire and parts of Kent, there is very little archaeological evidence for settlement during the Middle Iron Age c. 300-100 BC, though we should bear in mind that this may have been partly related to the contemporary archaeological invisibility of settlement structures. During the course of the Late Iron Age archaeological evidence for occupation in these regions increases substantially.[139] If we follow contemporary opinion amongst Iron Age scholars and reject the possibility that this increase was due to population movements from northern France then it is best accounted for by an influx of people from surrounding regions of Britain, although population expansion amongst the pre-existing local populations, who are hard to detect archaeologically, is a further possibility.[140]

Warfare and unrest in northern Gaul throughout the second and the first half of the first centuries BC may have been a reason underlying the payments of gold coin from northern France into southeast Britain. As we have discussed (see pp. 10-13), these payments were principally made in order to strengthen social and political ties, and probably helped secure aid from British groups in warfare on the near continent. The precise conflicts are largely unknown to us, though there are several historical references that hint at violence in northern Gaul prior to the Gallic wars.[141] The Gallic wars themselves appear to have directly led to a major transfer of gold (Gallo-Belgic E and D) from northern France to Britain.

Another factor underpinning connective change in the Southern North Sea and Eastern Channel system was the growth in gold mining in central France which directly underlay the increasing appearance of gold coinages in Gaul. The gold deposits of Limousin in the Massif Central were exploited on a considerable scale from the fourth century BC onwards, but there was a major expansion of activity, involving large-scale open-cast mining, during the second and first centuries BC.[142]

The increasing trade apparent in the Atlantic system from the later second century BC onwards was principally stimulated by contemporary economic and political expansion in the Roman world. There appears to have been a sizeable increase in Italian wine production during the second century BC, which is evidenced through an examination of amphorae on Mediterranean shipwrecks. Greco-Italic amphorae, which were produced between c. 350-130 BC, are present on sixty-nine wrecks, whilst Dr.1A amphorae, which were produced during the shorter period c. 150-75/50 BC, have been identified on fifty-four.[143] Southern France was annexed as a Roman province (Gallia Transalpina) in c. 124-121 BC and this appears to have catalysed trade between Italy and southwestern France. Trade along the Atlantic seaways of France, extending up to south-central Britain, linked indirectly into these developing trade networks and was stimulated by them.[144]

A final reason for increasing connectivity in both the Southern North Sea and Eastern Channel system and in the Atlantic system may have been improvements in shipping technology, though assessments of prehistoric shipping technology must be extremely tentative due to

---

[133] Hawkes and Dunning, 1931; Allen 1960; Evans 1890; Hawkes 1931; 1968; Rodwell 1976; see: Cunliffe 2005; Burnett 1996.

[134] *B.G.* V.12.

[135] *B.G.* II.4.

[136] Cassius Dio *Historia Romana.* 39.1.

[137] Hill 2007, 26, 28, Tab. 2; Hawkes and Dunning 1931, Fig. 7; Cunliffe 2005, 149-152, Fig. 7.1; 2009.

[138] Cunliffe 2004; 2005; 2009; Hill 2007.

[139] Hill 2007; Bryant and Niblett 2001, 109-110; Bryant 2007; Hamilton 2007.

[140] Hill 2007.

[141] Caesar *B.G.* I.1, 28-54, II.3-4, 8, 15, 17, VI. 2, 24, VII.59, VIII.6; Strabo *Geog.* 4.4.3.

[142] Cauuet 1995; 2004; Cauuet *et al.* 1999.

[143] Parker 1992, 17; Loughton 2003.

[144] Cunliffe 1984a; 1988a; 2005, 600-601; Fitzpatrick 1989; Woolf 1993b; Loughton 2009, 78-80.

the limited archaeological evidence for prehistoric shipping in British waters.

The two main archaeologically attested boat types in use in the waters around the British Isles during prehistory were logboats and sewn-plank vessels.[145] There has been debate over the ability of such ships to conduct open sea voyages.[146] Boats constructed in this manner would probably have been best suited to riverine, estuarine or fairly short coastal voyages. As McGrail points out, there is no evidence that these vessels were propelled by any means other than paddling and their shape, lack of sheer and structure did not allow sufficient stability, freeboard and sea-kindliness for long open sea voyages.[147]
A further type of boat, which is harder to detect archaeologically, is the hide boat. This has been recorded by classical writers apparently relying upon Pytheas, who voyaged in British waters during the fourth century BC, and may well have been in use long before this date.[148] Boats constructed in this manner could be fairly seaworthy, but were limited in size due to the structural weakness of hides. Hide boats continued in use throughout the Later Iron Age; there is a gold model from Broighter, dateable to the first century BC, which certainly represents such a vessel.[149] There are also references to British hide boats by Classical authors from the mid-first century BC through to the third century AD.[150]

The Broighter model carries a sail, which, together with Caesar's description of the Venetic fleet, represents our earliest evidence for the use of sail in the waters of northwest Europe.[151] Given the poverty of evidence it is unclear whether the sail was a development of the first century BC. Most likely it was adopted in Atlantic waters following visits from Phoenician and other Mediterranean sailed vessels earlier in the first millennium BC.[152] The increasing application of this technology to native craft at the end of the first millennium BC may have contributed to an increase in the scale of maritime voyaging.

There was another change in shipping technology, which can probably be dated to the end of the first millennium BC, though the poverty of ships in the archaeological record makes this by no means certain. This concerns the appearance of sailed, iron-fastened, plank-built boats. These are first evidenced in Caesar's description of the Venetic fleet.[153] Such vessels are also attested from iconographic evidence and are depicted on first-century BC coins of the Atrebates from northern France and, slightly later, on early first-century AD bronze coins of Cunobelin, minted at Camulodunum, single examples of which have been identified at Camulodunum-Sheepen and at ten sites in East Kent (see cover image).[154] These represent the first attested examples of the so-called 'Romano-Celtic' ship type, which endured throughout the Roman period. This vessel type was evidently extremely seaworthy and had a large capacity and their development may well have played an important role in the increasing maritime connectivity evident at this time.[155]

2.2. The Eastern North Sea system

Introduction

In contrast to the Southern North Sea and the Channel there is very little evidence for contemporary long-distance maritime exchange occurring via the Eastern North Sea. Long-distance exchange was directed overland through central European 'intra-Germanic' gift exchange networks, but even these were of a small-scale nature. The explanation for the limited exchange in the Eastern North Sea system can in part be related to a previous phase of marine transgression, which meant settlement was absent along much of the northwest German coast. A limited shipping technology may also have played a role.

Imports to the Eastern North Sea coastal region

There are a few 'imported' copper-alloy vessels, present in northwest German and Scandinavian graves dated c. 150-1 BC **(Fig. 2.11)**. These include a number of bronze cauldrons with iron rims (Eggers type E4-6), which were probably produced in eastern France or southern Germany where finds appear to concentrate.[156] Several of these have been encountered in graves along the lower Elbe, dated, on the basis of associated native brooches, to the early to mid-first century BC.[157] Vessels of Italic manufacture (E18-22) are also present in the lower Elbe region. These occur in graves of the mid-first century BC, which are apparently chronologically distinct from and later than the earlier E4-6 horizon.[158] 'Imported' copper-alloy vessels are rare in Scandinavia, although examples are known from a few sites.[159]

On the basis of their distribution it is highly probable that these vessels arrived via overland routes through Central Europe. 'Intra-Germanic' gift exchange networks are the

[145] Examples of the former vessel include the Brigg logboat of c. 1000 BC and the Hasholme logboat of c. 300 BC (McGrail 1981, 248-9; 1990; 2001, 172-180; 2004, 59; Millett and McGrail 1987; Roberts 2004, 40). Prehistoric sewn-plank boats have been found at Caldicot (c. 1880-1690 BC), Kilnsea (1870-1670 BC), Dover (c. 1575-1520 BC), Ferriby (four vessels ranging in date between c. 1440/1310-410/350 BC), Goldcliff (c. 1000 BC) and Brigg (c. 820-790 BC) (McGrail 1990; 2001, 184-194; Van der Noort 2003, 2004a; Bayliss *et al.* 2004; Marsden 2004).
[146] McGrail 1990; 2001, 184-194; Van der Noort 2003; 2004a; Bayliss *et al.* 2004; Marsden 2004.
[147] McGrail 2001, 193-194.
[148] Pliny *H.N.* 4.104; Avienus *Ora Maritima*.
[149] McGrail 1990, 36-39; 2001, 181-183; Cunliffe 2009.
[150] Caesar *Bello Civili*. 1.54; Pliny *H.N.* VII.205-206; Cassius Dio *Historia Romana*. 48.18-19; Lucan *Pharsalia*. 4.130-138; Salinus *Polyhistor*. 2.3.
[151] *B.G.* III.13.
[152] Cunliffe 2009; McGrail 2001, 181-183, 196, 206-207.
[153] *B.G.* III.13; Strabo *Geog.* 4.4.1.
[154] Tomalin 2006, 35-36, Fig.4; McGrail 1990, 43-44.
[155] McGrail 1990, 44-46; 2001, 196-207; Cunliffe 2009.
[156] Wells 1994, 152; Erdrich 2001, 38-41; Hachmann 1990, 649-657.
[157] Laux, 1995; 85; Erdrich 2001, 38-41.
[158] Laux 1995, 85; Erdrich 2001, 41-42.
[159] Lund Hansen 1987, 126; Kunow 1983, Karte. 2; Wells 1994.

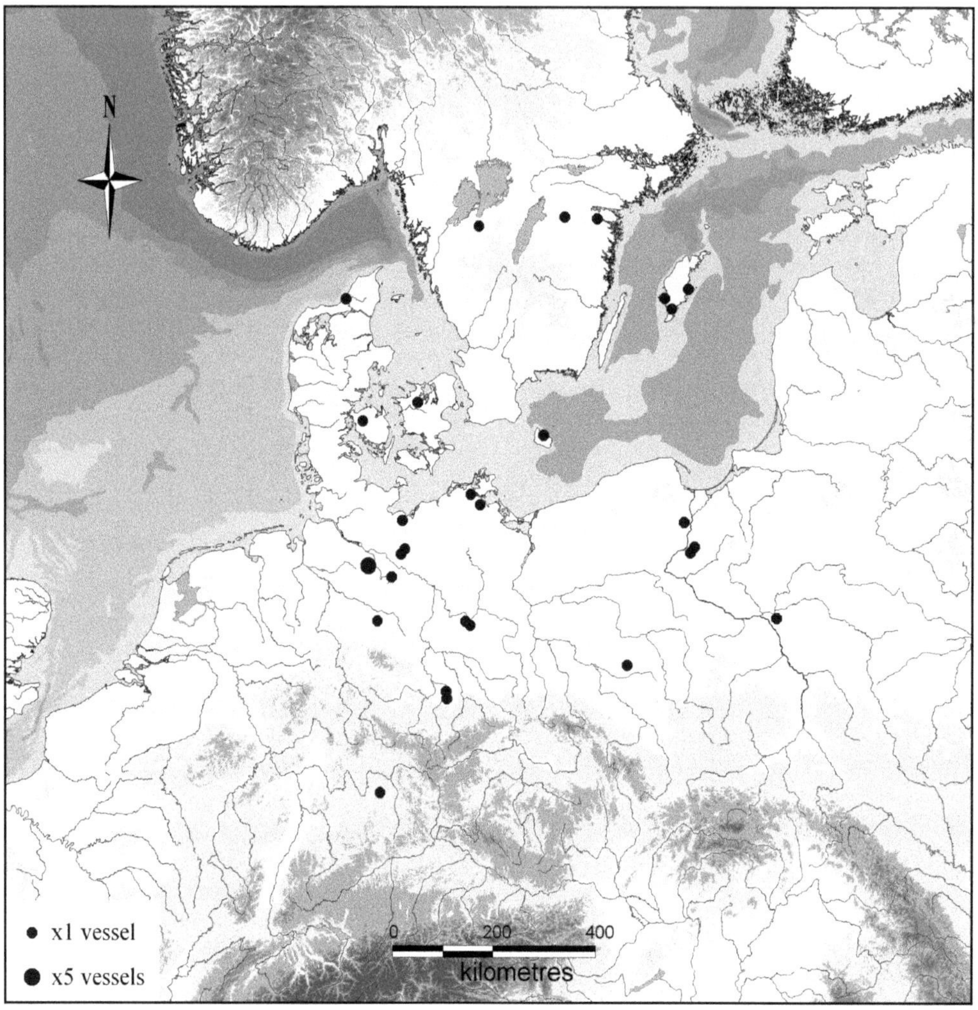

Fig. 2.11. Distribution of imported copper-alloy vessels in northern Europe c. 150-1 BC (after Kunow 1983, Karte 2).

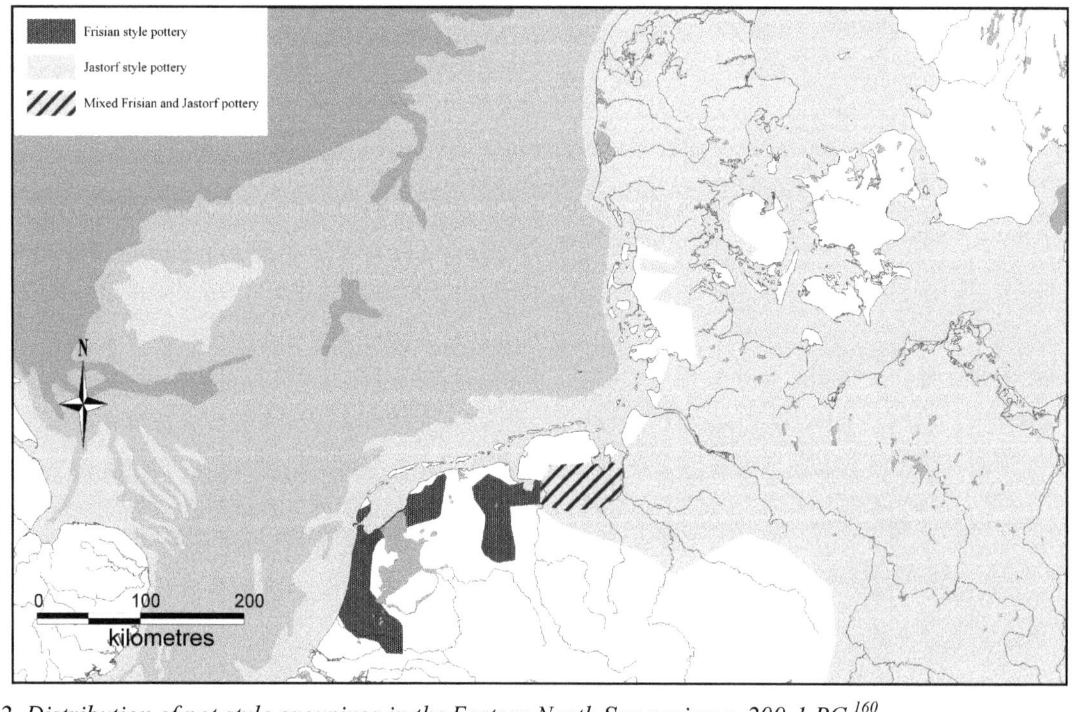

Fig. 2.12. Distribution of pot style groupings in the Eastern North Sea region c. 200-1 BC.[160]

[160] Data from: Taayke 1997, Abb. 5; Müller 2000, Abb. 2.

most plausible explanation for their appearance.[161] Certainly, the widespread distribution of contemporary Jastorf style pottery implies strong cultural connections across a wide area of Central and Northern Europe, which would almost certainly have been reinforced through the movement of people and objects (**Fig. 2.12**). The copper-alloy vessels may have initially entered these exchange networks as a result of peaceful interaction and exchange, though violent acquisition through warfare is a further strong possibility for which there is some historical record.[162] The Cimbi and Teutoni, who were probably of Danish origin, pillaged first Noricum and then Gaul, Spain and northern Italy at the end of the second century BC.[163] Caesar also records that 120,000 Germans from east of the Rhine had crossed this river and settled in eastern France in the years preceding his initial Gallic campaign of 58 BC.[164]

Other possible 'imports' include a small group of ornate copper-alloy cauldrons and display wagons from Denmark.[165] It is often argued that these were imported from 'Celtic' areas in southern Germany, but there is no reason why they could not have been local products. In any case they do not imply maritime links. The second- or first-century BC silver cauldron from Gundestrup in southern Jutland was probably of Thracian origin and, once again, would have travelled overland through Central Europe, either through gift exchange or as war booty obtained during the raids of the Cimbri and Teutoni.[166] A silver/billon stater of the Coriosolites, a tribe from northern Brittany, dated to c. 80 BC, was found at Bockhorn on the coast of Lower Saxony.[167] This is perhaps our only evidence of a long-distance maritime import from this phase. How and why it reached its destination is very hard to explain.

Exports from the Eastern North Sea region

Amber

There are several minor amber sources across Europe, in Romania, the Czech Republic, Poland and Sicily. However, the major accessible source is Baltic amber, which derives from an ancient forest which once grew on land, but now lies beneath the Baltic Sea. Deposits of Baltic amber are chemically indistinguishable from one another, although they can be distinguished from other types of amber. The main source of Baltic amber, and indeed the world's primary amber deposit, is located off the coast of the Samland peninsula and its surrounding bays in the eastern Baltic. Here amber is washed up on beaches in considerable amounts after winter storms, whilst in recent centuries it has also been mined and dredged from the seabed.[168] Amber is also encountered elsewhere in the Baltic and on the North Sea coast of Jutland. Small quantities can also be gathered from the beaches of northwest Germany and the northern Netherlands.[169] Amber is occasionally washed ashore on eastern Britain; during the nineteenth century, when large quantities of seaweed were collected from the Norfolk and Suffolk coasts for use as fertiliser, amber fragments were often recovered, several weighing over 0.5 kg.[170]

I have conducted a survey of the amber from Iron Age sites in Britain dated c. 800 BC-AD 43. There are forty-three amber objects, all beads, from nineteen sites of Iron Age date, located throughout the island (**Fig. 2.13**, Appendix 3). Obtaining more specific dates is difficult, but a total of five beads from five sites could be dated more closely to the Later Iron Age (175/150 BC-AD 43). Of these only a bead from Crosskirk broch in Scotland can probably be placed specifically in the period 175/150-50 BC, though several beads from the Middle to Late Iron Age Arras culture cemeteries in Yorkshire might also belong to this phase.[171] There is no survey of Iron Age amber in the regions of continental northwest Europe to the south and west of the Rhine, though amber does occasionally occur in this region; for example, a necklace of ten amber beads was found in a burial dated to around the end of the second century BC at Bois de Wérimont in Belgium.[172]

The amount of Iron Age amber known from Britain is very small. Many of these finds, including those from Scotland, probably derived from amber washed up on the British coast. Some material could have been 'imported' from the Eastern North Sea coast across the North Sea, although it may have arrived indirectly via the Low Countries or northern France. A possible mechanism for this might be low-level gift exchange, or the small scale movement of people. We should also bear in mind that during the Iron Age there was an important amber exchange route linking the eastern Baltic to central and southern Europe.[173] Some of the amber found in Britain need not have arrived from Eastern North Sea regions at all, but could have come indirectly from France, having ultimately travelled via the central European route.

Other exports

Aside from the extremely limited evidence for amber, one can only point to a handful of belt hooks of northwest German origin, which have been found south and west of the Rhine and may have travelled via the Eastern North Sea. These include an example from the Eastern River area of the Netherlands around Nijmegen, whilst a series of locally made beltplates from this region display strong stylistic links to the northwest German examples and

[161] Fitzpatrick 1993; Wells 1994, 157.
[162] C.f. Erdrich 2001, 77-79.
[163] Plutarch *Parallel Lives. Life of Marius*. 11-27; Florus *Epitome*. XXXVIII; Caesar. *B.G.* I.33.
[164] *B.G.* I.31-54.
[165] Hedeager 1992a, 43-45; Wells 1994.
[166] Taylor 1992; Bergquist and Taylor 1987.
[167] Berger 1985, 207-8; 1992, 35-36, Abb. 17.
[168] Beck and Shennan 1991, 16-19, 37; Lambert *et al.* 1988; Grimaldi 1996; Waterbolk and Waterbolk 1991.
[169] Waterbolk and Waterbolk 1991.
[170] Beck and Shennan 1991; Reid 1884; Foord 1890.
[171] Appendix 3. Objects Nos. 2-9, 41.
[172] Mariën 1980, 24, Fig. 4.
[173] Guštin 1996.

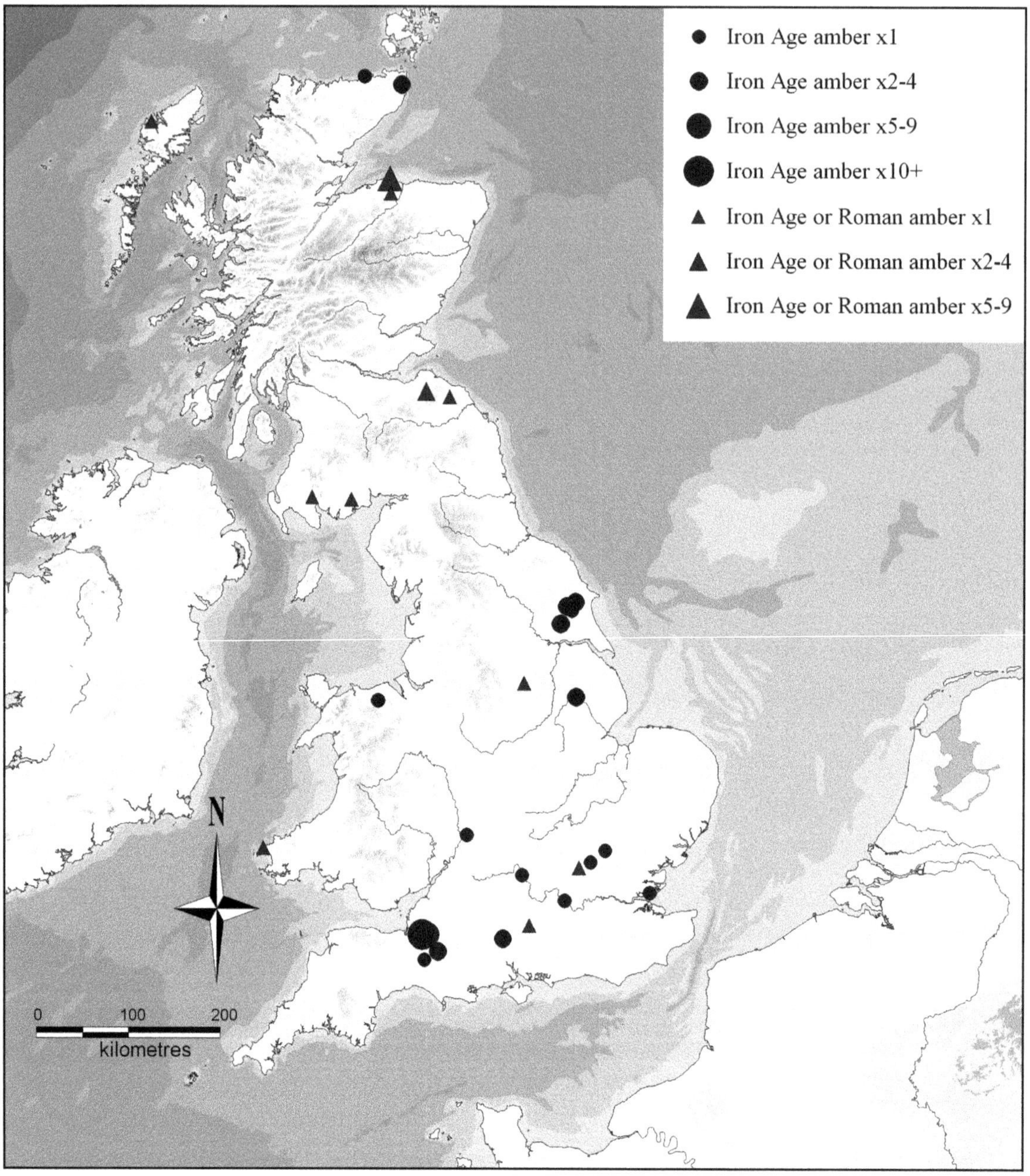

Fig. 2.13. Distribution of amber in Britain dating to the Iron Age (c. 800 BC-AD 43).

imply some degree of cultural contact, perhaps involving the transfer of people between the two areas.[174]

Synthesis

Archaeologically visible long-distance maritime exchange was extremely limited in the Eastern North Sea system between 175/150-50 BC. We can point to only a handful of objects which may in fact have moved via the North Sea: a silver billon coin from northern Brittany found on the northwest German coast, a beltplate of north German origin identified in the Eastern River area of the Netherlands and perhaps a few objects of amber found in Britain and Belgium. The long-distance transmission of objects, particularly copper-alloy vessels, via central European 'intra-Germanic' gift exchange networks was somewhat more common, but still very small-scale.

The determinants of connectivity

Sea level change

Since the beginning of the Holcene period and the rapid rise in sea-levels that accompanied the end of the Ice Age, the flat, low-lying coastal regions of the Eastern North Sea coast have been heavily influenced by a series of marine transgressions and regressions. In the northern Netherlands there was uninterrupted settlement from c. 600 BC until at least the late third century AD. The beginning of this settlement can be correlated with the onset of a marine regression from c. 800 BC, which allowed the coastal areas to be inhabited and flat settlements, such as Ezinge, to appear. In addition, the

[174] Roymans 2004, 113-118, Fig. 7.6; Ebel 1990.

salt marshes in parts of the northern Netherlands witnessed continuous expansion throughout the Late Iron Age and Roman period, owing to the long-term erosion of the former peat area in the western Wadden Sea.[175]

A phase of marine transgression (Dunkirk Ib) occurred c. 400 BC, according to dates obtained through C14 and pollen analysis of peat deposits from northwest Germany. The evidence suggests a strong and rapid sea level rise of c. 2.2 m, which is accompanied by the abandonment of settlement along the northwest German coast. In the northern Netherlands settlement continued, though artificial settlement mounds were built to cope with these rises and the associated risk of winter storm surges and flooding.[176]

From c. 150 BC, a regression phase began, which resulted in a fall in sea level, measured at c. 1.25 m. This regression facilitated the gradual re-inhabitation of the northwest German coastal region. Settlements on the Pleistocene area of the Elbe-Weser triangle, such as Flögeln and the Heidenschanze have occupation evidence dating back to c. 100 BC. The earliest evidence for flat settlements on the coastal marshes, meanwhile, dates to c. 50 BC, as at Feddersen Wierde. In Schleswig-Holstein the reoccupation of the coastal region was even slower, only beginning in the first century AD.[177]

The decline in sea level from c. 150 BC onwards thus facilitated the gradual colonization of the north German coastal region and possibly contributed to an expansion of settlement in the northern Netherlands.[178] This is of considerable importance to understanding connectivity in the Eastern North Sea system, as an increasing coastal population leads to a greater potential for maritime contacts. Whilst the regression began during this period, the expansion of settlement into the coastal regions was, however, a gradual process which continued into the following period. The impacts of this event upon maritime connectivity in the Eastern North Sea system were not immediately apparent, but very likely facilitated the increasing scale of exchange observable in the subsequent Roman period.

Shipping technology

Our evidence for prehistoric shipping technology in the waters of the Eastern North Sea coast suggests the existence of two main boat types: logboats, and sewn-plank boats. Examples of prehistoric logboats include Øgårde 3 (c. 3190 BC) and Verup I (c. 2770 BC) from Amose in Denmark.[179] The best example of a sewn-plank boat comes from the weapon deposit at Hjortspring, on Als in the Danish part of Schleswig, which was apparently laid down c. 350 BC. This would have accommodated ten paddlers on each side with a total crew of perhaps twenty-three. It bears a close resemblance to examples on Bronze Age rock carvings found throughout Scandinavia, which suggests that this technology developed much earlier. It was quite suitable for short, fair-weather, coastal voyages and a reconstructed vessel can cover c. 100 km on a long day's voyage in good conditions.[180] In contrast to the waters of the Southern North Sea, the Channel and the Atlantic, there is no evidence for the use of sail at this time and paddling would have been the main form of propulsion. Our earliest clear evidence for the use of sail in the native shipping traditions of northern Europe dates to the seventh century AD and comes from the Gotland picture stones, whilst our earliest excavated sailing vessels date to the eighth century AD.[181]

There is little evidence for any clear changes in shipping technology in northern waters during the period currently under consideration. Several boats dating to the Pre-Roman and Early Roman periods (c. 150 BC-AD 165) have been identified in northwest Germany, but these are almost all small dugout log boats, the largest of which would have been suitable for short coastal voyages.[182] These 'technologically limited' shipping traditions may help explain the apparently low levels of connectivity observed in the Eastern North Sea system during the Late Iron Age.

2.3. Maritime systems 175/150-50 BC: a comparison

A stark contrast is thus evident between the Southern North Sea and Channel systems and the Eastern North Sea system. Sizeable increases in connectivity are observed in both the Southern North Sea and Eastern Channel system and the Atlantic system from the mid- to late second century BC onwards. For the Atlantic system this can be related to the contemporary political and economic expansion of the Roman world. The growth of connectivity within the Southern North Sea and Eastern Channel system had more to do with 'non-Roman' factors, such as population increase in southeast Britain, a possible increase in warfare in northern Gaul and an expansion of gold mining in central Gaul. The overall growth in connectivity apparent in both these systems was probably also aided by the development of increasingly seaworthy ships and improved maritime technology, including the sail, towards the end of the first millennium BC.

The Eastern North Sea system is virtually bereft of evidence for long-distance maritime connectivity. This is in part due to the avoidance of North Sea coastal routes in favour of overland routes through Central Europe, though the lack of settlement in some coastal regions of the Eastern North Sea, due to an earlier phase of marine transgression, and a very limited shipping technology probably contributed as well. Having said this, the

[175] Dubois 1924; Behre 2004; 2007; Taayke 1997; Vos 1999.
[176] Behre 2004; 2007.
[177] Behre 2004; 2007; Schmid and Schuster 1999.
[178] Behre 2004; 2007; Taayke 1997.
[179] Christensen 1990; McGrail 2001.
[180] Kaul 2003; 2004; McGrail 2001, 191-192.
[181] McGrail 2001, 211-212.
[182] Teigelake 2006.

connectivity observable in these overland Central European routes is low and certainly not on the scale of the maritime links across the Southern North Sea and Channel. A broader explanation for this could be a cultural separation and an unwillingness, or inability, to participate in exchange relations with the regions in Mediterranean Europe and Central France, which were undergoing rapid economic expansion at this time.

3. North Sea and Channel connectivity 50 BC-AD 43

3.1. The Southern North Sea and Channel systems

Introduction

There was a considerable growth in connectivity in the Southern North Sea and Eastern Channel system in the aftermath of the Gallic wars, particularly from the late first century BC onwards. Some gold and silver entered southeast Britain as a result of payments made by the Roman state to British client rulers. A wide range of products, including wine, pottery, copper-alloy objects, olive oil and fish products, were imported to southeast Britain through trade in return for largely archaeologically undetectable British products, such as gold, silver, iron, agricultural products and perhaps salt and oysters. The principal determinants of this growth were the onset of client kingship relations between Rome and southeast Britain in the aftermath of the Gallic wars, the permanent presence of a large Roman army in northwest Europe from c. 16/13 BC onwards and economic growth in the Western provinces of the Empire.

The thriving trade networks of the Atlantic system which characterised the pre-Gallic war period were disrupted by the events of the Gallic wars and subsequently appear to have been somewhat peripheral to developments affecting the Southern North Sea and Eastern Channel system. Despite this, there is clear evidence for limited Atlantic trade during the second half of the first century BC and the early first century AD.

Continental imports

Coinage and metals

Following the Gallic wars very few precious metal coins produced by native groups on the continent reached Britain. There is, however, a notable group of imported 'Gallo-Belgic' bronze coins (over 300 have now been recorded) from southeast Britain. These coins date largely to the mid- to late first century BC and they appear to concentrate in Kent, Hertfordshire and around Chichester Harbour.[183] They presumably arrived through market trade.

[183] De Jersey 2006.

The only direct evidence relating to the import of gold from the Roman Empire to Britain concerns a handful of gold finger rings and bracelets, such as examples from the hoard at Alton in Hampshire that also contains Atrebatic staters dating to the early first century AD.[184] There is, however, indirect evidence that a considerable amount of gold was reaching southeast Britain from the Empire, but almost all of this was remelted and used for the manufacture of native British coinages.

Substantial gold coinages were issued in southeast Britain; estimates provided by Derek Allen, concerning the number of coin dies and the likely output of these dies, suggest that in the Hertfordshire-Essex region (the 'Eastern Kingdom') c. 1,000,000 gold coins were issued during the reign of Cunobelin (c. AD 10-40) that equate to c. 1,000 kg of fine gold.[185] Meanwhile, the coinage of Verica, his contemporary in East Sussex and Hampshire (the 'Southern Kingdom'), equates to c. 330 kg (**Fig. 3.1**).[186] The great majority of the gold used in these coinages probably derived from earlier imports of Gallo-Belgic coins.[187] Indeed, as discussed above (see pp. 12-13), the output of Gallo-Belgic E, which reached Britain in large quantities, probably approached c. 6,000 kg of fine gold. Metallurgical analyses indicate, however, that Gallo-Belgic coins were probably not the source of all of the inscribed coinages issued in Britain from the mid-first century BC onwards. The gold content of many coins from the Eastern Kingdom was mostly maintained between 39-41% gold, whilst other elements in the coins, such as copper and silver varied with little discernable pattern. This must have been achieved through the use of refined gold that was mixed with a variable copper-silver alloy. In all likelihood the source of this refined gold would have been the Roman Empire; the contemporary Roman gold coinage was c. 99% fine.[188]

There are indications that gold imports from the Empire may have increased as this period progressed;

[184] Abdy 2002, Fig. 3.
[185] Allen 1975. The best guide to the various Iron Age coinages of Britain is Rudd *et al.* Forthcoming. See also: Cunliffe 2005 and Van Arsdell 1989.
[186] Allen and Haselgrove 1979.
[187] John Sills, pers. Comm. 2010.
[188] Cowell 1992; Northover 1992, 239-253, Fig. 5.

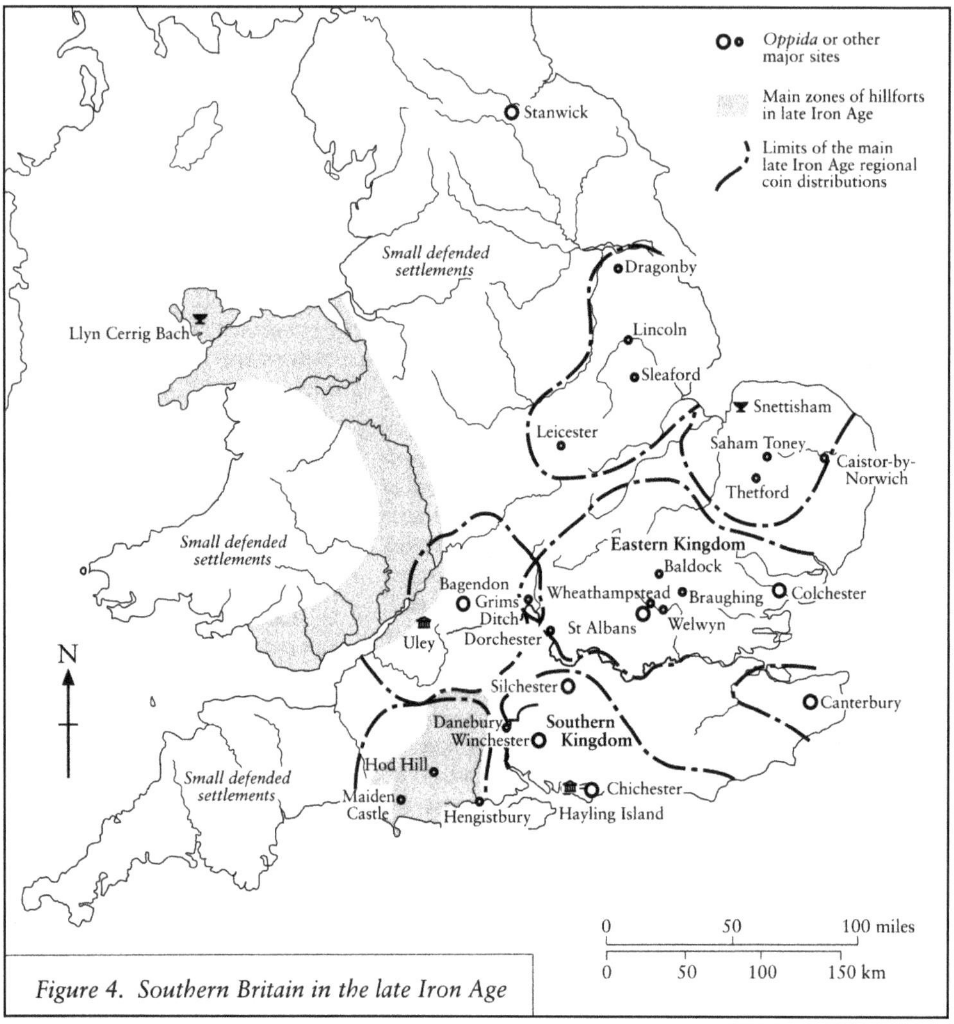

Fig. 3.1. Southern Britain in the Later Iron Age (Mattingly 2006, Fig. 4).

Fitzpatrick has noted that the earlier coins of Cunobelin, which were issued over perhaps fifteen years, equate to around two-thirds of the previous British dynastic series that were issued over a period of perhaps twice the length. Furthermore, the later issues of Cunobelin outnumber the earlier issues by c. 2:1, while on settlement sites Cunobelin's coins outnumber pre-Cunobelin coins by c. 3:1.[189]

Republican and early Imperial silver *denarii*, all minted at Rome, are well known from Britain. Most of these early *denarii* arrived in Britain after the Roman conquest. Indeed, Republican *denarii* were only specifically targeted by the state for remelting, due to their slightly higher precious metal content, during the reign of Trajan and prior to his reign they still formed a large proportion of the coin in circulation; Hoards deposited in the late first and early second centuries AD still typically contain c. 30-40% Republican issues.[190] However, Robertson's corpus of Roman coin hoards from Britain lists several *denarii* hoards that close with Republican or early Imperial issues.[191] There is a strong case for at least some of these hoards arriving in Britain prior to the Claudian invasion, although many scholars have assigned them to the early post-conquest phase.[192] Our clearest example of *denarii* in pre-conquest Britain is the East Leicestershire hoard, which contains c. 5,000 native British coins dating down to the early first century AD and includes well over 100 Republican and early Imperial *denarii*, along with a silver-gilded Roman cavalry helmet.[193] Aside from *denarii*, silver moved into Britain from the Empire in other forms; three silver vessels have been found in graves at Welwyn dated to the mid- to late first century BC.[194]

On the basis of metallurgical analyses, the native silver coinages that were increasingly struck in southeast Britain during the later first century BC were probably based on *denarii*, or other forms of silver, deriving from the Roman Empire.[195] The silver coinages of the Eastern and Southern Kingdoms are typically more than 96% fine, and silver of this quality was probably obtained

[189] Fitzpatrick 1992, 27.
[190] Abdy 2002, 19-21; Reece 2002, 17; Robertson 2000.
[191] Robertson 2000.
[192] Robertson 2000; Abdy 2002; Reece 2002.
[193] Hill *et al.* 2006.
[194] Smith 1912; Stead 1967, 21-23, 47.
[195] De Jersey 2001, 11; Northover 1992.

from the Empire where contemporary *denarii* were largely better than 95% pure.

Most of the gold and silver that came to southeast Britain from the Roman world can be explained in terms of political payments made by the Roman state to British client kings. Classical historical sources provide us with hints of the existence of political relations between Britain and Rome following Caesar's invasions of 55-54 BC. Caesar stated that he received hostages and payments of tribute from the British tribes.[196] Strabo, probably writing c. AD 18, noted that he had personally observed Britons in Rome and that Britons had been in Rome to pay court to Augustus, to establish embassies and to set up dedications at the Capitol.[197] Two British rulers are recorded as having fled to Augustus on the *Res Gestae*, whilst Adminius, who had been banished by his father Cunobelin, surrendered to Caligula during his abortive invasion attempt in AD 40.[198] In addition, one of the recorded motivations for Claudius's invasion of Britain was persuasion by a Briton named Bericus, who had been driven out of the island by an uprising.[199]

The iconography of the British Late Iron Age coinage, recently studied in detail by John Creighton, provides even stronger testament to the existence of direct political relationships between Rome and southeast Britain.[200] During the latter part of the Late Iron Age there were two main coin-issuing authorities in southeast Britain. First, the Southern Kingdom, whose coin distribution centres in Hampshire and Sussex, and second the Eastern Kingdom that has a coin distribution focused on Essex and Hertfordshire.[201] From c. 20 BC onwards dramatic iconographical changes occurred on the coinages of southeast Britain. Previously, during the second and first centuries BC, there were only very gradual changes in coin imagery, but from this date the changes were immense. The first coins bearing the legends of rulers in Latin script (in this case Commius) appeared in the southern kingdom from c. 50 BC onwards and from c. 20 BC they were commonplace on British coins. In addition, from c. 20 BC Romanized images began to appear on the coins.[202] As Creighton has demonstrated, this was not simply a case of copying Roman coins that were present in nearby Gaul or Germany.[203] Instead, the British coins display a highly specialised knowledge of the iconography that was being employed at Rome in the mid- to late first century BC to assert the power of Octavian/Augustus and facilitate the creation of his new position as Roman emperor.

At Rome this iconography was not restricted to coins, but was present on a range of material culture including statuary, decorative motifs on public and private architecture, pottery, precious stones and glass beads. Six key themes in this iconography have been outlined by Zanker: Octavian's inheritance and ability, Octavian's destiny, Actium, healing through piety and sacrifice, the Golden Age and, lastly, the new forum of Augustus and the Aeneid. Aside from the final theme, these are all recurring themes on the British coinage.[204] Much of this iconography was extremely subtle and complex, and it is unlikely that it would have been understood by the majority of the British audience. Witness, for example, the horseman depicted below a star on an early issue of Tincommarus.[205] Creighton has persuasively linked this into the imagery developing in Rome during the early stages of Octavian's assumption of power when he was depicted on a horse to strengthen his initially weak military credentials. The star, meanwhile, was to symbolise his connection to the deified Julius Caesar, or perhaps in the case of Tincommarus his deceased father Commius. On the coin of Tincommarus the legend reading *C.F.*, meaning son of Commius, clearly links into this theme as well.

The iconography employed on the coinages of southeast Britain from c. 20 BC onwards thus implies clear and strong direct political links to Rome. The best explanation for this is that British rulers had been brought up in Rome as hostages in the aftermath of the Caesarian campaign. They had had first-hand experience of the development of Augustus's iconography as he established himself as emperor. The British rulers subsequently returned home and applied this iconography themselves, probably as client kings. Certainly, this type of relationship seems to have been standard practice in the Roman world at this time.[206] The coinage of Juba of Mauretania shows clear connections with the imagery on the British coinage and can be explained through the presence of 'hostages' from this area at Rome.[207] In addition, the strong iconographic connections might also imply some form of direct link between Mauretania and Britain that very probably occurred in the context of meeting in Rome at the same time.[208]

The burial at Lexden, in the suburbs of modern-day Colchester in Essex, dates to c. 15-1 BC and contains all the trappings one might associate with a British client ruler. Amongst the grave goods were the remnants of a possible iron *sella curulis* (a folding chair – a symbol of Roman magisterial authority), a silver medallion of Augustus, cast from a coin of c. 17 BC, numerous imported bronze vessel-fittings and statuettes, and Roman chainmail.[209]

[196] *B.G.* IV.38, V.22-23.
[197] *Geog.* IV.5.2-3.
[198] *Res Gestae.* 6.32; Suetonius *Caligula.* 44.2.
[199] Cassius Dio *Historia Romana.* 60.19.
[200] Creighton 2000.
[201] Creighton 2000, 55-79, Fig. 3.8; Mattingly 2006, 68-80, Fig. 4; Haselgrove 1984a; Cunliffe 2005, Figs. 7.9, 7.16.
[202] Haselgrove 1996b, 71-72, 82, Tab. 6.1; Creighton 2000, 64-79, 101-125, Fig. A2.
[203] Creighton 2000, 80-125; c.f. Henig 1972.
[204] Zanker 1988; Creighton 2000, 94-125.
[205] Van Arsdell 1989, 375: S7; Creighton 2000, 101-105.
[206] Braund 1984.
[207] Creighton 2000, 117-124; Cassius Dio *Historia Romana.* 51.15.
[208] Creighton 2000.
[209] Foster 1986; Creighton 2000, 181-183; Niblett 2007.

Some of the rulers in southeast Britain were therefore client kings of Rome. This political relationship would have been backed up materially. Rome often acted to support its clients not simply with the threat of direct military action against their rivals, but also through payments of bullion and precious metals. Certainly, we read in Tacitus that during the first century AD Rome supported the power of the client kings of the central European Quadi and Marcomanni through payments of coin.[210] The payments to the British kings would have been made primarily to the two political centres in southeast Britain which were allied to Rome most strongly- the Southern and Eastern kingdoms- perhaps in order to ensure that British groups did not contribute to instability in Gaul in the aftermath of Caesar's campaigns, or during the German campaigns of Augustus (see pp. 42-45).

Brass objects began to appear in southeast Britain in some quantity from the late first century BC onwards. Brooches of Langton Down, Rosette and Thistle types were imported to Britain during the late first century BC and early first century AD and nearly all of them are made of brass.[211] Between 1997 and 2004 the Portable Antiquities Scheme recorded 118 Langton Down and 48 Rosette brooches, primarily from East Anglia, but with several examples also deriving from elsewhere in the southeast and from Lincolnshire and Yorkshire.[212] In addition, at least two of Tasciovanus's (ruler of the Eastern Kingdom c. 20 BC-AD 10) latest coin issues were brass.[213]

Brass was undoubtedly an import from the Roman world. It was an alloy of copper with c. 15-28% zinc, like tin-bronze it was suitable for wrought-working, but it gave a shinier golden finish.[214] Metallic zinc was very hard to produce and it appears to have been virtually unknown to the Romans.[215] However, the cementation process, which was discovered in the mid- to late first century BC, allowed the production of brass by heating finely divided copper metal in a closed crucible with zinc oxide or carbonate (calamine) and charcoal.[216] It is extremely unlikely that zinc ores, required for the cementation process, were mined in Britain prior to the Roman conquest. The brass objects known from Late Iron Age Britain were thus almost certainly based on imported metal, possibly based on the zinc ore deposits of northwest and southwest Spain.

A handful of copper-alloy vessels produced in Italian workshops also arrived in Britain. These include jugs of the Kærumgård type (E122) and Aylesford pans (E130), which have been found in graves at Aylesford in Kent and Welwyn in Hertfordshire. Both of these vessel types were found together in Welwyn Grave B which dates to the mid- to late first century BC.[217] In contrast to the gold and silver, political payments are a less suitable mechanism to account for the arrival of copper-alloy objects in Britain. Trade is perhaps more likely, though some brooches and copper-alloy vessels may have arrived through the movement of people.

Pottery

From c. 20/10 BC large-scale, specialized pottery industries began to develop in northern France, notably around Reims.[218] The products of these 'Gallo-Belgic' pottery industries reached southeast Britain in substantial quantities between c. 20/10 BC-AD 70/80 (**Fig. 3.2**).[219] A significant proportion arrived prior to the Claudian invasion; there is a very large assemblage at the Late Iron Age *oppidum* of Camulodunum (perhaps several thousand vessels), whilst smaller quantities derive from other *oppida* such as Braughing (651 vessels) Silchester, Canterbury, Leicester and Bagendon. Gallo-Belgic ware is also present in twenty-five cemeteries, or individual burials, of pre-conquest date and at Poole Harbour in Dorset.[220] The distribution clearly implies the use of routes across the Southern North Sea and Eastern Channel (**Fig. 3.2**).

Whiteware flagons and butt beakers from northern France are present at a few sites in southeast Britain, such as Silchester.[221] These will have arrived via the same route as the Gallo-Belgic wares. Micaceous Central Gaulish products, such as flagons, storage jars, cups and platters, which date between c. 30/20 BC and the early first century AD, have been noted at several British sites including Silchester, Braughing, Welwyn and Canterbury.[222] The continental distribution of this ware suggests a route to Britain via the north French coast, quite probably from around the mouth of the Seine.[223]

Italian *terra sigillata* (ITS) also reached southeast Britain in some quantity from the later first century BC onwards (**Fig. 3.3**). ITS was manufactured at Italian workshops, such as Arezzo and Pisa, but from c. 15 BC production of nearly identical vessels was also taking place at Lyon.[224] Analysis of the petrology and of the stamps on the British material has revealed that much was produced at Arezzo, but vessels from Puetoli, Pisa and Lyon have also been identified.[225] The earliest examples found in Britain are platters with radial stamps which date to c. 20 BC and on the basis of their stamps, the bulk of the British vessels were produced between c. 20 BC-AD 15, which coincides with the peak phase of output of the ITS

[210] Tacitus *Germania*. 15, 42.
[211] Bayley 1998, 14, Fig. 3.
[212] Worrell 2007, Tab. 2.
[213] Haselgrove 1996b, 73.
[214] Dungworth 1997b; Riederer 2002; Caley 1964; Bayley 1998.
[215] Craddock 1998. The only ancient reference to zinc (mock-silver) was by Strabo (*Geog*. XIII.56).
[216] Craddock 1998; 2009; Bayley 1998; Caley 1964.
[217] Stary 1995; Eggers 1966, 67-69; Carver 2001; Stead 1967; Boube 1991; Feugère and de Marinis 1991.
[218] Deru 1996.
[219] Timby and Rigby 2007; Fitzpatrick and Timby 2002, Fig. 14.4; Tyers 1996b; forthcoming.
[220] Timby and Rigby 2007; Cunliffe 2004, 7.
[221] Fitzpatrick and Timby 2002, 167.
[222] Tyers 1996b, 142-143; forthcoming; Fitzpatrick and Timby 2002, 163-167.
[223] Tyers 1996b.
[224] Ettlinger *et al*. 1990; Fülle 1997; Desbat *et al*. 1996.
[225] Hartley and Williams 1988, 94-96; Williams and Dannell 1978, 9.

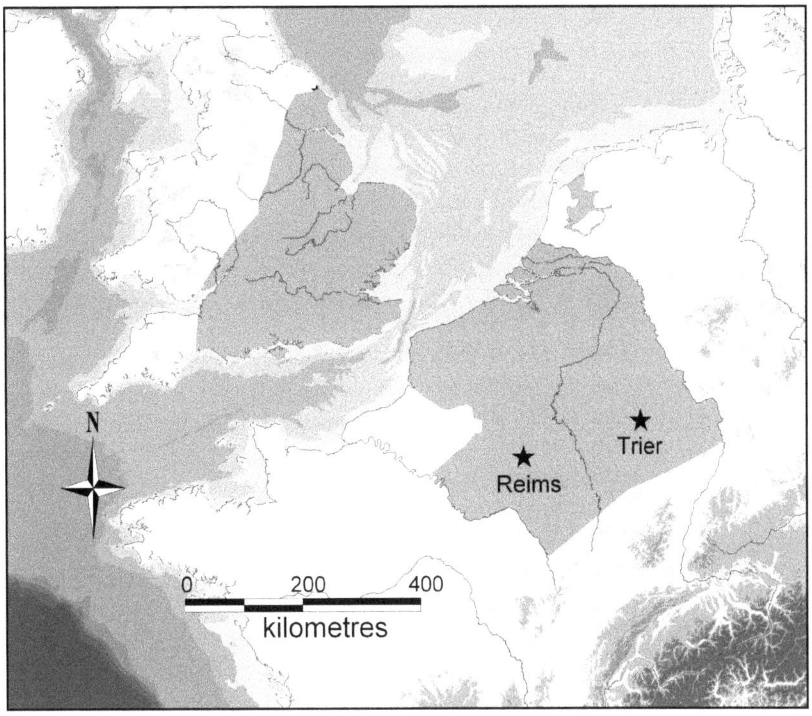

Fig. 3.2. Distribution of Gallo-Belgic wares (Modified from Fulford 2007, Fig. 5.2; Tyers 1996a, Fig. 200. See Timby and Rigby 2007).

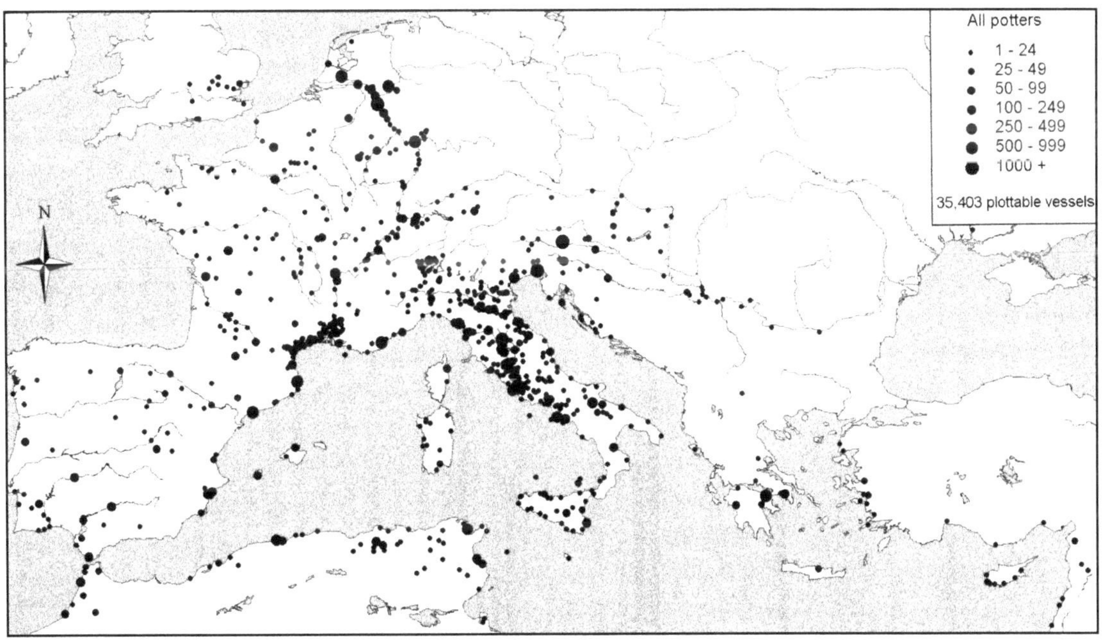

Fig. 3.3. Distribution of stamped ITS vessels (Oxé et al. 2000, Fig.4).

industries.[226] ITS has been identified on at least twenty-six sites in southeast Britain, principally in the Essex-Hertfordshire region. It is usually present at these sites in small amounts, though notable quantities are encountered at some *oppida*, for example, 64 vessels were found at Skeleton Green, Braughing, Hertfordshire, 50 vessels at Silchester and 80 sherds at Canterbury.[227] On the adjacent continent ITS occurs in large quantities at Roman military sites along the Rhine, but smaller amounts are also known from sites along the whole of the northern and western coasts of France (**Fig. 3.3**). The principal routes of ITS import probably lay across the Southern North Sea and Eastern Channel, but we cannot exclude

[226] Wickenden 1986, 53, Fig. 26.9; Oxé *et al*. 2000.

[227] Willis 2005, Appendices 6.6-6.7; Tyers forthcoming; Bird 1984, 129; 1995a; 2000, 183-187; Dannell 1981, 152-158, Tab. 1; Boon 1974, 40, Fig. 6.1-2.

smaller-scale movements via the Atlantic and Western Channel.

Small amounts of South Gaulish and Central Gaulish *terra sigillata* also reached Britain prior to the Claudian invasion. Wares from these sources probably began to arrive from c. AD 20; several decorated bowls and plain stamped vessels are known from Sheepen, near Colchester, that were produced in southern Gaul during the AD 20s and 30s. Although the contexts in which they were found are not securely pre-conquest it is probable that at least some of these vessels arrived from the near continent before AD 43. Excavations at the Silchester basilica yielded Central Gaulish Lezoux and Montans ware from layers that probably pre-date AD 43, and Lezoux ware has also been found at Fishbourne in a possible pre-conquest layer.[228] The contemporary continental distribution of Central Gaulish ware is restricted to western and northern France and does not extend north of the Somme, which implies a cross-Channel route, perhaps from around the mouth of the Seine.[229]

The imported pottery is an excellent candidate for market trade. The large quantities involved, particularly of Gallo-Belgic ware, are highly suggestive of a marketed product. Historical evidence also supports the existence of trade between Britain and the Roman world; Strabo, writing c. AD 18, implies its presence when he provides a list of objects that were imported to Britain from Gaul (ivory chains and necklaces, amber-gems, glass vessels and other petty wares), and those that were exported from it (grain, cattle, gold, silver, iron, hides, slaves and hunting dogs). Furthermore, he states that the tax duties paid on both imports and exports from Britain were so lucrative that, from an economic point of view, a Roman invasion of the island was a risk that was simply not necessary.[230] Indeed, Duncan-Jones has recently demonstrated that custom dues on trade at the Empire's external frontiers were typically 25% (see p. 93).

In addition, bronze coinage was minted in quantity, alongside the gold and silver coinages, in southeast Britain from c. 20 BC onwards, whilst over 300 imported Gallo-Belgic bronze coins, dating roughly to the second half of the first century BC, have also been identified in southeast Britain.[231] Whilst the high value coinages do not necessarily imply market relations, the low value bronze coinages are much better explained in terms of trade.[232] This is further supported by the distribution of bronze coins, which, in contrast to the more widely distributed precious metal coinages, is highly restricted and clusters at large settlement complexes, usually typified by large earthworks, known as *oppida*, which develop from c. 20 BC onwards. *Oppida* were centres of political power, but some probably functioned as market centres as well.[233] The fact that imported pottery concentrates at *oppida* further supports the suggestion that it was a marketed product.

Wine

The earliest Dressel 1B (Dr.1B) amphorae were probably produced around the turn of the second century BC; transitional Dr.1A/1B forms with consular dates of 97 BC and 90 BC have been found at Rome and Burriac in Spain respectively.[234] Like Dr.1A, Dr.1B primarily contained wine, which is evidenced by *tituli picti* (painted inscriptions) and residue analysis.[235] Dr.1B replaced Dr.1A as the dominant Italian wine amphorae type on Mediterranean shipwrecks between c. 100-75 BC. The latest Dr.1B from shipwrecks date to c. 50 BC (Plane 1) and 47 BC (Planier 3), though a few examples are known with consular dates which indicate that Dr.1B were still being produced in limited quantities down to c. 10 BC.[236]

Strong concentrations of Dr.1B are known from 'native' sites in the Seine basin and further north from the region of the Somme Valley, although there are a scatter of find-spots right along the entire continental coast between Brittany and the Strait of Dover (**Figs. 3.4-5**). Dr.1B appear in these regions from the early first century BC onwards, but there appears to be a notable increase at sites post-dating the Gallic Wars, as evidenced by the amphorae density at the *oppidum* of Pommiers in the Aisne Valley, which is three times in excess of the quantities at the earlier *oppidum* at Villeneuve-St-Germain. Even rural settlements, such as Beaurieux, had access to considerable numbers of amphorae at this time.[237] Aside from the rural site of Wange in central Belgium, Dr.1B are unknown at native sites to the north of northern France, southern Belgium, Luxembourg and the Moselle region of Germany. A few examples have been recorded at Roman military installations constructed during the early stages of Augustus's German campaigns (c. 20/15-10 BC), though here they are significantly outnumbered by Dr.1B's replacement type Dressel 2-4. These sites include Nijmegen in the eastern Netherlands, Velzeke and Liberchies in Belgium and several forts in Germany.[238]

Dr.1B are present at several sites in Britain with a particular concentration in the Essex-Hertfordshire region, though there is a smaller group of finds around the Solent (**Fig. 3.6**). In the Essex-Hertfordshire region Dr.1B are encountered in graves, at sites including Welwyn (Graves: 1 (five vessels); A (one vessel) and B (five vessels)), Sandon, Essex, (two vessels) and Thaxted, Essex, (one vessel). Dr.1B are also present at settlements, such as Heybridge on the Essex coast (forty-two Dressel

---

[228] Tyers forthcoming; Willis 2005, sections 6.4.2, 6.6.2; Dannell 1971; 1985, 83; Bird 2000, 183-7, 193-4.
[229] Delage 2001, Fig. 2,1.
[230] *Geog.* IV.5.2-3.
[231] Haselgrove 1996b, 81, Tab. 6.1; Creighton 2000, Fig. A.2; De Jersey 2006.
[232] Fitzpatrick 1992, 27; Haselgrove 1987a, 110, Figs. 6:1-6:3; 1992, 127-128; 1996b, 74-76; Holman 2005, 38-39.
[233] Haselgrove 1987, 110, Figs. 6:1-6:3; 1992, 127-128; 1996, 74-76; Holman 2005, 36-37; Bryant 2007; Bryant and Niblett 2001.
[234] Loughton 2003, 181.
[235] Loughton 2003, 182.
[236] Parker 1992, 32; Loughton 2003, 182; Sealey 1985, 26.
[237] Haselgrove 1996a, 169, 172-173, Tab. 1; Loughton 2009.
[238] Roymans 1990, Tab. 7.1

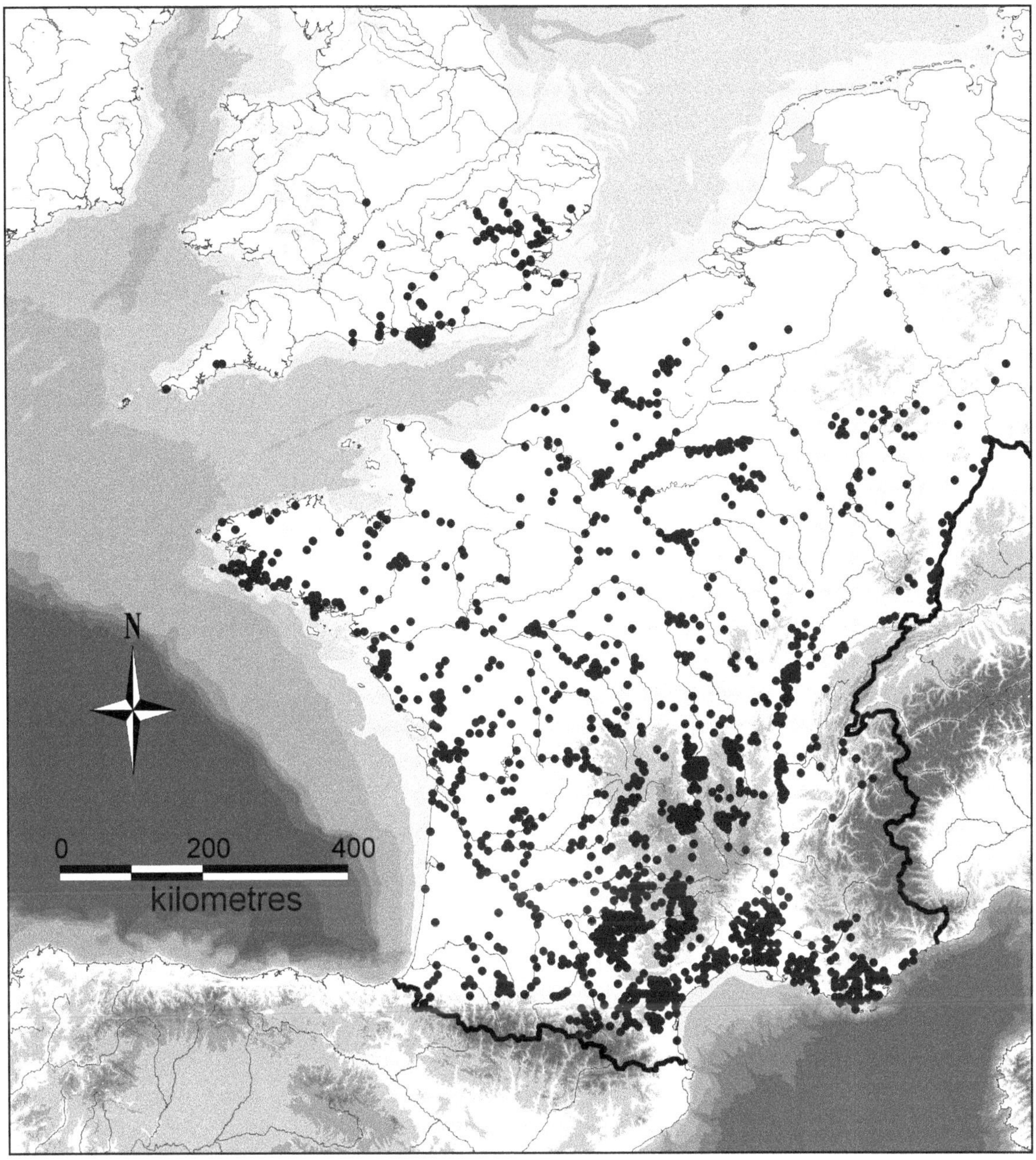

Fig. 3.4. Distribution of Republican amphorae in northwest Europe (France, Belgium, Luxembourg, the Netherlands, western Germany and Britain) (Sources: France: Loughton 2003, Fig. 7; Belgium, Luxembourg, the Netherlands and western Germany: Roymans 1990, Fig. 7.2; Britain: Carver 2001; Trott and Tomalin 2003; Cunliffe 2005, Fig. 17.28).

1 amphorae, predominantly Dr.1B), Sheepen in Essex (forty-six sherds of Dr.1B) and Braughing in Hertfordshire (well over one hundred Dr.1 sherds, including both Dr.1A and Dr.1B).[239] Contextually dated examples of Dr.1B in Britain are rare, though the main occupation at both Heybridge and Braughing began c. 50 BC, which provides a probable *terminus post quem* for the amphorae at these sites.[240] The Welwyn graves are dated c. 50-10 BC, a Dr.1B from Hertford Heath was deposited c. 30-15 BC, whilst a burial deposit containing Dr.1B at Heybridge has been dated to c. 10 BC.[241] At the Lexden burial near Colchester, which dates to c. 15-1 BC, Dr.1B are outnumbered by later Dressel 2-4 amphorae, which suggests that this type was being replaced by this time.[242] At Sheepen occupation only began c. AD 5.[243] Thus, the majority of the Dr.1B from southeast Britain were probably imported via northern France between c. 50-20/10 BC. As with the pottery, trade is the most likely mechanism to account for their appearance. The apparently 'late' date of some of the British material in contexts after the end of Dr.1B production is curious. It may suggest curation of wine, or empty amphorae, in Britain for some years after their import.

[239] Carver 2001.
[240] Carver 2001, 24-27.
[241] Carver 2001, 31, 101-103.
[242] Fitzpatrick 2003a, 14; Foster 1986.
[243] Carver 2001, 6.

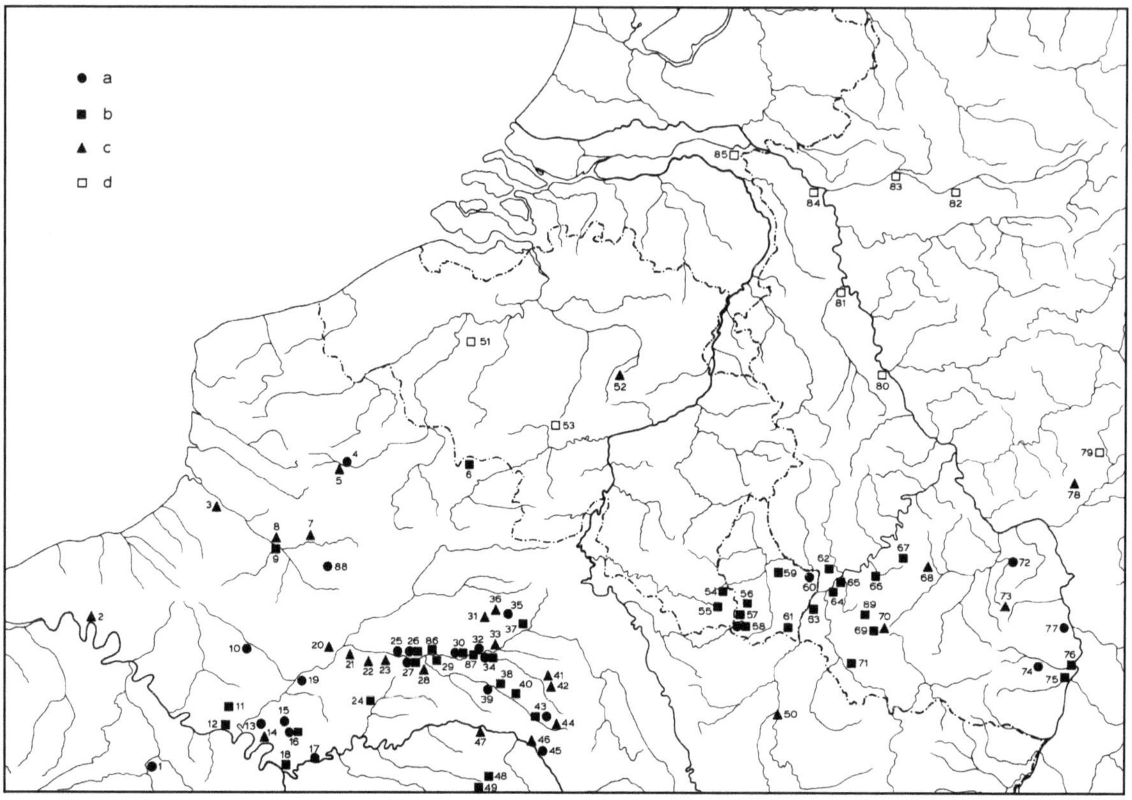

Fig. 3.5. Distribution of Dressel 1 amphorae in northern France, Belgium, the Netherlands, Luxembourg and western Germany (Roymans 1990, Fig. 7.2) a = Dr.1A; b = Dr.1B; c = Dressel 1, type unspecified; d = Dr.1B in Roman fort.

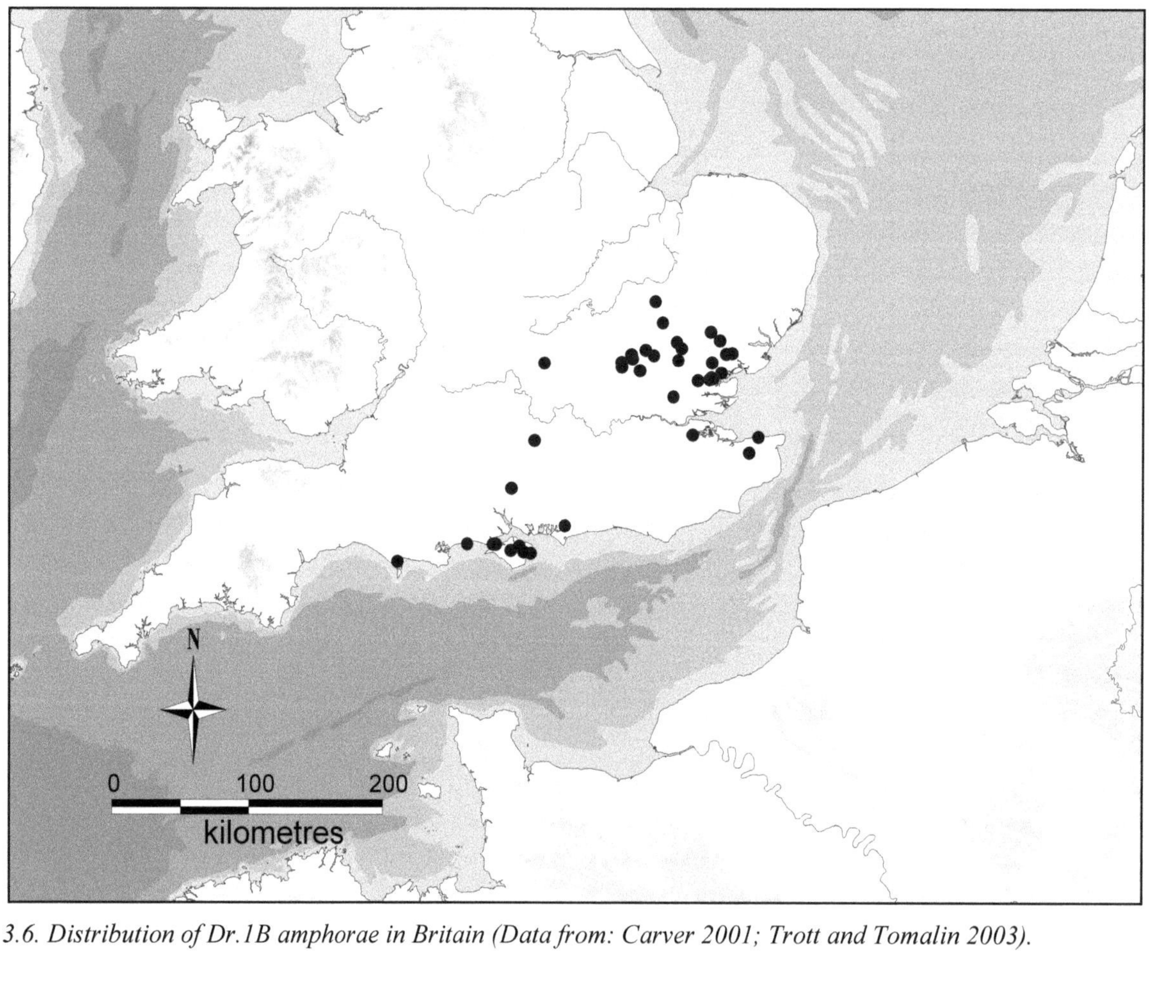

Fig. 3.6. Distribution of Dr.1B amphorae in Britain (Data from: Carver 2001; Trott and Tomalin 2003).

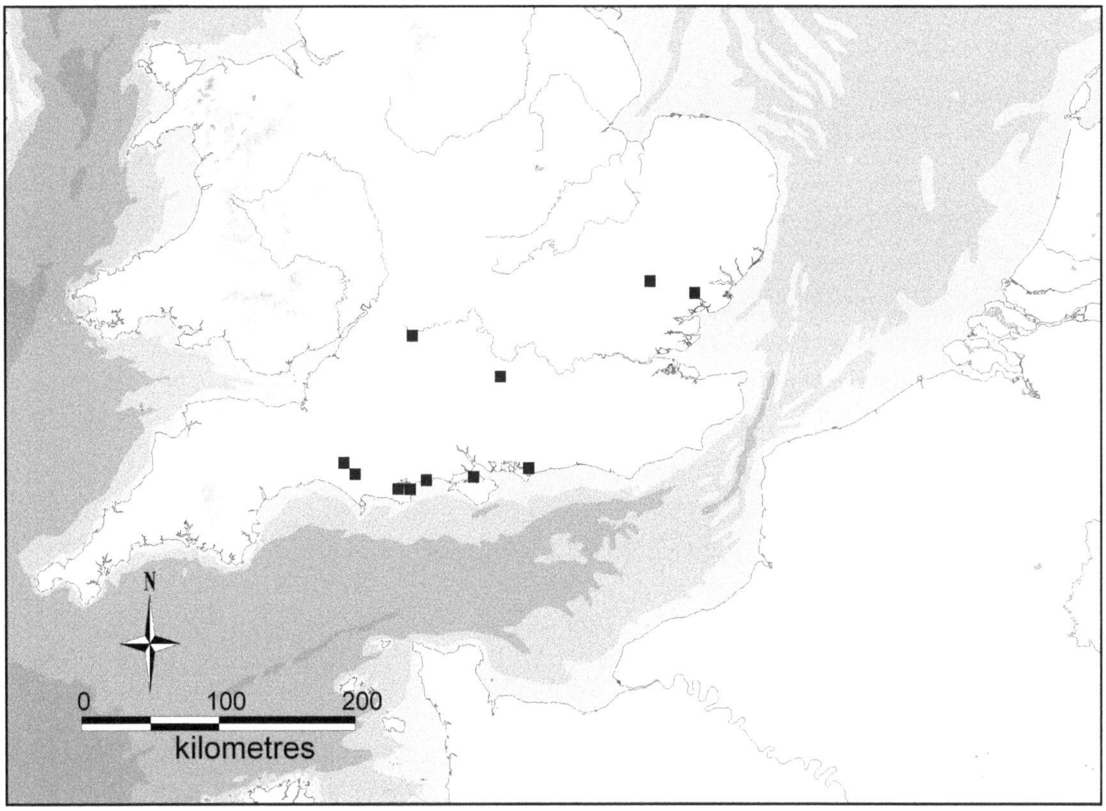

Fig. 3.7. British distribution of Pascual 1 amphorae (after Paul Tyers (URL accessed June 2010): http://www.potsherd.uklinux.net/atlas/Ware/PAS1).

The second, smaller group of British Dr.1B finds derive from the Solent coast, in particular the Isle of Wight, where at least six find-spots are known.[244] We should bear in mind that the prevalence of burials with grave goods in the Essex-Hertfordshire region, and their absence from south-central Britain, may have distorted the difference in size between the two groups.[245] The Solent group may have arrived after the Gallic wars, perhaps via western France, but given the known chronology of the Dr.1B type we cannot exclude the possibility that some, or all, of them were imported from Brittany alongside the Dr.1A during the first half of the first century BC.

By the late first century BC, the Dr.1B amphorae type had been replaced and the sources of the wine supplied to Britain widened. At this time Pascual 1 amphorae were traded to southern Britain in small quantities (**Fig. 3.7**). These had a capacity of c. 22 l and primarily transported wine from Catalonia in northeast Spain. On the basis of dated Mediterranean shipwrecks, the type was probably produced between c. 30 BC-AD 30. Finds are primarily concentrated in south-central Britain around the Solent, and they very probably arrived via an Atlantic route from southwest France where finds are common.[246]

Dressel 2-4 (Dr.2-4) amphorae began to be imported from the late first century BC onwards. These replaced the Dr.1B type and were first produced in Italy around the mid-first century BC. From the end of the first century BC, they were also being made in the eastern Mediterranean, southern France and Spain where they gradually replaced the Pascual 1 type.[247] Dr.2-4 had a better weight-to-volume ratio than the Dressel 1 and had certainly superseded them by c. 20 BC; for example, in the Roman forts built for the Augustan German offensive Dr.2-4 are far more important than Dr.1B.[248] Similarly, Dr.2-4 are twice as common as Dr.1B in the Lexden burial of c. 15-1 BC.[249] Dr.2-4 became one of the standard wine amphorae types for almost the entirety of the first century AD; although other contents such as *defrutum*, fish-products, olive oil and dates may also occasionally have been carried.[250]

In Britain the Dr.2-4 from Iron Age contexts are mostly of Italian origin and principally concentrate in the Essex-Hertfordshire region (**Fig. 3.8**).[251] The largest assemblage derives from Camulodunum-Sheepen, where forty-four examples have been identified.[252] On the continent Italian Dr.2-4 are well known at military sites along the Rhine, but also from civil sites in northern France and they

[244] Trott and Tomalin 2003, Fig. 12.
[245] Fitzpatrick 1985.
[246] Tyers 1996a; Fitzpatrick 1985; 2003a.

[247] Fitzpatrick 2003a, 14.
[248] Roymans 1990, 147, Tab. 7.1.
[249] Williams 1986.
[250] Tyers 1996a.
[251] Fitzpatrick 2003a, 14.
[252] Carver 2001, 26.

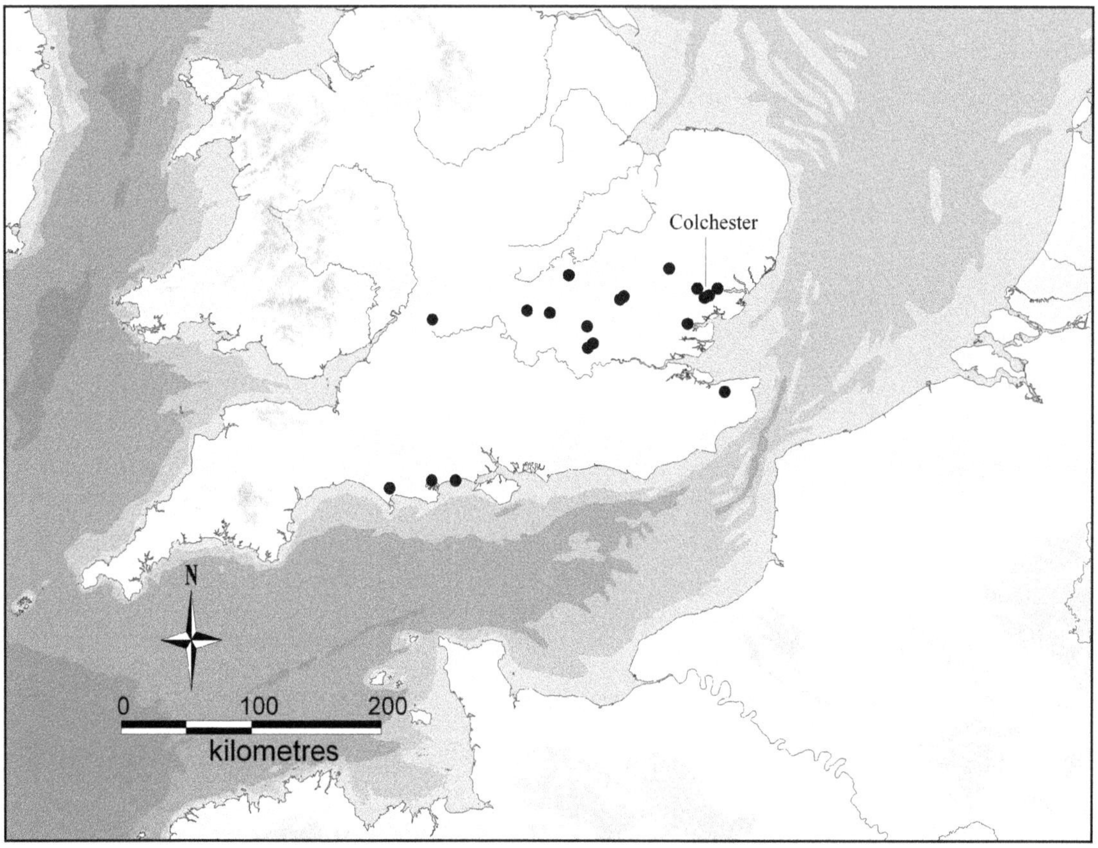

Fig. 3.8. Distribution of Dr. 2-4 on British Iron Age sites (after Carver 2001, Fig. 4). N.B. There are numerous Dr.2-4 from the Isle of Wight. These are as yet undated, but many could have arrived during the Iron Age (Trott and Tomalin 2003).

evidently came to southeast Britain via the Southern North Sea and Eastern Channel.[253]

A smaller group of Dr.2-4 found on the Dorset coast may have travelled alongside the Pascual 1 amphorae via an Atlantic route from southwest France, although a route via northern France or the Low Countries cannot be ruled out. A few other wine amphorae, such as the early flat-bottomed Gauloise types, which were produced in southern France, and Italian Camulodunum 139 flagons, which may have contained wine, are occasionally found in Pre-conquest contexts in southeast Britain.[254]

In comparison to Dr.1B, these later amphorae types reached Britain in much lower quantities. There was evidently a severe decline in wine amphorae importation that Paul Sealey has estimated may have been up to as much as three quarters.[255] The Mediterranean shipwreck evidence gives a similar picture, with a major late first-century BC fall in cargoes of wine amphorae; cargoes of wine amphorae are present on forty shipwrecks dated 75-25 BC (all of Dr.1B type), whilst they are found on only nine wrecks dated 25 BC-AD 25 (mainly Dr.2-4 type). This is despite the fact that the overall number of shipwrecks increased in the later period.[256]

[253] Tyers 1996a.
[254] Fitzpatrick 2003a.
[255] Sealey 2009; Fitzpatrick 2003a, 14. See: Carver 2001, 78-103.
[256] Parker 1990, Fig. 1; 1992, 16-18.

The reduction in wine amphorae found in Britain and in the Mediterranean does not mean, however, that there was a collapse in wine production and distribution towards the end of the first century BC. Italian viticulture did not undergo a sudden decline at this time.[257] Indeed, wine production even underwent expansion into other areas, such as Spain and Languedoc-Roussillon and Provence in southern France where viticulture was extended beyond the limited confines of Massalia during the later first century BC and into the early first century AD.[258]

Rather than a decline in wine production the evidence suggests that we are dealing with a shift in the types of container used to transport the wine. It was during the late first century BC that barrels came to be of great significance. The barrel had been used amongst some of the native peoples of southern France during the Iron Age, primarily for beer. From the late first century BC, however, it was utilised for transporting wine. The barrel certainly possessed advantages over the amphora for transport via the rivers and roads of France; it had a better weight-to-volume ratio, it could be easily rolled and

[257] Tchernia 1986; Panella and Tchernia 2002; Carandini 1985. Though Sealey (2009) has argued that the decline of wine amphorae imports to Britain is reflective of a decline in the wine trade caused by increased demand for, consumption of, and retention of Italian wine within Italy.
[258] Brun and Laubenheimer 2001, 206-207; Brun 2001; Buffat *et al.* 2001.

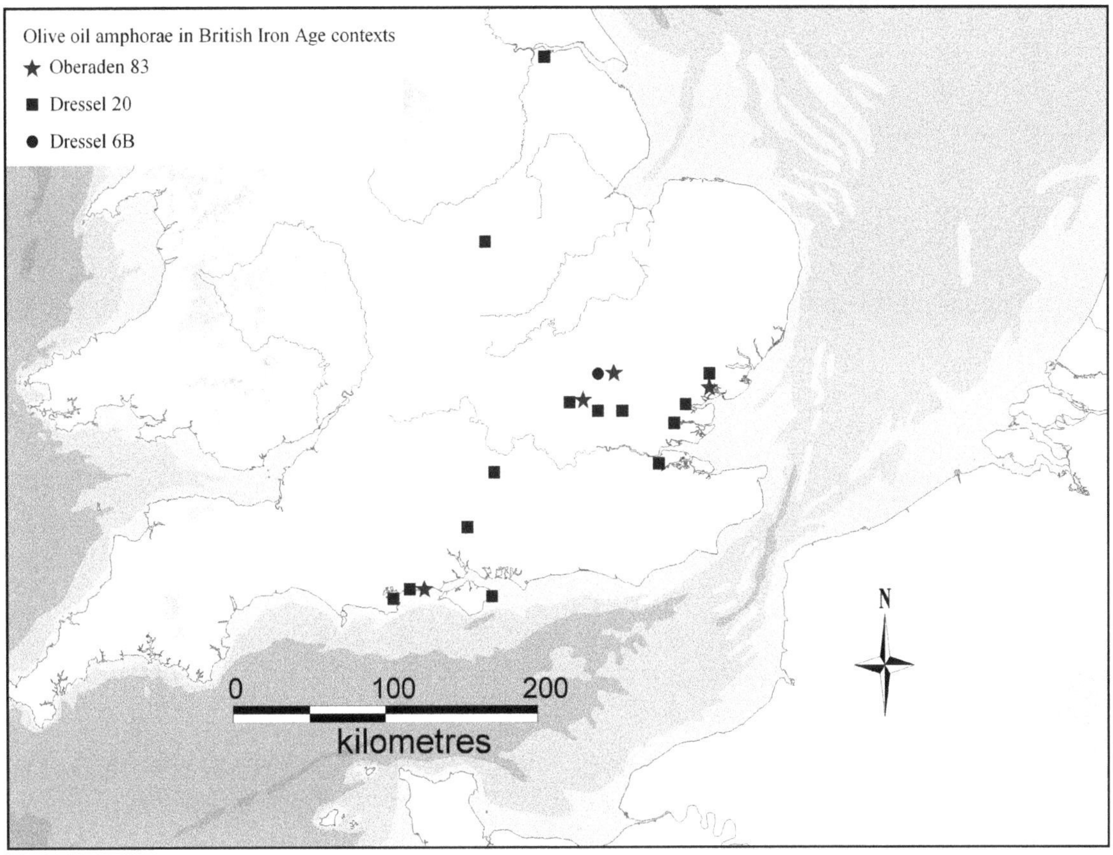

Fig. 3.9. Distribution of olive oil amphorae in British Iron Age contexts (after Fitzpatrick 2003a, Fig. 8).

moved during journeys with many changes and stages, and it was more durable than amphorae during bumpy road haulages. The amphora, by contrast, was perfectly suited for bulk sea transport, and it could be sealed more effectively, which prevented secondary fermentation of the wine, ensuring that a much finer product was delivered to its destination.[259]

Forty-six barrels have been found in late first-century BC contexts, most at military sites associated with the Augustan offensives in Germany. Many were made from wood that grew in central France, and indeed barrel-making centres are attested in the Lyon area from the late first century BC onwards. The absence of barrels from Late Iron Age contexts in Britain is not acceptable evidence that they were not imported as their preservation requires exceptional circumstances, such as waterlogging, and the majority of known examples were reused as well-linings in Roman military camps.[260] The switchover to barrels as the primary wine container in temperate Europe from the late first century BC onwards means that the contemporary decline in wine amphorae known from Iron Age Britain cannot simply be read as a decline in overall wine import. Very probably, wine would have continued to have been imported at a similar, and in all likelihood increasing, rate as the period progressed.

[259] Wilson 2009b; Marlière 2002, 185-192.
[260] Marlière 2002, 174-195, Fig. 212.1.

Olive oil

Some olive oil was traded to Britain prior to the Claudian invasion (**Fig. 3.9**). The earliest imports were Oberaden 83 amphorae, which bore olive oil from Baetica in southeast Spain. These are known from four British sites and probably began to arrive from the last decade BC.[261] Another early type found at Braughing, Herts, and possibly also at the nearby site of Skeleton Green, was the Dressel 6B. This began to be produced in the last decade BC and carried olive oil from Istria and other sites around the Adriatic.[262] The most common olive oil amphorae type identified at Iron Age sites in Britain, however, was the Dressel 20 (Dr.20), which replaced the Oberaden 83 from the Tiberian period (AD 14-37) onwards and was specifically designed to facilitate the bulk transport of olive oil by sea. Like the Oberaden 83 this was a Baetican type, and the overwhelming majority were manufactured at oil-producing centres in the Guadalquavir Valley.[263] Dr.20 are known from pre-Roman contexts on at least thirteen British sites.[264] It is hard to estimate the number of vessels involved, though multiple amphorae are implied at Braughing by records of Dr.20 assemblages (all weighing between c. 1-9 kg) at five separate excavations.[265] The mere presence of Dr.20

[261] Williams and Peacock 1979; 1983; Fitzpatrick 2003a; Wheeler and Wheeler 1936, Fig. 13, No. 29.
[262] Williams and Peacock 1983; Fitzpatrick 2003a, 17, Fig. 8.
[263] Etienne and Mayet 2004; Martin-Kilcher 1987.
[264] Fitzpatrick 2003a, 17, Fig. 8.
[265] Williams and Peacock 1983, Tab. 1.

sherds is enough to imply the sizeable consumption of olive oil at a site. These were very large vessels with a capacity of between 40-100 litres, commonly around 70-75 litres.[266]

The main foci of olive oil consumption in continental northwest Europe were the military forts along the Rhine and they were probably transhipped to southeast Britain via northern France or the mouth of the Rhine.[267] The olive oil amphorae from British sites around the Solent may have arrived via the Atlantic seaways, although, as with the southeast British examples, they may have come via the coast of northern France or the Low Countries.

Seafood

Amphorae of Dressel 7-11/ Beltrán I types, which transported Mediterranean fish products, are occasionally encountered on British sites. For example, Two Beltrán I amphorae have been recorded at King Harry Lane, Verulamium.[268] At Skeleton Green, Braughing, the bones of a Spanish mackerel (*Scomber colias*), which inhabits the waters off southern Europe, was found in a well, and can presumably be connected to the Spanish amphora sherd from the same context.[269]

British exports

Metals

A few examples of British gold and silver coins dated c. 20 BC-AD 60 are present on the continent, whilst British bronze coins dated c. 20 BC-AD 45 have been identified at fourteen different continental sites (**Fig. 3.10**). These were largely minted in southeast Britain, primarily in the Eastern Kingdom, and the vast majority cluster in northern France, which attests to particularly strong links across the Strait of Dover. Scattered examples are also present along the coast of Belgium and on the Lower Rhine, which hint at more limited maritime contacts between this region and Britain. Meanwhile, three bronze coins of the Eastern Kingdom have been found in western France around the Gironde, suggesting the operation of limited maritime routes along the Atlantic façade.

The number of coins is relatively small, but we can suggest that the majority were exported to the continent by trade. Strabo includes gold and silver, most probably in the form of coin, amongst Britain's exports, though the majority would presumably have been melted down; British coins had much lower precious metal contents than contemporary Roman coins, and they would not have been legal currency in the Empire.[270] Of course, some coins may have reached the continent as personal possessions, potentially even in the aftermath of the Claudian invasion. This may explain the slightly 'odd' coins present in the Lower Rhine region; a bronze coin of the Dorset-based Durotriges and a late (c. AD 40-45) silver coin of the Iceni have been identified at two rural settlements in the Dutch Eastern River area. These can perhaps be related to the return of Batavian auxiliaries who had acquired these objects during military service in Britain.[271]

Long-distance movements of iron are exceptionally hard to trace archaeologically due to the relative abundance of iron sources, corrosion problems associated with the metal and difficulties in accurately determining sources through chemical or physical means. To date we cannot actually point to any iron objects which were definitely exported from Britain. That said, we can tentatively suggest that iron was exported from Britain to the continent during this period. Strabo lists iron as one of Britain's exports and the presence of a huge Roman army in northwest Europe from the end of the first century BC onwards created a significant potential source of demand.[272] There was certainly increasing iron production in southeast Britain during the Late Iron Age; along the 15 km long Bulbourne Valley in Hertfordshire slag-tapping shaft furnaces and surface finds of slag have been noted on at least six sites, whilst there is evidence for Late Iron Age iron smelting on thirteen sites in the East Sussex Weald and at least eight sites in the East Midlands.[273]

Other exports

I have argued that much of the material imported into Britain during this period arrived through market exchange. For this reason we should expect a sizeable group of exports to have made their way to the continent. Our archaeologically attested exports, however, are extremely scant. Aside from metals (gold, silver and iron) Strabo lists grain, cattle, hides, slaves and hunting dogs as Britain's exports, which are of course virtually undetectable archaeologically, though we can surely expect them to have been transferred to the continent in quite notable quantities.[274] There is also evidence for substantial Iron Age and Roman-period salt exploitation in two of the main regions which received traded goods at this time, namely the north Kent and Essex coasts and the Portsmouth/Langstone/Chichester Harbour area of the Eastern Solent coast.[275] In addition, it is precisely these areas that constitute the principal oyster fisheries of England.[276] Such coastal resources may well have figured amongst Britain's exports.

Ports

There is little clear evidence pertaining to ports on the coast of the near continent. In southeast Britain our best candidate for a port in the Eastern Kingdom is Camulodunum, which is situated on the river Colne near the Essex coast (**Fig. 3.11**). This site had evidently

[266] Carreras Monfort 2000, Fig. 2; Peña 2007, 305; Tyers 1996a.
[267] Martin-Kilcher 1987; Remesal 1986; 1997.
[268] Williams 1989, 116.
[269] Partridge 1981, 57, 242-3, Fig. 22, 68.
[270] *Geog.* IV.5.2.

[271] Hassall 1970; Bird 2002, 258.
[272] *Geog.* IV.5.2.
[273] Morris and Wainwright 1995; Bryant 1999, 271-276, Tab. 6.7; Cleere and Crossley 1995, 52-56; Schrüfer-Kolb 2004, 52-54, Tab. 4, Fig. 31.
[274] *Geog.* IV.5.2-3
[275] Carver 2001; Rippon 2000, 58-64; Haselgrove 1982.
[276] Tomalin 2006, Fig. 3.

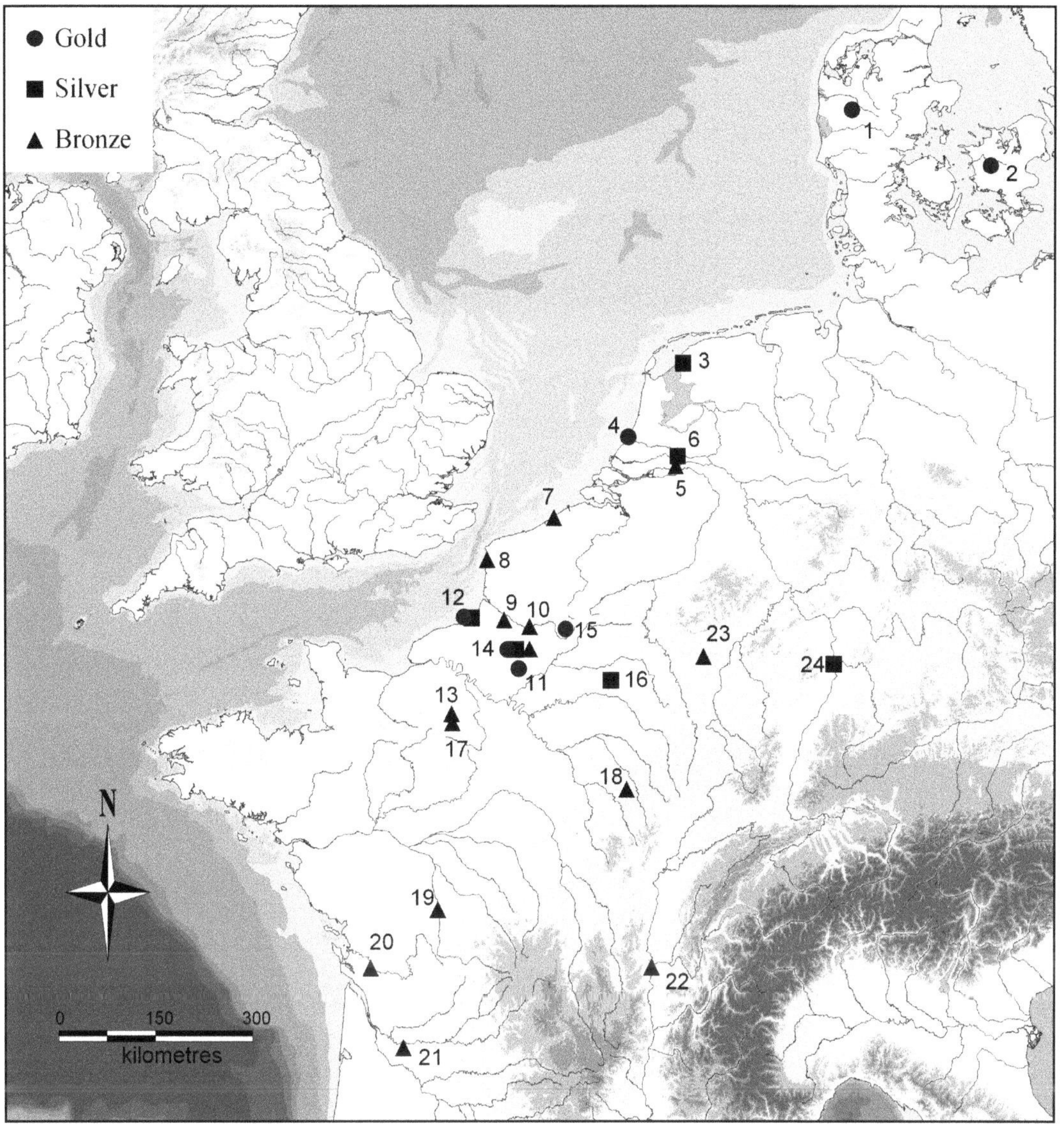

Fig. 3.10. Continental sites with British Celtic coins c. 20 BC-AD 60 (see Appendix 2).

developed as a major political centre by the end of the first century BC; large numbers of coins marked CAM or CAMV were struck from c. 20 BC, a huge and complex system of dykes began to be constructed c. 25 BC, whilst the Lexden tumulus with its numerous grave goods deriving from the Roman world is also sited here.[277] Excavations within the Camulodunum complex at the riverside site of Sheepen, occupied from AD 5 onwards, have revealed large quantities of continental pottery and Dr.2-4 wine amphorae.[278] Other sites in the Eastern Kingdom, such as the coastal site of Heybridge, were also engaged in direct trade with the continent.[279] Braughing in Hertfordshire, which has evidence for very large quantities of imported pottery and amphorae between c. 30/20 BC-AD 20/30, would very probably have had its imports transhipped via the Thames estuary and the rivers Rib and Lea.[280]

In the Southern Kingdom, meanwhile, the settlement complex around Chichester Harbour probably served as the principal port of entry (**Fig. 3.12**). Chichester/Selsey was one of the main *oppida* in the Southern Kingdom and a large dyke system cut off a substantial portion of the coast from the surrounding region.[281] Native gold coins and goldwork have been identified at Selsey, whilst early first-century AD imported pottery is present in the Chichester/Fishbourne area.[282] Chris Rudd has also demonstrated that this area is marked by a particular concentration of Late Iron Age coins and that several southern coin series were probably minted in the near vicinity.[283] The potential importance of this location is

[277] Van Arsdell 1989, 361-427; Creighton 2000, Fig. 6.6; Cunliffe 2005, 144-145, 161-163, Figs. 7.11-12; Hawkes and Crummy 1995.
[278] Niblett 1985, 1-5; Hawkes and Hull 1947, 46-51, 168-286.
[279] Carver 2001.

[280] Partridge 1981, 99-103, 152-195, 351-356; Bryant 1994, 62; 2007, 63-67; Bryant and Niblett 2001, 104.
[281] Cunliffe 2005, 172, Fig. 7.18; Bradley 1971; Creighton 2000, 192-197, Fig. 7.5.
[282] Manley and Rudkin 2005; Mattingly 2006, 76.
[283] Rudd 2006; Rudd *et al.* Forthcoming.

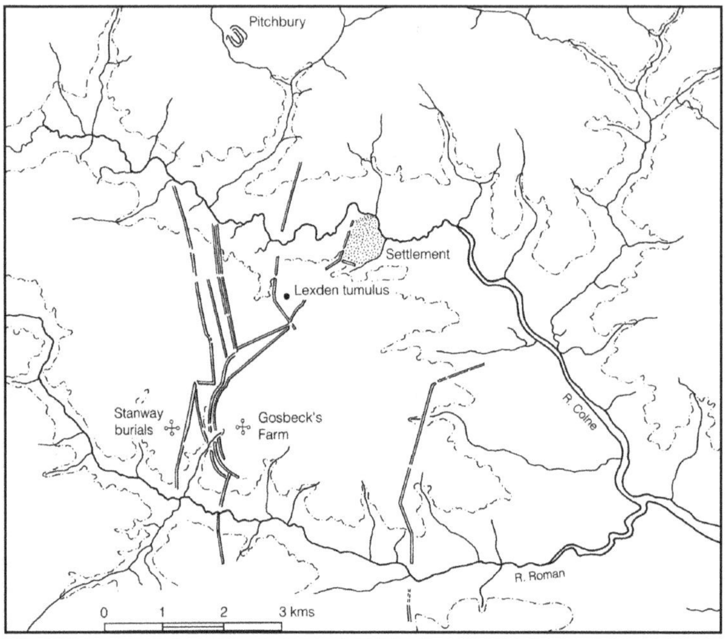

Fig. 3.11. Late Iron Age and early Roman settlement in the region of Camulodunum (Cunliffe 2005, Fig. 7.11, based on Hawkes and Crummy 1995).

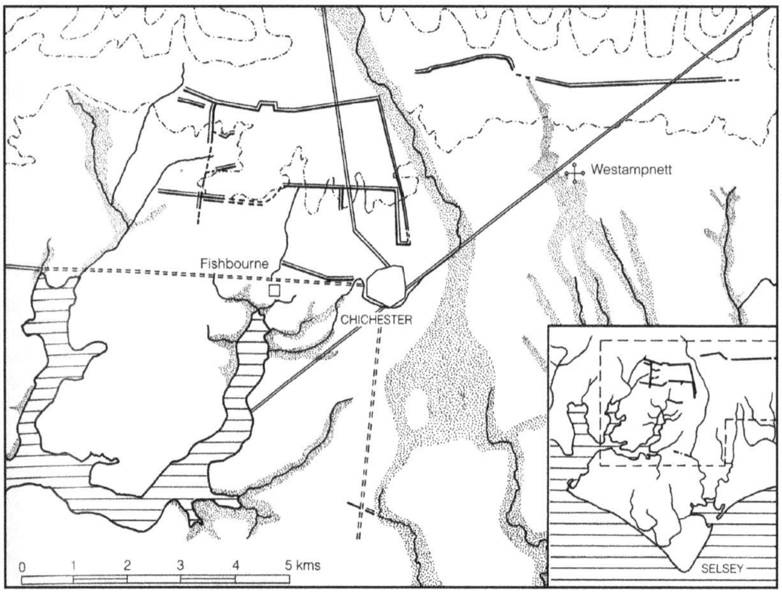

Fig. 3.12. Dykes in the Chichester region (Cunliffe 2005, Fig. 7.18, based on Bradley 1971).

further demonstrated by the nearby Late Iron Age and Early Roman temple on Hayling Island, whilst a magnificent palace was constructed at Fishbourne in the later first century AD.[284] In the Dorset region, whilst Hengistbury declined as a port after c. 50 BC, Poole Harbour seems to have increased in importance somewhat. Here, Pascual 1 wine amphorae, which attest to Atlantic links, are fairly common, whilst a wide range of Gallo-Belgic table wares, dated c. 15 BC-AD 50, imply direct, or indirect, connections with northern France via the Eastern Channel as well.[285]

[284] Cunliffe 1971; 1998.
[285] Cox and Hearne 1991; Cunliffe 2004, 7.

Synthesis

In the aftermath of Caesar's Gallic wars there was a gradual expansion in connectivity in the Southern North Sea and Eastern Channel system, increasing from the end of the first century BC onwards. Gold and silver were sent to southeast Britain by the Roman state in support of rulers in its two main client kingdoms: the Eastern Kingdom and, to a lesser extent, the Southern Kingdom. Other continental imports included objects of copper-alloy, olive oil, wine, fish products and most notably large quantities of pottery, such as Italian *terra sigillata*, Central Gaulish micaceous ware and particularly Gallo-Belgic ware. These principally came to Britain by market exchange which developed in the wake of the client kingship relations. In return for the traded imports a range of, primarily archaeologically undetectable, material was exported from Britain. This probably included gold, silver, iron, agricultural products, such as grain, cattle and hides, slaves, hunting dogs, salt and, perhaps, oysters.

Strabo listed the four principal routes between the continent and Britain and two of these concern the Southern North Sea and Eastern Channel system: a route departing from the mouth of the Rhine and a route departing from the mouth of the Seine. Strabo stated that those who voyaged to Britain from the regions near the Rhine did not set off from the Rhine itself, but from the territory of the Morini, who occupied what is now the Pas-de-Calais.[286] This appears to be backed up by the archaeological evidence, and is clearest in the map of British coin exports (**Fig. 3.10**), which demonstrate that Britain had much stronger connections with northern France, than with the Lower Rhine region. A number of sites in southeast Britain functioned as ports, or entrepôts. In the Eastern Kingdom we can point to Camulodunum, and to a lesser extent Heybridge, on the Essex coast, whilst sites in Hertfordshire, such as Braughing engaged in trade with the continent via the Thames estuary. The smaller-scale continental connections of the Southern Kingdom were probably focused on the *oppidum* at Chichester/Selsey.

The thriving trade relations in the Atlantic system which existed prior to the Gallic wars appear to have been disrupted by c. 60/50 BC. Atlantic trade continued however; Pascual 1 wine amphorae were certainly imported to southern Britain via the Atlantic. A small group of imports in south-central Britain including Dr.1B and Dr.2-4 wine amphorae, along with Baetican olive oil amphorae may also have arrived via Atlantic routes. A few finds of coins, minted in southeast Britain, in western France also hint at Atlantic routes. Two of Strabo's four routes between the continent and Britain also concern the Atlantic system: those that began at the mouths of the rivers Loire and Garonne.[287] Our best candidate for a port in south-central Britain is Poole Harbour, though other smaller sites may have engaged in trade with the continent as well.

The determinants of connective change

A particularly significant reason for the expansion of connectivity in the Southern North Sea and Eastern Channel system was the establishment of client kingship relations between the Roman state and British rulers in the Eastern and Southern Kingdoms, which began in the aftermath of the Gallic Wars (see pp. 29-30). The Roman state made payments of gold and silver to its British clients as part of these relationships. Furthermore, client kingship encouraged market trade by creating (generally) peaceable conditions in which traders could operate. Young members of the British elite would also have been sent to Rome as hostages. Being brought up in Rome probably impacted upon their dining habits, which became 'Mediterraneanized'. When these hostages returned to Britain they may have created a demand for Mediterranean food and drink and for 'Romanized' pottery from which to eat and drink. These elite practices may have influenced others in southeast Britain to adopt similar practices, further increasing the source of demand. As Creighton has noted, there is also evidence for other changes in diet at this time, which appear to have been influenced by contact with continental consumption practices. These include the introduction of wildfowl into the diet and eating increasing amounts of pig, which is very much a Roman habit.[288]

Another important reason underlying the increasing links between southeast Britain and the near continent was the stationing of a huge Roman army in the vicinity of the Rhine from c. 16/13 BC onwards. Between c. 16/13 BC-AD 9 this army comprised five or six legions (c. 25-30,000 men) along with a large number of auxiliary troops, whilst between c. AD 16-43 it comprised eight legions (c. 40,000 men) with, perhaps, an equal number of auxiliaries.[289] The presence in north-west continental Europe of a large army, many of whom were of Mediterranean origin (creating a demand for Mediterranean food, drink and dining equipment), that was paid with large quantities of coin, stimulated a sizeable trade with Mediterranean Europe via the rivers Rhône and Rhine.[290] A by-product of this was that there were more products in northwest continental Europe that were available to be traded with Britain. In addition, this military force's considerable requirements for agricultural products and iron may also have served to promote an increasing trade with southeast Britain.[291]

Furthermore, economic growth occurred throughout the Western Empire during the later first century BC meaning more mass-produced objects were available for trade. The reasons for this was probably related to the opening up of new markets, as vast swathes of Western Europe had come under Roman control during the campaigns of Caesar and Augustus, and also to the boost to the state finances and money supply afforded by the application of advanced mining technologies on mineral resources, particularly in Spain.[292] In addition, the now permanent presence of a huge Roman army in northwest Europe brought military contracts to the Western provinces along with the stimulating presence of large quantities of cash used to pay the Roman army and those who supplied them.

We witness expanding evidence for manufacturing in many regions. In northern France, for example, the Gallo-Belgic pottery industries began to produce on a large scale from c. 20/10 BC onwards.[293] In Spain, Portugal and Morocco, large-scale production of salted fish is first

[286] *Geog.* IV.5.2.
[287] *Geog.* IV.5.2.

[288] Creighton 2000, 214.
[289] Schönberger 1969, 145, 153; Tacitus *Annals*. II. 6-8.
[290] Whittaker 1994; Cherry 2007; Lo Cascio 2007; Leveau 2007.
[291] Salway 1993, 50; Millett 1990, 32-33; Whittaker 1994; Thomas and Stallibrass 2008; Cavallo *et al.* 2008.
[292] Wilson 2009a, 201.
[293] Deru 1996; Tyers 1996b; 2009.

attested in the later first century BC, whilst there is a major increase in facilities for olive oil and wine production in Spain and southern France at around the same time.[294] Meanwhile, the end of the first century BC also witnessed the huge expansion of the Italian *terra sigillata* industries.[295] Between c. 26-19 BC northwestern Spain was occupied and subdued by the armies of Rome and the gold mines of this region were brought rapidly into operation, perhaps, producing as much as one ton of gold per annum.[296]

The thriving Atlantic trading system of pre-60/50 BC appears to have been heavily disrupted by Caesar's campaigns in Brittany which involved the destruction of the Veneti (Caesar states that the whole population were sold as slaves following their revolt in 56 BC, so an example could be made of those who rebelled against Roman rule).[297] After the Gallic wars the Atlantic system was somewhat peripheral to the developments which impacted upon the Southern North Sea and Eastern Channel system and was less affected by them.

3.2. The Eastern North Sea system

Introduction

From the late first century BC onwards there was a connective increase in the Eastern North Sea system. Much of this can be related to the Roman military's occasional use of the North Sea for the large-scale transfer of troops and supplies to northwest Germany during the campaigns of the Augustan and early Tiberian period. These campaigns were abandoned following Germanicus's punitive expeditions of AD 15-16, in the wake of the disastrous massacre of Varus and his army at Kalkriese in AD 9. The Frisian territories in the northern Netherlands remained within the Empire beyond this date, but these were lost to the Empire following the Frisian revolt in AD 28.

Roman-native interaction took place, but much of this related to looting and the acquisition of war booty from defeated Roman military units by the natives, though luxury items were occasionally exchanged between Roman and native as political gifts. Near the Rhine, Frisian territory was integrated into the Empire down to the Frisian revolt and here taxation was gathered in the form of oxhides which were transferred, via Lake Flevo, to Roman military installations on the Lower Rhine. Evidence for market exchange is scarce, and once again it is largely restricted to the northern Netherlands. Some copper-alloy vessels may have reached northwest Germany via overland intra-Germanic gift exchange networks following trade on the upper Danube frontier.

The Roman military presence

In 16 BC Augustus made the decision to launch a major invasion of Germany.[298] This decision was in part related to the Augustan drive for military conquest and continual expansion of the Empire, and in part a reaction to unrest in Gaul in the years 31-28 BC and 20-19 BC, which had involved tribes from east of the Rhine, and, most pressingly, a need to avenge the defeat of a force under M. Lollius by a coalition of the Sugambri, Usipetes and Tencteri, in 17/16 BC, which resulted in the loss of the fifth legion's eagle.[299] Preparations for invasion were undertaken between 16-13 BC; these involved the construction of bases and a build-up of troops in the Rhine region (**Fig. 3.13**).[300]

A canal - the *Fossa Drusiana* - was dug at this time as well, which linked the Rhine to *Lacus Flevo* (the IJsselmeer) and thence to the North Sea. A *moles* (a groyne or jetty designed to divert water into the canal) was also constructed.[301] Some scholars have suggested that the *Fossa Drusiana* followed the course of the Vecht, beginning in the vicinity of the fort at Vechten.[302] It is more plausible, however, that it lay near the route of the modern Gelderse IJssel, although recent geological analysis indicates that the upper Gelderse IJssel channel itself only began to form c. AD 600 (**Figs. 3.13-14**).[303] Our only evidence for a major Roman fort in the Netherlands at the time of Drusus is the nearby site of Nijmegen.[304] In addition, Tacitus records that in AD 16 Germanicus's fleet assembled at the *Insula Batavorum* (Betuwe near Nijmegen) prior to sailing down the canal.[305] Perhaps most telling is the recovery of a first-century AD tombstone from the river Rhine near the mid-first-century AD fort at Carvium at the bifurcation of the Rhine and Waal.[306] This states that Carvium is near the mole (*Carvium ad molem*). There is also a possibility that there was a second canal, perhaps linking Lake Flevo with the North Sea via Friesland. Our evidence for this comes from Suetonius, who refers to the *Fossae Drusianae* (canals of Drusus).[307]

The offensives against Germany began in 12 BC with the emperor's stepson, Drusus, commanding armies against the Sugambri and Usipetes. In addition, a fleet was sent via the *Fossa Drusiana* to the eastern coast of the North Sea where an alliance was made with the Frisians, a raid prosecuted against the Chauci, and a naval battle successfully contested with the Bructeri on the river

[294] Trakadas 2005; Wilson 2006; Strabo. *Geog*. III.2.6; Haley 2003; Wilson and Marzano, pers. Comm. 2008; Brun and Laubenheimer 2001, 206-207; Brun 2001; Buffat *et al*. 2001.
[295] Kenrick 1993; Oxé *et al*. 2000, 36-38, Tab. II, Figs. 5-6.
[296] Wilson 2002; 2007, 111-113; 2009a; Howgego 1992, 7.
[297] *B.G.* III. 7-19; Cunliffe 1988a; 2005, 600-601.

[298] Wells 1972; Gruen 1996, 179-180.
[299] Cassius Dio *Historia Romana*. 47.49, 51.20-21, 54.11, 20; Velleius Paterculus. II.97; Suetonius *Augustus*. 23; Tacitus *Annals*. I,10. For differing views on the subject see: Wells 1972; 1999; Luttwak 1976; Gruen 1996, 178-188; Nouwen 2004; Drinkwater 2002; Glüsing 1989.
[300] Wells 1972; Gruen 1996, 180; Bosman and de Weerd 2004; Van Enckevort 2004.
[301] Suetonius *Claudius*. 1.2; Tacitus *Hist*. V.19; *Annals*. II.8.1, XIII. 53.
[302] Wells 1972, 111; Galestin 2003a, 479-480.
[303] Makaske *et al*. 2008.
[304] Van Enckevort 2004; Bosman and de Weerd 2004.
[305] Tacitus *Annals*. II. 6-8, 23-24.
[306] Bogaers and Rüger 1974, 90-92.
[307] Suetonius *Claudius*. 1.2; Huisman 1995.

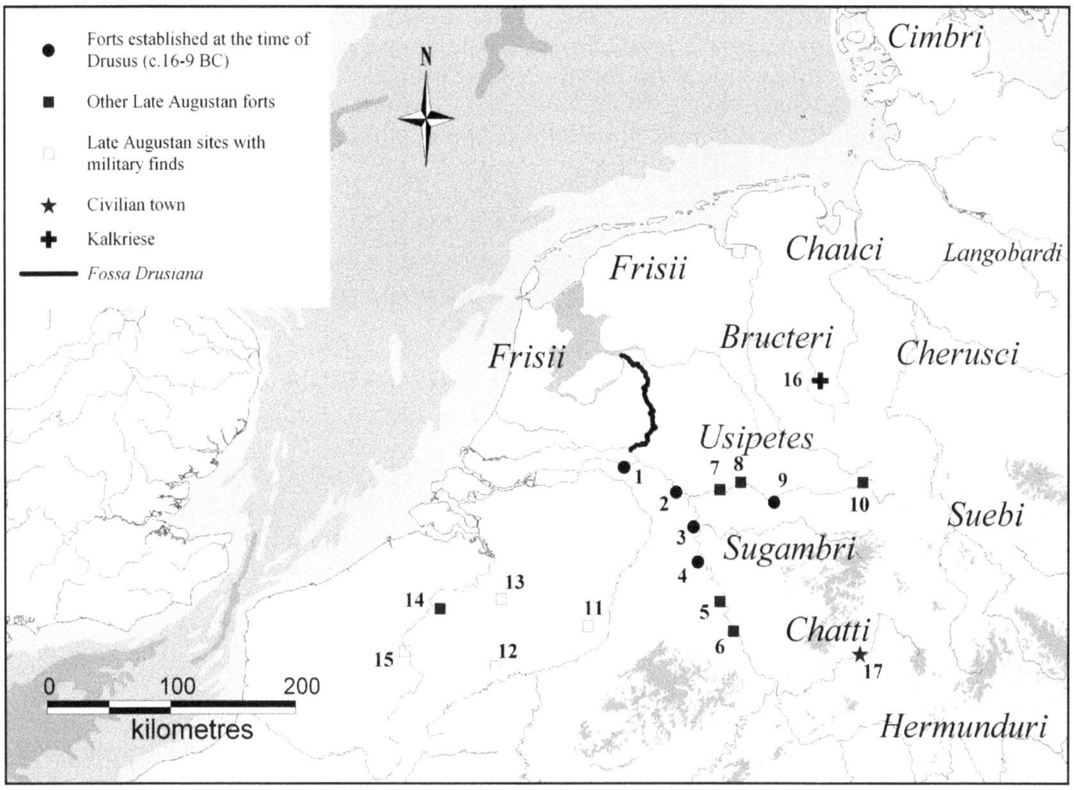

Fig. 3.13. Roman military sites in northwest Europe c. 16 BC-AD 9 (after Bosman and de Weerd 2004, Fig. 13 with modifications).
1. Nijmegen, 2. Xanten, 3. Moers-Asberg, 4. Neuss, 5. Cologne, 6. Bonn, 7. Holsterhausen, 8. Haltern, 9. Oberaden, 10. Anreppen, 11. Tongeren, 12. Liberchies, 13. Elewijt, 14. Velzeke, 15. Tournai, 16. Kalkriese, 17. Waldgirmes.

Ems.[308] Drusus's fleet probably sailed much further on an exploratory mission. There are several references to an Augustan fleet reaching Jutland, and perhaps even the Baltic – a voyage which significantly improved Roman knowledge of the Eastern North Sea coastal region.[309] Augustus's *Res Gestae* states that his fleet sailed from the mouth of the Rhine to the land of the Cimbri (Jutland), where the Cimbri, Charydes, Semnones and other unnamed tribes sought his friendship through envoys.[310] Pliny wrote that the greater part of the Northern Ocean had been navigated under Augustus, with his fleet reaching the promontory of the Cimbri (Jutland), thence either witnessing, or being informed of, an immense sea extending to Scythia and to regions numb with excessive moisture (ice and fog).[311] Tacitus was probably referring to the same event when he described an unsuccessful attempt by Drusus Germanicus to reach the northern Pillars of Hercules, which ancient writers suspected linked the Caspian Sea to the Ocean.[312] That these descriptions do indeed refer to Drusus's fleet, rather than a later voyage, is strongly supported by Tacitus naming Drusus Germanicus as being behind the venture. This was the name by which he refers to Drusus in his *Histories*, whilst other members of Drusus's family - Germanicus and Tiberius - were never referred to by him in this way.[313]

Following the voyage in 12 BC, the Roman campaigns were primarily directed overland against the Sugambri, Usipetes, Cherusci, Chatti and Marcomanni.[314] In AD 5, however, Tiberius, in conjunction with a land-based assault on the Chauci, Langobardi and many unnamed tribes in the vicinity of the Elbe, sent a fleet via the North Sea to the river Elbe. The fleet sailed up the Elbe, proving victorious over several native tribes, before reconnoitring with the army and providing them with supplies.[315]

In AD 9 Varus, the legate of the Rhine army, was in the process of making Germany between the Rhine and the Elbe into a province, but he, along with three entire legions and a large body of auxiliaries, was killed in an ambush by a coalition of German tribes led by the Cheruscan prince Arminius.[316] Recent archaeological excavations prove almost certainly that the location of

[308] Cassius Dio *Historia Romana*. 54.32; Suetonius *Claudius*. 1.2; Strabo *Geog*. 7.1.3; Tacitus *Germania*. 34.
[309] Though Strabo (*Geog*. 7.2.4) states that nothing is known of the Germans near the Ocean beyond the Elbe, although elsewhere (7.2.1) he is aware of envoys and a gift sent by the Cimbri to Augustus.
[310] *Res Gestae* 26; Cooley 2009.
[311] Pliny *H.N.* 2.67; Nicolet 1991, 87, 91-94.
[312] Tacitus *Germania*. 34; Nicolet 1991, 87, 91-94; Rives 1999, 263-264.
[313] *Hist*. 5.19; Nicolet 1991, 87, 91-94. Scholars in support of these events referring to the fleet of Tiberius in AD 5 include Grane (2007, 154) and Storgaard (2003).
[314] Wells 1972; Gruen 1996, 180-183.
[315] Velleius Paterculus. II.106.
[316] Cassius Dio *Historia Romana*. 56.18-24; Velleius Paterculus. II.117-120.

this battle was Kalkriese, near Osnabrück in Lower Saxony (**Fig. 3.13**).[317] This event led to the immediate withdrawal of all Roman forces to the west of the Rhine and the abandonment of the Rhine-Elbe province.[318]

In the year AD 15 Germanicus commanded the Rhine legions on a major punitive campaign against Arminius's coalition. He sailed, with four legions, through "the lakes" (probably the *Fossa Drusiana* and Lake Flevo) and thence along the North Sea coast to the mouth of the Ems, where he rendezvoused with the rest of the army and the cavalry, which had travelled overland. The land between the Ems and Lippe was ravaged, and the site of Varus's defeat was located, where the dead were buried and a monument erected to them. Arminius was then engaged in an indecisive battle, before the fleet conveyed Germanicus and his legions back to the Rhine for winter quarters.[319]

Over the winter of AD 15-16 a thousand vessels were constructed by shipwrights along the Rhine, and these were assembled at the *Insula Batavorum* (Betuwe) between the Rhine and Waal. In AD 16, supplies were sent forward, and the fleet then transported eight legions and allied auxiliaries through the *Fossa Drusiana*, the lakes and the high sea to the Ems, whence the fleet remained in the mouth of the river, on the west side. Arminius's coalition was defeated at Idisiaviso, east of the Weser, and Tacitus records a further successful battle after this. Some of the legions then returned to winter quarters on the Rhine by foot, the rest by ship. On the way back, the fleet was struck by a storm, scattering the ships, some as far as Britain, and sinking many with a great loss of life. The emperor Tiberius subsequently ordered a cessation of offensives beyond the Rhine, perhaps as a result of this accident, perhaps because he realised a conquest of Germany was futile, or maybe, as Tacitus suggests, simply out of jealousy towards his nephew Germanicus.[320] From this date onwards the territory of the Frisians, in the northern Netherlands, was the only area beyond the Rhine that was under Roman control, and this was lost following the Frisian revolt in AD 28.[321]

There is some archaeological evidence in the coastal regions of the Eastern North Sea that is best explained as resulting from a direct Roman presence. This concerns several sites that can probably be linked to the naval campaigns of Germanicus in AD 15-16.

Velsen is situated on the North Sea coast of North Holland at the mouth of the Oer-Ij, which was the northernmost branch of the Rhine (**Fig. 3.14**). It actually comprises two sites, Velsen 1 and Velsen 2, over 1km apart, though they probably formed part of the same complex. Both are undoubtedly Roman forts, with defences and earthen walls, and contain a wide range of material typically associated with a Roman fort, including Roman *militaria*, brooches, coins and other metal objects, wine amphorae, particularly Dressel 2-5 and Camulodunum 184, Dr.20, glass vessels and a wide range of coarse and fine wares, including Gallo-Belgic ware, ITS and South Gaulish *terra sigillata*. There was a harbour installation at Velsen 1, evidenced by moles, jetties and ship houses, and finds of lead at Velsen 2 may indicate ship repair here as well. The find material and the dates obtained through dendrochronology support a date of c. AD 14/16-43 for Velsen 1 and c. AD 39-43 for Velsen 2.[322] The site can probably be equated with the fortress Flevum, named by Tacitus as the place of refuge for the fleeing governor of the Frisians – Olennius – during the Frisian revolt in AD 28. Tacitus described Flevum as housing a considerable force of Romans and allies, who kept guard over the shores of the Ocean.[323]

Two sites, of a somewhat different character, also attest to a Roman military presence at the time of Germanicus further up the North Sea coast; these are Winsum-Bruggeburen in Friesland, and Bentumersiel, on the west bank of the Lower Ems in Lower Saxony, Germany (**Fig. 3.14**).[324] Both of these sites have evidence for native pottery and settlement throughout the Late Iron Age and Roman periods, until at least the second or third century AD. Winsum was raised on a mound in the typical fashion of native terp settlements, though, unusually, Bentumersiel was a flat settlement throughout its existence. What marks these settlements as atypical are large assemblages of Roman finds dating to the Late Augustan and Early Tiberian period.

At Winsum the pottery included ITS (nine vessels), South Gaulish *sigillata* (twelve vessels), Pompeian red ware, Gallo-Belgic ware and several other fine and coarse ware types. Fragments of a *dolium* were also present. The amphorae assemblage included Oberaden 83/Dr.20 (119 sherds, at least four different vessels) for olive oil, Haltern 70 (one rim fragment) for olives preserved in *defrutum*, Dr.7-11 (twenty-six wall fragments) for salted fish, and, for wine, Dr.2-4 (twelve wall fragments), Camulodunum 184 (eight wall fragments) and Gauloise flat-based amphorae (113 sherds, at least twenty vessels, representing a total of at least 500 litres of Gaulish wine). A closely comparable pottery and amphorae assemblage was also present at Bentumersiel. Both sites also possessed small coin assemblages and a wide range of

[317] In an area 6 km long and 1 km wide, over 5000 Roman finds, including 1300 pre-Tiberian coins and Roman *militaria*, have been made. There are, in addition, five pits containing the bones of humans and animals, and a turf, sand and limestone rampart, stretching over 400 m, which may have played a role in the Germanic ambush. See: Schlüter 1999a; 1999b; Wilbers-Rost 2003a; 2003b.

[318] Cassius Dio *Historia Romana*. 56.19-20; Velleius Paterculus. II.119-120.

[319] Tacitus *Annals*. I.60-63, 70.

[320] Tacitus *Annals*. II.6-26; Wells 1972, 7-8, 244-5, 249.

[321] Tacitus *Annals*. IV. 72.

[322] Bosman and de Weerd 2004; Bosman 1997; Morel 1988.

[323] *Annals*. IV.72.

[324] Galestin 2002a; 2002b; 2003a; 2003b; Ulbert 1977; Strahl 2006. Erdrich (2001, 89) argues that Bremen-Seehausen on the Lower Weser was also a Roman military camp or fleet station. There are four Augustan/Tiberian period Roman finds in the vicinity of Bremen: two brooches, a *gladius* sheath and a copper-alloy vessel. These need not imply a military base, however, and they could easily be war booty.

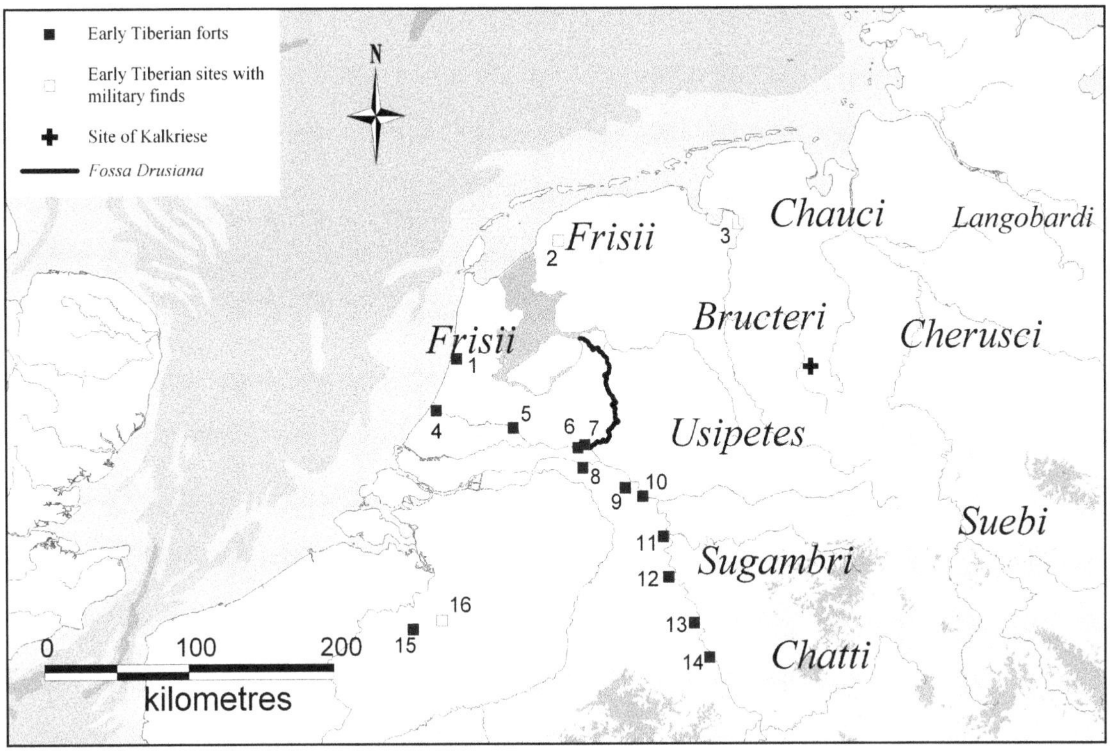

Fig. 3.14. Military sites in north-west Europe at the time of Germanicus' campaigns c. AD 15-16 (after Bosman and de Weerd 2004, Fig. 14 with modifications).
1. Velsen, 2. Winsum-Bruggeburen, 3. Bentumersiel, 4. Valkenburg, 5. Vechten, 6. Driel, 7. Meinerswijk, 8. Nijmegen, 9. Altkalker, 10. Xanten, 11. Moers-Asberg, 12. Neuss, 13. Cologne, 14. Bonn, 15. Asse, 16. Elewijt.

Roman copper-alloy objects, such as, brooches, lantern bases and steelyard weights. At Bentumersiel Roman *militaria* were also identified. All these finds can be broadly dated to the Late Augustan and early Tiberian period. The eight early Roman coins from Winsum, for example, are all pre-Tiberian, though some bear countermarks dating them to c. AD 14/15-22/23.[325]

Although there are no traces of Roman military earthworks at either site, and though Roman *militaria* are lacking from Winsum, there are extremely good grounds for linking these sites to a direct Roman military presence. The wide range of Roman articles is typical of contemporary Roman forts, and *militaria* are present at Bentumersiel. In addition, as we shall see later, imported Roman pottery and amphorae are virtually absent outside these sites. The dating of the find complexes, although by no means precise, suggests a connection with the naval campaigns of Germanicus in AD 15/16. Indeed, Bentumersiel's location, on the west bank of the Lower Ems, closely matches Tacitus's description of the place where Germanicus's fleet remained after conveying the legions to the Ems in AD 16. Roman occupation at both sites was short-lived and may have ceased by AD 16; however, the imprecision of the dating means occupation down to c. AD 30 cannot be ruled out for either site.[326]

Roman and native interaction

Not all of the 'imported' material found along the Eastern North Sea coast can be explained purely in terms of a direct Roman military presence; Roman material is often encountered in 'native' contexts along the Eastern North Sea coast, whilst 'native' material also found its way to the Empire south of the Rhine as well. It is clear that some form of interaction was taking place between Romans and natives.

Imports

There is a thin scatter of Republican and Augustan single coin finds (*denarii* (silver), *aes* (copper alloy) and very rarely *aurei* (gold)), and a handful of Augustan *denarii* hoards from the North Sea coastal regions of Germany.[327] A similar picture is evident in the northern Netherlands, though there are two *denarii* hoards, at Fyns in Friesland and Zoutkamp in Groningen, which both closed slightly later, in AD 37.[328] Silver vessels are occasionally encountered; three silver vessels are present amongst the grave goods of an early first-century grave at Hoby on Lolland in Denmark (**Fig. 3.15**).[329] At Hildesheim, near Hannover, a huge hoard of around seventy silver vessels, weighing a total of 54 kg, was discovered in 1868. The vessels in this hoard could well all be Augustan or earlier

[325] Galestin 2002a; 2002b; 2003a; 2003b; Ulbert 1977; Strahl 2006; Erdrich 2001.
[326] Tacitus *Annals*. II.8; Galestin 2002a; 2002b; 2003a; 2003b; Ulbert 1977; Strahl 2006; Erdrich 2001.
[327] Berger 1992; 1995.
[328] Galestin 2001, Tab. 1; Hiddink 1999, Fig. 7.4; Van der Vin 1996, Tab. 4.
[329] Storgaard 2003; Lund Hansen 1987, 195-196.

Fig. 3.15. The contents of the Hoby grave, Lolland, Denmark (Photo: National Museum of Denmark/Lennart Larsen).

in date, although it has been suggested that some of the vessels might be younger.[330] From c. AD 1 onwards, native objects of silver, primarily brooches and needles, first begin to appear on any scale in the *Barbaricum*.[331] These provide further testament to the import of silver, in the form of coins or vessels, from the Roman Empire, which must have provided the raw material for their production. Gold meanwhile is much rarer in the *Barbaricum* and does not yet seem to have been used for native objects on any scale.[332]

Most of the coins and silver vessels can best be explained in relation to the Roman military campaigns in Germany. Some of the coins could represent casual losses made by soldiers, but many were probably looted by the natives from defeated enemies; Varus's army must have carried a huge amount of coin, indeed, 1,300 pre-Tiberian coins have been identified at the Kalkriese battle site, and their distribution as war booty will have represented a major

330 Strong 1979; Wheeler 1954, 68-70; Grane 2007, 33-34; Jørgensen *et al.* 2003, 383-385; Gregarek 1997, 94-5; Erdrich 2001, 102-103; 2002, 83-91.

331 Eger 1995, 113; Cosack 1979, 29; Lund Hansen 2001, 157.

332 Eger 1995, 113.

injection of silver into native society. Despite insecurities with its dating the best interpretation of the Hildesheim treasure is that the find, or at least the bulk of it, represents war booty from the time of the German campaigns, most likely from Kalkriese itself. In Germanic society war booty was often dedicated to the gods in sacred places. We know this from the Danish weapon deposit finds and from references by Classical historians; however, this was not always the case, Tacitus specifically relates that some of the plunder from Varus's defeat was distributed to individuals.[333] The later (AD 37) *denarii* hoards from the northern Netherlands might indicate small-scale trade, although equally they might relate to a Roman military presence in the Claudian period at the time of Corbulo, they could be loot, or they could have been acquired by Frisians serving as Roman auxiliaries.

The silver vessels from Hoby, meanwhile, are best explained as political gifts. The name 'Silius' was inscribed on the bases of the larger silver vessels, and the group can perhaps be seen as a political gift made by Gaius Silius, who served as the legate of the four legions of the 'Upper army' of the Rhine between c. AD 14-21 and participated in Germanicus's campaigns in AD 15-16, to a, presumably important, native leader.[334]

Finally, we should mention two British gold coins found in Denmark and a British silver coin identified near the terp of Witmarsum in Friesland (**Fig. 3.10**). All three were minted c. 10 BC-AD 10. These may indicate some form of direct low-level contact across the North Sea; indeed, the coin from Vildbjerg in Jutland is a South Ferriby stater and these were minted and distributed around the Humber estuary. The coin from Friesland, a silver coin of the Dobunni, who occupied the Cotswold region, might have been obtained by a Frisian auxiliary serving in the Roman army in Britain at around the time of the Claudian invasion. Certainly, a tombstone from Watermoor in Gloucestershire, dated c. AD 45-70, records a cavalryman from a Frisian auxiliary unit who had died after twenty years service.[335]

Roman copper-alloy vessels, mostly produced in Italy, are present in several graves in the Lower Elbe region and also in Denmark dated, on the basis of native finds, c. AD 1-40. The quantities are small, but, certainly in Denmark, represent a notable increase in the number of 'imported' vessels when compared to graves dated prior to AD 1 (**Tab. 3.1, Figs. 3.16-17**).[336] The dearth of evidence pertaining to Roman vessels in the northern Netherlands during this phase and indeed in general throughout the Roman period is a curious phenomenon. Whilst it may reflect a genuine absence of such vessels, it is probable that their apparent rarity has more to do with the lack of a visible burial custom in this region.[337]

There is a marked increase in copper-alloy brooches of native manufacture in parts of the northwestern *Barbaricum* at this time, and this can almost certainly be connected with the contemporary rise in imports of copper-alloy, principally vessels, from the Empire, which provided the raw material for the production of these objects. Large numbers of native brooches, including, Armbrustfibeln and Rollenkappenfibeln types, were made in brass and bronze between c. AD 1-70. These concentrate heavily in graves around the Lower Elbe and Mecklenburg-Pomerania in Germany, and in Denmark. As with the copper-alloy vessels, the possible rarity of such brooches in the northern Netherlands may in fact be related to the lack of archaeologically visible burial customs.[338]

Many of the copper-alloy vessels probably reached the Eastern North Sea coast of the *Barbaricum* in connection with the Roman campaigns in this region. Some may have been obtained by the natives as war booty; Roman military units will have carried copper-alloy vessels amongst their equipment and an army the size of Varus's must have possessed them in huge quantities.

We should also bear in mind that other mechanisms of distribution probably played a role as well. Some of the vessels could well have arrived by way of Bohemia, where vessels concentrate, via overland intra-Germanic gift exchange networks.[339] The vessels may originally have entered Bohemia, which was the territory of the Marcomanni, by way of market trade. Indeed, Tacitus wrote that camp-followers and traders from the Roman provinces were present in Marcomannic territory in AD 19, having been lured there by trading privileges, and a desire to increase their wealth.[340] Some vessels may even have been presented to native leaders by Roman commanders as political gifts. Certainly, the five examples from the grave at Hoby, which form a banqueting set with the Roman silver vessels, could be placed in this category (**Fig. 3.15**).

A few Roman brooches have also been found in the Eastern North Sea region, the majority at settlements in Friesland.[341] These could be explained in terms of a direct Roman military presence in the region up to the Frisian revolt, though trade, or returning auxiliaries are other possibilities.

Roman swords (*gladii*) are present in several first-century AD weapon graves in central and eastern Jutland, whilst at Hedegård in central Jutland a Roman legionary's

[333] Tacitus *Annals*. I.57, 59; Caesar *B.G.* VI.17; Orosius. V.16; Worsaae 1865; Hagberg 1967, 65-69; Jørgensen 2003; Ilkjær 2003; Kaul 2003; Lund 2003.
[334] Tacitus *Annals*. I.31, 72, II.6-7, 25; Storgaard 2003; Lund Hansen 1987, 195-196.
[335] Boeles 1951, Fig. 27; Henig 1993, 45-46, Nr. 137.
[336] Kunow 1983; Lund Hansen 1987, 106-151, Figs. 73-100, Karte 2; Berke 1990; Grane 2007, 152-156; Storgaard 2003. Though see Erdrich (2001) for an alternative dating approach and Kehne (2003, 323-325), Grane (2007, 140-151) and Lund Hansen (2003a) for counter-criticisms of Erdrich's arguments.
[337] Fulford 1985, 101-102.
[338] Cosack 1979, 21-56, Karten 2-6; Erdrich 1999.
[339] Lund Hansen 1987; Hedeager 1978; 1987.
[340] *Annals*. II.62.
[341] Cosack 1979, Karten 2, 14; Galestin 2003b; Haalebos 1986; Erdrich 2001, 60.

Period	Date	Length of period in years	No. of imported copper-alloy vessels	No. of imported copper-alloy vessels per year
A	c. 150-1 BC	150	4	0.027
B1a	c. AD 1-40	40	21	0.525
B1b	c. AD 40-70	30	10	0.333
B2	c. AD 70-150/160	85	90	1.059
B2/C1a and C1a	c. AD 150/160-210/220	60	56	0.933
C1b	c. AD 210/220-250/260	40	113	2.825
C2	c. AD 250/260-310/320	60	30	0.5
C3	c. AD 310/320-375	60	2	0.033

Tab. 3.1. Rate at which copper-alloy vessels were deposited in Danish graves c. 150 BC-AD 375 (calculated using data from Kunow 1983, Karte 2; Lund Hansen 1987, Karten 16, 17, 19, 22, 24, 25, 30, 32).

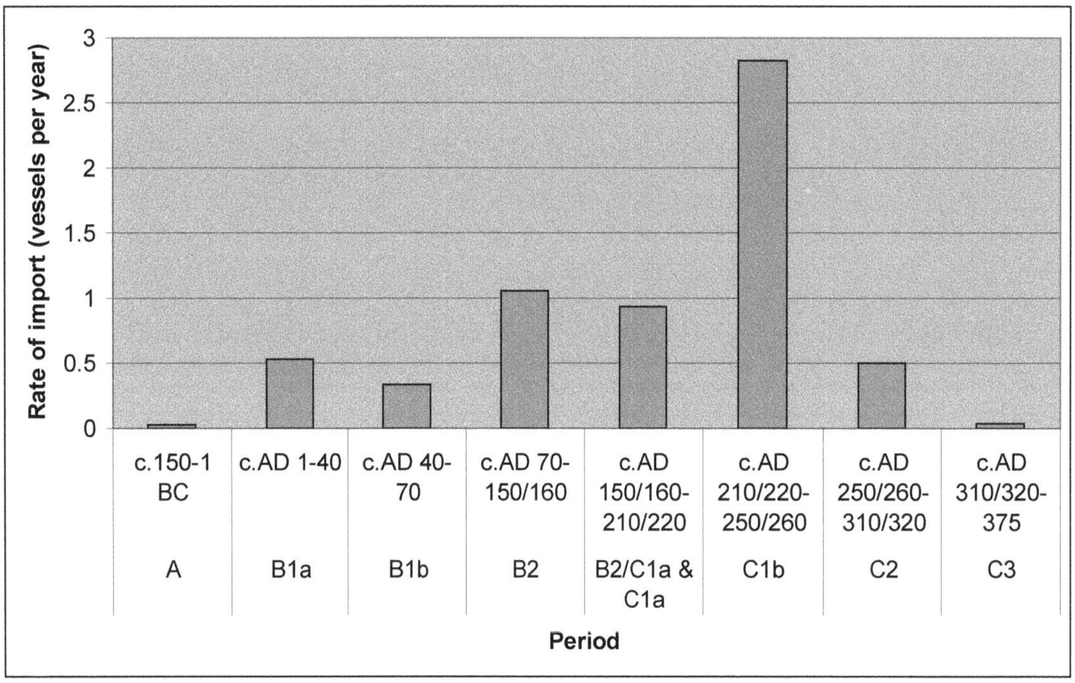

Fig. 3.16. Rate at which imported copper-alloy vessels were deposited in Danish graves c. 150 BC-AD 375.

dagger (*pugio*) was found in an early first-century AD burial that also contained a Roman copper-alloy vessel.

Another burial at Hedegård contained parts of a technically well-made chainmail suit, which was probably produced in the Empire, and chainmail has also been found in a first-century BC/first-century AD context at Putensen in Lower Saxony. These finds probably represent war booty obtained from the Roman army campaigning in Germany, although Grane has suggested that the Hedegård finds were political gifts.[342]

Aside from coinage and metals, other Roman objects are relatively uncommon. Outside of the Roman military installations, at Velsen, Winsum and Bentumersiel, imported amphorae are entirely absent, whilst pottery is rare, restricted solely to *terra sigillata*. In North Holland, which lay within Frisian territory, early first-century AD *terra sigillata* is present on a handful of settlements around Velsen. These finds were, however, very probably looted from the fort following its abandonment c. AD 43; in some cases sherds found at native settlements can be joined exactly to sherds from the fort.[343] In Friesland, meanwhile, *terra sigillata* sherds dating to the first half of

[342] Watt 2003; Grane 2007, 155, 170-1; Jørgensen *et al.* 2003, 386-387; Erdrich 2002, 151.

[343] Vons and Bosman 1988.

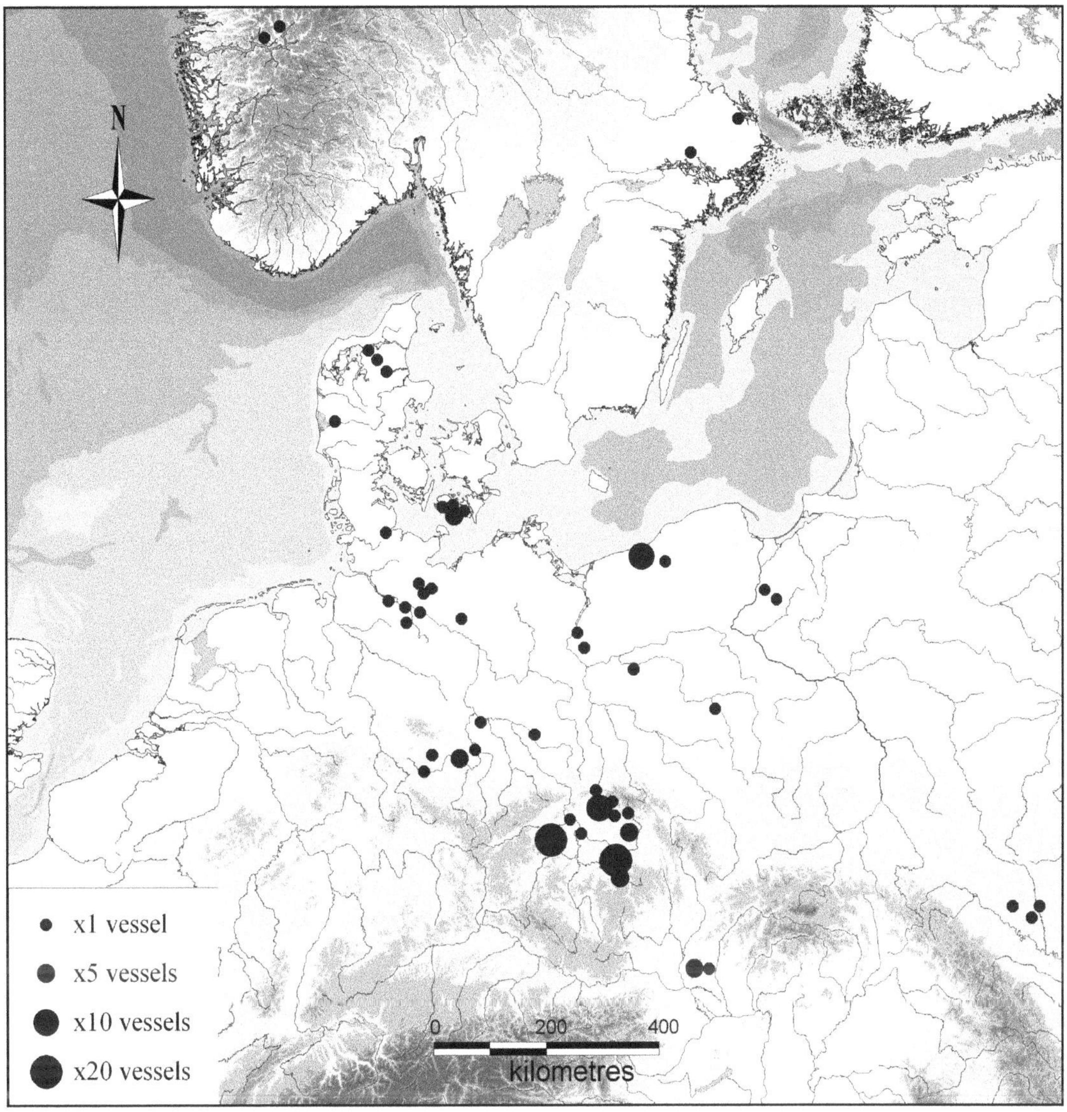

Fig. 3.17. Distribution of imported Roman copper-alloy vessels in period B1a (c. AD 1-40) (after Kunow 1983, Karte 8).

the first century AD are known from ten terpen along the Wijnaldum Ried ridge in Westergo and from five terpen in Oostergo.[344] These may be indicative of extremely limited market exchanges between the natives and the Roman world, though they might simply relate to the direct presence of the Roman military in the region. Aside from Bentumersiel, *terra sigillata* is absent in Lower Saxony, barring a single ITS vessel from Stelle, north of Osnabrück, and it is unknown in Schleswig-Holstein and Scandinavia.[345]

Lava querns are present along parts of the Eastern North Sea coast in some quantity. These derive from within the Empire at Mayen, on the middle Rhine, where several quarries with evidence for Roman-period working have been identified, though these cannot be dated with any precision.[346] The scale of Roman operations was vast and as many as 30,000 querns may have been produced per annum.[347] Over the course of the Roman period lava querns were imported to the northwest *Barbaricum* in large quantities (see p. 123). They are particularly well known from the three northern provinces of the Netherlands, where fragments or complete examples have been recorded from over one hundred settlements (Appendix 11). This includes twenty-one settlements in Groningen, twenty-nine in Friesland and thirty-one in Drenthe.[348] In addition, they are known from thirty-three sites in Lower Saxony, one in Schleswig-Holstein and one in Mecklenburg-Vorpommern, though they are entirely absent from Scandinavia.[349]

Determining the scale of lava quern supply is highly problematic; they are extremely friable and tend to break into numerous small pieces. This means that several

[344] Volkers 1991; 1999.
[345] Erdrich 2001, 151.
[346] Mangartz 1998; 2008; Bockius 2000; Hunold 2001; Peacock 1980; Crawford and Röder 1955; Hörter *et al.* 1951.
[347] Mangartz, pers. Comm. 2008.
[348] Ernst Taayke, pers. Comm. 2009.
[349] Taayke, pers. Comm. 2009; Erdrich 1995a, Abb. 9; 2002, 216-217; Voss 1998, 132.

hundred fragments may in fact derive from a single quern. It is also hard to assess chronology; fragments often occur residually in contexts much later than the time of their actual supply. There is, however, a change in quern design, which occurred around the middle of the first century AD, that provides an important insight into this issue. On the basis of C14 dating of settlement layers in the north Dutch terpen, we know that the so-called Brillerij type, which had a bi-concave upper stone, was in use between c. 200 BC-AD 50 and is largely restricted to layers dating to the late first century BC to first century AD. From c. AD 30-50, this was replaced by the Westerwijtwerd type, which had a flange at the outside of its upper stone, and this type continues to be found in the northern Netherlands up until the third century AD.[350]

Brillerij type querns have been found at thirteen sites in Groningen, seventeen in Friesland, sixteen in Drenthe and two sites in Lower Saxony (Feddersen Wierde and Mahlstedt).[351] This clearly demonstrates that significant quantities of lava querns were reaching the northern Netherlands, and to a much lesser extent northwest Germany, during this period. How they arrived is hard to determine. Their prevalence in the northern Netherlands implies that they are unlikely to be related solely to a Roman military presence. More likely they indicate some form of market exchange with the Lower Rhine regions of the Empire. Tacitus attests that the main route between Frisian territory and the Rhine, even for the Frisians themselves, was across "the lakes" (Lake Flevo) and there was very probably a maritime dimension to these exchanges, which may also have utilised the coastal waters of the northern Netherlands, though overland routes may also have been of importance.[352]

Exports

Evidence for 'exports' from the Eastern North Sea coast region to the Roman Empire is much more limited. A few bronze spurs of north Germanic workmanship have been identified in early first-century AD contexts at Nijmegen, outside the fortress on the Kops Plateau.[353] These must surely be connected to the presence of north Germanic auxiliary troops in the fortress. Certainly, Tacitus wrote that the Chauci provided auxiliaries to Germanicus for his campaigns in AD 15 and 16.[354]

Strabo records that the Cimbri sent the most sacred vessel in their country (presumably a copper-alloy, or silver cauldron) as a gift to Augustus. Of course, this need not have been presented directly to Augustus in Rome, more likely it was given to an important Roman military commander, or official, on his behalf at some point during the German campaigns. The Cimbrian envoys probably travelled by sea; Strabo states that after presenting their gift they 'set sail for home'.[355]

There is a little evidence that small quantities of native Frisian pottery made its way to Roman military installations. Handmade Frisian style pottery has been identified at Velsen (5% of the total), Haltern (two vessels), and to the south and west of the Rhine at Cologne (several vessels in Tiberian contexts), at the earliest fort at Valkenburg and at Xanten. These may have arrived with Frisian auxiliaries. Indeed, a former Roman auxiliary was recorded living in Frisian territory at the time of the Frisian revolt in AD 28.[356] Another possibility is that they represent low-level trade, perhaps in some sort of food product contained within the vessels. The vessel forms are not entirely clear, but they appear to be low jars with a wide mouth. These may have been suitable for food storage and transport as well as for dining.[357]

Tacitus wrote that Drusus had imposed on the Frisians a modest tribute of oxhides for military use. These payments continued until the time of the Frisian revolt in AD 28, when the Frisian governor at that time, Olennius, raised the tax to such an extent that the Frisians could not deliver enough cattle to meet it, and were forced to deliver land and slaves in their stead. This, according to Tacitus, was the primary cause of the Frisian revolt, after which the Romans were forced to leave Friesland and the payment of this tribute would have ceased.[358]

A piece of evidence that has traditionally been used to imply the operation of a substantial market exchange between the Frisians and the Empire is the wax tablet found at the native terp of Tolsum in Friesland. The original translation was thought to indicate the purchase of an ox from a native by individuals associated with the Roman military.[359] A recent re-investigation by Alan Bowman *et al.*, however, dispels this viewpoint.[360] The word thought to refer to an ox was mistranslated. The tablet is, in fact, the second half of a debt declaration between a slave, Carus, and an unknown debtor. The reverse bears the signatures of three witnesses, a legionary tribune, a Batavian soldier and a slave. The transaction is recorded as having taken place on the 23rd Feb AD 29. It must now surely be interpreted as originating in a Roman military context and can probably be related to the presence of a Roman force in Friesland during the events of the Frisian revolt. Though it dates a year later than Tacitus places the revolt, Bowman *et al.* suggest, with precedent, that he may have compressed the events of a prolonged revolt into a single year. Alternatively, the Romans may have maintained a limited military presence in Friesland immediately subsequent to the revolt.[361]

Amber reached the Roman Empire in increasingly large quantities from around the beginning of the first century AD onwards, though it appears to have travelled overland

350 Van Heeringen 1985; Taayke, pers. Comm. 2009.
351 Tayke, pers. Comm. 2009.
352 Tacitus *Annals*. XIII.54.
353 Van Enckevort 2004, 112, Fig. 8.
354 *Annals*. I.60, II.17.
355 *Geog*. 7.2.1.
356 Tacitus *Annals*. II.73.
357 Carroll 2001; Brandt 1983.
358 *Annals*. II.72.
359 Vollgraff, 1917; Whittaker, 1994; 113; Carroll, 2001; 322.
360 Bowman *et al*. 2009.
361 Tacitus *Annals*. II. 72-4; Bowman *et al*. 2009.

from the Danzig Bay area of the Baltic, via Central European trade routes.[362] Small quantities may have arrived in the Empire via the North Sea. Certainly, Pliny stated that during the campaigns of Germanicus (c. AD 15-16) the fleet encountered a North Sea island that was nicknamed *Glaesaria*, or 'amber island'.[363] Amber was imported to Britain in very small quantities between c. 50 BC-AD 43. Examples have been identified in contexts of this date at Skeleton Green, Braughing, Hertfordshire and at Bredon Hill in Worcestershire.[364] They probably arrived via northern France, rather than across the North Sea; Strabo stated that amber gems were amongst the items imported to Britain from *Celtica* (Gaul).[365]

Synthesis

The last decades BC and early decades AD witnessed some increase in connectivity between the Roman Empire south and west of the Rhine and the coastal regions of the Eastern North Sea; much of it can be assigned directly to the Roman military presence in the region from the beginning of Augustus's German campaigns onwards. Certainly, a Roman fortress at Velsen was occupied between c. AD 14/16-43, whilst the Roman military also utilized Winsum and Bentumersiel as bases at the time of Germanicus's campaigns in AD 15/16. These sites were evidently supplied by waterway, in the latter two cases, via the *Fossa Drusiana*, Lake Flevo and the Eastern North Sea.

There was also interaction between Roman and native, evidenced principally by imports of metalwork: copper-alloy vessels, coins and weaponry, but very little outside military contexts. Many of these finds can best be interpreted as representing war booty from Roman military campaigns in northwest Germany and the northern Netherlands. There are a few political gifts that can also be linked into these campaigns. The Roman dining service from Hoby was probably presented by the Roman general Silius to an important native leader at the time of Germanicus's expeditions. Political gifts were not a one-way phenomenon and we have written evidence that Cimbrian envoys, who had travelled by sea, presented a metal vessel to Augustus, or one of his representatives (see p. 50).

The Romans imposed taxation and tribute on some of the native peoples in the Eastern North Sea coastal regions. The Chauci had to deliver auxiliary troops at the time of Germanicus. Between c. 12 BC-AD 28 the Frisians were subject to a tax in oxhides, which were destined for use by the Roman military on the Lower Rhine. Latterly this tax extended to the provision of slaves as well. Evidence for market exchange is much more limited and is largely restricted to the northern Netherlands. Here, large quantities of imported lava querns provide our best indication of trade with the Lower Rhine region of the Empire, which would have taken place via Lake Flevo and possibly the *Fossa Drusiana*. A handful of finds of *terra sigillata* found in the same region may also indicate market exchange, though a connection to a Roman military presence cannot be ruled out. It is hard to point to exports other than hides; a few finds of Frisian pottery from Roman military installations might have been traded, though they might also have arrived with Frisian auxiliaries. Some of the copper-alloy vessels from northwest Germany may have arrived via overland intra-Germanic gift exchange networks following trade on the upper Danube frontier.

3.3. Maritime systems c. 50 BC-AD 43: a comparison

The Southern North Sea and Channel systems can be clearly distinguished from the Eastern North Sea system and, barring a few British coins found along the Eastern North Sea coast, there is negligible evidence for cross-North Sea linkage. In common with each other, both systems witness a connective expansion from the end of the first century BC onwards. There are, however, notable differences. The scale of the Southern North Sea and Channel systems far exceeds their counterpart, and the form the connectivity takes in each system is also highly distinct. In the Southern North Sea and Eastern Channel system fairly large-scale political payments of gold and silver were made by the Roman state to British client kings. The majority of exchange in both the Southern North Sea and Eastern Channel system and in the Atlantic system, meanwhile, was of market type. In contrast, in the Eastern North Sea system most connections can be explained by the direct presence of the Roman army and the looting of their equipment and possessions by natives as war booty. Political gifts were occasionally exchanged between Roman and native and taxation was of some importance in linking the Frisian area, of the northern Netherlands, to the Lower Rhine. Most notably, market exchange was extremely scarce, and can only account for the movement, via Lake Flevo, of some articles between the northern Netherlands and the Lower Rhine.

The reasons for these differences were largely political. In southeast Britain, generally positive relations existed between the client kings and the Roman state, which facilitated a connection with Roman economic systems. Furthermore, the presence of these kings at Rome whilst young acquainted them with Mediterranean foodstuffs and dining habits and helped to drive importation of these products to Britain. In addition, these links built on the pre-existing social and economic connections with northern France, which had developed during the preceding phase. By contrast, in the Eastern North Sea system the lack of engagement of the natives with Roman economic systems can largely be related to their frequently hostile relations with the Empire.

The causes of connective change in the two regions are thus significantly different. In the Southern North Sea and Channel system connective change is best explained as

[362] Calvi 1996; 2005; Buora 1996; Pasquinucci 1978.
[363] *H.N.* XXXVII. 11.
[364] Appendix. 3. Objects Nos. 14, 39.
[365] *Geog.* IV.5.3.

being driven by the development of client kingship relations, a sizeable Roman military presence on the Rhine, and economic expansion in the Mediterranean provinces of the Western Roman Empire. In the Eastern North Sea region, meanwhile, the primary engine of change was the Roman military presence during the prosecution of the German campaigns up until the Frisian revolt.

4. North Sea and Channel connectivity AD 43-165

4.1. The Southern North Sea and Channel systems

Introduction

Following the Claudian invasion of Britain there was a huge rise in levels of connectivity in both the Southern North Sea and Eastern Channel and Atlantic systems, though greater in the former than in the latter. Vast quantities of products were shipped across these seaways as a result of payments and transfers of wealth made by the Roman state, and through private trade. There are, however, indications that the Roman state's payments were not balanced and that they pumped far more into Britain than they removed from it.[366] The main factors lying behind the connective changes are: Britain's political integration into the Empire; the Roman state's need to make payments to support a large British garrison; a growth in 'Romanized' consumer tastes within Britain; and economic growth in parts of the Western Empire.

Continental imports

Coinage and metals

From AD 43 vast amounts of coin were paid into Britain, principally as a result of payments made by the Roman state. There was a large body of troops in Britain from the invasion onwards (**Tab. 4.1**). The invading army probably constituted 40,000 men and whilst we cannot be precise about subsequent changes in the size of the garrison throughout the later first century, by the first half of the second century it evidently numbered c. 53,000, though we should bear in mind that this figure is based on all the recorded units being at full strength, which may not have been the case in practice. This latter figure is based on the fact that 63 or 64 auxiliary units are attested on inscriptions dated AD 98-146 and documentary evidence suggests that the theoretical strength of an auxiliary unit was 600 men. To this we may add three legions.[367] Since Augustus, legionaries were paid HS (= *sestertii*) 900 per year, which was increased to HS 1200 under Domitian and remained at this level down to the end of the second century AD.[368] Auxiliaries, meanwhile, were probably paid at about 5/6 the rate of legionaries.[369]

Date	No. of auxiliary units	No. of legions	Total theoretical size of garrison
AD 43	Unknown	4	40,000
AD 150	63/64	3	53,000
AD 210	60 + 10 *numeri*	3	55,000
AD 390	53	2	18,000

Tab. 4.1. Size of British military garrison (based on Breeze, 1984; 268 with alterations).

Soldiers would only have received a portion of their salary in cash; indeed, an Egyptian papyrus of AD 81 records that legionaries had only c. HS 150 cash available for spending.[370] Much of the soldiers' pay was deducted for the provision of equipment and other supplies. We can imagine that the state obtained some of these provisions through taxation in kind, but much would have been bought from civilian suppliers. In the case of the supply of the British garrison many of these payments would have been made to foreign enterprises, but the state also made purchases from British civilian producers as well. Indeed, this is archaeologically well exemplified by the Black burnished ware industry of Poole Harbour, which supplied large quantities of pots to the northern military garrisons between the early second and mid-fourth centuries, evidently by military contract.[371]

In addition to their pay soldiers could also expect a discharge bonus of HS 12,000 on completion of their military service.[372] Duncan-Jones estimates that each legion produced c. 120 veterans per year.[373] Officers, meanwhile, earned far more than the troops, probably

[366] Fulford 1984.
[367] Breeze 1984; Mattingly 2006, 130-131.
[368] Wilson 2009a; Lo Cascio 2007, 637.
[369] Speidel 1973; Hopkins 1980, 124; Lo Cascio 2007, 637.
[370] Cherry 2007, 733; Lo Cascio 2007, 637-638.
[371] Allen and Fulford 1996; Mattingly 2006, 517-518.
[372] Hopkins 1980, 124; Lo Cascio 2007.
[373] Duncan-Jones 1994, 34.

around 20% of the total spent on the military.[374] State expenditure also included the payment of senatorial and equestrian officials, which we can very roughly estimate at c. HS 2,000,000 per year. Certainly, we know that an early third-century AD governor of Africa was earning HS 1,000,000 per annum.[375]

Based on these figures we can very roughly estimate the Roman state's total annual expenditure on Britain at HS 53 million in the Claudian period and HS 87 million in the mid-second century AD (**Tab. 4.2**). The second estimate compares closely to Mattingly's calculation of annual British military costs at HS 90 million in the mid-second century AD.[376] Of course, we should bear in mind that, as discussed, not all of this was paid to Britain in coin, but a substantial portion must have been. State payments must principally have been made in precious metal coin. Walker has estimated that during the reign of Antoninus Pius (AD 138-161) the average import of *aes* was only HS 108,000 per annum, which, in terms of value, represents only c. 0.1% of the state's total annual expenditure on Britain (HS 87.4 million).[377] An examination of British hoards closing between AD 41-180 provides c. 500 *aurei* and more than 15,000 *denarii*, a ratio of 1:30, which is not too far away from the value ratio of 1:25 between these types of coins.[378] This strongly suggests that both gold and silver coins were heavily utilised as the media through which state payments were made.

	AD 43	AD 150
Legionary pay	18	18
Auxiliary pay	15	40
Retirement bonuses	11.5	15.8
Officer pay	6.6	11.6
State officials' pay	2	2
Total	53.1	87.4

Tab. 4.2. Britain's estimated cost to the Roman state (HS (= sestertii) million).

Not all coin arrived in Britain as a result of state expenditure; some arrived through trade. Although there are distinct regional differences in coin pools, particularly with low-value *aes*, which have been used to suggest a lack of integrated trade between the various regions of the northwest Empire, there are also considerable overlaps. As the evidence stands it cannot be used to reject the possibility of substantial inter-regional movement of coin through trade.[379] Loan payments were also made between private individuals; Cassius Dio reveals that Claudius provided loans to the foremost Britons, whilst Seneca had lent the islanders the gigantic sum of HS 40 million.[380] Of course, we should bear in mind that these loans, and quite possibly many payments associated with trading activity, may not actually have necessitated physical movement of coin at all. Recent studies have revealed that Roman financial systems were extremely sophisticated and relied heavily on the use of credit.[381]

Aucissa and Hod Hill brooches have been found at a wide range of British sites, both native and military, and are dated c. AD 43-70. Many were probably brought from the continent as personal possessions by invading troops, though some may have been traded.[382] After c. AD 70 imported brooches are extremely rare, which can probably be connected to a major expansion in Romano-British brooch production.[383] Copper-alloy vessels also arrived, which, on the basis of typology and of makers stamps on some vessels, came from manufactories in Italy and, increasingly as time went on, Gaul. Mid-first-century *paterae* (handled pans) of Eggers' types E154-155, E131 and E137-140 are certainly known from several British sites, whilst a bucket (E24) is present at Hod Hill. A larger group of late first- to mid-second-century copper-alloy vessels, primarily *paterae* (E139-144, E150), and pan and filter sets (E160, E162), have been found throughout Britain.[384] The imported vessels have a strong, though by no means exclusive, correlation with Roman military sites. Some of them probably arrived as personal possessions of troops sent to Britain from abroad, but trade is another possibility.

Pottery

From AD 43 continental pottery was imported to Britain in huge quantities; by far the most important imports were fine *terra sigillata* tableware. Enormous amounts of *sigillata* reached Britain from workshops in southern Gaul, principally La Graufesenque, between AD 43-110/120. The volume of pots involved is striking; Marsh recorded over 10,000 decorated and stamped South Gaulish sherds from London, whilst it is found in quantity at sites all over Britain (**Fig. 4.1**). There is a strong chronological pattern to South Gaulish Ware import; Marsh's study of large urban and military assemblages revealed little import in the AD 40s, but after AD 50 there was a major increase, with a peak between c. AD 70-85. This was followed by a dramatic

[374] Hopkins 1980, 124-125; Lo Cascio 2007, 637.
[375] Mattingly 2006, 493.
[376] Mattingly 2006, 493. Calculated as being 15% (the proportion of the total Roman forces in Britain) of Duncan-Jones's (1994) overall estimate of annual Roman military expenditure (c. HS 600 million) in the second century AD. Based on 15% of Hopkins (1980) figure of HS 400-500 million for total annual army pay, we arrive at a figure of HS 67.5 million. Other estimates of annual British military pay are: HS 27-40 million (Casey 1994a, 7), HS 32 million (Cherry 2007, 732) and HS 26 million (Millett 1990, 58).
[377] Walker 1988, 304-305.
[378] Calculated using data from Robertson 2000; Abdy 2002.
[379] Hopkins 1980; Duncan-Jones 1990; Howgego 1994; Walker 1988; Kemmers 2005.
[380] Cassius Dio *Historia Romana*. 62.2.
[381] Howgego 1992; Harris 1993; 2006; 2008; Andreau 1999; Temin 2001; Wilson 2009a; Bowman, 1994.
[382] Bayley and Butcher 2004; Eckardt 2005; Worrell 2007.
[383] Bayley and Butcher 2004.
[384] Eggers 1966; Moore 1973; McPeake and Moore 1978; Bennett and Young 1981; c.f. Kunow 1983; Lund Hansen 1987.

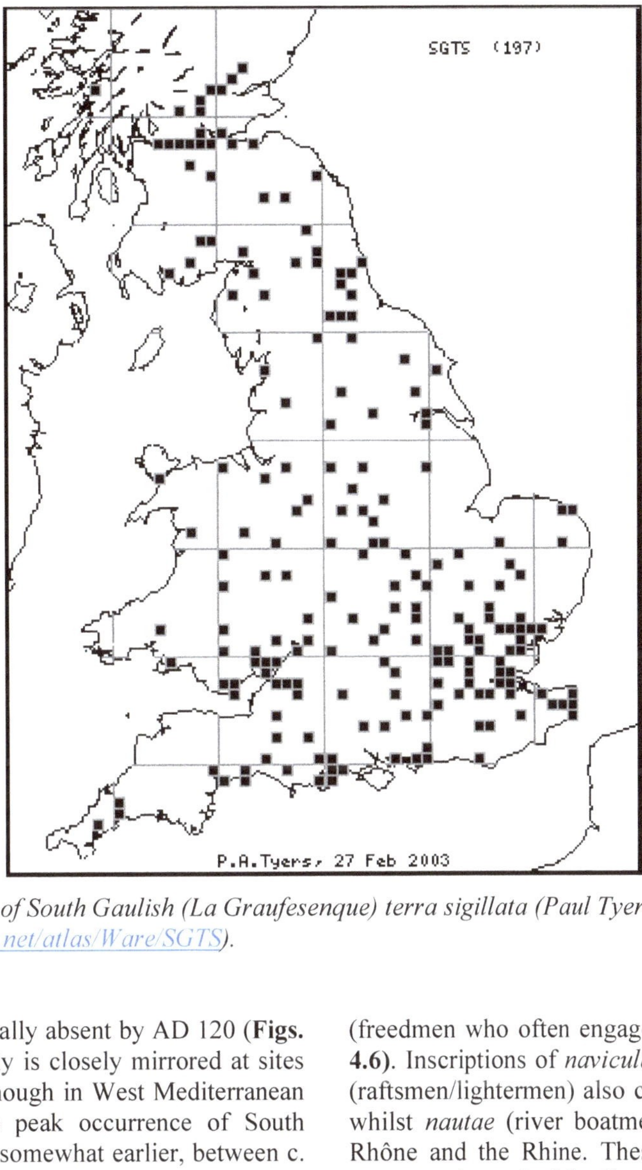

Fig. 4.1. British distribution of South Gaulish (La Graufesenque) terra sigillata (Paul Tyers (URL accessed June 2010): http://www.potsherd.uklinux.net/atlas/Ware/SGTS).

decline and the ware is virtually absent by AD 120 (**Figs. 4.2-3**). This pattern of supply is closely mirrored at sites on the adjacent continent, though in West Mediterranean regions of the Empire the peak occurrence of South Gaulish ware can be placed somewhat earlier, between c. AD 55-70 (**Fig. 4.4**).[385]

The British distribution of South Gaulish ware is so extensive that it is difficult to establish which ports were involved in the dissemination of this ware. The vast assemblage from London, however, points towards the importance of this site as the principal British entrepôt.[386] The prevalence of South Gaulish *sigillata* throughout the Western Empire makes it similarly hard to determine with precision how it reached Britain (**Fig. 4.5**). Atlantic routes via southwest and northwest France may well have been of importance; however, the majority probably arrived across the Southern North Sea and Eastern Channel from ports on the coast of north France, Belgium and the southern Netherlands.

A trade route of great importance linked the Mediterranean to northwest Europe via the valleys of the Rhône and Rhine and their tributaries. The significance of this route is clear from the distribution of inscriptions recording *negotiators* (traders), and *Seviri Augustales* (freedmen who often engaged themselves in trade) (**Fig. 4.6**). Inscriptions of *navicularii* (shippers) and *utricularii* (raftsmen/lightermen) also cluster along the river Rhône, whilst *nautae* (river boatmen) are distributed along the Rhône and the Rhine. These inscriptions first begin to appear at the end of the first century AD and the majority date to the second and early third century AD when the epigraphic habit, or practice of producing named inscriptions, was at its height.[387]

Eleven inscriptions found on the continent explicitly record trading contacts with Britain, although the dateable examples appear to fall in the late second and early third century (**Tab. 4.3**). Of these nine derive from northern Gaul or the Rhine provinces, with only two examples identified elsewhere (Bordeaux).

Following the reduction in South Gaulish ware import at the end of the first century AD, the products of the Central Gaulish industry at Les Martres became the dominant source of supply between c. AD 100-130. The quantities involved were generally low, however, and the ware was restricted to a small number of sites.[388] A sizeable assemblage at London indicates its

[385] Marsh 1981; Going 1992; Dannell 1999.
[386] Rhodes 1986; Marsden 1994, 19-21; Symonds 2000; Marsh 1981.
[387] Verboven 2007; Middleton 1979; Whittaker 1994, 106; MacMullen 1982; Hope 1997.
[388] Willis 2005; Marsh 1981; Delage 2001; Marsh 1981; Dickinson 1990, 213; 2000, 204.

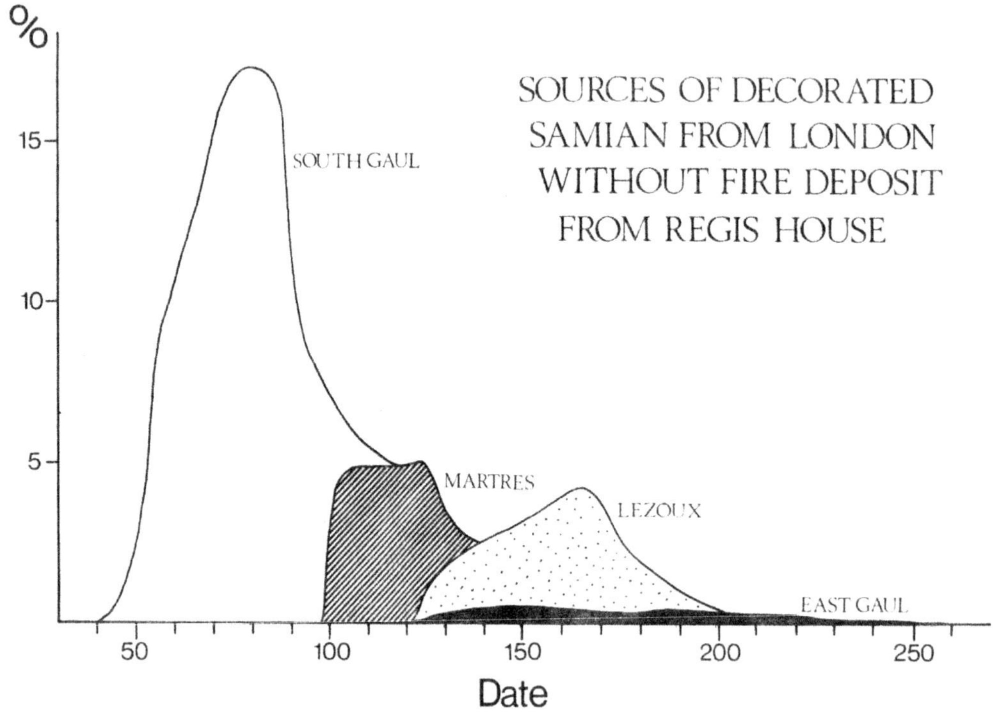

Fig. 4.2. London's terra sigillata supply (Marsh 1981, Fig. 11.7).

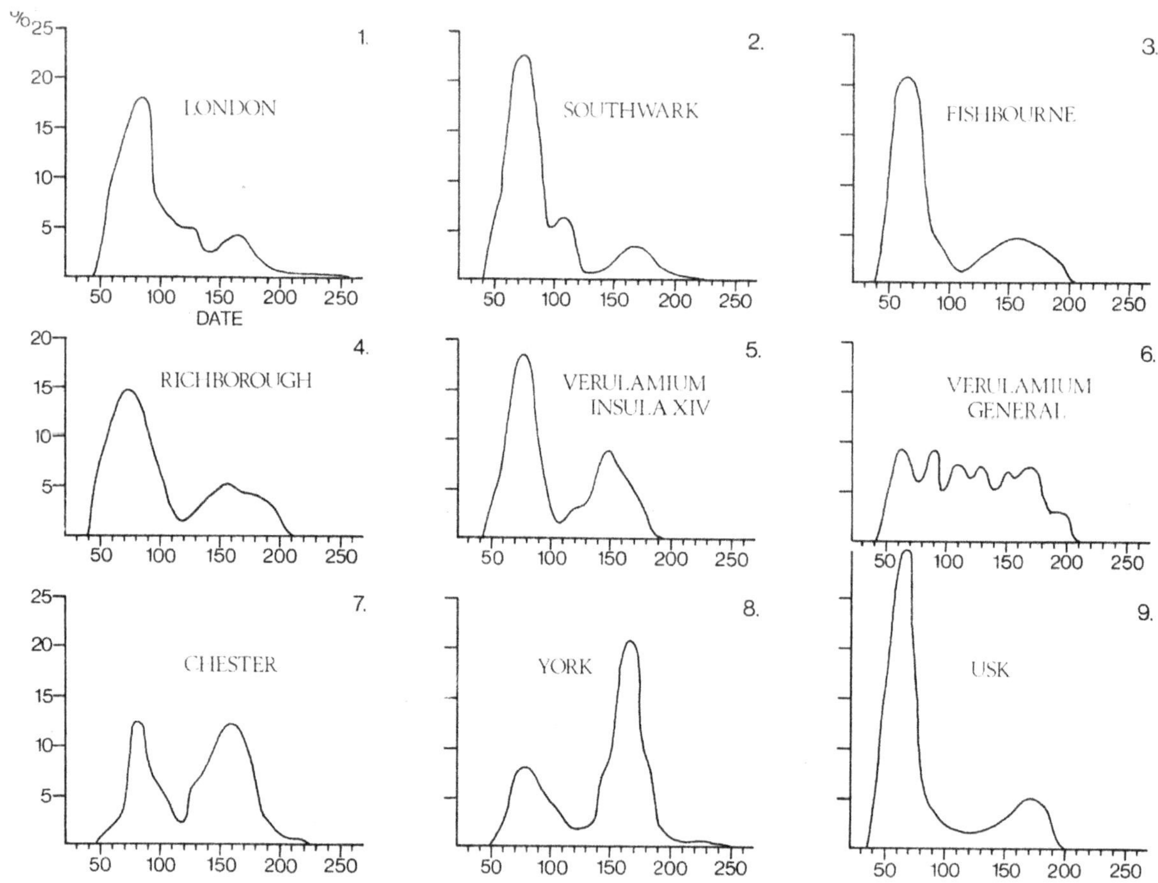

Fig. 4.3. Terra sigillata supply at various British sites (Marsh 1981, Fig. 11.8).

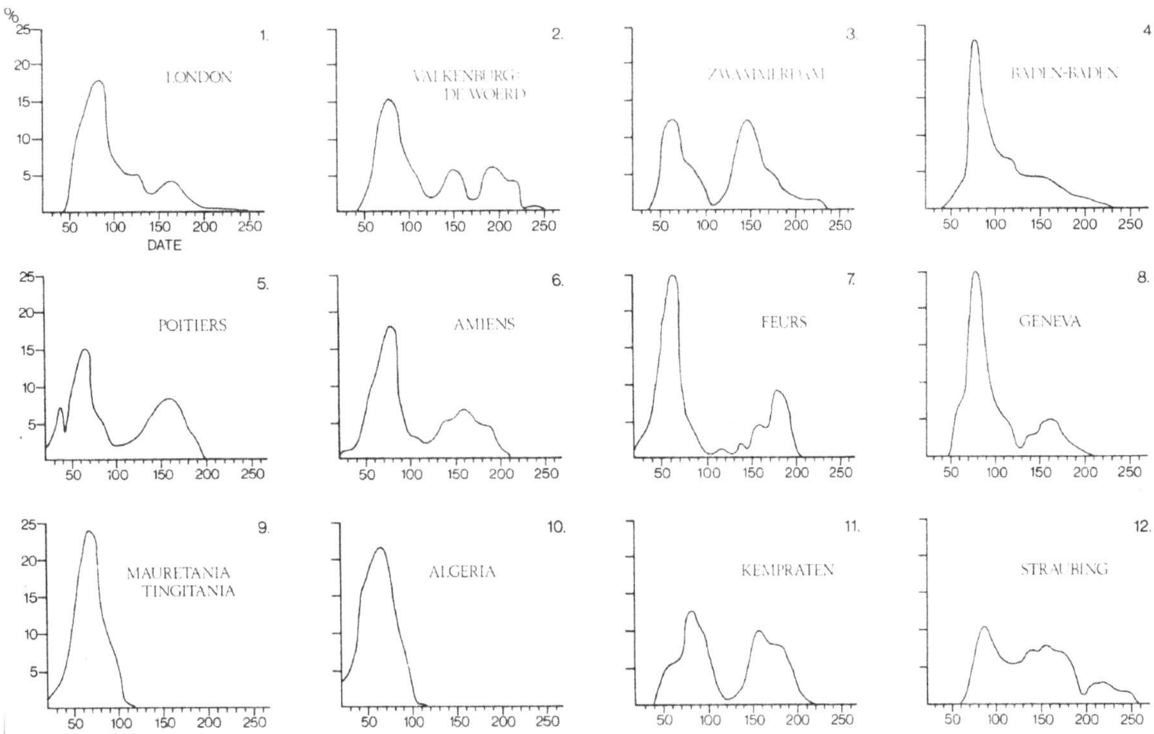

Fig. 4.4. Terra sigillata supply at various continental sites (Marsh 1981, Fig. 11.11).

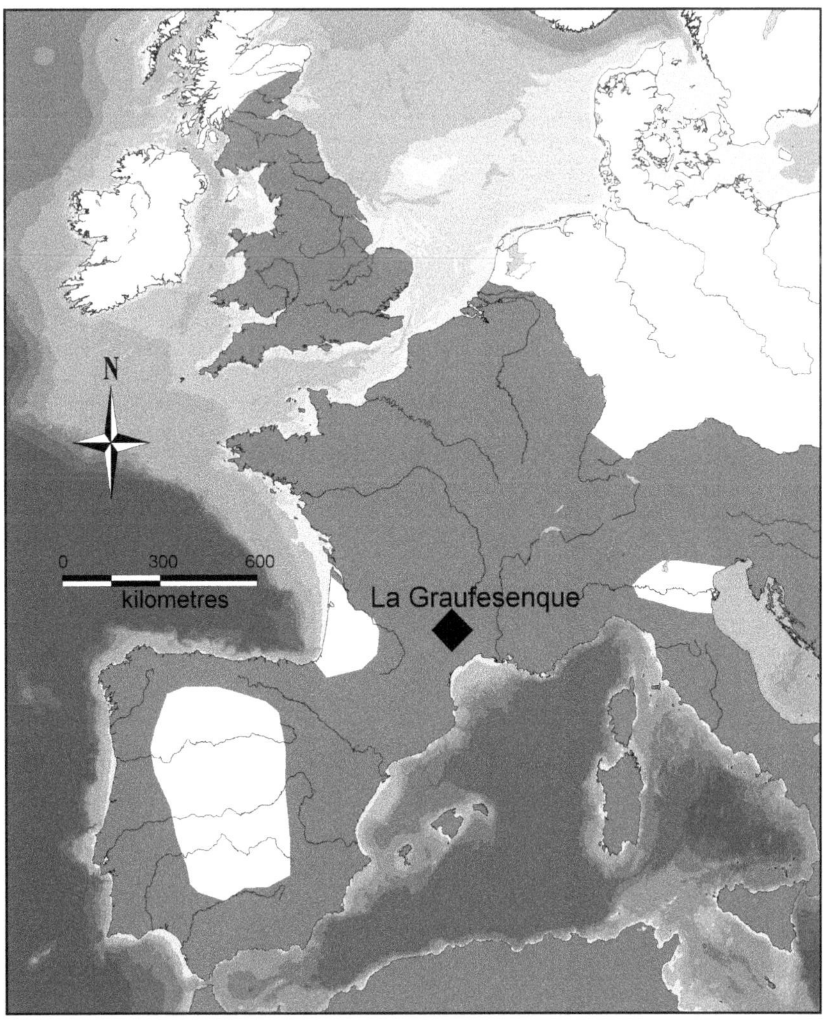

Fig. 4.5. Distribution of South Gaulish terra sigillata from La Graufesenque (after Tyers 1996b, Fig. 97).

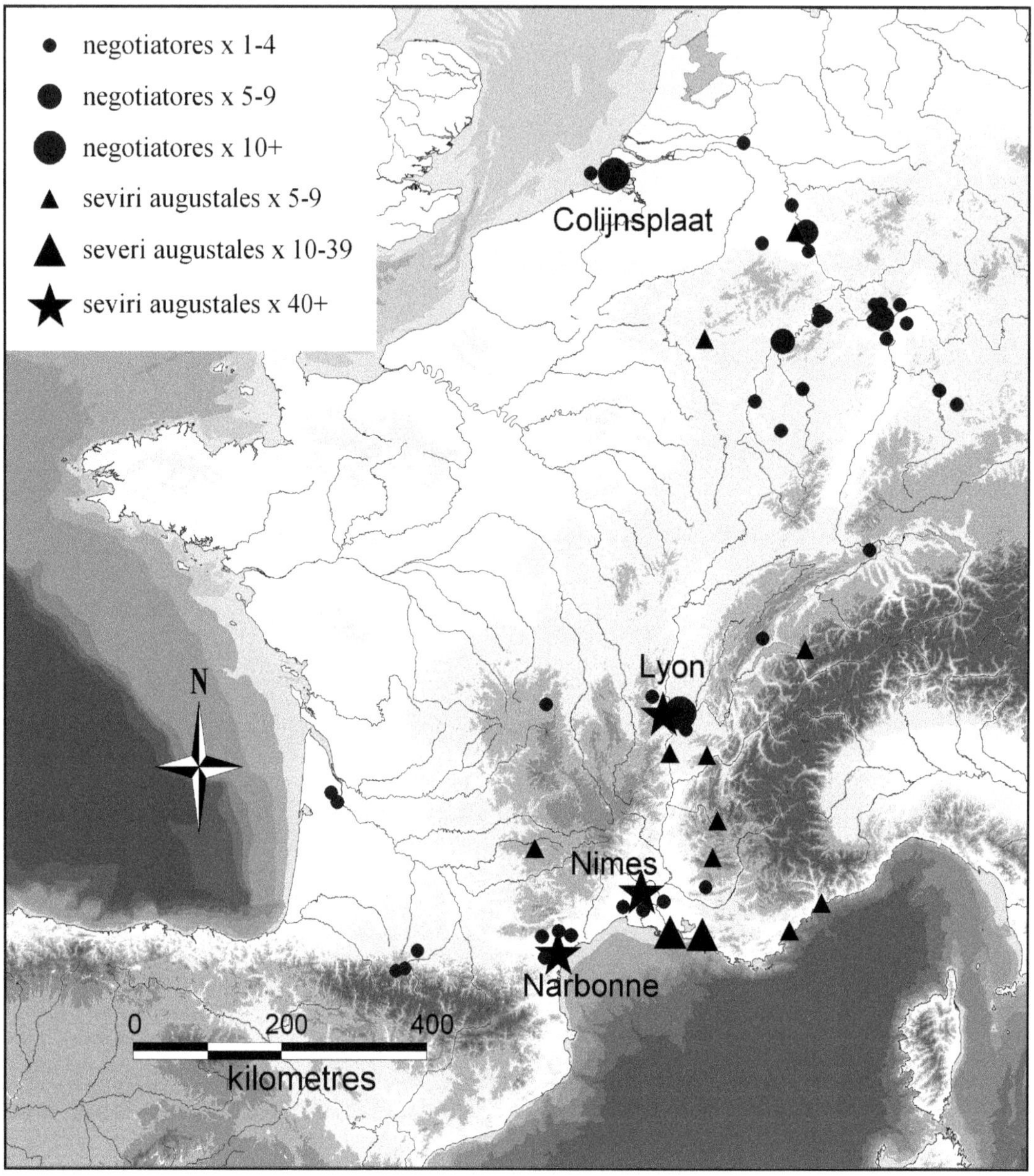

Fig. 4.6. Distribution in Gaul of inscriptions of negotiators (traders) and freedmen augustales who often took part in trade (after Whittaker 1994, Fig. 29 and Middleton 1979, Fig. 2).

probable importance as the main port of entry for this ware, but even here supply was never more than a quarter to a third of the maximum levels reached by South Gaulish ware.[389] Les Martres ware has a wide northwest European distribution.[390] It likely reached Britain via both the Southern North Sea and Eastern Channel and the Atlantic.

By the mid-second century AD Montans ware from Southern Gaul began to reach Britain in slightly increased quantities, but it was never especially common. It has a widespread, though low-density, distribution throughout Britain, both east and west. The densest concentrations appear to be at London and at military sites along the Antonine Wall.[391] On the continent Montans *sigillata* is restricted to western France and Iberia and it is virtually unknown east of the Seine. This clearly suggests that this ware came to Britain via Atlantic sea routes (**Fig. 4.7**).[392]

The overwhelming majority of mid-second century *sigillata* import derived from the Central Gaulish workshops at Lezoux. Lezoux products had been reaching southern Britain in very small amounts since the early first century AD, but they increased significantly from c. AD 120 and had become the most common *sigillata* imports by c. AD 130.[393] Studies of stamped and decorated Lezoux products consistently

[389] Marsh 1981; Rhodes 1986; 1989; Symonds 2000; Willis, 2005, section 6.2.
[390] Tyers 1996b, 113.
[391] Fulford forthcoming; Willis 2005, section 6.6, Appendix 6.8, Tab. 12.
[392] Tyers 1996b, 112-113.
[393] Marsh 1981; Willis 2005, section 6.2.

Find spot	Business	Origin of trader	Name	Date
Colijnsplaat, Zealand, Netherlands	*negotiator Britannicianus*		Arisenius Marius (lib)	Late second or early third century AD
Colijnsplaat, Zealand, Netherlands	*negotiator Britannicianus*	*cives Veliocassinius*	Placidus Viduci fil	Late second or early third century AD
Colijnsplaat, Zealand, Netherlands	*Negotiator cretarius Britannicianus*		M Secund(inius?) Silvanus	Late second or early third century AD
Colijnsplaat, Zealand, Netherlands	*Negotiator cretarius Britannicianus*			Late second or early third century AD
Colijnsplaat, Zealand, Netherlands	*negotiator Cantianus et Geserecanus*		Valerius Mar[...]	Late second or early third century AD
Cologne, Germany	*negotiator Britannicianus*		C Aurelius C L Verus	
Bonn, Germany	*reversus [e]x Britannia*		Asprius A[...]	
Cassel, Nord, France	*[negoti]ator [?vesti]arius ex [Provinci] a Brit[annia]*		Fufidius	
Marsal, Alsace, France	*negotiator vestia[rius ex Britannia?] superiore*			
Bourdeaux, France	*Neg[otiator] Britannicianus*	*civis Trever*	L Solimarius	
Bourdeaux, France	*sevir Augustalis* of both York and Lincoln		M Aurelius Lunaris	AD 237

Tab. 4.3. Inscriptions relating to trade between Britain and the continent (Based on Hassall 1978, Tabs. I-II; Stuart and Bogaers 2001).

indicate a steady growth in their presence on British sites from c. AD 120 to a peak between c. AD 160-170 (**Figs. 4.2-3**).[394] After this date supply graphs indicate a decline down to c. AD 200, following which Lezoux products totally disappear. Once again, this is the chronological pattern evidenced from continental sites as well (**Fig. 4.4**).[395] In considering the end of Lezoux importation to Britain we should bear in mind that there are a lack of well-dated assemblages in the second half of the second century AD, which means that the trend apparently indicated by supply graphs is by no means completely accurate. What we can say is that the supply of Lezoux products, and the output of the Lezoux industry in general, probably peaked around the mid- to late second century AD and suffered decline at some point in the second half of the second century AD. The data are at present not clear enough to judge exactly when in the second half of the second century this decline occurred and whether it was gradual, or, as in the case of La Graufesenque, rapid.[396]

Lezoux *sigillata* reached Britain in huge quantities. Marsh's study of *sigillata* supply generally indicates much higher rates of import for South Gaulish Ware during the late first century, but to some extent this is misleading (**Figs. 4.2-3**). Lezoux Ware appears to have been less significant than South Gaulish Ware at the major southern urban centres, such as London, but it is well known at northern military sites, such as York and Chester and it is also found on a wider range of smaller civil sites, in larger quantities than South Gaulish *sigillata* (**Tab. 4.4**).[397] Willis has also pointed out that there is a higher incidence of decorated bowls, upon which supply graphs principally rely, amongst South Gaulish products of the first century AD compared to the mid-second-century Lezoux industry.[398] These factors suggest that mid-second-century Lezoux import may in fact have approached the vast levels of earlier South Gaulish supply.

[394] Marsh 1981; Dickinson 2000; Bird 1999.
[395] Marsh 1981; though Willis has argued for continuously high import between AD 150-200 on the basis of contextually dated pottery groups.
[396] Michael Fulford, pers. Comm. 2010.
[397] Marsh 1981; Fulford 1991; Willis 2005, section 6.5.1; Rodwell 1987, 92-97.
[398] Willis 1998b, Tab. 4; Willis 2005, section 7.3.4.

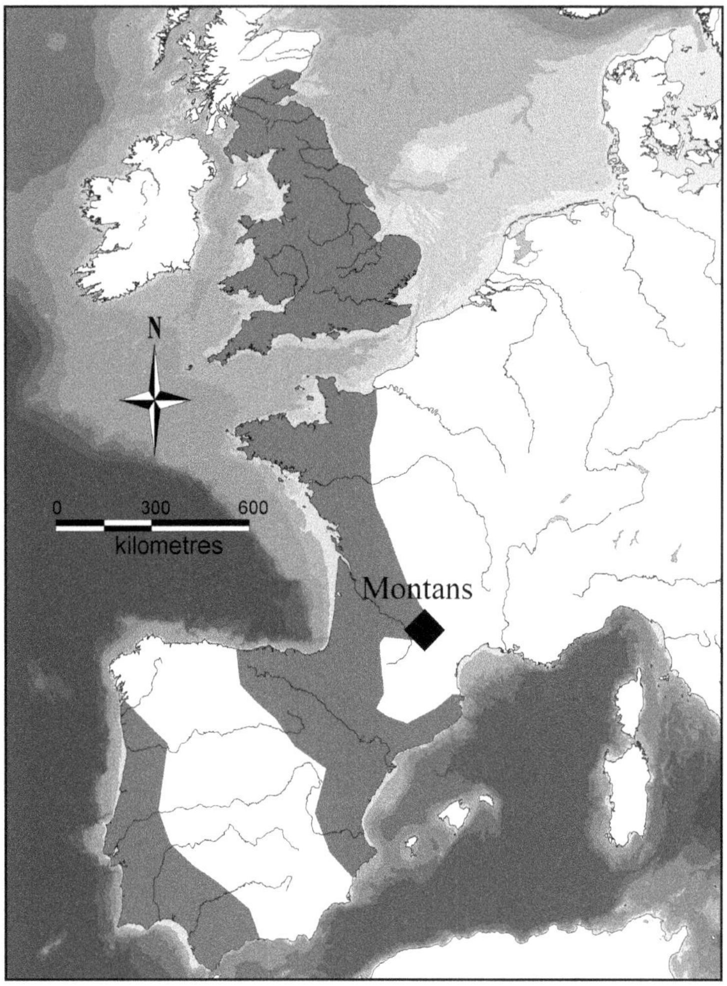

Fig. 4.7. Distribution of South Gaulish terra sigillata from Montans (after Tyers 1996b, Figs. 98).

Site	Site type	No of vessels	South Gaul (%)	Central Gaul (%)	East Gaul (%)	Reference
Alchester, Oxon	Small town	507	7	85	8	Booth *et al.* 2001; 277-285.
Asthall (Area A), Oxon.	Small town	228	9	82	9	Booth, 1997.
Asthall (Area B), Oxon.	Small town	168	1	98	1	Booth, 1997.
Hacheston, Suffolk	Small town	578	9	74	16	Blagg, *et al.* 2004; 150-158.
Scole, Norfolk	Small town	N/A (24kg)	8	75	13	Blagg, *et al.* 2004; 150.
Fosse Lane, Shepton Mallet, Somerset	Small town	445	12	77	10	Dickinson, 2001.

Tab. 4.4. Proportion of terra sigillata types from various British small towns.

Lezoux *sigillata* is found widely throughout Britain, though it is most common in the southeast, which suggests that the majority arrived via ports in the Thames estuary or east Kent (**Fig. 4.8**). At Pudding Pan, off Herne Bay on the north Kentish coast, over 400 *sigillata* vessels, mostly plain Lezoux Ware of the second half of the second century AD, have been recovered from the seabed and probably derive from a shipwreck.[399] Lezoux Ware had a wide distribution in the northwest continental Empire, though it is much rarer in the Rhine provinces,

[399] Walsh 2002.

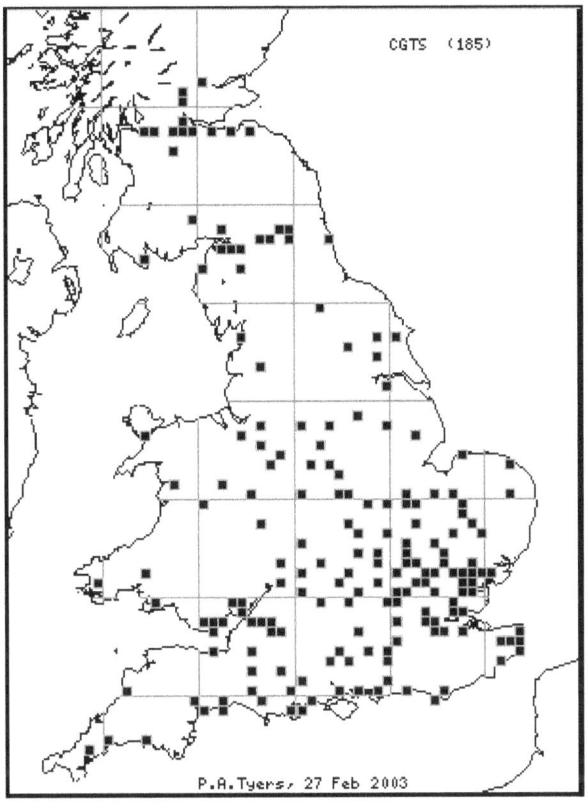

Fig. 4.8. British distribution of Central Gaulish terra sigillata (Paul Tyers (URL accessed June 2010): http://www.potsherd.uklinux.net/atlas/Ware/CGTS).

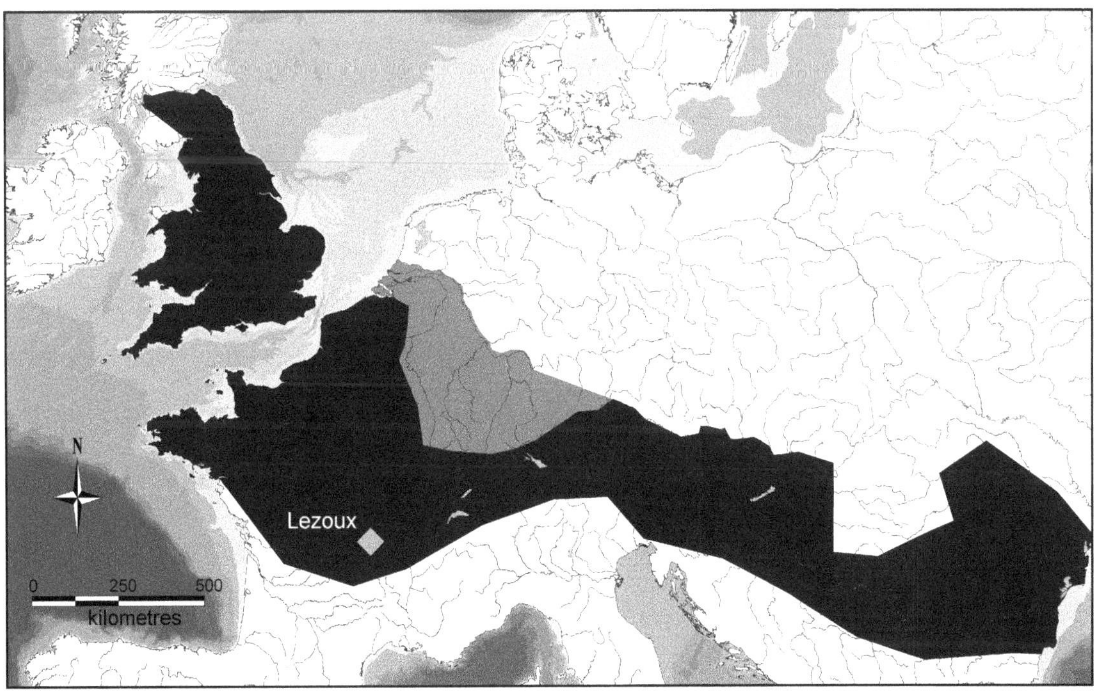

Fig. 4.9. General European distribution of Lezoux terra sigillata c. AD 140-160 (after Delage 2001, Fig. 2,5).

where the rise of the East Gaulish *sigillata* industries from the mid-second century AD onwards meant that it was effectively excluded (**Fig. 4.9**).[400] It was predominant in Belgica, however, which meant that it was almost certainly imported to Britain in quantity via the Southern North Sea and Eastern Channel. It could even have arrived via ports on the Scheldt estuary, which forms a dividing line between the principal Central and East Gaulish Ware distributions. Atlantic routes, particularly

[400] Tyers 1996b, 113.

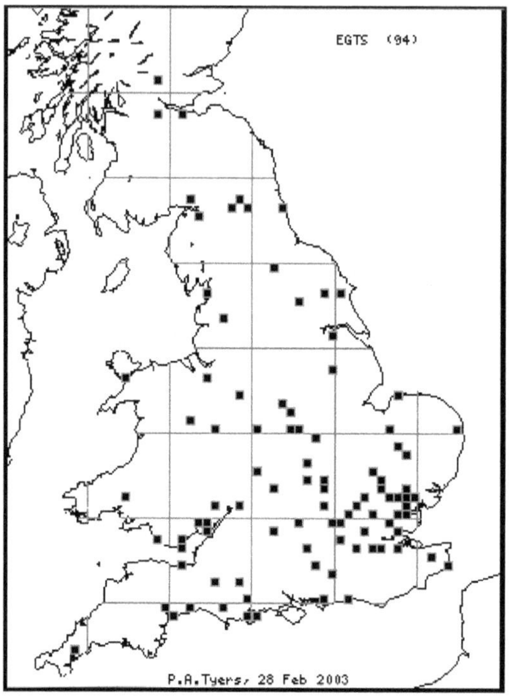

Fig. 4.10. British distribution of East Gaulish terra sigillata (Paul Tyers (URL accessed June 2010): http://www.potsherd.uklinux.net/atlas/Ware/EGTS).

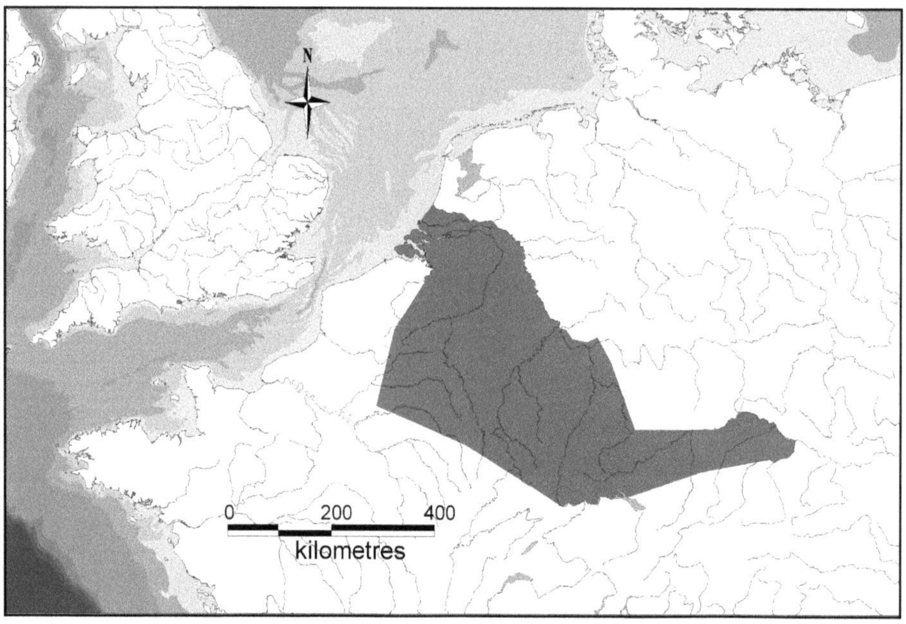

Fig. 4.11. Principal distribution of East Gaulish sigillata (after Woolf 1998, Fig. 7.6).

via the mouth of the Loire may also have been of importance.

East Gaulish *sigillata* was also imported into Britain between c. AD 120-260, though in much smaller quantities than Lezoux ware.[401] One of the main early sources was Blickweiler, though from c. AD 150 Trier and Rheinzabern became the dominant sources of supply.[402] There is little evidence that the scale of East Gaulish Ware supply to Britain varied much between the early second and mid-third century.[403] It is present at both military and civilian sites and is most commonly encountered in the Thames estuary region. Its continental distribution is largely restricted to the Rhine provinces and eastern Belgica, which means that it must have reached Britain across the Southern North Sea via the mouths of the Scheldt or Rhine (**Figs. 4.10-11**).[404]

[401] Marsh 1981; Willis 2005, section 6.7; Fulford forthcoming.
[402] *Ibid.*
[403] Marsh 1981, 204-205, Fig. 11.11,2.
[404] Tyers 1996b, 114; Fulford forthcoming.

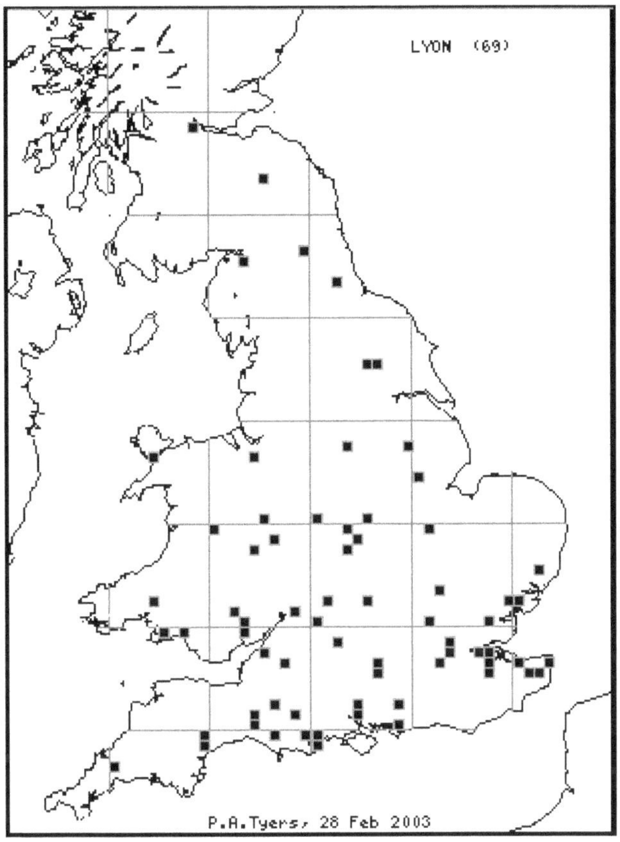

Fig. 4.12. British distribution of Lyon ware (Paul Tyers (URL accessed June 2010): http://www.potsherd.uklinux.net/atlas/Ware/LYON).

Terra sigillata would have reached Britain through trade, though the exact nature of this is debated. The fact that such large quantities were reaching Britain from a restricted number of production sites might suggest that this trade was underlain and supported by state contracts for military supply purposes. These would have involved the state paying the *sigillata* producers in exchange for the provision of large quantities of *sigillata*, which would then have been delivered to British military sites as pay in kind, or for purchase at a subsidised rate.[405] If this was the case, transport costs for *sigillata* would have been reduced; a passage by an early-third century author in the *Digest* states that goods for the use of the army were not liable for taxation, whilst this is also implied in a decree made by the emperor Hadrian.[406] The existence of these military supply lines may consequently have facilitated the traders' ability to exploit private civilian markets on a large-scale as well.

However, this interpretation is not entirely certain and we could in fact be dealing with an entirely free market trade, which involved private merchants targeting monetised sources of demand. *Terra sigillata* is, after all, extremely common at civil sites throughout the Western Empire, as in Britain, and a highly sophisticated private trade network was clearly in existence. The Vindolanda tablets also illustrate a striking degree of monetisation among military units on the north British frontier and demonstrate that a wide range of commodities were being paid for in cash.[407]

Numerous other pottery types were also traded to military and civilian consumers in Britain between AD 43-165; however, in contrast to the *sigillata* they were typically imported in much smaller quantities, perhaps in large part due to the rapid development of appropriate pottery industries within Britain.[408] The most notable of the other pottery imports were Gallo-Belgic wares, which had entered southeast Britain in significant quantities since c. 20/10 BC and continued to arrive down to c. AD 70/80 (see p. 30-32). Lyon ware also had a wide distribution throughout Britain c. AD 40-80, though in contrast to Gallo-Belgic wares, it is predominantly found at sites associated with the Roman military and in very small quantities (**Fig. 4.12**).[409] South Gaulish and Central Gaulish glazed wares are present at a handful of sites dated c. AD 40-70, whilst Spanish colour-coated wares and Pompeian red wares occur in contexts of c. AD 40-80. These wares are all well-known in the Rhineland and for the most part will have travelled to Britain via the Rhône-Rhine axis and thence across the Southern North

[405] C.f. Peacock and Williams 1986, 57-66; Whittaker 1994, 104-113; Fulford 1989a.
[406] *Digest.* 39.4.9.1. Paulus *Sentences, Book V*, 39.4.4.1; Paulus, *On the Edict, Book II.*

[407] Bowman 1994.
[408] Going 1992; Tyers 1996b; Swan 2002.
[409] Willis 2003; Tyers 1996b; forthcoming; Greene 1978; 1979.

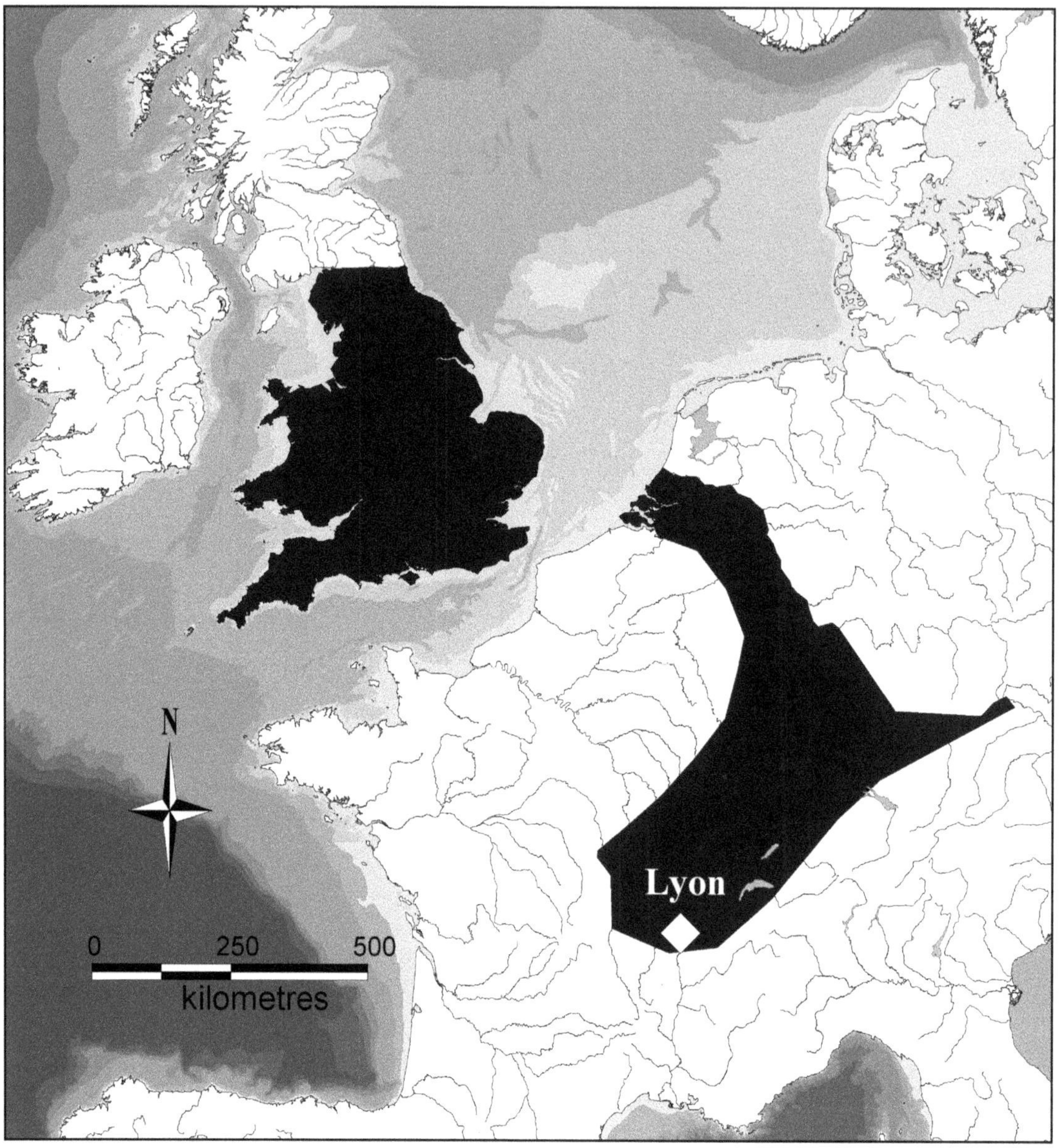

Fig. 4.13. Lyon ware distribution (after Tyers 1996b; Fig. 171).

Sea and Eastern Channel (**Fig. 4.13**).[410] Cologne ware reached a large number of British sites, principally around London and in east Kent, between c. AD 70/80-250. The continental distribution strongly suggests a route across the Southern North Sea from the mouths of the Scheldt and Rhine (**Fig. 4.14-15**).[411] Minor amounts of North Gaulish grey wares also came across the Strait of Dover to sites along the east coast of Britain between c. AD 70-250.[412] Central Gaulish black-slipped ware from Lezoux was shipped to Britain in large quantities c. AD 150-200 alongside the more prominent Lezoux *sigillata*, its British distribution clearly emphasises the importance of London and the Thames estuary and Kentish ports (**Fig. 4.16**).[413]

Mortaria were also imported; this includes a handful of examples from the Eifel in Germany (c. AD 40-70), Aoste in northern Italy (c. AD 50-85), the Rhône Valley (c. AD 50-100) and central Italy (c. AD 40-60), which most likely came to Britain via the Rhône-Rhine route. North Gaulish mortaria, which were principally produced between c. AD 55-100, were by far the most numerous imported mortaria. In Britain they are widespread, but the assemblages from Richborough, London and Colchester dominate the distribution map and evidently served as the principal ports of entry (**Fig. 4.17**). The continental distribution focuses on northern France and western Belgium, where they were probably produced, suggesting a trade route across the Strait of Dover. Between c. AD 150-200 a number of massive mortaria were imported to eastern Britain from Soller near Bonn. These were shipped across the Southern North Sea from ports at the mouth of the Rhine.[414]

[410] Tyers 1996b; forthcoming; Greene 1978; 1979.
[411] Anderson 1981; Tyers 1996b; forthcoming.
[412] Richardson and Tyers 1984; Tyers 1996b; forthcoming.
[413] Tyers 1996b; forthcoming.
[414] Tyers 1996b; forthcoming.

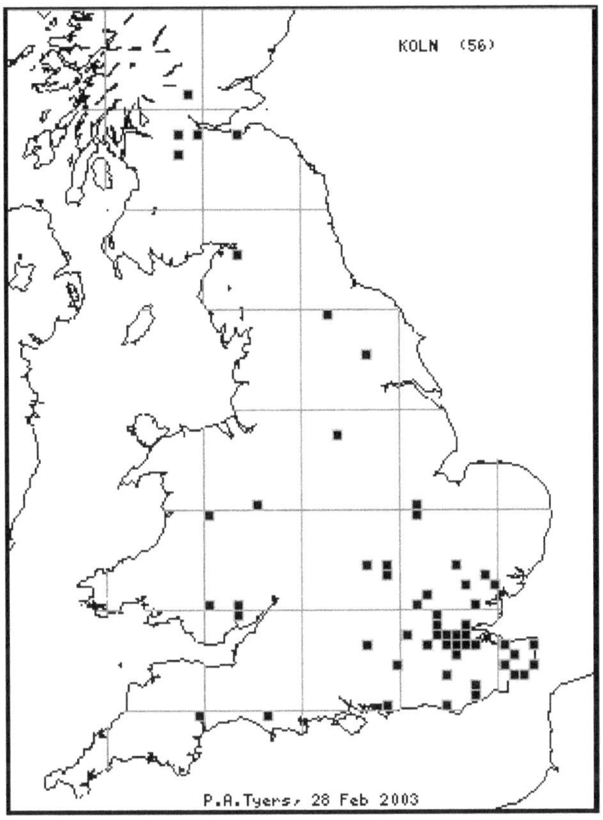

Fig. 4.14. British distribution of Cologne colour-coated ware (Paul Tyers (URL accessed June 2010): http://www.potsherd.uklinux.net/atlas/Ware/KOLN).

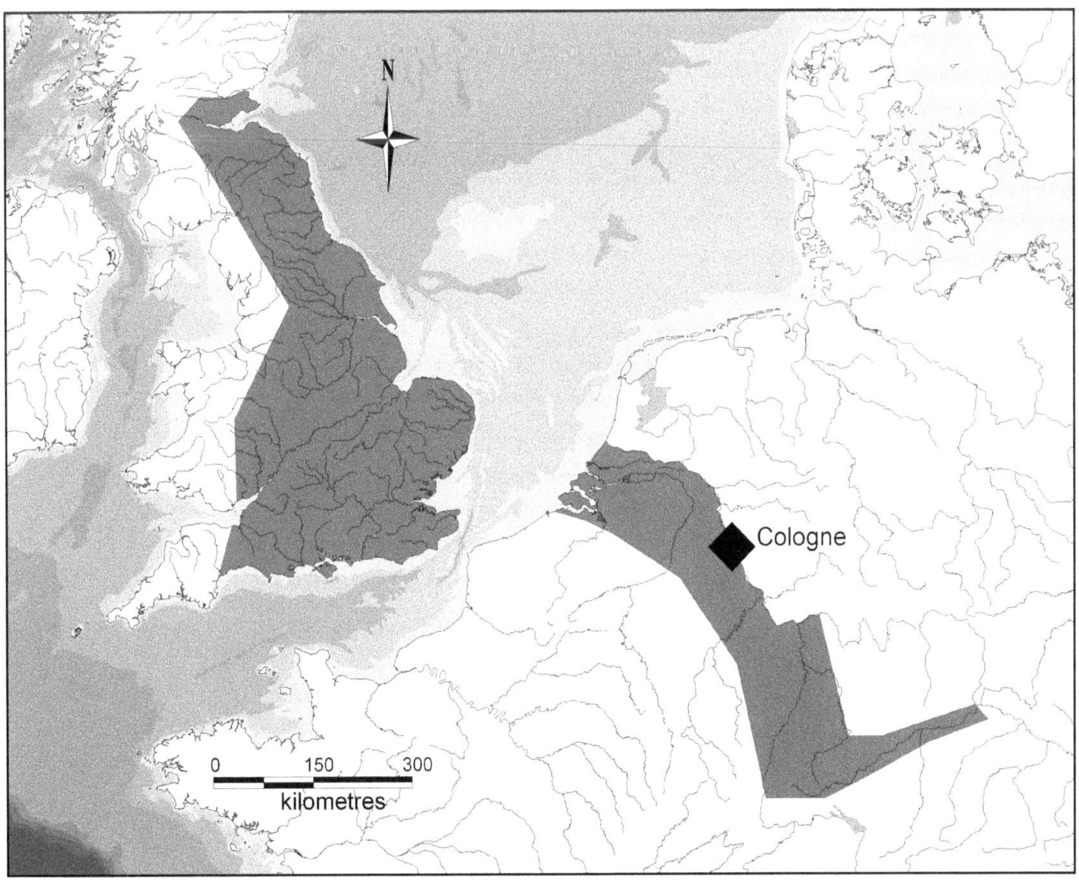

Fig. 4.15. Distribution of Cologne colour-coated ware (after Tyers 1996b, Fig. 168).

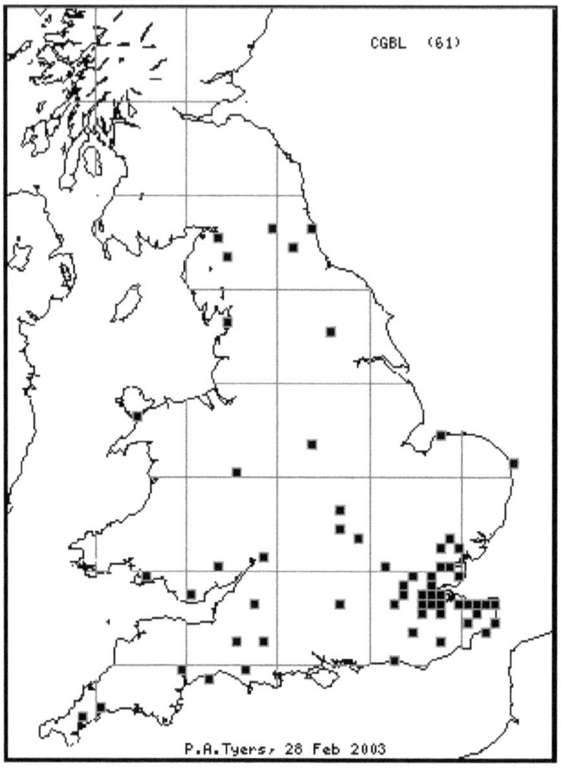

Fig. 4.16. British distribution of Central Gaulish blackslipped ware (Paul Tyers (URL accessed June 2010): http://www.potsherd.uklinux.net/atlas/Ware/CGBL).

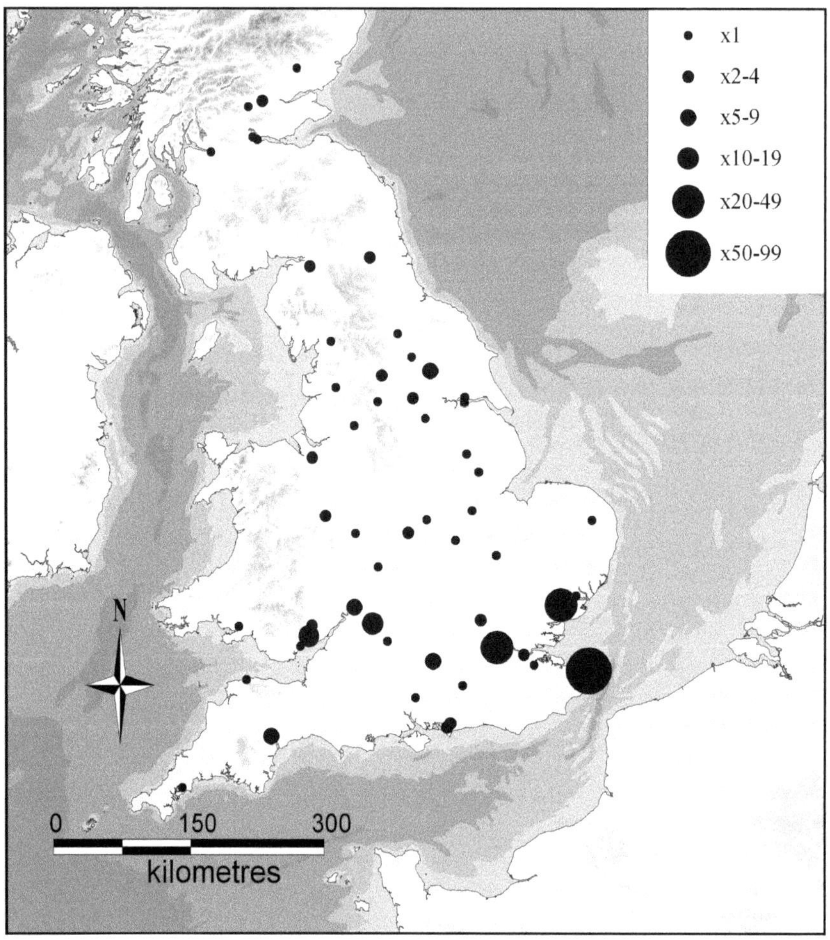

Fig. 4.17. British distribution of North Gaulish mortaria with stamps of the principal potters (after Tyers 1996b, Fig. 125).

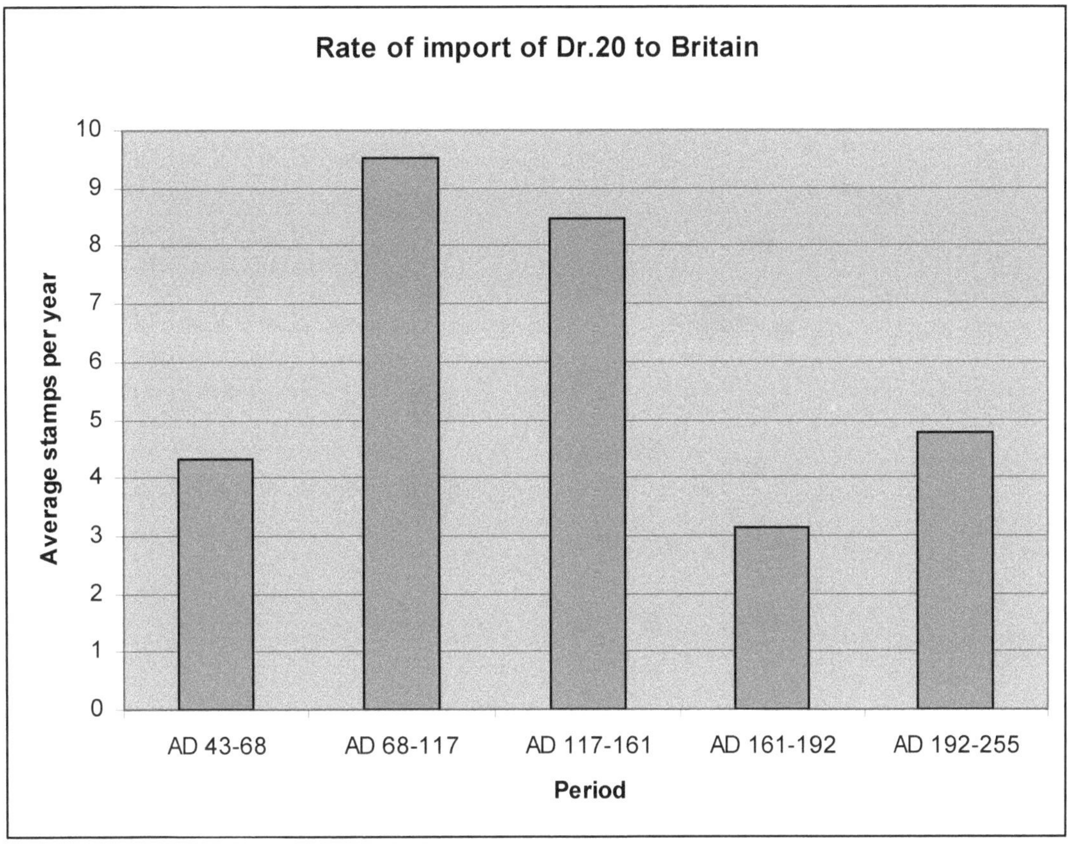

Fig. 4.18. Rate of import of stamped Dr.20 to Britain AD 43-255 (data from Carreras Monfort and Funari 1998, 250).

Period	Stamps	Average stamps per year
AD 14-68	108	2
AD 68-117	542	9.51
AD 117-161	373	8.48
AD 161-192	97	3.13
AD 192-255	300	4.76
AD 43-68	108	4.32

Tab. 4.5. Chronological variation of stamped Dressel 20s from Britain (Using data from Carreras Monfort and Funari 1998, 250).

Olive oil

Dressel 20 (Dr.20) amphorae, which carried olive oil from the Guadalquavir Valley in Baetica, southern Spain, are present at numerous Roman-period sites throughout Britain.[415] British amphorae assemblages are dominated by Dr.20, which typically constitute 70% or more by weight and 40-50% or more by sherd count (Appendix 9). In addition, Dr.20 regularly form a major component of total pottery assemblages; often over 30% by weight at Roman military and urban sites (Appendix 9). In considering these figures we must bear in mind that Dr.20 are exceptionally large containers, with the main types weighing between 28.4-37.2 kg, hence the survival, or partial survival, of only a few vessels at any given site is likely to have a major impact on that site's pottery assemblage by weight or sherd count.[416] However, on the other hand, their large volume (average 70-75 l (see p. 38)) implies the import of large quantities of olive oil.

Insights into the chronology of Dr.20 supply can best be gained by a study of stamps that occur on a sizeable minority of the amphorae. These stamps can often be dated fairly precisely. More than 1800 of these stamps have been recovered from Britain, of which over 1400

[415] Tyers 1996a; Williams and Peacock 1983; Carreras Monfort and Funari 1998.

[416] Carreras Monfort 2000, Fig. 2.

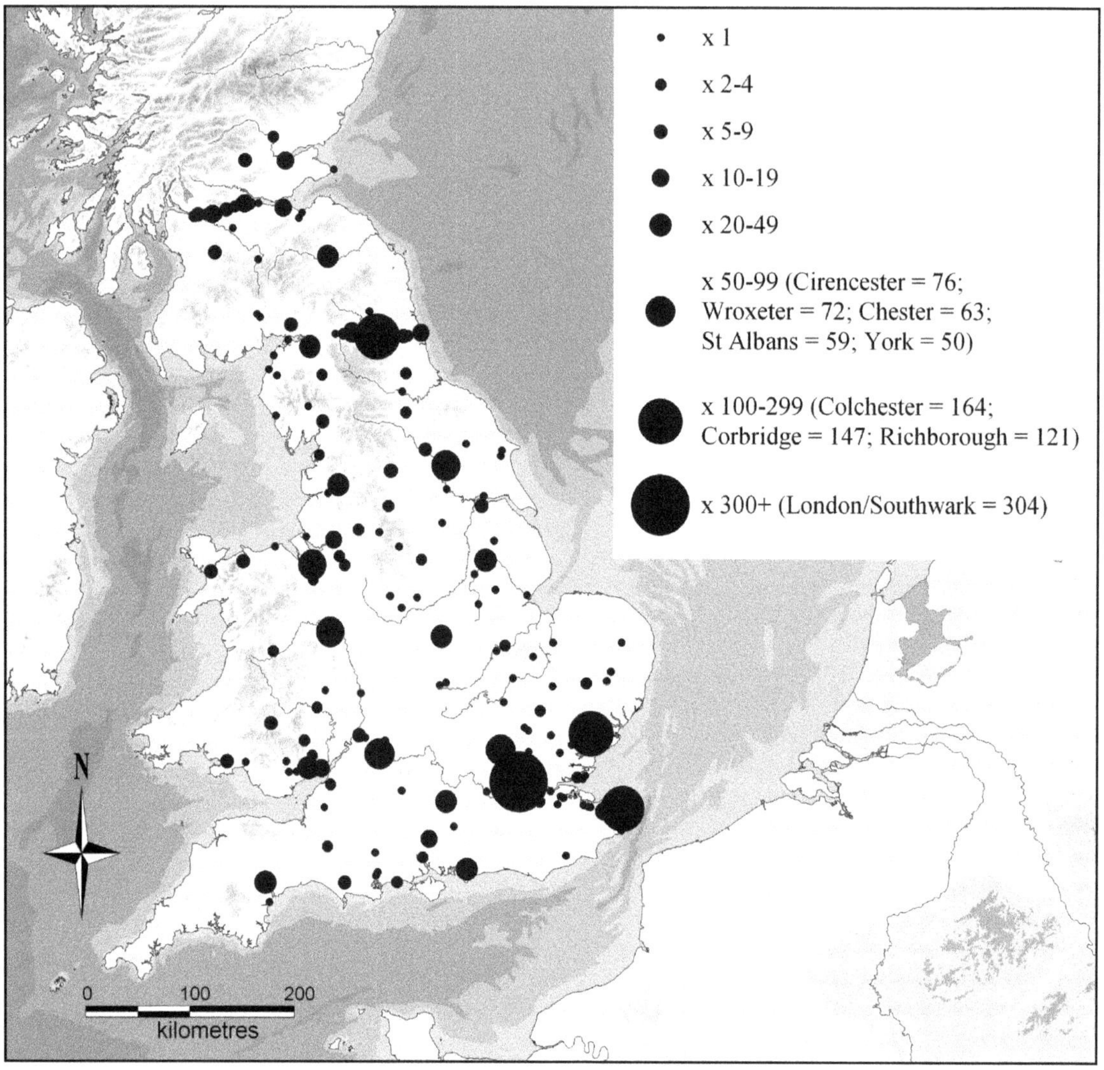

Fig. 4.19. Overall distribution of stamped Dr.20 in Britain (data from Carreras Monfort and Funari 1998).

can be closely dated (**Tab. 4.5, Fig. 4.18**).[417] Analysis demonstrates that during the Claudio-Neronian period Dr.20 came to Britain at a relatively low rate, but between AD 68-117 import more than doubled. The figures for the mid-second century (AD 117-161) are similarly high, which suggests Dr.20 continued to arrive at a fairly constant level until the late second century. These findings are further supported by the fact that Dr.20 sherds generally occur in greatest quantities in early to mid-second-century AD contexts and gradually decline after this date.[418]

The overall distribution of stamped Dr.20 shows that they were fairly prevalent throughout the Roman province of Britain, with concentrations noted in the southeast (particularly at London, Colchester and Richborough), around the Welsh borders and at Roman military sites in northern Britain (**Fig. 4.19**). Turning to examine their distribution more precisely by time period, we can see that Claudio-Neronian stamped Dr.20 are found in fairly small numbers throughout central and southern Britain (**Fig. 4.20**). Particularly high concentrations are present in the southeast at Colchester, London and Richborough and these three ports must have played important roles as entrepôts at this time.[419]

Stamped Dr.20 dated to AD 68-117 occur much more widely across Britain (**Fig. 4.21**).[420] In the southeast, significant quantities are present at Richborough and Colchester, but it is the dense concentration at London/Southwark that really stands out. London was clearly Britain's principal entrepôt for olive oil at this time, with many other British sites probably receiving their olive oil indirectly, following shipment by sea, or road, via London. The large number of stamps recovered

[417] Carreras Monfort and Funari 1998. N.B. Funari (1996; 2002) has also dated a much smaller number of the stamped Dr.20 from Britain according to a different chronological system (Claudio-Neronian, Flavian-Hadrianic, Antonine to the end of the second century AD, and third-century). His results suggest an overall peak in the short Claudio-Neronian phase, with fairly steady import through the next two phases and with a decline occurring in the final third-century phase.

[418] Carreras Monfort, pers. Comm. 2008. C.f. Williams and Peacock 1983; Carreras Monfort and Williams 2003, 64.

[419] Carreras Monfort and Funari 1998, 41, Fig. 28; Cunliffe 1968; Sealey 1985.

[420] Carreras Monfort and Funari 1998, 41, Fig. 29.

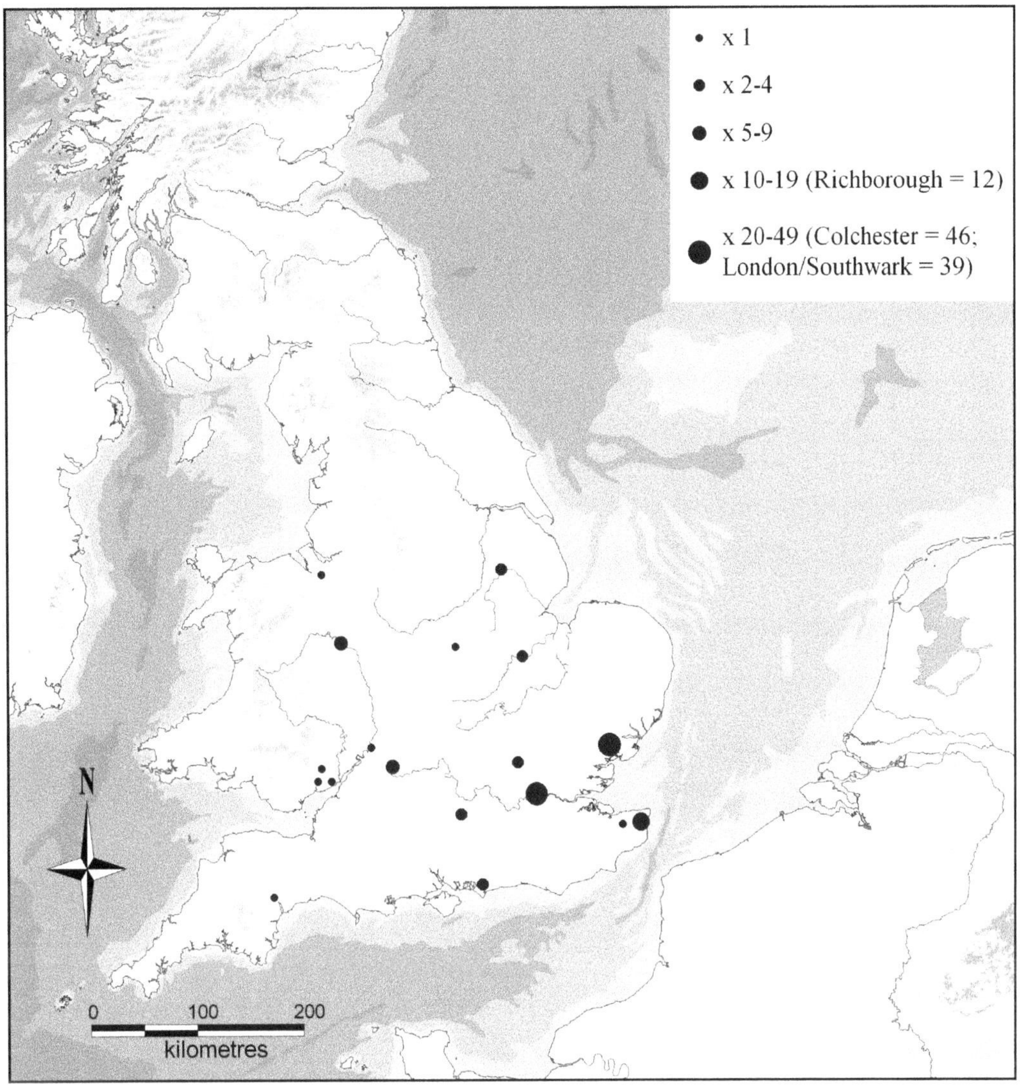

Fig. 4.20. Distribution in Britain of stamped Dr.20 dated AD 43-68 (data from Carreras Monfort and Funari 1998).

from western Britain may, however, suggest that some Dr.20 were shipped directly to the west coast from the continent, perhaps from Spain via an Atlantic route.

Stamped Dr.20 dating AD 117-161 are again present in some quantity in the southeast, though the relative number of examples recovered from the major ports, such as Richborough, Colchester, and in particular London, declines significantly when compared to the preceding phases between AD 43-117 (**Fig. 4.22**). This might have been down to Dr.20 being increasingly shipped directly from the continent to British ports nearer the military consumers on the northern frontier. London may well have retained its importance, however, and the reason for the decline could also be put down to more effective onward distribution, or perhaps in previous periods olive oil was more likely to be decanted from amphorae at London, whereas by the mid-second century Dr.20 were more often shipped on to the final destination through London. Large numbers of Dr.20 are known from the northern military frontier region, particularly along the Antonine Wall and Hadrian's Wall. The assemblage at Corbridge, at the point at which the main road from the south meets Hadrian's Wall, is the biggest in Britain from this phase, which suggests that the site was a particularly important collection and distribution centre for olive oil. Quantities of stamped Dr.20 from western Britain again raise the possibility of direct shipments from the continent to the west coast as well.[421]

A sizeable portion of the Dr.20 probably came to Britain direct from Baetica via the Atlantic seaways. Dr.20 were specifically designed for bulk transport by ship and an Atlantic route would have been far more cost-effective than overland routes. Some Dr.20 have even been found along the coasts of Brittany and Normandy.[422] A direct Atlantic route is also supported by considerations of stamped vessels; between AD 43-117 there are distinct differences in the group of stamps present in Britain and those present in Roman forts in Germany.[423] This is not to rule out the possibility that large numbers of Dr.20 did in fact arrive in Britain via the Rhône-Rhine route. There is

[421] *Ibid.* 47, Fig. 30.
[422] C.f. Fulford 2007; Whittaker 1994, 100-101
[423] Carreras Monfort and Funari 1998, 55-56, 266.

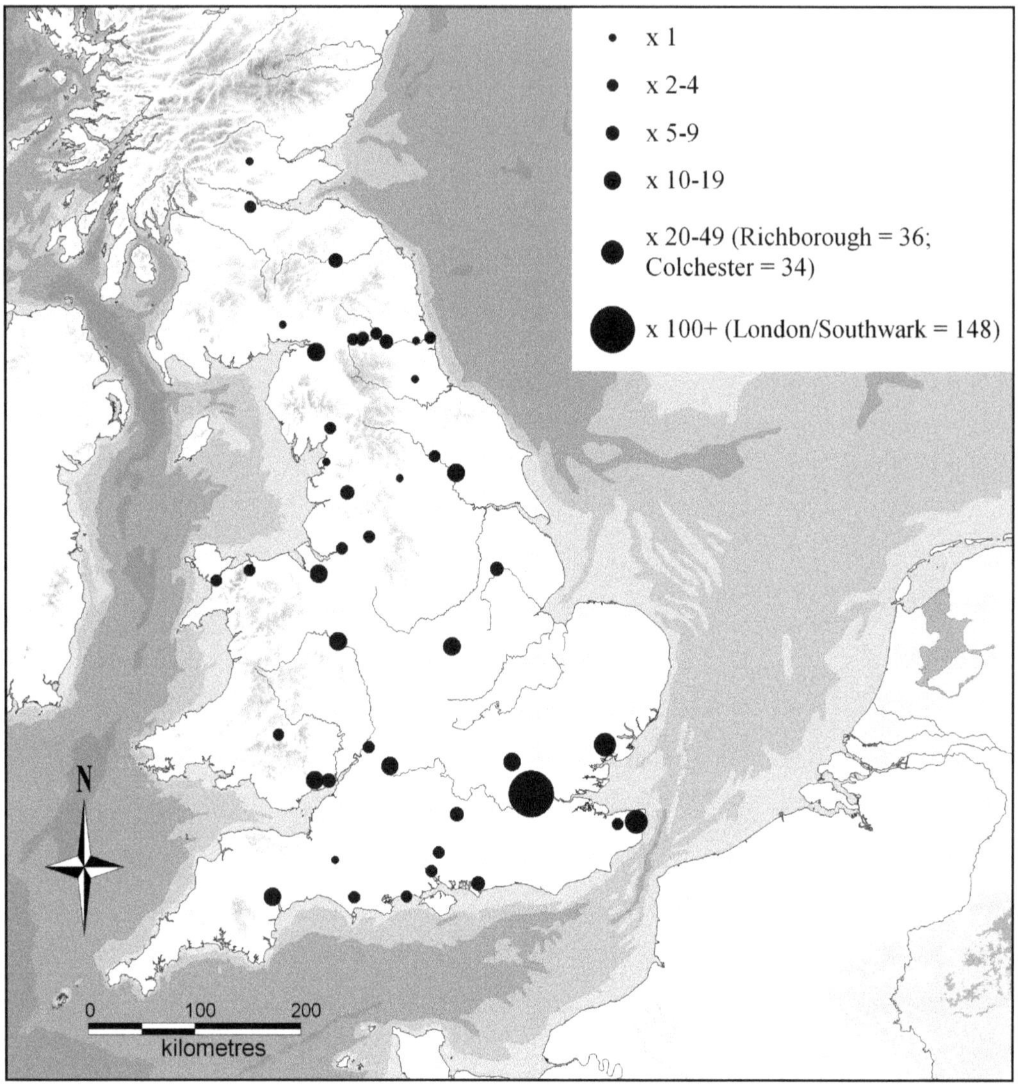

Fig. 4.21. Distribution in Britain of stamped Dr.20 dated AD 68-117 (data from Carreras Monfort and Funari 1998).

certainly a heavy concentration of Dr.20 along the valleys of the Rhône and Rhine.[424] Indeed, the differences between the stamps present in Britain and Germany are by no means absolute and there is considerable overlap. Of course, as Remesal-Rodríguez has pointed out, we should also bear in mind the possibility that olive oil was supplied to the German provinces via an Atlantic route as well as via the Rhône and Rhine.[425] Between AD 117-160 there are no longer any substantial differences between the stamps present in both Britain and Germany.[426] Whether this implies a common supply route via either the Rhône-Rhine, or, more likely, the Atlantic, is hard to judge.

Britain's olive oil supply was based around organised military supply routes and the Roman state acted as a bulk purchaser, placing contracts with the Baetican estates.[427] We know that the Roman state bought olive oil in bulk to supply the capital at Rome; the highly centralised and organised disposal of vessels at Monte Testaccio clearly implies this. The fact that many Dr.20 bore *tituli picti* (painted inscriptions), recording a range of information including the weight of the amphora and its contents, the names of the estate which provided the oil and the name of the merchant involved in shipping it, also suggests heavy state regulation. In fact, the construction of Monte Testaccio may well have been organised by the state in order to prevent fraudulent re-use of the marked vessels.[428] In Britain there is a heavy military focus to Dr.20 distribution and the military was probably the principal consumer; however, Dr.20 were reaching civil sites in quantity as well, particularly urban centres (see Appendix 9). They are often encountered at small towns and occasionally at rural sites. For example, at Little Oakley villa in Essex a minimum number of 22

[424] Keay and Williams 2005; Peacock and Williams 1986, 136; Tyers 1996a; Whittaker 1994, 100-101; Jones and Mattingly 1990, 196-7; Colls *et al.* 1977; Callender 1965.
[425] Remesal-Rodríguez 2002.
[426] Carreras Monfort and Funari 1998, 56, 266.
[427] Funari 1996; 2002; Carreras Monfort 2002; Carreras Monfort and Funari 1998; Remesal-Rodríguez 2002.
[428] Wilson 2009a.

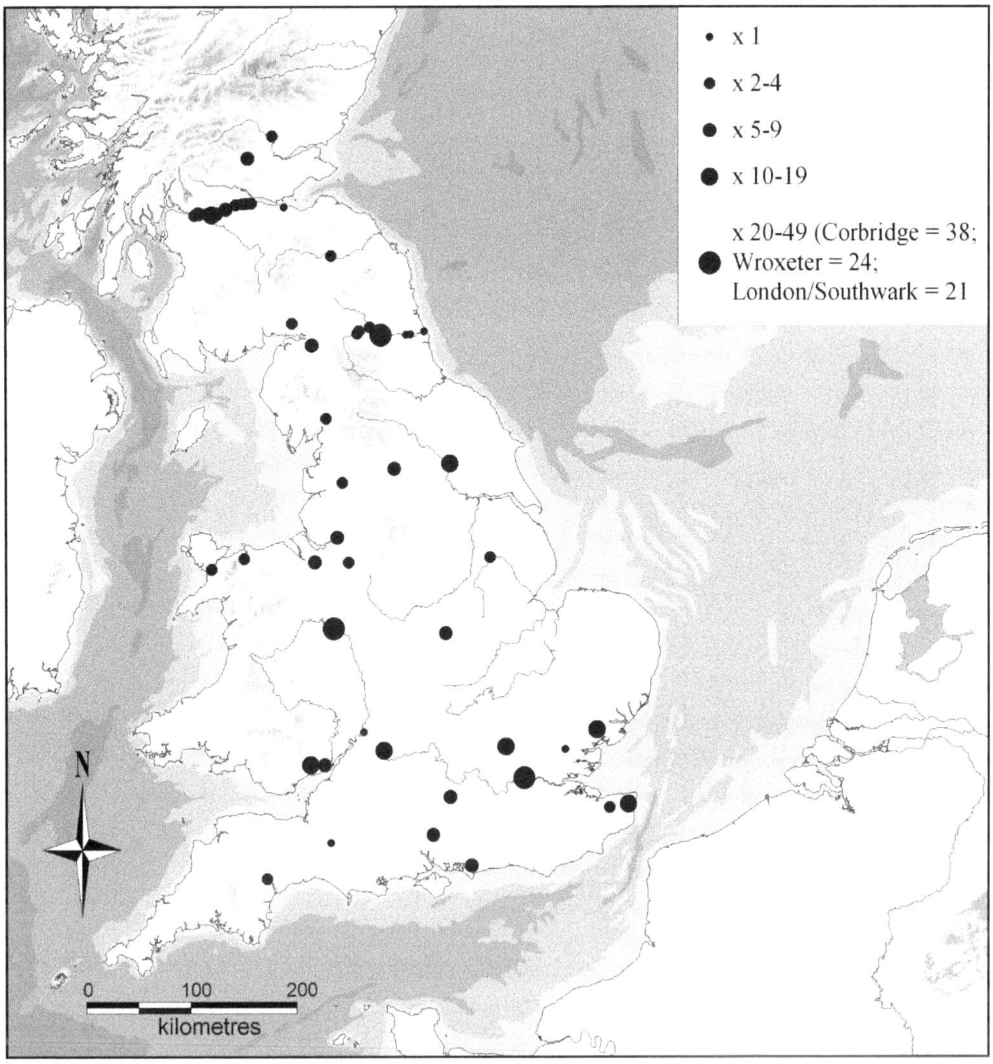

Fig. 4.22. Distribution in Britain of stamped Dr.20 dated AD 117-161 (data from Carreras Monfort and Funari 1998).

Dr.20 were identified, which represented over 1500 l of olive oil.[429] Clearly civilian markets were being exploited by traders alongside their official supply engagements.

Wine

Wine was also traded to Britain in large quantities following the Claudian invasion. Whilst numerous Dr.2-4 wine amphorae reached Britain during the preceding period (see pp. 35-36) they were imported, from Italy and Spain, in greatly increased quantity from the Claudian invasion down to the end of the first century AD or the early second century AD.[430] Camulodunum 184 amphorae, which were produced at various sites in the eastern Mediterranean and principally bore wine (although figs and honey were occasionally contained) are also found at large numbers of sites during this period and were certainly imported from the conquest until the mid-second century AD (**Fig. 4.23**).[431] The most important wine amphorae were the Gaulish flat-based types, almost all of which were manufactured at various locations in Languedoc and Provence in southern France. *Tituli picti* attest that wine was by far their most common content.[432] "Gauloise 4" (G4, also known as Dressel 30/Pélichet 47), which had a capacity of c. 37 l, became well-known from the Flavian period onwards and occur in Britain down to the mid-third century. They are typically the second most common Roman amphorae type in Britain, although they occur in much lower quantities than Dr.20.[433] They take second place in most London amphorae assemblages and at Canterbury they were the second commonest amphorae, forming 6.5% of the total Roman amphorae by weight.[434] At Colchester 117.4 kg of G4 were recovered, which formed 7.4% of the assemblage by weight, only marginally behind the Dressel 2-4 (7.5%), but well below the figures for Dressel 20 (66.3%).[435] G4 are even known in small quantities at

[429] Barford 2002, 136.
[430] Fitzpatrick 2003b; Tyers 1996a.
[431] *Ibid.*

[432] Laubenheimer 1985; Brun and Laubenheimer 2001, 208-9; Buffat and Pellecuer 2001, Fig. 48; Brun 2001.
[433] Tyers 1996b; Green 1980, 42; Carreras Monfort 2000, Fig. 53.
[434] Arthur 1986, 250; Rayner and Seeley 2002; Green 1980, 42.
[435] Symonds and Wade 1999, Tab. 3.1.

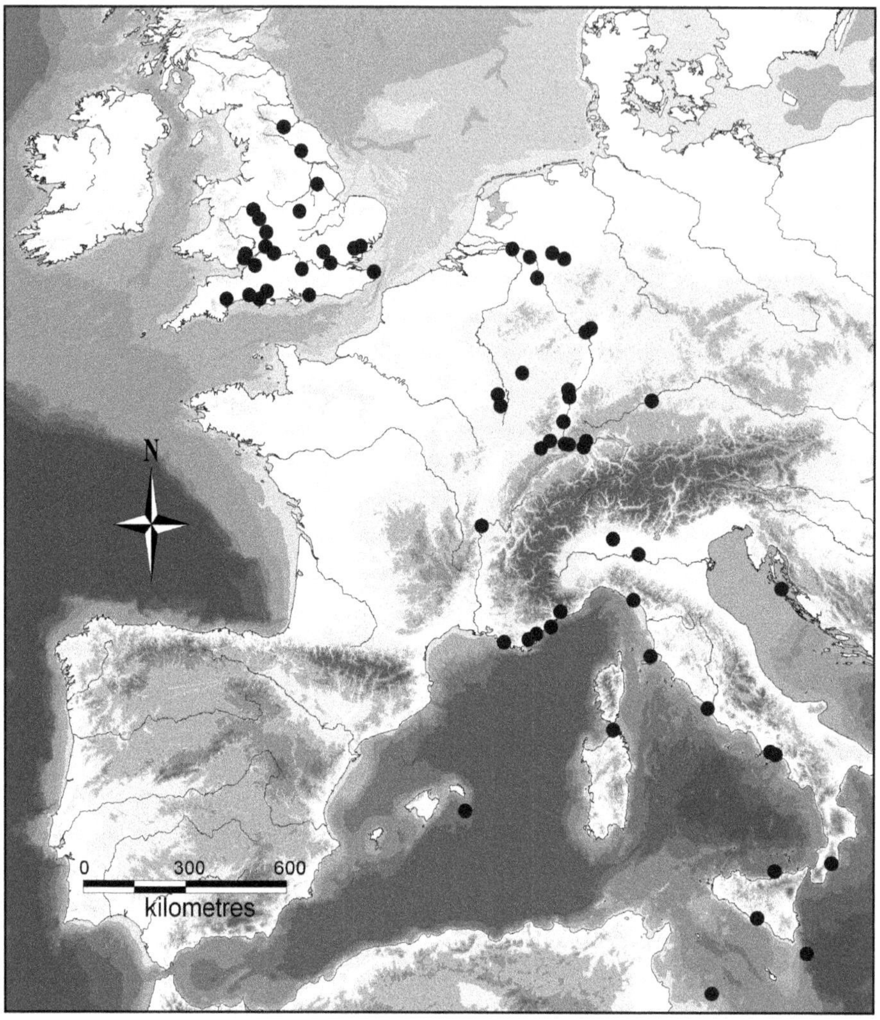

Fig. 4.23. West European distribution of Camulodunum 184 amphorae (after Tyers 1996a).

some rural sites, such as Highstead in Kent, and limited amounts reached northern military sites during the Flavian period.[436] All of these types of wine amphorae appear to have come to Britain via the the Rhône-Rhine route; on the continent examples concentrate heavily along this corridor (**Figs. 4.23-24**).[437]

Wine amphorae from minor sources are also known from Britain. These include an amphora produced in a fabric from Burgundy that has been identified in a mid-first-century AD context in London, whilst Cretan Dressel 43s, which probably carried wine, are known at a handful of British sites.[438] Dr.2-4 and G4 amphorae were also produced in Britain for a short period during the mid-first century AD at Brockley Hill and achieved a local distribution in the region north of London. Limited amphorae production was also taking place in London and at several other locations in the southeast from the mid-first century AD. Whether these productions related to local wine industries or to the transhipment of wine, which arrived from abroad is unclear.[439]

However, the volume of wine imported in amphorae is likely to have been only a small fraction of the total amount of wine that actually reached Britain; the majority was undoubtedly imported in barrels. Barrels are rarely detected archaeologically and their preservation depends on special circumstances, such as re-use in wells.[440] Nevertheless, 21 barrels from 6 British sites can be dated with some security to the second half of the first and the second century AD (and a further fifteen examples from Silchester also probably date to the first or second century AD), and on the basis of their typology and the types of wood used in their construction, such as silver fir for the Silchester barrels, they were almost certainly made in central or southern regions of France.[441] Including the British material (though excluding Silchester), 46 barrels can be dated to the first century AD, mostly the late first century AD, across Western Europe as a whole, whilst there are 33 from the second century AD (**Fig. 4.25**).[442] There is also considerable iconographic evidence attesting to trade of wine in barrels. This concentrates along the Rhône-Rhine axis.[443]

436 Arthur 2007, 237; Fitzpatrick 2003b.
437 Peacock 1978; Peacock and Williams 1986, 64; Tyers 1996a.
438 Laubenheimer 2003, 32-36; Williams 2003.
439 Symonds 2003; Desbat 2003, 49.
440 Marlière 2002, 174-175, 185, 195.
441 Marlière 2001; 2002.
442 Marlière 2002, 174, Figs. 211-212.
443 Marlière 2002.

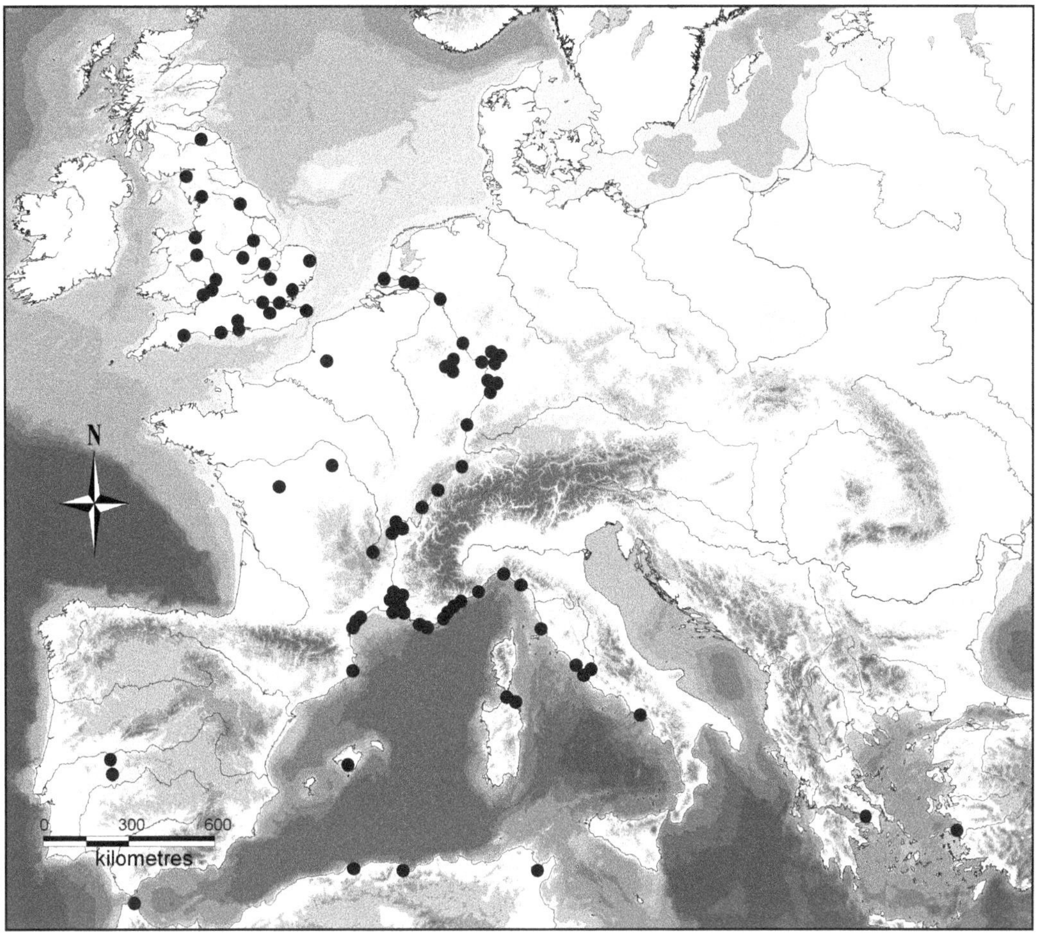

Fig. 4.24. Distribution of G4 amphorae (after Peacock and Williams 1986, Fig. 21).

The importance of the barrel in wine supply has been elucidated by Ejstrud's study of five amphorae assemblages from western continental Europe dated c. AD 30-70.[444] Ejstrud found that whilst the ratio of fish product to olive oil amphorae remained relatively constant across all the sites in the study, the relative proportion of wine amphorae varied significantly. At the southernmost sites, Rome and Lyon, wine amphorae comprised an average of 62% of the amphorae assemblages by volume. Further north, at Augst, Avenches and Nijmegen, meanwhile, wine amphorae comprised less than a third of the assemblages by volume. Whilst wine may simply have been consumed in smaller quantities relative to olive oil and fish products at the northern sites a more plausible explanation is that north of Lyon, which was a great centre of barrel-making, wine was primarily transported in barrels. Indeed, Ejstrud estimates that by solely taking account of amphorae the amount of wine arriving at Augst was underestimated by c. 90%.[445] Clearly barrels played the major role in wine transport to the northern provinces. What Ejstrud's study ignores is that barrels will also have played an important role as wine containers at this time in the southern regions too, as we can suggest from the low numbers of wine amphorae found on contemporary Mediterranean shipwrecks.[446]

[444] Ejstrud 2005.
[445] Ejstrud 2005.

Where did the barrelled wine come from? Aquitaine was probably a major source. Here wine production experienced significant growth during the second half of the first century AD and again during the mid-second century AD, yet amphorae production was very limited.[447] In the Tricastin of the middle-Rhône valley, one of the largest wine storehouses in the Roman world was built during the late first century AD, though here too there are no workshops for the production of amphorae.[448] Further north in central and northern France, where viticulture really begins during the second half of the first century, amphorae are also relatively rare and were almost certainly of secondary importance to the barrel.[449] Similarly, amphorae were rarely produced in the valleys of the Rhine and Moselle following the limited expansion of viticulture here during the mid-second century AD.[450] Indeed, even in southern France, where amphorae production is so well-attested, it is probable

[446] Parker 1990, Fig. 1.
[447] Balmelle *et al.* 2001; Brun and Laubenheimer 2001, 209-210, 212-213; Berthault 1997.
[448] Brun and Laubenheimer 2001, 209; Jung *et al.* 2001.
[449] Brun and Laubenheimer 2001, 210-212.
[450] Brun and Gilles 2001, 167, 178; Brun and Laubenheimer 2001, 213-214.

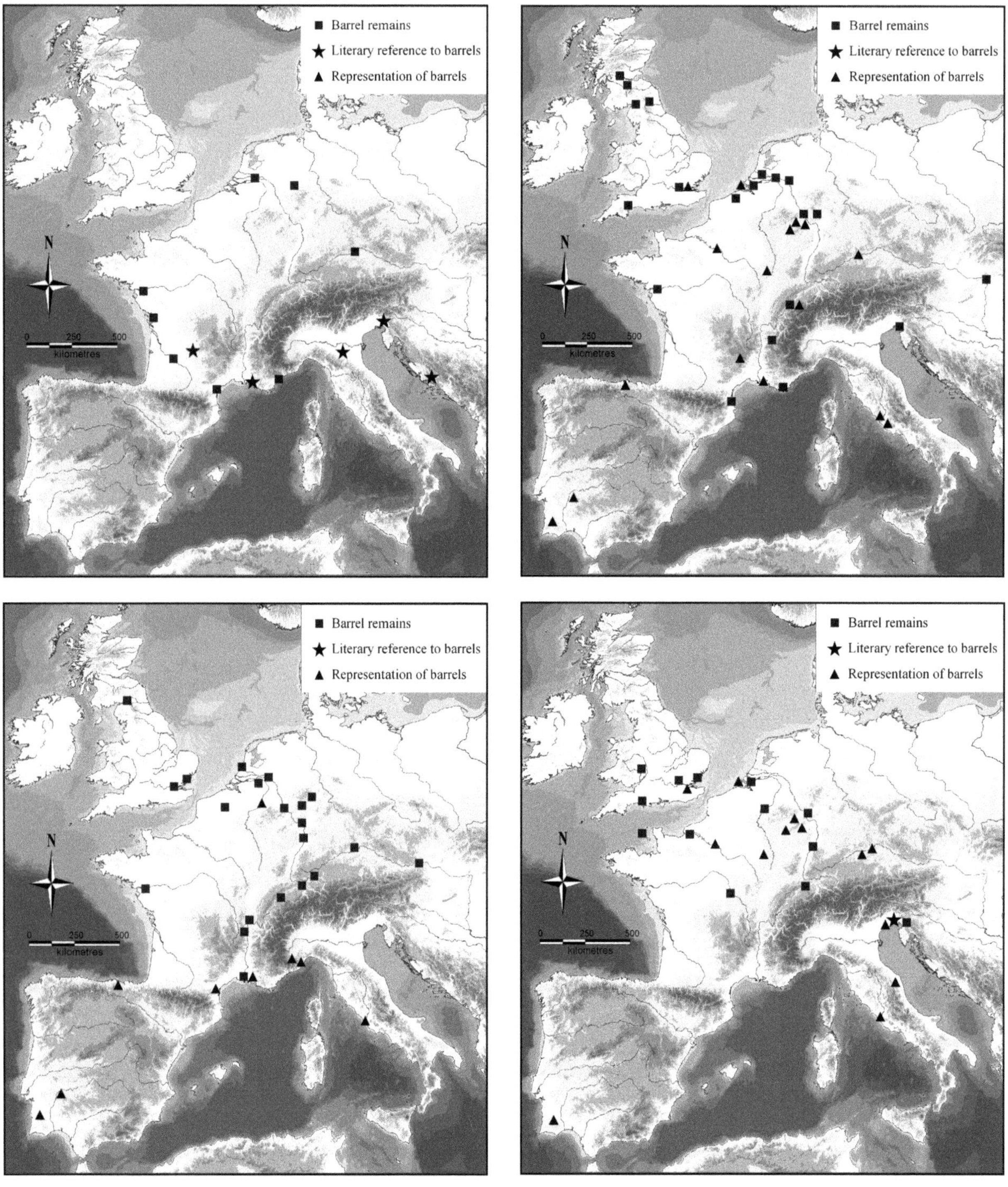

Fig. 4.25. Distribution of barrels and representations of barrels in Europe between the first century BC to fifth century AD. First century BC (top left), first century AD (top right), second century AD (bottom left), third to fifth centuries AD (bottom right) (after Marlière 2002, Fig. 212).

that much of the wine produced at the vast estates, where wine-making facilities were greatly expanded and improved during the second half of the first century AD and further in the mid-second century AD, would have been transported in barrels.[451] The wine trade in barrels to Britain would thus have involved Atlantic routes, from southwest France, and a route via the Rhône-Rhine and Southern North Sea and Eastern Channel.

As with olive oil, much barrelled wine was probably supplied to Britain in bulk through organised military supply following purchase by the state; the Roman army would have been a major consumer of wine, particularly since many troops in the British legions were recruited from Mediterranean provinces throughout the first and second centuries (see pp. 93-94). Large barrels have also

[451] Brun and Laubenheimer 2001, 207-209, 212-213; Brun 2001; Buffat and Pellecuer 2001.

been identified at a few northern British military sites.[452] In addition, wine was traded privately in large quantities to the civilian population. Barrels are present at several civil sites, such as Silchester and London.[453] In contrast to Dr.20, wine amphorae show relatively poor representation at military sites, where by the second century they are often absent, whereas they are relatively more common at civilian sites.[454] This is probably a result of private trading of high quality wines to individual consumers; several G4, such as those from Fos in southern France, bear *tituli picti* that record their contents as *Massicum*, a fine wine of Italian origin.[455]

Seafood

Salted fish product amphorae are found at several sites throughout Britain (**Figs. 4.26-27**). These principally concern Dressel types 7-11 and 38-39, which were produced down to the mid-second century and, on the basis of their fabrics, were largely manufactured in Spain, although some came from southern France.[456] From *tituli picti* and finds from Mediterranean shipwrecks we know that their principal contents were salted fish flesh (*salsamenta*) and various sauces produced from fish entrails and/or small fry, which were macerated with salt and fermented (*garum*, *liquamen*, *muria*, *allec* or *lymphatum*).[457] Other amphorae known from northwest Europe may also have carried fish sauce even though they are better known for other contents. For example, inscriptions on some Gauloise amphorae indicate that they too were occasionally used as fish product containers.[458]

In comparison to Dr.20, fish product amphorae form a relatively small portion of British amphorae assemblages; Williams and Peacock noted that fish product amphorae usually accounted for c. 10% by weight and sherd count, although they comprised 30% of an exceptional assemblage at Gloucester dating to the first half of the second century.[459] At Colchester 96.3kg of Dressel 7-11 amphorae were recovered, which comprised 6.1% of the amphorae assemblage of all periods by weight, not including the smaller quantities of other fish sauce amphorae also present at the site.[460] At Canterbury Dressel 7-11 accounted for 4.5% of the amphorae of all periods by weight and Pélichet 46s were also present.[461]

Within Britain fish product amphorae are found at civil sites in the south and seem to attest to private trade (**Figs. 4.26-27**). On the continent they are particularly well known from the Rhône-Rhine axis and a large number probably reached Britain from this route via the coasts of northern France, Belgium and the southern Netherlands.[462] Of course, Atlantic routes may also have been utilised and some probably reached Britain direct from southern Spain alongside the Dr.20.

Like wine, fish-products were also very probably transported in barrels. We do not know if they were employed at the west Mediterranean fish salting installations, but this is possible. In addition, fish salting installations in Brittany, which operated on a fairly sizeable scale from the late first century AD onwards, must have transported their products in barrels, as there is no evidence for amphorae production in their locality.[463] The general paucity of fish-product amphorae at British military sites is a curious phenomenon, which must presumably be explained by reliance on fish products transported in barrels, possibly from the western Mediterranean, Brittany or even from within Britain itself. As with olive oil some form of state contract is likely.

Other amphorae

Various amphorae which carried products other than olive oil, wine and salted fish, also reached Britain. Of greatest significance was the Haltern 70 (Ha.70) type, which has been identified at over 30 British sites dated c. AD 43-70/90 (**Fig. 4.28**). Ha.70 fabrics indicate production in Baetica and their principal contents, as attested by *tituli picti* and remains of olive stones within some examples, were olives preserved in *defrutum* (a grape product).[464] Their distribution indicates two possible supply routes: a Rhône-Rhine route, or an Atlantic route. The fact that examples have been discovered in Portugal and northwest Spain suggests the latter routes would have been of some importance for British supply. Examples may well have arrived with, and been traded alongside, the more numerous Baetican Dr.20.

One further amphorae type worth mentioning is the Richborough 527. This was traded to Britain from the mid-first century AD down to at least the early third century AD. Its origin was Lipari in the Aeolian islands north of Sicily and its contents appear to have been alum, which, as attested by Pliny, was mainly utilised as a mordant in dyeing wool, but perhaps also had a role in medicine.[465] Fifteen of these vessels have been noted in Britain, primarily in the southeast (**Fig. 4.29**). The continental distribution is incomplete, due to problems of recognition in the past, but examples are known throughout almost all of France, including the northwest coast and along the Rhône-Rhine axis, which opens the possibility to a route via either the Southern North Sea/Eastern Channel or the Western Channel/Atlantic.

---

452 Marlière 2002.
453 *Ibid.*
454 Bidwell and Speak 1994.
455 Desbat 2003, 49; Tchernia 1986, 283.
456 Martin-Kilcher 2003; Tyers 1996a; Tomber and Dore 1998, 84, 87, 107.
457 Martin-Kilcher 2003; Tyers 1996a; Trakadas 2005; Curtis 1991; 2005.
458 Davies *et al.* 1994, 18.
459 Williams and Peacock 1983.
460 Symonds and Wade 1999, Tab. 3.1.
461 Arthur 1986, 248-250.
462 Tyers 1996a; Martin-Kilcher 2003.
463 Wilson 2006.
464 Carreras Monfort 2003; Tyers 1996a.
465 *Ibid*; Pliny *H.N.* 35.52; Borgard *et al.* 2003; Tyers 1996a.

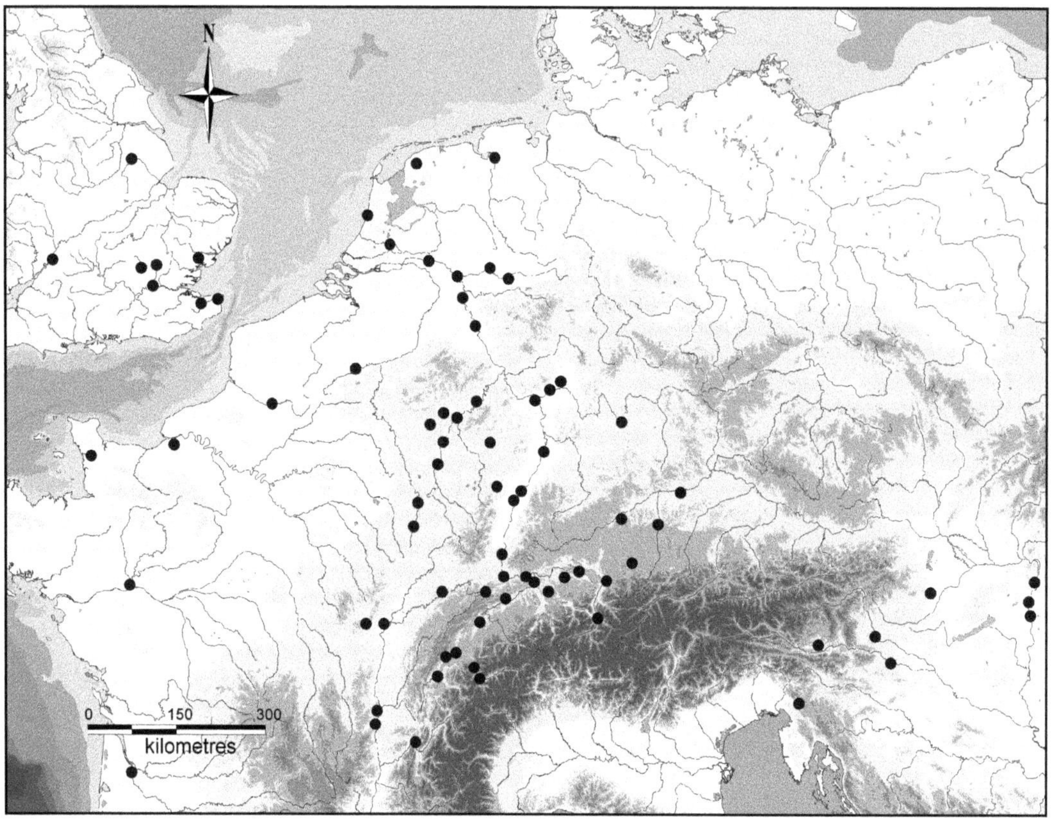

Fig. 4.26. Distribution of Iberian fish sauce amphorae in northwest Europe during the first century AD (after Martin Kilcher 2003, Fig. 11).

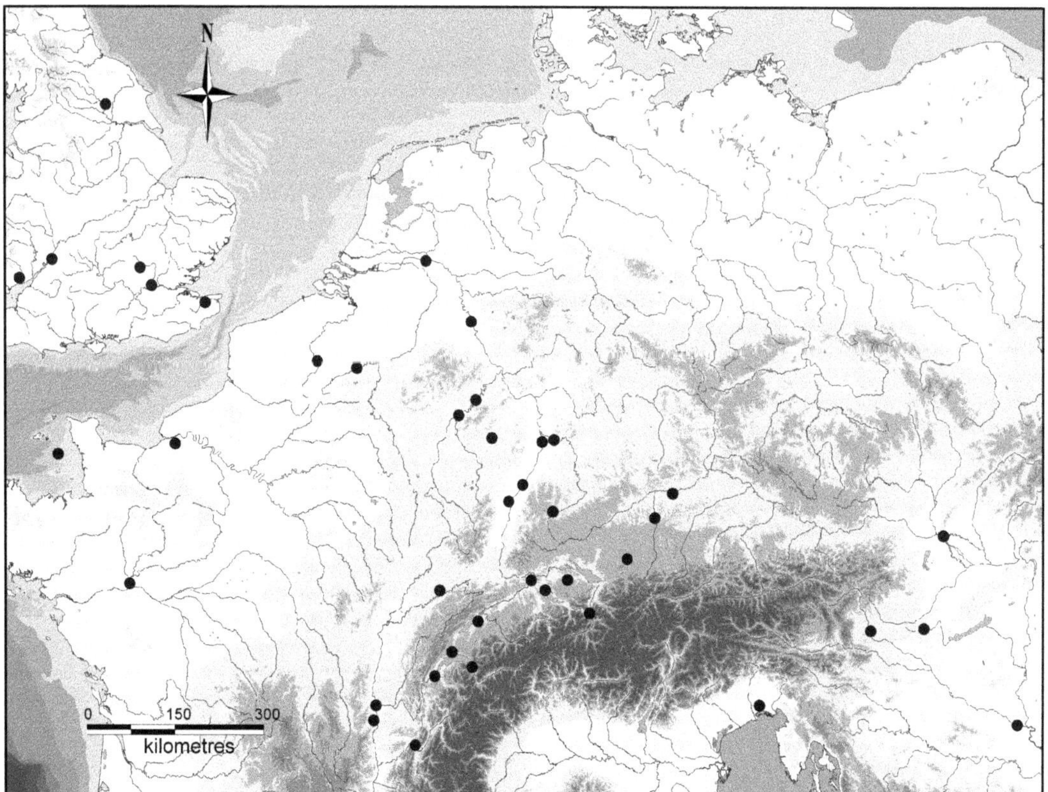

Fig. 4.27. Distribution of Iberian fish product amphorae in northwest Europe during the second century AD (after Martin Kilcher 2003, Fig. 12).

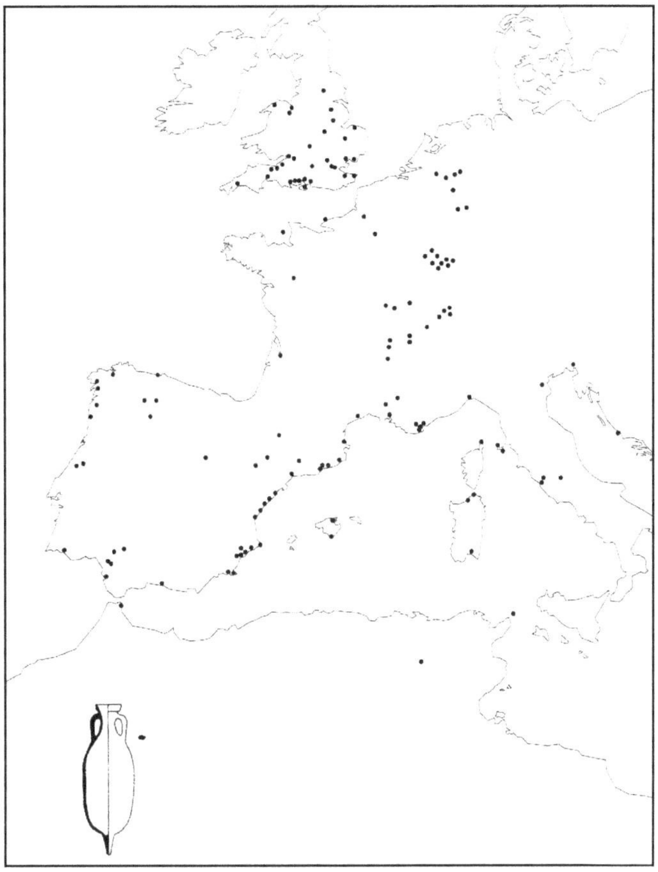

Fig. 4.28. Distribution of Ha.70 in the Western Roman Empire (Carreras Monfort 2003, Fig. 4).

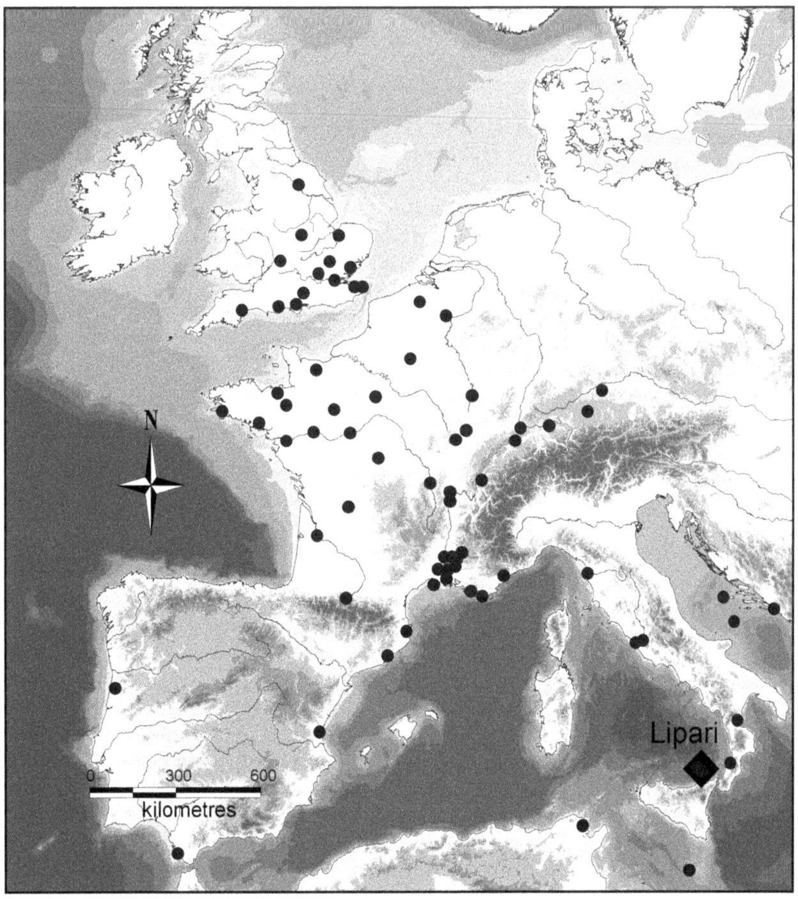

Fig. 4.29. Distribution of Richborough 527 amphorae (after Borgard et al. 2003, Fig. 4).

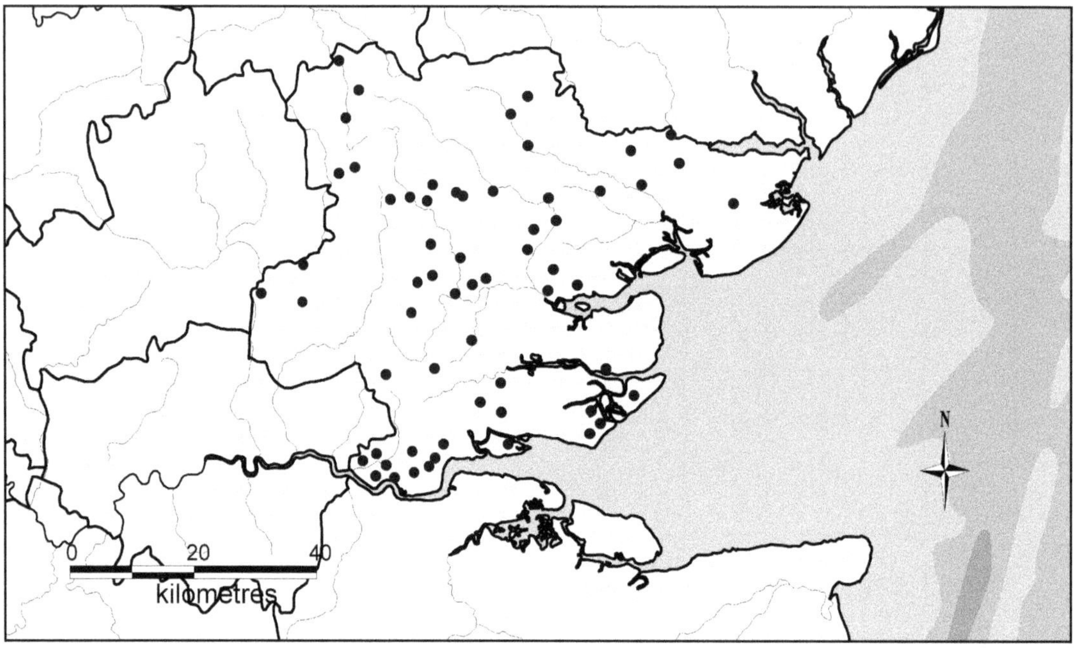

Fig. 4.30. The distribution of lava querns from Roman-period sites in Essex (data provided by Hilary Major 2007. Unpublished, but listed in Morris (2009, Appendix 11)).

Lava querns

Lava querns are relatively common finds at British sites dating to the Roman period. Almost all seem to derive from the quarries at Mayen on the Middle Rhine (See p. 49).[466] The only exceptions are two large donkey mills made from Auvergne lava, which were found in mid-first-century AD contexts at London and at Corfe Mullen in Dorset.[467] Their prevalence is somewhat curious given the exploitation of suitable local British minerals such as Millstone grit, Hertfordshire Puddingstone and various varieties of sandstone for quern production throughout the Late Iron Age and Roman period.[468] To date there has been no major survey of the lava querns found in Britain and indeed one is sorely needed. My own investigations suggest that they are most common in the southeast, particularly in Essex, Kent and Greater London. Based on data provided by Hilary Major I have investigated their occurrence in Essex where they are found on a wide range of site types, from urban Colchester, through small towns to villas and other rural settlements (**Fig. 4.30, Tab. 4.6**). Lava querns are also encountered on sites in numerous other southern counties, including Hertfordshire, Surrey, Bedfordshire, Buckinghamshire, Oxfordshire and Norfolk.[469] In addition, they are often found at military sites in northern England and Scotland.

Whilst we have to bear in mind the limitations in making accurate assessments of the lava quern supply (see pp. 49-50), it appears that they are fairly rare from secure pre-Flavian contexts. Small quantities certainly did arrive in the Claudio-Neronian period; for example, querns have been found in pre-Boudiccan layers at Colchester, whilst fragments from at least 32 different querns have been identified at Usk, which was occupied c. AD 55-75.[470] I argue, however, that the period c. AD 70-165 represented the peak of lava quern import to Britain. Supporting evidence for this view comes from London where lava querns are exceptionally common at sites dating to the late first and early second centuries AD. Excavations at sites of these dates within the City invariably reveal quern fragments, as, for example, at Billingsgate, Leadenhall Court, Roman Road/Parnell Road, Queen Street, Lincoln Road (Enfield), Aldgate, Morville Street and No.1 Poultry.[471] Indeed, the latter assemblage contained fragments from at least 1,000 lava querns dated c. AD 70-90.[472]

Site type	Number of sites in Essex with lava querns
Urban	1
Small town	8
Rural	52
Total	61

Tab. 4.6. Frequency of occurrence of lava querns in Essex by site type.

Lava querns are also well known from late first- to mid-second-century contexts at other urban sites in the southeast, such as St Albans and Colchester, and also at

[466] Peacock 1980.
[467] Williams-Thorpe and Thorpe 2007.
[468] King 1987; Shaffrey 2003.
[469] Many thanks to Ruth Shaffrey, Oxford Archaeology Unit, for her advice on this matter.

[470] Buckley and Major 1983; Manning *et al.* 1995, 214.
[471] McIlwain 1980; Milne and Wardle 1993, 83, Fig. 46.75; Mills 1984; Wilmott 1982, 61; Gentry *et al.* 1977, 179-181; Chapman and Johnson 1973, 51; McIsaac *et al.* 1979, 48; Rowsome, forthcoming.
[472] Rowsome, forthcoming.

small towns, as at Chelmsford, Braintree, and Elms Farm (Heybridge) in Essex and Staines in Berkshire.[473] A study of the large lava quern assemblage at Elms Farm indicates that deposition peaked c. AD 160 and a second-century AD peak is also evident in the Chelmsford material.[474] With the exception of Staines, none of the above small towns had any identifiable military background.[475] In addition, lava querns are regular finds in late first- to mid-second-century AD contexts at northern military sites. For example, they are present in late first-century AD contexts at Carlisle, whilst they are also known from Flavian occupation levels at Newstead and Strageath.[476] Furthermore, lava querns have been noted in Antonine deposits at Strageath and derive from forts along the Antonine Wall, such as Balmuidy and Bar Hill.[477]

London will have served as the main British entrepôt; in addition to the vast number of querns found here, there is also evidence for unfinished querns, which indicates that rough examples were imported here prior to finishing-off.[478] Once they arrived in London, querns will have been redistributed to other sites, principally by road and river, but also by sea. Querns may have arrived at other southeastern ports direct from the continent as well. The large mid-second-century assemblage from the small town at Heybridge, situated by the head of the Blackwater estuary suggests this site as one possible candidate, though they may equally well have reached this site indirectly via London. On the continent Mayen lava querns are prevalent throughout much of northwest Europe. They are widely distributed, reaching as far as Switzerland, though they primarily focus upon the river Rhine.[479] Consequently most of the lava querns will have reached Britain across the Southern North Sea via ports at the mouth of the Rhine and Scheldt.

Lava querns probably reached British military sites as a result of state contracts, though we cannot rule out the possibility that some querns reached military sites through private trade. The large number of querns from civil sites in southeast Britain is indicative of private trade on a substantial scale.

Other imports

Large quantities of glass vessels appear in Britain following the Claudian conquest; for example, excavations at Colchester between 1971-1985 revealed 6321 fragments of vessel glass, excavations at the Caerleon *canabae* c. 1300 glass vessel fragments, whilst work at 9 Blake Street in York uncovered 1571 glass fragments from a minimum of 115 vessels.[480] It is difficult to determine the extent to which we are dealing with direct imports of vessels from the continent and it is entirely possible that most of the glass vessels known from Roman Britain were in fact produced there, initially by craftsmen who had migrated from the continent. There is ample evidence for glass working in Britain, with c. 30 workshops identified across the province to date, several of which date back to the first and second centuries AD. These workshops are typically characterised by the presence of small glass furnaces, often found in association with crucibles used for melting glass, glass-working waste and occasionally collections of waste glass ready for recycling. Because of the ease with which glass could be recycled the amount of waste present at production sites is very small and it is extremely hard to tie down specific glass vessel products to particular workshops.[481]

Whether or not vessels were imported in quantity, virtually all of the glass found in Britain would have been imported in some form. Primary production of raw glass took place at only a few locations in the Roman world; scientific studies point to the Syro-Palestinian coast of the Eastern Mediterranean and to Egypt as the most important Roman glass making centres and this has also been backed up by finds of glass furnaces in these areas.[482] Pliny states that, in addition to the aforementioned areas, glass was also produced in Italy, Spain and Gaul.[483] Our only evidence for primary glass making in Britain, meanwhile, derives from Coppergate in York and dates to the late second century AD.[484] Glass blocks from the primary production sites were traded over long distances. Several examples have been noted on shipwrecks in the Mediterranean, including over 100 kg from a first-century AD wreck off Mljet in Croatia and 18 tonnes from the Embiez-Ouest wreck off southern France.[485] Much glass may therefore have been imported to Britain in block, rather than vessel, form, though at present we simply cannot determine if this was the case. Whatever form it arrived in we are probably dealing with private market trade.

Pipeclay figurines, the great majority of which were produced in the same region as Central Gaulish *terra sigillata*, were traded to Britain in substantial quantities alongside the *sigillata* between the end of the first century AD and the mid-second century AD.[486] About 400 examples are known from c. 120 sites (**Fig. 4.31**). Their import appears to have peaked by c. AD 150-160 and thereafter declined, probably ceasing before AD 200. Though they have a widespread distribution, which extends to military sites in northern Britain, they

[473] King 1987, 100-106; Buckley and Major 1983; Drury 1988, 144; Wickenden 1992, 89, Tab. 5; Humphery 2002, 119; Crouch and Shanks 1984, 109, Fig. 55.
[474] Hilary Major, forthcoming and pers. Comm. 2007; Drury 1988, 144.
[475] Eddy 1995.
[476] McCarthy 1990, 158-161; Curle 1911, 145, Pl. XVII; Frere and Wilkes 1989, 181-186.
[477] Frere and Wilkes 1989, 181-186; Miller 1922, 98; Robertson *et al.* 1975, 45.
[478] Chapman 1977, 41.
[479] Schäfer 2000.
[480] Cool and Price 1995; Evans 2000; Cool *et al.* 1995.
[481] Price 1978; 1995, 140; 1998; 2000; 2002; Allen 1998; Stern 2008.
[482] Stern 2008; Nenna *et al.* 1997; Gorin-Rosen 2000.
[483] *H.N.* 36.190.
[484] Jackson *et al.* 1998; Price 2002.
[485] Radic and Jurisic 1993, 122-123; Parker 1992.
[486] Though a small minority of the imported figurines were manufactured in the Rhine-Moselle region.

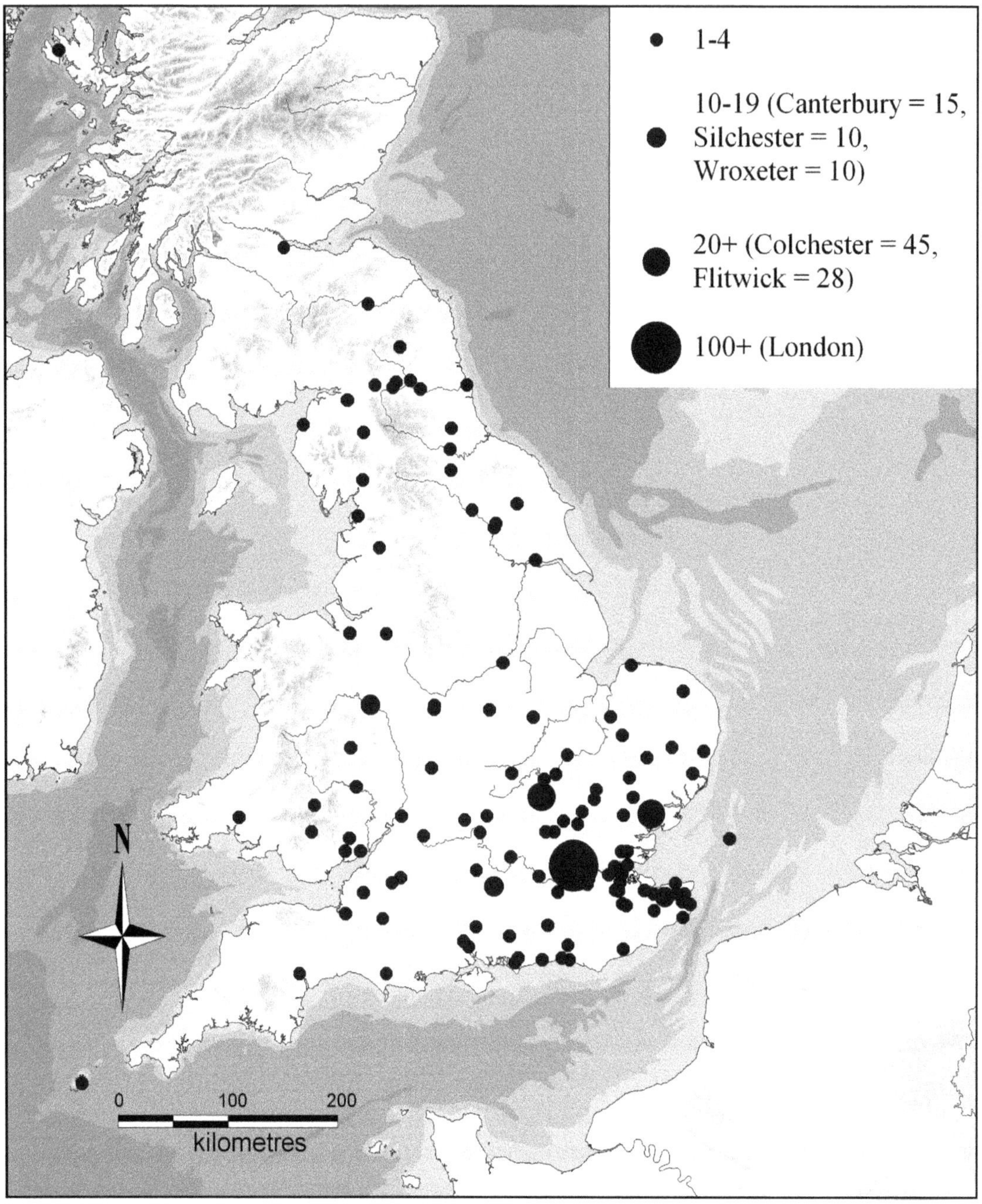

Fig. 4.31. British distribution of pipeclay figurines (after Bémont et al. 1993, Fig. 110) (Note the examples from the Scilly Isles (Fulford 1989b) and from Galloper Sands in the North Sea (Van Doorselaer 1973), which may well derive from shipwrecks).

primarily concentrate in southeast Britain and a very large group (c. 100) are known from London, which may have been the principal port at which they arrived, whilst 45 examples derive from Colchester.[487]

Small quantities of Italian marble, used as veneer, have been recovered from Neronian buildings at Canterbury and the bathhouse at Angmering in Sussex. At Fishbourne a wide range of Mediterranean marble veneers decorated the Flavian palace. Fragments of Egyptian porphyry have also been recovered from first-century AD contexts at Colchester and Rivenhall in Essex. The largest group of imported stonework derives from London; here marble veneers, from a wide range of Mediterranean stones, particularly from Eastern Mediterranean and Egyptian quarries, have been identified in contexts dating between the Neronian period and the early fourth century AD.[488] Stone from the Oise Valley in northern France was also utilised in the construction of the Flavian palace at Fishbourne and the Great Monument at Richborough.[489] Most imported

[487] Bémont *et al.* 1993, 245-250, Fig. 110; Austen 1991, 175-178; Milne 1985, 120-121.

[488] Pritchard 1986; Milne 1985, 106; Drummond-Murray and Thompson 2002, 65, 160.

[489] Fulford 2007, 65.

building stone was used in high-status buildings. Its import was presumably paid for by extremely rich individuals, or state officials.

The Roman army in Britain required a huge amount of basic agricultural provisions. Sauer has estimated that the 40,000-strong invasion army, its followers and animals would have needed c. 32,713 tonnes of grain per year.[490] To this one must add the vast livestock requirements for meat, for use as mounts and for transport, employment in sacrifices and for the construction of leather goods, such as tents.[491]

The extent to which the British garrison relied upon either imported or British produce is hard to assess, not least because we cannot distinguish between the essentially identical crops, and weeds associated with these crops, that grow in Britain and in continental northwest Europe. Some scholars have argued that during the initial decades of conquest the military's demand for agricultural products far outstripped the ability of British producers to provide them.[492] However, the requirements do not seem to have been beyond British agricultural capabilities; based on conservative use of the crop growing experiments at Butser Farm in Hampshire, Sauer estimates that the annual grain supply of the mid-first-century AD army could have been provided by an area of only 12.8 x 12.8 km (164 km^2), or by an area of 40.5 x 40.5 km if just 10% of the total grain product was requisitioned by the army.[493] Investigations of faunal and botanical remains from Roman forts, even as early as the Claudian period as at Alchester in Oxfordshire, suggest that the military relied heavily upon their immediate hinterland.[494]

However, a handful of grain deposits have been identified that were imported from Mediterranean regions. On the site of the forum in London a building burnt in the Boudiccan revolt (AD 61) contained a cereal deposit with 0.7% einkorn and also traces of lentils and bitter vetch, which strongly suggest a Mediterranean origin. A grain deposit at a store within a military annexe at Caerleon dating to the Flavian period contained lentils, which also imply a Mediterranean origin. Similarly, grain from a military warehouse in York dated c. AD 70-120 was probably imported from the same region.[495] This suggests that whilst the British garrison probably relied principally upon local agricultural produce, some imports, particularly of grain, were made on behalf of the state in order to feed the army.

[490] Sauer 2002; Rivet (1969, 189-198) estimates that the first-century AD army (excluding animals) consumed c. 15,000 tonnes of grain per year, whilst Millett (1990) proposed 8000-20,000 tonnes.
[491] Breeze 1984.
[492] Peddie 1997, 23-46; Fulford 1984; 1989a; Whittaker 1994, 103-104; Middleton 1979.
[493] Sauer 2002; Millett (1990) estimated an area of 14.1 x 14.1 km could meet the annual demands of the first-century army.
[494] Thomas and Stallibrass 2008, 9; Carrington 2008; Thomas 2008.
[495] Thomas and Stallibrass 2008; Straker 1984; Marsden 1987, 151-153; Helbaek 1964; Van der Veen 2008.

British Exports

Coinage and metals

As discussed above, there were large state payments of coin to Britain (pp. 53-54). Much coin will have been re-exported to the continent through private trade in exchange for imported goods, such as wine, *terra sigillata* and lava querns. As previously outlined, coin pools in the Western Empire display both distinctive regional differences as well as overlaps, which cannot be used to rule out significant long-distance movement of coin through trade. We should also bear in mind that long-distance trade need not necessarily have utilised physical coin as credit was heavily employed in the Roman world (see p. 54).

Aside from trade there were also substantial state-organised shipments of coin from Britain to the continental Empire. In the aftermath of the Claudian conquest the vast Late Iron Age gold and silver coinages of southeast Britain disappeared rapidly. Some of these were obtained by the Roman state as war booty or tribute and presumably melted down before being sent to the treasury and mint at Rome. Roman precious metal coin would also have been periodically returned to the central Rome mint.[496] This was undertaken by the British procurator who was in charge of finances and taxation within the provinces. *Denarii* were very probably recalled by the state in bulk during the reign of Trajan. At this time earlier Republican *denarii* which had much higher silver contents (c. 95%) than coins minted in Trajan's reign (mid-80%) disappear from the archaeological record.[497] State recall may also have occurred on lower levels at other times during the mid-second century AD. Pre-AD 64 *denarii* and those issued under Domitian had high silver contents and these are notably rare from hoards by the mid-second century AD.[498] However, some of these issues may in fact have been targeted for remelting by private individuals within Britain; the mid-second-century AD Snettisham jeweller's hoard included silver jewellery along with eighty-three *denarii* down to AD 154-155, which were presumably destined for the melting pot. Of the *denarii* seventy-four were from Domitian's reign.[499]

Britain was an important source of metals, though it was never worked to the same extent as the Iberian provinces, and these counted amongst the province's principal exports. Metals were of great value to the Roman state and they were exploited rapidly, and on a large-scale, following initial penetration of an ore-rich area by the Roman military. Gold was targeted at Dolaucothi in Wales by deep vein and hydraulic mining techniques. The main phase of state-organised extraction here was during the late first century AD down to c. AD 125 after which the mines were very probably leased out to civilian

[496] Howgego 1992; 1994.
[497] Reece 2002, 17.
[498] Abdy 2002, 27-29.
[499] Johns 1996, 213-215; 1997; Abdy 2002, 28-29.

	Mendips	S. Wales	Shrops.	NE Wales	Derbys.	Yorks.	Uncertain	Total
Claudius (AD 41-54)	1							1
Nero (AD 54-68)	3			1				4
Vespasian (AD 69-79)	13			5				18
Titus (AD 79-81)								
Domitian (AD 81-96)				1		2		3
Nerva (AD 96-98)							1	1
Unstamped, probably Flavian (AD 69-98)				18			1	19
Trajan (AD 98-117)						1		1
Hadrian (AD 117-138)	2		4		1	1	1	9
Antoninus Pius (AD 138-161)	3							3
M.Aurelius/Lucius Verus (164-169)	4							4
Sept. Severus (193-211)							3	3
Late third or fourth century AD					2		1 + 271	3 + 271
Unknown	3	1		1	23		3	31
Total	29	1	4	26	26	4	10 + 271	100 + 271

Tab. 4.7. Dates of lead pigs from various British ore-fields (data extracted from Stewart 2002, Tab. 5.6).

contractors.[500] Judging from the *Lex Vipasca*, a second-century AD contract for the running of the copper- and silver-mines at Aljustrel in Portugal, private contractors would have delivered 50% of the metal ore to the state in tax.[501] The Roman state would certainly have sent the gold obtained from Dolaucothi to the mint and treasury at Rome. Private contractors, meanwhile, may have traded their gold either within Britain or on the continent.

Lead was also targeted rapidly following the Roman conquest. Our principal evidence for lead mining derives from a large number of lead ingots, or pigs, many of which were stamped and can be precisely dated (**Fig. 4.32, Tab. 4.7**), though traces of hydraulic mining and gallery mines have been noted at various locations. In the Mendips lead mining was underway by AD 49, ore fields in northeast Wales, Yorkshire and perhaps south Wales were being exploited from at least the Flavian period onwards, and lead was certainly mined in Shropshire and Derbyshire by the early second century.[502]

As with gold, the Roman state was heavily involved in the operation of British lead mines, which is indicated by stamps attesting military units on several of the ingots, though private contractors would have been involved as well.[503] The distribution of British lead ingots implies that most British lead was consumed within the province itself, though there were exports. The Neronian lead ingot of Mendip origin found at Valéry-sur-Somme testifies to this (**Fig. 4.32**). This particular example was probably shipped across the Channel from Southampton Water as several first-century AD ingots of Mendip origin have also been located here. Brill and Wampler noted that a lead cistern from Pompeii had an isotopic composition most closely matched by British sources.[504] Furthermore,

[500] Burnham and Burnham 2004; Burnham 1997; Wilson 2002, 19-25; Bird 2001.

[501] Stewart 2002; Wilson 2009a, 176-178; Domergue 1983.

[502] Tylecote 1986; Whittick 1982; Boon 1991; Todd 1996; 2003; Carrington 2006; Timberlake and Kidd 2005; Jones and Mattingly 1990; Stewart 2002; Fulford 2004; Mattingly 2006; Fradley 2009.

[503] See footnote 502.

[504] Brill and Wampler 1967, 70.

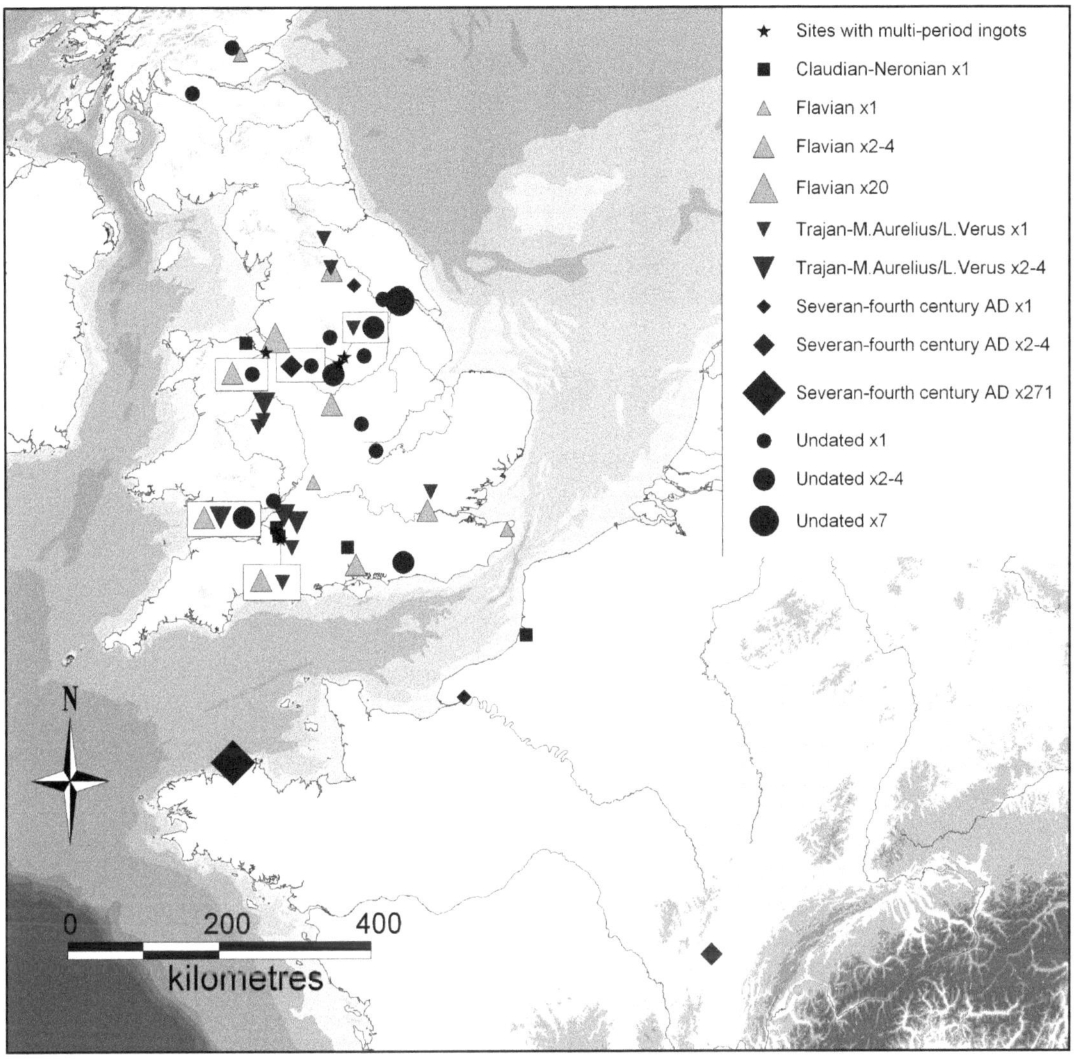

Fig. 4.32. Distribution and chronology of Romano-British lead pigs (data extracted from Stewart 2002, Tab. 5.6).

Pliny, writing c. AD 77, recorded that 'black lead' (lead) was so readily mined in Britain that a law had to be made limiting the amount that could be worked. One reason for this may have been to prevent exports undercutting the Spanish lead industry.[505] However, an analysis of a number of lead objects from Germany west of the Rhine indicates that British sources made no contribution at this early date with most lead in this region deriving from closer sources in the Eifel.[506]

Lead sources were not simply exploited for their lead. In the ancient world lead ores were the dominant source of silver. Whilst several British lead ingots are stamped *EX ARG*, which is best interpreted as 'from the lead-silver mines', questions have been raised over the extent to which silver was extracted from British ores. The mechanism involved would have been the cupellation process, which required the lead-silver mix to be melted in a furnace, whence lead was oxidised to litharge and either absorbed by a bone-ash layer, skimmed off, or lost as fume, whilst the silver was left unaltered. It has been argued that whilst silver might have been effectively extracted from Mendip and North Welsh lead by this means, the lower silver concentrations in the ores from Derbyshire, Yorkshire and Shropshire meant that cupellation of lead from these sources was simply not worthwhile.[507]

We should bear in mind, however, that a technological procedure known as Pattinson's process may well have been utilised in the Roman period and is possibly described by Pliny. This is a natural process which makes the extraction of silver from lead much more efficient. When newly smelted lead cools from a liquid state a layer of lead with a high concentration of silver forms near the surface. This layer could be skimmed off, providing lead with a high silver content ready for cupelling.[508] With the application of Pattinson's process considerable quantities of silver could have been extracted from the lead mined in Britain from AD 49 onwards, perhaps even from ores with a low silver concentration. The state sent much

[505] Pliny *H.N.* 34.49 (see also 34.47); Jones and Mattingly 1990, 179; Elkington 1976, 187-188.
[506] Durali-Mueller *et al.* 2007.
[507] Tylecote 1986; Jones and Mattingly 1990, 189-190; Elkington 1976.
[508] Pliny *H.N.* 33.31; Stewart 2002, 123-124.

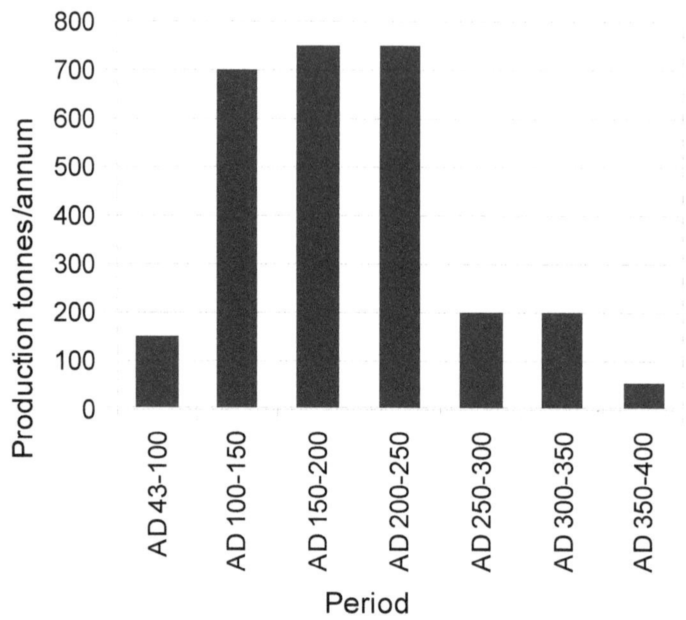

Fig. 4.33. Estimated iron production in the Weald (data from Cleere and Crossley 1995, 81).

	Iron Age with Roman	Iron Age with 1stC AD	1stC AD	2ndC AD	3rdC AD	4thC AD	5thC AD
Smelting	26	12	36	37	38	30	1
Certain	11	6	16	15	13	12	0

Tab. 4.8. Number of East Midlands sites with evidence for smelting (and of those, the ones which are certain) through time (after Schrüfer-Kolb 2004, Tab.4).

silver back to Rome, but the silver extracted by private contractors would have been marketed both within Britain and abroad.

There was a dramatic expansion in British iron production following the Roman conquest. In the Weald production had reached industrial proportions by the early second century AD (**Fig. 4.33**). Smaller-scale smelting also took place throughout Britain during the Roman period, with particular concentrations of activity in the Forest of Dean and in the East Midlands (**Tab. 4.8**). In the latter region one particular site, Laxton, probably produced c. 107 tonnes of iron per annum during the late first and early second centuries.[509]

The Wealden iron industry was evidently directly state-controlled and production was organised by the *Classis Britannica*. Tiles stamped CL.BR have been identified at five Wealden sites dating between the early second and third centuries AD. At Beauport Park, where the largest slag heap of all was probably situated (estimated at 100,000 tonnes equating to the production of 30,000 tonnes of iron), 1600 CL.BR tiles were recovered from the bath-house.[510] Elsewhere in Britain there may have been some state control of resources, though there was very likely substantial private production as well. The majority of British-produced iron was undoubtedly consumed internally within the province by both the Roman military and the civilian population; however, iron was probably exported to the adjacent continent as well.[511]

Surveys of the region lying between the Seine-Marne and the Rhine have produced only sparse evidence for Roman-period iron smelting in contrast to a greater prevalence of iron-working, though this may in part be due to lack of research because substantial ore resources do exist in this region.[512] These findings hint at the possibility that iron was imported here, through both state supply and private trade. British sources, particularly the Weald, would have been well-placed to meet these demands, although one must bear in mind that large-scale iron smelting took place elsewhere in the northwestern

[509] Cleere and Crossley 1995; Cleere 1976; Hodgkinson 1999; Taylor 2007, 36-37, 115-116, Fig. 4.12; Stewart 2002; Walters 1992; 1999; Fulford and Allen 1992; Schrüfer-Kolb 2004; Fulford 2006.

[510] Cleere and Crossley 1995; Peacock 1977; Mason 2003, 114-115, Fig. 47.

[511] British consumption: Manning 1985a; 1985b.

[512] Polfer 2000; Loridant 1999. *Contra* Serneels and Mangin 1996; Wightman 1985.

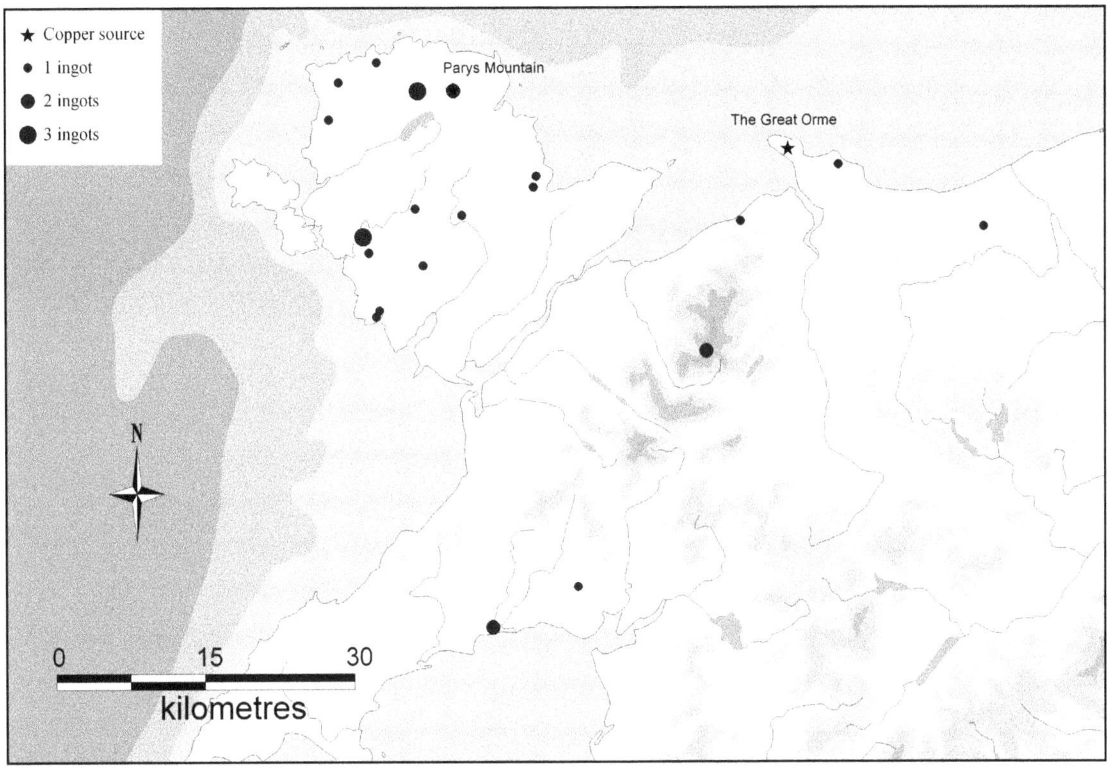

Fig. 4.34. Distribution of Roman-period copper ingots in North Wales (Data from Tylecote 1986, Tab. 10).

Empire, as in central and western France and at the Hüttenberg in southern Austria.[513]

Tin from the British southwestern peninsula was probably exploited following the Roman conquest; early Roman forts at Restormel Castle, Nanstallon and Calstock in Cornwall appear to have been located near tin deposits.[514] However, curiously Pliny, writing on tin, only mentions sources in northern Iberia.[515] The scale of British tin mining, and the question of tin export, is therefore unclear at present.

On the basis of inscribed but otherwise undated copper ingots we know that copper was mined in northwest Wales on a considerable scale, probably principally at Parys Mountain, by individuals who had leased the mines from the Roman state (**Fig. 4.34**).[516] The distribution of ingots hints at a fairly local exchange network; outside of northwest Wales only two copper ingots, both from Scotland, have been identified. However, we can suspect that copper from this source was melted down and consumed more widely and some may even have been exported. Finally, we should note the possibility that, despite the lack of direct evidence, zinc deposits in the Mendips were being exploited, alongside lead-silver ores, from the Claudian period onwards, though the probable existence of large-scale zinc-ore-mining in western Germany and in Belgium from the late first century onwards makes export unlikely.[517]

A number of British-style copper-alloy objects are present on the continent. I have noted 179 brooches of probable British type from the continent, the vast majority of which can be dated to between the late first and mid- to late second century AD (**Fig. 4.35**). These British-style brooches have extremely close parallels in Britain, and indeed they belong to a number of types, which occur in very large quantities on the island. Although British brooch types may appear to be well represented on the continent, in relative terms they are actually fairly rare, with brooches produced in local continental styles greatly outnumbering them in brooch assemblages.

Most of the British-style brooches derive from the northwestern parts of the continental Empire, from what would have been *Belgica* and the two German provinces, a sizeable, though by no means dominant, proportion from Roman military forts along the Rhine. Their distribution marks an important avenue of movement from Britain across the Southern North Sea and Eastern Channel to the north French, Belgian and south Dutch coasts, thence inland to Cologne and onwards along the Rhône-Rhine and Danube corridors where finds trail off. It is perhaps notable that British brooches do not follow the Rhine-Rhône back to the Mediterranean, though one must consider that my investigations favour areas with

513 Müller-Wille 1999; Serneels and Mangin 1996; Bielenin *et al.* 1998; Cech 2007; 2008.
514 Smart *et al.* forthcoming.
515 *H.N.* 34.97.
516 Tylecote 1986.

517 Pliny *H.N.* XXXIV.II; Craddock 2008; Durali-Mueller 2005; Willers, 1907; Davies 1935; Bayley 1998

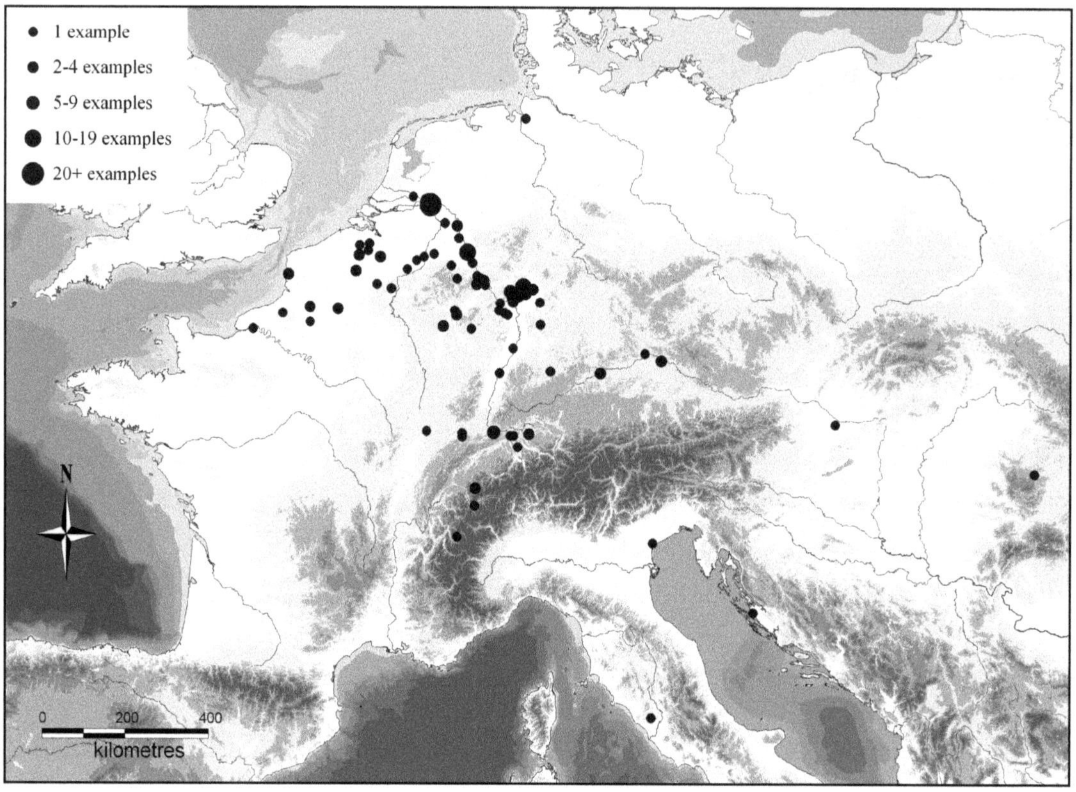

Fig. 4.35. Continental distribution of Romano-British brooches (see Appendix 6).

well-published brooch assemblages, such as western Germany and Switzerland.

A few of the British-style brooches may have reached the continent through an export trade in exotic British artefacts. It is probable that a much greater number moved with individuals as personal possessions. Some items may have been obtained by soldiers serving in Britain who subsequently returned to their homes on the continent, or were deployed abroad. Some may also have moved with British auxiliaries who were stationed on the continent from the mid- to late first century AD onwards. Some brooches were probably worn by British women who accompanied their husbands to the continent, indeed, several finds of brooches with possible female characteristics or associations have been made, although it must be admitted that the evidence linking specific brooch styles to particular genders is weak (Appendix 6).[518] We must also bear in mind the possibility that a significant number of British-style brooches were in fact manufactured on the continent by individuals working in British styles; however, in our present state of research this possibility can neither be confirmed, nor refuted.

There are several examples of British enamelled horse gear from the continent (**Fig. 4.36**). Whilst a few of these are pre-conquest in date, the majority were produced in the mid- to late first century AD. Other non-enamelled British products include a mid-first-century AD spouted bowl from Leg Piekarski in Poland bowl, and a mid-first-century AD mirror from Nijmegen. A distinctive group of enamelled copper-alloy vessels was produced in Britain between the late first century AD and the mid- to late second century AD. These included flasks, jugs, *alabastra* and, most common of all, *paterae* (pans), some of which bear stylised representations of Hadrian's Wall and a few even carry inscriptions listing the forts along the Wall (**Fig. 4.37**).[519] These items are most commonly encountered in northern Gaul and the Rhine provinces, though they are also known more widely throughout the Empire as well. Like the British brooches, trade cannot be ruled out, but a movement with individuals as personal possessions is more likely. One should also not rule out the possibility that a few of the artefacts were actually produced on the continent by mobile craftsmen working in British styles.

Other exports

Archaeological evidence for further British exports is lacking. We can suspect that archaeologically undetectable items, such as grain, cattle, hides, slaves and hunting dogs, listed by Strabo as Britain's pre-conquest exports featured heavily (see p. 38). Salt production and oyster-fishing were also prominent industries in Roman Britain, particularly at Poole Harbour and around the Thames estuary, and we might speculate that salt and oysters were exported as well.[520]

We have already seen that Romano-British agriculture was well capable of supporting the Roman garrison in the

[518] Tatiana Ivleva, (Leiden University), pers. Comm 2009; Southern 1989; Spaul 2000; Gillam 1984; Clay 2007, Fig. 1.

[519] Künzl 1995; 2008; Moore 1978; Bayley 1995.

[520] Rippon 2000; Tomalin 2006.

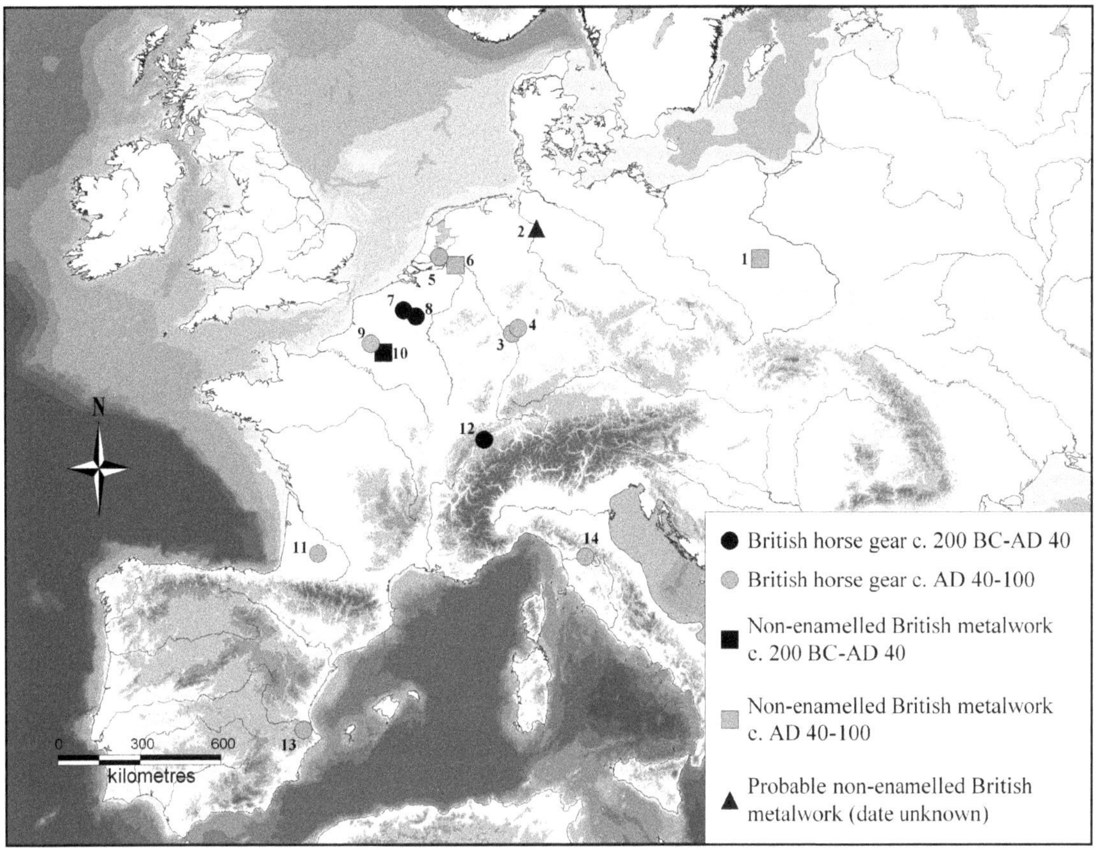

Fig. 4.36. The continental distribution of British horse gear and non-enamelled metalwork c. 200 BC-AD 100 (excluding brooches) (Appendix 7).

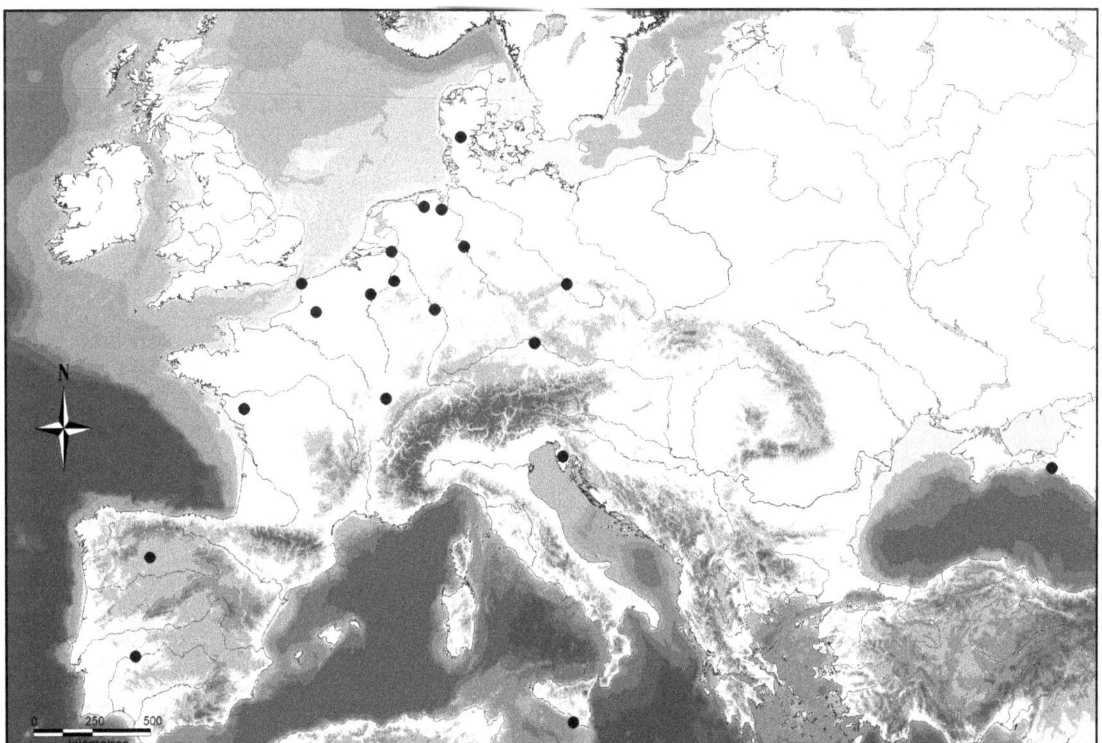

Fig. 4.37. Continental distribution of enamelled British metalwork (late first to mid-second century AD, excluding brooches and horse gear) (Appendix 8).

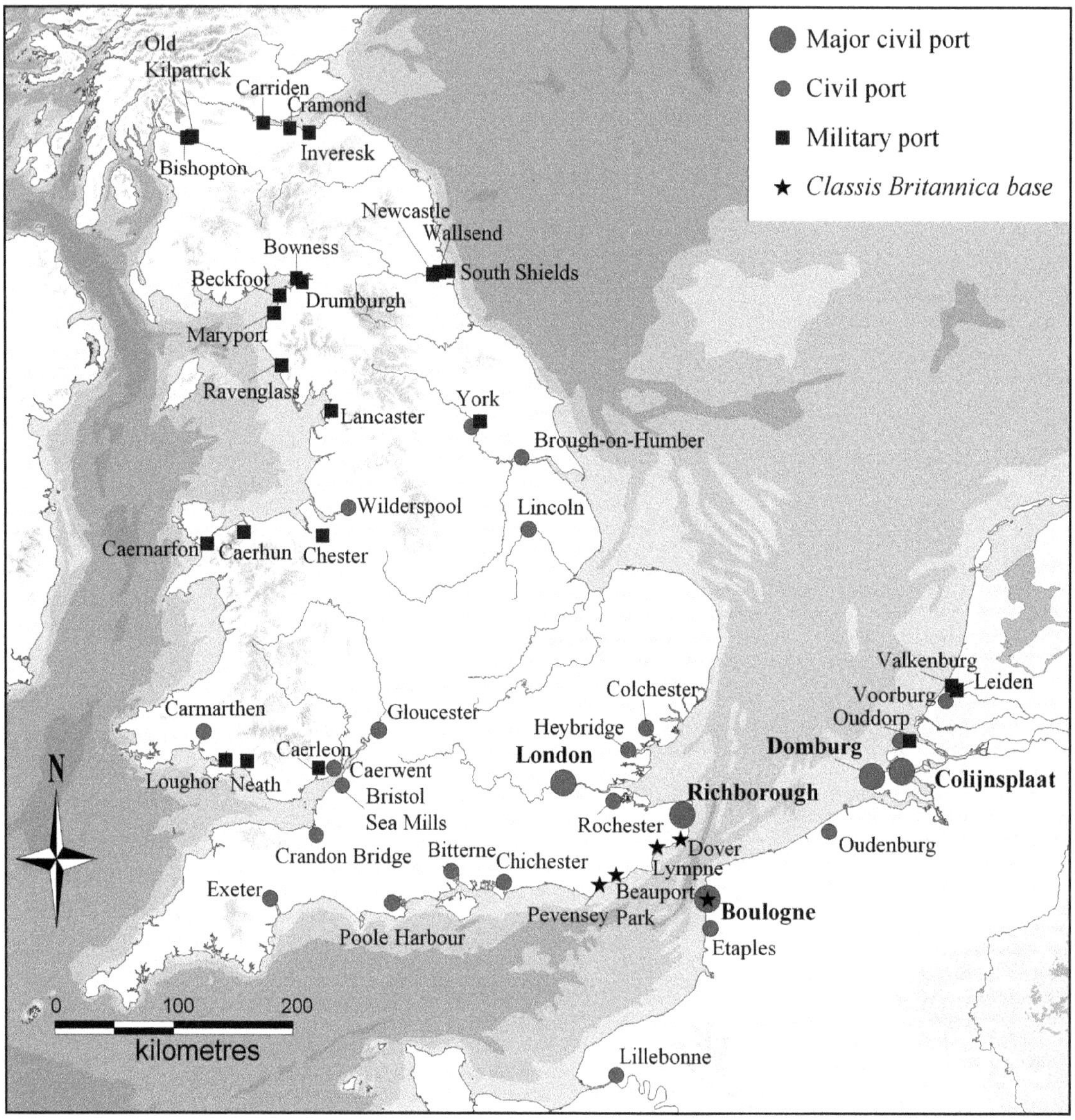

Fig. 4.38. The main second-century AD ports in Roman Britain and on the adjacent continent (For a full discussion of Romano-British ports see: Cleere 1978; Jones and Mattingly 1990, Map. 6:19; Mason 2003).

island, though grain was, on occasion, imported (see p. 81). It is possible that there was even enough of a surplus to export abroad. Roman forts in the Rhine delta appear to have imported a sizeable proportion of their cereals from outside their local region. There was little surplus cereal production at surrounding rural settlements and, furthermore, spelt wheat and bread wheat are amongst the most common cereals in archaeobotanical samples at the forts and these were not produced locally. Some cereals might well have reached the Rhine delta from Britain. These may have been obtained by the Roman state as tax in kind, or, alternatively, through state contract or trade on the private market. However, the Lower Rhine forts undoubtedly obtained the majority of their grain from the adjacent loess areas of the German Rhineland, the southern Netherlands, Belgium and northern France where there was a surplus production of mainly spelt wheat.[521]

Ports

The principal port of Roman Britain was undoubtedly London (**Fig. 4.38**). This had certainly developed as an important trading settlement by c. AD 50-55 and Tacitus described pre-Boudiccan London as being famed for its concentration of businessmen and saleable goods. London's development really took off in the Flavian period and it reached its peak in the early second century when its population probably numbered c. 50,000. Its Late Roman defences enclosed 128 ha, which was nearly twice the size of the next largest urban centre. In the late first century quays were constructed for at least 0.5 km along the north Thames waterfront, which facilitated deep-water berthing for large ships and these were renewed in the early second century, whilst a major new quay was constructed in the mid-second century. There is a huge concentration of imported products, including *terra sigillata*, lava querns, olive oil and wine amphorae in the city and it was evidently Britain's main entrepôt. It

[521] Cavallo *et al.* 2008; Groenman-van Waateringe 1989; Bloemers 1983; 1989.

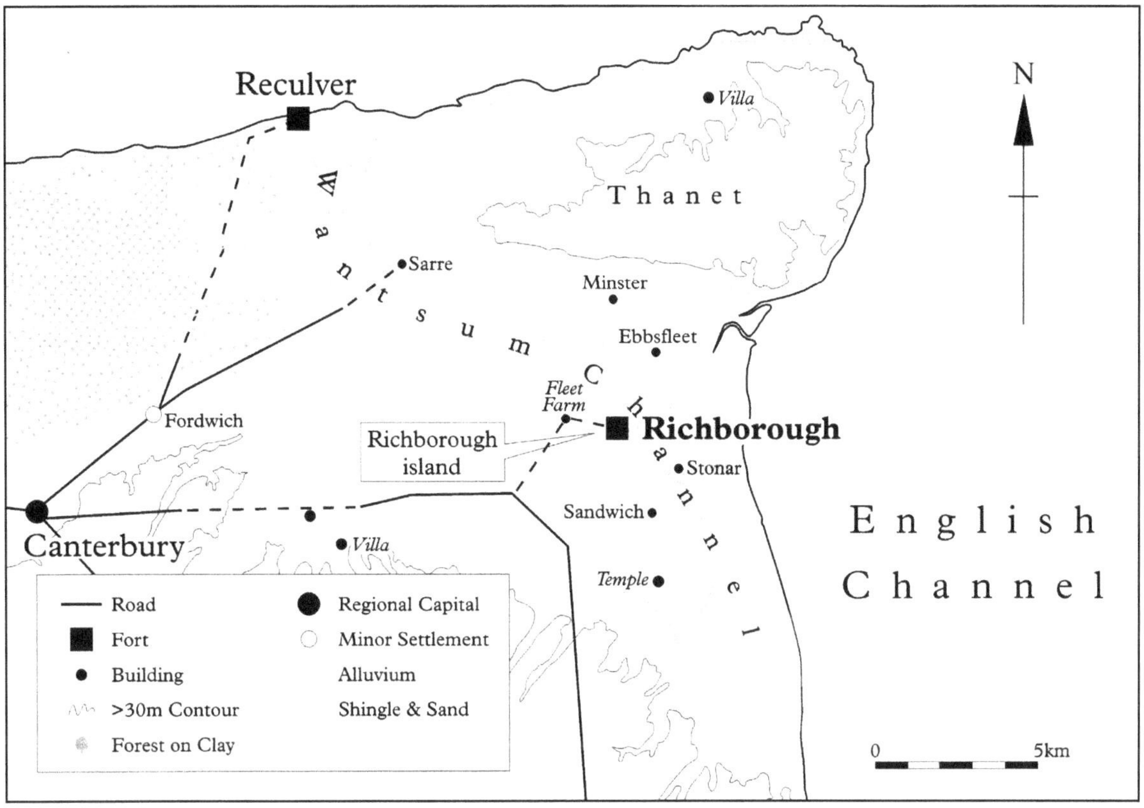

Fig. 4.39. Location map of Richborough in Roman east Kent (Millett and Wilmott 2003, Fig. 18.1).

probably played an important redistributive function with a large portion of the supplies destined for the military channelled through the city, before being re-directed to their destinations by road or by sea. In tandem with this it acted as the principal centre and focus for private, civilian trade.[522]

In Roman times Richborough lay in a sheltered anchorage provided by the Wantsum Channel (**Fig. 4.39**). It appears to have been the principal landing point of the Claudian invasion; excavations have revealed a defended Claudian beachhead protecting a 700m long stretch of the coast. The site was an important military supply base down to c. AD 75/85 and large ranges of granaries have been excavated here. A thriving civilian settlement developed at the site from the late first and into the second century AD.[523] The heavy concentration of imported goods in east Kent strongly implies that Richborough was a major trading centre. The site's gateway function is clear from the Great Monument, a huge 26 m high quadrifons arch clad in Carrara marble, constructed c. AD 85. Throughout the Roman world monumental arches were often built near main routes at the crossing of major geographical zones.[524]

In the southeast, aside from these two major civilian ports, the urban centres at Chichester, Rochester, Heybridge, Colchester and the possible site at Bitterne/Clausentum, all lay near the coast and participated in overseas trade to some degree.[525] In addition, Tomalin has recently drawn attention to a series of coastal villas which lay around the coasts of southern Britain. Several of these, most notably Brading on the Isle of Wight, possess a wide range of imports and will have traded by sea.[526]

The *Classis Britannica* had its principal British base at Dover, where a small fort (1.05 ha) was constructed c. AD 130/140 which overlay the unfinished remains of a defensive wall dated c. AD 120. Numerous tiles stamped CL.BR were found here and there is evidence for a 30 m long seawall, consisting of massive timber-framing with a shingle in-fill, which protected an inner-basin equipped with a timber waterfront. A pair of lighthouses was also built on the cliffs.[527] Further British *Classis Britannica* bases may have existed at Lympne and Pevensey, where stamped CL.BR tiles have been recovered. At the former site an inscription, dated c. AD 115-135, was recovered which was dedicated by a prefect of the British fleet.[528] Beauport Park was one of the principal iron producing sites of the Weald and possesses large numbers of CL.BR

[522] Tacitus *Annals*. 14.33; Drummond-Murray and Thompson 2002; Mattingly 2006, 265, 273-275; Marsden 1994; Miller *et al.* 1986; Jones 2004, 187.
[523] Cunliffe 1968; Millett and Wilmott 2003; Bushe-Fox 1949.
[524] Sauer 2002; Strong 1968.
[525] Cleere 1978; Mason 2003; Tomalin 2006.
[526] Tomalin 2006.
[527] Philp 1981; Rigold 1969; Peacock 1977; Tomalin 2006; Mason 2003, 107-111; Pearson 2002, 49-58.
[528] *RIB*. 66; Mason 2003, 113.

tiles. It lay near the former mouth of the Rother and was probably an important port for the transhipment of iron by the British fleet.[529]

A legionary fort was founded at York in AD 71 and an adjacent civil settlement developed alongside. York was situated on the river Ouse, where it was joined by the river Foss and landing structures and possible warehouses have been identified on the Foss. Large quantities of imported goods have been identified at York, although the evidence suggests that long-distance exchange at the site was most intensive during the late second and early third centuries. Civil sites at the mouth of the Humber, such as Brough-on-Humber and Old Winteringham may have served as transhipment ports for York.[530] South Shields, Wallsend and Newcastle were the ports for the eastern ends of Hadrian's Wall, whilst Carriden, Cramond and Inveresk were the ports for the eastern portions of the Antonine Wall.[531] The extent to which these northeastern sites received supplies direct from the continent is debatable. Most likely the majority of products were shipped indirectly via the ports of southeast Britain where the evidence for trade is more substantial. We should also bear in mind that many goods may have reached the northern frontier from the southeast by overland supply routes via the road network.

In southwest Britain civil ports had developed at Poole Harbour, Exeter, Crandon Bridge, Bristol Sea Mills, Gloucester, Caerwent and Carmarthen by the early second century. Meanwhile, there were large numbers of military sites situated along the Irish Sea coast, many of which probably fulfilled port functions.[532] Whilst the majority of Britain's continental contacts were undoubtedly directed via southeast Britain there were very probably direct supply routes linking into the Irish Sea from the Atlantic as well.[533] As discussed above, Baetican Dr.20 may well have been arriving in western Britain in bulk, as, perhaps, might have been other products, such as Ha.70 amphorae from southern Spain, wine in barrels from southwestern France, fish products from southern Iberia and Brittany and some *terra sigillata*.

Insights into western maritime supply networks are perhaps best achieved through consideration of a British product – Southeast Dorset Black burnished ware (BB1), which was manufactured in the Poole Harbour area in very large quantities (an estimated 1.3-1.7 million vessels were produced per year[534]). BB1 achieved a wide distribution throughout western Britain and reached sites along Hadrian's Wall in notable amounts (**Fig. 4.40**). The distribution patterns of BB1 raise a number of questions about exchange routes in western Britain. The ware is relatively rare on the Devon-Cornwall peninsula and significant quantities appear to have been transhipped in bulk across the Severn estuary, from ports such as Crandon Bridge, to south Wales and perhaps to northwest England and the western end of Hadrian's Wall. BB1 also has a strong distribution up the Welsh borders, which could imply an overland route as well.[535] Does this mean that maritime routes around the Devon-Cornwall peninsula and into the Irish Sea were avoided in Roman times and that goods imported from the continent were unloaded at Channel ports prior to overland distribution to the northern frontier? I suspect not. The absence of 'Roman' goods in Cornwall could principally be a result of this region being only weakly integrated into wider provincial marketing networks rather than an avoidance of maritime routes around the Cornish coast.[536] Although Fulford and Holbrook have portrayed the shipping route around Land's End as particularly hazardous, Jones has demonstrated that in historical times navigation around Land's End was commonplace and that ships doing so could take advantage of the tides in the Bristol Channel.[537]

Turning now to the adjacent continent, Boulogne (*Gesoriacum*) became an important port from the time of the Claudian invasion of Britain and is the most plausible embarkation point for the main part of the invasion force.[538] A large rectangular fort was constructed in the early second century AD, which would have held 4,000 men (**Fig. 4.41**). Considerable numbers of stamped CL.BR tiles are encountered here and on the basis of the fort's size (c. 400 x 300 m/12 ha), which dwarfs the fort at Dover, this was the main base of the *Classis Britannica*. To the west of the base there was a substantial urban civil settlement, 'the lower city', which occupied c. 60 ha along the banks of the Liane. Boulogne's importance is further highlighted by the orientation of the road network; it was linked directly to Cologne by a main road, which passed through the major urban centres at Cassel and Tongeren.[539] Elsewhere in northern France urban settlements at Étaples, at the mouth of the Canache, and the substantial 50 ha settlement at Lillebonne, by the mouth of the Seine, probably functioned as ports as well.[540]

At Oudenburg on the Belgian coast a trading settlement was established in the second half of the first century.[541] The south Dutch coast served as a major focus for maritime contacts with Britain. In Roman times the

[529] Cleere and Crossley 1995; Mason 2003, 114-115; Cleere 1978.
[530] Ottaway 1993; Monaghan 1997; Cleere 1978; Mason 2003, 126.
[531] Mason 2003, 130-134; Cleere 1978; Jones and Mattingly 1990.
[532] Jones 2009; Rippon 2008; Mason 2001; 2003; Biggins and Taylor 2004; Cleere 1978; Jones and Mattingly 1990.
[533] See Jones (2009) for the key discussion of the role of Britain's western seaways during the Roman period. A contrasting view is that of Fulford (2007), who has argued that the seaways of western Britain were little used and all but avoided throughout the Roman period.
[534] Mattingly 2006, 517-518.
[535] Allen and Fulford 1996; Allen *et al.* 2007; Fulford 2007; Tyers 1996b; forthcoming; Rippon 2008.
[536] Mattingly 2006, 45.
[537] Fulford 2007; Holbrook 2001; Jones 2009, 78-79. See also Fulford's (1989b) suggestion that material recovered from Nornour on the Scilly Isles represents a Roman shipwreck.
[538] Suetonius *Claudius*. 17; Frere and Fulford 2001; though see: Sauer 2002; Manley 2002; Black 2000.
[539] Seillier 2004; Brulet 1991; Belot and Canut 1994a; Peacock 1977; Mason 2003.
[540] Petit and Mangin 1994; Rogeret 1997, 328.
[541] Besuijen 2008, 58.

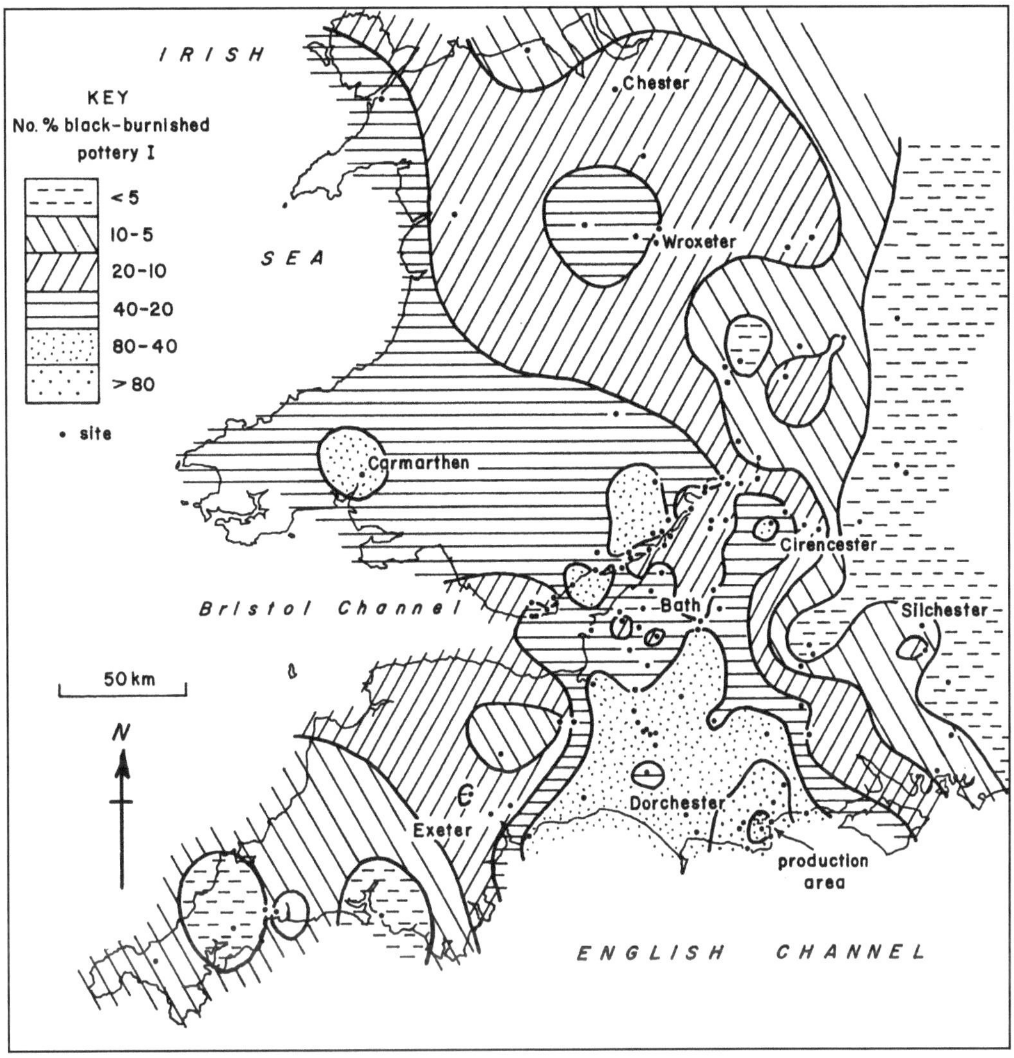

Fig. 4.40. Relative proportion of BB1 in southwest Britain (Allen and Fulford 1996).

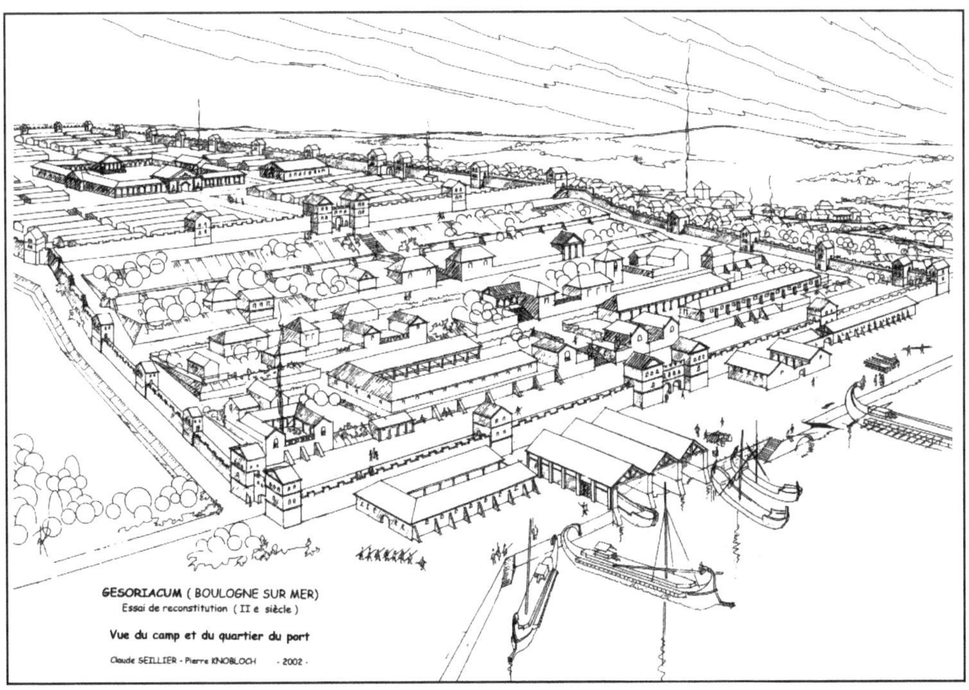

Fig. 4.41. The military camp and its port at Boulogne in the second century AD (Seillier, C. and Knobloch, P. In Seillier 2004).

Helinium, near what is now the mouth of the Scheldt, provided a huge sheltered inlet for shipping. It was the estuary of the Meuse and was directly linked to the Rhine following the construction of a 23-mile long canal by Corbulo in AD 47, which, according to Tacitus, was undertaken to avoid the perils of the Ocean. The Helinium was the boundary between Germania Inferior and Belgica and thus served as an outlet for trade from both provinces. A large number of altars dated to the late second and early third centuries were excavated at Domburg and dredged from the sea at the now submerged site of Colijnsplaat. These indicate significant trading links with Britain and it probable that these sites were important ports prior to the late second century as well (see pp. 109-110).[542]

Nearby at Ouddorp there is evidence of a military presence and stamped tiles of the *Classis Germanica.* There was also a *vicus* here dated c. AD 70-275 which possessed large amounts of imported pottery, some of British origin, and a channelled waterway.[543] Voorburg (Forum Hadriani) was a small urban site serving as the *civitas* capital of the Canninefates. It was evidently a significant port situated halfway along Corbulo's canal and excavations have revealed large quantities of imported pottery and amphorae as well as British BB1 and BB2 pottery.[544] Numerous Roman military forts were sited along the Old Rhine. Valkenburg and Leiden are those closest the entrance to Corbulo's canal.

Synthesis

Following the Claudian invasion there was a huge growth in connectivity between Britain and the continental Roman Empire as Britain became a Roman province. This is evident in both the Southern North Sea and Eastern Channel system and in the Atlantic system, though levels of connectivity in the former system were higher than in the latter. The increase was sudden from AD 43, following which there was steady expansion down to the Flavian period. Several scholars have suggested that Britain's continental contacts gradually declined at the end of the first and beginning of the second century as the province became more self-sufficient and requirements for imports diminished.[545] We have seen that this was not the case. Connectivity continued at a high level down to the late second century, at which point there was a major downturn.

Britain received a huge amount of imports between AD 43-165. Most of these were transported across the Southern North Sea and Eastern Channel, with a substantial portion travelling from Mediterranean provinces via the important Rhône-Rhine route. These imports included vast amounts of coin which arrived as a result of state payments to the army and state officials, as well as payments made to private British concerns who were given contracts to provide the army with supplies. In addition, much of the *terra sigillata* from the Southern, Central and Eastern Gaulish kilns arrived across these seaways, as did other pottery imports, such as Gallo-Belgic ware, Lyon ware, Cologne ware, Central Gaulish black-slipped ware and certain types of mortaria. Some Baetican olive oil, contained in Dr.20 amphorae, also reached Britain via this route as did wine in barrels and amphorae from southern and central France and elsewhere around the Mediterranean, Mayen lava querns, glass, occasionally grain, and perhaps some salted fish products in amphorae, and possibly barrels, from the western Mediterranean. These latter products would all have been traded to Britain; however, military contracts played an important role in the trade of several of these goods. The Roman state would have organised and paid for olive oil, wine, fish products, grain, and perhaps some pottery and lava querns, to be supplied in bulk to the British military garrison through contract. There was in addition a substantial private trade sector, which may have been stimulated by the existence of trade routes supplying contracted goods. Goods were privately traded to the British military garrison and there was a large civilian market in southeast Britain as well.

Imports were certainly arriving in bulk via the Atlantic seaways as well. These included a substantial portion of the Baetican Dr.20 olive oil amphorae, Baetican Ha.70 amphorae bearing olives in *defrutum*, wine in barrels from Aquitaine, fish products in amphorae, and possibly barrels, from Iberia and fish products in barrels from Brittany. Some of the *sigillata* from South and Central Gaul probably also arrived via these routes as well; the restricted continental distribution of Montans *sigillata* certainly implies Atlantic links with Britain. As with the Southern North Sea and Eastern Channel we are dealing with both state contracts and private trade.

Metals feature most prominently amongst Britain's exports, particularly silver, gold and some lead. Iron and copper may also have been exported. A fair number of British brooches and various other types of metalwork have been identified on the continent, particularly in Belgica and the German provinces, though this probably had more to do with movements of military personnel than with trade. Aside from metals, agricultural products, such as grain, as well as oysters and salt are possible candidates for export. Large quantities of the coin paid into Britain by the Roman state would also have been re-exported. Most of these articles, especially the metals, would have been either directly owned by the state, or acquired by the state through taxation. Their export therefore represented direct state payments; however, a substantial portion would also have been exported through private trade.

The evidence is highly suggestive that we are dealing with an imbalance in exchange. In contrast to the widespread evidence for imports to Britain, British exports are far less apparent, though we should bear in mind that this may in part be down to their archaeological invisibility. Private trade would, of course, have been

542 Tacitus *Annals*. 11.20; Besuijen 2008; Mertens 1977, 51; Stuart and Bogaers, 2001; Rippon 2000.
543 Besuijen 2008, 26-27; Trimpe Burger 1973.
544 Mark Driessen, pers. Comm. 2009.
545 Mattingly 2006, 500; Fulford 1984; 1989a; 1991; 2004, 314-315.

balanced, with continental imports presumably offset principally by payments of coin or credit by British consumers. The main 'gap' in exchange results from an imbalance in state payments. The Roman state pumped a huge amount of coin into Britain, and arranged for the military garrison to be supplied with large quantities of goods from private continental producers through contractual arrangements. The state was almost certainly unable to extract and export an equivalent range of goods from Britain.[546] Britain must have been held primarily for political rather than economic purposes.

These much greater levels of connectivity were facilitated by the creation of much better port infrastructure. In the Southern North Sea and Eastern Channel system the most important British ports were civil ports in the southeast, particularly London and Richborough, though the minor *Classis Britannica* base at Dover may have played a significant role as well. These sites not only drew in the bulk of the imports from the adjacent continent, but also acted as major conduits for Atlantic exchange as well. Further north, ports at Brough-on-Humber, York and at the eastern ends of Hadrian's Wall and the Antonine Wall may have received some imports direct from the continent, though it is highly likely that they were principally linked to the continent indirectly via the major southeastern ports. On the continental side, Boulogne housed the main base of the *Classis Britannica* and was also a large civil port. It was one of the main links between Britain and the continent. The south Dutch coast around the former Helinium was also of great significance; Domburg and Colijnsplaat may have functioned as ports at this time, whilst there was also a sizeable civil port at Voorburg on Corbulo's canal which linked the Rhine to the Helinium via the Maas.

In the Atlantic system there were a number of civil ports in southwest Britain, as well as many Roman military ports around the Irish Sea. I have argued that these ports were probably directly engaged in trading contacts with the Empire's continental Atlantic provinces via the Atlantic seaways.

The determinants of connective change

Political integration

Britain's integration into the Roman Empire drove this connective expansion. Taxes on trade with the continental Empire would undoubtedly have been reduced. Duncan-Jones has recently demonstrated that customs dues were 25% at the Empire's external frontiers, whilst they generally appear to have been 2.5% at provincial boundaries, although this latter rate did vary and figures of 5% and 2% have also been recorded.[547] A direct Roman military presence allowed traders to operate in greater safety and to penetrate deeper into the island. Furthermore, the Roman state improved the communication infrastructure within Britain. The rapid construction of the road network and also of the British fleet (*Classis Britannica*) will both have played important roles in facilitating increases in connectivity.[548] Urbanisation and the development of concentrated markets further catalysed trade.

State payments

Perhaps the most significant factor underlying the nature of connectivity were the payments made by the Roman state in coin to the large British garrison, as well as to state officials and private contractors supplying the Roman military. The military was also supplied in bulk with imported goods, such as olive oil and wine, paid for by the state. The Roman state also organised the removal of coin and mineral resources from Britain through taxation and in the latter case through direct ownership and extraction. These state payments had a knock-on impact as well. The injection of coin into Britain promoted private trade on a considerable scale. In addition, the trade networks utilised by contractual suppliers facilitated private trade, in part through allowing traders operating the official supply routes to bring extra goods with them, some of which they might even have been able to transport tax-free alongside the officially traded products, though laws were promulgated against this practice (see p. 63).

The growth of Mediterranean and 'Romanized' consumer tastes

A further factor was the growth in Mediterranean and 'Romanized' consumer tastes, which stimulated bulk imports of Mediterranean food and drink, such as olive oil, salted fish products and wine, as well as dining equipment, like the *terra sigillata* pottery. The principal agents of this 'consumer revolution' were the Roman military. An examination of tombstones recording the area of origin of British legionary recruits reveals that in the mid-first century AD they almost all derived from Mediterranean regions (**Tab. 4.9**). Mediterranean recruits continued to form a substantial portion of the British legions until well into the third century, though there was a trend towards increasing recruitment from colonies elsewhere in the Empire, particularly in Britain as time went on. Tombstones also reveal that many legionaries settled in Britain following the completion of their service (**Tab. 4.10**).[549] The urban settlements at Colchester, Lincoln, Gloucester and York were established as colonies for legionary veterans in the first century AD.[550] A scientific examination of bodies from a mid- to late second-century mass grave at Gloucester also revealed several individuals who probably grew up in the Mediterranean.[551] These Mediterranean individuals would not only have created a demand for Mediterranean and 'Romanized' products, but they would probably have catalysed demand amongst their families and amongst the wider Romano-British population.

546 Fulford 1984.
547 Duncan-Jones 2006.

548 For the road network see: Margary 1973; Davies 2002. For the *Classis Britannica* see: Mason 2003; Cleere 1977; Peacock 1977; Saddington 1990; 2007; McGrail 2001; Jones 2009.
549 Mann 1983; Hassall 2000; Holder 1982.
550 Mattingly 2006.
551 Simmonds *et al.* 2008.

Period	Italy	Narbonensis and Spain	Elsewhere in the continental Empire	British civil zone	British frontier zone camp
AD 43-69	5	4	0	1	0
AD 69-117	7	14	0	0	7
AD 117-193	0	5	0	1	3
AD 193-300	0	3	1	1	3

Tab. 4.9. Number of inscriptions recording the area of origin of British legionary recruits (using data from Mann 1983, Tab. 9).

Period	Settled in British civil zone	Settled in British frontier zone	Returned to homes outside Britain	Settled elsewhere on the continent
AD 43-117	0	3	1	2
AD 117-193	2	6	3	1
AD 193-300	1	7	2	1

Tab. 4.10. Number of inscriptions recording the area in which veterans of the British legions settled (using data from Mann 1983, Tab. 10).

Economic growth in the Western provinces

Increasing connectivity was also related to contemporary productive expansion in parts of the Western Empire. As we have seen, wine production throughout Gaul grew during the second half of the first century, and again in the mid-second century (see pp. 73-74). The Gaulish *sigillata* industries and other pottery industries throughout Gaul also flourished from c. AD 40/50 onwards (see pp. 54-66).[552] Studies of olive oil presses in Baetica also appear to indicate a phase of growth in the second half of the first century.[553] This economic expansion ensured products were available in bulk for long-distance trade with Britain. The reasons behind their growth may in part have been linked into the opening up of new markets in Britain following its incorporation into the Empire and the consequent provision of state contracts for the supply of the British garrison. More significant factors for growth in Gaul may have been increasing economic improvements and the Romanization of Gaulish consumer tastes.[554]

These four key factors contributed to increasing connectivity in both the Southern North Sea and Eastern Channel system and in the Atlantic system. As we have seen, however, levels of connectivity were higher in the former system than in its Atlantic counterpart. The main reason for this, and the reason for the probable continuation of this trend throughout the Roman period, was the fact that a large Roman military garrison was stationed along the Rhine from Augustan times onwards (see pp. 41-51). This garrison was well paid and its presence had contributed to the growth of manufacturing industries in adjacent regions, as well as stimulating the development of supply routes and communication infrastructure, such as roads, linking the Rhine to the Mediterranean via the river Rhône. The highly developed Rhône-Rhine route thus ensured that a sizeable proportion of Britain's continental contacts were directed across the Southern North Sea and Eastern Channel during this phase, though Atlantic routes were utilised as well.

4.2. The Eastern North Sea system

Introduction

In stark contrast to the Southern North Sea and Eastern Channel and Atlantic systems, there was very little maritime interaction in the Eastern North Sea system. Indeed, there appears to have been a characteristic lack of connectivity across the Lower Rhine frontier between the mid-first and mid-second centuries AD, a situation which can be contrasted heavily with the upper Danube frontier where significant trade was taking place between the Empire and barbarian tribes. In the northern Netherlands we can only point to a handful of imported objects, a few *denarii* and copper-alloy vessels, and perhaps some statuettes, lava querns and *terra sigillata*, which might have arrived through maritime trade, though overland routes may also have been utilised. Exports possibly included cattle hides and slaves. There are many copper-alloy vessels in northwest Germany and Scandinavia, but these were not the result of North Sea trade, rather, they came indirectly via the Elbe basin having entered the *Barbaricum* through trade on the upper Danube frontier. One of the main reasons for the paucity of connectivity in the Eastern North Sea system is the lack of cross-frontier political engagement due to enduring negative relations

[552] Woolf 1998; Marsh 1981; Greene 1978; 1979.
[553] Andrew Wilson and Annalisa Marzano, pers. Comm. 2008; Haley 2003.
[554] Woolf 1998.

from the Varus massacre and the Frisian revolt, a lack of desire to expand the Empire beyond the Rhine and the relative security of the Rhine frontier. The absence of any truly exotic goods in the northern Netherlands and northwest Germany also hampered trade. In contrast, the tribes of the upper Danube region were heavily engaged in political relations with the Empire, which extended to client kingship. They also controlled access to the trade in Baltic amber, an important luxury good.

Imports to the Eastern North Sea coastal region

Coinage and metals

A fair number of first- and second-century *denarii* have been found in the coastal regions of the northwest *Barbaricum*; however, as I shall discuss later, most of these *denarii* arrived in the late second century at which time the overwhelming majority of *denarii* hoards close (see pp. 113-114). There was probably a trickle of *denarii* into the northern Netherlands and northwest Germany prior to the late second century. A *denarii* hoard at Dronrijp in Friesland closed in AD 117, whilst the hoards at Barger-Oosterveen in Drenthe and Middels-Osterloog, not far from the coast of Ostfriesland in Lower Saxony, closed in AD 128 and AD 140 respectively.[555] They probably entered the *Barbaricum* through trade. Indeed, Tacitus, writing at the end of the first century AD, stated that the Germans living nearest the Roman frontiers used gold and silver in commerce, though they preferred silver as it was more convenient for buying cheap merchandise.[556] Whether these coins arrived by maritime trade is debatable. The north Dutch material may represent very low-level direct trade via Lake Flevo, whereas the coins from northwest Germany probably arrived via the Elbe basin having been traded across the upper Danube, or upper Rhine, frontier.

A few Roman silver vessels are present in the northwest *Barbaricum*; for example, there are a pair of silver pans and a pair of silver cups in the mid-second-century AD grave at Marwedel on the Lower Elbe.[557] These are likely to represent political gifts, which, as Tacitus attests, were presented by the Roman state to Germanic chieftains and ambassadors.[558] Once again a route via the Elbe basin is more likely.

Perhaps the most common Roman imports are copper-alloy vessels, which are present in a number of northwest German and Scandinavian graves dated c. AD 40-150/160 (**Figs. 4.42-43**). Initially vessels manufactured in Italian workshops were most common, but Gallic products became increasingly dominant over time.[559] The distribution pattern of these vessels suggests that they entered the *Barbaricum* across the upper Danube and were subsequently redistributed via inter-Germanic exchange networks. Trade is the most likely explanation for this; certainly, Tacitus records that the Hermunduri, who occupied northern Bavaria and Thuringia, were the only Germans allowed to trade with the Empire, not merely on the bank of the Danube, but far within the Empire's borders and at Augsburg – the capital of Raetia.[560] We might also suspect that the Marcomanni (from Bohemia) and the Quadi (from southwestern Slovakia and Moravia) also engaged in trade with the Empire. These two groups appear to have been clients of Rome (see p. 100) and copper-alloy vessels concentrate heavily in their territories. One further possibility is that some of the copper-alloy vessels from northern Europe were brought back by Germanic auxiliaries who served in the Roman forts along the Rhine. Our only evidence for this is the presence of Germanic Almgren type 101 brooches, which date between the late first and mid-second centuries AD, at several Roman forts along the Rhine. These are principally distributed in the Lower Elbe region.[561] Even in this case overland routes are more plausible than North Sea links.

The North Sea may have had a minor role to play; a late first- to mid-second-century grave on the island of Texel in the northern Netherlands contains four vessels, which were perhaps traded via the North Sea.[562]

Roman copper-alloy statuettes are known from several sites along the Eastern North Sea coast, particularly at terp settlements in Friesland where they are numerous (see p. 119). Statuettes are hard to date with precision and although it seems likely that the majority arrived during the later second or the first half of the third century AD, when there is greater evidence for connectivity in the Eastern North Sea system, it is entirely possible that some were imported, probably through trade, between the mid-first and mid-second century.

Other imports

Aside from a few coins, a handful of silver vessels, possibly a few statuettes and the copper-alloy vessels, which in the case of the northwest German material principally arrived via central European overland routes, there is precious little evidence for Roman material in the Eastern North Sea coastal regions. Roman pottery and amphorae are virtually absent. *Terra sigillata* from the second half of the first century AD is unknown and early second-century *sigillata* is extremely rare. There is some *sigillata*, particularly from Noord Holland and Friesland, that can be assigned production dates in the mid-second century AD; however, we should bear in mind that many of these mid-second-century products may in fact have arrived during the later second century AD, from which time there is a much larger quantity of *sigillata* and other Roman imports (see pp. 120-122).[563] Tacitus recorded

[555] Berger 1992, 122-150, Abb. 46; Galestin 2001; Van der Vin 1996.
[556] *Germania*. 5.
[557] Busch 1995, 204-206; Erdrich 2001, 96; 2002, 154; Eggers 1951, 177, Karte 48.
[558] *Germania*. 5.
[559] Kunow 1983; Lund Hansen 1987.
[560] *Germania*. 41.
[561] Böhme 1972.
[562] Kunow 1983, Karte 4; Woltering 1979, 106-107.
[563] Erdrich 2001; Volkers 1991.

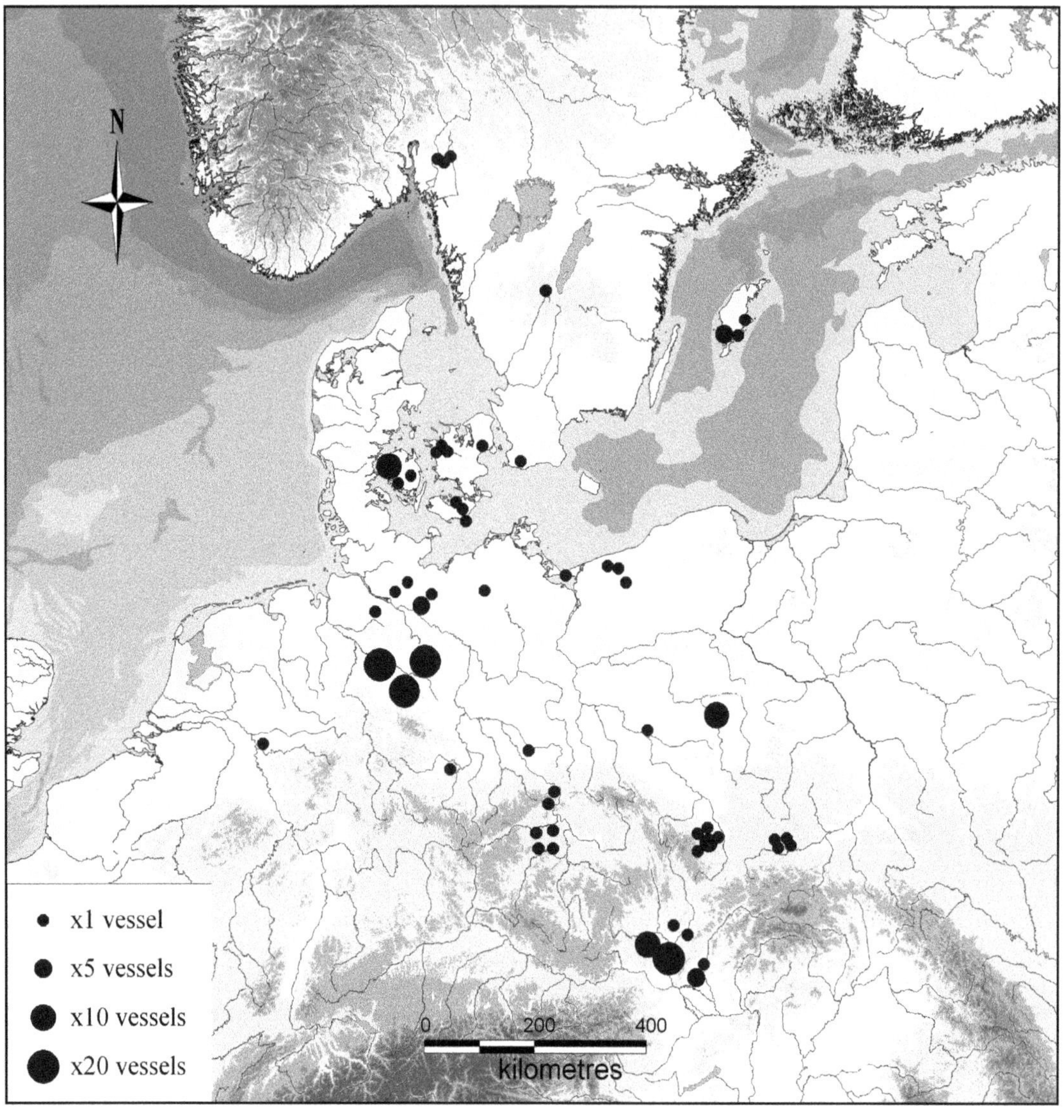

Fig. 4.42. Distribution of imported Roman copper-alloy vessels in period B1b (c. AD 40-70) (after Kunow 1983, Karte 9).

that the German tribes living nearest the Rhine and Danube bought wine, though there is no evidence that wine was traded in the northwest *Barbaricum*.[564] Of course it is possible that wine was imported in barrels, but the complete absence of amphorae implies that this would have been very small-scale. We should also bear in mind that lava querns, imported from quarries at Mayen on the middle Rhine, are known from Roman-period contexts at many settlements along the eastern North Sea coast. These are hard to date and we cannot rule out that some examples did arrive during this period; however, most of the dating evidence we do have points to import during the Augustan and Tiberian period in the northern Netherlands and in the later second century, and perhaps the early third, in the northern Netherlands and northwest Germany (see pp. 49-50, 123).

[564] *Germania*. 23.

Exports from the Eastern North Sea coastal region

Archaeologically undetectable items

Assessment of Germanic exports is extremely difficult due to the fact that they would principally have been archaeologically undetectable. We get some sense of the possibilities from passages by Cassius Dio referring to Germanic tribes providing goods to the Empire as a result of treaties made during the Marcomannic wars. The Quadi had to furnish the Romans with cattle and horses, whilst the Marcomanni had to provide the Romans with large quantities of grain.[565] A number of German loan-words have been identified in Latin: soap, amber, hides and goose. These may also have been exports.[566] Slaves may have been occasionally traded with the Empire; Tacitus states that in *Germania* slaves were disposed of

[565] Cassius Dio *Historia Romana*. 71.11, 72.2.
[566] Wild 1976; Hedeager 1978.

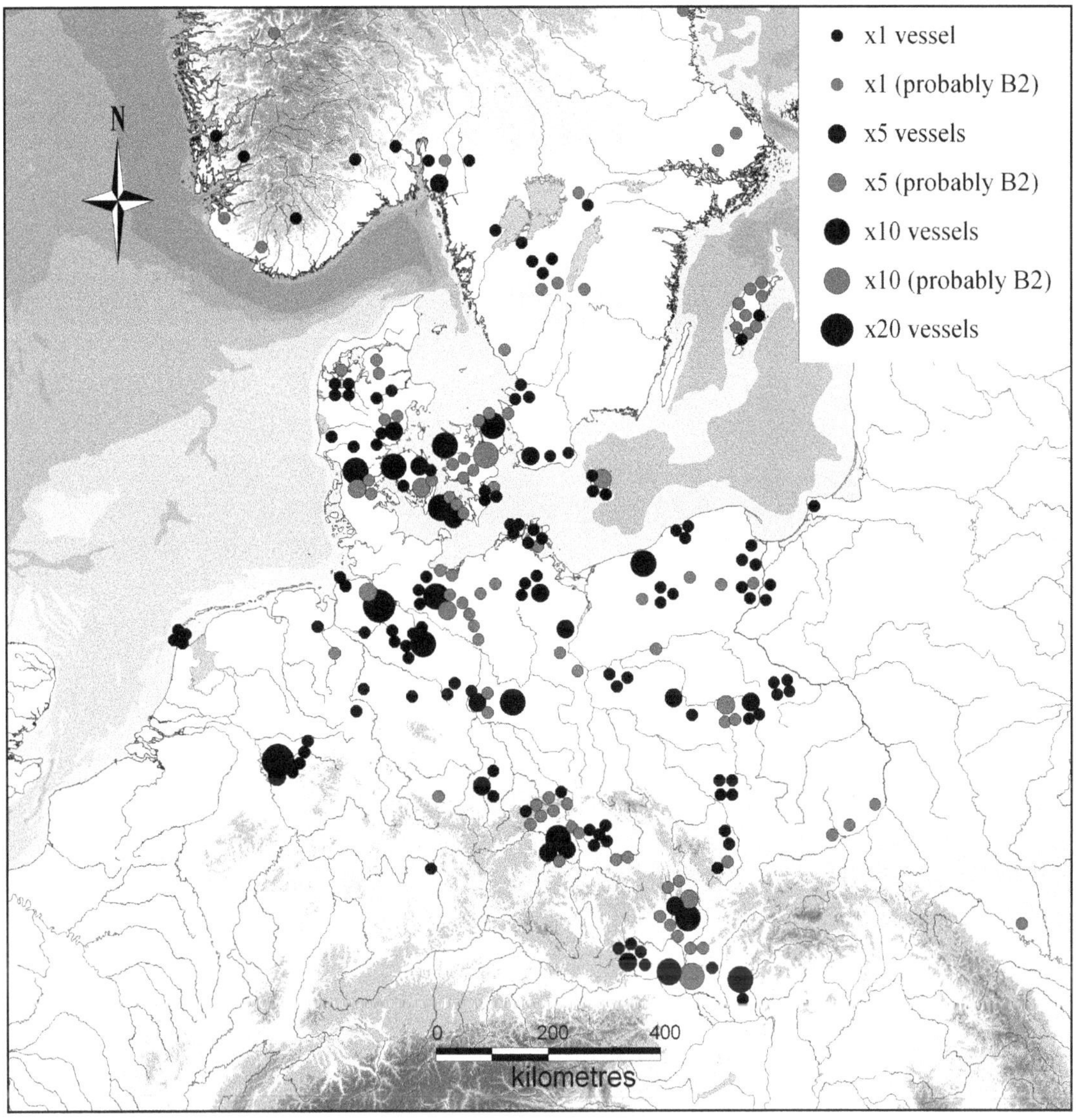

Fig. 4.43. Distribution of imported Roman copper-alloy vessels in period B2 (c. AD 70-150/160) (after Kunow 1983, Karte 4).

by trade.[567] He further states that the Frisii sold a group of former auxiliaries back to the Romans as slaves.[568]

Several scholars have suggested that the Roman army stationed on the lower Rhine frontier depended heavily upon agricultural goods supplied from across the frontier.[569] This was not necessarily the case. Zooarchaeological studies indicate that following the Roman occupation the local communities of the Rhine delta within the Empire produced a surplus of cattle, sheep and horses, and played the major role in providing the Roman army stationed here with animal products and meat.[570] A study of animal bones at sites along the Rhine also suggests that there was no import of livestock from outside the Empire, though of course this does not exclude hides.[571] Military sites in the Rhine delta received most of their grain from the adjacent loess areas within the Empire, such as Germany, Belgium and northern France (see p. 88). There was no necessary dependence upon supplies from beyond the frontier.

A number of scholars have also interpreted a particular passage of Tacitus to imply the presence of Roman traders "all over" the northern Netherlands in the late first century AD.[572] This is highly questionable. The passage concerned refers to the massacre of traders by a group of Canninefates and Frisians during the events of the Batavian revolt. Tacitus clearly describes this massacre taking place within the Empire on the Batavian Island in the Lower Rhine region. There is thus little to suggest a thriving export trade in agricultural products from the northern Netherlands. Any trade that was occurring was on an extremely low-level.

567 *Germania*. 24.
568 *Agricola*. 28.
569 Whittaker 1994, 113-131; Bloemers 1983.
570 Groot 2008.
571 Whittaker 2004; 8.
572 Tacitus *Histories*. 4.15; Whittaker 1994, 113; Carroll 2001; Cherry 2007, 731.

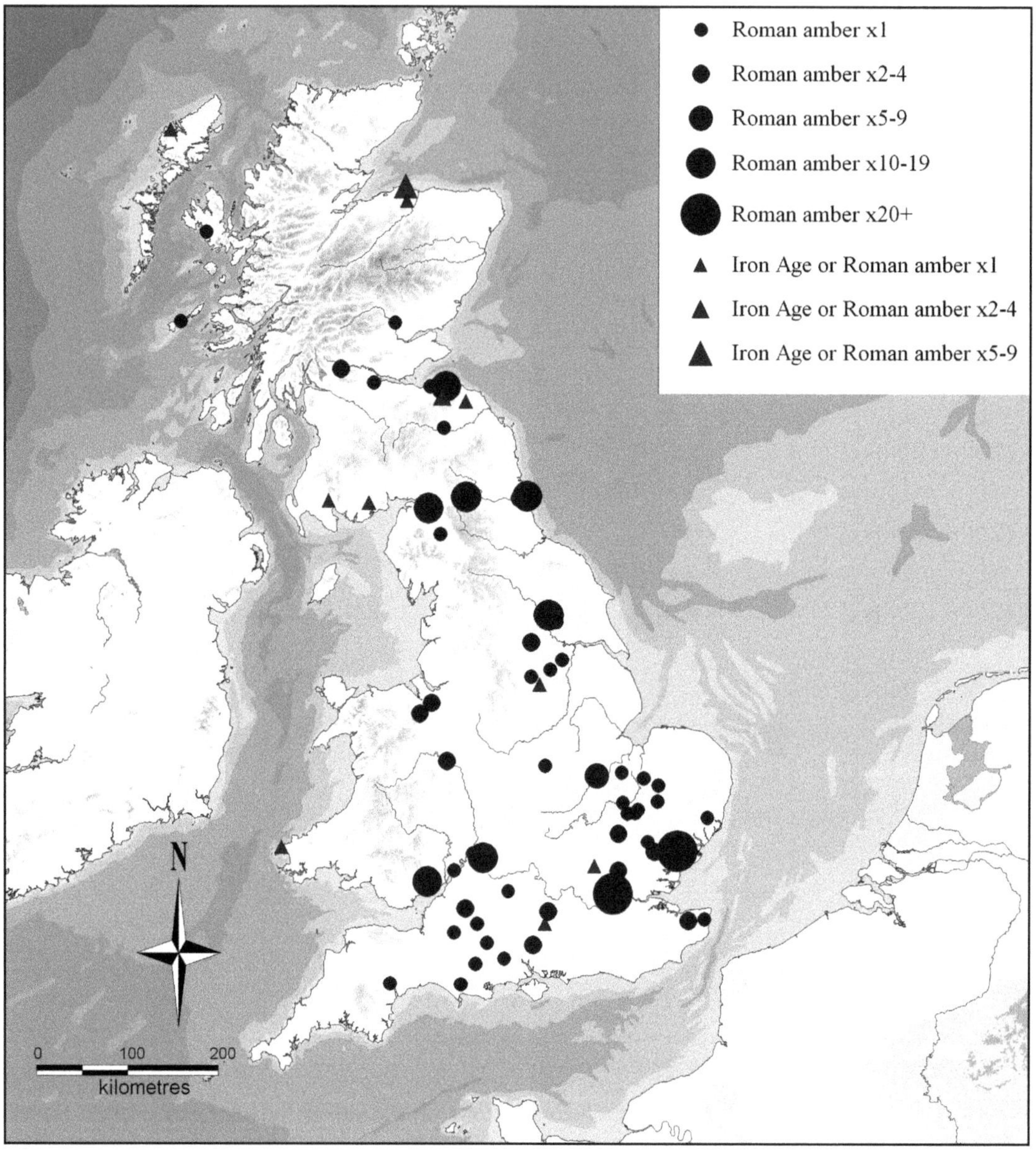

Fig. 4.44. Distribution of amber in Britain during the Roman period (c. AD 43-430) (Appendices 4-5).

Amber

Amber reached the Roman Empire in increasingly large quantities from around the beginning of the first century AD onwards.[573] Almost all of this amber came from the Danzig Bay area of the Baltic via overland central European trade routes. Evidence in support of this proposal can be found in contemporary Classical sources. For example, Pliny wrote that amber originated in the Northern Ocean and was brought by the Germans to the Roman city of Carnuntum, which lies in modern day Austria. He noted that during the reign of Nero, a Roman *eques* (knight) travelled to northern Europe via this route and there obtained a huge amount of amber that was used to decorate a gladiatorial exhibition in Rome.[574] On a distributional basis Roman amber finds are particularly prevalent in Hungary, Austria, Slovenia and northeast Italy, which lie at the end of this central European overland trade route. Indeed, huge amounts of intricately carved amber are known from Aquileia in northeast Italy at the head of the Adriatic and we can argue that this site was a specialised amber working centre at this time.[575]

I have conducted a survey of Roman-period (AD 43-430) amber from Britain, which has yielded 258 amber objects from 57 British sites of Roman-period date (**Fig. 4.44, Tab. 4.11-12**). In addition, there are 18 objects from 11 sites, which belong to either the Iron Age or Roman period. Amber of Roman-period date is distributed widely throughout Britain and several finds even derive from native sites in northern Scotland. The amber is found on a wide range of sites, with finds fairly equally split between military sites, urban sites and small towns or rural locations (**Tab. 4.13**).

[573] Calvi 1996; 2005; Buora 1996; Pasquinucci 1978.
[574] *H.N.* 37.11.

[575] Brown and Henig 1977; Calvi 1996; 2005; Buora 1996; Lista 2007.

Period	No. of amber objects	No. of sites with amber
Iron Age (800 BC-AD 43).	43	19
Roman (AD 43-430)	258	57
Iron Age or Roman (800 BC-AD 430)	18	11
Total	319	87

Tab. 4.11. Number of amber objects (N.B. one object = one bead, one ring etc) and the number of sites with amber from Britain during the Iron Age and Roman periods.

Period	No. of amber objects	No. of sites with amber
800-175 BC	7	5
175 BC-AD 43	5	5
AD 43-165	116	15
AD 165-260	3	3
AD 260-430	46	15

Tab. 4.12. Chronological change in the occurrence of amber on British Iron Age and Roman-period sites (dated by context).

Site type	No. of amber objects	No. of sites with amber
Military	65	16
Urban	120	11
Small town, rural or native	73	30
Total	258	57

Tab. 4.13. Site types on which amber occurs during the Roman period (AD 43-430).

This survey suggests that amber was not especially common in Britain during the Roman period. When compared to other periods we see that it exceeds the Neolithic (3 find sites) and the Middle and Late Bronze Age (4 and 17 find sites respectively), during which periods amber is fairly rare. It is exceeded by the Early Bronze Age, from which c. 2,000 amber objects have been identified from 93 different sites, mainly in Wessex, though c. 1,000 of these objects derive from a necklace in a single grave at Upton Lovell ('the Golden barrow').[576] The Roman period is greatly dwarfed by the Early-Middle Saxon periods (mid-fifth to eighth centuries AD) from which 18,000 amber beads are known from 106 different cemeteries.[577]

However, there is a clear increase in amber from British contexts of Roman-period date over those of Iron Age date (**Tabs. 4.11-12**). Not all of the Roman finds can be dated more specifically, but of those that can 116 amber objects from 15 sites can be assigned to the period AD 43-165 (**Tab. 4.12**). This represents a peak phase of amber import for the entire Iron Age and Roman period, although we should bear in mind that we are dealing with a relatively small sample and that 70 of these objects derive from a single necklace found in London.[578]

Most of the amber from Roman-period sites in Britain is in the form of simple beads, typically longitudinal or annular and it is hard to determine where these were manufactured. However, there are a few intricately carved objects, such as the cockle-shell from Chester, an amber ramshorn from Wroxeter, an amber finger ring and a mouse from Carlisle, which are paralleled in the material from Aquileia in northeast Italy and were almost certainly produced there.[579] These latter finds will definitely have been based on amber which reached the Empire via the central European amber-route and subsequently came to Britain via other regions of the Empire. The vast majority of the remaining amber will have travelled to Britain via the same route, perhaps mainly through trade, though some will have belonged to individuals who moved to Britain from the continent. There is little to suggest a North Sea trade route in amber, and even if small quantities did come to the Empire via this route it was dwarfed in significance by the main overland trade route.

[576] Beck and Shennan 1991.
[577] Brugmann 2004; Huggett 1988, 64-66, Fig. 1.
[578] Appendix 5, object Nos. 79-148; Chapman 1974.
[579] Appendix 5, object Nos. 15, 25, 26; 189; Calvi 2005, Tav. 22-32, 73, 75, 77, 84, 89, 92; Lista 2007.

Synthesis

Between the mid-first and mid-second centuries AD levels of maritime connectivity in the Eastern North Sea system were extremely low. In fact this lack of connectivity extended to the Empire's entire Lower Rhine frontier, in marked contrast to the upper Danube frontier where there were thriving trade relations between the Empire and the barbarian groups at the border.

There may have been very low-level trade between the Romans and the peoples of the northern Netherlands, some of which may have occurred via the North Sea, although overland routes may also have been utilised; the number of imports in this region are miniscule, we can point to a few *denarii*, a handful of copper-alloy vessels, and perhaps some statuettes and lava querns, though we generally lack characteristic trade items, such as pottery and amphorae, although small amounts of *terra sigillata* might have arrived in the mid-second century AD. Slaves and cattle hides may have been exported in return. There are large numbers of Roman copper-alloy vessels in Northwest German and Scandinavian graves, but these almost certainly arrived via overland routes, most likely through intra-Germanic gift exchange, following trade on the upper Danube frontier.

The determinants of connective change

There were several reasons for the general lack of engagement across the Lower Rhine frontier; firstly, relations between the Germans of this region and the Empire were essentially hostile following the defeat of Varus and the Frisian revolt in the early first century AD. The historical sources are fairly quiet on events on this frontier, but in AD 41 the Romans waged a campaign against the Chauci.[580] Around AD 47 the Chauci began to engage in piratical raids on the coast of Gaul in light vessels, though these were ultimately defeated by Roman forces under the command of Corbulo.[581] Corbulo subsequently established a fortress and garrison amongst the Frisians and arranged for the assassination of the leader of the Chauci, though the rage this caused amongst the Chauci led Claudius to call Corbulo back west of the Rhine.[582] Frisians and Chauci were also involved on the Batavian side during the Batavian revolt against Roman rule (AD 69-70).[583]

There also seems to have been no aim to further expand the Empire in northwest Europe, whilst the frontier here was relatively secure. These factors also contributed to a lack of cross-frontier engagement. Claudius initiated the construction of a chain of forts along the Rhine c. AD 47, whilst under Domitian linear defences were constructed along the entire German frontier, which were further strengthened and renewed in the early second century.[584] There was also a shift of troops away from the Rhine frontier and, increasingly over time, towards the Danube.[585]

For these reasons there was a lack of political engagement across the Lower Rhine frontier, which severely impeded trade. Furthermore, there was nothing of particular economic value that could be gained from the northwest *Barbaricum*. This was in contrast to other regions outside the Empire, such as India (spices), Saharan Africa (ostrich eggs and jewels) and central Europe (amber via the amber-route), which had luxury articles to offer and which engaged in thriving trade relationships with the Empire.[586]

In contrast, there was much greater connectivity across the upper Danube frontier. A large part of the reason for this was the existence of strong political relations, extending to client kingship, between the Empire and the groups immediately beyond the upper Danube frontier. This is supported by the literary sources: in the early first century AD the Romans allowed the followers of two exiled Marcomannic kings to settle in Moravia and provided them with a new ruler, Vannius of the Quadi.[587] During the Empire's civil wars of AD 69 the Quadi are recorded as supplying Vespasian with troops and as helping to protect the Empire's borders.[588] A coin issued by Antoninus Pius in the early 140s had the legend REX QUADIS DATUS, which indicates that he had installed a Quadian king, whilst Marcus Aurelius was asked to approve a Quadian king at the beginning of the Marcomannic Wars.[589] Tacitus also wrote that the power of the Marcomannic kings relied upon Roman influence, principally monetary payments.[590] Relations with these clients were not always peaceful as the Marcomanni refused to aid Domitian against the Dacians and defeated a subsequent Roman punitive campaign.[591]

In addition, it was the groups on the upper Danube who controlled access to the most important luxury article that the northern *Barbaricum* had to offer – amber. The availability of this product clearly stimulated an intense cross-frontier trade in the upper Danube region.

4.3. Maritime systems AD 43-165: a comparison

Both the Southern North Sea and Eastern Channel system and the Atlantic system underwent vast connective increases from the mid-first century AD onwards. In contrast, there was very little interaction between the Empire and the tribes of the northwest *Barbaricum* via the North Sea. The principal reasons for this strong

[580] Cassius Dio *Historia Romana*. 60.8.7.
[581] Tacitus *Annals*. 11.18.
[582] Tacitus *Annals*. 11.19-20.
[583] Tacitus *Histories*. 4.15, 4.79.
[584] Erdrich 2001; Wells 1978; Bogaers and Rüger 1974; Schönberger 1969; 1985; Luttwak 1976.
[585] Hassall 2000.
[586] Wheeler 1954; Mattingly 2003; Tomber 2008.
[587] Tacitus *Annals*. 2.63, 12.29; Velleius Paterculus *Historia Romana*. 2.108-110; Grane 2007, 49-51.
[588] Tacitus *Histories*. 3.5, 3.21.
[589] *Historia Augusta. Marcus Antoninus*. 14.3; Wilkes 2000, 583; Grane 2007, 51.
[590] *Germania*. 42.
[591] Cassius Dio *Historia Romana*. 67.7.

differentiation are political. Britain was integrated into the Roman Empire, which meant that all the coastal regions that bordered the Southern North Sea and Eastern Channel and, with the absence of Ireland and Scotland, the Atlantic façade were now part of the same wider political entity. The Roman state pumped resources into Britain in support of its army and also extracted products from it. Furthermore, Britain's entry into the Empire greatly facilitated private trade by reducing customs taxes and helping to ensure the safety of traders. The presence of Mediterranean troops and veterans in Britain also increased demand for imported food, drink and dining equipment.

The lack of cross-frontier engagement in the Eastern North Sea was very much due to political factors. Rome and the northwestern barbarians appear to have had little interest in engaging politically throughout the mid-first to mid-second centuries and this disrupted connectivity. Whether we can link changes in the situation in the Southern North Sea and Eastern Channel and Atlantic systems with the Eastern North Sea system is debatable. One might suspect that the choice of Britain as a target for invasion by Claudius was influenced by the lack of suitable targets for expansion elsewhere along the northwest frontier. The conquest and occupation of Britain by a large part of the Roman army may have further contributed to a lack of further Roman interest beyond the Lower Rhine frontier, but it would be wrong to push these points too far.

5. North Sea and Channel connectivity AD 165-260

5.1. The Southern North Sea and Channel systems

Introduction

There was a major decline in Britain's connections with the continent in the later second century AD, with no significant recovery occurring in the first half of the third century AD. This is despite the fact that this is precisely the period of the well-known Nehalennia inscriptions. The decline affected exchange via the Southern North Sea and Eastern Channel as well as via the Atlantic seaways. Other scholars have proposed a range of explanations for why contact between Britain and the rest of the Empire decreased. These include the notions that imports principally declined because British products increasingly took their place, that demand for Mediterranean food stuffs and dining equipment declined over time as the army became increasingly local in origin, and the suggestion that the Roman state had lost interest in Britain following the Severan military campaign to the island.[592]

I argue, however, that the rapid and dramatic evidence for declining connectivity during the later second century AD, which had been preceded by a relatively constant high level of contact between the late first and mid-second century AD, must principally be explained by a significant economic slump and a reduction in levels of production and manufacture which affected the Roman Empire from the late second century AD onwards. The principal causes of this slump were the Antonine plague, which reduced population levels and work forces in many parts of the Empire, and the Marcomannic wars and subsequent troubles with barbarian peoples, which were exacerbated by the devastating impact of the plague upon Roman military strength. This warfare resulted in some devastation within the Empire, but, more importantly, huge quantities of coin and bullion were lost to the Empire through political payments and bribes paid to the barbarian peoples. This contributed to a severe debasement of the coinage and had a knock-on effect upon trade and economic activity throughout the Empire.

[592] Mattingly 2006, 500; Fulford 1989a; 1991; 2004, 314-314, 323; Carreras-Monfort and Funari 1998.

Continental imports

Coinage and Metals

As in the preceding period, coins were shipped to Britain in quantity and on a regular basis as pay for the large body of troops and the state officials stationed on the island.[593] There is no evidence that troops were withdrawn from Britain in quantity prior to the mid-third century AD. In contrast, there are records for several new units being posted to the island. According to Cassius Dio 5,500 Sarmatian auxiliaries were transferred to Britain in AD 175, whilst new auxiliary units (*cunei* and *numeri*) increasingly appear on the northern British frontier from the early third century AD onwards (**Tab. 4.1**).[594] Whilst substantial state payments were still reaching Britain the inherent value of the coins involved fell substantially.

The *denarius* had been continuously and gradually debased from the reign of Nero. However, in the reign of Marcus Aurelius *denarii* were still c. 65-70% pure silver and contained c. 2 g of silver. The silver content fell more dramatically during the later second century AD, most notably in AD 194-195 when Septimius Severus reduced it to c. 48%. A further major change occurred under Caracalla who introduced the *Antoninianus* or radiate in AD 214. This was valued at the price of two old *denarii*, but contained only 1.5 times as much silver. The radiate was briefly discarded by Severus Alexander (AD 222-238), but came back and had effectively replaced the *denarius* by AD 244. By AD 260 the silver coinage was extremely base and contained only c. 5-8% silver, about 0.1-0.2 g.[595] The amount of gold in the gold coinage, which had declined only slightly since its establishment under Augustus, dropped dramatically throughout the first half of the third century AD from 7.3 g in AD 200 to 4.79 g in AD 250. This principally concerned a reduction in the overall size of the coin as the level of fineness was maintained at c. 99% down to AD 250.[596]

[593] Abdy 2002, 29-36.
[594] Dio Cassius *Historia Romana*. 71.16; Breeze 1984; Birley 2007.
[595] Wilson 2007, 116-117, Fig. 2; Hitchner 2009; Reece 2002, 19-20; Abdy 2002, 31; Casey 1994a, 9-11.
[596] Wilson 2007, 113, Fig. 1.

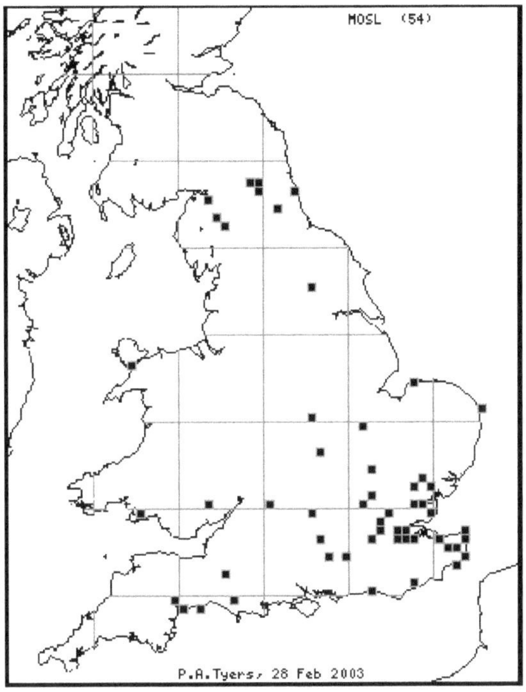

Fig. 5.1. British distribution of Trier ware (c. AD 180-250) (Paul Tyers (URL accessed June 2010): http://www.potsherd.uklinux.net/atlas/Ware/MOSL).

The volume of *aes* coinage reaching Britain began to decline gradually during the later second century AD and this will have had a negative effect upon low-level trade. Coin from the reign of Marcus Aurelius is relatively well represented on British sites and was evidently imported at a similar, albeit slightly reduced, rate to *aes* of the late first to mid-second century AD. Coins of Commodus are rarer, but still present in some quantity, whilst there is an even greater drop c. AD 193-197. *Aes* coinage minted c. AD 197-260 is exceedingly rare in Britain meanwhile.[597]

There are hints of a decline in the number of continentally produced copper-alloy vessels known from Britain. Despite their prevalence on the adjacent continent pan and filter sets (E161) and Hemmoor buckets, which were produced in Belgica and the Rhine provinces, are rare in Britain (**Fig. 5.10**).[598] A few mid-second- to early third-century Knee brooches of continental origin have also been noted in Britain. A survey of Knee brooches from Britain reveals that over half of the provenanced examples derive from military sites.[599] Whilst some might have arrived through trade, their fairly strong military associations imply that many arrived as personal possessions with troops travelling from the Rhine-Danube frontier regions.

Pottery

Lezoux *sigillata* probably continued to be traded to Britain in appreciable quantities down to c. AD 200, but, as discussed above, there was a downturn in importation, which may have been either gradual or rapid, during the second half of the second century (see p. 59). East Gaulish *sigillata* continued to be traded throughout the later second century and beyond the decline of Lezoux imports down to c. AD 260, but, in comparison to the levels of import of South Gaulish ware in the late first century and Lezoux ware in the mid-second century, East Gaulish ware was supplied at a low rate (see p. 62). Other pottery was also traded to both civil and military locations in Britain, principally via the Southern North Sea and Eastern Channel. Soller mortaria, Central Gaulish black-slip ware and North Gaulish ware continued to arrive in small but notable quantities until the early third century (see p. 64), whilst Trier black-slipped ware reached many British sites between c. AD 180-250 (**Fig. 5.1**).[600]

Olive oil

The later second century AD saw a pronounced decline in the amount of olive oil reaching Britain relative to during the late first to mid-second century (**Tab. 4.5, Fig. 4.18**). There is then an increase in the stamped Dr.20 dated AD 192-255 compared to those dated AD 161-192. At first glance this implies a recovery in olive oil importation, but a consideration of late second- and early third-century stamped Dr.20s from Monte Testaccio in Rome has revealed a change in the rate of stamping over time. Whilst only 40-50% of second-century Dr.20s bore stamps, this figure rose to 60-75% during the third century.[601] Our figures for import into Britain at this time cannot therefore be taken to indicate a rise in olive oil import and, in all likelihood, hint at import at a roughly similar rate throughout the late second and early third

[597] Walker 1988, 299-301; Abdy 2002, 37; Reece 2002, 44.
[598] Eggers 1966, 76, 90; Gerrard 2009.
[599] Bayley and Butcher 2004, 179-181; Eckardt 2005.
[600] Tyers 1996a; forthcoming; Richardson and Tyers 1984.
[601] Carreras Monfort, pers. Comm. 2008.

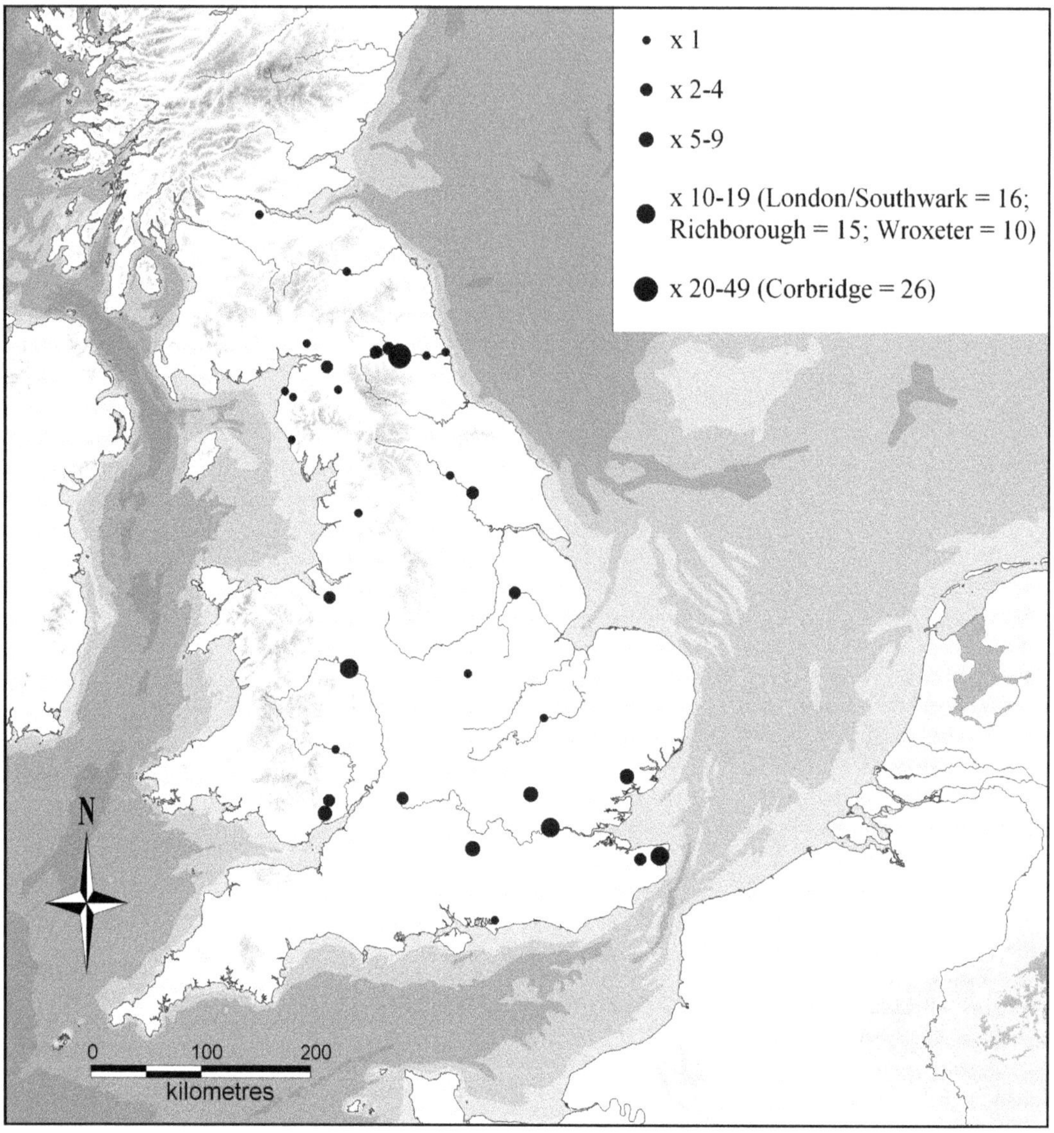

Fig. 5.2. Distribution in Britain of stamped Dr.20 dated AD 161-192 (data from Carreras Monfort and Funari 1998).

centuries.[602] This chronological pattern corresponds extremely closely to that obtained from analyses of stamped Dr.20 in the Rhine provinces of the Empire, namely a large number of stamps dating between the late first and the mid-second century AD, with a decline in the second half of the second century and a slight rise in the first half of the third century.[603]

Stamped Dr.20 vessels dated AD 161-192 are well known from Hadrian's Wall, whilst high densities of stamps are also present along the Welsh borders and in the southeast (**Fig. 5.2**). Much olive oil probably reached Britain direct by sea from Baetica via the Atlantic, though some may also have been imported across the Southern North Sea and Eastern Channel having been brought up via the Rhône-Rhine corridor. Assessment of this issue is difficult; a study of stamps does show distinctive differences between Britain and Roman forts in Germany, which supports differences in supply, probably due to the use of Atlantic routes to supply Britain. However, there is also considerable overlap in the stamps, which means we cannot rule out an important Rhône-Rhine link as well. We should also bear in mind that the German forts may in fact have received much of their olive oil via the Atlantic seaways; indeed, sites in southern France appear to lack certain stamps which are present in both Germany and Britain at this time.[604]

The British distribution of the stamped Dr.20 dated AD 192-255 shows a heavy concentration at Roman forts along Hadrian's Wall and also at Cramond and Carpow in the Scottish Lowlands (**Fig. 5.3**). Considerable quantities are also known from sites along the Welsh borders, at York and Lincoln, and in the southeast, with London, Colchester and east Kent once more having significant numbers of stamps. There are no major differences

[602] Using figures from Tab. 4.5 the relative rates of Dr.20 import can be recalculated according to the changing rate of stamping as c. 7.0 per year between AD 161-192 versus c. 7.1 per year between AD 192-255.
[603] Remesal-Rodríguez 1986; 1997; 2002, 305.
[604] Carreras Monfort and Funari 1998, 267. C.f. Remesal-Rodríguez 2002.

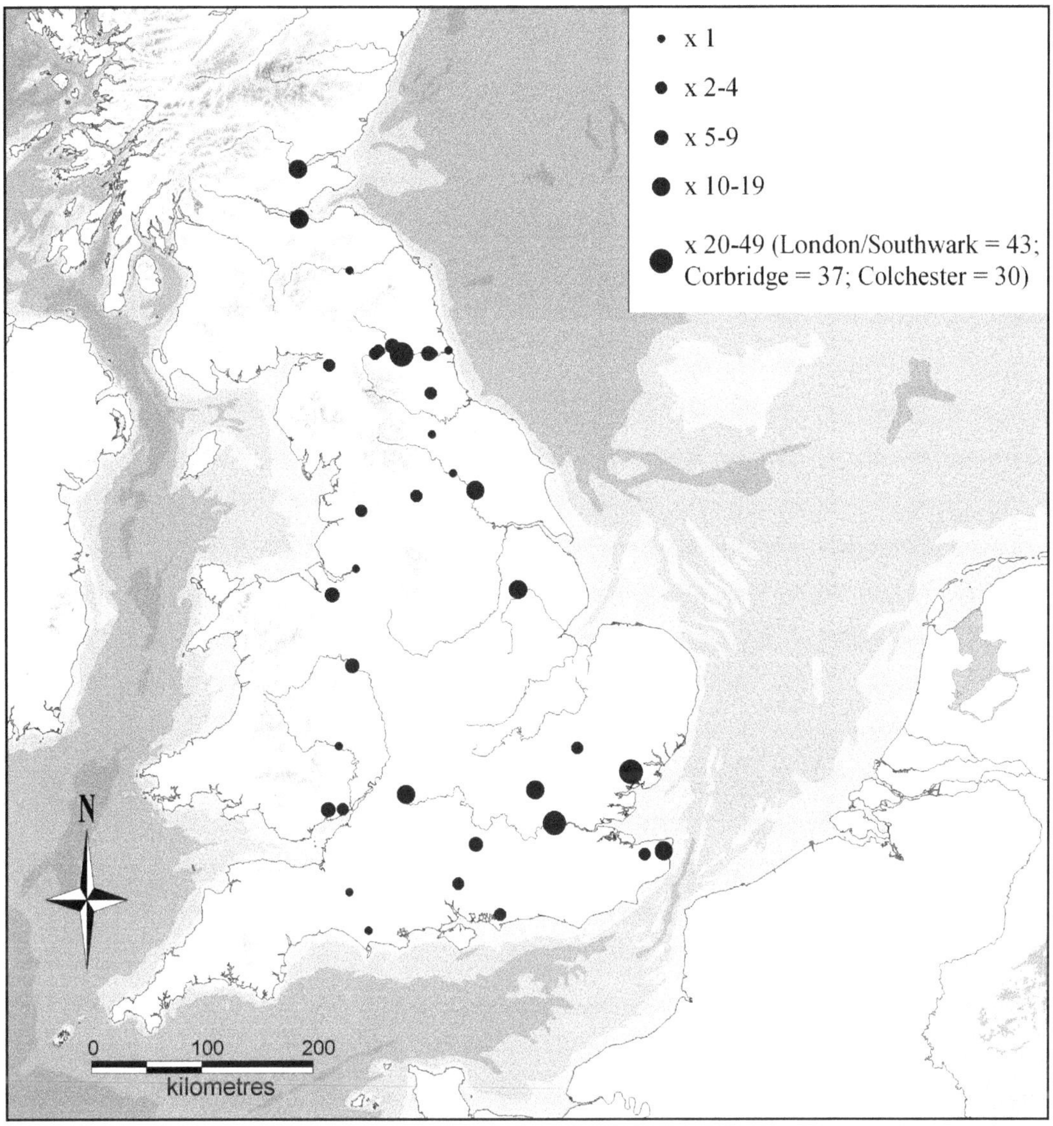

Fig. 5.3. Distribution in Britain of stamped Dr.20 dated AD 192-255 (data from Carreras Monfort and Funari 1998).

between the Dr.20 stamps from Britain, the German provinces and southern France between AD 192-255.[605] This might hint at the operation of similar supply mechanisms for Baetican olive oil across Western Europe, with either the Rhône-Rhine route or the Atlantic route perhaps coming to dominate supply.

Wine

Imported G4 amphorae are found at numerous British sites of late second or early third-century date; for example, at Exeter G4 comprise about 20% of the later second- and third-century amphorae assemblage.[606] At New Fresh Wharf in London, which contains material dating to the late second- and first half of the third-centuries AD, there was 22.9 kg of G4 in comparison to 55.6 kg of Dr.20.[607] Here the G4 accounted for 16.4% of the amphorae. Wine amphorae produced in Campania in Italy have also been identified at several late second- and third-century British sites, principally northern military sites.[608] In addition, G12 amphorae are known at a few sites along the south east coast of Britain in late second- or third-century AD contexts. Whilst limited British G12 production is known, the majority were produced in Normandy and they almost certainly carried wine from this region.[609]

As in the preceding period, most wine came to Britain in barrels from production facilities in southern, central and southwest France, with smaller-scale imports arriving from northern Gaul and the Rhine provinces. In Britain, some twelve barrels have been recovered from four sites of the late second and first half of the third century, which compares closely to the number of examples known from the mid-first to mid-second century.[610] Marlière notes a slight decline in the overall number of

[605] Carreras Monfort and Funari 1998, 57, 268.
[606] Holbrook and Bidwell 1991, Tab. 14.
[607] Richardson 1986, Fig. 76.
[608] Tyers 1996b; Arthur and Williams 1992.
[609] Tyers 1996b; Laubenheimer 2003, 39-44, Fig. 15, Symonds 2003, 58.
[610] Marlière 2002, T1-8, 29-30, 33, 51.

barrels from second-century AD contexts in Western Europe (thirty-three examples) when compared to the first century (forty-six examples), with a further decline coming in the third century (twenty-seven examples).[611] However, we should not read too much into this as the sample sizes are small and, as discussed above, the recovery of barrels is highly dependent upon favourable conditions of preservation. An examination of the incidence of representations of barrels on stone carvings, meanwhile, indicates a substantial increase over time, with the majority of these representations dating to the second half of the second and first half of the third centuries.[612] Goatskin bottles, which are virtually undetectable archaeologically, may also have been used to transport wine during this period and these are depicted on the late second- or early third-century relief of a trader from Mainz.[613] However, we should bear in mind that the occurrence of barrels and goatskins on stone carvings is also by no means a reliable measure of levels of trade. It is clear that the epigraphic habit, or the practice of producing named inscriptions and carvings relating to trade, in fact peaked in the late second and early third centuries AD, and this does not necessarily relate to the scale of the trade itself.[614]

Indeed, there is indirect evidence to suggest that there was a contemporary decline in the wine trade; in overall terms the apogee of viticulture in Gaul was the early to mid-second century AD and there is clear evidence for a productive slump in several regions in the latter decades of the second century and in the early third century. In Provence, Languedoc and the Tricastin several wine producing establishments were abandoned at this time, whilst palynological evidence suggests that towards the end of the second century vineyards were increasingly going out of use and were being replaced by open meadows and arable cultivation.[615] In Aquitaine, meanwhile, there is less evidence for decline and the majority of wine producing installations appear to have continued in use until the middle of the third-century.[616]

Much of the wine from southern and central France, and the lesser products of northern Gaul and the Rhine provinces, probably came to Britain through a trade focused on the Rhône-Rhine corridor and thence to Britain across the Southern North Sea and Eastern Channel. The stone carvings depicting barrels, many of which were set up by wine-traders, cluster heavily in central France and around the southern and western tributaries of the Rhine.[617] Indeed, two altars dating to this period found at Colijnsplaat at the mouth of the Scheldt, a port with known connections to Britain, were dedicated by wine traders, and bear depictions of vines and barrels.[618] The wine from Aquitaine would have travelled to Britain in barrels via an Atlantic route. The funerary stele of a barrel-maker found in Bordeaux might be coupled with a monument made from British millstone-grit, set up there in AD 237 by a trader whose origin was noted as York and Lincoln, to imply that this port played a role in the British-Aquitanian wine trade.[619]

Seafood

There is reduced evidence for the import of fish-products from the Mediterranean to the northwestern Empire during this period, certainly in comparison to the first- and early second-centuries AD. Fish-product amphorae post-dating the mid-second century AD are exceptionally rare.[620] This may be coupled with the fact that there was a substantial fall in production in the western Mediterranean in the early third century, with the aggregated vat capacities of salting factories in Lusitania, Baetica and Mauretania Tingitana decreasing by almost 2/3.[621]

However, there is evidence for salted fish processing on a vast scale along the coast of Brittany. The sites of Douarnenez-Plomarc'h 2 and 1 respectively represent the second and fourth largest factories by vat capacity in the entire Roman world. Whilst the Armorican salting factories began to operate during the first half of the first-century AD, they underwent a dramatic increase in productivity from the middle of the second-century AD onwards. The known aggregate vat capacity for the period AD 151-200 is almost $1000m^3$, which is almost five times the aggregate capacity of the vats during the period AD 101-150, which is c. $200m^3$. This vast output continues into the early third century with the aggregate vat capacity during the period AD 201-250 estimated at c. 900 m^3.[622]

The vast output of the Breton installations far exceeded local demand and much must have been destined for export to other parts of north-west Europe. The products were not exported in amphorae. Whilst some may have moved in pots, the majority will have been transported in barrels, which are hard to detect archaeologically.[623] Despite the absence of direct evidence, one can assume that fish products from Brittany were reaching Britain in quantity via the seaways of the Western Channel. The absence of fish bones at most British sites suggests a preference for sauces (*garum*, *liquamen* and *allec*), rather than the salted fish.[624]

There is also evidence for the limited production of fish sauces in Belgium and the southern Netherlands, as well as in Britain, from at least the late second century AD onwards. Several sites in Belgium and the southern Netherlands, as well as in Britain, engaged in the

[611] Marlière 2002, 174, Figs. 211-212.
[612] Marlière 2002, 175, Fig. 212.
[613] Marlière 2002, 187, Fig. 13
[614] MacMullen 1982; Hope 1997.
[615] Brun and Laubenheimer 2001, 212, 214-215; Brun 2001; Buffat and Pellecuer 2001; Jung *et al.* 2001.
[616] Brun and Laubenheimer 2001, 214; Balmelle *et al.* 2001.
[617] Marlière 2002, Fig. 128.
[618] Stuart and Bogaers 2001, A8, A41.
[619] Marlière 2002, R35; Hassall 1978, 42, Tab. II.8.
[620] Martin-Kilcher 2003, Figs. 11-12.
[621] Wilson 2006, Fig. 3.
[622] Wilson, 2006.
[623] *Ibid.* 534,
[624] Cool 2006, 237; Rippon 2000, 220-221; Barrett *et al.* 2004.

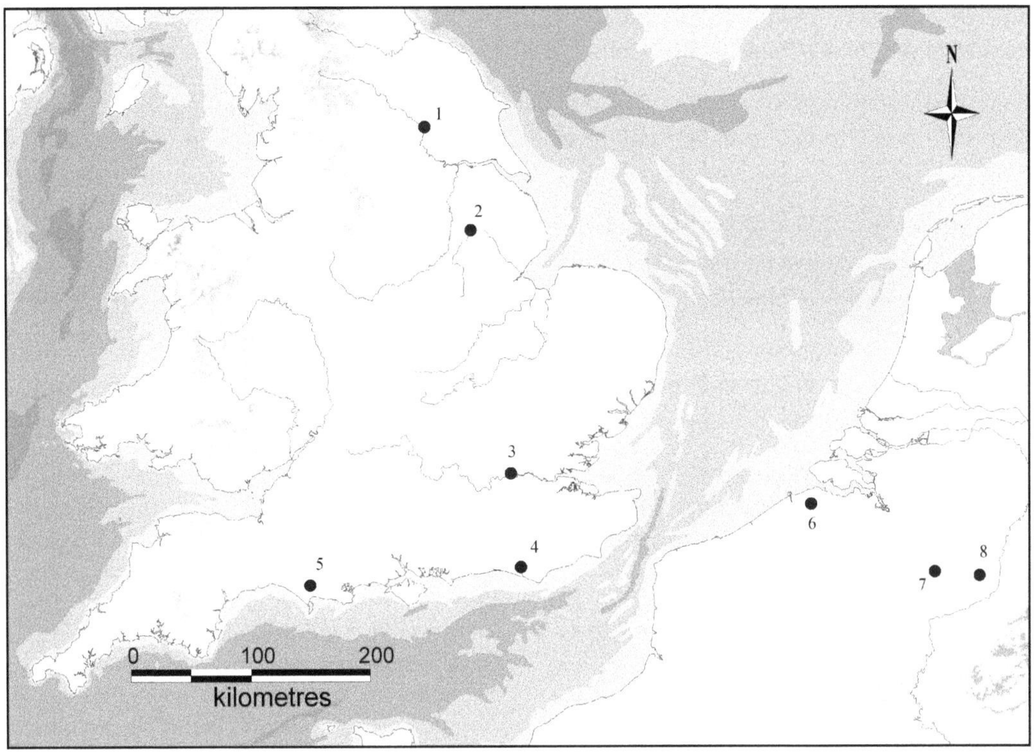

Fig. 5.4. Late second- to fourth-century allec production sites in Britain and the near continent (1. York, 2. Lincoln, 3. London, 4. Beddingham, 5. Dorchester, 6. Aardenburg, 7. Tienen, 8. Tongeren) (Data from: Jones 1988; Dobney et al. 1996, 54-56; Bateman and Locker 1982; Hamilton-Dyer 2008; Vanderhoeven et al. 2001; Lentacker et al. 2004; Van Neer et al. 2005; Van Neer and Lentacker 1994; Immerzeel 1990, 183; Stuart and Bogaers 2001).

production of fish sauces, probably *allec*, from the late second century onwards (**Fig. 5.4**). These are characterised by the presence of large numbers of small fish from the family *clupeidae*, sometimes in association with kilns or buildings with large-scale processing facilities. The finds are unparalleled in the Medieval period and are unlikely to represent the remains of fish-gutting, or other forms of processing.[625]

These small-scale products may also have been traded in barrels across the Southern North Sea and Eastern Channel; certainly, three inscriptions from Colijnsplaat, dated to the second half of the second or early third century attest to the presence of individuals trading in *allec*.[626] Of course they might equally well have been involved in the trade of *allec* produced in Brittany.

Lava querns

Several scholars have suggested a major decline, even a possible cessation of lava quern import in the later second century.[627] Lava quern fragments are widespread in contexts dating to the late second century or the first half of the third century AD and later. For example, lava has been found in contexts of these dates at London, Stonea Grange in Cambridgeshire, Alcester in Warwickshire, Ilford, Stagsden, Harlow and Great Dumnow in Essex and Ravenglass in Cumbria.[628] Determining whether or not these are merely residual or whether they in fact indicate continued import is difficult. Given the frequency of later finds it should not be ruled out that the import of querns continued, though at a somewhat reduced rate.

British Exports

Coinage and metals

As the coinage was increasingly debased the state probably organised the rounding up of old *denarii* through taxation and sent them back to the mint at Rome. Older *denarii* with a higher silver content would facilitate the production of more new *denarii*, or radiates, with a lower silver content. Indeed, by the mid-third century the radiate was being stamped over old *denarii*, which resulted in a doubling of profit by the state.[629] The thoroughness of this process is indicated by the rarity of hoards with significant quantities of *denarii* closing later than AD 260. In the M1 Motorway hoard, which closed in AD 270, there were 435 *denarii* and radiates, but only one coin pre-dated the Severan period.[630] One should also bear in mind that many *denarii* would have been melted down by private individuals within Britain. Similar

[625] Hamilton-Dyer 2008, 4.
[626] Stuart and Bogaers 2001, A34, A39, B44.
[627] Peacock 1980; Hilary Major, pers. Comm. 2007; Allen *et al.* 2007, 185.
[628] Chapman and Johnson 1973, 51; Farid 2000, 120; Jackson and Potter 1996, 517-518; Booth 2001, 260; Dawson 2000, 93; Medlycott 2000, 61; Lavender 1997, 87; Potter 1979, 94.
[629] Wilson 2007, 116; Casey 1994a, 11.
[630] Abdy 2002, 32-36.

processes probably occurred with the gold coinage too.[631] Coin continued to leave Britain through trade as well.

Changes in the scale of British lead-silver mining are hard to assess. The latest known stamped lead ingots from Britain date to AD 164-169; however, an ingot from Châlons-sur-Sâone in France bears a stamp of the emperor Septimius Severus and Legio VI, which was stationed at York. This may derive from a British source, as might very similar pigs from nearby Alouettes and another example from Lillebonne (**Fig. 4.32**).[632] The decline in the number of stamped ingots during this period is often taken as reflecting a shift from mining under the auspices of state officials to private enterprises.[633] A change in the structure of lead-silver mining may well have occurred in Britain at this date, indeed there are many undated pigs, particularly from northern England (**Fig. 4.32, Tab. 4.7**). The key question, however, is whether there was a decline in the scale of mining output between these dates. The evidence is very scanty, but we can suspect that there was. Most of our positive evidence for lead-silver mining dates to the late first and second centuries AD. This presumably had a knock-on effect on the scale of British silver exports. Lead exports may also have declined, though we have seen that some British lead was possibly being exported in the Severan period.

The main traces for gold-mining at Dolaucothi date to the late first and early second centuries; however, the settlement was occupied until the fourth century and it is certainly likely that mining on a reduced scale, in underground galleries rather than by opencast hydraulic working, was still undertaken by private contractors. A portion of this gold was exported.[634]

Late second- and early third-century British copper-alloy brooches are rare on the continent, although probable examples are present at Zugmantel, Regensburg, Cologne, Zugmantel and Straubing in Germany and Schaerbeek in Belgium (Appendix 6). This is principally due to a major decrease in British brooch production at the end of the second century, which can probably be explained as a change in fashion, with brooches no longer being worn as standard dress.[635]

Iron production in Roman-period Britain very probably reached its maximum output between the mid-second and mid-third centuries (see p. 84, **Fig. 4.33, Tab. 4.8**). Most of this iron was consumed internally, but exports to the adjacent continent probably continued throughout this period.

Ports

There are strong archaeological indications that London suffered a decline in population during the second half of the second century. Excavations have revealed that in many parts of the city building sequences were interrupted at this time and deposits of so-called 'dark earth' (probably soil from gardening) overlay earlier Roman sequences. The coin sequence at Southwark, south of the river Thames, shows a sudden and marked dip between AD 161-192. This hints at a drop in settlement at this time.[636] Despite these signs of decline London maintained its role as Britain's main port throughout this period (**Fig. 5.5**). Major new oak-timber quays were constructed at Custom House in the late second century and at New Fresh Wharf c. AD 235-245. The fill of the quay at New Fresh Wharf contained sherds from a wide range of imported amphorae and pottery which had arrived in London during the late second and early third centuries AD and were probably discarded wares from nearby warehouses. These included numerous finds of Dr.20 (55.6 kg) and G4 (22.9 kg) amphorae, as well as a huge amount of Lezoux ware dated AD 170-180, East Gaulish *sigillata* and Trier Ware.[637] Richborough continued as a port, with imports, such as Dr.20 amphorae, well known; however, the settlement suffered a decline in the late second century as buildings and roads fell out of use, whilst the volume of imported *sigillata* fell dramatically.[638]

The *Classis Britannica* base at Dover seems to have been abandoned c. AD 180 and whilst it experienced a short phase of intensive occupation between c. AD 200-210, after this it was demolished and abandoned and saw no further occupation until c. AD 275-280.[639] This is presumably to be connected with a shift in the fleet's activities to the earliest shore forts, which were constructed at about this time. Excavations at the shore fort of Reculver in Kent reveal that the first phase of construction belongs to the years AD 185-195, though the fort was left unfinished and was only completed around twenty years later. Shore forts at Brancaster and Caister-on-Sea in Norfolk are similar to Reculver in that they have internal bastions, unlike the later sturdier shore forts that possess external bastions, and their construction was probably contemporary with Reculver.[640] A role for these forts as holding points and bases for supplies destined for the Roman military on the northern frontier, particularly during and after Septimius Severus's campaigns to northern Britain between AD 208-211, has been suggested and this is plausible.[641] Certainly, at Brancaster and Caister-on-Sea the considerable cattle-bone deposits are biased towards non-meat-bearing bones, which imply that meat was processed at, and exported from, these sites in quantity.[642]

[631] Wilson 2007, 113, Fig. 1.
[632] Stewart 2002, 211; Fulford 2007, 317-318.
[633] Tylecote 1986, 61; Fulford, 2007, 317-318.
[634] Burnham and Burnham 2004.
[635] Bayley and Butcher 2004, 207.
[636] Perring 1991, 76-89; Roskams 1991; Swain and Williams 2008; Sheldon 1981; Drummond-Murray and Thompson 2002, Fig. 114.
[637] Miller *et al.* 1986; Marsden 1994.
[638] Millett and Wilmott 2003, 188; Cunliffe 1968; Fulford 2007, 64; Carreras Monfort and Funari 1998.
[639] Mason 2003, 109; Pearson, 2002, 55, 58; Philp 1981.
[640] Philp 2005; Allen and Fulford 1999; Cunliffe 1977; Pearson 2003.
[641] Darling and Gurney 1993; Allen and Fulford 1999; Pearson 2005; Cotterill 1993.
[642] Hinchliffe and Green 1985; Darling and Gurney 1993; Pearson 2005, 83; Cotterill 1993.

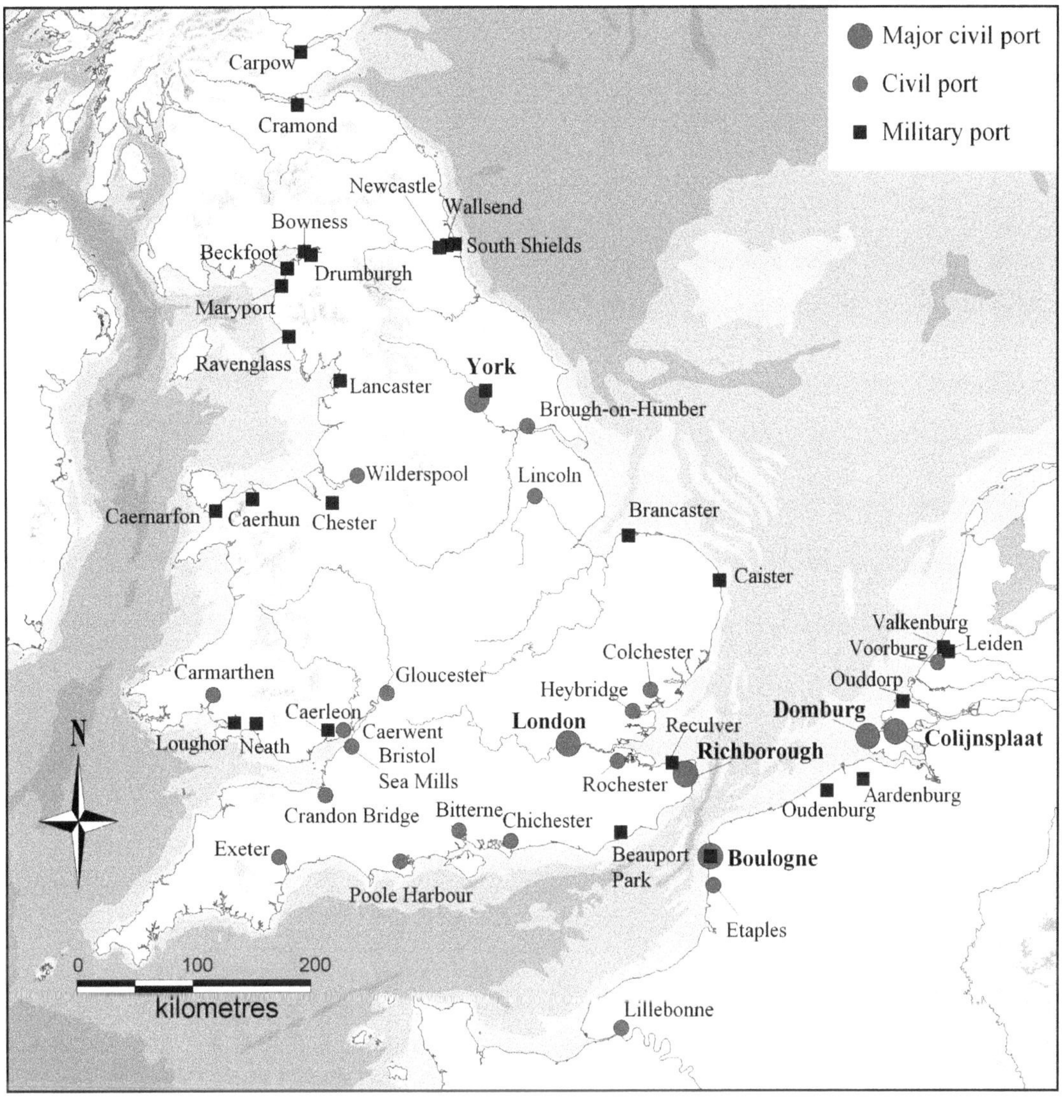

Fig. 5.5. The main ports of the early third century AD in Roman Britain and on the adjacent continent.

In the north, the ceramic evidence suggests that York underwent expansion from c. AD 180 onwards and it is during the late second and early third century AD when the evidence for long-distance exchange at this site is most intensive.[643] South Shields, at the mouth of the Tyne, was a major maritime supply depot for the northern army in the early third century, probably initially in connection with the Severan campaigns. Twenty new granaries were built at this time. At South Shields Baetican Dr.20 olive oil amphorae sherds are well known from early third-century contexts, whilst coarse pottery of Black-burnished ware 2 (BB2) type, produced at various locations around the Thames estuary, reached the site in great quantities throughout the third century AD.[644] The imports, such as the Dr.20, probably did not arrive directly from the continent. Instead, the finds of BB2 indicate transhipment up the east coast of England via the Thames estuary region. For a short time during the Severan campaigns several large forts were occupied on the east coast of Scotland, at Carpow on the Tay and Cramond on the Firth of Forth.[645] Like South Shields these probably served as military supply depots receiving goods from southeast England by sea.

On the continent the important naval base and civil fort at Boulogne continued in use throughout the late second and early third centuries, though the naval base shows signs of being partially closed down during the course of the third century.[646] The civil ports at the mouth of the Rhine and Scheldt, such as Voorburg and Domburg and Colijnsplaat display signs of vibrancy. From the latter two sites more than 150 altars have been recovered, which date to the late second or early third century; at Domburg the coin series peaked AD 180-218, whilst inscriptions from Colijnsplaat bear consular dates of AD 188, 193, 223, 227 (and possibly 222). These altars were dedications, principally to the goddess Nehalennia, made in thanks for successful trading ventures. They attest to considerable trading activity; traders in *allec*, pottery, salt and wine are all recorded. Much of this trade was

[643] Monaghan 1997; Ottaway 1993.
[644] Bidwell and Speak 1994; Dore and Gillam 1979.
[645] Pearson 2002, 53.
[646] Seillier 2004; Brulet 1991; Pearson 2002, 55.

evidently directed across the Southern North Sea between the Rhineland and northern Gaul, and Britain. Of the twenty dedicants at Colijnsplaat who list their origin the vast majority came from the Rhine provinces, or northern Gaul. Meanwhile, of the six altars whose dedicants record trade with a specific region, five name Britain, two of whom specify themselves as pottery traders (**Tab. 4.3**). Of the British traders one was a *negotiator Cantianus et Geserecanus*, which meant that his ships alternated between Kent, Boulogne and Colijnsplaat. One altar lists a [*negotiator*] *Gallicaus*, or a trader with Gaul.[647]

Synthesis

Both the Southern North Sea and Eastern Channel system and the Atlantic system suffered a downturn in connectivity during the late second century, and there was no significant recovery in the first half of the third century.

Imports declined in the Southern North Sea and Eastern Channel system; precious metal coin continued to arrive in quantity as state payments, but the quality of the coin declined dramatically. The state sent far less *aes* coin to Britain. There is also evidence to suggest a decline in traded goods, such as pottery, wine, lava querns and the portion of olive oil that arrived by this route. In the Atlantic system the volume of olive oil imports declined substantially. The wine imports in barrels from southwest France does not appear to have been affected, whereas there is a notable rise in salted fish production in Brittany, much of which must have been exported.

British exports included re-exports of coin collected by the state through taxation and also exported through private trade. There are hints that British non-ferrous mining declined in the later second century, which would have had a knock-on effect upon exports of metal, though this apparent 'decline' may simply be the result of the state increasingly handing the operation of the mines over to private contractors who did not stamp their ingots with official dates. Iron production, meanwhile, remained at a high level and some of this would have been exported by the state and by private individuals. As in the preceding period, other exports are hard to assess because of their archaeological invisibility, but we can suspect that agricultural products, salt and oysters may have been exported from Britain.

Similar ports were involved in the Atlantic system in this period as in the preceding period. In the Southern North Sea and Eastern Channel system the main British civil ports at London and Richborough show signs of decline, but probably retained their important position. There was a reorganisation of east-coast British military supply in the late second or early third century, possibly in connection with Severus's British campaigns. The minor *Classis Britannica* base at Dover was abandoned and new coastal bases were established at Reculver in east Kent and at Caister and Brancaster in East Anglia. South Shields at the eastern end of Hadrian's Wall became a major maritime supply depot, whilst the northern port of York also underwent expansion from the late second century onwards. On the continent, civil ports at the mouth of the Rhine/Maas were heavily engaged in trade with southeast Britain in the late second and early third centuries.

The determinants of connective change

The replacement of Mediterranean imports with local northwest European and British products may have played some role in the late second-century connective decline.[648] This is best apparent with regard to salted fish-products, which were produced in greatly increased amounts in northwest Europe during the later second century (see pp. 106-107). We also get our first clear evidence for viticulture in Britain during the second century, albeit on a small-scale.[649] However, whilst 'import replacement' may have played some role it does not fully explain why there was a contemporaneous fall-off in imports to Britain of Central Gaulish *sigillata*, olive oil, and lava querns. Indeed, we should not rule out that the late second-century rise of fish-salting installations in northwest Europe and the contemporary development of viticulture in Britain was in fact a response to declining import from southern Europe.

The increasing trend to recruit soldiers from near to their stations may have played a minor role in the decline in long-distance trade. It has been suggested that soldiers lost their taste for Mediterranean food products over time.[650] This fails to fully explain why the decline came suddenly in the late second century. There is no evidence that recruitment patterns shifted dramatically at this time. Indeed, soldiers were still recruited into the British legions from Mediterranean provinces and it is unlikely that consumption patterns within Britannia suddenly shifted at this time (**Tabs. 4.8-9**). We must search elsewhere for the key determining factors.

One of the principal causes of the economic slump was the Antonine plague, the symptoms of which, described by Galen, a physician and medical writer who lived at the time of the plague, are consistent with smallpox, though they do not rule out other possibilities.[651] The demographic and economic impact of the plague has been an issue of vigorous debate in recent years, and I argue that it had a significant impact.[652] It is recorded in numerous historical accounts; according to the *Historia Augusta* and Ammianus Marcellinus, the plague originated in the east, in Babylonia, and was brought to the Empire by Lucius Verus's army on its return from the Parthian war of AD 162-166.[653] Aelius Aristides wrote

[647] Stuart and Bogaers 2001; Hassall 1978.

[648] Mattingly 2006, 500.

[649] Brown *et al.* 2001.

[650] Mattingly 2006, 500-501; Carreras-Monfort and Funari 1998.

[651] Duncan-Jones 1996, 116; Littman and Littman 1973; Galen, Kuhn. 4.788, 10.360-63.

[652] C.f. Duncan Jones 1996; 2002; Lo Cascio 2010; Bruun 2007; Scheidel 2009; Wilson 2009b; 2009c.

[653] *Historia Augusta. Lucius Verus.* 8.1-2; Ammianus Marcellinus. 23.6.24.

that in the year AD 165 a plague infected him and many others in the city of Smyrna on the Mediterranean coast of Anatolia.[654] Whilst he managed to recover, large numbers died from the disease. By AD 166 the great plague had reached Rome, which caused Galen to flee to Pergamum.[655]

Severe plagues were a relatively regular occurrence in the ancient world, which led to familiarity and insensitivity; Duncan-Jones noted that Livy mentioned a serious epidemic afflicting Rome every 8.25 years on average between 490-292 BC and every 4.8 years in Livy's more detailed narrative for the years 212-165 BC.[656] However, judging by the historical sources, the Antonine plague was long-lasting and had a particularly devastating impact throughout the Empire.[657] Jerome states that in the year AD 168 a polluting disease had taken hold of many provinces and affected Rome.[658] At the end of this same year the physician Galen was at Aquileia with the army when the plague grew fiercer and killed the majority of the troops there.[659] In the *Historia Augusta* various passages describe the grave pestilence, which carried off thousands of civilians, soldiers and nobles at the time of the Marcomannic wars both prior to and after Lucius Verus's death in AD 169.[660] Its devastation of the army led Marcus Aurelius to spend three years conscripting new troops at Carnuntum; he enrolled several new legions and, besides this, slaves, gladiators and bandits were enlisted, whilst German auxiliaries were also hired.[661] Jerome, meanwhile, records that in the year AD 172 the plague reduced the Roman army almost to extinction.[662] Eutropius states that at the time of the Marcomannic wars all of the Roman armies perished from the pestilence, along with a large part of the population in Rome, Italy and the provinces, whilst Ammianus Marcellinus notes that at the time of Lucius Verus and Marcus Aurelius an incurable disease polluted everything with contagion and death, from the frontiers of Persia to the Rhine and to Gaul.[663] There was some exaggeration here, but a serious epidemic is clearly being described. The plague possibly reappeared in AD 189, affecting Rome, Italy and perhaps the entire Empire.[664] This latter event was the worst outbreak of disease known by Cassius Dio and according to him it often killed 2000 people a day at Rome.[665]

The Antonine plague had a major demographic impact upon the Roman Empire. An epidemiological model has predicted that a highly virulent form of smallpox could have induced a total death-toll of 25% of the Empire's population, whilst another study has posited a population loss of between 14-20% between AD 165-189.[666] Such approaches are highly speculative, though there is proxy evidence to suggest that there was a significant population decline in certain parts of the Empire at this time. Duncan-Jones analysed the detailed documentary evidence from Egypt and plausibly suggested that there was a dramatic fall in rural population during the later second century as a result of the Antonine plague, though this view has been challenged.[667]

The demographic impact of the plague in other provinces of the Empire where we lack such detailed documentary sources is harder to assess. Duncan-Jones has argued that a severe decline in the number of year-dated army diplomas after AD 167 can be related to plague-induced casualties amongst the military. This does appear likely, though Roxan and Greenberg have pointed out that the decline coincides closely with a reduction in the rights afforded to veterans by such diplomas.[668] Jongman has argued that the population of Italy began to decline in the second half of the second century AD, whilst a study of site occupation in Gaul indicates a peak of population in the mid- to late second century AD with a decline underway before the end of the second century.[669]

In Britain, at Gloucester, a recently excavated mid- to late second-century mass-grave contained the remains of ninety-one individuals without signs of trauma, and this can perhaps be interpreted as a plague pit, although the fact that some skeletons are incomplete means this is not certain and we may be dealing with a reburial of remains from a cemetery elsewhere.[670] There is also a notable rise in the number of coin hoards in Britain during the reign of Marcus Aurelius, which represents the peak for the entire period of the Principate, and indeed, a late second-century peak in coin hoards is the standard pattern observable across Western Europe.[671] This might well be related to a significant rise in mortality, perhaps a result of plague, which meant that the recovery rate of hoards was much lower at this time. We must of course bear in mind that the debasement of the precious metal coinage from the later second century AD onwards meant that older higher quality coinage might well have been preferentially hoarded, which would lead to an over-representation of *denarii* hoards closing in the reign of Marcus Aurelius. There are also signs that urban populations in parts of Britain declined. As we have seen, London suffered population decline in the second half of the second century (see p. 108). Harvey Sheldon has suggested that there was a fall in the intensity of occupation at other settlements in southeast England,

[654] *Or.* 48.38-44; Duncan Jones 1996, 116.
[655] Galen, Kuhn. 19.15.
[656] Duncan-Jones 1996, 109-111.
[657] For a full discussion of the historical sources see: Duncan-Jones 1996; Gilliam 1961.
[658] Jerome, AD 168, ed. Helm p.206.
[659] Galen, Kuhn. 19.17-18.
[660] *Historia Augusta. Lucius Verus.* 8.1-2; *Marcus Aurelius.* 13.3-6, 17.2, 21.6.
[661] Orosius. 7.15.5-6; *Historia Augusta. Marcus Aurelius.* 21.6.
[662] Jerome, AD 172
[663] Eutropius. 8.12.2; Ammianus Marcellinus. 23.6.24.
[664] Cassius Dio *Historia Romana.* 72.14.3; Herodian *Roman History.* 1.12.
[665] *Historia Romana.* 72.14.3.

[666] Scheidel 2002, 99-100; Littman and Littman 1973.
[667] Duncan-Jones 1996; Greenberg 2003; Scheidel 2002; Bagnall 2002.
[668] Duncan-Jones 1996, 124, Fig. 6; Greenberg 2003; 414-415, Fig. 1; Roxan 1981.
[669] Jongman 2009, 124; Lewit 1991; 2005.
[670] Simmonds *et al.* 2008; Esmonde Cleary 2009.
[671] Abdy 2002, 9, 25; Casey 1994a, 54, Fig. 9; Guest and Popovitch 2000.

such as Staines, at the same time, whilst following a fire at Verulamium c. AD 155-160 recovery in many parts of the city was delayed for fifty years or longer.[672]

The Antonine plague would have had a heavily disruptive impact upon economic activity, not just by reducing the consumer base, but also by decimating workforces. Mortality or flight induced by the Antonine plague appears to be the most plausible explanation for the cessation of mining activity at Rio Tinto by c. AD 180, at the gold mines of northwest Iberia during the late second or early third centuries and possibly at some of the largest gold mines in Dacia, which were abandoned c. AD 166-167. The metal deposits at these locations were by no means exhausted, though, as Wilson has pointed out, if work stopped at the Spanish mines, even for a short time, the mining galleries would flood and a large input of labour would have been required to drain them and to bring the mines back into operation.[673] We might ask whether workforces were similarly affected elsewhere. During the late second century and early third centuries productive output was reduced in the Central Gaulish *sigillata* industry, the wine industries of southern and central France, the fish-salting installations of the western Mediterranean and probably also at the olive oil estates in Baetica (see pp. 103-107).[674] This may have had much to do with the direct impact of the Antonine plague. Economic decline was not restricted to Western Europe; a detailed chronological survey of the African red-slip pottery industry indicates that, following rapid growth from the early second century AD to a peak in the mid-second century AD, the industry shows signs of having suffered decline, or at the very least stagnation, during the second half of the second century.[675]

The second main cause of the connective decline was the increasing debasement of the coinage, which had a strong impact upon monetary confidence, economic activity and trade.[676] This was due to two main factors; firstly, there was an intense increase in warfare with barbarian peoples during the reign of Marcus Aurelius, principally along the middle and upper Danube frontier in the major conflict known as the Marcomannic wars (AD 166-180).[677] The root cause of this conflict, as mentioned in the *Historia Augusta*, was barbarians deep within the *Barbaricum* displacing and driving on other tribes, which led to an increasing pressure on the Danube frontier.[678] This was most likely a result of the beginning of a migration of peoples, later known as the Goths, from the Baltic towards the Black Sea, which caused the displacement of other barbarian groups.[679] Indeed, the Wielbark culture, which was present around the Vistula delta of northern Poland from the first half of the first century AD onwards and is thought to correspond to the Goths, begins to shift towards the southeast at precisely this time.[680] However, the Antonine plague, which was ravaging the Roman army at this time, encouraged barbarian incursions and severely hampered the ability of the Roman army to deter them. As discussed in greater detail below the military problems of the Marcomannic wars led the Roman state to turn to diplomacy as a tool to ensure the security of their borders. Enormous quantities of *denarii* were used to secure treaties and buy peace with barbarian peoples (see pp. 113-114). Secondly, the fact that operations at the Empire's principal bullion mines had ceased, or declined, as a result of the Antonine plague exacerbated the shortage of precious metal.

We should also bear in mind one final possibility. That is that the decline in connectivity between Britain and the continental Empire from the late second century onwards had much to do with the Roman state introducing a series of cost-saving measures, such as ending or reducing certain military supply contracts in the Western Empire. If this was indeed the case, and proving it is difficult, then the Roman state's need to make these savings should in any case be viewed in the context of the aforementioned disruption caused by the Antonine plague and the Marcomannic wars, in particular the pressure on the state's money supply caused by the payment of large subsidies to barbarian peoples.

5.2. The Eastern North Sea system

Introduction

In contrast to the Southern North Sea and Channel systems, during the later second century there was a sudden expansion in exchange between the Rhine regions of the Empire and the Eastern North Sea coast, following the minimal contacts of the post-Tiberian period. Much of this exchange took place through North Sea maritime routes, via the mouths of the Rhine and Lake Flevo, though overland routes were also of considerable importance. This exchange involved a late-second century injection of *denarii* into the northwest *Barbaricum* as political payments from the Roman state. There was also a thriving trade, involving substantial imports of *terra sigillata*, copper-alloy vessels and lava querns, and smaller amounts of *aes* coin and statuettes, into Eastern North Sea coastal regions, whilst exports to the Empire probably included agricultural products, fish, re-exported coin and perhaps small quantities of amber. In the Frisian occupied areas of the northern Netherlands this trade continued at a high-level down to c. AD 260. In Groningen and northwest Germany, meanwhile, it appears to have been terminated prior to AD 200. The

[672] Sheldon 1981; Niblett 2001, 112-126.
[673] Wilson 2002; 2007; 2009a; 2009c; Scheidel 2009; Jones 1980; Howgego 1992; Domergue 1990.
[674] Marsh 1981; Woolf 1998; Brun and Laubenheimer 2001; Brun 2001; Buffat and Pellecuer 2001; Jung *et al.* 2001; Wilson 2006; Andrew Wilson and Annalisa Marzano, pers. Comm. 2008; Haley 2003.
[675] Fentress *et al.* 2004; Wilson 2009b.
[676] Scheidel forthcoming.
[677] Cassius Dio *Historia Romana*. 71; *Historia Augusta. Marcus Aurelius*; Birley 2000; 2001; Friesinger *et al.* 1994; Grane 2007, 45-80; Böhme 1975; Lennartz 1969.
[678] *Historia Augusta. Marcus Aurelius*. 14.1.
[679] Storgaard 2003, 115-116; Godłowski 1984; Birley 2000, 166; Wilkes 2000, 584; 2005, 225; Grane 2007, 54-55; Wilkes 2005, 225.
[680] *Ibid.*

key factors underlying these changes were again the Marcomannic wars and Antonine plague, which had weakened the Empire's frontiers and stretched its military forces. This led the Roman state to politically re-engage with the peoples beyond its northwest frontier and to establish treaties, which necessitated cash payments to the barbarians. The existence of peace stimulated and facilitated trade. In the Frisian areas peaceful relations appear to have been maintained down to c. AD 260, though in Groningen and northwest Germany hostile relations probably re-emerged by the end of the second century, which disrupted trade links.

Imports to the Eastern North Sea coastal region

Coinage and metals

There was an influx of silver *denarii* to the Eastern North Sea coastal regions of the *Barbaricum* during the later second century AD. In the north Dutch provinces of Friesland, Groningen and Drenthe eleven out of the thirteen *denarii* hoards which post-date AD 37 close in the period AD 160-194.[681] Of the seventeen post-Augustan *denarii* hoards in the northwest German states of Lower Saxony and North Rhine-Westphalia which are large enough (12-1145 coins) for chronological analysis fifteen close in the relatively short period AD 168-198, whilst one closes in AD 215.[682]

This pattern is repeated across the entire north European *Barbaricum*. In total c. 70,000 silver *denarii* are known, from c. 200 hoards and 850 single finds, principally from Poland and Eastern Europe. Whilst the coins themselves have dates ranging throughout the first and second centuries AD, the hoards principally have closing coins of the late second century AD, from the reign of Marcus Aurelius to the early years of Septimius Severus, and there is a sharp cut-off after this date.[683] The material also shows strong parallels with the Scottish hoards, although, the latter have a slightly greater concentration in the Severan period and into the early third century AD.[684]

It is extremely likely that the vast bulk of the *denarii* entered the *Barbaricum* in the late second century AD.[685] Berger has demonstrated that the hoards from northwest Germany, which close with *denarii* of the late second century, have exactly the same composition as late second-century hoards found within the northwestern Empire.[686] The bulk could not have arrived very far into the third century, for whilst some early third-century silver coins are present in the *Barbaricum* they are fairly rare.[687] In addition, systematic debasement of the silver coinage ensured that within the Empire earlier *denarii* with higher silver contents were rapidly and systematically withdrawn from circulation for remelting into greater numbers of new coin during the early third century. Indeed, second-century *denarii* become rare in coin hoards within the Empire closing in the 230s and 240s, and are virtually absent from the 250s.[688]

Some of the *denarii* arrived in the *Barbaricum* as booty from raiding undertaken at the time of the Marcomannic wars. There is no reason why a portion of the *denarii* found in northwest Germany might not have been obtained during raids, such as those of the Chauci or Chatti on Belgica c. AD 170-175.[689] Some may also have arrived through trade. However, the main mechanism through which the vast bulk of the *denarii* flooded into the *Barbaricum* was through political payments made by the Roman state to buy peace and stability along the Empire's increasingly insecure northern borders. These political payments occurred in the context and aftermath of the Marcomannic wars and the Antonine plague, which had stretched the Empire's military capacity to a degree not previously experienced (see pp. 110-112). These factors ensured that northern barbarians were now much better placed to demand, and receive, monetary payments from the Roman state in exchange for peace. These payments are certainly attested in the literary sources.[690]

The *denarii* from the northern Netherlands can plausibly be seen as political payments; the establishment of some form of treaty between the Roman state and the peoples of the northern Netherlands at about this time is implied by the presence of Frisian auxiliary units in Britain from at least the early third century AD. A Frisian auxiliary unit, a *cuneus Frisiorum*, is known from an inscription at Housesteads fort, in northern Britain, during the reign of Alexander Severus, along with two other units, which probably derive from across the Lower Rhine frontier, the *numerus Hnaudifridi* and *Germ(ani) cives Tuihanti*. An inscription from Vindolanda dating to the time of Alexander Severus also records a *numerus [G]er[man]orum*(?) or *Fr[is]orum*(?). A mid-third-century inscription from Papcastle records a *cuneus Frisionum Aballavensium*, whilst an undated, presumably third-century, inscription from Binchester records the *cuneus Fris(iorum) Vinovie(nsium)*.[691] Furthermore, c. 200 sherds of handmade black, burnished pottery, known as Housesteads ware, have been identified at four of the forts along Hadrian's Wall: Housesteads, Birdoswald, Vindolanda and Burgh-by-Sands (and possibly Castlesteads). Housesteads ware has been dated from the third to sixth centuries AD and whilst it was produced from local clay sources, it shows strong stylistic similarities to the Frisian pottery style of the northern

[681] Galestin 2001, Tab.1.
[682] Berger 1992, 133-146, Abb. 49.
[683] Bursche 1989; 1996; 2006; Bolin 1929; see various articles in Aillagon 2008.
[684] Hunter 2007; Fig. 20.9; Robertson 2000.
[685] *Contra* Lind 1988; 1991.
[686] Berger 1992; 1996, 57; Reece 2008.
[687] Van der Vin, 1996, 365, Tab. 4; Berger 1992, 161-164, Abb. 56; 1995, 106; Bursche 1996, 37; 2006.
[688] Berger 1996, 58; Horsnæs 2003; Robertson 2000.
[689] *Historia Augusta. Didius Julianus*. 1.7.
[690] Marcus Aurelius. AD 171: Cassius Dio *Historia Romana*. 71.11-12. AD 179: Cassius Dio *Historia Romana*. 71.19. Commodus. AD 180: Herodian *Roman History*. 1.6.8-9. Caracalla. AD 213: Cassius Dio *Historia Romana*. 78.14. Severus Alexander. AD 234: Herodian *Roman History*. 6.7.9.
[691] *RIB* 1.882-883, 1036, 1593-1594, 1576; Birley 2007; Clay 2007; Tomlin and Hassall 2003.

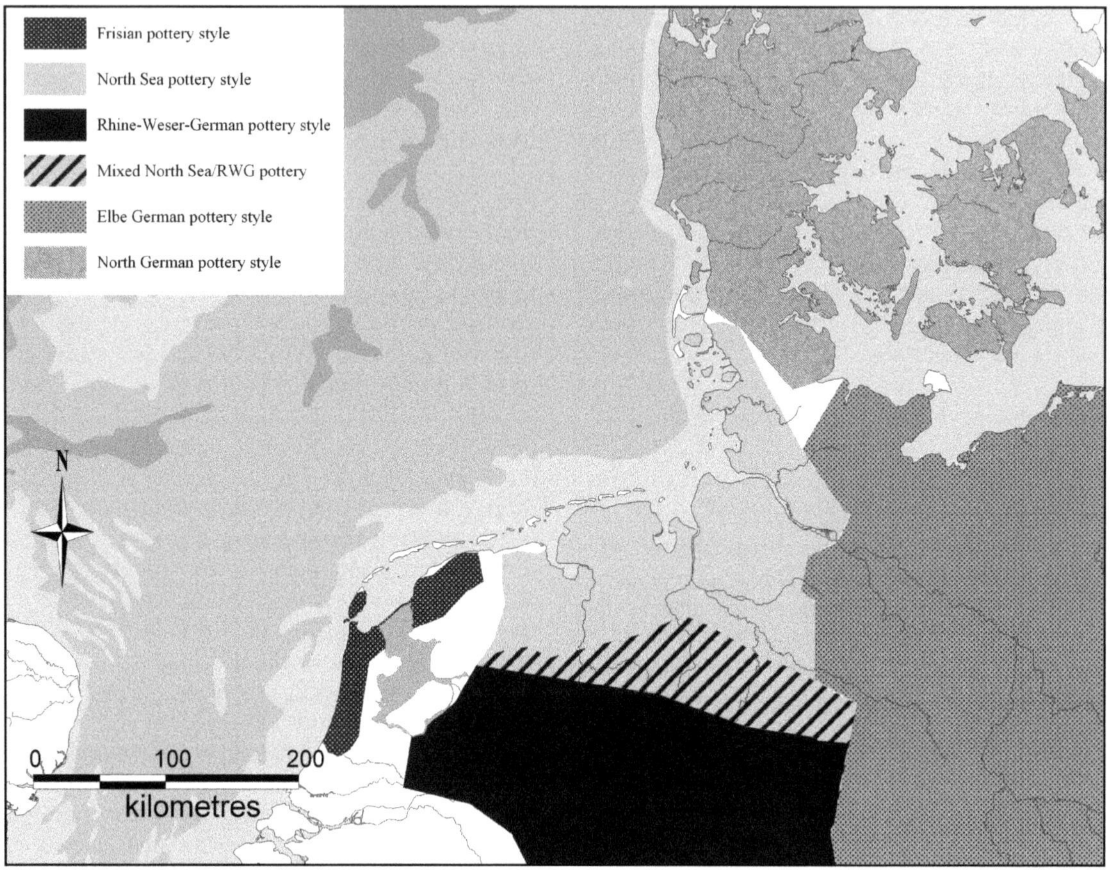

Fig. 5.6. Pottery style groups in the Eastern North Sea region c. AD 1-250 (Data from: Taayke 1997, Abbs. 7-8; Mildenberger 1989, Abb. 10-11; Schmid 1981, Abb. 116).

Netherlands, particularly that of Noord Holland (**Fig. 5.6**).[692]

The probability is that the majority of the *denarii* from northwest Germany also arrived directly as political payments designed to secure peace with the Germanic tribes of this region, particularly the troublesome Chauci and Chatti. Some of the payments to the Chauci were probably transferred via the North Sea by either Roman, or more likely, Chaucian 'envoys'.

Consideration will now be given to the south Scandinavian material. There is a notable group of *denarii* from Denmark (1572 *denarii* excluding Bornholm) and of the twenty recorded Danish *denarius* hoards thirteen close between AD 161-195, whilst a further six close between AD 199-223.[693] Of even greater significance is the sudden occurrence of large quantities of gold and silver ornaments, particularly silver brooches and gold arm and finger rings, and military fittings in third-century graves and weapon deposits throughout southern Scandinavia.[694] These objects were of Scandinavian manufacture, but they attest to a large influx of precious metal, which must ultimately have derived from the Roman Empire, from at least the end of the second or beginning of the third century AD.

Other Roman imports reached southern Scandinavia in quantity as well. There is a huge peak in the number of imported copper-alloy and glass vessels found in Danish graves dating to the first half of the third century AD (**Fig. 3.16**). The imports of this date were almost exclusively manufactured in the northwestern continental parts of the Roman Empire, in either Belgica or the Rhine provinces. Within Scandinavia these vessels are largely restricted to Denmark and overwhelmingly concentrate in rich graves on southeast Zealand, which appears to have the densest concentration of these goods from the entire *Barbaricum* (**Figs. 5.7-8**).[695] Roman long-swords (*spathae*), many of which bear Roman makers-names, or stamps, also reached Scandinavia in large quantities. They are present in several Danish weapon deposits that date to the first half of the third century. Ilkjær has demonstrated that weapon deposits of this date represent the remains of defeated armies who had invaded western Denmark from Norway, or western Sweden. 193 *spathae* have been recovered from Illerup deposits A and B and at least 66 have been excavated at Vimose C. This suggests that Roman swords would have been relatively commonplace amongst the equipment of northern

[692] Jobey 1979; Wilmott 2009, 273-275; Carol van Driel Murray, pers. Comm. 2006; Ernst Taayke, pers. Comm. 2007.

[693] Kromann 1989, 26; Horsnæs 2003; 2008; Nielsen 1989.

[694] Lund Hansen 1995, 209-240; 2001; Plahter *et al.* 1995; Storgaard 2003; Jørgensen *et al.* 2003; Ilkjær, 2002, 100; Carnap-Bornheim and Ilkjær 1996-7; Pauli Jensen *et al.* 2003.

[695] Lund Hansen 1987.

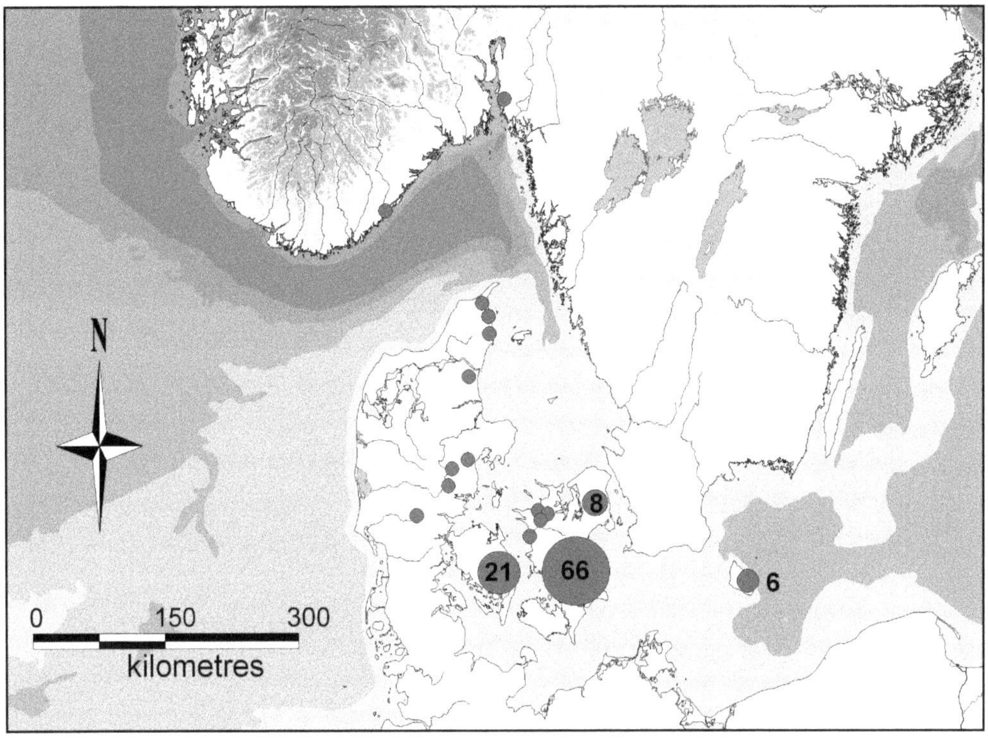

Fig. 5.7. Distribution of copper-alloy vessels in southern Scandinavia during phase C1b (c. AD 210/220-250/260) (after Lund Hansen 1987, Karte 25).

barbarian armies at this time. Compare, for example, the number of swords found at Illerup A and B (193) to the number of lance and spearheads (1228) found at the same sites.[696]

The key question is: how did this material get to Scandinavia? Several scholars have suggested that it came to southeast Zealand via a direct North Sea route that was instigated by the Romans. According to these views the Roman imports are either seen as political payments sent by the Roman state to the Baltic in order to secure an alliance with a south Scandinavian power based on Zealand, or as articles of trade.[697] I find these interpretations unlikely. The Roman state would surely not have sent large quantities of goods by ship all the way to the Baltic in order to actively cultivate an alliance with barbarians. Trade is also unlikely; in contrast to parts of the *Barbaricum* closer to the Roman frontiers where trade was probably occurring, *terra sigillata* is rare in Scandinavia. Perhaps more significantly, the one product which might actually have stimulated such a long-distance trade was amber and this only reached the northwestern Empire in fairly small quantities, nowhere near the levels at which it is found at Aquileia and other places along the central European amber route (see p.124).

Another strong possibility, which may in future turn out to be correct, is that the Roman material reached Scandinavia indirectly via intermediate Germanic groups following trade in the border areas. Whilst an examination of the distribution maps of imported Roman copper-alloy and glass vessels from late second- and, particularly, early third-century contexts across the *Barbaricum* suggests that there was a special concentration in Scandinavia we should bear in mind that this may be more a factor of representivity than a reflection of the real situation (**Fig. 5.8**).[698] Roman copper-alloy and glass vessels and swords, as well as precious metal objects, predominantly appear in areas with archaeologically visible burial traditions, particularly richly furnished inhumations, which in the early third century are mainly encountered on Zealand. Weapon deposits are also a Scandinavian phenomenon. The apparent Scandinavian concentration of these types of import may therefore be misleading and Roman vessels and swords might well have been just as, or more common, in the central parts of the *Barbaricum* where they are less well represented archaeologically. A re-mapping of the late second- and third-century Hemmoor bucket vessel type suggests that the Scandinavian concentration may actually be less significant than often assumed (see **Fig. 5.10**). A clear way of illustrating these dangers is the fact that more third-century Roman copper-alloy vessels and swords are currently known from Scandinavia than from within the Empire itself.

These problems of representivity mean that we must be wary about arguing for a direct connection, but I suspect that one did exist. Even bearing in mind these limitations the group of early third-century imports from Scandinavia

[696] Rald 1994; Ilkjær 1990; 2002; 2003; Lund Hansen 2003b.
[697] Lund Hansen 1987; Grane 2007; Storgaard 2003; Bursche 2008.
[698] Lund Hansen 1987; Eggers 1951; Fulford 1985; Hedeager 1978; 1987.

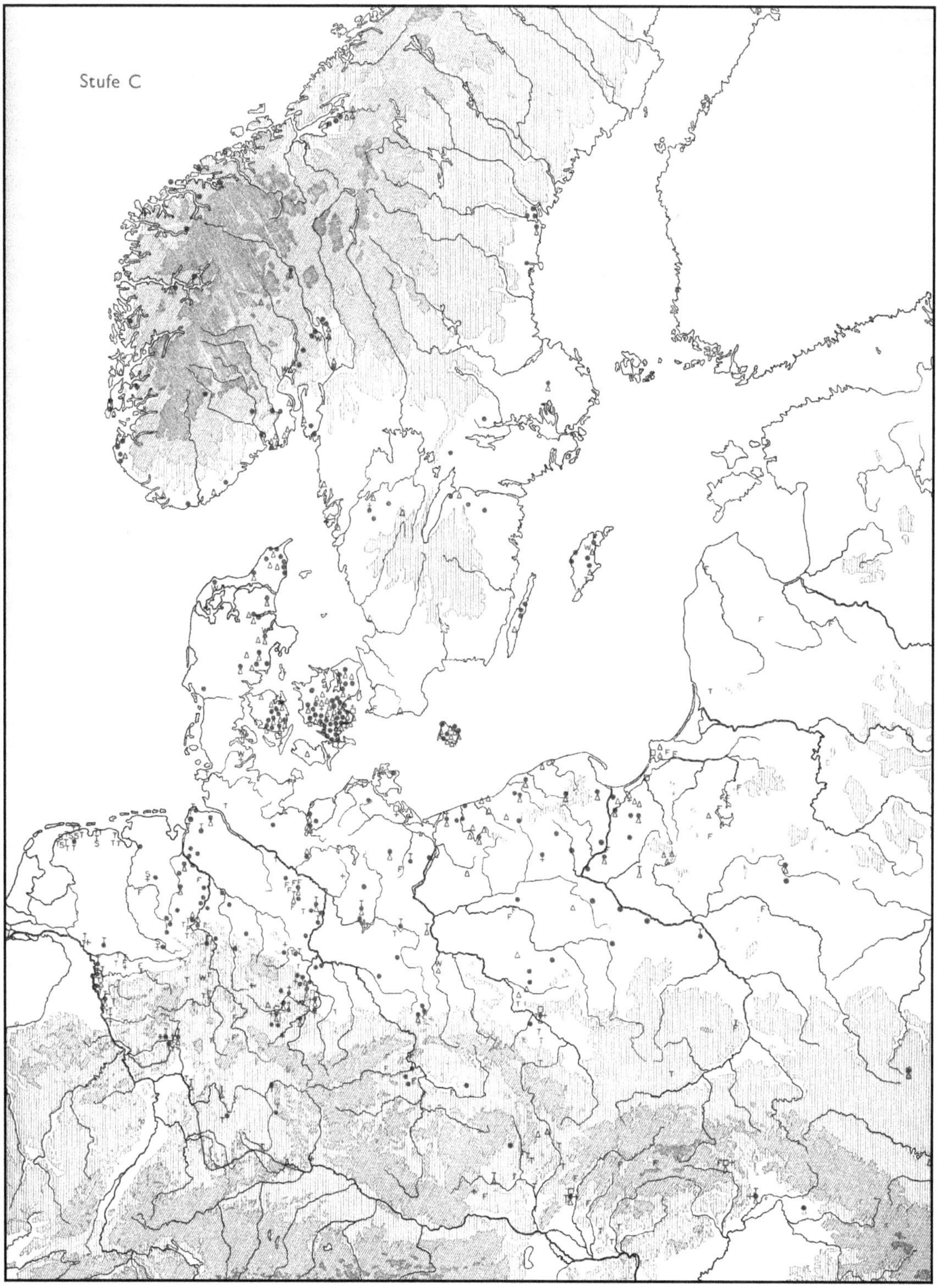

Δ = Glass vessel; • = Bronze vessel; W = Weapon; T = *Terra sigillata*; F = *Fibula*;
S = Statuette.

Fig. 5.8. Eggers (1951, Karte 6) distribution map of Roman imports in the Barbaricum during the Later Roman Iron Age (c. AD 150/160-375).

does appear to be particularly large and varied.[699] Furthermore, there are several cultural features which suggest that individuals from southern Scandinavia were present in the Roman frontier region at this time. These include the development of runic script; the earliest known runic inscription is on a wooden comb in the Vimose 2 weapon deposit, which is dated to the beginning of the second half of the second century AD. Further early inscriptions, apparently recording owners or makers names, have also been identified on a handful of weapons from the early third-century weapon deposits at Illerup, Vimose and Thorsbjerg and on five silver rosette

[699] Lund Hansen 1987, 144-151.

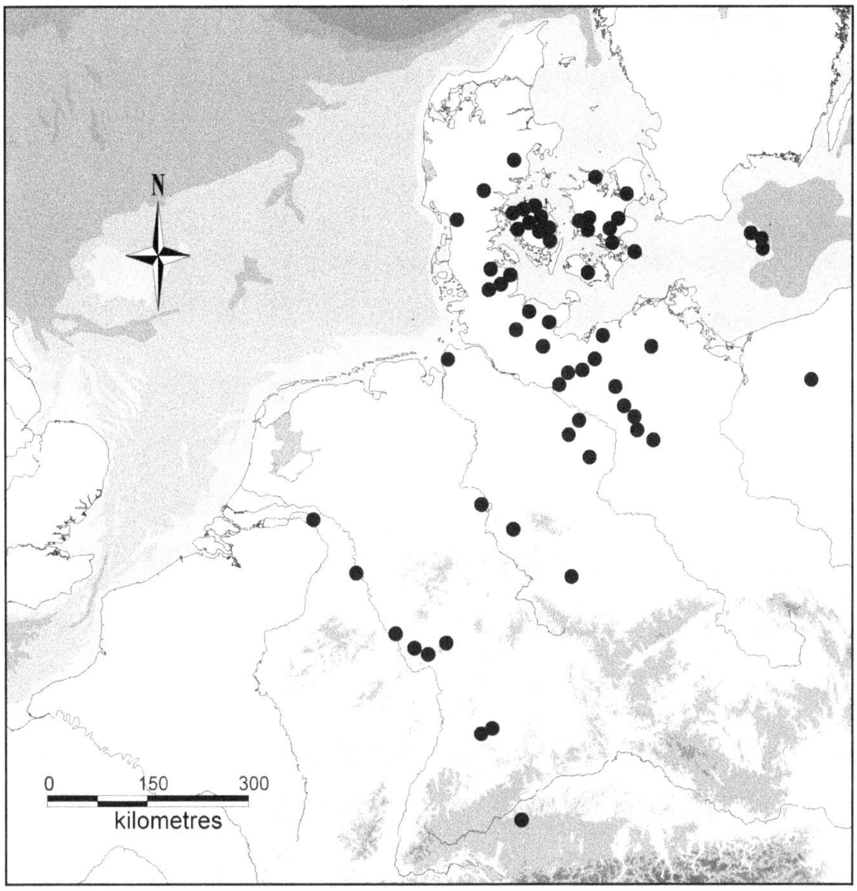

Fig. 5.9. Sites with Almgren VII, Series 4 brooches (after Böhme 1972, Abb. 4).

brooches from third-century women's graves throughout the Baltic. Whilst there are many notable differences, the runic alphabet was undoubtedly derived from the Latin alphabet, specifically the old Roman cursive script of pre-AD 200.[700] In addition, sections of late second- or third-century stone roads have been excavated at two sites in Denmark that are seemingly based on, and inspired by, Roman models.[701] Evidence from the weapon deposits also suggests that from the later second century Scandinavian armies began to develop organisational features similar to the Roman army, such as including archers, cavalry and surgeons.[702]

Rather than viewing this direct contact as occurring through Roman instigated political subsidies or trade, we should surely see it as being instigated by the Scandinavians themselves. That the Roman imports represent booty from Scandinavian raids on the Empire is one possibility that should not be dismissed outright, but the most plausible suggestion is that Scandinavians came to the Empire to serve as auxiliaries in the Roman army and subsequently returned home, bringing Roman goods with them.[703] Certainly, there are considerable numbers of late second- and third-century North Germanic brooches in the Roman forts along the Rhine and in the *Agri Decumates* (**Fig. 5.9**). Their North Germanic distribution includes southern Scandinavia and they clearly attest to the presence of North Germanic mercenaries, possibly of Scandinavian origin, along the Rhine *limes*.[704] Runes are also best explained as originating in a Roman military context where literacy would have been pervasive, particularly amongst the officers.[705]

It is possible that the Scandinavians maintained these links via a direct North Sea route, but I suspect an overland route to have been far more likely. The most probable context for the origin of the relationship was the Marcomannic wars, when Scandinavians were probably amongst the barbarian forces attacking Rome's Danube frontier. Evidence for this comes from the rich grave at Mušov in Moravia, which represents the burial of a powerful barbarian leader. Two gold pendants amongst the grave goods are best paralleled in Denmark and may represent the presence of a Scandinavian woman in the grave.[706] Furthermore, the gold Kolben arm ring type, which was produced in Scandinavia from at least the early third-century AD onwards, had its origin in the Ukraine and appears to have been a symbol of rank amongst the Sarmatian aristocracy.[707] There is also a

[700] Rausing 1992; Moltke 1985; Stoklund 2003.
[701] Nørgård Jørgensen 2003.
[702] Pauli Jensen *et al.* 2003; Frölich 2003.
[703] C.f. Grane 2007; Rausing 1987; 1992; Storgaard 2001; 2003.
[704] Böhme 1972; Beckmann 1995; Grane 2007.
[705] Rausing 1992; Stoklund 2003.
[706] Peška 2008; Grane 2007, 62-80; Storgaard 2003, 116.
[707] Lund Hansen 2001, 160-163; Storgaard 2003, 116.

Sarmatian ornament in one of the early third-century AD graves at Himlingøje on Zealand.[708] During the Marcomannic wars, Scandinavian forces probably entered into a treaty arrangement with Rome whereby one of the conditions was delivery of troops for service in the Roman army. This practice of barbarian groups providing troops for the Romans is well attested in the historical records of the Marcomannic wars.[709]

Further support for the direct overland route is that the Germanic elite of the Later Roman period was highly mobile and that Scandinavian peoples were well capable of covering long distances overland. Clear evidence comes from graves of the second half of the third century AD, which demonstrate a strong link between southern Scandinavia, specifically Funen, and Thuringia in central Germany (see p. 143). Furthermore, very strong direct relations were maintained over long distances between the Goths in southeast Europe and people from Denmark during the second half of the third and the fourth centuries (see p. 143).

Lastly, we should bear in mind that the Stevns peninsula of southeast Zealand, where the majority of Roman imports concentrate, does not appear to be well situated for controlling Scandinavian trade, or political contacts, with the Roman world, which come from the North Sea. Surely the location of Stevns and the power of the southeast Zealand elite are much better seen in terms of contact with the nearby north German coast and the subsequent overland routes to the Roman frontier.

Thus, the Scandinavian material is probably not of direct relevance to a consideration of North Sea connectivity. Whilst we should not entirely rule out the possible existence of a late second- and early third-century maritime link between the mouth of the Rhine and the Baltic, I propose that the strong connections between Scandinavia and the Roman Empire are best seen in terms of direct overland links, involving the participation of Scandinavian troops as auxiliaries in the forts of the Rhine *limes* during the later second and early third century as a result of treaties established during the Marcomannic wars, and which saw the subsequent movement of troops between the Rhine and Scandinavia via the modern German parts of the *Barbaricum*.

Roman copper-alloy (*aes*) coins, specifically *sestertii* (159 examples), are present in the northern Netherlands in some quantity. These primarily date to the Antonine period down to c. AD 190 with a few early third-century examples.[710] A*es* coins of this period have also been found along the northwest German coast in small quantities.[711] In contrast to the precious metal coins, the presence of *aes* coin in these regions is best explained through trade with the Empire. Bursche has formerly argued that some of a large group of *aes* from Lithuania dating c. AD 170-253 reached their destination from the Rhineland via a direct North Sea/Baltic trade route; however, a north Italian origin for these coins now seems more probable, though the matter is by no means resolved.[712]

In his detailed study of the imported material from the northern Netherlands and the northwest German states of Lower Saxony and Schleswig-Holstein, Erdrich suggests that a very large quantity of copper alloy vessels reached the region in the late second century AD (c.f. **Figs. 5.8, 5.10**). These consisted primarily of Hemmoor buckets (E55-65), which were regularly used as urns for cremation burials in northwest Germany, but also certain types of pans and filters (E161) and other types of buckets and basins as well (E44-49, 79-87).[713] Finds of Hemmoor buckets within the Empire suggest that the type was produced in Belgica and the Rhine provinces between the mid- to late second century AD and the mid- to late third century AD, whilst they are encountered in graves outside the Empire dated throughout the third century AD.[714] There is thus nothing inherent in the dating of the vessels to restrict them solely to the later second century AD. Erdrich makes this suggestion on the basis of the associated *terra sigillata*, which in coastal northwest Germany and the north Dutch province of Groningen ceases c. AD 200. In this he is probably correct, but we cannot apply this dating to Friesland, where fragments of copper-alloy vessels have been noted amongst settlement finds, as *terra sigillata* continues to arrive in quantity here down to c. AD 260. In Friesland copper-alloy vessels were probably arriving throughout the late second and early to mid-third century.

Erdrich has argued that the copper-alloy vessels principally reached the northwest *Barbaricum* as a result of political payments and as the personal possessions of auxiliaries who had returned home after service in the Roman army.[715] There may be something in this, but it is unlikely that the Frisian material can be related to returning mercenaries, as these are epigraphically attested in northern Britain whilst the copper-alloy vessels were clearly produced in northern Gaul and the Rhine provinces. Erdrich suggests that Chaucian soldiers were stationed on the Danube *limes* following their defeat by Didius Julianus, but this fails to explain why the copper-alloy vessels derive from the northwestern Empire. It is unlikely that the Roman state would have stationed Chaucian soldiers on the Rhine limes, which they had just been attacking.

I believe trade is the most likely explanation. The presence of fairly large numbers of copper-alloy vessels in the northern Netherlands and northwest Germany together with other material, such as *terra sigillata* and

[708] Storgaard 2003, 172.
[709] Cassius Dio *Historia Romana*. 71.11-13, 16, 72.2-3; *Historia Augusta. Marcus Aurelius*. 21.7.
[710] Van der Vin 1996, 361, Tab. 4; 1999; 2000, 636.
[711] Berger 1992, 152-156, 164-170, Abb. 54, 57; 1995, 106; Kromann, 1989, 265; 1995, Fig. 13.3-13.4.
[712] Bursche 1989; 1996; 2006; Reece 2008; Sidrys 2001.
[713] Erdrich 2001, 44-47, 103-128.
[714] Erdrich 1995a; 1995b; 2001, 44-47; Notte 1989; Bodart 1997, 162-163; Mould 2004; Berke 1990, 47-8; Werner 1936; Lund Hansen 1987.
[715] Erdrich 2001.

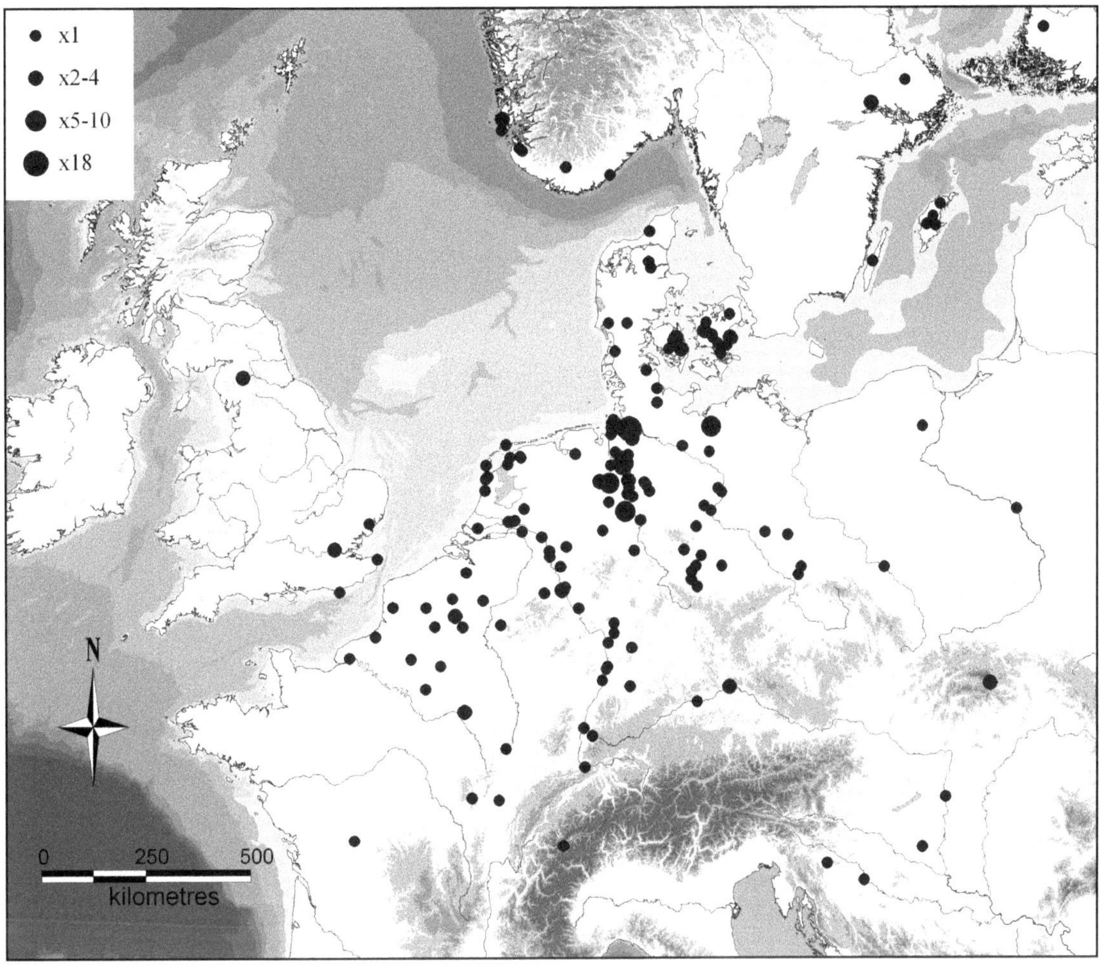

Fig. 5.10. Distribution of Hemmoor buckets (E55-65, excluding E63) (Data from Notte 1989; Erdrich 1995a, Abb. 8; Lund Hansen 1987, 461-462; Mould 2004, 374-376; Gerrard 2009; Bodart 1997; Kramer 2001).

lava querns, supports this. Much of this trade probably took place via the North Sea; there is a strong distribution of vessels along the north Dutch and northwest German coasts. In addition, a Hemmoor bucket found on the seabed off the Frisian island of Terschelling is likely to derive from a shipwreck.[716] The distribution also suggests that part of the material from the north-west German coast arrived overland, via the Lippe and Weser valleys. Of course, we should bear in mind that some of the northwest German material may actually have arrived as a result of late second-century raiding by Chauci and Chatti on Belgica and the Lower Rhine provinces. A huge hoard of more than 700kg of iron, copper-alloy (including dozens of copper-alloy vessels) and silver has been dredged from the middle-Rhine at Neupotz and is dated to the 270s.[717] This almost certainly represents loot from an Alamannic raid, which sunk as the raiders were crossing back across the Rhine. The hoard has parallels elsewhere, such as nearby Hagenbach, and demonstrates that one of the principal aims of Germanic raids was to obtain as much metal from within the Empire as possible.

Other copper alloy objects imported from the Roman Empire include statuettes. A particularly large number have been recovered from settlements (terpen) in the coastal regions of the northern Netherlands, principally Friesland. Statuettes are also occasionally found in northwest Germany, though the distribution here does not necessarily imply a maritime supply route (**Fig. 5.11**). The majority of examples date from the second to the mid-third centuries AD, although first-century examples are also known. They primarily appear to have been made in the northwestern part of the continental Empire, though a horse and rider statuette recently found in Friesland might well belong to the series of rider-god statuettes produced in eastern Britain and have been brought back by a Frisian auxiliary who served in Britain.[718]

A few enamelled plate brooches of the late second and third centuries are present in Friesland and northwest Germany.[719] Some of these were probably imported via the North Sea, probably through trade, though some may have been obtained by Chaucian raids, or represented the personal possessions of individuals who had spent time in

[716] Kramer 2001.
[717] Historisches Museum der Pfalz Speyer 2007; Künzl 1993; Grane 2007, 106-107.

[718] Busch 1995, 289-323; Galestin 1994; Evert Kramer (Friesmuseum), pers. Comm. 2007; Mackintosh 1995.
[719] Thomas 1966, Taschenkarte 1; Galestin 2003a, 473; Erdrich 1999, 176; 2001, 60.

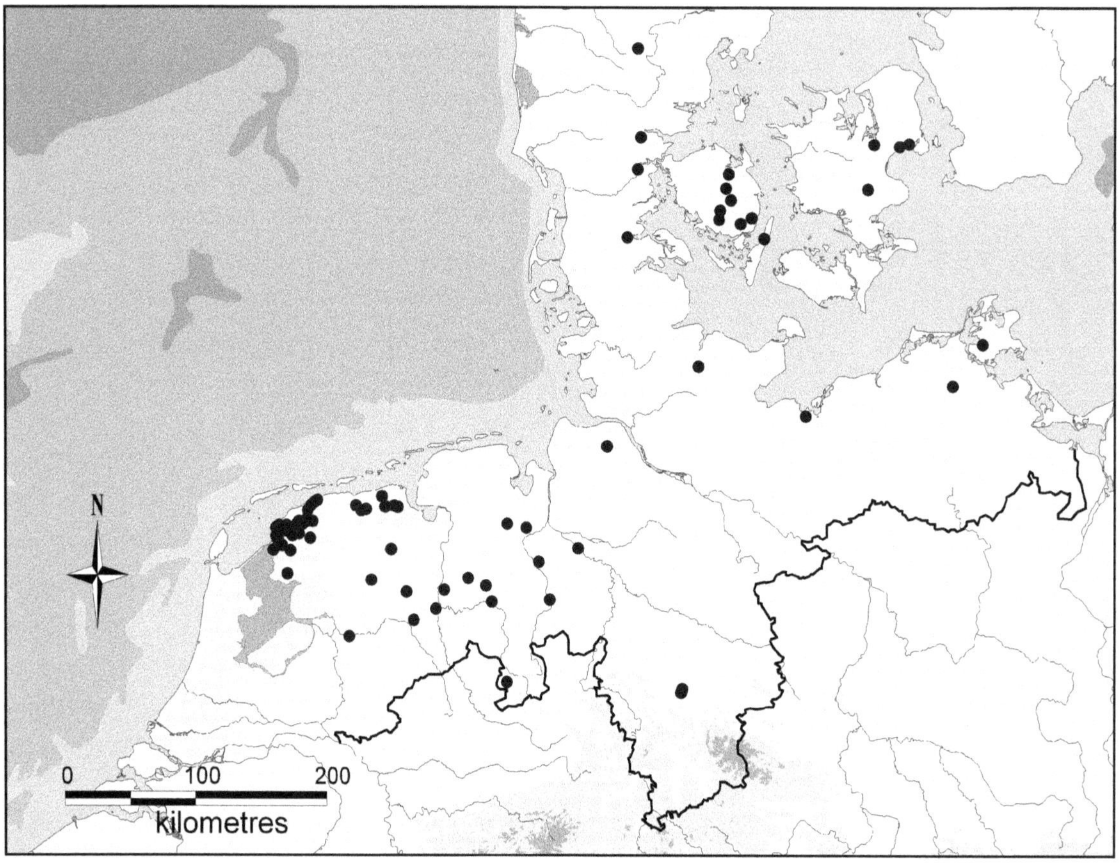

Fig. 5.11. Distribution of Roman statuettes in part of the northwest Barbaricum (the Netherlands north of the Rhine, Lower Saxony, Mecklenburg-Vorpommern, Schleswig-Holstein and Denmark) (Data from Zadoks-Josephus Jitta et al. 1967; Galestin 1994; Erdrich 2002, 217; Voss 1998, 132-133; Erdrich and Carnap-Bornheim 2004, 127; Salskov Roberts 1994).

the Empire, perhaps as auxiliaries. An enamelled plate brooch from a grave at Loxstedt on the coast of Lower Saxony is likely to be of British origin, though examples of this type have been identified in the continental northwest Empire as well (**Fig. 4.35**). How it got to Lower Saxony is hard to ascertain. One might speculate that it arrived as a result of a Chaucian raid on the southeast British coast.

Pottery

In the coastal regions of the northern Netherlands and Lower Saxony fairly large quantities of *terra sigillata* have been found, primarily in settlement mounds (terpen), but in Lower Saxony vessels were often used as cremation urns as well (**Tab. 5.1**). From Friesland c. 2,600 sherds, 472 with decoration, have been recovered from c. 80 terpen. It is rare to find sherds which came from the same vessel, which suggests the movement of considerable numbers of pots. Slightly smaller quantities of *sigillata* are known from Noord Holland, Groningen and Lower Saxony, whilst the ware is very rare north and east of the Elbe.

It is worth bearing in mind that the relatively high figures from Friesland are primarily a result of the quarrying away of the terpen for use as fertiliser during the nineteenth and early twentieth centuries. Workmen were rewarded for each piece of *sigillata* that they found, doubly so for decorated pieces.[720] It is highly probable that the largely unexcavated terpen in Lower Saxony actually contain comparable quantities. Indeed, large-scale excavation at Feddersen Wierde revealed over 200 sherds.[721] In Groningen, meanwhile, the major excavation at Ezinge produced over 100 sherds.[722]

Erdrich's study of the dates derived from stamped and decorated wares indicates that in Lower Saxony and Groningen *terra sigillata* supply was a phenomenon of the last third of the second century, with a cut-off occurring before AD 200 (**Tab. 5.2**).[723] These regions were occupied by the Chauci (c.f. **Fig. 5.6**). In the Frisian-occupied regions of Friesland and Noord Holland, meanwhile, *terra sigillata* supply continued at a high rate down to c. AD 260, though much more so in Friesland than in Noord Holland.[724] Whilst small quantities of mid-second-century wares are present in all the afore-mentioned regions the majority probably arrived in the later second century along with the larger amounts of later second-century material.

[720] Volkers 1999, 151.
[721] Erdrich 2002, XXI-02-14/3.3-3.38.
[722] Glasbergen 1944.
[723] Erdrich 2001, 50-58, 103-131.
[724] Galestin 2005, 222 and Tab. 2; Volkers 1991.

	No. of sherds	No. of vessels	No. of decorated sherds	No. of sites with *terra sigillata*
Noord Holland	?	?	65	?
Friesland	c. 2600	?	472	c. 80
Groningen	c. 400	c. 300	75	15
Lower Saxony	?	?	51	84
Schleswig-Holstein	?	?	13	5

Tab. 5.1. Terra sigillata finds from the coastal provinces of the northern Netherlands and northwest Germany (Data from: Galestin and Volkers 1992, Tab. 1; Volkers 1999; Galestin 2005; Erdrich 2001, 50-51, 151-163, Tab. 3; 2002, 212-213; Erdrich and Carnap-Bornheim 2004, 123-124; Glasbergen 1944).

	AD 145-165	AD 160-190	AD 190-210	AD 210-230	AD 230-270
Noord Holland	9	17	3	3	1
Friesland	18	70	33	55	26
Groningen	2	13	2	0	1
Lower Saxony	3	15	1	0	1

Tab. 5.2. Number of dateable Trier terra sigillata sherds in the northern Netherlands and Lower Saxony (After Galestin 2010, Tab. 2. Based on data from: Erdrich 2001, 56, 129; Volkers 1991).

Volkers has argued that the Frisian *terra sigillata* was looted from abandoned Roman forts along the Lower Rhine *limes* during the Late Roman and Early Medieval periods. This argument was made on the basis of excavations at Wijnaldum, which is the only Frisian terp to have undergone excavation according to modern archaeological methods. Here *terra sigillata* was absent from layers pre-dating the Late Roman period. Indeed, out of twenty-nine sherds, which could be contextually dated, none was found to be earlier than AD 250 and twenty were found in early Medieval contexts.[725] But the looting hypothesis should be dismissed however. The prevalence of *terra sigillata* at sites right along the North Sea coast, including Roman-period settlements and graves in Lower Saxony, tells against it. More likely the presence of *terra sigillata* in chronologically late contexts at Wijnaldum is to be explained by disturbance of earlier layers, or by the curation of pots and sherds, which, judging by the many instances of sherd reuse, seem to have been accorded a special role by the inhabitants of the terpen.[726]

The vast majority of *terra sigillata* in Friesland and Noord Holland derive from the East Gaulish industries, in particular Trier and Rheinzabern, with only twenty-seven sherds from Friesland deriving from the Central Gaulish workshops at Lezoux. A study of the percentage of wares from different sources, and of the different form-types, suggests that the *terra sigillata* from Noord Holland and Friesland compares closely to native settlements, such as Rijswijk, which lie in the southern Netherlands within the borders of the Empire. Meanwhile, clear differences are apparent in the *terra sigillata* assemblages of these 'native' sites and those of the Roman military within the Lower Rhine region.[727] This demonstrates that the *terra sigillata* from Noord Holland and Friesland arrived at its destination via similar supply mechanisms as at the native sites in the southern Netherlands within the Empire. In this case trade with the Lower Rhine region via the North Sea and Lake Flevo is certain. A few sites possess particularly large assemblages, for example, twelve sites in Friesland have over 50 sherds, including six with over 100 sherds. At the top is Cornjum, near the mouth of the former Middelzee, with 572 sherds, whilst Hatsum I and Hatsum II, which are situated in central Westergo, have 367 and 250 sherds respectively. These sites may have played an important role in the marketing of the ware within Friesland and its onward distribution to other sites.[728]

Meanwhile, in Lower Saxony and Groningen, whilst there is a predominance of East Gaulish wares, Central Gaulish ware is present in curiously large quantities, comprising 27 and 20 % of the total decorated wares respectively.[729] This high proportion of Central Gaulish ware is not paralleled in Friesland or Noord Holland, or indeed, at native sites in the southern Netherlands within

[725] Volkers 1999, 152, Tab. 2.

[726] C.f. Galestin 2010, 71-72.

[727] Volkers 1991, Tab. 1; Erdrich 2001, 112-115, Tabs. 7-8.

[728] Galestin and Volkers, 1992; Galestin 2005, 224, Tab. 3; 2010.

[729] Erdrich 2001, 50-51.

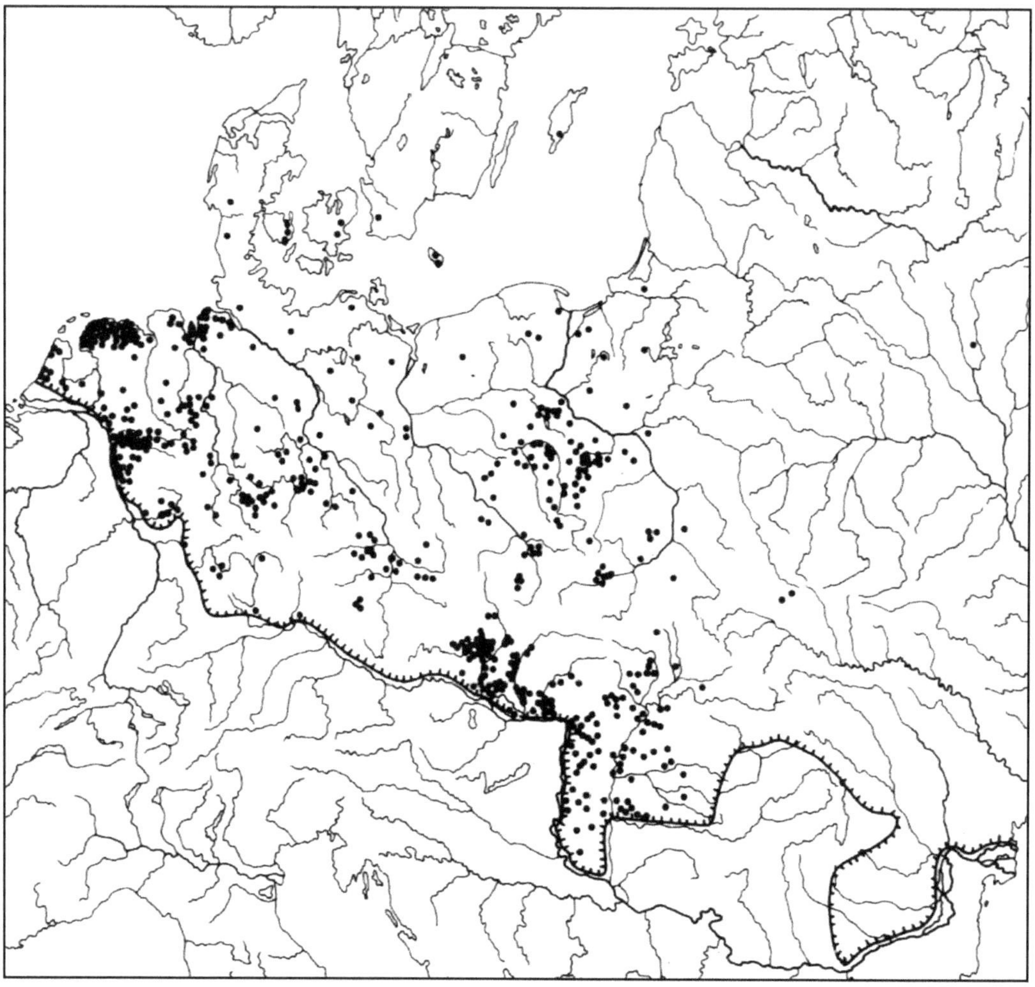

Fig. 5.12. Distribution of terra sigillata in the Barbaricum (Lund Hansen 1987, Fig. 127, after Godlowski 1985, Abb. 2).

the Empire. On this basis Erdrich has argued for a direct link between this area of the North Sea coast and the Middle Danube, where Central Gaulish and East Gaulish wares are present in similar proportions to Groningen and Lower Saxony.[730] He argues that this *sigillata* was brought back by Chaucian auxiliaries who had served in the Roman army, though I have already raised objections to this theory (see p. 118). I propose that the Central Gaulish ware was in fact obtained by the Chauci from either the Rhine provinces, where Central Gaulish ware was in fact present in significant quantities throughout the second century AD, or the coastal regions of Belgica, or, less likely, Britain, where this ware was dominant. Perhaps it was booty from the Chaucian raids in the early 170s, though a Chaucian trade link with these areas is possible as well. The bulk of the East Gaulish ware, meanwhile, was obtained by the Chauci through similar trade mechanisms as the East Gaulish ware in the northern Netherlands. Much of it probably came by sea, but the presence of notable quantities of *terra sigillata* along the Lippe and Weser valleys suggests that overland trade routes played a contributory role as well (see **Fig. 5.12**).

Aside from the *terra sigillata*, imported Roman pottery is, surprisingly, extremely rare in the northwest *Barbaricum*, though excavations at Wijnaldum in Friesland turned up a late second- to mid-third-century Trier ware vessel, a flagon frequently encountered at Nijmegen, and Roman tiles of second- to third-century date, which may have arrived as ships' ballast.[731] The main exception is Noord Holland, nearest the Imperial frontier. Here a number of coastal sites possess small assemblages of wheel-thrown Roman pottery, which probably arrived by sea from the mouths of the Rhine or Scheldt. The majority of this is Lowlands Ware, a coarse wheel-thrown pottery with a sandy fabric, typically reduced, but sometimes oxidised. This has recently been petrologically provenanced to the Bergen-op-zoom region near the Scheldt estuary in the southern Netherlands and is distributed throughout the North Sea coastal regions of Belgium and the southern Netherlands. Lowlands Ware was produced between c. AD 70 and the fourth century AD, though production reached a peak between the second to mid-third centuries. Most of the Lowlands Ware found at Den Burg on Texel can be dated to phases belonging to the late second century AD onwards.[732]

[730] Erdrich 2001, 115-117, Tab. 10.

[731] Galestin 1999.

[732] De Clercq and Degryse 2008; Van der Linden, forthcoming.

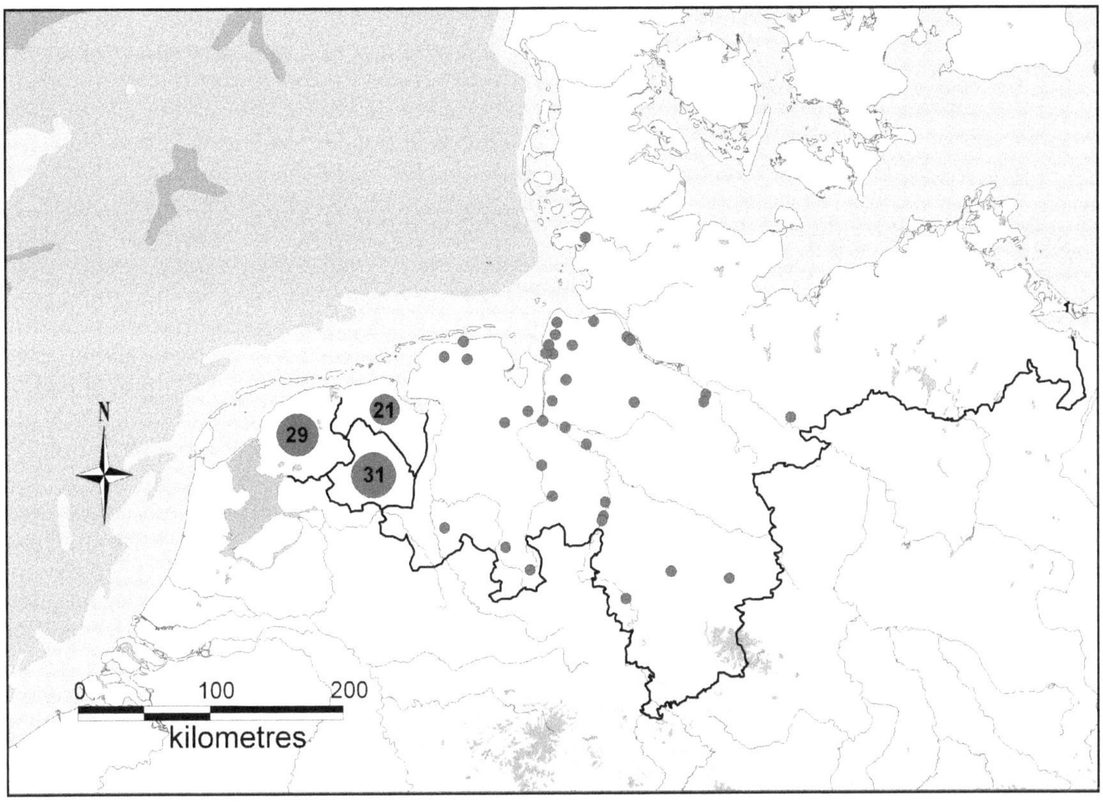

Fig. 5.13. Late Iron Age and Roman-period sites with lava querns in part of the northwest Barbaricum (see Appendix 11). Constructed using data provided by Ernst Taayke (Noordelijk Archeologisch Depot Nuis, pers. Comm. 2009) and from Erdrich (1995a, Abb. 9; 2002, 216-217) and Voss (1998, 132).

Lava querns

Lava querns from the quarries at Mayen on the middle Rhine were also imported to the northwest *Barbaricum* via the North Sea (**Fig. 5.13**). I have previously discussed the evidence for a considerable import of lava querns to the northern Netherlands during the Late Augustan and Tiberian period (see pp. 49-50); however, some querns clearly post-date that episode. The Westerwijtwerd type, with a flange at the outside of its upper stone, developed c. AD 30/50 and has been noted at numerous sites in the northern Netherlands and at a few locations in northwest Germany (see Appendix 11).[733] Precise contextual datings from these regions are rare and whilst two examples from the northern Netherlands appear to belong in the first century AD, the majority lie in the second and third centuries AD.

In addition, lava fragments at Feddersen Wierde have been found in association with *terra sigillata* dated to the late second century AD, whilst fragments are also found in an erosion layer dating to the late second to early third century AD.[734] On this basis we can propose that the majority of the lava querns from northwest Germany and a large number of examples from the northern Netherlands were imported during the late second, and perhaps the early third, century AD.

The quantities involved are hard to assess, but appear to have been considerable. The lava quern assemblage at Feddersen Wierde, for example, comprised 116 fragments, weighing over 150 kg.[735] It is best to interpret these querns in terms of trade. A coastal trend in their distribution suggests the importance of a North Sea maritime supply route; however, the presence of many finds inland in Drenthe and Overijssel in the eastern Netherlands, and along the Weser and its tributaries, implies that overland trade routes were also of great importance.

Exports from the Eastern North Sea coastal region

Coinage

An important re-export from the northwest *Barbaricum* may well have been the precious metal coinage, which, as discussed above (see pp. 113-114), was paid to barbarian groups by the Roman state in order to secure treaties and peace arrangements. These payments probably played an important role in facilitating these groups' entry to and participation in the Empire's monetised markets.

Agricultural products and fish

The most important exports from the Eastern North Sea coastal regions were probably traded agricultural products, grain and, more importantly, hides. As noted in the preceding chapter (see p. 97), the Roman military in

[733] Ernst Taayke, pers. Comm. 2009.

[734] Erdrich 2001, 117-120.

[735] Haarnagel 1979, 280; Erdrich 2001, 119.

the Lower Rhine region principally relied on grain imported from southern Belgium and northern France, but possibly from other areas within the Empire as well. Meat and hides, meanwhile, derived primarily from local communities in the Lower Rhine region. In the context of the peace treaties established in the aftermath of the Marcomannic wars the sources of hide supply may well have been extended across the frontier to include the communities of the northwest *Barbaricum*.

There are certainly hints that both population and agricultural production were increasing in the Eastern North Sea coastal regions throughout the second and into the first half of the third century. This meant that more products were potentially available for trade with the Empire; for example, on the basis of dateable native pottery, Taayke has demonstrated that in the north Dutch provinces of Friesland and Groningen there were increases in the number of occupied settlements from the pre-Roman Iron Age onwards, reaching a peak in the second and early third century AD prior to a serious decline in the second half of the third century AD.[736] Analysis of the number and size of settlement structures at Feddersen Wierde, in the coastal marshes of the Elbe-Weser triangle, suggests that population steadily increased from c. 40 at its foundation in the first century BC to a peak of c. 300 in the late second and early third centuries AD. The number of cattle similarly rises from c. 100 at the time of the settlements origin to a maximum of 443 in the late second and early third century.[737]

Fish also appear to have been exported from the northern Netherlands at this time. A votive stone found at Beetgum terp in Friesland was dedicated to the goddess HLUDANA by a group of *conductores piscatus*. These were very probably individuals from within the Empire who were engaged in supplying areas within the Empire with fish caught off the coast of the northern Netherlands. It is unclear whether the members of the *conductores piscatus* fished these waters themselves, or whether they purchased the fish from native fishermen. The presence of the word DEA dates the inscription to the time of the Nehalennia inscriptions of the late second and early third century.[738]

Amber

Several scholars have proposed that during the late second and early third century amber reached the northwest Empire in quantity via a direct Baltic-North Sea route, which circumvented and replaced the overland central European route following the disruptions of the Marcomannic wars.[739] Amber is certainly known in contexts of this date at sites in the Lower Rhine region of the Empire; for example, there are c. 246 Roman-period amber objects, primarily beads, in the Cologne museum, which probably derive from Cologne, and whilst most of these cannot be dated with precision a significant proportion of those that can appear to belong to the late second century AD or afterwards.[740] Carved amber objects have also been identified in late second-century AD graves at Heerlen in the southern Netherlands and at Noirmont in Belgium and from a third-century grave at Esch in the southern Netherlands.[741] However, the amount of amber found in the northwest Empire is simply too small to support the suggestion of a major re-orientation of the amber supply route. It pales in comparison with the massive quantities of amber excavated at Aquileia and elsewhere along the central European amber route. Suggestions that this latter route was abandoned due to the disruptions of the Marcomannic wars are also unfounded; amber continued to arrive via the central European route down to the mid-third century, although apparently on a decreasing scale.[742] Some of the small quantities of amber found in the Rhineland probably arrived indirectly from other parts of the Empire having ultimately travelled across Central Europe to the Danube; however, some may well have arrived via overland trade across the Rhine border. A small amount may even have been traded via the North Sea coastal regions of the northern Netherlands and northwest Germany.

In Britain, meanwhile, amber appears to be very rare in contexts of this period. There are only three objects from three sites which are securely of this date. However, this decline may be somewhat exaggerated. As Chris Going has pointed out, contexts of the first half of the third century AD are hard to recognise in the British archaeological record, primarily on account of the lack of pottery and coins that can be securely assigned to this phase.[743] There is nothing to suggest a direct trade route across the North Sea and, as in earlier phases, the amber finds from Britain will have arrived indirectly from elsewhere in the Empire.

Synthesis

The later second century witnessed a major increase in the scale of maritime connectivity in the Eastern North Sea system. This principally involved exchange between the Lower Rhine region of the Empire and the Eastern North Sea coast of the *Barbaricum* via the mouth of the Rhine and Lake Flevo. In the Frisian occupied areas of Noord Holland and Friesland, exchange with the Empire continued at a high level down to c. AD 260. In northwest Germany, meanwhile, there appears to have been a cut-off in contacts with the Empire sometime before AD 200.

In both of these areas a sizeable number of *denarii* entered in the later second century. These are best explained in terms of political payments made by the Roman state in order to secure peace treaties in the context of the Marcomannic wars and Antonine plague,

[736] Taayke 1996, 200; Gerrets 1999, 333.
[737] Randsborg 1991, Fig. 42; Haarnagel 1979; Kossack *et al.* 1984.
[738] Galestin 1997; 2005; Boeles 1951, Pl. 17.
[739] Lund Hansen 1987; Storgaard 2003; Bursche 1996.
[740] La Baume 1968.
[741] Mariën 1980, 260, 277, 279, Figs. 178, 194, 197; Lund Hansen 1987, 235-238, Fig. 151.
[742] Calvi 1996; 2005; Buora 1996; Lista 2007; La Baume 1968.
[743] Going 1992.

which had left the Empire's northern frontiers vulnerable. Other imports followed, including a small quantity of *aes* coin, statuettes and large numbers of lava querns, copper-alloy vessels and *terra sigillata* pottery, which virtually all derive from the northwestern parts of the continental Empire, particularly the Rhine provinces. These ceased to reach northwest Germany by AD 200, but continued to flow into Friesland until c. AD 260. All of these imports are best interpreted in terms of trade, although some of the northwest German material may have arrived as booty from Chaucian and Chattian raids. Exports, meanwhile, are harder to identify. We may suggest that Roman coin was re-exported, whilst agricultural products, particularly hides, and some fish, are a further strong possibility. Very small quantities of amber may also have entered the Empire via the coastal regions of the Eastern North Sea. The principal mechanism for the transfer of these exports was trade.

Finally, we must point out that whilst the North Sea routes were very important in the connections evident between the north Dutch and northwest German coasts and the Rhine regions of the Roman Empire they were not exclusively so. Overland exchange routes via the Eastern Netherlands and the Lippe and Weser valleys also played a not inconsiderable role. Recently many scholars have argued for the existence of a direct North Sea route to the Baltic through which large quantities of material reached a barbarian power on southern Zealand via either trade or political subsidies; however, I argue that this occurred via overland routes to the Rhine.[744] Transfer to southern Scandinavia via intermediate Germanic groups following trade in the border regions is one strong possibility, but I favour a direct connection that involved Scandinavian mercenaries serving as auxiliaries on the Rhine frontier and subsequently returning home across Germany.

The determinants of connective change

As in the Southern North Sea and Eastern Channel and the Atlantic systems, the principal determinants of connective change in this period were the dual effects of the Marcomannic wars and the Antonine plague (see pp. 110-112). These events conspired to leave the Empire's northern frontiers weakened and vulnerable. In an attempt to secure the frontiers both Marcus Aurelius and Commodus conceded to barbarian demands and made treaties with barbarian peoples that necessitated large payments of silver coin. This practice extended to the peoples across the Empire's northwest frontier with whom the Empire was now forced to engage with, having had minimal contact with them following the events of the Late Augustan-Tiberian period – the Varus battle and the Frisian revolt.[745]

The development of these peace treaties facilitated substantial cross-frontier trade relations. To a certain extent this trade may also have been stimulated by the injection of precious metal coin into the northwest *Barbaricum* as political payments, which contributed to the participation of the barbarians in the monetised market systems of the Empire. The continuation of trade between the Empire and the Frisian-occupied areas of the northern Netherlands down to c. AD 260 suggests that peaceful relations endured between these groups until the mid-third century. One problem is the apparent rupture in connections between northwest Germany and the Empire prior to AD 200. The explanation probably relates to a degeneration of relations between these two parties by the end of the second century. We know that Caracalla waged war against various Germanic tribes across the Rhine in AD 213, as did Maximinius in AD 235. The battlefield of Kalefeld, in southeast Lower Saxony, can probably be linked into Maximinius's campaign (see p. 113).

5.3. Maritime systems AD 165-260: a comparison

During the late second century AD connectivity in both the Southern North Sea and Eastern Channel and the Atlantic systems underwent a downturn from which they never recovered. State payments into, and possibly extractions from, Britain and overseas private trade all seem to have declined. I have related this to a major economic slump that affected the wider Empire, the causes of which were the Antonine plague, which led to demographic decreases and population flight, and the loss of precious metal as a consequence of vast payouts made to barbarian tribes during and after the Marcomannic wars and decreasing mining activity within the Empire. These latter factors led to devaluations in the coinage which accelerated over time and directly affected economic activity and trade.

The Eastern North Sea system, meanwhile, experienced significantly increasing connectivity during the late second century, with trade between the Frisians and the Empire continuing down to c. AD 260. Connectivity in the Eastern North system was, however, still well below the Southern North Sea and Eastern Channel and Atlantic systems. The reason for the change was the Roman military crisis caused by the Marcomannic wars, which led to a weakening of Rome's northern frontiers and consequently forced the Empire to engage politically with the barbarians beyond the northwestern frontiers. This took the form of cash payouts and trade followed in the wake of peace.

There is thus a clear link between connective change in both regions. Disease and warfare contributed to declining economic activity within the Empire, whilst at the same time forcing the Empire to engage politically with groups beyond its frontier. The principal agents of change were the Antonine plague and the Marcomannic wars, with the former event playing a major contributory role in the latter.

[744] Lund Hansen 1987; Grane 2007; Storgaard 2003; Bursche 1996; 2008.
[745] C.f. Erdrich 2001.

6. North Sea and Channel connectivity AD 260-409

6.1. The Southern North Sea and Channel systems

Introduction

Both the Southern North Sea and Eastern Channel and the Atlantic systems witnessed significant levels of connectivity during the Late Roman period, with a severe cut-off occurring after AD 409 following Britain's secession from the Roman Empire. It is hard to say whether connectivity underwent a change in scale in the Late Roman period. What is clear is that there was a substantial change in the nature of connectivity. There are far fewer imported products in Britain during the Later Roman period, though there is a large quantity of imported coin, principally found in civilian areas in southern Britain. Meanwhile, very large quantities of agricultural products were exported from Britain, as a result of taxation in kind, state purchase and probably purchase by private individuals. Evidently the northwestern continental Empire depended heavily upon Britain for its grain supply. The main factors underlying the Late Roman changes in connectivity were: political divisions occurring within the Empire, which disrupted internal long-distance trade networks; reductions in the British military garrison, which freed up a greater proportion of British agricultural surplus for export; increasing barbarian invasion and piracy, which led to economic and demographic decline in northern Gaul, particularly in rural areas, which led the military garrison and urban centres of this region to turn to Britain for their supplies; sea level rises, which intensified demographic and economic decline in coastal areas of the southern North Sea; and economic growth in central and southwest England, which was underlain by demands for a secure source of agricultural produce to feed the northwestern Empire and the consequent injection of coin to pay for this produce.

Continental imports

Coinage and Metals

Britain received large quantities of coin from continental mints between AD 260 and 406, with the exception of a ten-year gap during the revolt of Carausius and Allectus (AD 286-296) when Britain was separated from the central Empire. A study of coin site finds from Britain indicates that there were severe fluctuations, but these clearly coincided with the numerous changes in the precious metal content of the Late Roman coinage, which directly affected its value (**Fig. 6.1**). Put simply, large numbers of coins were lost when the coinage contained particularly low quantities of precious metal, whereas when the coinage was improved smaller quantities were lost as a consequence. Because of these extreme fluctuations it is very hard to assess any changes in the monetary value of coin imported to Britain during the course of the later third to early fifth centuries, or indeed in relation to the earlier part of the Roman period when a fairly stable, good-quality precious metal coinage formed the backbone of the Empire's monetary economy.

By AD 260 the currency system established under Augustus, which was based upon a tri-metallic division into gold, silver and copper-alloy coin had completely broken down.[746] The silver coinage had become so base (c. 5% silver by AD 260 dropping to c. 1% by AD 270) that a separate copper-alloy coinage could no longer be maintained.[747] Between AD 260-275 there was a huge import of base radiates into Britain from the mints of the breakaway Gallic Empire at Cologne and Trier.[748] Site finds and hoards from Britain invariably show a distinctive peak for coins minted within this period (**Fig. 6.1**).[749] However, whilst there really was a vast import of coin at this time we should bear in mind that the size of this peak is probably somewhat exaggerated. This coin was devalued by the Aurelianic reform and the measures of Probus, which led to it being hoarded and discarded in large quantities.[750] In addition, one must bear in mind that the radiate coins of AD 260-275 were very small and this ensures a high representation amongst site finds as they would have been much easier to lose, and harder to recover once lost, than larger examples (an *as* weighed c. 10g, whilst a radiate weighed c. 2-3g).[751]

[746] Casey 1994a, 38; Reece 2002, 46.
[747] Reece 2002, 20, 48.
[748] Weder 1997-8; Besly and Bland 1983; Bland and Burnett 1988.
[749] Abdy 2002, 9.
[750] Casey 1994a, 56; Abdy 2002, 43; Reece 2002, 48.
[751] Abdy 2002, 39.

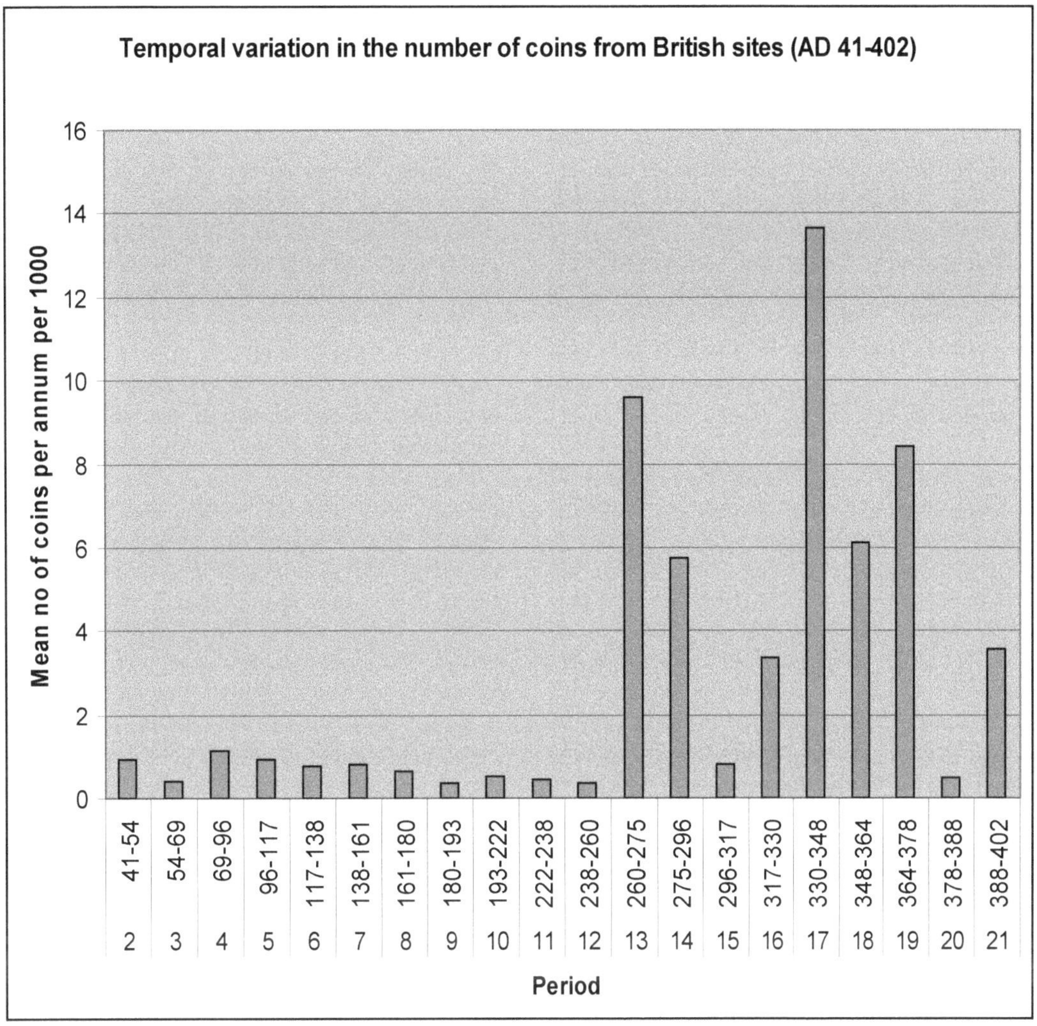

Fig. 6.1. Annual rate of coin loss (per 1000 coins total) on 140 British sites (AD 41-402) (data from Reece 2002, 145).

From AD 275 there was a decline in coin loss of imported coin. This can be connected to Aurelian's coinage reform of c. AD 273/274, which restored the silver content of the radiate coinage to c. 4-5%.[752] Although the site finds do show a large number of coins from this date these are primarily unofficially minted barbarous radiates, which were produced down to c. AD 330 as a response to the lack of official supply of low-value coin, which was required to facilitate everyday monetary transactions within the province.[753] At the time of Carausius and Allectus's breakaway regime (AD 286-296) there was a complete cessation of coin imports to Britain as the usurpers minted their own coins in Britain.[754]

Base coins minted between AD 296-330, which contain c. 2-4% silver (the *follis* or *nummus*), are found in relatively small quantities at British sites. These coins were minted at several locations in the Western Empire and whilst London was the main mint supplying Britain, Trier and Lyon were also of importance.[755] One reason for the relatively low numbers of *folles* is that they were large coins (initially 10g). This not only gave them a comparatively high value, which perhaps led to a low rate of import, but also meant that they were easy to recover and hence are under-represented amongst site finds.[756]

AD 330-348 marks the highest peak of site coin finds in Britain for the entire Roman period. Enormous quantities of base coin from a number of continental mints, most notably Trier, Lyon and Arles are found in Britain.[757] Once again we should bear in mind that the size of these coins probably played an important part in this picture. They were very small, only 1.5g, which not only gave them a very low value, but contributes heavily to their strong loss-patterns on archaeological sites.[758]

From AD 348 onwards there was a considerable reduction in the quantity of base coin reaching Britain, which was down to the coins becoming larger and more valuable. In AD 348 the billon coinage was reformed and the silver contents improved.[759] A series of copies of the

[752] Casey 1994a, 38; Reece 2002, 22-23.
[753] Casey 1994a, 38-40; Abdy 2002, 47-48; Reece 2002, 48-49, 56-57.
[754] Reece 2002, 51-54, 129.
[755] Fulford 1977, 65-70, Fig. 10.
[756] Casey 1994a, 42; Abdy 2002, 48; Reece 2002, 26-27.
[757] Reece 2002, 28-30, 57-58, 137; Fulford 1977, 68.
[758] Casey 1994a, 42; Reece 2002, 57
[759] Casey 1994a, 44; Abdy 2002, 51-55; Reece 2002, 30-34, 58-62

Constantinian coinage, the so-called 'Fallen Horseman copies' were manufactured between AD 350-370 as a response to the lack of official coin.[760] Around AD 357-363 silver was excluded from the bronze coinage altogether and from now on a tri-partite system of very pure gold and silver together with bronze was re-established.[761] The Valentinianic period (AD 364-378) saw a large influx of low-value bronze.[762] There is a curious lull in supply, of the bronze coinage at least, between AD 378-388, but there was a further substantial import from AD 388, with a sudden cut-off at the beginning of the fifth century. The final bronze and silver coin came to Britain in AD 402, whilst the latest gold coins are from AD 406.[763]

In Britain the second half of the fourth century and the beginning of the fifth century is marked by a remarkable concentration of precious metal hoards. Of all the known Roman silver coin hoards which close between AD 388-410, 80% derive from Britain.[764] An early fifth-century AD hoard from Hoxne in Suffolk included 580 coins of gold and 14,205 of silver, along with 200 other gold and silver objects. The objects it contained primarily dated from the mid-fourth to the beginning of the fifth century AD. [765] Further major treasures of this date have been found at Eye, Thetford, Mildenhall and Water Newton, whilst they are also encountered beyond the frontier, where they presumably represent loot from barbarian raids, as at Coleraine in Northern Ireland and at Traprain Law in Scotland where a vast late fourth-century treasure was discovered.[766]

These finds might well represent a contemporary influx of precious metal to Britain; Reece notes that in 357 and 363, respectively, the Empire suddenly began to mint high-quality coin in gold and silver in quantity.[767] What is more, it is under Julian in AD 360 that we get our first record of the troops being paid a donative of five *solidi* and a pound of silver (totalling nine *solidi* in value) upon the accession of the emperor, a practice which appears to have become standard throughout the Later Roman Empire, though the sparse literary record means that we cannot be certain whether this practice was in fact instituted prior to Julian.[768] Twenty silver ingots, some bearing mint marks from Trier and Rome, have been identified in the British Isles from fourth- and early fifth-century contexts.[769] A possible reason for this phenomenon, at least in relation to gold, might have been the Roman Empire's ability to gain access to new sources of precious metal. Indeed, there are several regulations in the Theodosian Code, most formulated AD 365-392, that relate to gold mining in the Eastern Empire.[770] In addition, gold coins of this period contain platinum, which suggests that a new source was being exploited, a good candidate for which is sub-Saharan Africa.[771]

Of course the main reason for the particularly high representation of precious metal in Britain during the final years of Roman rule must be related to the onset of increasingly unstable and violent conditions.[772] A further factor was the decline of the Roman tax system and also of precious metalworking in the fifth century. This ensured that objects and coin from the end of the Roman period were less often melted down and re-worked than in earlier times, which meant that they were available for circulation until well into the fifth century.[773]

Prior to the mid-third century the principal mechanism through which coin entered Britain was army pay. From the second half of the third century on, however, there are strong hints that this changed. The Roman army in Britain was substantially reduced during the Late Roman period. The *Notitia Dignitatum* is a list of Late Roman military dispositions. Whilst it underwent revisions down to c. AD 428 the British section was compiled in the 390s.[774] From this document we can ascertain that the British garrison comprised one legion and eight auxiliary units under the command of the Count of the Saxon Shore and one legion and thirty-six auxiliary units under the command of the *Dux Britanniarum*. Excavations at Late Roman forts in Britain suggest that the unit sizes were substantially smaller than during the early Roman period. Auxiliary units appear to have been reduced from 500 during the *Principate* to c. 200-300 men in the fourth century. The legions, meanwhile, were down from 5-6,000 to 1,000. This gives us a figure of c. 12,000 frontier troops (*limitanei*). A field army of nine units under the command of the *Comes Britanniarum* is also listed. These units would have been somewhat larger, which perhaps gives us c. 6,000 *comitatenses* and an estimated total of c. 18,000 for the British garrison in the 390s, well below the c. 50-55,000 troops stationed in the island prior to the mid-third century (see p. 53, **Tab. 4.1**).[775]

Whether this is an accurate estimate of the garrison size is debatable as the *Notitia* makes no mention of units in Wales and in northwest England, despite the fact that forts there show continuing occupation throughout the fourth century. The field army might well have been a temporary posting ordered in by Stilicho to reinforce Britain at a time of crisis.[776]

Despite notable limitations the *Notitia Dignitatum* can be used to suggest that by the end of the fourth century the

---

[760] Reece 2002, 57-59, Casey 1994a, 44-46.
[761] Casey 1994a, 44; Abdy 2002, 51-55; Reece 2002, 30-34, 58-62
[762] Casey 1994a, 46; Reece 2002, 59-62.
[763] Casey 1994a, 46-48; Abdy 2002, 56; Reece 2002, 36, 59-62.
[764] Abdy 2002, 62; Laycock 2008, 138; Fulford 1996, 166, Fig. 5.
[765] Bland and Johns 1995; Abdy 2002, 58-61.
[766] Bland and Johns 1995, 16-17; Johns and Potter 1983; Painter 1977a; 1977b; Curle 1923; Abdy 2002, Fig. 39.
[767] Reece 2002, 31.
[768] Jones 1964, 623-630; Southern and Dixon 1996, 76-82.
[769] Tylecote 1986, Tab. 41; Abdy 2002, 57-58.
[770] Edmonson 1989, 86, 92; *CTh* 10.19, I.32.5.
[771] Wilson 2007, 122-123; Callu *et al.* 1985, 105; Garrard 1982.
[772] Laycock 2008, 138.
[773] Abdy 2002, 62.
[774] Mattingly 2006, 238; Wood 1990; Hassall 1977; Birley 2005, 401-404; James 1984.
[775] *Notitia Dignitatum Occidentis.* 28; James 1984; Southern 2004; Mattingly 2006, 238-247.
[776] Mattingly 2006, 238-247; Birley 2005, 401-404; Mann 1977.

British garrison was well below its pre-mid-third century levels. The main reductions probably came in the second half of the third century. The garrisons in the north were severely depleted in the later third century and many forts were abandoned then. Inscriptions found on the continent also suggest that sections of the British garrison were being removed to fight in civil and foreign wars on the continent during the mid-third century and that they were not subsequently returned.[777]

A second, and more significant, reason why army pay was less important in the transfer of coin to Britain in the Late Roman period was a major change in the system through which soldiers were paid. For the majority of the Principate the army received a sizeable proportion (perhaps 1/5 or 1/6) of their pay in cash (see pp. 53-54); however, from the later third century onwards, soldiers and officers were paid almost entirely in kind, that is their wages were commuted from cash into clothing, equipment and particularly food, which the state had levied as taxes, produced in state factories or purchased from private individuals.[778]

An Egyptian papyrus dated to AD 299 and 300 suggests that soldiers were still receiving an official salary in cash, with legionaries and troopers of the *alae* receiving 600 *denarii* a year, infantrymen in the cohorts 400 *denarii* a year and auxiliaries 200 *denarii*. These sums were unchanged since the Severan period and because of severe inflation they were practically nominal by the end of the third century. Soldiers also received annual donatives which were presented on the dates of the emperor's birthday, accession day and consulates. These totalled 7500 *denarii* a year for legionaries and 1250 a year for auxiliaries, though the value of these payments was extremely low as well. Of much greater significance, however, was the accession payments mentioned above, which appear to have become standard from the accession of Julian in AD 360.[779] This would have involved a significant transfer of precious metal to the British garrison in the later fourth century.

The small size of the British garrison and the fact that almost all its pay was received in kind prior to the late fourth century means that we must look to other mechanisms to help explain the large volumes of coin found in Britain. We must also bear in mind that in Britain the Late Roman period saw a relative shift in coin site finds away from military areas towards the civilian areas in the south. Under the Principate coin finds were biased towards military sites, whilst from the late third century they occur on civil sites in large numbers. They even penetrate rural communities in numbers from this date and particularly in the mid-fourth century.[780] To some extent this may simply indicate a greater monetisation amongst the civilian rural population, but the main reason for the arrival of high volumes of coins in civilian areas must result from high levels of overseas trade, or through payments for state contracts.[781] As I shall discuss below it was the export of British agricultural products which accounted for the main injections of coin to Britain throughout this period.

There is limited evidence for the import of copper-alloy vessels to Britain during this period. In contrast to the continent, third-century vessel hoards are notably absent. However, there is a small group of fourth-century hoards. These primarily contain vessels of British manufacture, though a few imported examples may be noted from these hoards and from a few other sites besides. Late Roman frying pans of Coptic origin have been identified at four sites in southeast Britain. The *basin à bord godronné* type, which has been found at four British sites, very probably originated in the region between the Seine and the Rhine, whilst a handful of other vessels from British sites also derive from this area.[782] In addition, there are a few Westland cauldrons, which were probably imported to Britain from northern Gaul or the Rhineland between the third and early fifth centuries. Westland cauldrons of probable third- to fourth-century type (Type 1) have been identified at Prestwick Carr in Northumberland, Wooton in Surrey, Loveden Hill, in Lincolnshire, and Burwell, in Cambridgeshire.[783] A clear Type 2C vessel (dated c. AD 300-500) is present in the Late Roman vessel hoard from Draper's Gardens in London, whilst a probable vessel was noted at the Roman cemetery at Brougham in Cumbria.[784] They reached Britain from the adjacent continent via the Southern North Sea or Eastern Channel. How they arrived is unclear; possibly through trade, though they may have been personal possessions of troops or other individuals who moved between the continent and Britain.

Crossbow brooches were the main brooch type in use throughout the Western Empire during this period, and were 'imported' to Britain in small quantities. The brooches may be divided into types on the basis of their constructional and decorative features. Type 1 is dated c. AD 280-320, Type 2 to c. AD 300-365, Type 3/4 to c. AD 325-410, Type 5 to c. AD 350-415 and Type 6 to c. AD 390-460.[785] Crossbow brooches belonging to all these types have been identified in Britain, primarily in the south but also in the vicinity of Hadrian's Wall.[786] Types 5 and 6 are represented by a handful of examples, whilst there are only c. 10 brooches from Type 2. Types 1 and 3/4 are best represented with c. 30 examples each. These proportions generally mirror the patterns observable in the different regions of Western Europe, although Type 1 is slightly over-represented in Britain, whilst Type 3/4 is slightly under-represented.[787] This tells us,

[777] James 1984; Southern 2004.
[778] Jones 1964, 623-630; Southern and Dixon 1996, 76-82; Hopkins 1980, 116, 123-124.
[779] Jones 1964, 623-630; Southern and Dixon 1996, 76-82.
[780] Reece 1991; 1995; Toomey 2003, Figs. 56-57.
[781] C.f. Fulford 1996; 2004, 324.
[782] Eggers 1966, 90-93; Kennett 1969; Gerrard 2009.
[783] Dahlin Hauken 2005, 94.
[784] Gerrard 2009; Mould 2004, 206-208.
[785] Swift, 2000a, 13-24, Tab. A; Pröttel 1988; Keller 1971.
[786] Swift, 2000a, Figs. 12-16; Laycock 2008, 102-103, Fig. 45.
[787] Swift 2000a, Fig. 17.

unsurprisingly, that most crossbow brooches arrived during the late third and fourth centuries.

A European-wide examination of the different foot-patterns present on Type 3/4 indicates that the vast majority bore one of three particular patterns. The best explanation is that these brooches were mass-produced in Danubian regions where these foot-patterns are most common and occur on a larger proportion of brooches than in the western provinces. In Britain only about a third of Type 3/4 brooches bear this pattern, the rest having a wide variety of different patterns.[788] This suggests that whilst some of the brooches were imported from Danubian regions the majority were produced on a small-scale in Britain, or in continental Europe west of the Rhine. The imports clearly came from the frontier regions of the Empire and reached southeast Britain via the Southern North Sea or Eastern Channel. The probable reason for their arrival was that they moved as personal possessions with troops or officials who had been transferred between Britain and the continent.

Military copper-alloy belt buckles and belt fittings have been identified at large numbers of British sites of the Late Roman period. The vast majority were produced in Britain between c. AD 370 and the early fifth century (see p. 134), but some examples were also imported from the continent.[789] The imported fittings belong to types which concentrate heavily on the continent in the region between the Loire and the Rhine and to the south of the upper and middle Danube; to judge from the distribution they were probably produced in these regions, although one should bear in mind that this coincides exactly with the distribution of large Late Roman-period cemeteries.[790] The argument for continental manufacture is further strengthened by the standardisation of forms across Europe and by the employment of complex manufacturing techniques, such as chip-carving, which imply manufacture at a restricted number of centres.[791] A connection to the Late Roman military workshops, or *fabricae*, attested in exactly these regions of the continent in the *Notitia Dignitatum* has much to recommend it.[792] Accurately establishing the chronology of the belt-fittings is tricky. The problem has been tackled by Sommer, who established a relative chronology that was reinforced by associations with crossbow brooches.[793] Meanwhile, Böhme also attempted to date the belt-fittings by means of their associations in graves between the Loire and the Elbe.[794]

We can thus see that a small number of continentally produced belt-fittings probably began to arrive in southeast England during the first half of the fourth century AD; buckles of Sommer's Sorte 1 Form A have been found on four sites in southeast Britain and on western European sites these are dated c. AD 310-350.[795] Other types of imported buckle occasionally found in Britain can be dated broadly to the fourth century as a whole.[796] From c. AD 370 to the early fifth century there was an increase in the numbers of imported belt fittings reaching southeast Britain, most notably the chip-carved sets.[797] However, one must not overemphasise the scale of this import as the quantities involved were fairly small. They probably attest to the presence of troops in Britain who had previously been stationed along the Rhine-Danube frontier on the continent, with an influx of such troops apparently coming in the later fourth century, presumably in relation to the expeditions of Count Theodosius and Stilicho.

Pottery

Some pottery was imported to Britain from the continent during this period, though it was largely restricted to three main classes: Argonne ware, Mayen ware and *Céramique à l'éponge*, whilst German marbled flagons are also occasionally identified.[798] Pottery imports in the Late Roman period were far below the levels of earlier times.

Argonne ware was produced in northern France just to the east of Rheims and obtained a fairly wide distribution in the northwest continental regions of the Empire. Small amounts are known from a number of sites in Britain, predominantly concentrating in East Kent and around the Thames estuary (**Fig. 6.2**). The main supply routes evidently ran across the Strait of Dover, though there is a smaller group of finds from the British Solent coast as well. The British examples were imported between the late third and the beginning of the fifth centuries.[799] Notably, there is a complete absence of the distinctive fifth-century types, which often possess grey, reduced cores and bear roller-stamped Christian symbols.[800]

Mayen ware was produced in the Eifel region of Rheinland-Pfalz and its continental distribution is centred upon the Rhine region. Its British distribution is similar to that of Argonne ware, with, if anything, a stronger clustering in East Kent and around the Thames estuary; indeed, 90% of the British material derives from Canterbury, Richborough, Colchester and London (**Fig. 6.3**). The supply routes would therefore have focused on the Southern North Sea and the Strait of Dover. On the continent the Mayen ware industries were active between c. AD 300-450, but the bulk of the British finds occur in

788 Swift 2000a, 43-49, 73-78, Figs. 48-49; 2000b, 47-48.
789 Laycock 2008, 113-134, Figs. 48, 51, 54; Böhme 1986; Hawkes and Dunning 1961.
790 Swift 2000a, Figs. 229-248; Hawkes and Dunning 1961, 10-21, Fig. 3; Böhme 1974; Karte. 11-18; 1986. Abb. 3, 22, 24.
791 Böhme 1974, 97; Sommer 1984, 102; Hawkes and Dunning 1961, 12.
792 Bishop and Coulston 2006, 238-240, Fig. 146; James 1988.
793 Sommer 1984, 59, 74.
794 Böhme 1987, Abb. 38, 40.
795 Swift 2000a, 190, Figs. 231-232.
796 Swift 2000a, 192, Fig. 233.
797 Swift 2000a, 192-204, Figs. 236, 238, 239, 244, 246; Böhme 1974, Karte 11; 1986, Abb. 3, 11, 14, 18; 1987, Abb. 38; Barber and Bowsher 2000, 206-208; Laycock 2008.
798 Fulford 1977; 1978; Tyers 1996b; forthcoming; Fulford and Bird 1975 (fabric 1 only).
799 Fulford 1977; 1978; Tyers 1996b; forthcoming.
800 Bayard 1990; Dijkman 1992; Boeles 1951.

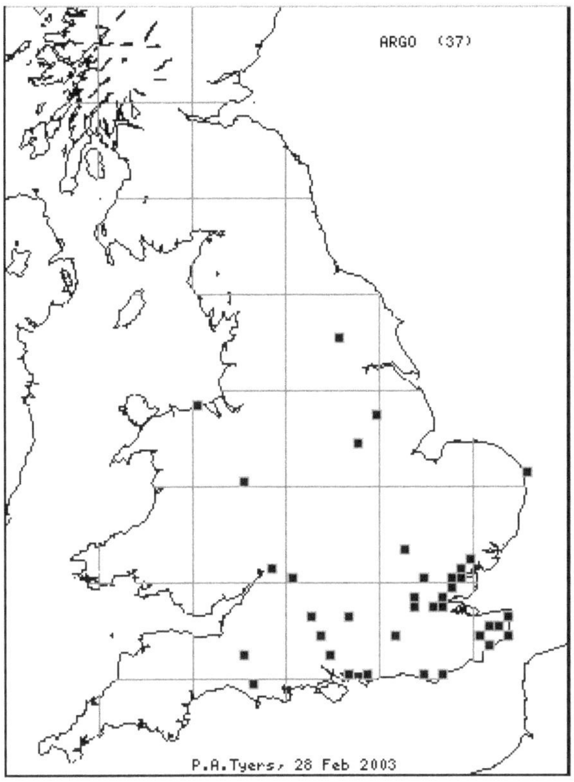

Fig. 6.2. British distribution of Argonne ware (Paul Tyers (URL accessed June 2010): http://www.potsherd.uklinux.net/atlas/Ware/ARGO).

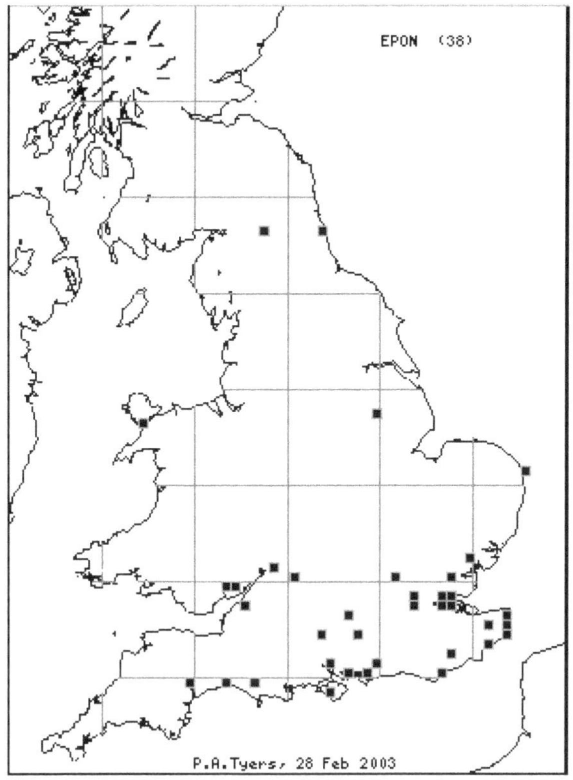

Fig. 6.4. British distribution of Céramique à l'éponge (Paul Tyers (URL accessed June 2010): http://www.potsherd.uklinux.net/atlas/Ware/EPON).

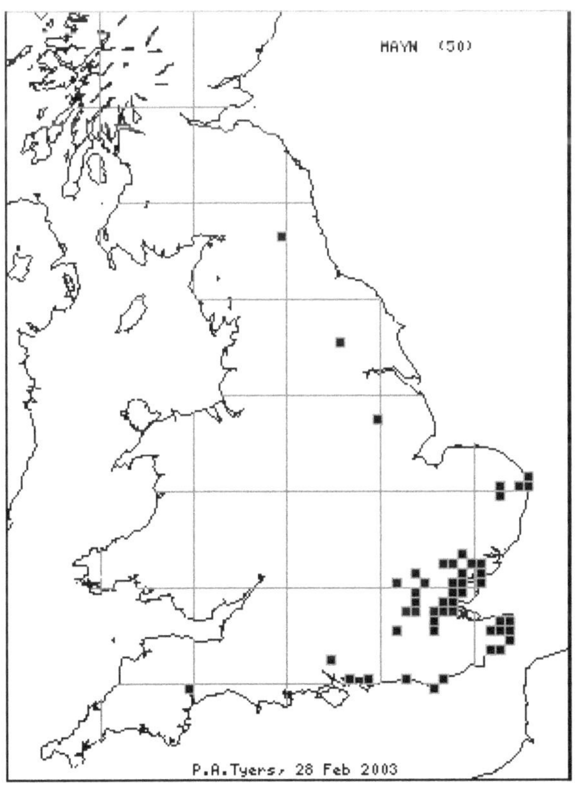

Fig. 6.3. British distribution of Mayen ware (Paul Tyers (URL accessed June 2010): http://www.potsherd.uklinux.net/atlas/Ware/MAYN).

mid- to late fourth-century contexts.[801] German marbled flagons, meanwhile, were manufactured in the Middle Rhine, or Lower Moselle Valleys and are found along the middle and Lower Rhine. The British distribution is entirely restricted to the East Kent/Thames estuary region and consists of vessels of third- and fourth-century dates. Like the Mayen ware the supply route centred on the Southern North Sea and the Strait of Dover.[802]

The third main ware was *Céramique à l'éponge*, which was produced in western France, probably near Civaux in Vienne, and its continental distribution covers northwest France, principally the area between the Gironde and the Loire. The examples found in Britain appear to be fourth-century in date and they are found around the southern coast of Britain (**Fig. 6.4**). They attest to a fairly notable Atlantic or Western Channel link.[803]

As in the earlier phases of Roman Britain the pottery imports arrived through trade. Its distribution suggests a predominantly civilian trade focused on the communities living in southeast Britain, though the wares are certainly present at many of the Shore forts as well. Their probable low-value, which gave them poor resilience to transport costs, and the existence of thriving Romano-British pottery industries in southern Britain limited their penetration inland.

[801] Fulford 1977; 1978; Tyers 1996b; forthcoming; Fulford and Bird 1975 (fabric 1 only).
[802] Tyers 1996b; forthcoming.
[803] Fulford 1977; 1978; Tyers 1996b; forthcoming.

Olive oil

The supply of Baetican olive oil to Britain suffered around the mid-third century AD. The latest known Dr.20 stamps date to this time and, indeed, the latest known *tituli picti* on Dr.20 anywhere in the Roman world come from Monte Testaccio in Rome and date to AD 255.[804] Henceforth, Baetican olive oil barely reached Britain at all. Thinner-walled Dr.23 amphorae replaced Dr.20 as containers for the transport of Baetican oil and these were in production from the second half of the third century up until the late fifth or early sixth, but examples have only been noted on two British sites. An unstratified vessel was found at the small town of Heybridge in Essex, whilst four Dr.23 rims derive from Winchester.[805]

North African olive oil began to reach Britain in increasing quantities from the early third century onwards, but the amounts involved were low in comparison to Baetican oil imports between c. AD 43-255.[806] Indeed, at the British sites where they are present North African amphorae typically comprise less than 5% of the total olive oil amphorae.[807] Sporadic examples of North African olive oil amphorae had reached Britain since at least the late first or early second century AD, but they became increasingly common from the early third century onwards and principally occur in third- and fourth-century contexts.[808] They appear to have been imported down to the end of Roman rule as most examples from Exeter derived from later fourth-century deposits, whilst they have been encountered in early fifth-century contexts at London, Mucking and Gloucester.[809] Later examples arrived in western Britain during the late fifth and early sixth centuries, but these are beyond the scope of this study.[810]

In terms of distribution, North African amphorae of the third to early fifth centuries AD have mainly been found at major civil sites, in particular, London, York, Leicester and Exeter. The majority of findspots lie in the south and east of Britain, particularly at sites near the coast. They are very rare on military sites and are apparently absent from the shore forts of the east coast. In the north, around Hadrian's Wall, North African amphorae are known only from Carlisle.[811] A few examples of North African amphorae are present in Gaul, which means that a minor overland route supplying Britain via the Southern North Sea and Eastern Channel coast of the continent cannot be ruled out; however, the disproportionately large British distribution and the high number of finds at southwest British sites, such as Exeter, surely implies that, as in the Early Medieval period, the majority of North African olive oil was reaching Britain via the Atlantic seaways.[812] The British distribution clearly implies a free-market trade dominated by the civilian market.

Wine

Imported wine amphorae are extremely rare in Britain during the Late Roman period, though a handful of G4 and Campanian types may have arrived during the second half of the third century.[813] Some wine probably continued to arrive in barrels; certainly barrels, which possibly contained wine, were present in the Guernsey shipwreck, which sank in the AD 280s and, judging by finds of British pottery on board, was operating between ports in Britain and western France.[814] However, as with the amphorae there is also a declining incidence of barrels from British sites, with only six examples from three Late Roman sites.[815] This corresponds to the general pattern throughout Western Europe, where only twenty-seven barrels can be dated to the third century, whilst only eight are known from the fourth- and fifth-centuries (**Fig. 4.25**). The incidence of pictorial representations of barrels in the Empire also declines.[816] This provides very tentative proxy evidence for a decline in the trade of wine in barrels.

Lending further support to this view is the fact that there was a dramatic decline in wine production in the main western production centres in southern France and in Aquitaine from around the middle of the third century onwards.[817] One particular region, the Moselle Valley, did see a considerable expansion of viticulture during the latter half of the third century, reaching a peak in the fourth century. This region had at least ten sites associated with wine production, many of which were equipped with screw presses, vats and large storage houses with under-floor heating for the fermentation of wine.[818] Whether any of this wine actually reached Britain is debatable; the nearby Western Imperial capital at Trier was presumably the principal consumer.

Seafood

Around the middle of the third century there is a distinct change in Mediterranean fish-product amphorae forms, apparently paralleling the contemporary decrease in container form evident in the shift from Dr.20 to Dr.23 olive oil amphorae.[819] Amphorae types dating from the later third century onwards are extremely rare in Britain and the northwest of the Empire.[820] The declining trade with the north is also highlighted by the fact that the output of most of the west Mediterranean fish-salting installations was well below the peak levels attained during the second half of the first and second centuries AD, although operations did continue at most sites until

[804] Carreras Monfort and Funari 1998; Dressel 1899; Williams and Carreras 1995, 234.
[805] Wickenden 1986, Fig. 26, 19; Carreras Monfort and Williams 2003.
[806] Williams and Peacock 1983; Williams and Carreras 1995.
[807] Carreras Monfort and Funari 1998, Tab. 1; Williams and Carreras 1995, Tab. 1.
[808] Williams and Carreras 1995; see: Green 1986, 102; Richardson 1986, Fig. 76; McCarthy 1990, 204.
[809] Williams and Carreras 1995, 234; Peacock 1972.
[810] Fulford 1989c.
[811] Williams and Carreras 1995; Tyers 1996a; Peacock 1972.
[812] See Tyers 1996a for the continental distribution.
[813] Tyers 1996a.
[814] Rule and Monaghan 1993, 99-100, 129; Marlière 2002, T57-70.
[815] Marlière 2002, T21-24, 26, 50.
[816] Marlière 2002, 174, Fig. 212.
[817] Brun and Laubenheimer 2001, 215-216.
[818] Brun and Gilles 2001.
[819] Martin-Kilcher 2003, 76.
[820] *Ibid.* 82.

the fifth-century.[821] However, Britain did receive sporadic Mediterranean imports. For example, at Great Holts Farm, Boreham, Essex, deposits dated to the late third or early fourth century contained Spanish mackerel alongside scad.[822] Here is evidence for import of Mediterranean fish to a high-status British rural site at a fairly late date.

Imports from Brittany, across the Western Channel/Atlantic, probably continued at a high level into the second half of the third century; however, analysis by Andrew Wilson suggests that the fish-salting facilities in Brittany suffered a severe contraction by the first half of the fourth century, which must correspond to a fall in cross-Channel trade in these products.[823]

Lava querns

Although lava querns are often found in contexts securely dated to this time, it is hard to prove that we are not simply dealing with residual fragments from earlier phases of import. For example, fragments are known from graves in the Late Roman cemetery at Poundbury, Dorset and in the Eastern cemetery of London and they are also present in late third- and fourth-century contexts at several other sites, including London, Colchester, Chelmsford, Braintree, Great Chesterford and Aveley in Essex.[824] Lava querns are even found at rural sites in the north at this time, such as the villas of Rudston and Dalton Parlours in Yorkshire.[825] It is not out of the question that a limited trade in lava querns did occur across the Southern North Sea during the latter years of Roman rule. Indeed, it is very likely that imported lava was used in the construction of Walton Castle shore fort, which was built in the later third century.[826]

British Exports

Coinage and metals

Throughout the late third and fourth centuries, quantities of coin, particularly those containing precious metal, will undoubtedly have been returned from Britain to the mints on the continent for re-coinage. This coin will have been collected by state officials in Britain via the medium of taxation and then shipped to the mints.

Between c. AD 286-296 coin was minted in Britain under the breakaway regime of Carausius and Allectus. These coins are relatively rare on the continent, perhaps surprisingly so considering the fact that, for a time at least, Carausius's authority extended well into northern Gaul.[827] Following Britain's re-integration into the Empire *folles* were minted on the island between AD 296-326. The principal mint was at London, although another mint probably operated for a short while at either Colchester or Gloucester.[828] Between these dates British minted coin is very common in northwestern parts of the continental Empire. Fulford's studies have shown that in north French coin assemblages they account for c. 25-40% of the coins dated AD 296-326. They also form a smaller, but still sizeable, proportion of contemporary coin assemblages in the Rhineland.[829] Such large-scale, rapid transfers of coin are probably best accounted for by state shipments of coin from the British mints to the continent, though civilian trade should not be ruled out. What the state was using these coins to pay for is open to question; they may have been made in exchange for bulk imports of continental goods to Britain, probably for the use of the army. However, the Roman state may simply have used coins from the various mints in the northwest Empire to pay its soldiers and officials and to purchase goods from private individuals, regardless of where these individuals were stationed, or where the goods were destined for.

In contrast to the first and second century, we lack clear evidence for gold mining in Britain, but if gold continued to be exported at all, the quantities would have been small. Direct evidence for lead-silver mining is also absent, though numerous lead coffins throughout southern Britain hint at the existence of a thriving industry.[830] Of course we should bear in mind that much of this lead may actually be accounted for by recycling of the substantial amounts that were present in earlier Roman public buildings.[831] Whether Late Roman lead-mining extended to the primary production of small amounts of silver destined for export is unclear, but certainly possible.

Lead was being exported from Britain; lead-isotope analysis of lead objects from Trier and Martberg in Germany indicates that some material dating to the second half of the third or fourth century was made from lead sourced in the south Pennines around Matlock or Ashby-de-la-Zouch.[832] In addition, the cargo of a third- or fourth-century shipwreck at Ploumanac'h off the coast of Brittany comprised some 271 lead ingots weighing c. 22 tonnes. Some were stamped CIVTBR or CBRIGAN (*Civitas Brigantium*) and others ICIIN P (*Iciinorum plumbum*) and CIVTICENORP (*Civitas Icenorum plumbum*).[833] Whilst the *Civitas* of the Brigantes, in northern England, did contain lead sources, there were none in the territory of the Iceni in Norfolk. The ingots from this latter region would therefore have been formed from remelted lead, or perhaps represent lead from other sources that was transhipped through Norfolk.

Some copper-alloy objects were also exported from Britain to the continent. Swift's analysis of bracelets from

[821] Trakadas 2005, 52, 54, 60, 65; Wilson 2006, 534-536, Fig. 3.
[822] Locker 2003, 200.
[823] Wilson 2006, Fig. 4.
[824] Sparey-Green 1987, 105; Barber and Bowsher 2000, 241, 348, 354; Buckley and Major 1983, 73-76; Gentry *et al.* 1977, 179-181; King 1987, 100; Wickenden 1992, 89; Crummy 2002; Lavender 1997, 87; Garwood 2004, 19; Foreman and Maynard 2002, 148.
[825] Stead 1980, 120-3; Buckley and Major 1990.
[826] Allen and Fulford 1999, 169-170; Pearson 2002a, 58.
[827] Casey 1977, Fig. 1-2; 1994b, Figs. 3, 13.
[828] Reece 2002, 51, 129.
[829] Fulford 1977, Fig. 10.
[830] Jones and Mattingly 1990, Map 8:34.
[831] Rogers 2005.
[832] Durali-Mueller *et al.* 2007.
[833] L'Hour 1987; Stewart 2002, 217.

sites throughout the western Empire indicates that several types were very probably made in Britain. Most convincing are bracelets of cogwheel type, which primarily date to the late fourth century. Whilst these are known in large quantity from British sites they are very rare on the continent, though examples are known from Oudenburg and Tongeren in Belgium. Multiple-motif bracelets, which date throughout the fourth century, are also found predominantly in Britain, although they appear at nineteen sites on the adjacent continent between the Loire and the Rhine. An example from Trier is identical to a bracelet found at Rushall Down in Wiltshire, which suggests production in the same workshop.[834]

Swift goes further and argues that several other bracelets of mid-third to early fifth-century date, which have been found on the continent, were also made in Britain. These include bracelets with type 1 snakeshead terminals, imitation bead decoration and strip bracelets with a5, a8, a10, a14, b1, b3, b10, b12, b15, b47 and e2 decoration. The majority of bracelets belonging to these types have been found in Britain and the continental examples were very probably exported, though we should bear in mind the possibility that some were produced on the continent by mobile craftsmen. These bracelets have been found in small numbers in the region between the Loire and the Rhine, with a few also found on sites along the upper Danube. A notably strong British link can be observed in the Oudenburg bracelet assemblage where seven bracelets of probable British origin have been found in four graves. The Oudenburg bracelets show particular similarities to examples found at Portchester with a b12 bracelet bearing an identical decoration to an example found at the British site. Eight bracelets of British type also derive from Augst in Switzerland.[835]

Certain types of zoomorphic belt fittings which were produced in Britain during the late fourth and early fifth century are very occasionally encountered on the continent. A buckle of Hawkes and Dunning Type IA has been identified at Bruggenum, Limburg in the Netherlands, buckles of Hawkes and Dunning Type IB derive from Iruña-Veleia in the Spanish Basque country, Barcelona and Krefeld-Gellep in western Germany, a Hawkes and Dunning Type IIA buckle was also found at Iruña, whilst Laycock has noted another British buckle from Argeliers near the French-Spanish border.[836] As Laycock and others have pointed out, these buckles were very probably brought to the continent as the personal possessions of soldiers during the campaigns of the British usurper Constantine III (c. AD 406/407-410/411) (see pp. 138-139).

Tin exploitation in southwest Britain seems to have peaked during the Late Roman period. Our evidence for this comes from the size of the pewter (a tin alloy, typically containing c. 35-95% tin mixed with lead) industry in southern Britain. Over 400 pewter vessels and c. 100 small pewter objects have been recovered from southern Britain with the vast majority in contexts dating to c. AD 260-430.[837] In addition, our only secure Roman tin ingot, a 17.9 kg example from Carnanton in Cornwall, is of late third- or fourth-century date.[838] Dungworth's analyses of elemental variation in northern English copper-alloy objects dating from the first to the fourth centuries AD also indicates that the average tin content reached a peak in the fourth century.[839] Furthermore, sediment analysis suggests that hydraulic tin-mining was taking place on southern Dartmoor between the fourth and seventh centuries AD.[840]

This productive increase probably underlay a small-scale export trade in pewter and tin-alloy to the continent across the Southern North Sea and Eastern Channel. Despite the notable corrosion problems associated with this material, over 100 pewter vessels have been identified at Late Roman sites on the adjacent continent, primarily from cemeteries in northern France, but also from Belgium and the southern Netherlands. Whether the vessels themselves were British exports is unclear as some seem to have construction techniques, such as the application of sheet-silver surfaces, which have not been recognised amongst the British material. Nonetheless, I suspect that the material upon which they were based was exported. Indeed, ten Roman tin-alloy ingots recovered from the Thames in the nineteenth century hint at the possibility of tin-alloy export in ingot form.[841]

There was a pronounced decline in Wealden iron production in the second half of the third century. Output fell by almost three-quarters from c. 750 tonnes per annum between c. AD 150-250 to c. 200 tonnes per annum between c. AD 250-350 (**Fig. 4.33**). There is very little evidence for smelting during the fourth century and none whatsoever for the fifth century.[842] As argued in previous chapters, whilst most Wealden iron was probably consumed within Britain, some was probably exported. The rapid reduction in output from the mid-third century onwards must have impacted upon this export.

Elsewhere in Britain the evidence for decline is more gradual. In the Forest of Dean, for example, whilst many iron production sites fell out of use at the end of the second century, or during the course of the third, several major sites continue in use, whilst a few were even established, during the fourth century and into the early fifth.[843] In the East Midlands there is little evidence for decline, with a similar number of smelting sites in operation throughout the Roman period, although only one smelting site can be dated to the fifth century

[834] Swift 2000a; 2000b; Sas 2004.
[835] Swift 2000a; 2000b; Sas 2004.
[836] Laycock 2008; 2009; Hawkes and Dunning 1961; Böhme 1986; Gil *et al.* 2000; Aurrecoechea 1996; Sommer 1984, 24-5, Sorte 1, Form C, Typ d, Variant 6.

[837] Beagrie 1989.
[838] Stewart 2002, 229; Warner 1967.
[839] Dungworth 1997b, Tab. 3.
[840] Thorndycraft *et al.* 2004.
[841] Beagrie 1989.
[842] Cleere and Crossley 1995, 84-86.
[843] Stewart 2002, Tab. 5.5; Walters 1992; 1999; Fulford and Allen 1992.

(**Tab. 4.8**). Indeed, the production site at Clipsham, which largely operated during the fourth century, possesses a slag heap of c. 12,000 m^3, which equates to a large estimated output of 120 tonnes per annum.[844] Whilst much of the iron from these latter two industries was probably destined for internal British consumption, a proportion might well have been exported alongside agricultural products obtained from the same regions of the country.

Pottery

From c. AD 280 small quantities of southeast Dorset BB1 began to reach sites in Normandy. By the fourth century there was a large-scale export to Normandy and examples also reached the Breton shore forts and as reached as far as Bordeaux, with BB1 also present at several coastal sites along the continental coast of the Eastern Channel and Southern North Sea. Malcolm Lyne's recent investigations show that over 1,000 BB1 pots have now been identified in Normandy; a fourth-century assemblage from Bayeux had over 300 BB1 pots comprising 15-20% of the material, whilst a fourth-century assemblage from Lillebonne possessed 40% BB1.[845] The evidence suggests a significant Late Roman trade in BB1 vessels focused on the Western Channel. We are clearly dealing with some sort of trade and there is reason to believe that it may have taken the form of a military contract; BB1 is particularly encountered at military sites and shore forts on the continent. Furthermore, it is extremely likely that military contracts had ensured the supply of large quantities of BB1 to the northern British frontier since the early second century.[846]

Other British pottery is less well known on the continent, though this is perhaps in part down to problems with recognition. There is a thin scatter of Romano-British pottery at coastal sites in northern France, Belgium and the southern Netherlands, though the overall quantities involved are fairly low.[847] Detailed pottery analysis has been undertaken at the shore fort of Oudenburg in Belgium and notable quantities of Romano-British pottery, including BB1, BB2, New Forest, Nene Valley, Hadham, Alice Holt-Farnham, Pevensey and Dales ware have been encountered in late third- and fourth-century levels.[848] British pottery is also well known from the shore fort at Aardenburg in the southern Netherlands.[849] These finds probably represent a low-level trade, focused particularly on military sites and the shore forts.

Agricultural products

Five separate historical authorities attest to Julian's efforts (as Caesar) to restore shipments of grain from Britain to the Rhineland in AD 358-359 following their apparent disruption by Frankish tribes (the Salii and Chamavi) inhabiting the Rhineland. The volume of grain shipped by Julian was evidently vast; Zosimus says that Julian built 800 boats larger than galleys for this undertaking, whilst another source cites 600 ships. Ammianus and Libanius state that Julian was restoring the grain route, which as a result of the Frankish disruptions had recently been diverted overland in wagons at great expense, presumably via the north French coast.[850] This all supports the contention that there were sizeable exports of grain from Britain to the Rhineland during the fourth century and very likely in the late third.[851] This grain export was clearly of major concern to the Roman state. It would have been obtained by the Roman state through taxing British producers in kind and also through wholesale purchasing from private producers (see pp. 128-129). The undertaking of transport across the Southern North Sea was possibly in the hands of private shippers, though it may have been shipped by state-owned ships or naval forces. Private trade may also have been of considerable importance.

Textiles were probably exported from Britain in quantity, although the fact that they virtually never survive in the archaeological record limits any real assessment of this issue. The Edict of Diocletian from AD 301 lists British woolen capes (*byrri*) and rugs (*tapetia*), which suggests that they would have been amongst Britain's leading exports.[852] Private trade seems most likely for these products, though it is not impossible that, as with grain and other agricultural goods, the state had contracts with British textile producers to provide goods or uniforms for some of its continental forces.

Jet and shale

In the latter part of the Roman period, from c. AD 180 onwards, sizeable quantities of objects, principally jewellery and small domestic items, were produced in northern England from black materials sourced across this region, such as jet, cannel coal and shale, which typically require chemical analysis to distinguish from one another. In addition, Kimmeridge shale was worked in significant quantities throughout the Late Iron Age and Roman periods at the Isle of Purbeck in Dorset. Objects made from black materials are also well known from later Roman contexts on the continent, particularly in the Rhine provinces of the Empire. An important series of light microscopy analyses has revealed that the black objects from the Rhine provinces were not British exports, but were made from locally sourced jet. Similarly, jet was being exploited for what were largely local industries in Hungary, France and Spain. Whilst it is possible that some jet and shale was exported from Britain to the continent, on the basis of present analyses exports cannot be demonstrated and we must conclude that if they did occur then they would have been relatively small-scale. Certain stylistic similarities

---

844 Schrüfer-Kolb 2004, 126.

845 Malcolm Lyne, pers. Comm. 2007; forthcoming; Allen and Fulford 1996, Fig. 11; Tuffreau-Libre *et al.* 1995.

846 Allen and Fulford 1996.

847 Fulford 1977; 1978; Belot and Canut 1994b.

848 De Clercq, pers. Comm. 2007; Vanhoutte *et al.* 2009; Hollevoet 2004.

849 De Clercq, pers. Comm. 2007.

850 Julian *Ep. ad. Ath.* 279D, 280A, B, C; Libanius. *Or.* 18.82-83, 87; Ammianus 18.2.3-4; Eunapius Frag. 12; Zosimus 3.5.2; Birley 2005, 423-424; Ireland 1986, 147-149.

851 Fulford 1996; 2004, 324.

852 *Edict of Diocletian.* 19.28-29, 48; Wild 1978.

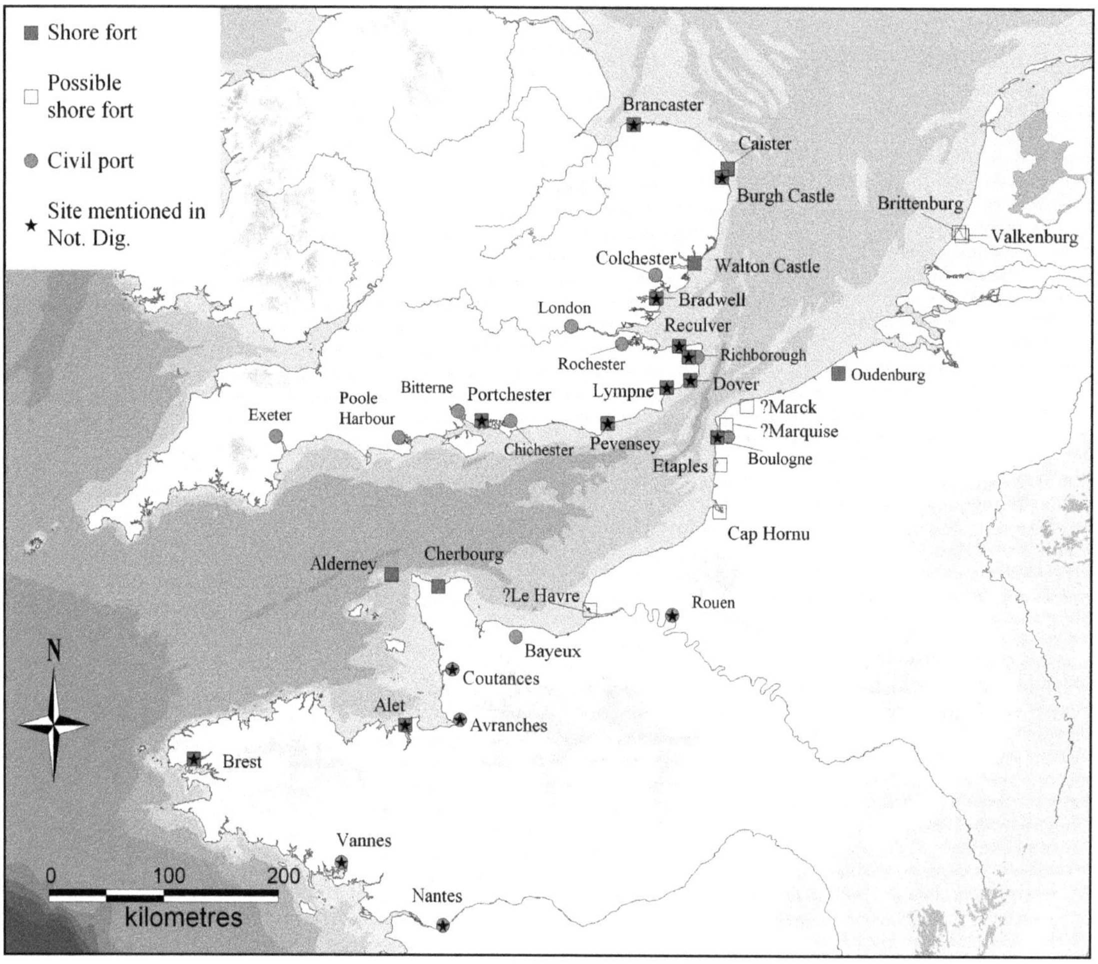

Fig. 6.5. Distribution of Late Roman shore forts and ports.

between jet objects from York and the Rhine provinces do suggest the possibility that craftsmen moved between these two industries however.[853]

Ports

During the second half of the third century civilian ports along the coasts of Britain and the northwest continental Empire either underwent a major decline or were replaced by strong fortifications. At London there is a concentration of Late Roman imports and it was probably the most important port in Britain at the time, but there was a major decline in comparison to earlier periods. There is no evidence for the construction of new riverside quays or warehousing and the massive late second- and early third-century quays were allowed to silt up during the latter half of the third century and were robbed out during the early fourth century. A riverside wall was constructed c. AD 255-270 which suggests an increased security risk from the sea.[854] Richborough possessed a Late Roman shore fort, which will be dealt with below, however I suspect it probably served as a significant civil port in the Late Roman period as well. It very probably served as the main port of entry for the sizeable quantities of traded imported pottery found in East Kent. Although little is known of Late Roman civilian Richborough aerial photography has indicated the presence of an urban focus between the third-century fort and amphitheatre.[855]

Along the South Dutch and Belgian coast civil settlements and most forts were abandoned in the late third century; these included Aardenburg, Voorburg, Oudorp on Goree, Domburg and Colijnsplaat and the other sites on the south of the Maas estuary. The abandonment of all these sites can be placed c. AD 270 and, as discussed below, can be connected to increasing Germanic invasions combined with the effects of a steadily rising sea level.[856] Whilst a shore fort was constructed at Boulogne in the later third century the civil settlement continued outside its walls.[857]

The later third century witnessed the construction of numerous shore forts around the Empire's Southern North Sea and Channel coasts (**Fig. 6.5**). In Britain the shore forts are located in the southeast spread between Portchester on the Solent and Brancaster on the Wash. Whilst Caister, Reculver and Brancaster were built in the

[853] Allason Jones 1996; 2002; Allason Jones and Jones 1994; 2001; Allen *et al.* 2007.
[854] Marsden 1994, 105-108.
[855] Millett and Wilmott 2003.
[856] Besuijen 2008; Brulet 1991; Lendering 2000; Trimpe Burger 1973; Mertens 1977.
[857] Seillier 2004.

later second or early third century the remainder belong to the later third century. Dating evidence is scarce, though Richborough and Portchester probably belong to the 280s, whilst a coin associated with construction deposits at Pevensey gives a *terminus post-quem* of AD 293, which is supported by the use of timbers dated by dendrochronology to AD 280-300. An association with an anti-invasion scheme undertaken by Allectus, and his predecessor Carausius, seems the best explanation for their construction. Subsequently they would have served as naval bases, both for the defence of British coastal waters against barbarian pirates and as secure bases for the transshipment of products, in particular British grain, to the continent.[858]

There were also large numbers of Late Roman forts and heavily fortified towns along the Southern North Sea and Channel coast of the continent (**Fig. 6.5**). Whilst the chronologies of the continental shore forts have not been precisely determined they principally appear to have been works of the mid- to late third century.[859] Like the British examples their functions would have been defence against barbarian piracy and acting as secure transshipment points for state supplies. Insight into the latter issue may be gained from investigations at the fourth-century fort at Valkenburg near the mouth of the Old Rhine, which possessed three large wooden granaries, which might hint at a connection to the supply of British grain.[860] Similarly, the site of Katwijk-De Brittenburg in South Holland has long since been lost to the sea, but a drawing of 1581 appears to depict a Late Roman shore fort with external bastions, within which lay stone foundations for probable granaries (**Fig. 6.6**).[861]

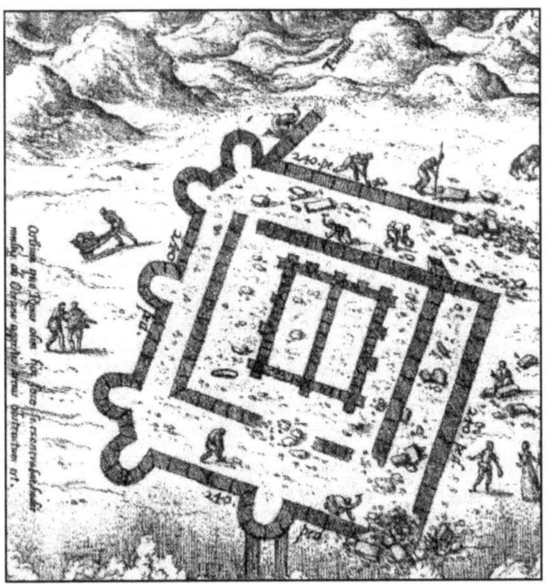

Fig. *6.6. Katwijk-De Brittenburg (drawing made by Abraham Ortelius in 1581).*

[858] Pearson 2002; 2005; 2006; Mason 2003, 155; Fulford and Tyers 1995; Cunliffe 1975; Cotterill 1993; White 1961; Wood 1990; Johnson 1976; Johnston 1977; Maxfield 1989.
[859] Brulet 1989; 1991; Seillier 2004; Mertens 1977; Lendering 2000; Mason 2003; Johnson 1976.
[860] Groenman van Waateringe 1986; Lendering 2000.
[861] Parleviet 2002; Hessing 1995; De Weerd 1986; Grane 2007, 110.

Most of the shore forts are listed as the bases of military units on the *Notitia Dignitatum*, which probably reflects the state of the garrisons at the end of the fourth century (see p. 128). The *Notitia* splits the shore forts up into three separate commands: The *Comes Litoris Saxonici* was in charge of nine garrison sites around the southeast coast of Britain (Brancaster, Burgh Castle, Bradwell, Reculver, Richborough, Dover, Lympne, Pevensey and Portchester).[862] The *Dux Belgicae Secundae* commanded three units, including the *Classis Sambricae* (the Fleet of the Somme), which was probably based at the mouth of the Somme and is also attested by stamped tiles from Etaples, a unit based at the unknown site of Marcis, which is probably Marck or Marquise in the Pas-de-Calais and a loaned unit based at Portu Epatiaci, which is also unknown, but might also be Etaples.[863] Finally the *Dux Tractus Armoricani* controlled some ten sites on the west French coast between the mouth of the Seine and the mouth of the Loire.[864]

The fragmentation of these commands was probably a long-standing affair, as the Carausius and Allectus episode had made it too dangerous to arrange for a wider naval command. Nevertheless, there were clearly strong organisational links between the different sections; these are best evidenced at the extremely well-excavated forts of Portchester and Oudenburg. Connections are clearly apparent in the jewellery, which implies the presence of numerous British women at the latter site, who had presumably moved with a unit posted from Portchester, or another of the British shore forts (see p. 134). Recent analysis has also revealed a large quantity and wide range of British pottery at Oudenburg (see p. 135).

Synthesis

During the second half of the third century there was substantial connectivity in the Southern North Sea and Eastern Channel system and the Atlantic system, although it is hard to assess its scale relative to preceding periods.

In terms of continental imports to Britain, the Southern North Sea and Eastern Channel system had a large influx of coin and precious metal. Some of this was to pay the army and state officials, particularly the flow of precious metal in the late fourth century which seems to have coincided with the introduction of vast accession donatives under the emperor Julian. However, a decline in the garrison size coupled with a shift to payment in kind in the late third century meant that army pay was not an overly significant factor. The majority of coin arrived as a result of private trade with, or state payments to, private civilian concerns who supplied products, principally agricultural goods, such as grain, to military and urban centres in the Rhineland. Aside from the coin there were few imported goods; some military equipment arrived with soldiers who had been posted to Britain from

[862] *Notitia Dignitatum Occidentis*. 28; Ireland 1986, 143-144; Hassall 1977.
[863] *Notitia Dignitatum Occidentis*. 38; Hassall 1977; Mason 2003, 160.
[864] *Notitia Dignitatum Occidentis*. 37; Hassall 1977.

the continent. Some pottery, Mayen ware and Argonne ware, arrived in southeast Britain through private trade. The quantities are notable, but tiny when compared to imported pottery of the earlier Roman phases.

Aside from probable traded imports of coin, the amounts of imports reaching Britain via the seaways of the Atlantic and Western Channel were fairly low. Olive oil arrived from North Africa, whilst *Céramique à l'éponge* came from western France. Severely dwindling quantities of wine from Aquitaine and seafood from Brittany may have been imported as well. These were probably all privately traded.

Britain exported a large amount of agricultural goods, particularly grain. These were obtained by the state through taxation in kind and on the market from private producers and also through private trade before subsequently being shipped across the Southern North Sea and Eastern Channel to consumers in the Rhine basin. Other exports across the Southern North Sea and Eastern Channel included small amounts of pottery, which probably represent low-level private trade, as well as jewellery and military equipment, which probably left with its wearers as personal possessions. Small amounts of iron, lead and tin/tin-alloy were probably shipped out of Britain by the state, though some of these metals may have been privately traded as well.

There were also British exports across the Western Channel, which may have included agricultural products, but are most apparent in the form of southeast Dorset BB1 pottery, found in large quantity in Normandy and also present at Breton shore forts. State contracts or supply mechanisms probably account for this distribution, though some private trade cannot be ruled out.

In the Southern North Sea and Eastern Channel private trade would have operated out of the declining civilian ports, such as London and Richborough in Britain, whilst Boulogne and inland ports well up the Rhine would have been important on the continent. Civilian traders may even have organized transport from the shore forts, on, or alongside, naval vessels for protection. The sizeable state movements may also have utilized the civilian ports, but a more important role must be assigned to the shore forts, which probably served as secure holding and transshipment points.

In the Atlantic and Western Channel civilian ports, such as Exeter and Poole Harbour, were important on the British side, whilst civilian ports extending down the French coast as far as the Mediterranean may also have played a role. In Normandy and Brittany shore forts received notable quantities of BB1 from Dorset.

The determinants of connective change

Political division within the Empire

Several phases of political division in the Late Roman period affected the northwestern parts of the Empire and impacted upon connectivity across the Channel and North Sea. The first major division occurred between AD 260-274 with the establishment of the Gallic Empire. Postumus, who had been given an important military command on the Rhine frontier, fell out with and killed the heir of the co-emperor Gallienus and proclaimed an independent Gallic Empire, which initially comprised Britain, the Germanies, Gaul, Spain and possibly Raetia. Postumus successfully repulsed Gallienus's attacks, but was killed by his own troops in AD 268. His eventual successor, Tetricus, soon lost Gallia Narbonensis, Gallia Aquitania and Spain and was eventually defeated by Aurelian in AD 274, following which the western Empire was reunited.[865]

The political divisions that occurred at the time of the Gallic Empire might well have disrupted long-distance trade in the western Empire; the decline of the Aquitanian wine industries at this time may have had something to do with the loss of markets in various parts of the Empire. The virtual cessation of large-scale Baetican olive oil export by the mid-third century might also have in part been related to the loss of markets in Italy, from which it never recovered, though, as noted, the decline probably actually pre-dates the Gallic Empire.

The second major political division was the revolt of Carausius and Allectus between AD 286-297. In AD 286 the co-emperor Maximian sentenced to death Carausius, the commander of a fleet charged with ridding the seas of Belgica and Armorica of Frankish and Saxon pirates, on the charge of intentionally letting the barbarians plunder, so that he could intercept them and embezzle their booty on their journey back. Carausius proclaimed himself emperor and seized control of Britain and northern Gaul. Maximian's attempts at defeating Carausius were initially unsuccessful, though by AD 293 he had taken northern France and Boulogne, which led to Carausius's assassination and replacement by one of his own officers, Allectus. By AD 296 the Caesar Constantius Chlorus had organised a two-pronged naval invasion and successfully retaken Britain for the Empire.[866] The separation and isolation of Britain from much of the rest of the Empire for an eleven-year period clearly interrupted connectivity, with a major decline in private trade and state supply the inevitable outcome.

The third, and most decisive break of all, came at the beginning of the fifth century. In AD 406 or 407 the British army proclaimed Constantine III emperor, probably in response to a huge barbarian invasion across the frozen Rhine which not only threatened Britain

[865] Drinkwater 1987; 2005; Wilkes 2005.
[866] For the historical sources see: Birley 2005, 371-393; Ireland 1986, 126-136. For summaries see: Salway 1993, 207-232; Frere 1978, 376-382; Casey 1994b.

directly, but, as Fulford has pointed out, probably disrupted Britain's exports on which the wealth of the province principally depended.[867] Constantine left Britain with the field army and won over the remnants of the army in Germany and Gaul and also secured much of Gaul and Spain. In AD 409, in the absence of Constantine and much of the field army, the people in Britain threw off Roman rule and freed their cities from barbarian invaders. Constantine was defeated in AD 410/411 and when Honorius regained control of the Gallic provinces in AD 411 he was unable, or unwilling, to reunite Britain with the Empire.[868] This had a catastrophic effect on Britain's connections with the Empire; state payments were no longer received in exchange for British agricultural products and army pay ceased. In the wake of this a dramatic economic collapse followed and the island split into numerous small militarised kingdoms.[869]

Changes in the British garrison

As discussed above (see pp. 128-129), there was a significant reduction in the British garrison from the mid-third century onwards. This meant that a much smaller portion of the British agricultural surplus was required to feed the British military garrison and meant that exports to the continent could increase.

Barbarian invasions.

From the mid-third century onwards the Western Empire experienced previously unknown levels of violence and invasion from the barbarian peoples living to the north and east of the river Rhine and in Britain, from peoples in Scotland and Ireland as well. What made these invasions even worse was the fact that the Empire was plagued by civil war in the mid-third century. Furthermore, from the mid-third century onwards new and more aggressive barbarian peoples were placing immense pressure on the Empire's other frontiers, in particular the Goths on the lower Danube and the Persians in the east, which put the Roman army under great strain.[870]

In the second half of the third century the principal aggressors from across the Rhine are named in historical sources as the Franks and the Alamanni, though we should be wary about giving too much credence to the ethnic affiliations provided by Classical authors. The Rhineland came under extreme barbarian pressure in AD 253, though Gallienus appears to have been able to hold the frontier.[871] In AD 260, however, there was a major invasion of Gaul and Spain by the Franks and of Gaul, Raetia and Italy by the Alamanni.[872] These groups again invaded and devastated a weakened Gaul in the aftermath of the defeat of the Gallic Empire, though they eventually suffered a heavy defeat from the emperor Probus in AD 277-278.[873] The Franks are also recorded as terrorising the sea under Probus, so there may have been a heavy element of seaborne piracy in their incursions.[874]

In AD 285 or 286 Maximian defeated a force of Heruls and Chaibones who had attacked the Lower Rhine, probably by sea. The former peoples can possibly be placed on Sealand in Denmark, the latter were either Saxons or Franks.[875] By AD 286 historical sources attest that the coasts of Belgica and Armorica were infested with Frankish and Saxon pirates, which Carausius was specifically appointed to clear.[876] Carausius is said to have employed barbarians in his fleet and trained them for seamanship, whilst Allectus is explicitly recorded as having Franks in his army. Following Allectus's defeat in battle, these Franks fled to London and began to loot the city, which was spared by the timely arrival of Constantius Chlorus. Of course we should bear in mind that the panegyrics which attest to all this might in fact have distorted the truth in order to portray Carausius and Allectus in a bad light.[877]

During the following half century the northwestern Empire does not appear to have been marked by serious warfare, perhaps because of the success of Diocletian's reorganisation of the military, or perhaps because of the victories obtained by Constantius over the Franks and Alamanni in the 290s. The resettlement of barbarian peoples as *laeti* on land in northern Gaul may also have temporarily relieved the pressure.[878] There was, however, a serious outbreak of Frankish piracy, which affected the Empire's coast as far as Spain between AD 306-313.[879]

After c. AD 350 barbarian invasions once again become more frequent; the Franks and Alamanni overran the Rhine frontier in the mid-350s and Julian's heavy response alarmed the Saxons, who attacked the Empire by sea and temporarily seized the Batavian island.[880] In AD 360 there was a major invasion of Britain by the Scots, or Attacotti, and the Picts.[881] AD 367 was marked by serious incursions by multiple barbarian groups, which was labelled the barbarian conspiracy; Britain was attacked by Picts, Scots, Attacotti and Saxons, whilst the Franks and Saxons raided the coast of Gaul. Count Theodosius was sent to Britain with 2000 troops and successfully dealt with the problem.[882]

---

867 Fulford 2004, 324; Birley 2005, 457-459; Thompson 1977.

868 Orosius 4.40.4; Zosimus 5.27.2-3, 31.4, 32.3, 43.1-2, 6.1-3; *Narratio de imperatoribus domus Valentinianae et Theodosianae MGH AA* IX, *Chron. Min.* i.630; Procopius *De bello vandalico* 3.2.31, 37-38; Birley 2005, 455-465; Thompson 1977; Mattingly 2006, 530; Ward-Perkins 2005.

869 Esmonde Cleary 1989; Laycock 2008; Mattingly 2006, 529-539; Cooper 1996; Wickham 2005, 306-310.

870 Wilkes 2005; Drinkwater 2005.

871 Zosimus 1.30; Drinkwater 1987, 88; 2005, 43; Wilkes 2005, 222.

872 Victor 33.3; Eutropius 9.8; Orosius 7.22.8; Drinkwater 1987, 23-24, 88-89; 2005, 43-44; Haywood 1999, 49-51.

873 *Historia Augusta. Probus.* 12.3; Zosimus I.68.1; Haywood 1999, 51.

874 *Pan. Lat. vet.* 8(5). 18.3; Birley 2005, 391.

875 *Pan. Lat. vet.* 2(10).5.2-3; *Pan. Lat. Vet.* 3(11).7.1; Drinkwater 2007, 180-181; Haywood 1999, 60.

876 Eutropius 9.21; Aurelius Victor 39.20.

877 *Pan. Lat. vet.* 8(5).12.1, 16-17; Birley 2005, 388-393; Haywood 1999, 61-62.

878 *Pan. Lat. vet.* 8(5).8.1-9.4; Wilkes 2005, 231; Haywood 1999, 64; Birley 2005, 380; Nixon and Rodgers 1994, 120-121.

879 *Pan. Lat.* 4.17.1; Haywood 1999, 64.

880 Zosimus 3.5.2, 6.1-4; Haywood 1999, 66-67.

881 Ammianus Marcellinus 20.1.1; Birley 2005, 424-426.

882 Ammianus Marcellinus 27.8, 28.3; 30.7.9-11; Birley 2005, 427-440; Laycock 2008, 109-134.

Bartholomew has suggested that there is no literary evidence to support the involvement of Saxons in attacks on Britain during the barbarian conspiracy and this view has recently become extremely popular, added to by scholars who assert that contemporary Germanic ship technology was insufficient to successfully mount long-distance pirate raids.[883] The latter point will be dealt with below, where it is asserted that Germanic ship technology was suitable for undertaking such raids (pp. 148-149). We should also bear in mind that the accuracy of these literary sources with regard to their ethnic attributions of barbarian groups is highly dubious. In fact they do seem to suggest that Saxons were involved in attacks on Britain during AD 367; as Birley has pointed out, a passage of Ammianus clearly referring to the events of 367 is best read as including the Saxons amongst the list of hostile peoples harrying Britain.[884] Furthermore, a reference inserted into a late fourth-century translation of Josephus' *Jewish War* discusses fighting against Scots and Saxons as part of a British campaign, very likely the events of 367-368.[885] Claudian also describes Count Theodosius conducting naval campaigns around the British coast and includes a statement that the Orkneys ran red with Saxon blood.[886] The Saxon shore commands (*Litus Saxonicus*) attested in the *Notitia Dignitatum* also surely imply the onset of a major Saxon threat by at least the end of the fourth century.

In the latter decades of the fourth century the Saxons begin to come to the fore in historical accounts of invasion. In AD 370, having passed the difficulties of the Ocean, the Saxons attempted to invade northern Gaul, but were repulsed.[887] Stilicho undertook defensive measures in Britain c. AD 398, which probably involved sending troops. Claudian, writing of this the following year, stated that the sea was now safer with the Saxons tamed and that Britain was secure now that the Picts were broken. The same writer recorded that prior to Stilicho's intervention Britain had been suffering at the hands of the Scots and Picts and from hostile Saxon pirates who had arrived on all coasts with the winds.[888] The huge invasion of Vandals, Alans and Suebians into Gaul across the frozen Rhine in AD 405 or 406 has been dealt with briefly above. Our final consideration is the mention in the Gallic Chronicle of AD 452 that Britain was devastated by an invasion of Saxons in AD 408, presumably the barbarians that Zosimus records endangering Britain's cities, which prompted the people in the island to cast off Roman rule.[889]

Drinkwater has argued that in the west the barbarian invasions of the Late Roman period were small-scale affairs, which were greatly exaggerated in the historical sources in order to promote the interests of the Roman elite.[890] He suggests that the invasions cannot have been as bad as they were portrayed and that the barbarians were in fact being exploited by Rome; I argue, however, that they had a devastating impact. There is widespread evidence for depopulation and economic decline in large parts of northwest Europe from the late third century onwards and this must principally be assigned to the effects of barbarian invasion.[891]

Throughout Gaul towns had become small, heavily fortified affairs by the late third century. Whilst during the early Empire *civitas* capitals were typically large, undefended settlements of c. 100 ha, by the later Empire their walled areas comprised a mere 4-10 ha, though there are indications that sizeable areas may have been occupied outside the walls. Towns also appear to have declined in number; a survey of small towns in northern Gaul shows a decline from 87 sites in the early third century to 56 by the end of the century.[892]

There was also a severe decrease in rural settlement; Belgium and northwest France are virtually devoid of fourth-century villas, in stark contrast to the early imperial period to which hundreds of examples have been assigned. The only real concentrations in northern Gaul are restricted to the localities of the major cities, such as Trier, Cologne, Tongres and Paris.[893] The coastal plain of Belgium, which had witnessed a major phase of settlement expansion in the early third century, was almost completely deserted by c. AD 260/270.[894] The Roman parts of the Netherlands were also virtually empty by the end of the third century, with settlements in the west abandoned c. AD 260/270, whilst survey reveals an abandonment of 70% of settlements in the Dutch Eastern river region in the mid-third century. Pollen evidence from the latter region also reveals a contemporary decrease in arable cultivation, coupled with an increase in woodland. Fourth- and fifth-century artefacts are extremely rare in the coastal areas of Belgium and the Netherlands.[895]

This image of depopulation and deserted land in northern Gaul is lent support by the historical sources, which record barbarian peoples, labelled as *laeti* and *foederati*, being brought in to settle and cultivate the land. They first appear in the panegyrics of the late third century, for example, under Maximian in AD 288 defeated Franks were brought into the Empire to farm the deserted corn lands of the Nervii and Treveri, whilst the deserted lands of the Ambiani, Bellovaci, Tricasses and Lingones are recorded as again growing green under barbarian

883 Bartholomew 1984; c.f. Cotterill 1993; Pearson 2002; 2005; Laycock 2008, 169.
884 Ammianus Marcellinus 26.4.5; Birley 2005, 427-428.
885 Birley 2005, 432.
886 Claudian *De III cons. Honorii.* 52-8, *De IV cons. Honorii*; Birley 2005, 437-438.
887 Ammianus Marcellinus 28.5.1-2; Birley 2005, 441-442.
888 Claudian *In Eutrop.* 1.391-393; *De Cons. Stil.* 2.247-255; Birley 2005, 452-453.
889 *Chron. Gall.* a.452, MGH AA IX, *Chron. min.* i. 654: 62; Zosimus 6.5.2-6.1; Birley 2005, 455-460.
890 Drinkwater 2007.
891 C.f. Ward-Perkins 2005.
892 Wightman 1981; Esmonde-Cleary 1989; Johnson 1983a; Haywood 1999, 55.
893 Fulford 1996; Van Ossel 1992; Esmonde-Cleary 1989.
894 Rippon 2000, 141; Thoen 1978, 235; 1981.
895 Rippon 2000, 141-146, Fig. 27; Louwe Kooijmans 1980, 129; Henderikx 1986, 478; Vos and Van Heeringen 1997, 67-68; Willems, 1981, 76, Fig. 23; 1984, 143, Fig. 137.

tillage.[896] Chamavi and Frisii also seem to have been captured and sent to till deserted lands as *laeti* following Constantius's campaigns to the Rhine-Scheldt delta in AD 293.[897] Panegyrics of AD 307 and 310 state that Frankish tribes were uprooted and settled in deserted tracts of Gaul so that they might maintain the peace of the Empire through agriculture and military service.[898] Ammianus also refers to *laeti* on the west side of the Rhine at the time of Julian, whilst the *Notitia Dignitatum* lists settlements of *laeti* in Gaul.[899]

There was decline elsewhere in northwest Europe as well; in Brittany many coastal villas were abandoned c. AD 270-280, while others survived at a reduced level. Pollen samples also indicate a reduction in cultivation and an encroachment of forest.[900] The Roman territory beyond the upper Rhine and Danube, the *Agri Decumates*, was also abandoned by Roman forces c. AD 260, probably as a result of barbarian invasions, though the contemporary civil wars probably played an important role as well.[901]

Coastal areas of eastern Britain also underwent a late third-century economic and demographic decline. In Sussex and Kent many coastal villas were abandoned in the mid- or late third century.[902] Occupation in southeast Essex and eastern Suffolk had also declined by the Late Roman period.[903] Rippon notes a general decline in settlement and economic activity around the coastal marshes of southeast Britain, which began, in some cases, in the later second century, but hastened in the third and fourth centuries.[904] The pottery industries, which had flourished in the coastal regions of southeast Britain during the Antonine period, such as the Upchurch industry in Kent, the BB2 industry and the Colchester potters, had declined to be of only local concern by the mid-third century and, unlike the pottery industries of central and western England, did not recover.[905] These changes may have had much to do with sea level rise, though piracy probably played a role as well. For example, Godmanchester suffered major fire damage at the end of the third century and scattered, disarticulated human bones, some gnawed by dogs or wolves, lay on top of third-century deposits, which is suggestive of a massacre.[906]

Barbarian invasion and piracy not only disrupted and threatened communications, particularly undefended private trade, but it was also the principal cause of a severe demographic and economic decline in much of northwest Europe, particularly in rural areas. This led to the surviving urban centres and military forces of this area turning to Britain for supplies as central and western Britain were comparatively unaffected by barbarian invasions.

Sea-level rise

Sea-level rise also contributed, alongside barbarian invasion and piracy, to economic and demographic decline in coastal areas. This rise was a result of the Dunkirk II marine transgression, which was one of a number of long-term transgressions and regressions in sea level which affected the North Sea basin. A new study of peat deposits from the North Sea coast of Germany places the onset of the Dunkirk II transgression at c. AD 50. Sea level gradually rose to a peak c. AD 300 of 0.87 m above German Ordnance Datum at Mean High Water - a substantial overall rise considering that Mean High Water had stood at 0.65 m below German Ordnance Datum in the late first century BC. By c. AD 350 a minor regression phase was underway.[907]

We do not know that the Dunkirk II transgression affected all of the coastal areas of the North Sea equally, or even at the same time; however, by the Late Roman period it had a major impact upon the coastline of the Southern North Sea. For example, the Belgian coastline appears to have retreated ten miles in some areas.[908] A poet referring to Constantius's campaign to the Rhine-Scheldt delta in AD 293 described the land as thoroughly soaked, drenched with water and marshy and stated that it was hardly land at all.[909] On Voorne and Putten in Zeeland, a number of the sites abandoned c. AD 260 were covered with flood silts, which were themselves sealed by a peat layer C14 dated to the mid- to late third century AD.[910]

In Britain too there is palaeoenvironmental evidence for an increase in marine flooding and a sea level rise during the Late Roman period from several wetland areas of Britain, such as the Severn estuary, Romney Marsh, the Fenland, Lincolnshire and the Humber. In these regions Roman-period sites are often covered by over 1 m of alluvium.[911] In the Fens the coastline in places retreated over 30 miles further than the modern coast of the Wash.[912]

Economic growth in southwest and central England

The final factor underlying connective change in the Late Roman period was the ability of southwestern and central England to undergo economic growth and produce large agricultural surpluses for export. There was a major expansion of villas in the southwest, particularly in the

[896] *Pan. Lat. vet.* 8(5).21; Hawkes and Dunning 1961, 7; Williams 1997, 50-51.
[897] *Pan. Lat. vet.* 8(5).8.1-9.4; Birley 2005, 380; Nixon and Rodgers 1994, 120-121.
[898] *Pan. Lat. vet.* 7.4.2, 6.5.3; Nixon and Rodgers 1994; Hawkes and Dunning 1961, 7.
[899] Ammianus 20.8.13; James 1984, 172; Hawkes and Dunning 1961, 7.
[900] Haywood 1999, 54-55; Galliou 1981.
[901] Drinkwater 1987, 89; Wilkes 2005, 223. This is the most plausible theory though there is considerable debate on this topic: Grane 2007, 90-103; Kuhnen 1992; Theune 2004; Fischer 1999; Strobel 1999.
[902] King 2004, 357; Drewett *et al.* 1988, 218; Mattingly 2006, 388.
[903] King, 2004, 359; Williamson 2005, 13; Newman 1992, 32.
[904] Rippon 2000, 138-141, Tab. 4.
[905] Going 1992.
[906] Haywood 1999, 64-65; Green 1975.
[907] Behre 2007.
[908] Thoen 1978; Haywood 1999, 49.
[909] *Pan. Lat. vet.* 8(5).8; Birley 2005, 380; Nixon and Rodgers 1994, 120-121.
[910] Rippon 2000; 141; Brinkkemper *et al.* 1995.
[911] Rippon 1997; 2000, 138-141; Van de Noort 2004b, 107-129; Long *et al.* 1998.
[912] Simmons 1980; Haywood 1999, 49.

Cotswolds and Dorset, beginning in the late third century and reaching its apogee in the first half of the fourth century.[913] Upex has also noted that in the Nene Valley and central-eastern England settlements show signs of expansion in the late third and first half of the fourth century, with decline here only coming in the late fourth century.[914]

The main reason for this growth was the existence of relatively peaceful and settled conditions in the interior of England, which suffered far less from barbarian invasion than other parts of the northwestern Empire. In contrast, the unstable conditions on the continent led consumers here increasingly to turn to Britain as a source of food, which the Roman state probably ensured by making large cash payments to the British producers and arranging safe transport for the supplies.[915]

The growth in agricultural production is also mirrored by a major expansion in British pottery industries, particularly at Oxford, the New Forest, Much Hadham, the Nene Valley, Alice Holt and southeast Dorset BB1, from the mid-third century onwards, although, as discussed above, these were mainly consumed internally within Britain.[916] The growth of these pottery industries was clearly related to the influx of coin to the civilian areas of Britain during the Late Roman period. Going has outlined the main phases of growth, in the mid-third and mid- to late fourth century, which seem to coincide with the main injections of bulk, low-value coin, thus maximising the potential number of people who could gain access to coin and participate in monetised market relations.[917] The growth of the pottery industries was also probably influenced by the decreased availability of continental imports, particularly *terra sigillata*, which although hardly imported at all during the first half of the third century was in fact curated and kept in widespread circulation until well into the third century.[918]

6.2. The Eastern North Sea system

Introduction

In the mid-third century there was a cessation in maritime trade between the Empire and the Eastern North Sea coast of the *Barbaricum*. Connections between the coastal areas north and south of the Rhine continued, however. There was a marked change in mechanism, with some material now being transferred from the Empire to the Eastern North Sea coast through Frankish and Saxon piracy, whilst objects were moved between both areas as a result of posting Frankish and Saxon soldiers in northern Gaul and settling Germanic peoples in this area as *laeti* and *foederati*. There are several main reasons behind these changes. These include the contemporary political and military weaknesses within the Empire and the economic decline of northern Gaul and the Rhine provinces. In addition, social and economic changes amongst the barbarian peoples were important factors. New and larger tribal entities emerged, iron production intensified, ship-building technology improved and a sea-level rise caused increasing pressure on coastal communities. These factors all led the Saxons and Franks to turn increasingly to piracy and to seek new land within the Empire's boundaries.

Imports to the Eastern North Sea coastal region

Coinage and metals

To some extent the patterns of coin import to the eastern coasts of the North Sea show similarities to the pattern of coin import to Britain, that is, more coin arrived at times when the precious metal content was low. There is a notable concentration of base-silver radiates in the northern Netherlands and northwest Germany which date to c. AD 260-274.[919] Thereafter base coins are rare in Friesland, which suffered a severe demographic decline in the later third century (see p. 149). In northwest Germany, particularly the region between the lower Elbe and Weser rivers (the Elbe-Weser triangle), meanwhile, base coins continued to arrive in numbers into the first half of the fourth century, with a sizeable group dating to the time of the tetrarchy and a large peak in the Constantinian period, following which there was a decline, with a cut-off c. AD 355, after which bronze coin came in only small quantities.[920] Whether this cut-off actually reflects a contemporary change in the degree or type of contact between the peoples of the North Sea coast and the Empire is hard to ascertain as it coincides with the period when silver was excluded from the bronze coinage and a tripartite coinage system was established (c. AD 357-363. See p. 128, **Fig. 6.1**). With its, admittedly tiny, silver content removed the bronze coin may have appealed far less to Germanic peoples.

Gold *aurei* and *solidi* minted at Trier reached the northwest *Barbaricum* in fair quantity during the second half of the fourth and the beginning of the fifth century.[921] Interestingly, this also parallels the British situation where gold became more prevalent as well. Precious metal reached the Eastern North Sea coast in other forms as well. A hoard of Roman silver, which probably dates to the fourth century AD, was found in 1861 near Winsum terp in Friesland. Now almost entirely lost, it consisted primarily of vessels and included a compacted mass of almost pure silver weighing c. 3 kg.[922] Roman silver finds from Lower Saxony include the 1.4 kg late fourth-century decorated silver plate found near the coast

[913] Mattingly 2006, 397-400, 499; Fulford 1996; 2004; King 2004; Millett 1990.
[914] Upex 2008, 240-242.
[915] See Fulford 1996; 2004.
[916] Going 1992; Young 1977; Fulford 1975; Howe *et al.* 1980; Tyers 1996b; forthcoming.
[917] Going 1992.
[918] Willis 2005.
[919] Van der Vin 1996, 365-366; 1999; Berger 1992, 164-170, Abb. 57; 1995, 106.
[920] Van der Vin 1996, 365-366; 1999; Berger 1992, 187-196, Abb. 62; 1995, 106-109, Karte 4.
[921] Berger 1992, 161-164, 171-187, Abb. 55, 59-60; 1995, 109, Karte 3; Van der Vin 1996, 366, Tab. 4; 2000, 636; Bloemers 1983, 198-200, Figs. 8.30-8.31; Kromann 1989; 1995, Fig. 13.4.
[922] Galestin 1993.

at Altenwalde and the three stamped silver ingots of Theodosius I (AD 378-395) and Valentinian III (AD 425-455) found further inland at Dierstorf.[923]

Some of the finds of coin and precious metal probably represent booty obtained in the historically well-attested Saxon and Frankish pirate raids on the coasts of the Empire (see pp. 139-141). However, some of the material will have arrived as a result of people from the Eastern North Sea coast serving as soldiers, *foederati* or *laeti* in northern Gaul from the later third century and subsequently returning to their homelands. In addition, a substantial contact, involving the exchange of goods and the movement of people between the Germanic peoples south and north of the Rhine probably developed during this period and some material will have reached the Eastern North Sea coast in this fashion. Trade with the Roman Empire proper does not seem to have been occurring.

Large quantities of precious metal were also reaching Scandinavia; a substantial proportion of this derived from the Eastern Empire and arrived alongside other material, such as large quantities of glass from the Black Sea coast, via overland routes across Eastern Europe, most probably as a result of strong political and cultural contact with the Goths and participation alongside these peoples in wars in the Black Sea region.[924] Some coin did reach Denmark via western routes; for example, 11 *solidi* from a hoard at Gudme ending AD 355 were minted at Trier.[925] However, these probably arrived overland. Indeed, a strong link is apparent between graves on Fyn and the exceptionally rich Hassleben-Leuna group of graves from Thuringia which date to the second half of the third century.[926] Despite this we cannot rule out the possibility that some precious metal reached Scandinavia from the Empire via the North Sea. The Heruli, who possibly came from Denmark, were involved in a probable maritime raid on the Lower Rhine with a tribe of Saxons or Franks in AD 285 or 286.[927]

There are hardly any imported Roman copper-alloy vessels from the Eastern North Sea coastal regions of the northern Netherlands and northwest Germany that can be assigned to the second half of the third century or afterwards.[928] This is the general pattern observable throughout the western *Barbaricum*, where despite the arrival of some vessels in central Germany and Scandinavia during the second half of the third century, the fourth century is characterised by a dearth of imports.[929] The main exception to this rule is Norway, where Westland cauldrons are fairly common in fourth- and fifth-century graves. These were probably produced somewhere in the Western Empire.[930] Lund Hansen has argued that the Norwegian finds in fact reached their destinations indirectly via the Danish region. She attributes the rarity of these vessels in Denmark to the contemporary lack of a furnished grave custom from the fourth century onwards.[931] This must be correct; certainly large quantities of Gothic glass from Norway must have come via Denmark or elsewhere in the Baltic.

A number of belt fittings produced in the Roman frontier region between c. AD 370-430 are found in the northwest *Barbaricum*, particularly in graves in the Elbe-Weser triangle. These were surely obtained by Saxons and Franks serving as soldiers, *foederati* or *laeti* in northern Gaul and then returning home.[932] Belt fittings of British origin are rare in these regions, though a Hawkes and Dunning Type 1B belt plate was found in a cremation burial at Westerwanna in the Elbe-Weser triangle. This was undoubtedly a late fourth- or early fifth-century product of the Cotswolds region. It presumably arrived as a personal possession of a Saxon soldier who had obtained it during service in Britain during the Late Roman, or more probably, the early post-Roman period, though booty from a pirate raid cannot be ruled out.[933]

There are a handful of bracelets in Lower Saxony which arrived from the northwestern parts of the Empire. These include a fourth-century strip bracelet with punched circle and dots separated by lines from Altenwalde, originating from either Britain or the region between the Seine and the Rhine.[934] A clear British late fourth-century cogwheel bracelet is present in a cremation burial at Westerwanna.[935] The bracelets probably arrived with their wearers, though this is not certain. They may represent women from Britain, and perhaps another part of the northwestern Empire, who arrived as the partners of Saxon soldiers who had seen service abroad, or who may have been seized during Saxon pirate raids.

Chainmail has been recovered from several sites along the coast of northwest Germany in late third- to early fifth-century contexts. Fragments were occasionally deposited in the cremation burials of both men and women, where they may have served to provide ritual protection.[936] This chainmail was probably a product of the Empire and will most likely have been obtained by Saxon soldiers through service in the Roman military, or as booty; we cannot, however, completely rule out the possibility that it was locally made.

[923] Busch 1995, 232-233, 258-259; Erdrich 2002, 192-193.
[924] Zosimus 1.42-43, 46; Storgaard 1994; 2003; Lund Hansen 1987; Kromann 1989; 1994; Horsnæs 2008; Vang Petersen 1994; Bursche 1996.
[925] Horsnæs 2008; Kromann 1989.
[926] Becker 2008; Werner 1973; Storgaard 2003; Grane 2008; Hedeager 1992a, 158, Fig. 3.40; 1992b; 287.
[927] *Pan. Lat. Vet.* 2(10).5.2-3; *Pan. Lat. Vet.* 3(11).7.1; Drinkwater 2007, 180-181; Haywood 1999, 60.
[928] Erdrich 2001, 128-135.
[929] Lund Hansen 1987.
[930] Dahlin Hauken 2005; Bollingberg and Lund Hansen 1995; Lund Hansen 1987.
[931] Lund Hansen 1987, 190, 214-215, 224.
[932] Böhme 1974; 1986.
[933] Laycock 2008; 2009; Böhme 1986, Abb. 30; Quillfeldt and Roggenbuck 1985, Grab 701b, Taf. 122; Busch 1995, 274-275; Erdrich 2002, XXI-02-27/1.60, Taf. 120.6.
[934] Observed in Museum Harburg. For distribution see: Swift 2000a, 136, Fig. 184.
[935] Zimmer-Linnfeld 1960, 40, Taf. 35, 256c.
[936] Busch 1995, 276-277; Erdrich 2002, 215; Erdrich and Carnap-Bornheim 2004, 126.

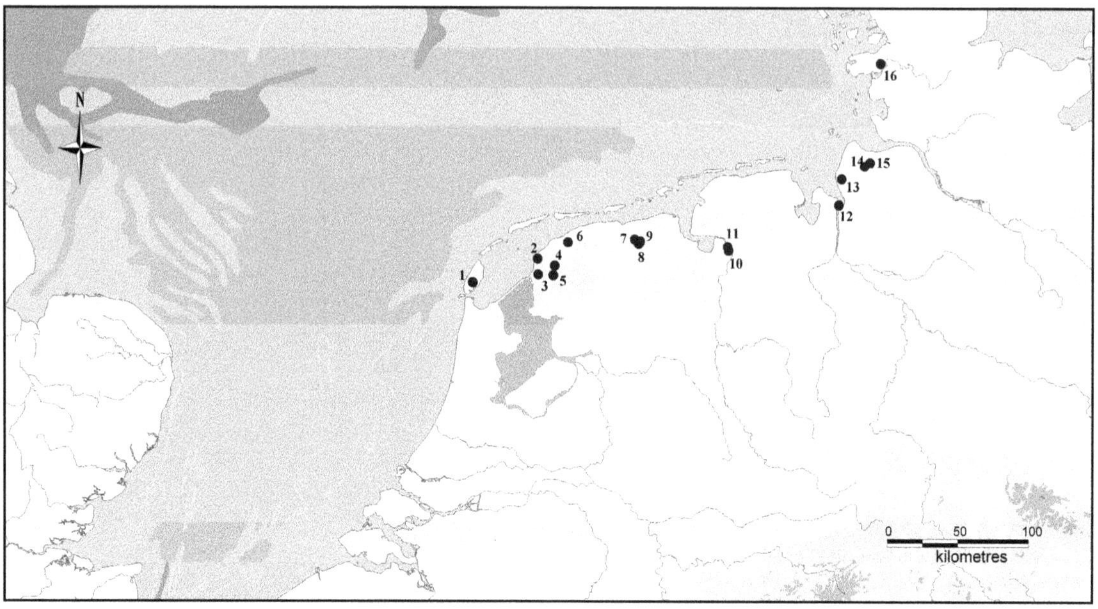

Fig. 6.7. Sites north of the Rhine with Romano-British pottery c. AD 260-430. 1. Den Burg, 2. Wijnaldum, 3. Witmarsum, 4. Winsum, 5. Oosterend, 6. Hijum, 7. Ezinge, 8. Brillerij, 9. Oostum, 10. Bentumersiel, 11. Jemgum, 12. Einswarden, 13. Feddersen Wierde, 14. Westerwanna, 15. Nordleda, 16. Tofting.

Pottery

There were a handful of pottery imports during the Late Roman period, though these were far below the levels at which East Gaulish *terra sigillata* arrived during the late second and early third century. The Late Roman imports include Mayen ware, which has been found in small quantities at Den Burg and Schagen-Muggenburg on the Noord Holland coast and at Wijster in Drenthe.[937] Whilst fifth-century Argonne ware is known at several sites in the northern Netherlands, fourth-century examples appear to be absent.[938] I have recorded at least twenty-one Romano-British pottery vessels from sixteen sites between the Rhine and the Eider (**Figs. 6.7-9**, Appendix. 10). The majority, perhaps all, of these vessels can be assigned to the period AD 260-430. They reached the Eastern North Sea coast directly from southern Britain; as discussed above, Romano-British pottery is fairly rare in continental parts of the Empire. The British distribution of the wares concerned shows a distinct southern bias. Whilst BB1 is widespread, New Forest ware derives almost exclusively from the Channel coast of England, Oxford ware is most common in central and southern England, Hadham ware in southeast England, whilst Nene Valley ware is found throughout central and eastern England. This pottery may have been obtained in Saxon and Frankish pirate raids on the coasts of southeast England, though it is possible that many pots were transported with Saxon mercenaries returning home from service in England during the post-Roman period.

Other pottery imports include wheel-thrown *terra-nigra*-like pedestal bowls of Chenet type 342/Gellep 242, which date to the late fourth and early fifth century and have been identified at numerous sites along the coast of the northern Netherlands and northwest Germany. These were probably produced in the region south of the Rhine, as they are also found here, though at present their production region cannot be ascertained with any security.[939] In addition, many fragments of wheel-thrown funnel-shaped bowls, in so-called *terra nigra*-like ware, are found at sites in the northern Netherlands. At Wijnaldum, some twenty fragments were excavated, the majority of which derived from fourth-century contexts, whilst c. 150 sherds were found at Wijster in Drenthe. It cannot be ruled out that these bowls represented a local adoption of Roman wheel-throwing techniques and indeed, local handmade pottery of the third and early fourth century bears a strong similarity to their forms. However, the bowls are paralleled at sites such as Rijswijk, De Bult in the southern Netherlands and given the relative rarity of the ware in the northern Netherlands they are probably best seen as an import from south of the Rhine.[940] *Terra-nigra*-like ware does not necessarily represent trade with the Roman Empire. These vessels were probably manufactured in the areas settled by barbarian *laeti* and *foederati* and their appearance further north is best connected with intra-Germanic exchange, or as personal possessions connected with the movement of Franks and Saxons from one side of the Rhine to the other.

Exports from the Eastern North Sea coastal region

Metalwork

A sizeable number of brooches manufactured in the northwest *Barbaricum* begin to appear in graves in northern Gaul between c. AD 370-450. The Germanic brooches concerned are simple crossbow brooches,

[937] Diederik 2002, 50, afb. 31; Van Es 1967, 169-172.
[938] Boeles 1951; Glasbergen 1944.
[939] Erdrich 2002, 213-214; Bloemers 1983, 193, Fig. 8.27.
[940] Galestin 1999; Van Es 1967, 158-168.

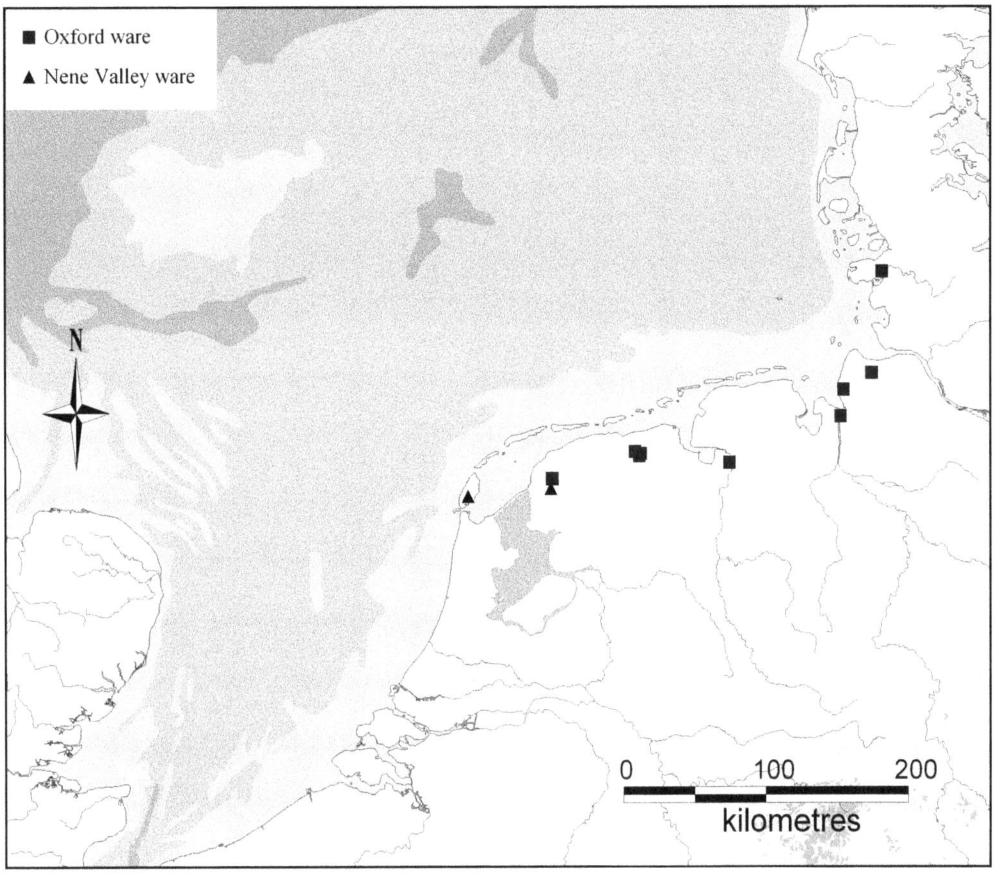

Fig. 6.8. The distribution of Oxford and Nene Valley wares north of the Rhine.

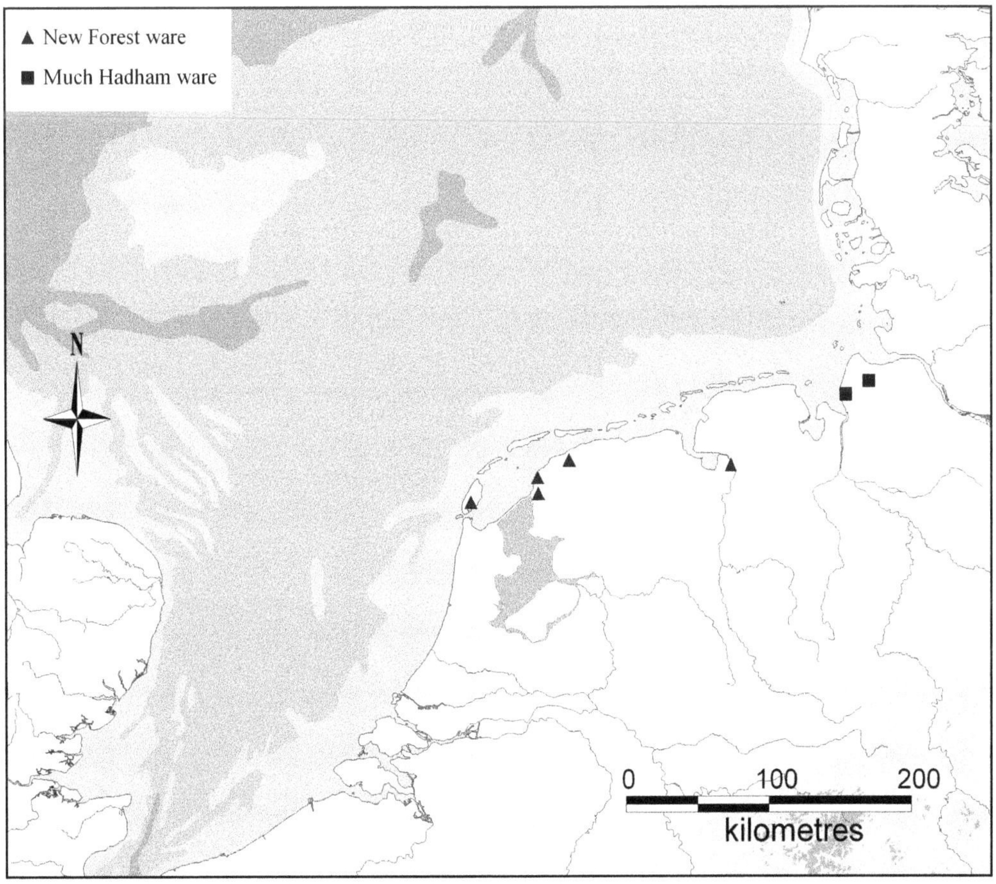

Fig. 6.9. The distribution of New Forest and Much Hadham wares north of the Rhine.

tutulus brooches and supporting arm brooches with a trapezoid footplate. They represent a brooch tradition clearly foreign to northern Gaul and are strongly paralleled in the northwest German region, most notably in the Elbe-Weser triangle, though examples are also known in the northern Netherlands. The majority of these brooches were very probably produced in these latter regions, though some, most notably the mercury-gilt (niello) tutulus brooches would have been made in the region between the Loire and the Rhine, perhaps in Gallo-Roman workshops, utilising the foreign tradition.[941] These brooches clearly attest to the presence of Saxon and Frankish women in northern Gaul. The context for their arrival would have been the widespread appearance of Germanic soldiers, *laeti* and *foederati* in northern Gaul, which must have accelerated from the later fourth century onwards. Indeed, between AD 370-450 a large group of weapon graves appears between the Rhine and the Loire, which are strongly paralleled in the Elbe-Weser triangle and represent Germanic recruits from beyond the Rhine.[942]

In contrast, 'Germanic' brooches of the second half of the fourth and the beginning of the fifth century AD are notably much rarer in Britain than in northern Gaul. Such brooches are not entirely absent, indeed, a brooch derived from the Almgren VII series has been identified at Kirmington in Lincolnshire. This has its best parallels in the northern Netherlands and northwest Germany and most likely dates to the later third or early fourth century.[943] Two tutulus brooches of unparalleled type have been identified at Abingdon and a fine silver example has been found in a late fourth- or early fifth-century grave in the Eastern cemetery of London. The latter example has traces of niello-inlay and typologically belongs to the Cortrat-Oudenburg type, which on distributional grounds was almost certainly produced in the region between the Loire and the Rhine in a 'Germanic' style.[944]

It was only during the middle third of the fifth century that brooches originating in the coastal regions of northwest Germany, or possibly the northern Netherlands, began to reach southeast Britain in quantity. These include supporting-arm brooches of Mahndof and Perlberg type, of which c. 30 British examples are known, early equal-arm brooches, early cruciform brooches and certain types of decorated plate brooch.[945] These brooch types are hard to date precisely. Whilst they have formerly been considered as early fifth-, or even late fourth-, century in date, they should probably be placed in the middle third of the fifth century. The admittedly limited evidence for associations in northwest German graves indicates that they are rarely found with simple crossbow brooches, tutulus brooches or supporting-arm brooches with a trapeze-shaped foot and are thus very likely to be chronologically later. In addition, these brooch types are virtually absent from the north French material, which again suggests a chronological separation and that such types are unlikely to date to the beginning of the fifth century or earlier.[946] The brooch evidence indicates that the beginnings of Anglo-Saxon population movements to Britain began in the mid-fifth century and not before. By the later fifth and early sixth century Germanic-style brooches are known in large quantities from southern and eastern Britain; however, given their sheer quantity it is probable that most of these later brooches would actually have been produced in Britain, albeit drawing upon foreign styles.[947]

Pottery

Pottery does not seem to have been exported from the Eastern North Sea coast to the Empire during this period. Whilst Myres argued that Saxon pottery first appeared in Britain at the end of the fourth century, the evidence now best supports a date in the mid-fifth century, as with the brooches.[948] Even then this Saxon pottery was very probably made in Britain rather than being directly imported from abroad. Catherine Hills has demonstrated that despite the strong typological similarities there are in fact distinct differences in the decoration of pots from the Spong Hill cemetery in Norfolk and the pottery from cemeteries in the Elbe-Weser triangle.[949]

Amber

Small quantities of amber may have reached the northwestern Empire via a North Sea route during the Late Roman period. Amber of this date is known from Cologne, whilst a collar comprising hundreds of amber beads has been found in a late third-century AD context at Niederzier-Hambach in North-Rhine Westphalia.[950] The overland central European amber routes declined in the late third century and the Aquileian amber industry finally collapsed.[951] However, amber is still well known from central and eastern European sites beyond the Imperial frontier at this date and amber was probably still entering the Empire across the Danube border.[952]

A small, but notable, group of amber can be detected in British contexts dating to this period (**Tab. 4.11**). Some of this could certainly have arrived from the Eastern North Sea coast. Indeed, there appears to have been an expansion in amber usage in northwest Germany (and indeed across the whole of northern Europe) around this time. Several graves in the Late Roman and Migration period cemetery at Westerwanna contain simple amber

[941] Böhme 1974; 1986; 2007.
[942] Böhme 1974; 1986; Todd 1998, 464-465, Fig. 8.
[943] Erdrich, pers. Comm. 2006; Everson and Knowles 1978; Dark 2000, Fig. 3.
[944] MacGregor and Bolick 1993, 81-82; Barber and Bowsher 2000, 183-184; Böhme 2007, 13-14, Figs. 5-6.
[945] Evison 1977; *Portable Antiquities Scheme Annual Report* 2005/6, 62-64; McLean and Richardson 2007; Tyler 1990; 1995; *Portable Antiquities Scheme Annual Treasure Report* 2003, 57-58; MacGregor and Bolick 1993; Böhme 1974; 1986; Bruns 2003.
[946] Evison 1977; Böhme 1974; 1986; Bruns 2003.
[947] McLean and Richardson 2007.
[948] Myres 1969; 1977; Myres and Green 1973; Leahy 2007, 63-65, 89-123.
[949] Hills 1999.
[950] Horn 1987, Taf. 13.
[951] Pasquinucci 1978; Calvi 1996; 2005; Buora 1996; Lista 2007.
[952] Pasquinucci 1978; Bliujiene 2001.

beads.[953] However, the amount of British material is relatively small and there is no reason why it could not have arrived indirectly from the Empire; indeed, two amber beads from the Late Roman cemetery at Lankhills in Winchester were found in graves belonging to a group of foreign individuals who very probably originated in the Upper Danube province of Pannonia.[954]

Synthesis

The Late Roman period, from the second half of the third to the beginning of the fifth century, was marked by a substantial decline and the virtual disappearance of the considerable North Sea trade which had characterised the late second and early third century. However, some material continued to be exchanged via the North Sea, though now through the mechanisms of Saxon and Frankish piracy and the movement of Saxon and Frankish soldiers, *foederati* and *laeti* into northern Gaul, some of whom subsequently returned to their homelands. As in the preceding periods, the contacts were principally directed along the Eastern North Sea coast with the mouths of the Rhine and Scheldt linking most strongly to the coastal regions north and east of the Rhine; however, the Late Roman period saw increasing contacts with the Channel coast of Gaul and to some extent southeast Britain as Germanic pirates extended their areas of operation and large numbers of Germanic soldiers, *foederati* and *laeti* were settled in Gaul between the Loire and the Rhine.

The imports to the Eastern North Sea region included fair amounts of coin and some silver treasure. Roman military belt-fittings are present in several late fourth- and early fifth-century graves in the Elbe-Weser region, whilst a handful of bracelets from this region were probably obtained from Britain, or other parts of the northwestern Empire. There are also a few finds of Roman chainmail. Some pottery was imported from southeast Britain, probably as a result of pirate raids, though it may have arrived in the post-Roman period, whilst pottery from the Lower Rhine region probably reached the north Dutch and German coasts as a result of contact with related Germanic *foederati* and *laeti* in the former area.

Our best evidence for 'exports', meanwhile, comes from women's brooches of the later fourth and early fifth centuries in northern Gaul, though these actually represent the movement of Saxon and Frankish women into this region alongside male Germanic soldiers. A small amount of amber may also have reached the Empire via the Eastern North Sea, most probably through the movement of people who had it amongst their personal possessions.

The determinants of connective change

Political and social change

Several factors underlie the connective change observable in the Eastern North Sea system from the mid-third century onwards. First, the political fragmentation within the Empire and the increased pressure of Gothic and Persian attacks on its Danube and Eastern frontiers respectively led to a weakness in its western frontiers, which created greater opportunities for barbarian raiding and piracy in the west and also a greater reliance upon barbarian forces for the defence of these frontiers (see pp. 138-141). Economic decline in northern Gaul also meant that there were fewer goods to trade, the mass-produced East Gaulish *terra sigillata* and Hemmoor buckets, which were traded to the *Barbaricum* in large quantities during the late second and first half of the third century, were now absent and were not truly replaced.

Social changes within the northwest *Barbaricum* also had an important impact; new and larger barbarian groupings emerged in the third century: the Saxons, the Franks and the Alamanni. These were all confederations of pre-existing smaller tribes and their emergence resulted in barbarian groups now being able to mount sustained co-operative attacks on the Empire in which large numbers of troops could be mobilised.[955]

Intensification of Germanic iron production

The Later Roman period also appears to be marked by an intensification of iron production throughout the northwest *Barbaricum*. This facilitated the production of more iron weaponry and more clinker-built ships, which greatly increased the capacity for piracy. For example, at Snorup, in southwest Jutland, survey has detected some 8000-9,000 slag pit furnaces in an 80 km^2 region and Smeklova and Voss estimate that up to 150,000-200,000 furnaces may in fact exist in the region. Most of the excavated examples have been radiocarbon dated to AD 330-570, although a few may date back as far as AD 250. Each smelt appears to have yielded c. 40-60 kg of iron, which gives us an output of c. 1.3-2.25 tonnes of iron per year based on the number of detected furnaces, though based on the estimated number this rises to c. 25-50 tonnes per annum (**Tab. 6.1**).[956] Whilst this is not vast by the standards of iron smelting sites within the Empire, such as the Weald, it still attests to considerable production. Other areas of the northwest *Barbaricum*, particularly northwest Germany and the Eastern Netherlands, also underwent an intensification of iron production based on slag pit furnaces in the fourth and fifth centuries and the details of several production sites are presented in **Tab. 6.1**.

[953] Zimmer-Linnfeld 1960, Graves: 399, 821, 1067, 1166, 1208, 1230, 1552, 1593; Lund Hansen, 1976; 1995, 217-222, Figs. 8.8-9; Fonnesbach-Sandberg 2006; Bliujiene 2001; Swift 2003; Tempelmann-Maczynska 1985.
[954] Appendix 5, object Nos. 156-157.

[955] Todd 1998; Haywood 1999, 41-49.
[956] Voss 2003; Smekalova and Voss 2003; Rasmussen *et al.* 2006

Site	Total iron production (t)	Years of operation	Iron production (t/a)
Storbekken, Norway	15-30	AD 300-500	0.075-0.15
Snorup, Denmark (recorded sites)	320-540	AD 330-570	1.3-2.25
Snorup, Denmark (estimated)	6000-12000	AD 330-570	25-50
Göhlen, Mecklenburg-Vorpommern	20	AD 300-500	0.1
Joldelund, Schleswig-Holstein	7	AD 300-500	0.035
Heeten, Overijssel, Netherlands	15	AD 310-345	0.43

Tab. 6.1. Estimated iron production (tonnes per annum) at selected sites in the northwest Barbaricum (Calculated using data from: Müller-Wille 1999, 210; Voss 2003, 498, 504; Smekalova and Voss 2003; Rasmussen et al. 2006; Wollschläger 1992; Jöns 1997, 175; 1999, 253-254, 256; Groenenwoudt and van Nie 1995; Verlinde and Erdrich 1998).

Improvements in Germanic ship technology

Technological improvements to Germanic shipbuilding techniques also contributed to increasing piracy and maritime mobility amongst Germanic peoples. As previously discussed, during the pre-Roman and earlier part of the Roman period the shipping traditions along the Eastern North Sea coast and the Baltic consisted of fairly simple log boats and sewn-plank vessels (see p. 25). These had relatively small capacities and were probably unsuitable for long sea-voyages. Whilst we have no direct evidence for the ships used by the Frankish peoples who occupied the land around the mouth of the Rhine during the Late Roman period, we can safely assume that they had adopted the styles of carvel-built vessels propelled by oar and sail typified by Late Roman warships found on the Rhine, such as the five late fourth-century examples from Mainz.[957] In the Baltic, meanwhile, large clinker-built boats began to appear during the course of the second century AD and had become commonplace by the third and fourth centuries. These had overlapping planks fastened with iron nails and were more seaworthy and structurally more stable, which allowed them to be built to greater sizes.[958] Whilst there is a lack of relevant boat finds from the North Sea coast of Germany we must strongly suspect that the peoples living here shared in the clinker-built traditions. Certainly, several examples of vessels constructed in this technique, including the Sutton Hoo ship, are known from Anglo-Saxon contexts in England.[959]

The earliest known clinker-built boat is an oak vessel found at Nydam bog in eastern Schleswig-Holstein. Only a few fragments of this vessel have been recovered, but sections of planking reveal that it was clearly clinker-built. Dendrochronology indicates that it was constructed from trees felled c. AD 190. A clinker-built boat of pine was also excavated at Nydam by Conrad Engelhardt in 1863. Unfortunately this was around the time of the second war of Schleswig and the boat was burnt for firewood by Prussian soldiers the following year, though estimations based on Engelhardt's rough measurements suggest that the vessel was c. 19 m long, 3 m wide and 1 m deep with capacity for twenty-two oarsmen. Recent excavations have uncovered further fragments of the vessel, including a large side-rudder, and a shield board associated with the boat has been dated to AD 296, which suggests a date of c. AD 300 for the vessel. The fact that it was constructed from pine, which was not common in Denmark at this time, is suggestive that it was built further north in Scandinavia.[960]

The most famous vessel found at Nydam is the complete oak ship. This was constructed from trees felled c. AD 310-320, though it was probably deposited in the lake in the mid-third century. The ship was built from oak obtained from within a region comprising Schleswig-Holstein, Denmark and Scania. Its current dimensions are c. 23.7 x 3.75 x 1.20m, although the planking has probably shrunk in breadth by 13-14% over time, so the sides would originally have been somewhat higher. Several oar tholes have been recovered and there would have been room for fourteen oarsmen on each side. The ship had a fairly large capacity and possessed a deadweight of c. 7.6 tonnes.[961]

Aside from the Nydam vessels finds of clinker-built ships of Roman date are scarce; a clinker washstrake dated c. AD 320 was identified on an extended logboat from Bjorke in Sweden, and we can point to two boats of probable third- or fourth-century date from Valderøy and Halsnøy in western Norway, which, whilst not clinker-built, were constructed from overlapping planks that were sewn together.[962] However, an examination of nausts

[957] Haywood 1999; 70-76; Rupprecht 1982; Höckmann 1993.
[958] McGrail 2001, 207-211.
[959] Haywood 1999, 93-110; Bruce-Mitford 1974; 1975; McGrail 2001.
[960] Rieck 2003.
[961] Rieck 2003; McGrail 2001, 208-210.
[962] McGrail 2001, 208.

(boathouses) from the Norwegian coast indicates that large boats, the size of the biggest Nydam ship or larger, and very probably of clinker-construction, were commonplace from the second half of the second century onwards. Several hundred nausts are present along the south and west coasts of Norway and they were constructed between the Roman and Medieval periods to provide shelter for boats on these exposed sections of the coast. Investigations have revealed several nausts which were constructed in the second, third and fourth centuries. These structures are typically c. 30 m long and c. 5m wide, which demonstrates that large ships were far more prevalent than the ship finds alone would suggest.[963]

Whilst the sailed carvel vessels which the Franks probably possessed would have been suitable for long-distance raiding there has been considerable debate about the ability of the early clinker-built ships to undertake piratical attacks upon the coasts of the Roman Empire. Under oars the large Nydam vessel would have been capable of travelling thirty-six nautical miles a day in favourable conditions and it would have had to have landed at night.[964] If a vessel of this type were equipped with a sail then its ability to engage in piracy against the Southern North Sea and Channel coasts of the Empire would have been vastly improved.[965] There is no actual evidence for the use of sail on any of the Roman-period clinker vessels found around the Baltic. In addition, the earliest clear evidence for the use of the sail in Scandinavia derives from the seventh and eighth centuries.[966] That is not to say that sail was not used on such vessels. The hull of the largest Nydam boat was strong enough for a simple sail to have been fitted. Trials of an experimental model of the similar Sutton Hoo vessel, which was also sail-less, also suggest it would perform effectively with a light mast and square sail.[967] Furthermore, there are several references to the Saxons and Franks co-operating with each other on raids against the Roman Empire (see pp. 139-141). As the Franks were very probably using sail this would certainly provide a context for the adoption and use of sail by groups further to the north. A passage by Claudian published in AD 400 and referring to Stilicho's measures to defend Britain in c. AD 398 records Britain as no longer having to watch on all her coasts for the Saxon who came with the dangerous winds.[968] This may hint at the use of sail amongst the Saxons.

Whether or not the sail was employed on the clinker-built boats of the Saxons and the people further to their north it is clear that these boats were technologically suitable for long-distance raiding. In Scandinavia a group of finds known as weapon deposits represent the remains of defeated invading armies, which were deposited by the victors in a lake in order to give thanks to their gods throughout the Roman and Migration periods. Some sites were used on more than one occasion and contain the equipment of several chronologically distinct armies. The vast majority of these deposits derive from eastern Jutland and they reach a dramatic peak during the third century AD. Studies of the equipment have revealed the area of origin of the defeated armies. During the first half of the third century most of the deposits contain the equipment of armies from southern Norway and western Sweden, whilst from the second half of the third century the majority of the remains belong to armies attacking from central Sweden, probably around the Lake Mälaren region.[969] The distances covered by these seaborne armies were considerable and are certainly of the same order as the distance between northwest Germany and the Strait of Dover. The shipping technology developed at this time was therefore eminently suitable for Saxon pirates to direct raids against Roman areas of the Southern North Sea and Channel.

Sea level rise

Finally, the rising sea level also played a contributory role. As we have seen, sea levels around the North Sea were rising from c. AD 50 onwards, probably reaching a maximum around AD 300 (see p. 141). This probably resulted in severe problems in the coastal districts of the Eastern North Sea. In Friesland there was evidently a major demographic collapse in the second half of the third century. Sites were abandoned and Frisian pottery disappears by c. AD 250. The Frisian people left this area and were probably incorporated into existing Frankish settlements in Gelderland and Overijssel, which increase in size at this time, though stylistically Frisian pottery is unknown from this, or any other, region.[970] Some Frisians were evidently accepted into the Empire as *laeti*, indeed a panegyric recording Constantius Chlorus expeditions in the Rhine-Scheldt region records this explicitly.[971] Small groups of new peoples moved into the Frisian area from the German areas further east, and they are represented by the presence of pottery styles from this area in the second half of the third century, though there is hardly any evidence at all for occupation in Friesland during the fourth century.[972]

The northwest German area may also have been affected. A decline in population at Feddersen Wierde, evidenced by a decrease in the overall number and size of structures and the stalling space for cattle, occurred from the second half of the third century onwards and this may have been connected to sea level rise.[973] The increasing pressure placed on the coastal communities by the rising sea may well have been a contributory factor in their turning to piracy, or seeking to settle new lands within the boundaries of the Empire.

---

963 Myhre 1985; Stylegar and Grimm 2005; Grimm 2001.
964 Haywood 1999, 107; Crumlin-Pedersen 1990; Cotterill 1993.
965 Haywood 1999, 93-110.
966 McGrail 2001, 211.
967 Haywood 1999, 93-110.
968 Claudian *De Cons. Stil.* 2.247-255; Birley 2005, 452-453.
969 Ilkjær 1990; 2002; 2003; Lund Hansen 2003b.
970 Taayke 1997; 1999; Rippon 2000.
971 *Pan. Lat. vet.* 8(5).8.1-9.4; Birley 2005, 380; Nixon and Rodgers 1994, 120-121.
972 Taayke 1997; 1999; Rippon 2000.
973 Kossack *et al.* 1984; Haarnagel 1979; Randsborg 1991, Fig. 42.

6.3. Maritime systems c. AD 260-409: a comparison

In the Late Roman period the Southern North Sea and Eastern Channel and Atlantic systems both appear to witness a decline in levels of private trade, whilst the balance of state payments appears to shift from a bias towards imports into Britain to exports from Britain. In the Eastern North Sea system trade relations with the Empire seem to have ceased, but there were still significant levels of connectivity, with piracy and population movements increasing.

There was clearly a link between changes in the two systems. The principal agent was increasing barbarian pressure on the Empire from beyond the northwest frontiers. As we have seen, this extended to maritime piracy. This led to devastation and population decline in large parts of northern Gaul and the Rhine provinces, which contributed to the increasing dependence of the army and cities of these areas upon Britain for supplies and troop withdrawals from Britain. In addition, it facilitated further barbarian incursions and contributed to the resettlement of barbarian groups south of the Rhine in large numbers.

7. Conclusions

Overview

In this study I have set out a model for how connectivity in the North Sea and Channel should be interpreted and understood during the Late Iron Age and Roman periods. I have proposed that there were three maritime systems operating in the waters of the North Sea and Channel, which were principally structured by geography, in particular the existence of short open-sea crossings and coastal routes. These systems were: the Atlantic system, encompassing the Western Channel and Europe's Atlantic seaboard; the Southern North Sea and Eastern Channel system, focusing on the Strait of Dover; and the Eastern North Sea system, which stretched from the mouth of the Rhine to the North Sea coast of Denmark. These three systems were all to some extent coherent, although the Atlantic and Southern North Sea and Eastern Channel systems displayed considerable overlap. Maritime connectivity in each of these systems was highly variable over time in terms of the mechanisms of exchange employed and particularly in terms of the scale and strength of exchange. This variability was principally a result of wider political and economic changes, which often had simultaneous effects upon all three systems, though the precise nature of these effects was often different in each of the systems.

175/150-50 BC

In both the Atlantic and in the Southern North Sea and Eastern Channel systems the onset of the Late Iron Age represented a period of reconnection to the continent following a lull in exchange during the Middle Iron Age. The Atlantic system is characterised by imports to Britain of Italian wine in Dr.1A amphorae, along with some Breton coins and pottery. British exports probably included tin, agricultural products and slaves. These articles were traded between Brittany and western France and the area of the British coast just west of the Solent, probably focusing on the major port-of-trade at Hengistbury Head. The reasons for the growth in this trade were economic growth in Roman Italy, Roman political expansion into southern Gaul, and the extension of trade networks linking the Classical world to southwest France and, probably indirectly, to the Atlantic façade of western France and southwest Britain. This Atlantic trade was heavily disrupted by Caesar's violent conquest of Brittany in the 50s BC.

In the Southern North Sea and Eastern Channel there was a huge influx of gold 'Gallo-Belgic' coins, minted in northern France, into southeast Britain. This injection must principally be explained in terms of social and political payments made by individuals or groups in northern France. Securing military aid from British groups in conflicts on the continent was probably one of the main purposes of these payments. The determinants of these links were a population increase in southeast Britain, a growth in warfare on the near continent and increasing exploitation of gold resources in central Gaul. In contrast, evidence for maritime exchange in the Eastern North Sea system is virtually non-existent. This corresponds to the trend observable in northwest Europe to the north and east of the Rhine in general; long-distance exchange was limited and where it did take place, it focused on overland routes, principally the Elbe basin. The reason for this appears to have been a contemporary lack of settlement in coastal regions and a limited shipping technology.

50 BC-AD 43

Following Caesar's conquest of Gaul the Atlantic trading networks were severely disrupted as a consequence of the violence of the Roman army in Brittany. They did not disappear completely, however, as wine in amphorae and possibly some olive oil continued to reach Britain via Atlantic trade. The picture is very different in the Southern North Sea and Eastern Channel; here a thriving trade gets underway, with wine, olive oil and particularly Gallo-Belgic pottery imported to southeast Britain in quantity, in exchange for products recorded by Strabo as: grain, cattle, hides, gold, silver, iron and hunting dogs. We should probably add salt and perhaps oysters to this list. The main reason for the development of this trade was the extension of client kingship relations to Britain. This created peaceful, if asymmetrical, relations, which facilitated the flow of goods, whilst the presence of young British hostages in Rome, and perhaps other Mediterranean cities, engendered a taste and demand for Mediterranean products which they brought back with them to Britain. The British client rulers were also supported by considerable payments of gold and silver from the Roman state. These subsidies were melted down and contributed to the production of vast native British coinages which bear iconography extremely similar to that being employed in Rome on a range of media by Augustus through which he asserted his power and his right to rule as emperor. A further reason for the expansion of trade was the late first-century growth in large scale manufacturing in the Empire's western provinces.

The Eastern North Sea played an important role in the Roman invasions of Germania between 12 BC-AD 16. A canal – the Fossa Drusiana – was constructed by Drusus to link the Rhine to Lake Flevo (the IJsselmeer) in the northern Netherlands and thence to the North Sea. In 12 BC a fleet was sent by this route to the Ems and then appears to have undertaken an exploratory mission as far as Denmark. This route was certainly employed for a large-scale supply mission in AD 5 and was used to deploy a large part of Germanicus's armies to the Ems in AD 15-16. In northwest Germany Roman-native interaction appears to have been limited to warfare and Roman material was obtained by natives principally as war booty, although there are hints at precious vessels occasionally being presented as political gifts by both sides. The Frisian-occupied areas of the northern Netherlands were temporarily integrated into the Empire and cattle hides were collected as tax from the Frisians and sent to the military bases on the Rhine. There are also hints that an extremely small-scale trade began to develop; however, these exchange systems were interrupted by the Frisian revolt of AD 28.

AD 43-165

Following the Claudian invasion of Britain there was a major expansion of connectivity across both the Southern North Sea and Eastern Channel system and the Atlantic system, which were heavily linked. Levels of connectivity were greater, however, in the former system than in the latter. In terms of imports to Britain there was a huge injection of coin to Britain across the waters of the Southern North Sea and Eastern Channel. These were principally the result of payments made by the Roman state to fund the vast British military garrison and to pay their officials stationed in the island. A wide range of imported products, including *terra sigillata*, wine, olive oil, fish products, lava querns and occasionally agricultural produce, also came to Britain via the Southern North Sea and Eastern Channel, often having first travelled overland through Europe via the valleys of the rivers Rhône and Rhine. Britain also received imports via the Atlantic seaways, though somewhat less than arrived across the Southern North Sea and Eastern Channel. Atlantic imports included a large proportion of the olive oil from southwest Spain, Spanish amphorae bearing olives in *defrutum*, some *terra sigillata*, wine in barrels from Aquitaine and probably some fish products from Brittany. Many of these imported goods reached Britain as a consequence of direct contracts between the Roman state and producers, principally to supply the British military; however, there was a very substantial private trade as well, which targeted both civilian and military consumers.

Coin, much of which was injected into Britain by the state in the first place, was one of Britain's principal (re-) exports through private trade. Other products exported from Britain included metals, particularly silver and gold, with some lead, iron and copper probably being exported as well. Archaeologically invisible goods, such as agricultural produce, salt and oysters, may also have been exported. Some of these products were extracted from Britain by the state, either through direct ownership of the resource, or through taxation, but a portion left through private trade as well. Whilst private trade was balanced it appears extremely likely that there was a significant imbalance in the Roman state's payments to, and extractions from, Britain. The Roman state pumped far more into Britain than it was getting out of it.

Connectivity was principally directed through a number of important ports. There were a number of sizeable civil ports along the continental coast of the Southern North Sea and Eastern Channel, in both northern France and around the mouth of the Meuse. In addition to its role as a civil port Boulogne also functioned as the principal base of the British fleet, the *Classis Britannica*. The main ports of southeast Britain were the civil sites of Richborough and, particularly, London. These served as the main conduits for Britain's continental links in the Southern North Sea and Eastern Channel system and, in addition, 'sucked in' a substantial amount of trade from the Atlantic system as well. There were, however, a number of civil and military ports along the western Channel and Irish Sea coast of Britain that were in direct contact with the continent via the Atlantic seaways.

The principal reasons for the changes in connectivity following the Claudian invasion were Britain's political integration into the Empire, the Roman state's requirements to supply the large military garrison stationed in the island through both cash payments and contractually supplied products, and the growth in 'Romanized', or Mediterranean, consumer tastes, which, in the most part, was the result of the presence of large number of troops and veterans of Mediterranean origin in Britain. Economic growth (certainly extensive, possibly intensive) in the Western provinces during the second half of the first century also facilitated the increasingly high levels of trade and was, in turn, probably stimulated by it. The main reason that connectivity was greater in the Southern North Sea and Eastern Channel system than in the Atlantic system was because a large, well-paid Roman army had been stationed along the Rhine since Augustan times. This had stimulated industry in adjacent regions, as well as supply routes and communication infrastructure, which linked the Rhine garrison to the Mediterranean via the river Rhône. These developments along the Rhône-Rhine corridor ensured that Britain was particularly strongly linked to the continent across the Southern North Sea and Eastern Channel in this period and throughout Roman times.

In contrast, connectivity in the Eastern North Sea system was negligible. A handful of Roman coins and copper-alloy vessels, and perhaps some lava querns, statuettes and mid-second-century *terra sigillata*, may have reached the northern Netherlands through maritime trade, whilst slaves and cattle hides might occasionally have been exported. A notable group of copper-alloy vessels from northwest Germany and southern Scandinavia reached their destinations indirectly through inter-Germanic gift exchange systems. These would originally have entered the *Barbaricum* following trade on the upper Danube frontier.

The main reason for this lack of connectivity was political; following the Varus massacre and the Frisian revolt essentially negative relations endured between Rome and the peoples of the northwestern *Barbaricum*. In addition, Rome no longer attempted to expand its borders in this region, linked in part perhaps to the successful conquest of Britain, whilst its frontiers here were relatively secure. There were also no truly exotic goods which could be obtained from across this frontier which hampered trade. This was in stark contrast to the upper Danube frontier where there was a thriving Roman-barbarian trade. Here political alliances, extending to client kingships, were in place, whilst the barbarian groups here controlled access to the *Barbaricum*'s main exotic product, Baltic amber.

AD 165-260

There was a severe connective downturn in both the Southern North Sea and Eastern Channel system and in the Atlantic system during the late second century and connectivity failed to recover significantly in the early third century. This is principally evidenced through declining imports. In the Southern North Sea and Eastern Channel system there is direct and proxy evidence to suggest that the main traded imports, *terra sigillata*, wine, olive oil and lava querns, all fell sharply in volume during the later second century. Similarly, there was a major decline in olive oil imports in the Atlantic system, though the wine trade with Aquitaine appears to have been largely unaffected, whilst there was probably an expansion in trade in fish products from Brittany. It is hard to assess Britain's exports, though there are hints that British non-ferrous mining experienced a down-turn in the late second century.

The late second-century connective decline may be related in part to the increasing replacement of long-distance imports with products produced locally in northwest Europe. Certainly, fish products were produced in Britain and throughout northwest Europe on an increased scale during the late second century, whilst small-scale viticulture is first attested in Britain during the second century; however, we might ask why other imports, such as olive oil and lava querns decreased simultaneously. Perhaps the British and northwest European production of fish products and wine was a response to declining long-distance trade. Another possibility is that there was a change in consumer tastes over time and that Mediterranean foodstuffs and dining equipment were no longer required in Britain, but again this cannot be the full explanation; there is no evidence for a sudden change in military recruitment patterns and Mediterranean troops were still recruited into the British legions at this time.

The principal causes of the decline appear to have been the Antonine plague and the increasing debasement of the coinage. Historical sources attest that the Antonine plague had a severe impact throughout the Roman Empire between AD 165-189. This would not only have reduced the consumer base, but heavily disrupted production by killing off workforces and inducing flight. The Roman precious metal coinage was increasingly debased throughout the late second and particularly in the third century. This will have had a major impact upon trade as the inherent value of the coin declined well below its face value. The main reasons for this debasement were the contemporary decline, and virtual cessation, of non-ferrous mining in Spain, which was probably caused by the impact of the Antonine plague upon the workforces. Of more immediate significance was the Roman state's practice of making vast payments of precious metal to barbarian peoples outside the Empire, which will be picked up further in the ensuing discussion of the Eastern North Sea system.

By contrast, there was a sudden surge in connectivity in the Eastern North Sea system during the late second century. Sizeable quantities of *denarii* reached the northern Netherlands and northwest Germany in the late second century, probably as a result of political payments made by the Roman state to ensure political treaties with barbarian groups. Trade followed in the wake of these payments with fairly large quantities of *terra sigillata*, lava querns and copper-alloy vessels known from settlements along the coasts of the northern Netherlands and in northwest Germany, although we should bear in mind that some of the German material may have arrived as a result of historically attested raids and that some may have been traded overland via the Lippe Valley. Germanic exports are hard to detect archaeologically, though we might suspect that some coin was re-exported and that cattle-hides and fish were traded as well. In the Frisian occupied areas of the northern Netherlands trade continued on a sizeable level down to c. AD 260; however, in northwest Germany there appears to have been a cut-off in contact with the Empire just prior to AD 200, which we can probably assign to the onset of hostile relations between the Empire and the barbarian groups of this area.

The main reasons for the growth in connectivity in the Eastern North Sea system are political. We know from historical sources that the Antonine plague had a severe impact upon the Roman military. This was a major contributory factor to the longevity and difficulties encountered by Marcus Aurelius and Commodus in bringing the Marcomannic wars to a close. The Antonine plague and Marcomannic wars led to a weakening of Rome's northern frontiers and forced the Empire to engage politically with northern barbarian peoples. This took the form of cash payouts and trade followed in the wake of these peace treaties. Connective changes in both the Southern North Sea and Eastern Channel system, the Atlantic system and in the Eastern North Sea system were thus underlain by the same principal agents: the Marcomannic wars and, more importantly, the Antonine plague.

AD 260-409

It is hard to judge whether or not there was any change in the scale of connectivity in the Southern North Sea and Atlantic systems from the mid-third century onwards. There was, however, a substantial change in the nature of this connectivity. A huge influx of coin from continental mints came to Britain, principally across the Southern North Sea and Eastern Channel. This must principally be explained in terms of sizeable state payments made to private civilian producers in southwest and central England in exchange for products, particularly grain, which were exported to feed the military garrison and urban centres in northwest continental Europe, though private trade may have been important in this respect as well. In contrast to earlier phases other imports were much rarer. In the Southern North Sea and Eastern Channel system we may point to small quantities of privately traded pottery: Mayen ware and Argonne ware. In the Atlantic system there were small-scale imports of North African olive oil, *Céramique à l'éponge* pottery from western France and severely diminishing amounts of wine from Aquitaine and seafood from Brittany. As mentioned, Britain exported large quantities of agricultural produce, particularly grain, through state contract and probably private trade and perhaps through taxation in kind as well. Iron and tin-alloy were also probably exported to the continent through state transfer and private trade. BB1 was shipped in bulk across the Western Channel from Poole Harbour to towns and military sites in Brittany and Normandy through similar mechanisms.

Most coastal sites in Belgium and the southern Netherlands were abandoned in the late third century, although some military ports at the mouth of the Rhine were probably in receipt of grain from Britain, whilst ships also sailed to Britain from ports further up the Rhine. Elsewhere, in addition to civil ports a series of coastal fortifications known as shore forts began to appear on the continental shores of the Southern North Sea, the Channel and Atlantic coasts of France and in southeast Britain from the late third century. These functioned as naval bases for defence against piracy and intra-Empire conflicts and also acted as secure transhipment points for traded and state-contracted goods.

The main reason for these changes was the deepening crisis of the Empire during the third century. Inter-Empire conflicts disrupted pre-existing long-distance exchange networks. Barbarian invasion and piracy led to a major economic and demographic decline in northern Gaul, which led to a dependence upon supplies from central and southwest Britain, which was less affected by barbarians. Continuing sea level rise contributed to this decline in coastal areas, particularly around the North Sea. Another factor was the substantial decline in the British garrison from the mid-third century onwards as a result of military crises elsewhere in the Empire. This not only reduced the state's requirements to supply the British garrison, but also freed up a greater proportion of the British surplus for export. We may also posit economic growth in central and southwest Britain, evidenced in the Late Roman fluorescence of villas and the pottery industries, as a further factor underlying the observed changes, though this was itself heavily underpinned by the near continent's increasing dependence upon Britain. Britain's secession from the Empire in AD 409 led to a sudden and almost complete cut-off in connectivity in both the Southern North Sea and Eastern Channel system and in the Atlantic system.

In the Eastern North Sea system there was a cessation of trade between the peoples of the North Sea coast of the *Barbaricum* and the northwest continental Empire by c. AD 260. Connections continued, however, though there was a marked change in the mechanisms of exchange. Roman material, such as a sizeable group of coins and silver treasure is encountered along the eastern North Sea coast of the *Barbaricum*. Belt-fittings, chainmail and pottery produced within the Empire are also encountered here. Female brooches originating in northwest Germany are also encountered in northern Gaul. This material is best explained through reference to settlements of Germanic peoples as *laeti* and *foederati* in northern Gaul from the mid- to late third century onwards. It was either transferred as a result of people moving, or through intra-Germanic exchange networks. Some was very probably the result of piracy. It is highly likely that maritime routes were heavily utilised in these 'exchange' networks. There are also vague hints at some sort of contact between Germanic peoples of the North Sea coast and southeast Britain; there are several finds of Late Romano-British pottery in the northern Netherlands and northwest Germany, whilst a British-made buckle and belt-plate are also present here. Piracy is a possible mechanism, though we should bear in mind that these objects may well have reached their destinations in the mid-fifth century at which time contacts between the North Sea coast of Germany and Britain become more readily apparent.

The reasons for these changes are similar to the determinants of change in the Southern North Sea and Eastern Channel system and the Atlantic systems. By the mid-third century political weaknesses within the Empire and concerted barbarian attacks along most of the Empire's northern and Eastern frontiers lead to stretching of the Roman military forces and greater opportunities for barbarian raiders across the northwest frontiers, which led in turn to rural depopulation in northern Gaul and meant that the Empire resettled barbarian peoples in this region as *laeti* and *foederati*. Social change within the *Barbaricum* fed into this as tribes coalesced into larger entities, such as the Franks and Saxons, which had a greater capacity for coordinated offensive action against the Empire. An intensification of iron production in the northwestern *Barbaricum* also meant more iron weapons and ships could be produced. Improvements in north Germanic ship construction technology also increased the capacity for raiding and maritime movements. Finally, a rise in the North Sea's level, which reached its maximum c. AD 300, caused pressure on tribes living in coastal regions and influenced their decision to turn to piracy and to seek new lands within the Empire.

Wider conclusions

A number of wider conclusions emerge from this study. Firstly, it is clear that connectivity in all three of the maritime systems of the North Sea and Channel experienced major changes over time and were vulnerable to wider political and economic changes.

Throughout this study the influence of wider political and economic factors has been made clear. A number of events have emerged as being of particular significance. We saw how Roman economic and political expansion had important repercussions upon connectivity in the Atlantic system during the second century BC. Caesar's campaigns in Gaul and Britain caused disruption in the Atlantic system, but the formulation of client kingship relations between groups in southeast Britain and the Empire in the aftermath of this conflict, and particularly during the Augustan period, stimulated a growth in connectivity across the Southern North Sea and Eastern Channel. The Roman army made use of the eastern North Sea, for the purposes of supply, troop movements and exploration during the Augustan German campaigns. The sea may also have been utilised in extracting taxation from the northern Netherlands and in a very small-scale trade between the Empire and the Frisian peoples following the latter's brief integration into the Empire following the Augustan invasion. These contacts were, however, sharply arrested after the defeat of Varus and his army at Kalkriese in AD 9 and the Frisian revolt in AD 28. These events contributed to a long phase of minimal contacts between the Empire and the northwest *Barbaricum* in the Eastern North Sea system.

The Claudian invasion of Britain resulted in an enormous up-surge in connectivity in both the Southern North Sea and Eastern Channel system and the Atlantic system. This was principally the result of the Roman state's requirements to pay and supply its army, which in turn stimulated a high volume of private trade. A major check to connectivity in these two systems came in the later second century. Connectivity declined suddenly and the main cause of this must be the Antonine plague on reducing both consumer bases and workforces and the effects that the plague and the contemporary Marcomannic wars had upon the Empire's money supply. In the Eastern North Sea system the effects of the plague and the Marcomannic wars are equally apparent. In this case the military crisis experienced by the Empire during the late second century led to a political re-engagement with barbarian peoples beyond its northwest frontiers in order to ensure the security of this frontier.

The impact of the Empire's mid-third-century crisis is also readily detectable. Political and military turmoil within the Empire coupled with concerted barbarian invasions led to economic and demographic decline in northern Gaul and the resettlement of Germanic *laeti* and *foederati* in this region. This in turn led the army and urban centres of northwest continental Europe to increasingly depend on Britain for basic supplies, particularly agricultural products. In the Eastern North Sea system these factors ensured that trade between the Empire and the barbarians ceased, whilst objects continued to move as a result of piracy, through the movement of *laeti* and *foederati* and through intra-Germanic exchange. Britain's secession from the Roman state in AD 409 caused the virtual collapse of state-contracted trade and private trade in the Southern North Sea and Eastern Channel system and in the Atlantic system. This event marks the end of the present study.

Viewed in comparative terms, it appears that we can contrast the maritime systems of the North Sea and Channel with the Mediterranean. Horden and Purcell demonstrated that the Mediterranean saw much greater continuity with high levels of connectivity maintained over the *longue durée*. The reason for this was economic necessity caused by geography; the existence of highly variable inter-annual rainfall patterns amongst the microregions of the Mediterranean coast meant that communities had to engage in exchange for their own survival.[974] This factor was not present in the North Sea and Channel where exchange was far more vulnerable to political requirements and economic shifts. Moreover, the North Sea and Channel were subject to more extreme weather conditions than the Mediterranean, and for more of the year; making sailing that much more difficult and hazardous.

Surveys of exchange and interaction across the *longue durée*, such as those of Cunliffe and Horden and Purcell, have played down the importance of short- and medium-term changes. My work has demonstrated that, at least in the context of my study, short- and medium-term change can be of great significance. I argue that greater account needs to taken of change on these shorter times scales.

Nevertheless, *longue durée* surveys do provide us with extremely important insights and I believe that, to be understood most effectively, change does need to be interpreted within a long-term context. Certainly, there are hints that the three maritime systems proposed here for the North Sea and Channel during the Late Iron Age and Roman period did persist over the *longue durée*, at least until c. AD 1500 when the discovery of the New World led to fundamental alterations in the existing exchange networks.[975] The three systems I have outlined are potentially visible throughout Later Prehistory. For example, in his detailed survey of the Late Bronze Age and Early Iron Age metalwork from northwest Europe, O'Connor concluded that there were extremely strong

[974] Horden and Purcell 2000; 2006.
[975] Cunliffe 2001.

contacts between southeast Britain (notably the Thames Valley) and northern France (particularly the valleys of the Seine, Somme and Oise) across the Southern North Sea and Eastern Channel.[976] Other work, meanwhile, has made it abundantly clear that important maritime exchange networks operated in the waters of the Atlantic and the Eastern North Sea throughout prehistory.[977]

Following the end of the Roman period it becomes immediately apparent that the Eastern North Sea system began to overlap with the Southern North Sea and Eastern Channel system to a much greater degree. Nonetheless, there are hints that the three maritime systems continued operating to some degree. The distribution of exchange articles, such as sceattas, suggests that during the Middle Saxon period the Eastern Channel, notably the emporium at Hamwic, was very much part of the thriving Southern North Sea maritime trading networks.[978] During this same period, meanwhile, the communities of the Eastern North Sea seem to have been principally linked into the Southern North Sea trading network via the great emporium at Dorestad on the Rhine, rather than engaging in large-scale trade directly across the North Sea.[979] It may also prove possible to identify the three maritime systems proposed in this volume in the Late Medieval period when wine was traded between western France and England, English wool with Flanders, and the Hanseatic League operated in the eastern and southern North Sea.[980] It is apparent though that the degree to which each of the systems overlapped with one another varied over the course of time. At certain times, such as the Viking period, the systems may even have broken down completely. An investigation of North Sea and Channel connectivity over the course of the *longue durée* would certainly warrant further study.

Finally, I propose that there is a need for future studies to take greater account of change on different scales. Works that integrate short- and medium-term changes into the bigger *longue durée* picture will surely have the maximum informative potential.

---

976 O'Connor 1980.

977 C.f. Cunliffe 2001; 2005; 2009; Clark 2004; 2009; Fontjin 2009; Bradley 2007; Butler 1963; Sheridan 2007. For the eastern North Sea distribution of red Helgoland flint objects see: Hartz and Segschneider 2006; Beuker 1988; 1990.

978 Hodges 1982; 2000; Naylor 2008; Parkhouse 1997; Loveluck and Tys 2006.

979 Heidinga 1999.

980 Lloyd 2005; Cunliffe 2001; Fulford 1978; Friedland 1991; Kirby and Hinkkanen 2000.

Appendix 1. British Celtic coins from the continent c. 120-20 BC

Coin No.	Site No.	Site	Lat.	Long.	Material	Type	Date	Find details	References
1	1	Duderstadt, Niedersachsen, Germany	51:31 N	10:16 E	Gold	British Qb stater. Issued by the Atrebates/Regni of the Selsey/Silchester region (John Sills (Celtic Coin Index), pers. Comm. 2008).	c. 50 BC ±5 years.		*FRMD* VII-4-9; p. 141; Berger 1985, 208, Abb. 6 (N.B the photo of the coin is incorrectly labeled as the example from Nienburg).
2	2	Wijk bij Duurstede, Utrecht, Netherlands.	51:58 N	5:21 E	Silver	Silver coin of the Iceni. (c.f. Van Arsdell, 1989; 655-1. Uninscribed Boar Type).	c. 35-25 BC.		Paul Belien (Geldmuseum Utrecht), pers. Comm. 2008.
3	3	Helden, Limburg, Netherlands.	51:19 N	6:00 E	Silver	Billon coin of the Durotriges c. 58-30 BC.	c. 58-30 BC.		Paul Belien (Geldmuseum Utrecht), pers. Comm. 2008.
4	4	Hesdin, Pas-de-Calais, France.	50:22 N	2:02 E	Gold	Whaddon Chase Type stater of the Catuvellauni (c.f. Van Arsdell 1989, 1476-5).	c. 55-45 BC.		Delestrée *et al.* 2003, 16.
5	5	Saint-Laurent-Blangy, Pas-de-Calais, France.	50:18 N	2:48 E	Potin	Potin, Class I, Type L.	Late second-mid-first century BC.	Early Roman fortlet.	Gruel and Haselgrove 2007, Tab. 14.1; Delestrée *et al.* 2003, 17.
6	6	Vron, Somme.	50:19 N	1:45 E	Potin	Potin, Class II, Type O-P.	Mid-first century BC.	Rural sanctuary.	Gruel and Haselgrove 2007, Tab. 14.1.
7-8.	7	Liercourt-Erondelle, Somme, France.	50:03 N	1:53 E	Potin	Two Potins, Class I, Type L.	Late second to mid-first century BC.	Early Roman camp.	Gruel and Haselgrove 2007, Tab. 14.1; Delestrée *et al.* 2003, 15.
9	8	Camp Rouge, Somme, France.	50:00 N	2:00 E	Bronze	Uninscribed cock bronze of Cottam's (1999) Type 2. Probably produced near Chichester.	Mid-to late first century BC.		Gruel and Haselgrove 2007, 251.
10	9	Chilly, Somme, France.	49:48 N	2:46 E	Potin	Potin, Class I, Type L.	Late second to mid-first century BC.	Rural sanctuary.	Gruel and Haselgrove 2007, Tab. 14.1; Delestrée *et al.* 2003, 12-13.
11-12.	10	Bois-l'Abbé, Seine Maritime, France.	50:00 N	1:19 E	Gold	Two British Qa coins (Pers. comm, John Sills (CCI), 2008).	c. 40s BC.	Rural sanctuary.	Delestrée *et al.* 2003, 13; CCI 97.0677-97.0678.

Coin No.	Site No.	Site	Lat.	Long.	Material	Type	Date	Find details	References
13-15	11	Fesques, Seine-Maritime, France.	49:47 N	1:29 E	Potin	Three Potins, Class I.	Late second to mid-first century BC.	Found at rural sanctuary.	Gruel and Haselgrove 2007, Tab. 14.1; Delestrée *et al.* 2003, 11-12.
16-17	12	Mont-César, Bailleul-sur-Thérain, Oise, France.	49:23 N	2:14 E	Potin	Two Potins, Class II, Type P.	Mid-first century BC.	*Oppidum* and/or sanctuary.	Gruel and Haselgrove 2007, Tab. 14.1; Delestrée *et al.* 2003, 12.
18	13	Rouvroy-les-Merles, Oise, France.	49:39 N	2:21 E	Potin	Potin, Class II, Type M-N.	Mid-first century BC.	Sanctuary complex & Roman fortress.	Gruel and Haselgrove 2007, Tab. 14.1; Delestrée *et al.* 2003, 15.
19	14	Saint-Pierre-Sur-Dives, Calvados, France.	49:01 N	0:02 W	Silver	Silver coin, Durotrigan E (c.f. Mack 317; Van Arsdell 1989, 1235-1).	c. 58-45 BC.		Allen 1960, 242.
20	15	Bennecourt, Yvelines, France.	49:02 N	1:34 E	Potin	Potin, Class II, Type M.	Mid-first century BC.	Found at rural sanctuary.	Gruel and Haselgrove 2007, Tab. 14.1; Delestrée *et al.* 2003, 12.
21	16	Coulommiers, Seine-et-Marne, France.	48:49 N	3:05 E	Gold	Atrebatic stater of Commius (c.f. Mack 92; Van Arsdell 1989, 350-1).	c. 45-30 BC.		Allen 1960, 208.
22	17	Chateaudun, Eure-et-Loire.	48:04 N	1:20 E	Gold	British Qa (John Sills (CCI), pers. Comm. 2008).	c. 40s BC.		CCI (Cetic Coin Index) 95.3064.
23-26	18	Corent, Auvergne, France.	45:40 N	3:12 E	Potin	Four Potin coins, Class II, Type O-P.	Mid-first century BC.	Late La Tène and early Roman sanctuary.	Gruel and Haselgrove 2007.
27	19	Rozel, Jersey.	49:14 N	2:03 W	Silver	Silver coin of the Durotriges.	c. 65-30 BC.	Hoard.	Boudet and Noldin 1989, Fig. 3.
28	19	Rozel, Jersey.	49:14 N	2:03 W	Silver	Silver coin inscribed Ammi/Sec of probable British type.	Mid-first century BC.	Possibly intrusive to the hoard.	Gruel and Haselgrove 2007, 250, note 7.

Coin No.	Site No.	Site	Lat.	Long.	Material	Type	Date	Find details	References
29-49	20	Le Câtillon, Jersey.	49:12 N	2:03 W	2 Gold & 19 Silver	One Durotrigan A gold stater, Chute Type, 65-58 BC (c.f. Van Arsdell 1989, 1205-1); one gold quarter stater; nineteen silver or billon coins, including at least six Durotrigan E, 58-45 BC (c.f Van Arsdell 1989, 1235-1, 1242-1), four Durotrigan thin silver type, 65-45 BC (c.f. Van Arsdell 1989, 1280-1) and a silver version of Durotrigan A. Chute Type (c.f. Van Arsdell 1989, 1205-1).	c. 65-45 BC (Hoard dated to mid-late first century BC).	Hoard.	Van Arsdell 1989, 539; Haselgrove 1987a, 317-321; Gruel and Haselgrove 2007, 249-250.

Appendix 2. British Celtic coins from the continent c. 20 BC-AD 60

Coin No.	Site No.	Site	Lat.	Long.	Material	Type	Date	Find details	References
1	1	Vildbjerg, Jutland, Denmark	56:11 N	8:46 E	Gold	South Ferriby stater/British K of the Corieltavi.	c. 10 BC-AD 10.		Thomsen 1952. CCI (Celtic Coin Index) 680016.
2	2	Munke-Bjergby, Zealand, Denmark	55:30 N	11:31 E	Gold	Stater of Tasciovanus-Sego. An east Kent series of Sego with Tasciovanus as overlord.	10 BC-AD 10.		Thomsen 1952. CCI 730225.
3	3	Near Witmarsum, Friesland, Netherlands.	53:06 N	5:28 E	Silver	Silver coin of the Dobunni (c.f. Van Arsdell 1989, Nos. 1074-1/1078-1, Pl. 30).	c. 10 BC-AD 10.	Metal detector find.	Paul Belien (Geldmuseum Utrecht), pers. Comm. 2008.
4	4	Katwijk, South Holland, Netherlands	52:12 N	4:24 E	Gold	Stater of Cunobelinus (c.f. Allen 1975, 15, No. 94).	c. AD 10-43.	Found on the beach in 1664 in the remains of the Brittenburg (an eroded Roman fortification).	Professor Nico Roymans, pers. Comm. 2008; Collection Nederlands Geld en Bankmuseum, Utrecht, inv. nr. 12295.
5	5	Est-Tieflaar, mun. Geldermalsen, Netherlands.	51:51 N	5:19 E	Bronze	Bronze coin ascribed to the Durotriges.	c. 20 BC-AD 45.	Found at the rural settlement at Est-Tieflaar.	Professor Nico Roymans, pers. Comm. 2008.
6	6	Wijk bij Duurstede, Utrecht, Netherlands.	51:58 N	5:21 E	Silver	Silver coin of the Iceni. (c.f. Van Arsdell 1989, 750-1. Ecen Symbol Type).	c. AD 40-45.		Paul Belien (Geldmuseum Utrecht), pers. Comm. 2008.
7	7	Ostende, Belgium.	51:13 N	2:55 E	Bronze	Bronze coin of Tasciovanus.	20 BC-AD 10		Boudet and Noldin 1989, Fig. 3; Allen 1960, 224.
8	8	Boulogne, France.	50:43 N	1:37 E	Bronze	Bronze coin of Cunobelinus.	c. AD 10-43.		Boudet and Noldin 1989, Fig. 3; Allen 1960, 235.
9	9	Airaines, Somme, France.	49:58 N	1:57 E	Bronze	Bronze coin of Cunobelin. Trinovantian, minted at Camulodunum (c.f. Van Arsdell 1989, 1977-1).	c. AD 10-20.		Delestrée *et al.* 2003, 15-16.

APPENDIX 2. BRITISH CELTIC COINS FROM THE CONTINENT c. 20 BC-AD 60

Coin No.	Site No.	Site	Lat.	Long.	Material	Type	Date	Find details	References
10	10	Daours, Somme, France.	49:54 N	2:27 E	Bronze	Bronze of Cunobelin. Trinovantian minted at Camulodunum (c.f. Van Arsdell 1989, 2105-1).	c. AD 20-43.	Gallo-Roman villa occupied first-second century AD.	Delestrée *et al*. 2003, 15.
11	11	Mont-César, Bailleul-sur-Thérain, Oise, France.	49:23 N	2:14 E	Gold	Stater of Cunobelinus (c.f. Mack 1964, 210-211).	c. AD 10-40.	*Oppidum* and/or sanctuary.	Delestrée *et al*. 2003, 12.
12	12	Bois-l'Abbé, Seine Maritime, France.	50:00 N	1:19 E	Gold	Kentish Quarter stater of VOSENOS (c.f. Van Arsdell 1989, 185-1).	c. 10-5 BC.	Rural sanctuary.	Delestrée *et al*. 2003, 13.
13	12	Bois-l'Abbé, Seine Maritime, France.	50:00 N	1:19 E	Silver	Dobunni Irregular Series, Class L (c.f. Van Arsdell 1989, 1170-1/1171-1).	c. 15 BC-AD 30.	Rural sanctuary.	Delestrée *et al*. 2003, 13.
14-15	13	Breteuil, Oise, France.	48:50 N	0:55 E	Bronze	Two bronze coins of the Trinovantes. Tasciovanus's third coinage (c.f. Van Arsdell 1989, 1810-1).	c. 15-10 BC.		Delestrée *et al*. 2003, 16.
16	13	Breteuil, Oise, France.	48:50 N	0:55 E	Bronze	Bronze coin of the Trinovantes. Cunobelinus (c.f. Van Arsdell 1989, 2091-1).	c. AD 20-43.		Delestrée *et al*. 2003, 16.
17	13	Breteuil, Oise, France.	48:50 N	0:55 E	Bronze	Bronze coin of the Trinovantes. Cunobelinus (c.f. Van Arsdell 1989, 2081-1).	c. AD 20-43.		Delestrée *et al*. 2003, 16.
18	14	Vendeuil-Caply, Oise, France.	49:37 N	2:18 E	Gold	Gold with bronze. Ancient forgery of a stater of the Trinovantes. Cunobelin Linear Type (c.f. Van Arsdell 1989, 1925-2).	c. AD 10-20.	Rural sanctuary.	Delestrée *et al*. 2003, 13-15.
19	14	Vendeuil-Caply, Oise, France.	49:37 N	2:18 E	Silver	Atrebates, Tincommius Second Coinage (c.f. Van Arsdell 1989, 383-1 variant).	Late first century BC.	Rural sanctuary.	Delestrée *et al*. 2003, 13-15.

Coin No.	Site No.	Site	Lat.	Long.	Material	Type	Date	Find details	References
20	14	Vendeuil-Caply, Oise, France.	49:37 N	2:18 E	Bronze	Bronze of Cunobelin. Trinovantian minted at Camulodunum (c.f. Van Arsdell 1989, 1977-1).	c. AD 10-20.	Rural sanctuary.	Delestrée *et al.* 2003, 13-15.
21	15	Vermand, Aisne, France.	49:52 N	3:09 E	Gold	Gold/bronze stater of Cunobelinus (c.f. Mack 203; Van Arsdell 1989, 2010).	c. AD 20-43.		Allen 1960, 235.
22	16	Reims, Haute-Marne, France.	49:15 N	4:02 E	Silver	Icenian-K (c.f. Van Arsdell 1989, 764-1).	c. AD 45-50.		Delestrée *et al.* 2003, 16.
23-24	17	Verneuil-sur-Avre, Eure, France.	48:44 N	0:56 E	Bronze	Two British bronze coins (no further details).	c. 20 BC-AD 45.		Boudet and Noldin 1989, Fig. 3.
25	18	Vertault, Côte d'Or, France.	47:55 N	4:21 E	Bronze	Bronze coin of Cunobelin.	c. AD 10-43.		Allen 1960, 235; Boudet and Noldin 1989, Fig. 3.
26	19	Civaux, Vienne, France.	46:27 N	0:40 E	Bronze	Bronze coin of Tasciovanus.	c. 20 BC-AD 10.		Boudet and Noldin 1989, Fig. 3.
27	20	Saintes, Charente-Maritime, France.	45:45 N	0:38 W	Bronze	Bronze coin of Cunobelinus.	c. AD 10-43.		Boudet and Noldin 1989, Fig. 3.
28	21	Doulezon, Gironde, France.	44:47 N	0:00 E	Bronze	Bronze imitation of a gold stater of Cunobelin.	c. AD 10-43.		Boudet and Noldin 1989.
29	22	Lyon, France.	45:46 N	4:50 E	Bronze	Bronze coin of Cunobelin.	c. AD 10-45.	Found in excavation of Gallo-Roman layer.	CCI 930144.
30	23	Titelberg, Luxembourg	49:32 N	5:52 E	Bronze	Uninscribed bronze coin. Later Kentish type.	Probably c. 20 BC-AD 40.		Gruel and Haselgrove 2007, 250.
31	24	Ludwigshafen-Rheingonheim, Germany	49:27 N	8:25 E	Silver	East Anglian uninscribed type (c.f. Van Arsdell 1989, 790-1).	Mid-first century AD, probably c. AD 60.	Single find from the Roman fort.	*FMRD* IV. 2; p. 339, No. 2210.1; Haselgrove 1977, 111.

Appendix 3. Amber from British Iron Age sites (800 BC-AD 43)

Site No.	Object No.	Site	Lat.	Long.	Details	Context date	Find details	References	Location
1	1	Windsor area, Berkshire, England.	51:28 N	0:36 W	Brooch decorated with amber and glass beads.	c. 400 BC.	Unknown.		
2	2 to 3	Dane's Graves, East Yorkshire, England.	54:03:20 N	0:26:48 W	Two amber beads.	Mid/Late Iron Age.	Arras culture cemetery. Barrow 5.	Stead 1979, 80, 99; Beck and Shennan 1991, 105-7, 160-1.	British Museum, acc. No. 76.2-12.10.
2	4	Dane's Graves, East Yorkshire, England.	54:03:20 N	0:26:48 W	Bronze brooch with possible amber inlay.	Mid/Late Iron Age.	Arras culture cemetery. Barrow 95.	Stead 1979, Fig. 24, No. 5.	
3	5	Kirkburn, East Yorkshire, England.	53:58:59 N	0:30:09 W	Amber bead.	c. 450-250 BC.	Arras culture cemetery. Found around neck in grave K6. The grave also contained a rare La Tène I import.	Stead 1991, 93.	
4	6	Market Weighton, East Yorkshire, England.	53:51:53 N	0:40:05 W	Amber ring.	Mid/Late Iron Age.	Arras culture cemetery. Burial A4- The 'Queens barrow'.	Stead 1979, 86, 98; Beck and Shennan 1991, 105-7, 163, Fig. 11.7, 2.	
4	7	Market Weighton, East Yorkshire, England.	53:51:53 N	0:40:05 W	Fragment of an amber ring.	Mid/Late Iron Age.	Arras culture cemetery. Barrow burial.	Stead, 1979; 86, 98; Beck and Shennan, 1991; 105-7; 163.	
5	8 to 9	Wetwang Slack, East Yorkshire, England.	54:01:10 N	0:34:35 W	Two amber beads on an iron brooch.	Mid/Late Iron Age.	Arras culture cemetery. Burial 250.	Beck and Shennan 1991, 105-7, 176-7, Fig. 11.16, 1.	
6	10	Southend, Essex, England.	51:32:7 N	0:42:2 E	Amber bead.	Late Iron Age.	Iron Age settlement. High in Iron Age occupation levels at Elms Road, Site 44.	Beck and Shennan 1991, 105-7, 170, Fig. 11.10, 6.	
7	11	Danebury, Hampshire, England.	51:08:15 N	1:32:21 W	Amber bead.	c. 550-450 BC.	Iron Age hillfort. Found in a pit	Cunliffe 1984b, 396, Fig. 7.42.	
7	12	Danebury, Hampshire, England.	51:08:15 N	1:32:21 W	Amber bead.	400-300 BC.	Iron Age hillfort. Found in a pit	Cunliffe 1984b, 396, Fig. 7.42.	

Site No.	Object No.	Site	Lat.	Long.	Details	Context date	Find details	References	Location
7	13	Danebury, Hampshire, England.	51:08:15 N	1:32:21 W	Amber finger ring.	300-100/50 BC.	Iron Age hillfort. Found in a pit	Cunliffe 1984b, 396, Fig. 7.42.	
8	14	Skeleton Green, Hertfordshire, England.	51:53:57 N	0:01:33 E	One third of a large amber bead.	c. 10 BC-AD 20.	Large Late Iron Age settlement. Layer of occupation material lying on the surface of cobbled path to building VII. Period I, Phase iii.	Partridge 1981, 112, Fig. 58,56.	
9	15	Welwyn Garden City, Hertfordshire, England.	51:48:02 N	0:12:09 W	Half a large amber bead.	Late Iron Age.	Late Iron Age cremation burial.	Stead 1967; Beck and Shennan 1991, 105-7, 176 and Fig. 11.14, 4.	
10	16 to 17	Fiskerton, Lincolnshire, England.	53:14 N	0:26 W	Two amber beads.	c. 600-250 BC.	Ritual site. Found in excavation of timber causeway dated 510±70 BC and 330±70 BC (HAR-4472 and HAR-4471).	Beck and Shennan 1991, 105-7, 158, Fig. 11.5, 6.	
11	18	Radley, Oxfordshire, England.	51:41:14 N	1:14:27 W	Amber bead.	Early Iron Age.	Found during excavations of pits containing early Iron Age pottery	*South Midlands Archaeology* 13 (1983): 141-2.	
12	19 to 22	Cadbury Castle, Somerset, England.	51:01:28 N	2:31:54 W	Four amber beads.	Probably Iron Age.	Hillfort.	Barrett *et al*. 2000, 190, Fig. 96.	
13	23 to 27	Glastonbury Lake Village, Somerset, England.	51:10:16 N	2:46:56 W	Five amber beads.	Iron Age.	Iron Age settlement. From four different occupation mounds.	Beck and Shennan 1991, 105-7, 158, Fig. 11.6, 1.	
14	28	Ham Hill, Somerset, England.	50:57:06 N	2:44:41 W	Amber bead.	Probably Iron Age.	Hillfort. From site iii, north spur. Bronze Age and particularly Iron Age finds are known from this site, although the associations of the amber are unknown.	Beck and Shennan 1991, 105-7, 160, Fig. 11.6, 2.	Somerset Museum, Taunton. Additions to the Museum 1915.

APPENDIX 3. AMBER FROM BRITISH IRON AGE SITES (800 BC-AD 43)

Site No.	Object No.	Site	Lat.	Long.	Details	Context date	Find details	References	Location
15	29	Meare, Somerset, England.	51:10:16 N	2:47:03 W	Amber bead.	Probably Iron Age.	Iron Age settlement. Isolated find from quarry on west side of roadway leading from Council Houses to Meare Heath.	Beck and Shennan 1991, 105-7, 164.	
15	30 to 31	Meare, Somerset, England.	51:10:16 N	2:47:03 W	Two amber beads.	Iron Age.	Iron Age settlement. Iron Age occupation material from Meare Lake Village.	Beck and Shennan 1991, 105-7, 164-5, Fig. 11.9, 1.	
15	32 to 34	Meare, Somerset, England.	51:10:16 N	2:47:03 W	Three amber arc-pendants.	Iron Age.	Iron Age settlement. Iron Age occupation material from Meare Lake Village.	Beck and Shennan 1991, 105-7, 164-5, Fig. 11.9, 1.	
15	35 to 38	Meare, Somerset, England.	51:10:16 N	2:47:03 W	Four amber beads.	Probably Iron Age.	Iron Age settlement. Near Peacock Farm, ¾ mile NE of Meare Lake Village.	Beck and Shennan 1991, 105-7, 165.	
16	39	Bredon Hill, Worcestershire, England.	52:02:05 N	2:05:39 W	Amber bead.	Probably early first century AD.	Iron Age hillfort. Last period of the inner entrance.	Hencken 1939, 86, Fig. 12,4.	
17	40	Henllan, Dyfed, Wales.	53:12:03 N	3:27:47 W	Amber bead.	Iron Age.	Hillfort/promontory fort.	Beck and Shennan 1991, 105-7, 192, Fig. 11.22, 3.	National Museum of Wales, acc. No. 53.267/1.
18	41	Crosskirk broch, Caithness, Scotland.	58:36:23 N	3:40:05 W	Amber bead or pendant.	Probably second or first century BC.	Native broch. In a shell deposit in the broch, phase two.	Fairhurst 1984, 119, Ill. 70,763; Hunter 1998, Tab. 10.	
19	42 to 43	White Gate broch, Caithness, Scotland.	58:32 N	3:07 W	Two amber beads.	Probably pre-Roman Iron Age (second half of first millennium BC).	Native broch.	Heald and Jackson 2001, 134; Hunter 1998, Tab. 10.	
	44 to 125	Unknown, England.			82 amber beads, some facetted, forming a gradated necklace.	Probably Iron Age.			Cambridge Museum of Archaeology and Anthropology. IDNO: Z 22288.

Appendix 4. Amber from British sites dating to either the Iron Age or the Roman period

Site No.	Object No.	Site	Lat.	Long.	Details	Context date	Find details	References	Location
1	1	Stratton Park, Easton Down, Hampshire, England.	51:15:07 N	1:07:59 W	Amber bead.	Late Iron Age or very early Roman.	Sealed beneath the Roman Road between Winchester and Silchester. MARC3 site R1, SU 539 408.	Beck and Shennan 1991, 105-7, 155.	
2	2	Gorhambury, Hertfordshire, England.	51:45:14 N	0:22:58 W	Amber bead.	Late Iron Age or Roman.	Late Iron Age and Roman settlement	Neal *et al.* 1990, 160, No.1005.	Verulamium Museum, St Albans.
3	3	Sutton Common, South Yorkshire, England.	53:21 N	1:13 W	Amber bead.	Iron Age or Roman.	Iron Age marsh fort/ enclosure.		Doncaster Museum.
4	4	Porth y Rhaw, Pembrokeshire, Wales.	51:55:17 N	5:14:33 W	Amber bead.	Iron Age or Roman.	Hillfort. Found in excavations by Peter Crane of Cambria Archaeology.		
5	5	Edin's Hall broch, Berwickshire, Scotland.	55:50 N	02:22 W	Annular amber bead.	Probably c. 100 BC-AD 400.	Native broch.	Dunwell 1999, 333-5, Ill. 20, 5; Hunter 1998, Tab. 10.	
6	6	Dowalton crannog, Dumfries and Galloway, Scotland.	54:57:42 N	4:28:52 W	Amber bead.	Iron Age or Roman.	Native crannog.	Stuart 1865, 121; Hunter 1998, Tab. 10.	
7	7 to 8	Long Yester camp, East Lothian, Scotland.	55:52:40 N	2:43:40 W	Two amber beads.	Iron Age or Roman.	Native fort, broch and settlement.	Dunwell 1999, 335; Hunter 1998, Tab. 10.	
8	9	Buittle, Kirkcudbrightshire , Scotland.	54:56:31 N	3:51:56 W	Amber.	Iron Age or Roman.	Native settlement.	Fraser Hunter, pers. Comm. 2007.	Stewartry Museum.
9	10	Birnie, Moray, Scotland.	57:35:28 N	3:16:55 W	Amber bead.	Iron Age or Roman.	Native settlement. Found during 2006 excavations.	Fraser Hunter, pers. Comm. 2007.	
10	11 to 17	Covesea, Moray, Scotland.	57:43:08 N	3:17:43 W	Seven amber beads.	Iron Age or Roman.	Native cave settlement. Found in a mixed occupation layer in the cave.		National Museum of Scotland, Edinburgh. NMAS acc No. HM204, 206-8.

APPENDIX 4. AMBER FROM BRITISH SITES DATING TO EITHER THE IRON AGE OR THE ROMAN PERIOD

Site No.	Object No.	Site	Lat.	Long.	Details	Context date	Find details	References	Location
11	18	Dun Bharabhat, Cnip, West Lewis, Outer Hebrides, Scotland.	58:12:53 N	6:57:24 W	Amber bead.	Fourth century BC to first century AD.	Native settlement. Reg. no. 085. Context 184-secondary occupation.	Harding and Dixon 2000, 28, Fig. 12, 7.	

Appendix 5. Amber from British sites dating to the Roman period (AD 43-430)

Site No.	Object No.	Site	Lat.	Long.	Details	Context date	Find details	References	Location
1	1 to 3	Stanfordbury, Bedfordshire, England.	52:02:30 N	0:19:60 W	Three amber beads.	c. AD 40-70.	Amongst the grave goods of the Stanfordbury burial.	Beck and Shennan 1991, 105-7, 172, Fig. 11.12, 3.	Cambridge Museum of Archaeology and Anthropology. IDNO: 1883.765.III.1.
2	4	Bottisham, Cambridgeshire, England.	52:13:24 N	0:15:31 E	Amber bead.	Roman.	Possibly associated with Romano-British settlement in the area. Found with 15 blue glass beads and one buff clay bead.		Cambridge Museum of Archaeology and Anthropology. IDNO: 1947.560.
3	5	Chesterton Camp, Cambridgeshire, England.	52:13:07 N	0:08:29 E	Amber bead.	Roman.	Possibly from the Roman fort.		British Museum. Registration No. 1882,0621.130. PRN: BCB51812.
4	6 to 11	Durobrivae, Cambridgeshire, England.	52:32:50 N	0:20:39 W	Bracelet of six amber beads.	Early fifth century AD.	Small town. Found in a girls(?) grave in Late Roman cemetery.	Hatton and Wall 2006, 14-19, Fig. 7; Burnham *et al.* 2000, 411.	
5	12	Grandford March, Cambridgeshire, England.	52:34:36 N	0:02:57 E	Possible fragment of amber.	Roman.	Romano-British settlement. March, 1962, Layer 2, Trench G, donated by Timothy Potter.		British Museum. Registration No. 1985,0503.734. PRN: BCE101601.
6	13	Hempsalls Fen, Willingham, Cambridgeshire, England.	52:18:52 N	0:03:50 E	Large circular amber bead.	First half of third century AD.	Rural hoard. Found with bronzes and other beads in glass, jet and stone.	Rostovtseff 1923, 94, No. 10, Fig. 4,2.	Cambridge Museum of Archaeology and Anthropology. IDNO: 1918.160.9-15.
7	14	Swaffham Prior, Cambridgeshire, England.	52:15:09 N	0:18:03 E	Small multi-facetted bead, possibly of amber.	Roman.	Unknown. Roman period rural settlement and a villa are in the area.		Cambridge Museum of Archaeology and Anthropology. IDNO: Z 26643.

APPENDIX 5. AMBER FROM BRITISH SITES DATING TO THE ROMAN PERIOD (AD 43-430)

Site No.	Object No.	Site	Lat.	Long.	Details	Context date	Find details	References	Location
8	15	Chester, Cheshire, England.	53:11:5 N	2:53:5 W	Fragments of a carved amber cockle shell. Made in Aquilea (c.f. Brown and Henig 1977).	Roman.	Roman legionary fort. Royal Infirmary. Site code: CHE CRI 92. SF no. 79.		
8	16	Chester, Cheshire, England.	53:11:5 N	2:53:5 W	Possible amber bead.	Roman.	Roman legionary fort. Context (1216) SF 9684, fill of a rubbish pit in amphitheatre area A.		
8	17	Chester, Cheshire, England.	53:11:5 N	2:53:5 W	Amber finger ring.	Roman.	Roman legionary fort. Old Market Hall excavations 1967-9. SF no. 669A.		
8	18	Chester, Cheshire, England.	53:11:5 N	2:53:5 W	Incomplete amber bead.	Roman.	Roman legionary fort. Crook Street excavations 1973-4. SF no.487.		
9	19	Carlisle, Cumbria, England.	54:53:43 N	2:56:18 W	Small annular bead.	Roman.	Roman fort. Castle Street.		Tully House Museum.
9	20 to 24	Carlisle, Cumbria, England.	54:53:43 N	2:56:18 W	Five assorted amber beads.	c. AD 140-180.	Roman fort. The Southern Lanes.	McCarthy 2000, 96, Nos. H1-5, Fig. 57.	Tully House Museum.
9	25	Carlisle, Cumbria, England.	54:53:43 N	2:56:18 W	Amber finger ring decorated with the head of Minerva.	Roman.	Roman fort.	McCarthy *et al.* 1982.	Tully House Museum.
9	26	Carlisle, Cumbria, England.	54:53:43 N	2:56:18 W	Amber knife handle carved in the form of a mouse eating.	Roman.	Roman fort.	McCarthy *et al.* 1983.	Tully House Museum.
9	27 to 28	Carlisle, Cumbria, England.	54:53:43 N	2:56:18 W	Two amber beads.	AD 83-94.	Roman fort. Annetwell Street.	McCarthy 2000, 96.	
10	29	Old Penrith, Cumbria, England.	54:40 N	2:45 W	Amber spindle whorl or bead.	Roman.	Roman fort.	Austen 1991, 110, No. 24, Fig. 48	
11	30	Exeter, Devon, England.	50:43:19 N	3:32:01 W	Fragment of an amber cylinder bead.	Roman.	Roman fort and urban site.	Holbrook and Bidwell 1991, 271, Fig. 125,1.	

Site No.	Object No.	Site	Lat.	Long.	Details	Context date	Find details	References	Location
12	31	Dorchester, Dorset, England.	50:42:52 N	2:25:48 W	Amber pendant of Baltic Berlock form (c.f. Lund Hansen, 1995, 217-222, Figs. 8.8-9; Bliujiene 2001).	Probably c. AD 300.	Urban site. Found in a female inhumation in Fordington Hill cemetery. On a necklace with glass, bone and pearl beads.	Henig 1984.	Dorset County Museum.
13	32	Hod Hill, Dorset, England.	50:53:47 N	2:12:28 W	Amber bead.	Roman.	Possibly associated with the Conquest-period Roman fort.		British Museum. Registration No. 1892,0901.1418. PRN: BCB13085.
14	33 to 34	Braintree, Essex, England.	51:52:52 N	0:33:24 E	"Some small amber beads".	Probably c. AD 260-430.	Small town. Found with glass beads near the right elbow of a skeleton in a limestone coffin. East-west alignment of the body, head at the west suggests that it may be Romano-Christian.	Beaumont 1900.	
15	35	Colchester, Essex, England.	51:53:23 N	0:54:04 E	Amber bead.	Roman.	Urban site/Roman fort.		British Museum. Registration No. 1870,0402.315. PRN: BCB51793.
15	36	Colchester, Essex, England.	51:53:23 N	0:54:04 E	Amber bead.	Roman.	Urban site/Roman fort.		British Museum. Registration No. 1870,0402.314. PRN: BCB13119.
15	37	Colchester, Essex, England.	51:53:23 N	0:54:04 E	Amber bead of Baltic berlock form (c.f. Lund Hansen 1995, 217-222, Figs. 8.8-9; Bliujiene 2001).	c. AD 200-250.	Urban site. From the Joslin collection (grave groups from either the Beverley Road district or from the west end of Colchester). From grave 97/12 find no.64.	May 1930, 280, Pl. LXXXVII, 97.	
15	38 to 39	Colchester, Essex, England.	51:53:23 N	0:54:04 E	Two armlets of amber.	c. AD 50-100.	Urban site/Roman fort. From the Joslin collection. Grave 29/47, no.275.	May 1930, 260.	

APPENDIX 5. AMBER FROM BRITISH SITES DATING TO THE ROMAN PERIOD (AD 43-430)

Site No.	Object No.	Site	Lat.	Long.	Details	Context date	Find details	References	Location
15	40	Colchester, Essex, England.	51:53:23 N	0:54:04 E	Amber pendant carved in the shape of an African man's head.	AD 260-430.	Urban site. Found in grave in Late Roman Butt Road cemetery.	Henig 1984; Crummy 1983, Fig. 54, No. 1802.	
15	41 to 54	Colchester, Essex, England.	51:53:23 N	0:54:04 E	Thirteen amber beads and one amber pendant.	AD 260-430.	Urban site. Found in various graves in the Late Roman Butt Road cemetery.	Crummy 1983, Nos. 559, 634-635, 647-649, 806, 903, 957, 959, 1348, 1419-20, 1802.	Colchester Museum.
16	55	Finchingfield, Essex, England.	51:58:03 N	0:26:59 E	Amber bead.	Roman.	Roman villa. Found in Roman building SMR number 1493. Occupation from late 1stC AD through to at least the late 4thC.		
17	56 to 72	Birdlip, Gloucestershire, England.	51:49:38 N	2:05:42 W	Necklace with seventeen amber beads.	c AD 50.	In Conquest-period grave enclosed by limestone slabs, associated with female inhumation. Mirror and other grave goods.	Beck and Shennan 1991, 105-7, 149, Fig. 11.2, 2.	
18	73	Cirencester, Gloucestershire, England.	51:42:51 N	1:57:60 W	Melon bead possibly made from amber.	Roman.	Urban site. Roman amber Cirencester No.6. 1857.		Cirencester Museum. A88b.
18	74	Cirencester, Gloucestershire, England.	51:42:51 N	1:57:60 W	Small annular bead of possible amber.	Roman.	Urban site. Found at the Cirencester Excavation Committee excavation at Dollar Street, Cirencester in 1966.		Cirencester Museum.
19	75	Gloucester, Gloucestershire, England.	51:51:56 N	2:14:55 W	Fragment of amber.	Roman.	Urban site. A8366a from the New Market Hall site in Gloucester dug in 1966-7.	Hassall and Rhodes 1974, 75.	

Site No.	Object No.	Site	Lat.	Long.	Details	Context date	Find details	References	Location
20	76	Lydney Park, Gloucestershire, England.	51:43 N	2:32 W	Amber bead.	Fourth century AD.	Religious site. Found in the core of one of the original walls of the temple. Several coins of late-third- and fourth-century dates were found in a similar position in the structure.	Wheeler 1932, 84, Fig. 18, 81.	
21	77	London, Greater London, England.	51:30:48 N	0:05:20 W	Waste amber.	Roman.	Urban. 23-25 Austin Friars, London. EC2. Site record AST87[567]<231>.		
21	78	London, Greater London, England.	51:30:48 N	0:05:20 W	Silver tutulus brooch with amber bead.	Late fourth to early fifth century AD.	Urban. Eastern cemetery. In a Germanic woman's grave- B374. Found with a triangular bone comb.	Barber and Bowsher 2000, 183-184.	
21	79 to 148	London, Greater London, England.	51:30:48 N	0:05:20 W	Necklace with seventy amber beads on a preserved flax string. Sixty-four of the beads are ellipsoid and they are divided into seven groups by six barrel disc spacer beads.	AD 50-150.	Urban. From bed of the river Walbrook, Old Jewry.	Chapman 1974, 273-274.	Museum of London.
21	149	London, Greater London, England.	51:30:48 N	0:05:20 W	Amber bead.	Probably early second century AD.	Urban. Upper Walbrook.	Maloney 1990, 82.	
21	150	London, Greater London, England.	51:30:48 N	0:05:20 W	Amber bead.	c. AD 95-100.	Urban. Leadenhall Court.	Milne and Wardle 1993, 77.	
22	151	Armsley, Fordingbridge, Hampshire, England.	50:56:36 N	1:45:55 W	Amber bead.	Roman.	Romano-British settlement.		Salisbury and South Wiltshire Museum.

APPENDIX 5. AMBER FROM BRITISH SITES DATING TO THE ROMAN PERIOD (AD 43-430)

Site No.	Object No.	Site	Lat.	Long.	Details	Context date	Find details	References	Location
23	152 to 154	Silchester, Hampshire, England.	51:21:27 N	1:04:56 W	Three amber beads.	Roman.	Urban site.		Museum of Reading.
23	155	Silchester, Hampshire, England.	51:21:27 N	1:04:56 W	Carved amber fly.	c. AD 260-430.	Urban site. Found in a late Roman pit 1293.	Fulford *et al.* 2006, 124-125, Fig. 75.	
24	156	Winchester, Hampshire, England.	51:03:45 N	1:18:54 W	Amber bead.	c. AD 340-370.	Urban site. Lankhills cemetery. Object no. 436, in the burial of a young girl- Grave 323. This grave belongs to group of foreign burials, which probably represents a group of people originating from Pannonia.	Clarke 1979, 295-6, Fig. 86K.	Winchester Museum.
24	157	Winchester, Hampshire, England.	51:03:45 N	1:18:54 W	Amber bead.	Fourth century AD.	Urban site. Lankhills Cemetery. In Grave 336. Belongs to a Pannonian burial group.	Swift 2000b, 74.	Winchester Museum.
24	158 to 159	Winchester, Hampshire, England.	51:03:45 N	1:18:54 W	Necklace with glass, amber, coral and (?) ivory beads.	Late fourth or early fifth century AD.	Urban site. A pit dug in the garden of the latest phase of a Roman house contained the necklace and over fifty coins down to c.387.	Frere *et al.* 1988, 318.	
25	160 to 161	Canterbury, Kent, England.	51:16:39 N	1:04:50 E	"Twelve amber and glass beads".	Early fifth century AD.	Urban site. A large pit cut the final courtyard surface and contained two adults, two children and a dog. This grave contained jewellery typical of the latest Roman period.	Grew *et al.* 1980, 366.	Canterbury Museum.
26	162	Richborough, Kent, England.	51:17:29 N	1:19:27 E	Half a large circular amber bead.	c. AD 40-85.	Roman fort. Found in a pit.	Bushe-Fox 1928, 31, Pl. XIV, Fig. 2,11.	

Site No.	Object No.	Site	Lat.	Long.	Details	Context date	Find details	References	Location
27	163	Leicester, Leicestershire, England.	52:38:05 N	1:07:47 W	Amber earring.	Roman.	Urban site. Jewry Wall. Unstratified.	Kenyon 1948, 271, Fig. 94, 10.	
28	164	Southery, Norfolk, England.	52:31:38 N	0:23:15 E	Amber bead.	Roman.	Unknown. Romano-British settlements in the area.		British Museum. Registration No. 1880.1124.79-82. PRN: BCB12755.
29	165	Weeting, Norfolk, England.	52:27:52 N	0:36:55 E	A small scrap of amber, probably a small amber beach-pebble.	Fourth century AD.	Rural site. Found in farm building.	Gregory 1996, 25.	
30	166 to 169	Vindolanda, Northumberland, England.	54:59:28 N	2:21:37 W	Four amber beads.	c. AD 105-125.	Roman military site.	Birley and Greene 2006, 50-52.	
30	170 to 172	Vindolanda, Northumberland, England.	54:59:28 N	2:21:37 W	Three amber beads.	c. AD 140-212.	Roman military site.	Birley and Greene 2006, 50-52.	
30	173	Vindolanda, Northumberland, England.	54:59:28 N	2:21:37 W	One amber bead.	c. AD 200-212.	Roman military site.	Birley and Greene 2006, 50-52.	
30	174 to 176	Vindolanda, Northumberland, England.	54:59:28 N	2:21:37 W	Three amber beads.	c. AD 212-300.	Roman military site.	Birley and Greene 2006, 50-52.	
31	177	Wheldrake, North Yorkshire, England.	53:53:48 N	0:57:50 W	Amber bead.	Third century AD.	Rural settlement. Found during 2002 excavations by Northern Archaeology Associates at Millfield Farm.		
32	178 to 185	York, North Yorkshire, England.	53:57:28 N	1:04:56 W	A necklace or bracelet with eight amber beads and many blue glass beads.	Probably c. AD 260-430.	Urban site/legionary fortress. Railway cemetery. Railway excavations of 1874.		York Museum.
32	186	York, North Yorkshire, England.	53:57:28 N	1:04:56 W	Annular amber bead.	c. AD 280-360/400.	Urban site/legionary fortress.	Cool *et al.* 1995, 1545-1546, 1649, No. 5821, Fig. 722.	

APPENDIX 5. AMBER FROM BRITISH SITES DATING TO THE ROMAN PERIOD (AD 43-430)

Site No.	Object No.	Site	Lat.	Long.	Details	Context date	Find details	References	Location
32	187	York, North Yorkshire, England.	53:57:28 N	1:04:56 W	Amber bead with lentoid cross-section.	First half of the second century AD.	Urban site/legionary fortress.	Cool *et al.* 1995, 1545-1546, 1649, No. 5822, Fig. 722.	
33	188	Wroxeter, Shropshire, England.	52:40:27 N	2:38:43 W	Amber finger ring.	Roman.	Roman fort/urban site.	An image of the ring can be found on the Darwin Country website (www.darwincountry.org); image number sy3974.	Shrewsbury Museum.
33	189	Wroxeter, Shropshire, England.	52:40:27 N	2:38:43 W	Carved amber ramshorn.	c. AD 56-90.	Legionary fortress. 90/24, sf6241.	Webster 2002, 127, Fig. 4.27, 212.	
34	190	Bath, Somerset, England.	51:22:51 N	2:21:34 W	Annular amber bead.	Roman.	Religious site. From the sacred spring.	Cunliffe 1988c, 23, Fig. 12, 49.	Bath Museum.
34	191 to 192	Bath, Somerset, England.	51:22:51 N	2:21:34 W	Two amber beads.	Probably Roman.	Unprovenanced. Religious site.		Bath Museum.
35	193	Shepton Mallet, Somerset	51:10:25 N	2:31:59 W	Annular amber bead.	Roman.	Small town. Cannard's Grave.		Somerset County Museums Service (in store) Ref No: 1/1996/5203.
36	194	Rossington Bridge, South Yorkshire, England.	53:28:48 N	1:03:30 W	Annular amber bead.	Roman.	Settlement/pottery production site.	Buckland *et al.* 2001, 22-24, Fig. 2, 32.	Doncaster Museum.
37	195	Sandtoft, South Yorkshire, England.	53:33:52 N	0:52:29 W	Annular amber bead.	Probably fourth century AD.	Late Roman settlement.	Samuels and Buckland 1978, 65-75, Fig. 7,3.	
38	196	Templeborough, South Yorkshire, England.	53:25 N	1:21 W	Small amorphous lump of amber.	Roman.	Roman fort.	May 1922, 54, Pl. 40,1.	
39	197	Hacheston, Suffolk, England.	52:11 N	1:22 E	Unworked piece of amber	Late third or fourth century AD.	Small town.	Blagg *et al.* 2004, 149, No. 395.	

Site No.	Object No.	Site	Lat.	Long.	Details	Context date	Find details	References	Location
40	198	Icklingham, Suffolk, England.	52:19:26 N	0:36:06 E	Amber bead.	c. AD 400.	Large Romano-British settlement. Part of the Icklingham hoard.	Liversidge 1968, 139, Fig. 52a.	Cambridge Museum of Archaeology and Anthropology. IDNO: 1947.1860 A-K.
41	199 to 204	South Shields, Tyne and Wear, England.	55:00 N	1:25 W	Six amber beads.	Roman.	Roman fort.	Bidwell and Speak 1984, 33-34.	
41	205 to 206	South Shields, Tyne and Wear, England.	55:00 N	1:25 W	Two amber buttons or beads.	Roman.	Roman fort.	Bidwell and Speak 1984, 33-34.	
41	207	South Shields, Tyne and Wear, England.	55:00 N	1:25 W	Octagonal amber brooch (?) setting with facetted edges.	Roman.	Roman fort.	Bidwell and Speak 1984, 33-34.	
41	208	South Shields, Tyne and Wear, England.	55:00 N	1:25 W	Fragment of an amber ring or bracelet of D-shaped section with grooves incised across the width.	Roman.	Roman fort.	Bidwell and Speak 1984, 33-34.	
41	209	South Shields, Tyne and Wear, England.	55:00 N	1:25 W	Amber bracelet of pear-shaped section, decorated across the outer (wider) face with incised lines.	Probably second or third century AD.	Roman fort.	Bidwell and Speak 1984, 33-34.	
42	210 to 211	Wallsend, Tyne and Wear, England.	54:59 N	1:32 W	Two annular amber beads.	Roman.	Roman fort.	Allason Jones, L. pers. Comm. 2007.	
43	212	Castleford, West Yorkshire, England.	53:43 N	1:21 W	Amber fingerring with broken, plain, D-sectioned hoop, expanding towards a bezel.	Roman.	Fort/vicus.	Cool and Philo 1998, 253, Fig. 108, 1-2.	

Site No.	Object No.	Site	Lat.	Long.	Details	Context date	Find details	References	Location
43	213	Castleford, West Yorkshire, England.	53:43 N	1:21 W	Oval-sectioned amber bead	Roman.	Fort/vicus.	Cool and Philo 1998, 253, Fig. 108, 1-2.	
44	214	Wanborough, Wiltshire, England.	51:32 N	1:42 W	Amber bead.	Roman.	Small town.	Anderson *et al*. 2001, 172, No. 15, Fig. 68, 15.	Devises Museum.
45	215	Westbury, Wiltshire, England.	51:15 N	2:11 W	Large amber bead.	Roman.	Romano-British settlement.	Cunnington and Goddard 1934, 177. No. 5. 614, Pl. LV, 5.	Devises Museum.
46	216	Withy Beds, Wiltshire, England.	51:05 N	2:02 W	Amber bead.	Roman.	Romano-British settlement.	Cunnington and Goddard 1934, 193-194, No. 491.	Devises Museum.
47	217 to 218	Ffrith, Clwyd, Wales.	53:05:26 N	3:04:14 W	"Amber beads".	Roman.	Roman settlement possibly associated with nearby lead mining.	Davies 1949, 230-231.	
48	219 to 225	Caerleon, Gwent, Wales	51:37 N	2:57 W	Seven amber beads, perhaps part of a single necklace.	c. AD 70-120.	Roman legionary fortress. From a drain.	Zienkiewicz 1986, 152-4, Fig. 50, 1-7.	National Museum of Wales.
48	226	Caerleon, Gwent, Wales	51:37 N	2:57 W	Amber finger ring.	Roman.	Found near Caerleon Roman legionary fortress at Great Bulmore Farm.		National Museums and Galleries of Wales. Accession code 84.44H.
48	227 to 233	Caerleon, Gwent, Wales	51:37 N	2:57 W	A portion of an amber necklace, comprising seven beads: three annular, one ring-shaped, two large mis-shapen beads and one large lenticular bead.	Second century AD.	Found near Caerleon Roman legionary fortress at Twin Oaks Sawmills on the Usk Road. Cremation burial.	Zienkiewicz 1986, 152.	National Museum of Wales.
49	234	Newstead, Borders, Scotland.	55:35:58 N	2:41:57 W	Amber bead.	Flavian or Antonine.	Roman fort.	Curle 1911, 337.	

Site No.	Object No.	Site	Lat.	Long.	Details	Context date	Find details	References	Location
50	235	St Germains, East Lothian, Scotland.	55:57:44 N	2:54:46 W	Amber bead (possibly a phallic pendant).	Probably Roman.	Native settlement. Unstratified.	Hunter 1998, Tab. 10; Alexander and Watkins 1998, 236-8, Ill. 18, 310.	
51	236 to 242	Traprain Law, East Lothian, Scotland.	55:57:49 N	2:40:15 W	Seven amber beads.	Roman.	Native hillfort.	Hunter 1998, Tab. 10.	
51	243	Traprain Law, East Lothian, Scotland.	55:57:49 N	2:40:15 W	Fingerring with amber bezel.	Roman.	Native hillfort.	Hunter 1998, Tab. 10.	
51	244	Traprain Law, East Lothian, Scotland.	55:57:49 N	2:40:15 W	Angular fragment of amber.	Roman.	Native hillfort.	Hunter 1998, Tab. 10.	
51	245	Traprain Law, East Lothian, Scotland.	55:57:49 N	2:40:15 W	Large amber bead.	Late first to early second century AD.	Native hillfort. Found in the lowest level of the excavations. These date primarily to the Iron Age and contain first century AD samian and a coin of Hadrian.	Curle 1915, 179.	
51	246	Traprain Law, East Lothian, Scotland.	55:57:49 N	2:40:15 W	Discoid bead of amber.	Possibly Roman.	Native hillfort. Found during backfill, (unstratified).	Curle and Cree 1916, 109-110, Fig. 26,16.	
51	247	Traprain Law, East Lothian, Scotland.	55:57:49 N	2:40:15 W	Annular amber bead.	Third century AD.	Native hillfort.	Curle 1920, 82, Fig. 11,16.	
51	248	Traprain Law, East Lothian, Scotland.	55:57:49 N	2:40:15 W	Small discoid amber bead.	Third century AD.	Native hillfort.	Curle 1920, 82, Fig. 11,17.	
51	249	Traprain Law, East Lothian, Scotland.	55:57:49 N	2:40:15 W	Bead of amber.	Late first early second century AD.	Native hillfort.	Cree 1924, 254.	
51	250	Traprain Law, East Lothian, Scotland.	55:57:49 N	2:40:15 W	Perforated tapering amber bead.	Second to fourth century AD.	Native hillfort. Found during excavations near the quarry, from the secondary occupation deposit underlying the Cruden wall.	Cruden 1940, 58; Dunwell 1999, 333-5.	

APPENDIX 5. AMBER FROM BRITISH SITES DATING TO THE ROMAN PERIOD (AD 43-430)

Site No.	Object No.	Site	Lat.	Long.	Details	Context date	Find details	References	Location
52	251	Dun Ardtreck, Skye, Inner Hebrides, Scotland.	57:19 N	6:24 W	Triangular amber bead.	Early/mid-second century AD.	Native settlement. Found at the phase II/III transition. Find no A.1965.771.	MacKie 2000, 329, 387, Ill. 28, 24, No. 39.	
53	252	Dun Mor Vaul, Tiree, Inner Hebrides, Scotland.	56:32 N	6:48 W	Fragment of probable amber.	Second century AD.	Native broch. Found in ash spread (context kappa).	MacKie 1974, 133; Hunter 1998, Tab. 10.	
54	253	Ardoch, Perthshire, Scotland.	56:31: 21 N	3:28:02 W	Amber bead.	Flavian or Antonine.	Roman fort.	Christison and Anderson 1898, 453.	
55	254 to 255	Underhoull, Unst, Shetland.	60:42:56 N	0:56:28 W	Two amber beads.	Roman.	Native broch. From the Broch-period horizon.	Small 1967, 234-5, Fig. 9.	
56	256	Fairy Knowe, Buchlyvie, Stirlingshire, Scotland.	56:06:54 N	4:17:37 W	Fragments of an amber bead.	Probably c. AD 70-140.	Native settlement.	Hunter 1998.	
56	257	Fairy Knowe, Buchlyvie, Stirlingshire, Scotland.	56:06:54 N	4:17:37 W	Fragments of a small unknown amber object. The fragments have a flat base, a rounded square corner and the sides slope slightly. It is not an annular bead or pendant.	Probably c. AD 70-140.	Native settlement.	Hunter 1998.	
57	258	Falkirk, Stirlingshire, Scotland.	55:59:50 N	3:47:19 W	Amber bead.	Roman.	Roman fort. Excavations at Hodge Street.	Batey 1993; 11.	Falkirk Museum.
	259	Unknown, England.			Amber bead.	Probably Roman.			British Museum. Registration No. 1877,0116.36. PRN BCB13169.

Appendix 6. Romano-British brooches on the continent

Brooch No.	Site No.	Site name	Lat.	Long.	Hull type	Hull group	Female associations	References
1	1	Heerlen, Limburg, Netherlands	50:54 N	5:59 E	T199	Plate	Umbonate	Spitaels 1969, Cat. No. 857 (many thanks to Sarnia Butcher for providing details of Spitaels thesis).
2	2	Maastricht, Limburg, Netherlands	50:51 N	5:41 E	T157	8 (Backworth)		Spitaels 1969, Cat. No. 863.
3	3	Nijmegen, Gelderland, Netherlands	51:50 N	5:52 E	T143A	7	Loop	Spitaels 1969, Cat. No. 745; Van Buchem 1941, Pl. XIV.5.
4	3	Nijmegen, Gelderland, Netherlands	51:50 N	5:52 E	T145B	7	Loop	Spitaels 1969, Cat. No. 746.
5	3	Nijmegen, Gelderland, Netherlands	51:50 N	5:52 E	T145B	7		Spitaels 1969, Cat. No. 747.
6	3	Nijmegen, Gelderland, Netherlands	51:50 N	5:52 E	T148B	7 (Lamberton Moor)	Loop	Spitaels 1969, Cat. No. 744.
7	3	Nijmegen, Gelderland, Netherlands	51:50 N	5:52 E	T148B	7 (Lamberton Moor)	Loop	Spitaels 1969, Cat. No. 750.
8	3	Nijmegen, Gelderland, Netherlands	51:50 N	5:52 E	T148B or C	7 (Lamberton Moor)	Loop?	Spitaels 1969, Cat. No. 751.
9	3	Nijmegen, Gelderland, Netherlands	51:50 N	5:52 E	T148 or 149	7 (Lamberton Moor)	Loop?	Spitaels 1969, Cat. No. 748.
10	3	Nijmegen, Gelderland, Netherlands	51:50 N	5:52 E	T154A	8 (Backworth)		Spitaels 1969, Cat. No. 738.
11	3	Nijmegen, Gelderland, Netherlands	51:50 N	5:52 E	T157	8 (Backworth)	Loop	Spitaels 1969, Cat. No. 739.
12	3	Nijmegen, Gelderland, Netherlands	51:50 N	5:52 E	T157	8 (Backworth)	Loop	Spitaels 1969, Cat. No. 740.

Brooch No.	Site No.	Site name	Lat.	Long.	Hull type	Hull group	Female associations	References
13	3	Nijmegen, Gelderland, Netherlands	51:50 N	5:52 E	T157	8 (Backworth)	Loop	Spitaels 1969, Cat. No. 741.
14	3	Nijmegen, Gelderland, Netherlands	51:50 N	5:52 E	T157	8 (Backworth)	Loop	Spitaels 1969, Cat. No. 742.
15	3	Nijmegen, Gelderland, Netherlands.	51:50 N	5:52 E	T157	8 (Backworth)		Spitaels 1969, Cat. No. 743.
16	3	Nijmegen, Gelderland, Netherlands	51:50 N	5:52 E	T173B	9		Spitaels 1969, Cat. No. 837.
17	3	Nijmegen, Gelderland, Netherlands	51:50 N	5:52 E	T173A	9		Spitaels 1969, Cat. No. 838.
18-19	3	Nijmegen, Gelderland, Netherlands	51:50 N	5:52 E	T267	Flate	Two brooches joined by chain	Spitaels 1969, Cat. Nos. 733, 735.
20	3	Nijmegen, Gelderland, Netherlands	51:50 N	5:52 E	T267	Flate	Umbonate	Spitaels 1969, Cat. No. 736.
21	3	Nijmegen, Gelderland, Netherlands	51:50 N	5:52 E	T267	Plate	Umbonate	Spitaels 1969, Cat. No. 737.
22	3	Nijmegen, Gelderland, Netherlands	51:50 N	5:52 E	T200	Plate		Spitaels 1969, Cat. No. 731.
23	3	Nijmegen, Gelderland, Netherlands	51:50 N	5:52 E	T143	7	Loop	Van Buchem 1941, Pl. XIV.4.
24	3	Nijmegen, Gelderland, Netherlands	51:50 N	5:52 E	Unclassified. Probably a rare variety of enamelled T-shaped brooch.	7		Van Buchem 1941; Pl. XIV.1.

Brooch No.	Site No.	Site name	Lat.	Long.	Hull type	Hull group	Female associations	References
25	4	Wijk bij Duurstede, Utrecht, Netherlands	51:59 N	5:21 E	T157	8 (Backworth)	Loop	Van Der Roost 1988 (reconstruction of decoration on bow in Lamberton Moor style is questionable).
26	5	Zetten, Gelderland, Netherlands	51:56 N	5:43 E	T158	8 (Backworth)		Böhme 1970.
27-28	6	Blicquy, Hainaut, Belgium	50:35 N	3:41 E	T148B	7 (Lamberton Moor)	Two brooches	Spitaels 1969, Cat. Nos. 42-43.
29	7	Destelbergen, East Flanders, Belgium	51:04 N	3:47 E	T166	8		Spitaels 1969, Cat. No. 586.
30	8	Fallais, Liege, Belgium	50:37 N	5:10 E	T200	Plate		Feacham 1951, Fig. 2,27; Spitaels 1969, Cat. No. 227.
31	9	Flavion, Namur, Belgium	50:15 N	4:42 E	T148C	7 (Lamberton Moor)	Probable loop	Spitaels 1969, Cat. No. 449.
32	10	Hofstade, East Flanders, Belgium	50:58 N	4:02 E	T166	8		Spitaels 1969, Cat. No. 592.
33-34	11	Schaerbeek, Brussels, Belgium	50:51 N	4:23 E	T259	Plate	Two brooches	Mariën 1980, 276, Fig. 189.
35	12	Thuin, Hainaut, Belgium.	50:20 N	4:17 E	T157	8 (Backworth)		Böhme 1970; Spitaels 1969, Cat. No. 205.
36	13	Tongeren, Limburg, Belgium	50:47 N	5:27 E	T148C	7 (Lamberton Moor)	Probable loop	Bayley and Butcher 2004, 255; Spitaels 1969, Cat. No. 148C.
37	14	Velzeke, East Flanders, Belgium	50:53 N	3:46 E	T166	8		Spitaels 1969, Cat. No. 598.
38	14	Velzeke, East Flanders, Belgium	50:53 N	3:46 E	T166	8		Spitaels 1969, Cat. No. 605.
39	15	Waasmunster-Pontrave, Waasland, Belgium	51:06 N	4:04 E	T166C	8		Spitaels 1969, Cat. No. 613.
40	16	Dalheim, Remich, Luxembourg	49:32 N	6:15 E	T145A	7		Bayley and Butcher 2004, 255; Spitaels 1969, Cat. No. 684.
41	16	Dalheim, Remich, Luxembourg	49:32 N	6:15 E	T267	Plate		Spitaels 1969, Cat. No. 683.
42		Unkown, Luxembourg			T157	8 (Backworth)		Spitaels 1969, Cat. No. 722.

Brooch No.	Site No.	Site name	Lat.	Long.	Hull type	Hull group	Female associations	References
43	17	Aime, Savoie, France	45:33 N	6:39 E	T93	5		Feugère 1985, 146, Pl. 159, 2013.
44	18	Amiens, Somme, France	49:54 N	2:18 E	T166	8		Hattatt 1987, 140, No. 971.
45	18	Amiens, Somme, France	49:54 N	2:18 E	T162	8		Hattatt 1987, 144, No. 980.
46	19	Catillon, Nord-Pas-de-Calais, France	49:29 N	0:37 E	T200	Plate		Feacham 1951, Fig. 2,29; Megaw and Megaw 2001a.
47	20	Étaples, Pas-de-Calais, France	50:31 N	1:39 E	T153-160	8 (Backworth)		Dilly 1978, 164.
48	20	Étaples, Pas-de-Calais, France	50:31 N	1:39 E	T90	5		*Hull Corpus* Plate 284.
49	21	Fesques, Seine-Maritime, France	49:47 N	1:29 E	T93A	5		Canny and Dilly 1997, 184, 191-2, No. 49.
50	22	Mandeure, Doubs, France	47:27 N	6:48 E	T157	8 (Backworth)		Böhme 1970.
51	23	Montbéliard, Doubs, France	47:31 N	6:48 E	T157	8 (Backworth)		Lerat 1957, No. 29.
52	24	Seveux, Haute-Saône, France	47:33 N	5:45 E	T168+	8		Lerat 1957, 269, Pl. 14.
53	25	Vendeuil-Caply, Oise, France	49:37 N	2:18 E	T148B or C	7 (Lamberton Moor)	Loop	Dilly and Jobic 1993, 382, 395, No. 232, Fig. XVII.
54	26	Vermand, Aisne, France	49:52 N	3:09 E	T94A	5		Dilly and Sallandre 1978, 148, No. 31, Pl. VI.
55	26	Vermand, Aisne, France	49:52 N	3:09 E	T168	8		Dilly and Sallandre 1978, 155, No. 39, Pl. VII.
56		Unknown, Picardy, France			T157	8 (Backworth)	Loop	Dilly 1978, No. 24; Böhme 1970.
57		Unknown, Picardy, France			T148B	7 (Lamberton Moor)	Loop	Dilly 1978, No. 25.
58		Unknown, Picardy, France			T149B	7 (Lamberton Moor)	Loop	Dilly 1978, No. 26.

Brooch No.	Site No.	Site name	Lat.	Long.	Hull type	Hull group	Female associations	References
59		Unknown, Picardy, France			T149B	7 (Lamberton Moor)	Loop	Dilly 1978, No. 27.
60		Unknown, France			T157	8 (Backworth)		Fauduet 1999, No. 46, Pl. VII.
61		Unknown, France			T200	Plate		Feacham 1951, Fig. 4, 31.
62	27	Alzey, Germany	49:45 N	8:07 E	T157	8 (Backworth)		Böhme 1970
63	28	Bad Kreuznach, Germany	49:50 N	7:52 E	T157	8 (Backworth)		Böhme 1970
64	29	Bingen, Germany	49:58 N	7:54 E	T90	5		Exner 1939, Group I. A. 4.
65	30	Blankenheim, Germany	50:26 N	6:39 E	T173A	9		Recorded in *Hull Corpus* description of T173A.
66	31	Bonn, Germany	50:44 N	7:06 E	T148B	7 (Lamberton Moor)	Loop	Collingwood 1930, 56, Fig. 13.
67	32	Burghöfe, Germany	48:39 N	10:47 E	T158	8 (Backworth)	Loop	Ortisi 2002, 34, Taf. 17, No. 282.
68	32	Burghöfe, Germany	48:39 N	10:47 E	T145	7		Ortisi 2002, 34, Taf. 17, No. 281.
69	33	Cologne, Germany	50:56 N	6:57 E	T149B	7 (Lamberton Moor)	Loop	Collingwood 1930, 56, Fig. 13; Exner 1939, Group I. A. 1, Taf. 6, 1; Ingo Martell, pers. comm. 2007.
70	33	Cologne, Germany	50:56 N	6:57 E	Possible T162	8		Ingo Martell, pers. comm. 2007.
71	33	Cologne, Germany	50:56 N	6:57 E	T162	8		Ingo Martell, pers. comm. 2007.
72	33	Cologne, Germany	50:56 N	6:57 E	T157	8 (Backworth)	Loop	Böhme 1970; Ingo Martell, pers. comm. 2007.
73	33	Cologne, Germany	50:56 N	6:57 E	T166	8		Exner 1939, 79, Group 1. B. 23; Ingo Martell, pers. Comm. 2007.
74	33	Cologne, Germany	50:56 N	6:57 E	T158	8 (Backworth)		Ingo Martell, pers. Comm. 2007.
75	33	Cologne, Germany	50:56 N	6:57 E	T157	8 (Backworth)		Ingo Martell, pers. Comm. 2007.
76	33	Cologne, Germany	50:56 N	6:57 E	T158	8 (Backworth)		Ingo Martell, pers. Comm. 2007.

Brooch No.	Site No.	Site name	Lat.	Long.	Hull type	Hull group	Female associations	References
77	33	Cologne, Germany	50:56 N	6:57 E	T157	8 (Backworth)		Ingo Martell, pers.comm. 2007.
78	33	Cologne, Germany	50:56 N	6:57 E	T168	8		In the Ashmolean Museum, Oxford, but deriving from Cologne. Mentioned in the *Hull Corpus* description of T168.
79	33	Cologne, Germany	50:56 N	6:57 E	T267	Plate	Umbonate	Exner 1939, 113-114, Group 4:52
80	33	Cologne, Germany	50:56 N	6:57 E	T267	Plate	Umbonate	Exner 1939; 115, Group 4:57, Taf.17,4.
81	33	Cologne, Germany	50:56 N	6:57 E	T259	Plate		Exner 1939, 102, Taf. 13,1.
82	33	Cologne, Germany	50:56 N	6:57 E	T259	Plate		Exner 1939, 102, Taf. 13,1.
83	34	Diersheim, Germany	48:39 N	7:53 E	T157	8 (Backworth)		Böhme 1970.
84	35	Eich, Germany	50:26 N	7:21 E	T157	8 (Backworth)		Böhme 1970
85	36	Flonheim, Germany	49:47 N	8:02 E	T166	8		Exner 1939, Group 1. B. 23.
86	37	Heddernheim, Germany	50:10 N	8:39 E	T96-103	6		Böhme 1970.
87	37	Heddernheim, Germany	50:10 N	8:39 E	T96-103	6		Böhme 1970.
88	37	Heddernheim, Germany	50:10 N	8:39 E	T96-103	6		Böhme 1970.
89	37	Heddernheim, Germany	50:10 N	8:39 E	T157	8 (Backworth)		Böhme 1970; Collingwood 1930, Fig. 8.
90	37	Heddernheim, Germany	50:10 N	8:39 E	Associated with T149	7 (Lamberton Moor)		Exner 1939, Taf. 6,4; *Hull Corpus* Pl. 518.
91	37	Heddernheim, Germany	50:10 N	8:39 E	Unclassified	Unclassified	Loop	Exner 1939, Group 1. B. 23, Taf. 7,11.
92	37	Heddernheim, Germany	50:10 N	8:39 E	T267-268	Plate	Umbonate	Fischer 1998, 217, No. 20, Abb. 150.
93	37	Heddernheim, Germany	50:10 N	8:39 E	T163	8		Discussion of T163 in the *Hull Corpus* mentions example(s) from Heddernheim; Riese 1898, 41.
94	38	Heldenbergen in der Wetterau, Germany	50:14 N	8:52 E	T148A	7 (Lamberton Moor)	Loop	Czysz 2003, 347, Taf. 4, B71.
95	38	Heldenbergen in der Wetterau, Germany	50:14 N	8:52 E	T148-9	7 (Lamberton Moor)	Probable loop	Czysz 2003, 347, Taf. 4, B72.

Brooch No.	Site No.	Site name	Lat.	Long.	Hull type	Hull group	Female associations	References
96	39	Hesselbach, Germany	49:34 N	9:05 E	T96-103	6		Böhme 1970
97	40	Hofheim, Germany	50:05 N	8:27 E	T157	8 (Backworth)		Böhme 1970
98	41	Kobern, Germany	50:19 N	7:28 E	T200	Plate		Feacham 1951, Fig. 3,26.
99	42	Köngen, Germany	48:41 N	9:22 E	T162	8		*Hull Corpus* Plate 595.
100	43	Loxstedt, Germany	53:28 N	8:39 E	T259	Plate		Unpublished. In Landesmuseum Hannover: Inv. No. 7232.
101	44	Mainz, Germany	49:59 N	8:16 E	Unclassified	7		Collingwood 1930, 56, Fig. 13.
102	45	Mainz-Weisenau, Germany	49:59 N	8:18 E	T157	8 (Backworth)	Loop	Böhme 1970
103	46	Mayen, Germany	50:20 N	7:13 E	T157	8 (Backworth)		Böhme 1970; Exner 1939, Taf. 7, 9.
104	46	Mayen, Germany	50:20 N	7:13 E	T148 or 149	7 (Lamberton Moor)	Probable loop	Exner 1939, 72-73, Group I. A. 1.
105	47	Moers-Asberg, Germany	51:26 N	6:39 E	T149B	7 (Lamberton Moor)	Loop	Bechert 1973, Taf. 9, No. 88.
106	47	Moers-Asberg, Germany	51:26 N	6:39 E	T112-119	7		Bechert 1973, Taf. 9, No. 87.
107	48	Möhn, Germany	49:50 N	6:35 E	T163	8		*Hull Corpus*; Hettner 1901, Taf. 4,18.
108	49	Neuss, Germany	51:12 N	6:42 E	T149B	7 (Lamberton Moor)	Loop	Exner 1939, 72-73, Group I. A. 1. Taf. 6.2, 5.1.
109	50	Nideggen, Germany	50:41 N	6:29 E	T39	3	Loop	Exner 1939, 84, Taf. 5,10.
110	51	Pont, Germany	51:29 N	6:18 E	T145	7		Cüppers 1962, 348, Grab 103, Abb. 30,d.
111	52	Praunheim, Germany	50:09 N	8:38 E	T149B	7 (Lamberton Moor)	Probable loop	Exner 1939, 72-73, Group I. A. 1, Taf. 6,3.
112	53	Regensburg, Germany	49:01 N	12:06 E	T271	Plate		Lamprecht 1906, Pl. IV, 7.
113	54	Rheinzabern, Germany	49:07 N	8:17 E	T158	8 (Backworth)		Böhme 1970
114	55	Saalburg, Germany	50:17 N	8:35 E	T99	6		Böhme 1970, No.1, Abb. 1,1.
115	55	Saalburg, Germany	50:17 N	8:35 E	T100C	6		Böhme 1970, No. 2, Abb. 1,2.
116	55	Saalburg, Germany	50:17 N	8:35 E	T100C	6		Böhme 1970, No. 3, Abb. 1,3.

Brooch No.	Site No.	Site name	Lat.	Long.	Hull type	Hull group	Female associations	References
117	55	Saalburg, Germany	50:17 N	8:35 E	T100C	6		Böhme 1970, No. 4, Abb. 1,4.
118	55	Saalburg, Germany	50:17 N	8:35 E	T100C	6		Böhme 1970, No. 5, Abb. 1,5.
119	55	Saalburg, Germany	50:17 N	8:35 E	T100C	6		Böhme 1970, No. 6, Abb. 1, 6.
120	55	Saalburg, Germany	50:17 N	8:35 E	T100C	6		Böhme 1970, No. 7, Abb. 1, 7.
121	55	Saalburg, Germany	50:17 N	8:35 E	T157C	8 (Backworth)	Loop	Böhme 1970, No. 8.
122	55	Saalburg, Germany	50:17 N	8:35 E	T158	8 (Backworth)	Loop	Böhme 1970, No. 11, Abb. 1,11.
123	55	Saalburg, Germany	50:17 N	8:35 E	T158	8 (Backworth)		Böhme 1970, No. 13, Abb. 1,12.
124	55	Saalburg, Germany	50:17 N	8:35 E	T158	8 (Backworth)		Böhme 1970, No. 14, Abb. 1,13.
125	55	Saalburg, Germany	50:17 N	8:35 E	153C	8 (Backworth)		Böhme 1970, No. 15, Abb. 1,14.
126	55	Saalburg, Germany	50:17 N	8:35 E	Unclassified	Unclassified		Böhme 1970, No.18, Abb. 1,17; Exner 1939, 78, Taf. 7.7.
127	56	Stockstadt am Main, Germany	49:59 N	9:04 E	T166	8		Exner 1939, Group 1. B. 23, Taf. 7,10.
128	57	Straubing, Germany	48:53 N	12:34 E	T100C	6		Bayley and Butcher 2004, 253; Walke 1965, Taf. 94,14.
129	57	Straubing, Germany	48:53 N	12:34 E	T148A	7 (Lamberton Moor)		Walke 1965, Taf. 94,15.
130	57	Straubing, Germany	48:53 N	12:34 E	T259	Plate		Walke 1965, Taf. 95,29.
131	58	Tholey, Germany	49:29 N	7:04 E	T148 or 149	7 (Lamberton Moor)	Probable loop	Exner 1939, 72-73, Group I. A. 1.
132	59	Trier, Germany	49:45 N	6:38 E	T148 or 149	7 (Lamberton Moor)	Loop	Collingwood 1930, 56, Fig. 13; Exner 1939, Group I. A. 1.
133	59	Trier, Germany	49:45 N	6:38 E	T148 or 149	7 (Lamberton Moor)		Collingwood 1930, 56, Fig. 13.
134	59	Trier, Germany	49:45 N	6:38 E	T157	8 (Backworth)		Böhme 1970

Brooch No.	Site No.	Site name	Lat.	Long.	Hull type	Hull group	Female associations	References
135	59	Trier, Germany	49:45 N	6:38 E	T145	7		Gose 1972, 151, Abb. 286,30; Collingwood 1930, Fig. 13.
136	60	Waldorf, Germany	50:29 N	7:13 E	T267	Plate	Umbonate	Exner 1939, 113-114, Group 4:52, Taf. 17,3.
137	61	Weissenthurm, Germany	50:25 N	7:27 E	T148 or 149	7 (Lamberton Moor)	Probable loop	Exner 1939, 72-73, Group I. A. 1.
138	62	Wiesbaden, Germany	50:05 N	8:15 E	T157	8 (Backworth)		Böhme 1970
139	62	Wiesbaden, Germany	50:05 N	8:15 E	T158	8 (Backworth)	Loop	Böhme 1970
140	63	Zugmantel, Germany	50:11 N	8:12 E	T153-160	8 (Backworth)		Böhme 1970
141	63	Zugmantel, Germany	50:11 N	8:12 E	T153-160	8 (Backworth)		Böhme 1970, No. 12, Abb. 1,10.
142	63	Zugmantel, Germany	50:11 N	8:12 E	T259	Plate		Böhme 1972, No. 988; Exner 1939, 102.
143	63	Zugmantel, Germany	50:11 N	8:12 E	T39	3		Böhme 1970, No. 16, Abb. 1,16; Exner 1939, 84, Taf. 8, 11.
144	63	Zugmantel, Germany	50:11 N	8:12 E	T173A	9		Böhme 1970, No. 17, Abb. 1,15.
145	63	Zugmantel, Germany	50:11 N	8:12 E	T271	Plate		Böhme 1972, No. 1132, Taf. 29.
146		?Kassel, Germany			Unclassified	Unclassified	Loop	Bieber 1915, 98, Taf. LVI, No. 468.
147		?Kassel, Germany			T100C	6		Bieber 1915, 99, Taf. LVI, No. 472.
148		?Kassel, Germany			T157	8 (Backworth)	Loop	Böhme 1970; Bieber 1915, 98, Taf. LVI, No. 467.
149		Unknown, Hess, Germany			T157	8 (Backworth)		Böhme 1970.
150		Unknown, Pfalz, Germany			T144 or T145	7		Bernhard 1980, 30, Taf. 9.9.
151		Unknown, middle-Rhine, Germany			T157	8 (Backworth)		Böhme 1970.
152		Unknown, middle Rhine Germany			T158	8 (Backworth)		Böhme 1970.
153		Unknown, Germany			T157	8 (Backworth)		Böhme 1970.
154	64	Augst, Switzerland	47:32 N	7:43 E	T158	8 (Backworth)		Riha 1979, 81, No. 281, Taf. 11.

Brooch No.	Site No.	Site name	Lat.	Long.	Hull type	Hull group	Female associations	References
155	64	Augst, Switzerland	47:32 N	7:43 E	T149B	7 (Lamberton Moor)	Loop	Riha 1979, 158-159, No. 1391, Taf. 47.
156	64	Augst, Switzerland	47:32 N	7:43 E	Unclassified	7		Riha 1979, No. 1393, Taf. 47.
157	64	Augst, Switzerland	47:32 N	7:43 E	T90	5		Riha 1979, 67, No.192; Bayley and Butcher 2004, 244.
158	64	Augst, Switzerland	47:32 N	7:43 E	T267	Plate	Umbonate	Riha 1979, No. 1595, Taf. 60.
159	64	Probably Augst, Switzerland	47:32 N	7:43 E	T158	8 (Backworth)		Ettlinger 1973, 109, Typ. 38, No. 3.
160	65	Baden, Switzerland	47:28 N	8:18 E	T267	Plate	Umbonate	Ettlinger 1973, Taf. 27.12.
161	66	Lunnern, Switzerland	47:15 N	8:25 E	T100C	6		Ettlinger 1973, 109, Typ. 38, No. 7, Taf. 12,7.
162	67	Martigny, Switzerland	46:28 N	7:11 E	T92	5		Rey-Vodoz 1986, 160, No. 89, Pl. 6. Br. Inv. 78/16. K 0845.
163	67	Martigny, Switzerland	46:28 N	7:11 E	T90 (possible)	5		Rey-Vodoz 1986, Pl. 4,57.
164	68	Oberwinterthur, Switzerland	47:30 N	8:45 E	T157	8 (Backworth)	Loop	Rey-Vodoz 1998, 19, FB 54, Planche. 4, 54.
165	68	Oberwinterthur, Switzerland	47:30 N	8:45 E	T145	7		Rey-Vodoz 1998, 32, FB 265, Planche. 15,265.
166	68	Oberwinterthur, Switzerland	47:30 N	8:45 E	T268	Plate	Umbonate	Rey-Vodoz 1998, 34, FB 282, Planche. 16,282.
167	69	Saxon, Switzerland	46:08 N	7:10 E	T149B	7 (Lamberton Moor)	Loop	Ettlinger 1973, 109, Typ. 38, No. 8.
168	70	Vindonissa, Switzerland	47:28 N	8:12 E	T113	7		Ettlinger 1973, 109, Typ. 38, No. 5, Taf. 12, 9.
169		Unknown, Switzerland			T149B	7 (Lamberton Moor)	Loop	Ettlinger 1973, 109, Typ. 38, No. 1, Taf. 12,8.
170		Unknown, Switzerland			T148-9	7 (Lamberton Moor)	Probable loop	Ettlinger 1973, 109, Typ. 38, No. 2.
171	71	Zadar, Croatia	44:07 N	15:15 E	T144-5	7		C.f. Ortisi 2002, 34.
172	72	Gilău, Romania	46:45 N	23:23 E	T-shaped	7	Loop	Isac 1995, 125, No. 54, Pl. X.
173		Unknown, Romania			T200	Plate		Vincent Megaw (pers. Comm).

Brooch No.	Site No.	Site name	Lat.	Long.	Hull type	Hull group	Female associations	References
174	73	Györ-Homokgödör	47:41 N	17:38 E	T200	Plate		Feacham 1951, Fig. 3,43.
175		Unknown, Hungary			T267	Plate	Umbonate	Sellye 1939, 53, Pl. V,1.
176	74	Morlupo, Italy	42:08 N	12.30 E	T157	8 (Backworth)		Böhme 1970
177	75	Venice, Italy	45:26 N	12:20 E	T157	8 (Backworth)		Böhme 1970
178	76	Thamusida, Morocco	34:20 N	6:29 W	T149B	7 (Lamberton Moor)	Probable loop	Gerharz 1987, Abb. 14,78.
179	77	Volubilis, Morocco	34:04 N	5:33 W	T158	8 (Backworth)		Gerharz 1987, Abb. 14,79.

Appendix 7. British horse gear and non-enamelled metalwork (excluding brooches) from continental sites (c. 200 BC-AD 100)

Site No.	Site	Lat.	Long.	Date	Description	Find details	References	Location
1	Leg Piekarski, Turek, Poland	52:00 N	18:37 E	Mid-first century AD.	Strainer bowl.	In a grave.	Megaw 1963; Jope 2000 (incorrectly argues for a partly foreign origin).	
2	Dörverden, Niedersachsen, Germany	52:51 N	9:14 E	Late Iron Age or Roman.	Unparalleled object, but stylistically it is likely tc be British. Copper-alloy rings with stylised animal (fish?) decoration.		Zimmermann 1969; Spratling, pers. Comm. 2007.	Landesmuseum Hannover.
3	Ober Olm, Hesse, Germany	49:56 N	8:11 E	Mid-first century AD.	Horse gear. Enamelled quadrilobe-strap union. No wear, therefore a new piece.	Found in a field.	Spratling 1972, 117-118; Henry 1933, Fig. 12,1; Lemann-Delerive *et al.* 1986, Fig. 13.	Mittelrheinisches Landesmuseum No. V930.
4	Hofheim am Taunus, Hesse, Germany	50:05 N	8:27 E	Mid-first century AD.	Horse gear. Westhall terret/crescentic-flangec terret.	Found in excavations of the Claudian-Neronian *Erdkastell.*	Spratling 1972, 405, Cat. No. 67; Palk 1992, No. 195; Ritterling 1913, 175, Nr. 15, Taf. XIII.37.	
5	Vechten, Netherlands	52:04 N	5:11 E	First century AD.	Horse gear. Pendant.	From the Roman fort of *Fectio.*	Spratling 1972, No. 227.	
6	Nijmegen, Netherlands.	51:50 N	5:52 E	Mid-first century AD.	British mirror.	Military site. Nijmegen 1926/27, cemetery L, grave 29.	Bogaers 1967, 75; Lloyd Morgan 1981, 111-116; Jope 2000, 136; Spratling, pers. Comm. 2007.	Nijmegen Museum.
7	Blicquy, Hainault, Belgium	50:35 N	3:41 E	Second to first century BC.	Horse gear. Linchpin.	Religious site. Major sanctuary and workshop area.	Demarez and Leman-Delerive 2001.	
8	La Courte, Hainaut, Belgium	50:25 N	4:13 E	First century BC.	Mini-terret. c.f. Stead 1991, 44-47, Figs. 37-38.		Spratling 1972, 51, 53; pers. Comm. 2007; Mariën 1961, 49, No. 61, Fig. 20.	
9	Paillart, Oise, France	49:40 N	2:19 E	Mid-first century AD.	Horse gear. Strap-union. Palk (1992) Type IIA.	Found near a rural Roman road at La Haute Bailly.	Lemann-Delerive *et al.* 1986; Palk 1992, No. 452; Spratling, pers. Comm. 2007.	

Site No.	Site	Lat.	Long.	Date	Description	Find details	References	Location
10	Compiègne, Oise, France	49:25 N	2:50 E	Late first century BC to early first century AD.	Handle of a mirror of British type. Very similar to examples from Colchester, Great Chesterford and Dorton, Buckinghamshire. In these examples the mirror disc is held by a handle with three discs decorated with enamel or coral.	Found in the river Oise.	Guillaumet and Schönfelder 2001.	
11	Eauze, Gers, France	43:52 N	0:06 E	Mid- to late first century AD.	Horse gear. Enamelled crescentic flanged terret.		Palk 1992, No. 193; Bateson 1981, 8, 117.	
12	La Tène, Switzerland	47:00 N	7:01 E	Second century BC.	Horse gear. Strap-union, probably British.	Ritual lake deposit.	Vouga 1923, Pl. VIII, 49; Spratling 1972, 112-113.	
13	Játiba, Valence, Spain	38:59 N	0:31 W	Mid- to late first century AD.	Horse gear. Knobbed-terret with red and blue enamel.	Roman town.	Santa-Olalla 1935, 203-204; Spratling 1972, 417, No. 90; Megaw and Megaw 2001a.	
14	Florence, Tuscany, Italy	43:46 N	11:15 E	Late first century AD.	Horse gear. Strap-union.	No secure provenance. Probably Tuscany.	Spratling, pers. Comm. 2007; Henry 1933, Fig. 21,1.	Uffizi, Florence.
15	Fayum, Egypt			Mid- to late first century AD.	Horse gear, but may not be British. Enamelled crescentic flanged terret.		Henry 1933, Fig. 22,2; Palk 1992, No. 194. Megaw and Megaw 2001a; Bateson 1981, 8, 117; Spratling, pers. Comm. 2007.	
16	No provenance, probably Germany.			Mid- first century AD.	Horse gear. Westhall terret/crescentic-flanged terret. With a Roman-type attachment.		Spratling, pers. Comm. 2007.	Römisch-Germanisches Zentralmuseum Mainz.
17	No provenance, possibly France.			(Late?) first century BC.	The Mayer mirror. Engraved with curvilinear and sub-triangular patterns.	Collected by Joseph Mayer in Paris shortly before 1854.	Fox 1958, 40, 84-105, 147-148, Pl. 56, A1, A2, Pl. 57a; Spratling 1972, No. 358.	City Museum, Liverpool.

Appendix 8. British enamelled metalwork (excluding horse gear and brooches) from continental sites

Site No.	Site	Date	Description	Find details	References
1	Nehasitz, Bohemia.	Late first to early second century AD.	Enamelled pan. Type West Lothian.		Moore 1978; Eggers 1951; Künzl 1995.
2	Maltbæk Mose, Jutland, Denmark.	Late first to early second century AD.	Enamelled pan. Type West Lothian. Red and green enamel.	Bog-find.	Moore 1978; Eggers 1951; Lund Hansen 1987; Jørgensen 2003, 389; Künzl 1995.
3	Vehner Moor, Oldenburg, Lower Saxony, Germany.	Late first to early second century AD.	Enamelled pan. Type Vehner Moor. Red and green enamel.	Part of a bog deposit, which included textiles.	Moore 1978; Eggers 1951; Erdrich 2002, Taf. 127.1; Künzl 1995.
4	Bentumersiel, Lower Saxony. Germany.	Late first to early second century AD.	Enamelled seal-box. Stylised 'N'-motif. c.f. seal-boxes from Lincoln (Megaw and Megaw 2001b, Fig. 392), Thirsk (Haverfield 1905, Fig. 35), Caerleon (Evans 2000, 357) and Chesters (Henry 1933, Fig. 46).	Native settlement.	Ulbert 1977, 41, 53, No. 53, Abb. 3, Taf. 4, 15; Erdrich 2002, XIX-12-3/2.33.
5	Bad Pyrmont, Lower Saxony, Germany.	Late first to early second century AD.	Enamelled pan. Type Vehner Moor. Blue, green and red enamel.	Hoard, large deposit of metalwork at a spring.	Teegan 1997a; 1997b; 2003; Moore 1978; Eggers 1951; Erdrich 2002, XX-03-2/1.1, Taf. 126; Künzl 1995.
6	Bingen, Rhineland-Palatinate, Germany.	Late first to mid-second century AD.	Enamelled pan with chequerboard pattern of blue and white enamel.	Roman settlement.	Henry 1933, 116, Fig. 28,2; Moore 1978.
7	Straubing, Bavaria, Germany.	Late first to early second century AD.	Enamelled belt plate with buckle. Blue triangles with yellow points. c.f examples from Richborough (Bushe-Fox 1949, Pl. XXXIII, 73) and Caerleon (Fox 1940, 128, Fig. 6, 10).	Roman fort.	Walke 1965, Taf. 97, 8.
8	Nijmegen, Netherlands.	Late first to early second century AD.	Globular handled flask with enamel decoration. An exact match to the moulds found at the Castleford workshop in Yorkshire (Bayley 1995).	Roman fortress/urban settlement. Cemetery of Ulpia Noviomagus between the voorstadslaan and Sperwerstraat. Ulp.1982.437me. Grave 8 no.36.	Koster 1997, 82-83, No. 110.

Site No.	Site	Date	Description	Find details	References
9	Heerlen, Limburg, Netherlands.	Late first to mid-second century AD.	Alabaston. A unique piece, but probably a British product.	Roman settlement on main road between Tongeren and Cologne. Has a large bath complex.	Künzl 1995, 42.
10	Namur, Namur, Belgium.	Late first to early second century AD.	Enamelled pan. Type Vehner Moor. Green and blue enamel.	Roman settlement. Found in La Plante cemetery.	Moore 1978; Künzl 1995.
11	Ambleteuse, Pas-de-Calais, France.	Late first to mid-second century AD.	Enamelled vessel with ring-handle and two dolphin supporters.	Found with coins of Tacitus (AD 270-273).	Moore 1978, 327; Künzl 1995, 42.
12	Amiens, Somme, France.	(?Early to) mid-second century AD.	Enamelled pan. Type Rudge. Stylised depiction of Hadrian's Wall.	Roman urban settlement.	Moore 1978; Künzl 1995.
13	La Guierche, Angoulême, France.	Late first to early second-century AD.	Flask with blue, orange and green enamel.	Found with coins of Laelianus and Tetricus (AD 268-273).	Moore 1978, 327; Henry 1933, 145, Fig. 45,4.
14	Rochefort, Jura, France.	Late first to early second century AD.	Enamelled pan. Type Vehner Moor. Blue, green and red enamel.		Moore 1978; Künzl 1995.
15	Probably found between Leon and Zamora in northern Spain.	(?Early to) mid-second century AD.	Enamelled pan. Type Rudge. Stylised depiction of Hadrian's Wall. Red, blue and green enamel.		Moore 1978; Künzl 1995; 2008, 222.
16	Probably from Mérida, Extremadura, Spain.	Late first to mid-second century AD.	Two enamelled barrel-cups. Paralleled at Selbourne in Britain.	Roman urban settlement.	Künzl 1995, 42.
17	Pinquente, Istria, Italy.	Late first to early second century AD.	Globular handled flask with blue, orange and red enamelled decoration. Similar to those produced at the Castleford workshop in Yorkshire (Bayley 1995).		Henry 1933, 143, Pl. 1; Moore 1978, 327; Künzl 2008, 24.
18	In the sea off Camarina, Sicily, Italy.	Late first to early second century AD.	Enamelled alabastron (cosmetic vessel/unguent container). c.f. example from the Bartlow Hills, Essex/Cambs (Künzl 2008, 24-25).	Shipwreck find.	Künzl 2008, 24.
19	Gorgippia, Krasnodar Krai, Russia.	Late first to early second century AD.	Decorated enamelled strigils (oil scrapers). Similar to decoration on Castleford moulds (Künzl 2008, 24).	Urban settlement.	Künzl 1995, 46; 2008, 24;

APPENDIX 8. BRITISH ENAMELLED METALWORK (EXCLUDING HORSE GEAR AND BROOCHES) FROM CONTINENTAL SITES

Site No.	Site	Date	Description	Find details	References
19	Gorgippia, Krasnodar Krai, Russia.	Late first to early second century AD.	Enamelled alabastron (cosmetic vessel/unguent container). c.f. example from the Bartlow Hills, Essex/Cambs (Künzl 2008, 24-25).	Urban settlement.	Künzl 1995, 46; 2008, 24.
20	Unknown, probably northern France.	Late first to mid-second century AD.	Jug with red, green, yellow, orange and blue enamel. Probably British.	In Mainz Museum. Possibly from a grave in France. Found with the enamelled handled pan (below).	Künzl 1995, 40-42, Abb. 2-3; 2008, 27.
20	Unknown, probably northern France.	Late first to mid-second century AD.	Enamelled handled flat-pan. Probably British.	In Mainz Museum. Possibly from a grave in France. Found with the enamelled jug (above).	Künzl 1995, 40-42, Abb. 4-5; 2008, 27.
21	Unknown, probably Germany.	Late first to mid-second century AD.	Flask with blue and red enamel.	In Landesmuseum Bonn.	Moore 1978, 327; Henry 1933, 143, Pl. 2.
22	Benevento, Campania, Italy.	Roman	Uncertain if this is British. Cup with blue and white enamel.		Moore 1978, 327; Henry 1933, 108, Fig. 23,1.

Appendix 9. Dressel 20 olive oil amphorae from a sample of British sites

Site name	Site type	Minimum number of vessels	Dr.20 weight (kg)	% of total amphorae by weight	% of total pottery by weight	Dr.20 sherd count	% of total amphorae by sherd count	% of total pottery by sherd count	Reference
Vindolanda	Military		98.28	95.35	30.1				Bidwell 1985, 182
Brougham	Military			100		16	100		Cool 2004, 335
Milecastle 35, Sewingcastle	Military			100		139	100		Bidwell and Speak 1994
Newcastle	Military		18.19	93.3					Bidwell and Speak 1994, 214
Housesteads	Military			100		39	100		Bidwell and Speak 1994
Manchester	Military		46.66	95.7					Gregory 2007
South Shields (*Principa* site), Tyne & Wear	Military		46.7		54.3				Bidwell and Speak 1994.
Old Penrith, Cumbria	Military		69.2			488	98.8		Bidwell and Speak 1994, 214.
York (fortress- 9 Blake Street)	Military					296		1.54	Monaghan 1993, Tab. 117.
York (General Accident site)	Urban/ military		103.94	72.7	30.1	379	53.2		Williams 1990, Tab. 22
York (5 Rougier Street)	Urban/ military		29		30.9	137	47.2		Williams 1990, Tab. 22
Colchester	Urban/ military		1052.78	66.3	18.6	2837	44.1	2.1	Symonds and Wade 1999, 137, Tab. 3.1
Exeter	Urban/ military		110.78	59.6					Holbrook and Bidwell 1991, Tab. 14
Cirencester	Urban		162.4	74					Williams and Peacock 1983, Tab. 1
Chichester	Urban		279.56	83.84					Carreras 2000, Fig.1
New Fresh Wharf, London	Urban		56.6	40.4	10.9				Richardson 1986, 96-138
Folly Lane, Verulamium	Urban	16	99.38	97.3					Williams 1999, 286-7
Canterbury, Kent	Urban			68					Arthur 1986, 245.
Clausentum, Hants	Small town		28.28	78					Williams and Peacock 1983, Tab. 1
Droitwich, Worcs	Small town		17.33	78					Williams and Peacock 1983, Tab. 1
Staines, Surrey	Small town			96					Arthur 1986, 245.

APPENDIX 9. DRESSEL 20 OLIVE OIL AMPHORAE FROM A SAMPLE OF BRITISH SITES

Site name	Site type	Minimum number of vessels	Dr.20 weight (kg)	% of total amphorae by weight	% of total pottery by weight	Dr.20 sherd count	% of total amphorae by sherd count	% of total pottery by sherd count	Reference
Stonea, Cambs	Small town		42.1	79.7	6.1	368	76.8		Keay and Carreras 1996, 435-440
Fosse Lane, Somerset	Small town		58.4		18	1029	92.1	4	Evans 2001, Tab. 3.
Deansway, Worcs	Small town		18.27	91	7.3				Williams 2004.
Chelmsford, Essex	Small town		7.8		1.3				Going 1987.
Hacheston, Suffolk	Small town					1122		7	Arthur 2004, 162
Chignall Villa, Essex	Rural		3.2		1.3	66		0.3	Wallace and Turner-Walker 1998, 99
Little Oakley, Essex	Rural	22							Barford 2002, 136
Poundbury, Dorset	Rural		9.8	66					Williams and Peacock 1983, Tab. 1
Dragonbury, Lincs	Rural		70.4	96					Williams and Peacock 1983, Tab. 1
Kenchester, Gloucs	Rural		41.5	78					Williams and Peacock 1983, Tab. 1
Lechlade, Gloucs	Rural		1.75	68					Williams and Peacock 1983, Tab. 1
Highstead, Kent	Rural					19		0.8	Arthur 2007, 237
Keston Villa, Kent	Rural	3		100		147	100	0.45	Cooper and Parfitt 1991, 196

Appendix 10. Romano-British pottery from sites north and east of the Rhine

Site No.	Vessel No.	Site	Lat.	Long.	Description	Reference	Location
1	1 to 2	Den Burg, Texel, Netherlands	53:03:14 N	4:47:46 E	Several sherds of Southeast Dorset black-burnished ware 1 (BB1). Differences between rim sherds 46.1837 and 67.42 indicate that at least two different vessels are present. Both are everted-rim cooking jars of Holbrook & Bidwell's (1991, Fig. 28) type 20.1. Obtuse-angled lattice decoration is present on some of the sherds. Type dates to late third or fourth century AD.	Fulford 1977; 1978.	Noord Holland Depot, Woormerveer/ Ecomare Museum, Texel. Sherd Nos: 46.1837; 40.1583; 56.50; 58.09; 65.29; 66.08; 67.42; 85.16B; also a loose fragment marked- 'los indoors').
1	3	Den Burg, Texel, Netherlands	53:03:14 N	4:47:46 E	New Forest ware. Purple metallic colour-coated beaker with the distinctive grey fabric and black inclusions of Fulford's (1975) fabric 1a variant. The New Forest industry dates AD 260 to the late fourth century.		Noord Holland Depot, Woormerveer. Sherd No.1833
1	4	Den Burg, Texel, Netherlands	53:03:14 N	4:47:46 E	Nene Valley mortarium. Off-white fabric with a slightly pinkish core and characteristic black iron-slag grits. Second- to fourth-century date.		Noord Holland Depot, Woormerveer. Sherd No. 57.19
2	5	Wijnaldum, Friesland, Netherlands	53:11:41 N	5:27:35 E	New Forest colour-coated beaker base (reused as cup). No context.		NAD Nuis. 144-54
3	6	Witmarsum, Friesland, Netherlands	53:06:08 N	5:27:59 E	New Forest colour-coated indented beaker. Body sherd. No context.		NAD Nuis 131-100
4	7	Winsum Bruggeburen, Friesland, Netherlands	53:09:09 N	5:37:57 E	Oxford ware brown-slipped bowl Young (1977, 159, Fig. 58) type C45. Type dated AD 240/250-400.	Galestin 2002, 440, Nr. 31, Fig. 3.31.	Groningen University c/o Marjan Galestin
5	8	Oosterend, Friesland, Netherlands	53:05:49 N	5:37:10 E	Nene Valley beaker of late third- to fourth-century type. c.f. Howe *et al.* 1980, No. 49. No context.	Boeles 1951, 157, Pl. XXIII. No.1 (mis-identified as Moselkeramik).	Friesmuseum. 159-1
6	9	Hijum, Friesland, Netherlands	53:17:28 N	5:45:56 E	Probable New Forest red-slipped bowl. Body-sherd reused as spindle-whorl. No context.		Friesmuseum. 25-39

Site No.	Vessel No.	Site	Lat.	Long.	Description	Reference	Location
7	10	Ezinge	53:18:32 N	6:26:30 E	Body sherd of an Oxfordshire mortarium with white slip on a hard red fabric with a grey core; rounded quartz grits; fourth century. Unstratified.	Fulford 1977.	NAD Nuis. 1925 VIII 132
7	11	Ezinge	53:18:32 N	6:26:30 E	Oxford red-slipped bowl. Body sherd. Young type 51.		NAD Nuis, 1926-VII.214(1)
8	12	Brillerij, Groningen, Netherlands	53:16:59 N	6:28:59 E	Oxford necked bowl with two bands of rouletting on the body; from the fourth-century phase of the terp	Fulford 1977.	NAD Nuis. 1926/VI 96
9	13	Oostum, Groningen, Netherlands	53:17:52 N	6:29:54 E	Oxford red-slipped bowl. Body sherd. Young type 51 (Oxfordshire Dr.38). From the phase of the terp dated AD 325-350; 1913/6 11.	Fulford 1977.	NAD Nuis
10	14	Bentumersiel, Lower Saxony, Germany	53:14:39 N	7:23:31 E	Probable Oxford red-slipped ware. Base fragment. Thick grey core. No context.		NIHK, Wilhelmshaven. Bls 73 strfd (?)
11	15	Jemgum, Lower Saxony, Germany	53:15:53 N	7:22:58 E	Probable New Forest colour-coated beaker base.		NIHK, Wilhelmshaven. J II
12	16	Einswarden, Lower Saxony, Germany	53:30:45 N	8:30:51 E	Probable Oxford red-slipped bowl. Large rim sherd with grey core. Young type 51.		NIHK, Wilhelmshaven. Einswarden E. J/S?. 28.4
13	17	Feddersen Wierde, Lower Saxony, Germany	53:39:57 N	8:32:35 E	Probable Much Hadham red slipped ware. Body sherd with two incised lines.	Erdrich 2002, XXI-02-14/3.35 (recorded as imitation *terra sigillata*).	NIHK, Wilhelmshaven. Feddersen Wierde, terra sigillata No.124 (St 135, N149, T B)
13	18	Feddersen Wierde, Lower Saxony, Germany	53:39:57 N	8:32:35 E	Probable Oxford red-slipped ware. Body sherd. It has a band of rouletting and a pink/grey core.	Erdrich 2002, XXI-02-14/3.38 (recorded as imitation *terra sigillata*).	NIHK, Wilhelmshaven. Feddersen Wierde Terra Sigillata No.104 (St 65, N-8, TB)
14	19	Westerwanna, Lower Saxony, Germany	53:44:30 N	8:46:46 E	Much Hadham red-slipped urn. Complete. c.f. Myres 1956, Group A (vessels ornamented with one or two lines of shoulder or belly bosses (grey and red wares); C20.3; Roberts 1982, Plate 27; Johnson 1983b, Fig. 40, No. 94 (in grey ware). Date of type AD 350 to early fifth century AD (Going, pers. Comm.). Used as cremation urn. No contents.	Busch 1995, 268-269 (recorded with photo as imitation *terra sigillata*); Quillfeldt von and Roggenbuck 1985, Taf. 59. Grab 285.	Museum Harburg

Site No.	Vessel No.	Site	Lat.	Long.	Description	Reference	Location
15	20	Nordleda, Lower Saxony, Germany	53:45:47 N	8:50:08 E	Oxford red-slipped bowl. Rim sherd. Young type C75.		Museum Burg Bederkesa (In group *Terra sigillata* Fst-Nr.11. Not individually numbered)
16	21	Tofting, Schleswig-Holstein, Germany	54:20:48 N	8:56:23 E	Oxford red-slipped, white painted bowl.	Fulford 1977; Erdrich 2002, XXIV-07-7/1.8, Taf. 18.14.	Schloß Gottorf, Schleswig-Holstein Landesmuseum.

Appendix 11. Lava querns in the northwest *Barbaricum*

List of sites in the northwest *Barbaricum* with lava querns

Data provided by Ernst Taayke (Noordelijk Archeologisch Depot Nuis, pers. Comm. 2009), with additions from: Erdrich 1995a, Abb. 9; 2002, 216-217; Voss 1998, 132.

Drenthe, Netherlands:

Balingerzand
Borger
Buinen
Dalen
Dalen-de Spil
Dalen-Molenakkers
Dwingeloo
Dwingeloo-Westeinde
Emmen P-west
Emmerveld
Erm
Exloo-Oude Dijk
Halfweg
Hoogeveen/Zuidwolde
Kerkenveld
Meppel
Midlaren
Noordbarge
Orvelte
Peelo
Peize
Rhee
Roden
Ruinen
Tynaarlo
Valtherveen
Vries
Wachtum
Wijster
Zeijen I
Zeijen II

Friesland, Netherlands:

Achlum-de Terp
Baard
Cammingaburen
Dronrijp
Dronrijp-Schatzenburg
Fochteloo
Goutum
Hijum
Jelsum
Klein Gietens
Leeuwarden-Bullepolder
Leeuwarden: Oldehove
Lichtaard-Staniaterp
Lions-Bolland
Lutjelollum
Miedum
Oosterbeintum
Oosterend
Scharnegoutum
Schelum
Stapert
Staveren
Stiens of Britswerd
Teerns
Tietjerk-Meenschar
Tritsum
Wanswerd/Birdaard
Warstiens
Winsum-Bruggeburen

Groningen, Netherlands:

Antum
Beijum
Brillerij
De Palen
Dorkwerd
Ezinge
Fledderbosscherpolder
Garreweer
Grijpskerk
Groningen: M'kerkhof 181
Helwerd
Heveskesklooster
Hoogkerk: Bangeweer (opgr. M&M)
Krassum
Paddepoel I
Paddepoel II
Paddepoel III
Raskwerd
Ten Boer
Westerwijtwerd
Wierhuizen

Lower Saxony and Bremen, Germany:

Arle, Aurich
Ashausen, Harburg
Baccum, Lingen, Emsland
Bardenfleth, Wesermarsch
Barnkrug, Stade
Barward, Cuxhaven
Brill, Wittmund
Dingen, Cuxhaven
Engter, Osnabrück
Estorf, Nienburg (Weser)
Feddersen Wierde, Cuxhaven
Flögeln Eekhöltjen, Cuxhaven
Fümmelse, Wolfbüttel
Grambke, Bremen.

Gross Meckelsen, Rotenburg (Wümme)
Landesbergen, Nienburg (Weser)
Lemke, Nienburg (Weser)
Mahlstedt, Oldenburg
Mahndorf, Bremen
Midlum, Cuxhaven
Oldendorf, Osnabrück
Ostbense, Ostfriesland
Oxstedt
Ritsch, Stade
Sarstedt, Hildesheim
Scharmbeck, Harburg
Tündern, Hameln-Pyrmont
Uthlede, Cuxhaven
Wohlstreek, Diepholz

Schleswig-Holstein, Germany:

Tofting

Mecklenburg-Pomerania, Germany:

Woosmer, Ludwigslust

List of sites in the northwest *Barbaricum* with Brillerij type lava querns

Data provided by Ernst Taayke (Noordelijk Archeologisch Depot Nuis, pers. Comm. 2009).

Drenthe, Netherlands:

Buinen
Dalen-de Spil
Dalen-Molenakkers
Dwingeloo
Erm
Halfweg
Kerkenveld
Noordbarge
Orvelte
Roden
Ruinen
Valtherveen
Vries
Wachtum
Zeijen I
Zeijen II

Friesland, Netherlands:

Achlum-de Terp
Dronrijp
Dronrijp-Schatzenburg
Fochteloo
Goutum
Jelsum
Leeuwarden
Lions-Bolland
Oosterbeintum
Scharnegoutum
Schelum
Stapert
Staveren
Tritsum
Wanswerd/Birdaard
Warstiens
Winsum-Bruggeburen

Groningen, Netherlands:

Brillerij
De Palen
Ezinge
Fledderbosscherpolder
Garreweer
Groningen: M'kerkhof 181
Helwerd
Heveskesklooster
Hoogkerk: Bangeweer (opgr. M&M)
Paddepoel I
Paddepoel II
Paddepoel III
Raskwerd

Lower Saxony, Germany:

Feddersen Wierde, Cuxhaven
Mahlstedt, Oldenburg

List of sites in the northwest *Barbaricum* with Westerwijtwerd type lava querns

Data provided by Ernst Taayke (Noordelijk Archeologisch Depot Nuis, pers. Comm. 2009).

Drenthe, Netherlands:

Balingerzand
Borger
Emmen P-west
Emmerveld
Erm
Hoogeveen/Zuidwolde
Peelo
Peize
Midlaren
Rhee
Tynaarlo
Valtherveen
Wijster

Friesland, Netherlands:

Cammingaburen
Hijum
Jelsum
Klein Gietens
Leeuwarden-Bullepolder
Leeuwarden: Oldehove

Lichtaard-Staniaterp
Lutjelollum
Oosterend
Stiens of Britswerd
Teerns
Tietjerk-Meenschar
Tritsum
Warstiens
Winsum-Bruggeburen

Groningen, Netherlands:

Antum
Beijum
Dorkwerd
Ezinge
Hoogkerk: Bangeweer
Krassum
Paddepoel I
Ten Boer
Westerwijtwerd
Wierhuizen

Lower Saxony, Germany:

Feddersen Wierde, Cuxhaven
Mahlstedt, Oldenburg
Sarstedt, Hildesheim
Tündern, Hameln-Pyrmont
Wohlstreek Diepholz

Bibliography

Abdy, R. A. 2002. *Romano-British Coin Hoards*. Princes Risborough, Buckinghamshire: Shire.

Aillagon, J.-J. (ed.), 2008. *Rome and the Barbarians. The Birth of a New World.* Venice: Palozzo Grussi.

Alexander, D. and Watkins, T. 1998. 'St Germains, Tranent, East Lothian: the excavation of Early Bronze Age remains and Iron Age enclosed and unenclosed settlements', *Proceedings of the Society of Antiquaries of Scotland* 128: 203-254.

Allason Jones, L. 1996. *Roman Jet in the Yorkshire Museum*. York: Yorkshire Museum.

Allason-Jones, L. 2002. 'The jet industry and allied trades in Roman Britain', in Wilson, P, and Price, J. (eds.), *Aspects of Industry in Roman Yorkshire and the North.* Oxford: Oxbow: 125-132.

Allason-Jones, L. and Jones, J. M. 1994. 'Jet and other materials in Roman artefact studies', *Archaeologia Aeliana* (Fifth Series) 22: 265-272.

Allason-Jones, L. and Jones, J. M. 2001. 'Identification of 'jet' artefacts by reflected light microscopy', *European Journal of Archaeology* 4 (2): 233-251.

Allen, D. 1998. *Roman Glass in Britain.* Princes Risborough, Buckinghamshire: Shire.

Allen, D. F. 1960. *The Origins of coinage in Britain: a Reappraisal.* Reprinted from: Frere, S. S. (ed.), *Problems of the Iron Age in Southern Britain.* London: Institute of Archaeology.

Allen, D. F. 1975. 'Cunobelin's Gold', *Britannia* 6: 1-19.

Allen, D. F. and Haselgrove, C. 1979. 'The gold coinage of Verica', *Britannia* 10: 1-17.

Allen, J. R. L. and Fulford, M. G. 1996. 'The distribution of South-East Dorset Black Burnished Category I Pottery in South-West Britain', *Britannia* 27: 223-281.

Allen, J. R. L. and Fulford, M. G. 1999. 'Fort building and military supply along Britain's eastern Channel and North Sea coasts: The later second and third centuries', *Britannia* 30: 163-184.

Allen, J. R. L. Fulford, M. G. and Todd, J. A. 2007. 'Burnt Kimmeridgian shale at Early Roman Silchester, south-east England, and the Roman Poole-Purbeck complex-agglomerated geomaterials industry', *Oxford Journal of Archaeology* 26 (2): 167-191.

Anderson, A. C. 1981. 'Some continental beakers of the first and second centuries AD', in Anderson, A. C. and Anderson, A. S. (eds.), *Roman Pottery Research.* BAR International Series 123. Oxford: 321-347.

Anderson, A. C. and Anderson, A. S. (eds.), 1981. *Roman Pottery Research.* BAR International Series 123. Oxford.

Anderson, A. S. Wacher, J. S. and Fitzpatrick, A. P. 2001. *The Romano-British 'Small-town' at Wanborough, Wiltshire: Excavations 1966-77.* London: Society for the Promotion of Roman Studies.

Andreau, J. 1999. *Banking and Business in the Roman World.* Cambridge: Cambridge University Press.

Arafat, K. and Morgan, C. 1994. 'Athens, Etruria and the Heuneburg: mutual misconceptions in the study of Greek-Barbarian Relations', in Morris, I (ed.), *Classical Greece: Ancient Histories and Modern Archaeologies*. Cambridge.

Arnaud, P. 2005. *Les routes de la navigation antique: itinéraires en Méditerranée.* Paris: Errance.

Arthur, P. 1986. 'Roman amphorae from Canterbury', *Britannia* 17: 239-258.

Arthur, P. 2004. In Blagg, T. Plouviez, J. and Tester, A. *Excavations at a Large Romano-British Settlement at Hacheston, Suffolk in 1973-4*. Ipswich: Suffolk County Council Archaeological Service.

Arthur, P. 2007. In Bennett, P. Couldrey, P and MacPherson-Grant, N. *Highstead near Chislet, Kent: Excavations 1975-1977.* Canterbury: Canterbury Archaeological Trust.

Arthur, P. and Williams, D. 1992. 'Campanian wine, Roman Britain and the third century A.D.', *Journal of Roman Archaeology* 5: 250-260.

Aubin, H. 1925. 'Der Rheinhandel in römischer Zeit', *Bonner Jahrbücher* 130: 1-37.

Aurrecoechea, J. 1996. 'Nuevas aportaciones al conocimiento de los contingents militares tardorromanos en Hispania: la guarnición de cinturón de origin Británico encontrada en Iruña', *Veleia* 13: 265-270.

Aurrecoechea, J. 1999. 'Late Roman belts in Hispania', *Journal of Roman Military Equipment Studies* 10: 55-62.

Auriemma, R. 1997. 'Le anfore africane del relitto de Grado. Contributo allo studio delle prime produzioni tunisine e del commercio di salse ed conserve di pesce', *Archeologia subacquea*. Studi, Richerche e Documenti II. Rome: 129-155.

Auriemma, R. 2000. 'Le anfore del relitto di Grado e il loro contento', *Mélanges de l'École Française de Rome. Antiquité. Paris* 112: 27-51.

Austen, P. 1991. *Bewcastle and Old Penrith: a Roman Outpost Fort and a Frontier Vicus: Excavations 1977-78*. Kendal: Cumberland and Westmorland Antiquarian and Archaeological Society.

Bagnall, R. S. 2002. 'The effects of plague: model and evidence', *Journal of Roman Archaeology* 15: 114-120.

Balmelle, C. Barraud, D. Brun, J.-P. Duprat, P. Gaillard, H. Jacques, P. Maurin, L. Petit-Aupert, C. Rigal, D. Robin, K. Roudié, Sillières, P. and Vernou, C. 2001. 'La viticulture antique en Aquitaine', in Brun, J.-P. and Laubenheimer, F. (eds.), 'La viticulture en Gaule', in *Gallia* 58: 129-164.

Barber, B. and Bowsher, D. 2000. *The Eastern Cemetery of Roman London: Excavations 1983-1990*. London: Museum of London Archaeology Service.

Barford, P. M. 2002. *Excavations at Little Oakley, Essex, 1951-78: Roman Villa and Saxon Settlement*. East Anglian Archaeology; Report No. 98. Chelmsford: Essex County Council.

Barrett, J. C. Freeman, P. W. M and Woodward, A. 2000. *Cadbury Castle, Somerset: The Later Prehistoric and Early Historic Archaeology*. London: English Heritage.

Bartholomew, P. 1984. 'Fourth century Saxons', *Britannia* 15: 169-185.

Bateman, N. and Locker, A. 1982. 'The sauce of the Thames', *London Archaeologist* 4 (8): 204-207.

Bateson, J. D. 1981. *Enamel-Working in Iron Age, Roman and Sub-Roman Britain. The Products and Techniques*. BAR British Series 93. Oxford.

Batey, C. E. 1993. *Discovery and Excavation, Scotland 1993*. Glasgow.

Bayard, D. 1990. 'L'ensemble du grand amphitheatre de Metz et la sigillée d'Argonne au Ve Siècle', *Gallia* 47: 271-319.

Bayley, J. 1995. 'Spoon and vessel moulds from Castleford, Yorkshire' in Mols, S. T. A. M. Gerhartl-Witteveen, A. M. Kars, H. Koster, A. Peters, W. J. Th. and Willems, W. J. H. (eds.), *Acta of the 12th International Congress on Ancient Bronzes, Nijmegen 1992*. Amersfoort: 105-111.

Bayley, J. 1998. 'The production of brass in Antiquity with particular reference to Roman Britain', in Craddock, P. T. (ed.), *2000 Years of Zinc and Brass* (revised edition). London: British Museum: 7-26.

Bayley, J. 2001. 'Non-ferrous metal technology in Britain in the earlier first millennium AD', in Polfer, M. (ed.), *L'artisanat romain: évolutions, continuités et ruptures (Italie et provinces occidentales)*. Monographies Instrumentum 20. Montagnac: Éditions Monique Mergoil: 69-77.

Bayley, J. and Butcher, S. 2004. *Roman Brooches in Britain*. London: The Society of Antiquaries.

Bayley, J. Mackreth, D. F. and Wallis, H. 2001. 'Evidence for Romano-British brooch production at Old Buckenham, Norfolk', *Britannia* 32: 93-118.

Bayliss, A. Groves, C. McCormac, C. Bronk Ramsey, C. Baillie, M. Brown, D. Cook, G. and Switsur, R. 2004. 'Dating', in Clark, P. (ed.), *The Dover Bronze Age Boat*. Swindon: English Heritage: 250-255.

Beagrie, N. 1989. 'The Romano-British pewter industry', *Britannia* 20: 169-191.

Beaumont, G. F. 1900. 'A Roman coffin found at Braintree', *Transactions of the Essex Archaeological Society* (New Series) 7: 401-402.

Bechert, T. 1973. *Funde aus Asciburgium. Heft 1. Römische Fibeln des 1. und 2. Jahrhunderts*. Duisburg und Rheinhausen.

Beck, C. and Shennan, S. 1991. *Amber in Prehistoric Britain*. Oxford: Oxbow.

Becker, A. 2002. 'Die Ausgrabungen in Lahnau-Waldgirmes' in Freeman, P. *et al.* (eds.), *Limes XVIII. Proceedings of the XVIIIth International Congress of Roman Frontier Studies held in Amman, Jordan (September 2000)*. BAR International Series 1084, I-II. Oxford: 461-465.

Becker, A. 2003. 'Lahnau-Waldgirmes. Eine Augusteische Stadtgründung in Hessen', *Historia* 52: 337-350.

Becker, A. Köhler, H.-J. and Rasbach, G. 1999. *Der römische Stützpunkt von Waldgirmes. Die Ausgrabungen bis 1998 in der spätaugusteischen Anlage in Lahnau-Waldgirmes, Lahn-Dill-Kreis*. Wiesbaden.

Becker, M. 2008. 'The Prince of Gommern (Germany)', in (ed) Aillagon, J.-J. *Rome and the Barbarians: the Birth of a New World*. Milan: Skira; New York: Rizzoli: 142-143.

Beckmann, B. 1995. 'Die germanische Funde in den Kastellen des Taunuslimes und ihre Beziehungen zum Fundgut in der Germania Libera', in Lund Hansen, U. 1995. *Himlingøje, Seeland, Europa: Ein Gräberfeld der jüngeren römischen Kaiserzeit auf Seeland, seine Bedeutung und internationalen Beziehungen*. Copenhagen: Det Kgl. Nordiske Oldskriftselskab: 410-413.

Behre, K. E. 2004. 'Coastal development, sea-level change and settlement history during the later Holocene in the Clay District of Lower Saxony (Niedersachsen), northern Germany', *Quaternary International* 112: 37-53.

Behre, K. E. 2007. 'A new Holocene sea-level curve for the southern North Sea', *Boreas* 36: 82-102.

Belot, E. and Canut, V. 1994a. *Céramiques des 2è et 3è s. de notre ère issues des fouilles du "Terrain Landrot" à Boulogne-sur-Mer*. Boulogne: Château-Musée Départment d'Archéologie Régionale Boulogne-sur-Mer.

Belot, E. and Canut, V. 1994b. 'Céramiques britanno-romaines découvertes à Boulogne et en Boulonnais' *Bononia* 25 (2è semester 1994): 9-17.

Bémont, C. Jeanlin, M and Lahanier, C. (eds.), 1993. *Les figurines en terre cuite gallo-romaines*. Documents d'Archéologie Française 38. Paris: Editions de la Maison des Sciences de l'Homme.

Bennett, J. and Young, R. 1981. 'Some new and some forgotten stamped skillets', *Britannia* 12: 37-44.

Beresford, J. 2005. *A Reassessment of the Ancient Sailing Season: the Case for Wintertime Seafaring on the Graeco-Roman Mediterranean*. Unpublished D.Phil thesis. University of Oxford.

Berger, F. 1985. 'Keltische Fundmünzen aus Niedersachsen', *Die Kunde. Niedersächsischer Landesverein für Urgeschichte. Neue Folge* 36: 207-215.

Berger, F. 1992. *Untersuchungen zu römerzeitlichen Münzfunden in Nordwestdeutschland. Stud. Fundmünzen Antike 9*. Berlin.

Berger, F. 1995. 'Römische Münzen in Norddeutschland', in Busch, R. (ed.), *Rom an der Niederelbe*. Hamburg: 99-111.

Berger, F. 1996. 'Roman coins beyond the northern frontiers: some recent considerations', in King, C. E. and Wigg, D. G. (eds.), *Coin Finds and Coin Use in the Roman World*. Berlin: Mann Verlag: 55-61.

Berger, F. 2008. 'Die römischen Fundmünzen in Niedersachsen und Westfalen. Kontext und Funktionen', in Bursche, A. Ciołek, R. and Wolters, R. (ed.), *Roman Coins Outside the Empire. Ways and Phases, Contexts and Functions. Proceedings of the ESF/SCH Exploratory Workshop Radziwill Palace, Nieborow (Poland), 3-6 September 2005*. Wetteren: Moneta: 105-111.

Bergquist, A. K. and Taylor, T. F. 1987. 'The origin of the Gundestrup cauldron', *Antiquity* 61: 10-24.

Berke, S. 1990. *Römische Bronzegefässe und Terra Sigillata in der Germania Libera*. Boreas, Beiheft 7. Münster.

Beuker, J. R. 1988. 'Die Verwendung von Helgoländer Flint in der Stein- und Bronzezeit', *Die Kunde* (NF) 39: 93-116.

Beuker, J. R. 1990. 'The importation of Heligoland-flint in the province of Drenthe (The Netherlands)', in Séronie-Vivien, M. R. and Lenoir, M. (eds.), *Le silex de sa genèse à l'outil. Actes du V° colloque international sur le silex. (Vth International Flint Symposium), Bordeaux, 17 sept.-2 oct. 1987. Cahiers du Quaternaire 17*. Volume II. Bordeaux: CNRS: 311-318.

Bernhard, H. 1980. 'Fundberichte aus der Pfalz. Frühgeschichte. 1976-1977', *Mitteilungen des Historischen Vereins der Pfalz* 78: 9-108.

Berthault, F. 1997. 'Production d'amphores vinaires dans la region du Langon (Vendée)', in *Actes du congrès de la Société française d'étude de la céramique antique en Gaule*. Le Mans; Marseille: SFECAG: 209-216.

Besly, E. and Bland, R. 1983. *The Cunetio Treasure-Roman Coinage of the Third Century AD*. London: British Museum.

Besuijen, G. P. A. 2008. *Rodanum: a Study of the Roman Settlement at Aardenburg and its Metal Finds*. Leiden: Sidestone Press.

Bidwell, P. T. 1985. *The Roman Fort of Vindolanda at Chesterholm, Northumberland*. London: Historic Buildings and Monuments Commission for England.

Bidwell, P. T. and Speak, S. 1994. *Excavations at South Shields Roman Fort. Volume I*. Newcastle: The Society of Antiquaries of Newcastle Upon Tyne with Tyne and Wear Museums.

Bieber, M. 1915. *Die Antiken skulpturen und Bronzen des Königl. Museum Fridericianum in Cassel*. Marburg.

Bielenin, K. Mangin, M. and Orzechowski, S. 1998. 'La sidérurgie ancienne et l'exploitation minière dans les Montagnes Sainte-Croix (Petite Pologne). III Archéométrie et histoire: les Montagnes Sainte-Croix et les regions productives européennes (fin de l'Âge du Fer- début du Moyen Âge)', *Dialogues d'Histoire Ancienne* 24 (1): 139-193.

Biggins, J. A. and Taylor, D. J. A. 'The Roman fort and *vicus* at Maryport: geophysical survey, 2000-2004', in Wilson, R. J. A. and Caruana, I. (eds.), 2004. *Romans on the Solway. Essays in Honour of Richard Bellhouse*. Kendal: 102-133.

Bird, D. 2001. 'Aspects of Roman gold mining: Dolaucothi, Asturias and Pliny', in Higham, N. (ed.), *Archaeology of the Roman Empire: a Tribute to the Life and Works of Professor Barri Jones*. Oxford: 265-75.

Bird, D. 2002. 'The events of A.D. 43: further reflections', *Britannia* 33: 257-263.

Bird, J. 1982. 'Overall summaries: The samian ware', in Bennett, P. Frere, S. S. and Stow, S. *Excavations at Canterbury Castle*. Maidstone: Canterbury Archaeological Trust and the Kent Archaeological Society: 158-159.

Bird, J. 1984. In Fulford, M. G. *Silchester. Excavations on the Defences 1974-80*. Britannia Monograph Series 5. London: Society for the Promotion of Roman Studies.

Bird, J. 1995a. In Blockley, K. Blockley, M. Blockley, P. Frere, S. S. and Stowe, S. *Excavations in the Marlowe Car Park and Surrounding Areas*. Canterbury: Canterbury Archaeological Trust.

Bird, J. 1999. In Symonds, R. P. and Wade, S. M. 1999. *Roman Pottery from Excavations in Colchester, 1971- 1986*. Colchester Archaeological Report 10. Colchester.

Bird, J. 2000. In Fulford, M. G. and Timby, J. *Late Iron Age and Roman Silchester. Excavations on the Site of the Forum-basilica 1977, 1980-86*. London: Society for the Promotion of Roman Studies.

Bird, J. and Williams, D. 1983. 'German marbled flagons in Britain', *Britannia* 14: 247-252.

Birley, A. R. 2000. 'Hadrian to the Antonines', in Bowman, A. K. Garnsey, P. Rathbone, D. (eds.), *Cambridge Ancient History. Volume 11. The High Empire A.D. 70-192*. Cambridge: Cambridge University Press: 132-194.

Birley, A. R. 2001. *Marcus Aurelius. A Biography*. London.

Birley, A. R. 2005. *The Roman Government of Britain*. Oxford: Oxford University Press.

Birley, A. R. 2007. 'Britain during the third century crisis', in Hekster, O. de Kleijn, G. and Slootjes, D. (eds.), *Crises and the Roman Empire: Proceedings of the Seventh Workshop of the International Network Impact of Empire* (Nijmegen, June 20-24, 2006). Leiden; Boston: Brill.

Birley, B. and Greene, E. 2006. *The Roman Jewellery from Vindolanda*. Greenhead: Roman Army Museum Publications.

Bishop, M. C. and Coulston, J. C. N. 2006. *Roman Military Equipment: from the Punic Wars to the Fall of Rome* (second edition). Oxford: Oxbow.

Black, E. W. 2000. 'Sentius Saturninus and the Roman invasion of Britain', *Britannia* 31: 1-10.

Blagg, T. F. C. 1981. 'Architectural patronage in the western provinces of the Roman Empire in the third century', in King, A. C. and Henig, M. (eds.), *The Roman West in the Third Century: Contributions from Archaeology and History*. Vol. 1. BAR International Series 109. Oxford: 167-188.

Blagg, T. F. C. 1990. 'Architectural Munificence in Britain: the evidence of inscriptions', *Britannia* 21: 13-31.

Blagg, T. F. C. Plouviez, J. and Tester, A. 2004. *Excavations at a Large Romano-British Settlement at Hacheston, Suffolk in 1973-4*. East Anglian Archaeology Report 106. Ipswich: Suffolk County Council Archaeological Service.

Bland, R. and Burnett, A. 1988. *The Normanby Hoard and other Roman Coin Hoards*. London: British Museum.

Bland, R. and Johns, C. 1995. *The Hoxne Treasure: an Illustrated Introduction* (third impression). London: British Museum.

Bliujiene, A. 2001. 'Lithuanian amber artefacts in the middle of the first millennium and their provenance within the limits of eastern Baltic region', in Butrimas, A. (ed.), *Baltic Amber*. Vilnius: Publishing Office of Vilnius Academy of Fine Arts: 171-194.

Bloemers, J. H. F. 1983. 'Acculturation in the Rhine/Meuse basin in the Roman period: A preliminary survey', in Brandt, R. Slofstra, J. (eds.), *Roman and Native in the Low Countries: Spheres of Interaction*. BAR International Series 184. Oxford: 159-209.

Bloemers, J. H. F. 1989. 'Acculturation in the Rhine/Meuse basin in the Roman period: Demographic considerations', in Barrett, J. C. *et al.* (eds.), *Barbarians and Romans in North-West Europe: from the Later Republic to Late Antiquity*. BAR International Series 471. Oxford: 175-197.

Bockius, R. (ed). 2000. *Steinbruch and Bergwerk: Denkmäler römischer Technikgeschichte zwischen Eifel und Rhein. Kataloghandbuch zu den Ausstellungen in den Museen von Mayen und Andernach. Vulkanpark-Forschungen* 2. Mainz.

Bodart, H. 1997. 'Le matériel en bronze découvert à Sains-du-Nord (Nord)', *Revue du Nord* 323: 161-166.

Boeles, P. C. G. A. 1951. *Friesland tot de elfde eeuw* (second edition). 's Gravenhage: M. Nijhoff.

Bogaers, J. E. 1967. 'Die Besatzungstruppen des legionslagers von Nijmegen im 2. Jh. n. Chr.', in *Studien zu den Militärgrenzen Roms. Vorträge des 6. Internationalen Limeskongresses in Süddeutschland*. Cologne/Graz: 54-76.

Bogaers, J. E. and Rüger, C. B. 1974. *Der niedergermanische Limes. Kunst und Altertum am Rhein* 50. Cologne.

Bohannan, P. 1996. 'Some principles of exchange and investment among the Tiv', in (eds.), Grinker, R. R. and Steiner, C. B. *Perspectives on Africa: a Reader in Culture, History and Representation*. Wiley-Blackwell: 119-128.

Böhme, A. 1970. 'Englische Fibeln aus den Kastellen Saalburg und Zugmantel', *Saalburg Jahrbuch* 27.

Böhme, A. 1972. 'Die Fibeln der Kastelle Saalburg und Zugmantel', *Saalburg Jahrbuch* 29: 5-112 and Taf 1-37.

Böhme, H. W. 1974. *Germanische Grabfunde des 4. bis 5. Jahrhunderts zwischen unterer Elbe und Loire*. Munich. C. H. Beck.

Böhme, H. W. 1975. 'Archäologische Zeugnisse zur Geschichte der Markomannenkriege (166-180 n.Chr)', *Jahresbericht Römisch-Germanisches Zentralmuseum* 22: 153-217.

Böhme, H. W. 1986. 'Das Ende der Römerherrschaft in Britannien und die Angelsächsische Besiedlung Englands im 5. Jahrhundert', *Jahrbuch des Römisch-Germanischen Zentralmuseums Mainz* 33: 468-574.

Böhme, H. W. 1987. 'Gallien in der Spätantike', *Jahrbuch des Römisch-Germanischen Zentralmuseums Mainz* 34: 770-773.

Böhme, H. W. 2007. 'Observations sur les fibulas Germaniques di IVe et Ve siècle découvertes à Vron (Somme)', *Revue Archéologique de Picardie* 2007. No.1/2: 5-30.

Bolin, S. 1926. *Fynden av romerska mynt i det fria Germanien*. Lund.

Bolin, S. 1929. 'Die Funde römischer und byzantinischer Münzen in freien Germanien', *Bericht der Römisch-Germanischen Kommission* 19: 86-145.

Bollingberg, H. J. and Lund Hansen, U. 1995. 'Roman cauldrons in Scandinavia; Major and minor element analyses', in Mols, S. T. A. M. Gerhartl-Witteveen, A. M. Kars, H. Koster, A. Peters, W. J. Th. and Willems, W. J. H. (eds.), *Acta of the 12th International Congress on Ancient Bronzes, Nijmegen 1992*. Amersfoort: 165-168.

Bonenfant, P. and Defosse, P. 1994. 'Les recherches paléosidérurgiques en Belgique: l'exemple de la forêt de Soignes au Sud-Est de Bruxelles', in Mangin, M. (ed.), *La sidérurgie ancienne de l'Est de la France dans son contexte européen*. Paris: Belles Lettres: 269-273.

Boon, G. C. 1974. *Silchester: the Roman Town of Calleva* (second edition). Newton Abbot.

Boon, G. C. 1991. '*Plumbum Britannicum* and other remarks', *Britannia* 22: 317-322.

Booth, P. M. 1997. *Asthall, Oxfordshire: Excavations in a Roman Small Town, 1992*. Oxford: Oxford Archaeological Unit.

Booth, P. M. 1998. 'Defining small towns in Roman Britain', *Journal of Roman Archaeology* 11: 613-623.

Booth, P. M. 2001. In Booth, P. M. and Evans, J. *Roman Alcester: Northern Extramural Area 1969-1988 Excavations*. York: Council for British Archaeology.

Booth, P. M. Evans, J. and Hiller, J. 2002. *Alchester. Excavations in the Extramural Settlement of Roman Alchester, Oxfordshire, 1991*. Oxford: Oxford Archaeology.

Borgard, P. and Cavalier, M. 2003. 'The Lipari origin of the 'Richborough 527'', in Plouviez, J. (ed.), *Journal of Roman Pottery Studies 10. Amphorae in Britain and the Western Empire*: 96-106.

Bosman, A. V. A. J. 1997. *Het culturele vondstmaterial van der vroeg Romeinse versterking Velsen 1*. Unpublished PhD thesis. University of Amsterdam.

Bosman, A. and de Weerd, M. 2004. 'Velsen: the 1997 excavations in the early Roman base and a reappraisal of the post-Kalkriese Velsen/Vechten dating evidence', in Vermeulen, F. Sas, K. and Dhaeze, W. (eds.), *Archaeology in Confrontation. Aspects of Roman Military Presence in the Northwest. Studies in Honour of Prof. Em. Hugo Thoen*. Gent: Academia Press: 31-62.

Boube, C. 1991. 'Les cruches', in Feugère, M. and Rolley, C. (eds.), *La Vaisselle tardo-républicaine en bronze*. Dijon: 23-45.

Boudet, R. and Noldin, J.-P. 1989. 'Une monnaie de l'âge de Fer de l'île de Bretagne, découverte à Doulezon (Gironde)', *Aquitania* 7: 177-181.

Bowman, A. K. 1994. *Life and Letters on the Roman Frontier: Vindolanda and its People*. London: British Museum.

Bowman, A. K. and Wilson, A. I. (eds.), 2009. *Quantifying the Roman Economy: Methods and Problems*, Oxford Studies in the Roman Economy 1.Oxford: Oxford University Press.

Bowman, A. K. Tomlin, R. S. O and Worp, K. A. 2009. '*Emptio Bovis Frisica*: The 'Frisian ox sale' reconsidered'', *Journal of Roman Studies* 99: 156-170.

Bradley, R. 1971. 'A field survey of the Chichester entrenchments', in Cunliffe, B. W. (ed.), *Excavations at Fishbourne. Vol. 1. The Site*. London: Society of Antiquaries: 17-36.

Bradley, R. 2007. *The prehistory of Britain and Ireland*. Cambridge: Cambridge University Press.

Bradley, R. and Edmonds, M. 1993. *Interpreting the Axe Trade: Production and Exchange in Neolithic Britain*. Cambridge: Cambridge University Press.

Brandt, R. 1983. 'A brief encounter along the northern frontier', in Brandt, R. and Slofstra, J. (ed.), *Roman and Native in the Low Countries. Spheres of Interaction*. BAR International Series 184. Oxford: 129-145.

Braudel, F. 1972. *The Mediterranean and the Mediterranean World in the Age of Phillip II*. New York: Harper and Row.

Braudel, F. 2001. *The Mediterranean in the Ancient World*. London: Allen Lane.

Braund, D. 1984. *Rome and the Friendly King. The Character of Client Kingship*. London: Croom Helm.

Breeze, D. 1984. 'Demand and supply on the northern frontier' in Miket, R and Burgess, C. (ed.), *Between and Beyond the Walls: Essays on the Prehistory and History of North Britain in Honour of George Jobey*. Edinburgh: John Donald: 264-286.

Brill, R. and Wampler, J. 1967. 'The isotope studies of ancient lead', *American Journal of Archaeology* 71: 63-77.

Brinkkemper, O. Duistermaat, H. Hallewas, D. P. and Kooistra, L. I. 1995. 'A native settlement from the Roman period near Rockanje', *Berichten Rijksdienst Oudheidkundig Bodemonderzoek* 41: 123-171.

Britnell, R. H. 2009. *Markets, Trade and Economic Development in England and Europe, 1050-1550*. Variorum Collected Studies Series. Farnham: Ashgate.

Brogan, O. 1936. 'Trade between the Roman Empire and the free Germans', *Journal of Roman Studies* 26 (2): 195-222.

Brown, A. G. Meadows, I. Turner, S. D. and Mattingly, D. J. 2001. 'Roman vineyards in Britain: stratigraphic and palynological data from Woolaston in the Nene Valley, England', *Antiquity* 75: 745-757.

Brown, D and Henig, M. 1977. 'Figured amber in the Ashmolean Museum, Oxford', in Munby. J and Henig, M. (eds.), *Roman Life and Art in Britain*. BAR British Series 41. Part I. Oxford: 21-24.

Bruce-Mitford, R. 1974. 'Snape boat' in Bruce-Mitford, R. (ed.), *Aspects of Anglo-Saxon Archaeology*. London.

Bruce-Mitford, R. 1975. *Sutton Hoo Ship Burial, I*. London: British Museum.

Brugmann, B. 2004. *Glass Beads from Early Anglo-Saxon Graves. A Study on the Provenance and Chronology of Glass Beads from Anglo-Saxon Graves*. Oxford: Oxbow.

Brulet, R. 1989. 'The continental Litus Saxonicum', in Maxfield, V. A. (ed.), *The Saxon Shore. A Handbook*. Exeter.

Brulet, R. 1991. 'Le Litus Saxon continental', in Maxfield, V. A. and Dobson, M. J. (eds.), *Roman Frontier Studies: Proceedings of the XVth International Congress of Roman Frontier Studies, 1989: Canterbury, England*. Exeter: University of Exeter Press: 155-169.

Brun, J.-P. 2001. 'La viticulture antique en Provence', in Brun, J.-P. and Laubenheimer, F. (eds.), 'La viticulture en Gaule' in *Gallia* 58: 69-89.

Brun, J.-P. 2004. *Archéologie du vin et de l'huile dans l'Empire romain.* Paris.

Brun, J.-P. and Gilles, K.-J. 2001. 'La viticulture antique en Rhénanie', in Brun, J.-P. and Laubenheimer, F. (eds.), 'La viticulture en Gaule', in *Gallia* 58: 165-179.

Brun, J.-P. and Laubenheimer, F. 2001. 'Conclusion', in Brun, J.-P. and Laubenheimer, F. (eds.), 'La viticulture en Gaule', in *Gallia* 58: 203-219.

Bruns, D. 2003. *Germanic Equal Arm Brooches of the Migration Period: a Study of Style, Chronology and Distribution including a Full Catalogue of Finds and Contexts.* BAR International Series 1113. Oxford: BAR Publishing.

Bruschi, T. and Wilkens, B. 1996. 'Conserves de poisson à partir de quatre amphores romaines', *Archaeofauna* 5: 165-169.

Bruun, C. 2007. 'The Antonine plague and the third-century crisis'', in Hekster, O. de Kleijn, G. and Slootjes, D. (eds.), *Crises and the Roman Empire: Proceedings of the Seventh Workshop of the International Network Impact of Empire (Nijmegen, June 20-24, 2006).* Leiden; Boston: Brill: 201-218.

Bryant, S. R. 1994. 'From chiefdom to kingdom' in Branigan, K. (ed.), *The Archaeology of the Chilterns: from the Ice Age to the Norman Conquest.* Sheffield: Chess Valley Archaeological and Historical Society: 49-66.

Bryant, S. R. 1999. *Settlement and Landscape in the Late Iron Age of Hertfordshire and the Northern Chilterns.* Unpublished PhD thesis. University of Sheffield.

Bryant, S. R. 2007. 'Central places or special places? The origins and development of '*oppida*' in Hertfordshire', in Haselgrove, C. and Moore, T. (eds.), *The Later Iron Age in Britain and Beyond.* Oxford: Oxbow: 62-80.

Bryant, S. R. and Niblett, R. 2001. 'The Late Iron Age in Hertfordshire and the north Chilterns', in Collis, J. (ed.), *Society and Settlement in Iron Age Europe.* Sheffield: J. R. Collis Publications: 98-110.

Buckland, P. C. Hartley, K. F. and Rigby, V. 2001. *The Roman Pottery Kilns at Rossington Bridge. Excavations 1956-1961. Journal of Roman Pottery Studies.* 9.

Buckley, D. G. and Major, H. J. 1983. 'Quernstones', in Crummy, N. *The Roman Small Finds from Excavations in Colchester 1971-9.* Colchester Archaeological Report 2. Colchester: 73-76.

Buckley, D. G. & Major, H. 1990. In Wrathmell, S. & Nicholson, A. P. (eds.), *Dalton Parlours: Iron Age settlement and Roman villa.* Wakefield: West Yorkshire Archaeology Service.

Budd, P. Gale, D. Pollard, A. M. Thomas, R. G. and Williams, P. A. 1992. 'The early development of metallurgy in the British Isles', *Antiquity* 66: 677-686.

Buffat, L. and Pellecuer, C. 2001. 'La viticulture antique en Languedoc-Roussillon', in Brun, J.-P. and Laubenheimer, F. (eds.), 'La viticulture en Gaule' in *Gallia* 58: 91-111.

Buora, M. (ed.), 1996. *Lungo la via dell'Ambra. Apporti altoadriatici alla romanizzazione dei territori del medio Danubio (I sec.a.C. - I sec.d.C.).* Udinese: Tavagnacco.

Burgess, C. and Shennan, S. 1976. 'The Beaker phenomenon: some suggestions', in Burgess, C. and Miket, R. (eds.), *Settlement and Economy in the Third and Second Millennia BC.* BAR 33. Oxford: 309-331.

Burnett, A. 1996. ''Gallo-Belgic' coins and Britain', in Raftery, B. (ed.), *Sites and Sights of the Iron Age.* Oxford: Oxbow: 5-11.

Burnham, B. C. 1997. 'Roman mining at Dolaucothi: the implications of the 1991-3 excavations near the Carreg Pumsaint', *Britannia* 28: 325-336.

Burnham, B. C. Keppie, L. J. F. Esmonde Cleary, A. S. Hassall, M. C. W. and Tomlin, R. S. O. 2000. 'Roman Britain in 1999', *Britannia* 31: 371-449.

Burnham, B. C. and Burnham, H. 2004. *Dolaucothi-Pumsaint: Survey and Excavation at a Roman Gold-mining Complex 1987-1999.* Oxford: Oxbow.

Bursche, A. 1989. 'Contacts between the Roman Empire and the mid-European Barbaricum in the light of coin finds', in Carradice, I. A. (ed.), *Proceedings of the 10th International Congress of Numismatics, London 1986.* Wetteren: 279-288.

Bursche, A. 1996. 'Contacts between the Late Roman Empire and North-Central Europe', *The Antiquaries Journal* 76: 31-50.

Bursche, A. 2006. 'Relations between the Late Roman World and Barbarian Europe in the light of coin finds', Paper delivered at the XIV International Economic History Conference, Helsinki 2006. Online article: http://www.helsinki.fi/iehc2006/papers1/Bursche.pdf

Bursche, A. 2008. 'Trade relations between Rome and the Barbarians', in Aillagon, J.-J. (ed.), *Rome and the Barbarians. The Birth of a New World.* Venice: Palozzo Grussi: 153-155.

Bursche, A. Ciołek, R. and Wolters, R. 2008. *Roman Coins Outside the Empire. Ways and Phases, Contexts and Functions. Proceedings of the ESF/SCH Exploratory Workshop Radziwill Palace, Nieborow (Poland), 3-6 September 2005.* Wetteren: Moneta.

Busch, R (ed.), 1995. *Rom an der Niederelbe.* Hamburg.

Bushe-Foxe, J. P. 1928. *Second Report on the Excavations of the Roman Fort at Richborough, Kent.* Oxford: Oxford University Press.

Bushe-Fox, J. P. 1949. *Fourth Report on the Excavations of the Roman fort at Richborough, Kent.* Oxford: University Press.

Butler, J. J. 1963. 'Bronze Age connections across the North Sea', *Palaeohistoria* 9.

Caley, E. R. 1964. *Orichalcum and Related Ancient Alloys.* American Numismatic Society. New York.

Callender, M. H. 1965. *Roman Amphorae: with an Index of Stamps.* London: Oxford University Press, for Durham.

Callu, J.-P. Brenot, C. Barrandon, J.-N. Poirier, J. 1985. 'Aureus obryziacus', in Morrisson, C. *et al.* (ed.), *L'or monnayé I. Purification et alterations de Rome à Byzance*. Paris: 81-111.

Calvi, M. C. 1996. 'Le ambre romane de Aquileia: aspetti e problemi', in Buora, M. (ed.), *Lungo la via dell'Ambra. Apporti altoadriatici alla romanizzazione dei territori del medio Danubio (I sec.a.C. - I sec.d.C.)*. Udinese: Tavagnacco: 13-20.

Calvi, M. C. 2005. *Le Ambre Romane di Aquileia*. Aquileia: Associazione Nazionale per Aquileia.

Canny, D. and Dilly, G. 1997. 'Les fibules de Fesques', in Mantel (ed.), Le Sanctuaire de Fesques. *Nord-Ouest Archéologie* 8: 185-198.

Carandini, A. (ed.), 1985. *Settefinestre: una villa schiavistica nell'Etruria romana*. Modena: Panini.

Carnap-Bornheim, C. and Ilkjær, J. 1996-7. *Illerup Ådal 5-8. Die Prachtausrüstungen*. Højberg: Jysk Arkæologisk Selskab.

Carreras Monfort, C. 2000. *Economía de la Britannia Romana: La Importación de Alimentos*. Barcelona.

Carreras Monfort, C. 2002. 'The Roman military supply during the Principate. Transportation and staples', in Erdkamp, P. (ed.), *The Roman Army and the Economy*. Amsterdam: Gieben: 70-89.

Carreras Monfort, C. 2003. 'Haltern 70: a review', in (ed.), Plouviez, J. *Journal of Roman Pottery Studies 10. Amphorae in Britain and the Western Empire*: 85-91.

Carreras Monfort, C. and Funari, P. P. A. 1998. *Britannia y el Mediterráneo: Estudios Sobre el Abastecimiento de Aceite Bético y africano en Britannia*. Barcelona.

Carreras Monfort, C. and Williams, D. F. 2003. 'Spanish olive oil trade in late Roman britain: Dressel 23 amphorae from Winchester', *Journal of Roman Pottery Studies* 10: 64-68.

Carrington, P. 2006. 'Towards a model of Roman society in Cheshire, first to third centuries AD', Online article: http://www.chesterarchaeolsoc.org.uk/R_cheshire_model.html

Carrington, P. 2008. 'Feeding the wolf in Cheshire: models and (a few) facts', in Stallibrass, S. and Thomas, R. (eds.), *Feeding the Roman Army: the Archaeology of Production and Supply in NW Europe*. Oxford: Oxbow: 18-30.

Carroll, M. 2001. 'Supplying the Roman fleet: native Belgic, Frisian and Germanic pottery from Cologne', *Journal of Roman Archaeology* 14: 311-324.

Carver, E. 2001. *The Visibility of Imported Wine and its Associated Accoutrements in Later Iron Age Britain*. BAR British Series 325. Oxford: BAR Publishing.

Casey, P. J. 1977. 'Carausius and Allectus- rulers in Gaul?', *Britannia* 8: 283-301.

Casey, P. J. 1994a. *Roman Coinage in Britain* (third edition). Princes Risborough, Buckinghamshire: Shire Archaeology.

Casey, P. J. 1994b. *Carausius and Allectus. The British Usurpers*. London: Batsford.

Cauuet, B. 1995. 'Celtic Gold Mines in West Central Gaul', in Morteani and Northover (eds.), *Prehistoric Gold in Europe*: 219-240.

Cauuet B. 2004. *L'or des Celtes du Limousin*. Limoges.

Cauuet, B. Szepertyski, B. and Diot, M.-F. 1999. 'L'exploitation de l'or en Gaule à l'Âge du Fer', in Cauuet, B. (eds.), *L'or dans l'Antiquité de la mine à l'objet*. Aquitania supplément 9. Talence: 31-70.

Cavallo, C. Kooistra, L. I. and Dütting, K. 2008. 'Food supply to the Roman army in the Rhine delta', in Stallibrass, S. and Thomas, R. (eds.), *Feeding the Roman Army: the Archaeology of Production and Supply in NW Europe*. Oxford: Oxbow: 69-82.

Cech, B. 2007. Archaeology in Hüttenberg. The *Ferrum Noricum* Project- Pre-Roman and Roman iron production. Online article: http://www.alpinespace.org/uploads/media/IRON ROUTE_Abstract_of_the_research_activities_WP 5_PP3.pdf

Cech, B. (ed). 2008. *Die Produktion von Ferrum Noricum am Hüttenberger Erzberg. Austria Antiqua* 2. Vienna.

Chapman, H. 1974. 'Three Roman objects from the City of London', *Transactions of the London and Middlesex Archaeological Society* 25: 273-277.

Chapman, H. 1977. 'The querns' in Jones, M. J. 'Archaeological work at Brough under Stainmore 1971-72: I. The Roman discoveries', *Cumberland and Westmorland Antiquarian and Archaeological Society* LXXVII: 41-42.

Chapman, H. and Johnson, T. 1973. 'Excavations at Aldgate and Bush Lane house in the City of London 1972', *Transactions of the London and Middlesex Archaeological Society* 24: 1-73.

Cherry, D. 2007. 'The frontier zones', in Scheidel, W. Morris, I. and Saller, R. P. (eds.), *The Cambridge Economic History of the Greco-Roman World*. Cambridge: Cambridge University Press: 720-740.

Christensen, C. 1990. 'Stone Age dugout boats in Denmark', in Robinson, D. E. (ed.), *Experimentation and Reconstruction in Environmental Archaeology*. Oxford: Oxbow: 119-142.

Christison, D. and Anderson, J. 1898. 'Account of the excavation of the Roman station at Ardoch, Perthshire, undertaken by the Society of Antiquaries of Scotland in 1896-97', *Proceedings of the Society of Antiquaries of Scotland* 32: 399-476.

Clark, G. 1944. *Prehistoric England* (third edition, Winter 1944-45). London: B. T. Batsford.

Clark, G. 1966. 'The invasion hypothesis in British archaeology', *Antiquity* 40: 172-189.

Clark, P. (ed.), 2004. *The Dover Bronze Age boat in context: Society and water transport in prehistoric Europe*. Oxford: Oxbow.

Clark, P. (ed.), 2009. *Bronze Age Connections: Cultural Contact in Prehistoric Europe*. Oxford: Oxbow.

Clarke, G. 1979. *Pre-Roman and Roman Winchester. Part 2, The Roman Cemetery at Lankhills*. Oxford: Clarendon Press.

Clay, C. 1989. 'The supply of bronze coin to Britain in the second century AD', *Numismatic Chronicle* 149: 209-224.

Clay, C. L. 2007. 'Before there were Angles, Saxons and Jutes: an epigraphic study of the Germanic social, religious and linguistic relations on Hadrian's Wall', in Gilmour, L. (ed.), *Pagans and Christians – from Antiquity to the Middle Ages Papers in Honour of Martin Henig, Presented on the Occasion of his 65th birthday*. BAR International Series 1610. Oxford: BAR Publishing: 47-63.

Cleere, H. F. 1976. 'Some operating parameters for Roman ironworks', *Institute of Archaeology Bulletin* 13: 233-246.

Cleere, H. F. 1977. 'The *Classis Britannica*', in Johnston, D. E. (ed.), *The Saxon Shore*. London: Council for British Archaeology: 16-19.

Cleere, H. F. 1978. 'Roman harbours in Britain south of Hadrian's Wall', in du Plat Taylor, J. and Cleere, H. (eds.), *Roman Shipping and Trade: Britain and the Rhine Provinces*. London: The Council for British Archaeology: 36-40.

Cleere, H. F. and Crossley, D. 1995. *The Iron Industry of the Weald* (second edition). Merton Priory Press.

Collingwood, R. G. 1930. 'Romano-Celtic art in Northumbria', *Archaeologia* 80: 37-58.

Collingwood, R. G. and Myres, J. N. L. 1936. *Roman Britain and the English Settlements*. Oxford History of England. Oxford: Clarendon Press.

Colls, D. Etienne, R. Lequément, B. Liou, B. and Mayet, F. 1977. 'L'épave Port-Vendres II et le commerce de la Bétique à l'époque de Claude', *Archaeonautica* 1. Paris.

Cool, H. E. M. 2006. *Eating and Drinking in Roman Britain*. Cambridge University Press.

Cool, H. E. M. Lloyd-Morgan, G. and Hooley, A. D. 1995. *Finds from the Fortress*. The Archaeology of York. The Small Finds 17/10. York: Council for British Archaeology, for the York Archaeological Trust.

Cool, H. E. M. and Philo, C. 1998. *Roman Castleford: Excavations 1974-85*. Wakefield: West Yorkshire Archaeology Service.

Cool, H. E. M. and Price, J. 1995. *Roman Vessel Glass from Excavations in Colchester, 1971-85*. Colchester Archaeological Report 8. Colchester: Colchester Archaeological Trust.

Cooley, A. 2009. *Res Gestae Divi Augusti: Text, Translation and Commentary*. Cambridge: Cambridge University Press.

Cooper, D. and Parfitt, K. 1991. In Philp, B. *et al*. *The Roman Villa Site at Keston, Kent: First Report (Excavations 1968-1978)*. Kent: Kent Archaeological Rescue Unit.

Cooper, N. J. 1996. 'Searching for the blank generation: consumer choice in Roman and post-Roman Britain', in Webster, J. and Cooper, N. J. (eds.), *Roman Imperialism: Post-Colonial Perspectives: Proceedings of a Symposium held at Leicester University in November 1994*. Leicester: School of Archaeological Studies: 85-98.

Cosack, E. 1979. *Die Fibeln der Älteren Römischen Kaiserzeit in der Germania libera (Dänemark, DDR, BRD, Niederlande, CSSR): Eine technologisch-archäologische Analyse. Teil I: Armbrustfibeln, Rollenkappenfibeln, Augenfibeln*. Göttinger Schriften zur vor- und frühgeschichte. Band 19. Neumünster: Karl Wachholtz Verlag.

Cottam, G. L. 1999. 'The 'cock bronzes' and other related Iron Age bronze coins found predominantly in West Sussex and Hampshire', *British Numismatic Journal* 69: 1-18.

Cotterill, J. 1993. 'Saxon raiding and the role of the Late Roman coastal forts of Britain', *Britannia* 24: 228-239.

Cowell, M. 1992. 'An analytical survey of the British Celtic gold coinage', in Mays, M. (ed.), *Celtic Coinage in Britain and Beyond; the Eleventh Oxford Symposium on Coinage and Monetary History*. BAR British Series 222. Oxford: BAR Publishing: 207-234.

Cox, P. W. and Hearne, C. M. 1991. *Redeemed from the Heath: The Archaeology of the Wytch Farm Oilfield 1987-90*. Dorchester.

Craddock, P. T. 1998. 'Zinc in Classical Antiquity', in Craddock, P. T. (ed.), *2000 Years of Zinc and Brass* (revised edition). London: British Museum: 1-6.

Craddock, P. T. 2008. 'Mining and metallurgy', in Oleson, J. P. (ed.), *The Oxford Handbook of Engineering and Technology in the Classical World*. Oxford: Oxford University Press: 93-120.

Crawford, O. G. S. and Röder, J. 1955. 'The quern-quarries of Mayen in the Eifel', *Antiquity* 29: 68-76.

Cree, J. E. 1924. 'Account of excavations on Traprain Law during the summer of 1923', *Proceedings of the Society of Antiquaries of Scotland* 58: 241-84.

Creighton, J. 2000. *Coins and Power in Late Iron Age Britain*. Cambridge: Cambridge University Press.

Crew, P. 1995. 'Aspects of the iron supply', in Cunliffe, B. W. *Danebury: an Iron Age Hillfort in Hampshire. Volume 6. A Hillfort Community in Perspective*. London: Council for British Archaeology: 276-284.

Crouch, K. R. and Shanks, S. A. 1984. *Excavations in Staines 1975-76. The Friends' Burial Ground Site*. London.

Cruden, S. H. 1940. 'The ramparts of Traprain Law: excavations in 1939', *Proceedings of the Society of Antiquaries of Scotland* 74: 48-59.

Crumlin-Pedersen, O. 1990. 'Boats and ships of the Angles and Jutes', in McGrail, S. (ed.), *Maritime Celts, Frisians and Saxons: Papers Presented to a Conference at Oxford in November 1988*. London: Council for British Archaeology: 98-116.

Crummy, N. 1983. *The Roman Small Finds from Excavations in Colchester 1971-9*. Colchester.

Crummy, N. 2002. 'Small finds and iron nails', 85-6 in Pearson, A. 'Excavations at 97-99 High Street, Braintree. *Essex Archaeology and History* 33, 78-88.

Cunliffe, B. W. 1968. *Fifth Report on the Excavations of the Roman Fort at Richborough, Kent*. Oxford.

Cunliffe, B. W. 1971. *Excavations at Fishbourne. Vol. 1. The Site*. London: Society of Antiquaries.

Cunliffe, B. W. 1975. *Excavations at Portchester Castle I: Roman*. London: Society of Antiquaries.

Cunliffe, B. W. 1976. 'The origins of urbanism in Britain', in Cunliffe, B. and Rowley, T. (eds.), *Oppida: the Beginnings of Urbanisation in Barbarian Europe*. BAR International Series 11. Oxford: 135-162.

Cunliffe, B. W. 1977. 'The Saxon shore- some problems and misconceptions', in Johnston, D. E. (ed.), *The Saxon shore*. London: Council for British Archaeology: 1-6.

Cunliffe, B. W. 1984a. 'Relations between Britain and Gaul in the first century BC and early first century AD', in Macready, S. and Thompson, F. H. (eds.), *Cross-Channel Trade between Gaul and Britain in the Pre-Roman Iron Age*. London: Society of Antiquaries: 3-23.

Cunliffe, B. W. 1984b. *Danebury: an Iron Age Hillfort in Hampshire. Volume 2. The Excavations 1969-1978: The finds*. London: Council for British Archaeology.

Cunliffe, B. W. 1987. *Hengistbury Head, Dorset. Volume 1. The Prehistoric and Roman Settlement, 3500 BC-AD 500*. Oxford.

Cunliffe, B. W. 1988a. *Greeks, Romans and Barbarians*. London.

Cunliffe, B. W. 1988b. *Mount Batten, Plymouth. A Prehistoric and Roman Port*. Oxford: Institute of Archaeology.

Cunliffe, B. W. (ed.), 1988c. *The Temple of Sulis Minerva at Bath. Vol. 2. Finds from the Sacred Spring*. Oxford.

Cunliffe, B. W. 1998. *Fishbourne Roman Palace*. Stroud: Tempus.

Cunliffe, B. W. 2001. *Facing the Ocean: the Atlantic and its Peoples 8000 BC-AD 1500*. Oxford: Oxford University Press.

Cunliffe, B. W. 2002. *The Extraordinary Voyage of Pytheas the Greek*. London: Penguin.

Cunliffe, B. W. 2004. 'Britain and the continent: networks of interaction', in Todd, M. (ed.), *A Companion to Roman Britain*. Oxford: Blackwell: 1-11.

Cunliffe, B. W. 2005. *Iron Age Communities in Britain: an Account of England, Scotland and Wales from the seventh century BC until the Roman Conquest* (fourth edition). London: Routledge.

Cunliffe, B. W. 2009. 'Looking forward: maritime contacts in the first millennium BC', in Clark, P. (ed.), *Bronze Age Connections: Cultural Contact in Prehistoric Europe*. Oxford: Oxbow.

Cunliffe, B. W. and de Jersey, P. 1997. *Armorica and Britain: Cross-Channel Relationships in the Late First Millennium BC*. Oxford.

Cunnington, M. E. and Goddard, E. H. 1934. *Catalogue of Antiquities in the Museum of the Wiltshire Archaeological and Natural History Society at Devises*. Devises.

Cüppers, H. 1962. 'Zwei kaiserzeitliche Brandgräberfelder im Kreise Geldern', *Bonner Jahrbücher* 162: 299-390.

Curle, A. O. 1915. 'Account of excavations on Traprain Law in the parish of Prestonkirk, county of Haddington in 1914', *Proceedings of the Society of Antiquaries of Scotland* 49: 139-202.

Curle, A. O. 1920. 'Report of the excavation of Traprain Law in the summer of 1919', *Proceedings of the Society of Antiquaries of Scotland* 54: 54-124.

Curle, A. O. and Cree, J. E. 1916. 'Account of excavations on Traprain Law in the parish of Prestonkirk, county of Haddington in 1915', *Proceedings of the Society of Antiquaries of Scotland* 50: 64-144.

Curle, A. O. 1923. *The Treasure of Traprain*. Glasgow.

Curle, J. 1911. *A Roman Frontier Post and its People: the Fort of Newstead in the Parish of Melrose*. Glasgow: James Maclehose and Sons.

Curtis, R. I. 1991. *Garum and Salsamenta. Production and Commerce in Materia Medica*. Leiden.

Curtis, R. I. 2005. 'Sources for production and trade of Greek and Roman processed fish', in Bekker-Nielsen, T. (ed.), *Ancient Fishing and Fish Processing in the Black Sea Region*. Aarhus: Aarhus University Press: 31-46.

Czysz, W. 2003. *Heldenbergen in der Wetterau. Feldlager, Kastell, vicus. Limesforschungen* 27. Mainz am Rhein: Verlag Phillipp von Zabern.

Dahlin Hauken, Å. 2005. *The Westland Cauldrons in Norway*. AmS-Skrifter 19. Stavanger.

D'Altroy, T. N. and Earle, T. K. 1985. 'State finance, wealth finance and storage in the Inka political economy', *Current Anthropology* 26: 187-206.

Dannell, G. B. 1971. 'The samian pottery', in Cunliffe, B. W. *Excavations at Fishbourne 1961-1969. Vol. 2. The Finds*. Leeds: 260-316.

Dannell, G. B. 1981. In Partridge, C. *Skeleton Green: a Late Iron Age and Romano-British Site*. London: The Society for the Promotion of Roman Studies.

Dannell, G. B. 1985. In Niblett, R. *Sheepen: an Early Roman Industrial Site at Camulodunum*. London: Council for British Archaeology.

Dannell, G. B. 1999. In Symonds, R. P. and Wade, S. M. *Roman Pottery from Excavations in Colchester, 1971- 1986*. Colchester Archaeological Report 10. Colchester.

Dark, K. 2000. *Britain and the End of the Roman Empire*. Stroud: Tempus.

Darling, M. J. and Gurney, D. 1993. *Caister-on-Sea: Excavations by Charles Green 1951-55*. Dereham.

Davies, B. Richardson, B. and Tomber, R. 1994. *A Dated Corpus of Early Roman Pottery from the City of London*. London/Walmgate: Museum of London and the Council for British Archaeology.

Davies, E. 1949. *The Prehistoric and Roman Remains of Flintshire*. Cardiff.

Davies, H. 2002. *Roads in Roman Britain*. Stroud: Tempus.

Davies, O. 1935. *Roman Mines in Europe*. Oxford.

Davies, O. 1948. 'The copper mines on Great Ormes Head, Caernarvonshire', *Archaeologia Cambrensis* 100: 61-66.

Dawson, M. 2000. *Iron Age and Roman Settlement on the Stagsden Bypass*. Bedfordshire Archaeology Monograph 3. Bedford: Bedfordshire County Archaeology Service.

De Clercq, W. and Degryse, P. 2008. 'The mineralogy and petrography of Low Lands Ware 1 (Roman lower Rhine-Meuse-Scheldt basin; the Netherlands, Belgium, Germany)' *Journal of Archaeological Science* 32 (2): 448-458.

De Jersey, P. 2001. 'Cunobelin's silver', *Britannia* 32: 1-44.

De Jersey, P. 2006. 'Belgic coins in Britain', in De Jersey, P. (ed.), *Celtic Coinage: New Discoveries, New Discussion*. BAR International Series 1532. Oxford: BAR Publishing: 117-137.

Delage, R. 2001. 'Les structures de production des ateliers de potiers à Lezoux du Ier au IVe s. Reflets de l'évolution des stratégies commerciales et de l'organisation du travail', in Polfer, M. (ed). *L'artisant romain: évolutions, continuitiés et ruptures (Italie et provinces occidentals)*. Monographies Instrumentum 20. Montagnac: Éditions Monique Mergoil: 117-135.

Delestrée, L.-P. Gendre, P. and Boisard, C. 2003. 'Monnaies celtiques de Bretagne insulaire trouvées en Gaule du Nord', *Cahiers Numismatiques* 155: 11-19.

De Ligt, L. 1993. *Fairs and Markets in the Roman Empire: Economic and Social Aspects of Periodic Trade in a Pre-industrial Society*. Amsterdam: J.C. Gieben.

Demarez, L and Leman-Delerive, G. 2001. 'A linch pin of British type found at Blicquy (Hainault, Belgium)', *The Antiquaries Journal* 81: 391-395.

Deru, X. 1996. *La céramique belge dans le Nord de la Gaule. Charactérisation, chronologie, phénomènes culturels et économiques*. Louvain-la-Neuve: Publications d'Histoire de l'Art et d'Archeologie de l'Université catholique de Louvain.

Desbat, A. 2003. 'Amphorae from Lyon and the question of Gaulish imitations of amphorae', in Plouviez, J. (ed.), *Journal of Roman Pottery Studies 10: Amphorae in Britain and the Western Empire*: 45-49.

Desbat, A. Genin, M. and Lasfargues, J. 1996. 'Les productions des ateliers de potiers antiques de Lyon. 1ère partie: Les ateliers précoces', *Gallia* 53: 1-249.

Desse-Berset, N. and Desse, J. 2000. '*Salsamenta*, *garum* et autres preparations de poisons. Ce qu'en dissent les os' *Mélanges de l'École Française de Rome. Antiquité*. Paris 112: 84-92.

Detsicas, A. P. (ed.), 1973. *Current Research in Romano-British Coarse Pottery: Papers given at a C.B.A. Conference held at New College, Oxford, March 24 to 26, 1972*. London: Council for British Archaeology.

De Weerd, M. D. 1986. 'Recent excavations near the Brittenburg: a rearrangement of old evidence', in Unz, C. *et al.* (eds.), *Studien zu den Militärgrenzen Roms III. 13. Internationaler Limeskongress, Aalen 1983*. Stuttgart: 284-289.

Dickinson, B.M. 1990 'The samian ware', in McCarthy, M. R. *A Roman, Anglian and Medieval Site at Blackfriars Street, Carlisle: Excavations 1977-9*. Kendal: Cumberland and Westmorland Antiquarian and Archaeological Society: 213-36.

Dickinson, B. 2000. 'Samian', in Buxton, K. and Howard-Davis, C. *Bremetenacum, Excavations at Roman Ribchester 1980, 1989-1990*. Lancaster: Lancaster University Archaeological Unit: 202-224.

Dickinson, B. 2001. 'Samian ware', in Leach, P. *Excavation of a Romano-British Roadside Settlement in Somerset. Fosse Lane, Shepton Mallet, 1990*. London: Society for the Promotion of Roman Studies: 144-149.

Dickinson, B. 2003. 'Samian ware', in Germany, M. *Excavations at Great Holts Farm, Boreham, Essex, 1992-94*. East Anglian Archaeology Report 105. Chelmsford: 156-157.

Diederik, F. 2002. *'Schervengericht' Een onderzoek naar inheems aardewerk uit de late derde en de vierde eeuw in de kop van Noord Holland*. AWN-Reeks No. 3.

Dietler, M. 1989. 'Greeks, Etruscans, and Thirsty Barbarians: Early Iron Age Interaction in the Rhone Basin of France', in Champion, T. C. (ed.), *Centre and Periphery. Comparative Studies in Archaeology*. London: Unwin Hyman.

Dijkman, W. 1992. 'La terre sigillée décorée à la molette à motifs chrétiens dans la stratigraphie maastrichtoise (Pays-Bas) et dans le nord-ouest de l'Europe', *Gallia* 49: 129-172.

Dilly, G. 1978. 'Les fibulas gallo-romaines du Musée Picardie', *Cahiers Archéologiques de Picardie* 5: 157-175.

Dilly, G. and Jobic, F. 1993. 'Les fibules de Vendeuil-Caply', in Piton (ed.), *Vendeuil-Caply. Nord-Ouest Archéologie* 5: 363-397.

Dilly, G. and Sallandre, S. 1978. 'Fibules du Vermandois', *Cahiers Archéologiques de Picardie* 5: 147-155.

Dobney, K. M. Jaques, S. D. and Irving, B. G. 1996. *Of Butchers and Breeds, Report on Vertebrae Remains from Various Sites in the City of Lincoln*. Lincoln.

Domergue, C. 1983. *La mine antique d'Aljustrel (Portugal) et les tables de bronze de Vipasca*. Paris: Diffusion E. de Boccard.

Domergue, C. 1987. *Catalogue des mines et des fonderies antiques de la Péninsule Ibérique*. Publications de la Casa de Velázquez. Série Archéologie; fasc. 8. Madrid: Boccard.

Domergue, C. 1990. *Les mines de la Péninsule Ibérique dans l'antiquité romaine*. Rome.

Dore, J. N. and Gillam, J. P. 1979. *The Roman Fort at South Shields: Excavations 1875-1975*. Newcastle: Society of Antiquaries.

Doswald, C. 1994. 'Les lingots de fer protohistoriques en Europe occidentale: problématique générale', in Mangin, M. (ed.), *La sidérurgie ancienne de l'Est de la France dans son contexte européen*. Paris: Belles Lettres: 332-343.

Dressel, H. 1879. 'Di un grande deposito di anfore rinvenuto nel nuovo quartiere del Castro Pretorio', *Bullettino della commissione archeologica communale di Roma* 7: 36-112, 143-195.

Dressel, H. 1899. *Corpus Inscriptionum Latinarum XV* pars I.

Drewett, P. Rudling, D. and Gardiner, M. 1988. *The South East to AD 1000*. Harlow.

Drinkwater, J. F. 1987. *The Gallic Empire. Separatism and Continuity in the North-western Provinces of the Roman Empire AD 260-274*. Stuttgart: Franz Steiner Verlag Wiesbaden GMBH.

Drinkwater, J. F. 2002. 'Prologue and epilogue. The socio-economic effect of Rome's arrival in and departure from Gaul', in Blois, L. de. and Rich, J. (eds.), *The Transformation of Economic Life under the Roman Empire*: 128-140.

Drinkwater, J. F. 2005. 'Maximinus to Diocletian and the 'crisis', in Bowman, A. K. Garnsey, P. and Cameron, A. (eds.), *The Cambridge Ancient History. Volume 12. The Crisis of Empire, A.D. 193-337*. Cambridge: Cambridge University Press: 28-66.

Drinkwater, J. F. 2007. *The Alamanni and Rome 213-496 (Caracalla to Clovis)*. Oxford: Oxford University Press.

Drummond-Murray, J and Thompson, P. 2002. *Settlement in Roman Southwark: Archaeological Excavations (1991-8) for the London Underground Limited Jubilee Line Extension Project*. London: Museum of London Archaeology Service.

Drury, P. J. 1988. *The Mansio and other Sites in the South-eastern Sector of Caesaromagus*. London: Chelmsford Archaeological Trust.

Dubois, G. 1924. 'Recherches sur les terrains quaternaires du nord de la France' *Mémoires de la Société Géologique du Nord* 8.

Duncan-Jones, R. P. 1990. *Structure and Scale in the Roman Economy*. Cambridge.

Duncan-Jones, R. P. 1994. *Money and Government in the Roman Empire*. Cambridge.

Duncan-Jones, R. P. 1996. 'The impact of the Antonine plague', *Journal of Roman Archaeology* 9: 108-136.

Duncan-Jones, R. P. 2002. *Structure and Scale in the Roman Economy* (fourth edition). Cambridge.

Duncan-Jones, R. P. 2006. 'Roman customs dues: a comparative view', *Latomus* T.65, 2006, Fasc. 1: 3-16.

Dungworth, D. B. 1996. 'The Production of Copper Alloys in Iron Age Britain', *Proceedings of the Prehistoric Society* 62: 399-421.

Dungworth, D. B. 1997a. 'Copper metallurgy in Iron Age Britain: some recent research', in Gwilt, A. and Haselgrove, C. (eds.), *Reconstructing Iron Age Societies*. Oxford: Oxbow: 46-50.

Dungworth, D. B. 1997b. 'Roman Copper Alloys: Analysis of artefacts from Northern Britain', *Journal of Archaeological Science* 24: 901-910.

Dunwell, A. 1999. 'Edin's Hall fort, broch and settlement, Berwickshire (Scottish Borders): recent fieldwork and new perceptions', *Proceedings of the Society of Antiquaries of Scotland* 129: 303-357.

Du Plat Taylor, J. and Cleere, H. (eds.), 1978. *Roman Shipping and Trade: Britain and the Rhine Provinces*. London: Council for British Archaeology.

Durali-Mueller, S. 2005. *Roman Lead and Copper Mining in Germany their Origin and Development through Time, Deduced from Lead and Copper Isotope Provenance Studies*. Unpublished PhD thesis, University of Frankfurt.

Durali-Mueller, S. Brey, P. G. Wigg-Wolf, D. Lahaye, Y. 2007. 'Roman lead mining in Germany: its origin and development through time deduced from lead isotope provenance studies', *Journal of Archaeological Science* 34 (10): 1555-1567.

Earle, T. K. 1977. 'A reappraisal of redistribution: Complex Hawaiian chiefdoms', in Earle, T. K. and Ericson, J. E. (eds.), *Exchange Systems in Prehistory*. New York: Academic Press.

Earle, T. K. 1997. *How Chiefs Come to Power: The Political Economy in Prehistory*. Stanford: Stanford University Press.

Ebel, W. 1990. 'Zu den Plattengürtelhaken der Ripdorfzeit südlich der Elbe', *Archäologisches Korrespondenzblatt* 20: 305-310.

Eckardt, H. 2005. 'The social distribution of Roman artifacts: the case of nail-cleaners and brooches in Britain', *Journal of Roman Archaeology* 18: 139-160.

Eddy, M. 1995. 'Kelvedon and the fort myth in the development of Roman small towns in Essex', in Brown, A. E. (ed.), *Roman Small Towns in Eastern England and Beyond*. Oxford: Oxbow: 119-128.

Edmonson, J. C. 1989. 'Mining in the later Roman Empire and beyond: continuity or disruption?', *Journal of Roman Studies* 79: 84-102.

Eger, C. 1995. 'Gewichte in der älteren römischen Kaiserzeit. Zum Einfluß des römischen uncialen Gewichtssystems in der Germania am Beispiel elbgermanischen Trachtzubehörs', in Busch, R. (ed.), *Rom an der Niederelbe*. Hamburg: 113-124.

Eggers, H.-J. 1951. *Der römische Import im freien Germanien*. Hamburg: Hamburgisches Museum für Völkerkunde und Vorgeschichte.

Eggers, H.-J. 1955. 'Zur absoluten Chronologie der römischen Kaiserzeit im Freien Germanien', *Jahrbuch des Römisch-Germanischen Zentralmusems* 2: 196-244.

Eggers, H.-J. 1966. 'Römische Bronzegefäße in Britannien', *Jahrbuch des Römisch-Germanischen Zentral-museums Mainz* 13: 67-164.

Ejstrud, B. 2005. 'Size matters: estimating trade of wine, oil and fish sauce from amphorae in the first century AD' in Bekker-Nielsen, T. (ed.), *Ancient Fishing and Fish Processing in the Black Sea Region*. Aarhus: Aarhus University Press: 171-181.

Ekholm, G. 1937. 'Handelsvägarna mellan Skandinavien och det Romerska Riket', *Scandia* 10: 149-164.

Elkington, H. D. H. 1976. 'The Mendip lead industry', in (eds.), Branigan, K. and Fowler, P. J. *The Roman West Country*. Newton Abbot: David and Charles: 183-197.

Erdrich, M. 1995a. 'Rom und die germanischen Stämme in Niedersachsen', in Busch, R. (ed.), *Rom an der Niederelbe*. Hamburg: 47-70.

Erdrich, M. 1995b. 'Zur Herstellung von Hemmoorer Eimern', in Mols, S. T. A. M. Gerhartl-Witteveen, A. M. Kars, H. Koster, A. Peters, W. J. Th. and Willems, W. J. H. (eds.), *Acta of the 12th International Congress on Ancient Bronzes, Nijmegen 1992*. Amersfoort: 33-38.

Erdrich, M. 1999. 'Continuity or discontinuity: Native and Roman metal finds', in Besteman, J. C. *et al.* (eds.), *The Excavations at Wijnaldum: Reports on Frisia in Roman and Medieval Times*. Volume 1. Rotterdam: A.A. Balkema: 171-183.

Erdrich, M. 2001. *Rom und die Barbaren: Das verhältnis zwischen dem Imperium romanum und den germanischen Stämmen vor seiner Nordwestgrenze von der späten römischen Republik bis zum gallischen Sonderreich*. Mainz am Rhein: Verlag Phillipp von Zabern.

Erdrich, M. 2002. *Corpus der römischen Funde im europäischen Barbaricum. Deutschland Band 4: Hansestadt Bremen und Bundesland Niedersachsen*. Bonn: Dr. Rudolf Habelt GMBH.

Erdrich, M. and Carnap-Bornheim, C. 2004. *Corpus der römischen Funde im europäischen Barbaricum. Deutschland Band 5: Freie und Hansestadt Hamburg und Land Schleswig-Holstein*. Bonn: Dr. Rudolf Habelt GMBH.

Esmonde Cleary, S. 1989. *The Ending of Roman Britain*. London: Batsford.

Esmonde Cleary, S. 2003. 'Civil defences in the West under the High Empire' in Wilson, P. (ed.), *The Archaeology of Roman Towns*. Oxford: Oxbow: 72-85.

Esmonde Cleary, S. 2009. 'Review of: Simmonds *et al.* 2008. *Life and Death in a Roman City: Excavation of a Roman Cemetery with a Mass Grave at 120–122 London Road, Gloucester*', *Britannia* 40: 389-390.

Etienne, R. and Mayet, F. 2004. *L'huile hispanique*. Paris: De Boccard.

Ettlinger, E. 1973. *Die Römischen Fibeln in der Schweiz*. Bern: Francke Verlag.

Ettlinger, E. Hedinger, B. Hoffmann, B. Kenrick, P. M. Pucci, G. Roth-Rubi, K. Schneider, G. Schnurbein, S. von, Wells, C. M. and Zabehlicky-Scheffenegger, S. 1990. *Conspectus formarum terrae sigillatae Italico modo confectae*. Materialien zur römisch-germanischen Keramik 10. Bonn: R. Habelt.

Evans, A. J. 1890. 'On a Late-Celtic urn-field at Aylesford, Kent', *Archaeologia* 52: 315-388.

Evans, E. 2000. *The Caerleon Canabae. Excavations in the Civil Settlement 1984-90*. London: Society for the Promotion of Roman Studies.

Evans, J. 2001. In Leach, P. *Fosse Lane, Shepton Mallet, 1990: Excavation of a Romano-British Roadside Settlement in Somerset*. London: Society for the Promotion of Roman Studies.

Everson, P. and Knowles, G. C. 1978. 'A tutulus brooch from Kirmington, Lincolnshire', *Medieval Archaeology* 22: 123-127.

Evison, V. I. 1977. 'Supporting-arm brooches and equal-arm brooches in England', *Studien zur Sachsenforschung* 1. Hildesheim: 127-147.

Exner, K. 1939. 'Die provinzialrömischen Emailfibeln der Rheinlande', *Bericht der Römisch-Germanischen Kommission* 29: 31-121.

Fairhurst, H. 1984. *Excavations at Crosskirk broch, Caithness*. Edinburgh: Society of Antiquaries of Scotland.

Farid, S. 2000. 'Excavation at Old Church Street, Kensington and Chelsea', *Transactions of the London and Middlesex Archaeological Society* 51: 115-141.

Fauduet, I. 1999. *Fibules préromaines, romaines et mérovingiennes du musée du Louvre, Département des antiquités grecques, étrusques et romaines*. Paris: Presses de l'ecole Normale Supérieure.

Feachem, R. W., 1951. 'Dragonesque fibulae', *The Antiquaries Journal* 31: 32-44.

Fentress, E. Fontana, S. Hitchner, R. B. and Perkins, P. 2004. 'Accounting for ARS: Fineware and Sites in Sicily and Africa', in Alcock, S. E. and Cherry, J. F. (eds.), *Side by Side Survey: Comparative Regional Studies in the Mediterranean World*. Oxford: Oxbow: 147-162.

Feugère. M. 1985. *Les fibulas en Gaul Méridionale*. Paris.

Feugère, M. and de Marinis, R. 1991. 'Les Poêlons', in Feugère, M. and Rolley, C. (eds.), *La Vaisselle tardo-républicaine en bronze*. Université de Bourgogne, Centre de recherches sur les techniques gréco-romaines 13. Dijon: 97-112.

Finley, M. I. 1973. *The Ancient Economy*. London: Chatto and Windus.

Fischer, T. 1999. 'Materialhorte des 3. Jhs. In den römischen Grenzprovinzen zwischen Niedergermanien und Noricum', in Tejral, J. (ed.), *Das mitteleuropäische Barbaricum und die Krise des römischen Weltreiches im 3. Jahrhundert*. Brno: 19-50.

Fischer, U. 1998. *Grabungen im Römischen vicus von Nida-Heddernheim 1961-1962*. Frankfurt.

Fitzpatrick, A. P. 1985. 'The distribution of Dressel 1 amphorae in north west Europe', *Oxford Journal of Archaeology* 4: 305-340.

Fitzpatrick, A. P. 1989. 'The uses of Roman imperialism by the Celtic barbarians in the later Republic', in Barrett, J. C. *et al.* (eds.), *Barbarians and Romans in North-West Europe: From the Later Republic to Late Antiquity*. BAR International Series 471. Oxford: 27-54.

Fitzpatrick, A. P. 1992. 'The roles of Celtic coinage in south-east England' in Mays, M. (ed.), *Celtic Coinage in Britain and beyond; the Eleventh Oxford Symposium on Coinage and Monetary History*. BAR British Series 222. Oxford: BAR Publishing: 1-32.

Fitzpatrick, A. P. 1993. 'Ethnicity and exchange: Germans, Celts and Romans in the late Iron Age', in Scarre, C. and Healy, F. (ed.), *Trade and Exchange in Prehistoric Europe*. Oxford: 233-44.

Fitzpatrick, A. P. 2001. 'Cross-Channel exchange, Hengistbury Head, and the end of hillforts' in Collis, J. (ed.), *Society and Settlement in Iron Age Europe*. Sheffield: J. R. Collis Publications: 82-97.

Fitzpatrick, A. P. 2003a. 'Roman amphorae in Iron Age Britain', *Journal of Roman Pottery Studies 10. Amphorae in Britain and the Western Empire*: 10-25.

Fitzpatrick, A. P. 2003b. 'The place of Gaulish wine in the military supply of amphorae-borne commodities to Roman Scotland', in Plouviez, J. (ed.), *Journal of Roman Pottery Studies 10. Amphorae in Britain and the Western Empire*: 60-63.

Fitzpatrick, A. P. and Timby, J. 2002. 'Roman pottery in Iron Age Britain', in Woodward, A and Hill, J. D. (eds.), *Prehistoric Britain: the Ceramic Basis*. Oxford: Oxbow: 161-172.

Fonnesbach-Sandberg, E. 2006. 'Torstorp Vesterby: a cemetery from the Late Roman Iron Age', *Journal of Danish Archaeology* 14: 109-125.

Fontjin, D. 2009. 'Land at the other end of the sea? Metalwork circulation, geographical knowledge and the significance of British/Irish imports in the Bronze Age of the Low Countries', in Clark, P. (ed.), 2009. *Bronze Age Connections: Cultural Contact in Prehistoric Europe*. Oxford: Oxbow: 129-148.

Foord, A. S. 1890. *Transactions of the Norfolk and Norwich Naturalists' Society*. 5: 92-5.

Foreman, S. and Maynard, D. 2002. 'A late Iron Age and Romano-British farmstead at Ship Lane, Aveley. Excavations on the line of the A13 Wennington to Mar Dyke road improvement, 1994-5', *Essex Archaeology and History* 33: 123-156.

Forster, R. H. and Knowles, W. H. 1911. 'Corstopitum: report of the excavations in 1910', *Archaeologia Aeliana* Ser. 3 Vol. 7: 143-267.

Foster, J. 1986. *The Lexden Tumulus. A Reappraisal of an Iron Age Burial from Colchester, Essex*. BAR British Series 156. Oxford.

Foster, J. 1996. 'Metalworking in the British Iron Age: the evidence from Weelsby Avenue, Grimsby', in Raftery, B. (eds.), *Sites and Sights of the Iron Age*. Oxford: Oxbow: 49-61.

Fox, A. 1940. The Legionary Fortress at Caerleon, Monmouthshire: Excavations in Myrtle Cottage Orchard, 1939. London: W. Pickering.

Fox, C. F. 1932. The Personality of Britain: its Influence on Inhabitant and Invader in Prehistoric and Early Historic Times. Cardiff: National Museum of Wales and the Press Board of the University of Wales.

Fox, C. 1958. *Pattern and Purpose: a Survey of Early Celtic Art in Britain*. Cardiff: National Museum of Wales.

Fradley, M. 2009. 'The field archaeology of the Romano-British settlement at Charterhouse-on-Mendip', *Britannia* 40: 99-122.

Frankenstein, S. and Rowlands, M. J. 1978. 'Early Iron Age Society in southwest Germany' *Bulletin of the Institute of Archaeology, University of London*. 15: 73-112.

Frere, S. S. Hassall, M. C. W. and Tomlin, R. S. O. 1988. 'Roman Britain in 1988', *Britannia* 20: 257-345.

Friesinger, H. Tejral, J. and Stuppner, A. (eds.), 1994. *Markomannenkriege. Ursachen und Wirkungen. VI. Internationales Symposium "Grundprobleme der frühgeschichtlichen Entwicklung im nördlichen Mitteldonaugebiet" Wien 23-26 November 1993*. Brno: Archäologisches Institut der Akademie der Wissenschaften der Tschechischen Republik.

Frere, S. S. 1978. *Britannia. A History of Roman Britain* (third edition). London: Routledge and Kegan Paul.

Frere, S. S. and Fulford, M. 2001. 'The Roman invasion of A.D. 43', *Britannia* 32: 45-55.

Frere, S. S. and Wilkes, J. J. 1989. *Strageath: Excavations within the Roman Fort, 1973-86*. London: Society for the Promotion of Roman Studies.

Frölich, A. 'The armamentarium of the army surgeon', in Jørgensen, L. *et al.* (eds.), *The Spoils of Victory: the North in the Shadow of the Roman Empire*. Copenhagen: Nationalmuseet: 342-343.

Fulford, M. G. 1975. *New Forest Roman Pottery*. BAR British Series 17. Oxford.

Fulford, M. G. 1977. 'Pottery and Britain's foreign trade in the Later Roman period', in Peacock , D. P. S. (ed.), *Pottery and Early Commerce. Characterization and Trade in Roman and Later Ceramics*. London: Academic Press: 35-84.

Fulford, M. G. 1978. 'The interpretation of Britain's late Roman trade: The scope of medieval historical and archaeological analogy', in du Plat Taylor, J. and Cleere, H. (eds.), *Roman Shipping and Trade: Britain and the Rhine Provinces*. London: The Council for British Archaeology: 59-69.

Fulford, M. G. 1984. 'Demonstrating Britannia's economic dependence in the first and second centuries', in Blagg, T. F. C. and King, A. C. (eds.), *Military and Civilian in Roman Britain: Cultural Relationships in a Frontier Province*. BAR British Series 136. Oxford: 129-142.

Fulford, M. G. 1985. 'Roman material in Barbarian society', in Champion and Megaw (eds.), *Settlement and Society: Aspects of West European Prehistory in the First Millennium BC*. Leicester: Leicester University Press: 91-108.

Fulford, M. G. 1989a. 'The economy of Roman Britain', in Todd, M. (ed.), *Research on Roman Britain 1960-89*. London: 175-201.

Fulford, M. G. 1989b. 'A Roman shipwreck off Nornour, Isles of Scilly?', *Britannia* 20: 245-249.

Fulford, M. G. 1989c. 'Byzantium and Britain', *Medieval Archaeology* 33: 1-6.

Fulford, M. G. 1991. 'Britain and the Roman Empire: the evidence for regional and long distance trade', in Jones, R. F. J. (ed.), *Roman Britain: Recent Trends*. Sheffield: J. R. Collis: 35-47.

Fulford, M. G. 1996. 'Economic hotspots and provincial backwaters: modelling the late Roman economy', in King, C. E. and Wigg, D. G. (eds.), *Coin Finds and Coin Use in the Roman World*. Berlin: Mann Verlag: 153-177.

Fulford, M. G. 2004. 'Economic structures', in Todd, M. (ed.), *A Companion to Roman Britain*. Oxford: Blackwell: 309-326.

Fulford, M. G. 2006. 'An industrial agglomeration in Britain', *Journal of Roman Archaeology* 19: 607-609.

Fulford, M. G. 2007. 'Coasting Britannia: Roman trade and traffic around the shores of Britain', in Gosden, C. Hamerow, H. de Jersey, P. and Lock, G. (ed.), *Communities and Connections: Essays in Honour of Barry Cunliffe*. Oxford: Oxbow: 54-74.

Fulford, M. G. Forthcoming. 'The pull of the north: Gallo-Roman sigillata in Britain in the second and third centuries', in Wilson, A. I. and Bowman, A. K. (eds.), *Trade, Commerce and the State in the Roman World*. Oxford Studies in the Roman Economy. Oxford: Oxford University Press.

Fulford, M. G. and Allen, J. R. L. 1992. 'Iron-making at the Chesters Villa, Woolaston, Gloucestershire: Survey and excavation 1987-91', *Britannia* 23: 159-215.

Fulford, M. G. and Bird, J. 1975. 'Imported pottery from Germany in Late Roman Britain', *Britannia* 6: 171-181.

Fulford, M. G. Clarke, A. and Eckhardt, H. 2006. *Life and Labour in Late Roman Silchester: Excavations in Insula IX since 1997*. Britannia Monograph Series 22. London: Society for the Promotion of Roman Studies.

Fulford, M. G. Timby, J. 2000. *Late Iron Age and Roman Silchester: Excavations on the Site of the Forum-Basilica 1977, 1980-86*. Britannia Monograph Series no.15. London: Society for the Promotion of Roman Studies.

Fulford, M. G. and Tyers, I. 1995. 'The date of Pevensey and the defence of an '*Imperium Britanniarum*'', *Antiquity* 69: 1009-1014.

Fülle, G. 1997. 'The internal organisation of the Arretine *terra-sigillata* industry: problems of evidence and interpretation', *Journal of Roman Studies* 87: 111-155.

Funari, P. P. A. 1996. *Dressel 20 Inscriptions from Britain and the Consumption of Spanish Olive Oil*. BAR British Series 250. Oxford: BAR Publishing.

Funari, P. P. A. 2002. 'The consumption of olive oil in Roman Britain and the role of the army', in Erdkamp, P. (ed.), *The Roman Army and the Economy*. Amsterdam: Gieben: 235-263.

Galestin, M. C. 1993. 'A fourth-century silver hoard from Winsum in the province of Friesland (The Netherlands)', *Bulletin Antieke Beschaving* 68: 257-261.

Galestin, M. C. 1994. 'A new Mars from the Netherlands', *Akten der 10. Internationalen Tagung über antike Bronzen*. Stuttgart: Konrad Theiss: 155-159.

Galestin, M. C. 1997. 'Romans and Frisians: analysis of the strategy of the Roman army in its connections across the frontier', in Groenman-van Waateringe, W. *et al.* (eds). *Roman Frontier Studies 1995: Proceedings of the XVIth International Conference of Roman Frontier Studies*. Oxford: Oxbow: 347-353.

Galestin, M. C. 1999. 'Roman wheelthrown pottery, terra nigra-like bowls and tiles', in Besteman, J. C. *et al.* (eds.), *The Excavations at Wijnaldum: Reports on Frisia in Roman and Medieval Times*. Volume 1. Rotterdam: A.A. Balkema: 157-169.

Galestin, M. C. 2001. 'The interpretation of Roman coin hoards', in Nijboer, A. J. (ed.), *Interpreting Deposits: Linking Ritual with Economy: Papers on Mediterranean Archaeology*. Groningen: 81-100.

Galestin, M. C. 2002a. 'Early Roman military activity on the Frisian coast', in Freeman, P. *et al.* (eds.), *Limes XVIII. Proceedings of the XVIIIth International Congress of Roman Frontier Studies held in Amman, Jordan (September 2000)*. BAR International Series 1084 (I). Oxford: BAR Publishing: 483-488.

Galestin, M. C. 2002b. 'Winsum-Bruggeburen, first report on the excavation. The Roman coins', *Palaeohistoria* 41/42 (1999/2000): 225-235.

Galestin, M. C. 2003a. 'Winsum-Bruggeburen, second report on the excavation. The Roman pottery', *Palaeohistoria* 43/44 (2001/2): 435-467.

Galestin, M. C. 2003b. 'Winsum-Bruggeburen, third report on the excavation. Bronze and other Roman finds', *Palaeohistoria* 43/44 (2001/2): 469-482.

Galestin, M. C. 2005. 'Barriers for barbarians?', in Visy, Z. (ed.), *Limes XIX. Proceedings of the XIXth International Congress of Roman Frontier Studies Pécs, Hungary, September 2003*: Pécs: 221-226.

Galestin, M. C. 2010. 'Roman artefacts beyond the northern frontier: interpreting the evidence from the Netherlands', *European Journal of Archaeology* 13 (1): 64-88.

Galestin, M. C. and Volkers, T. B. 1992. *Terpen en Terpvondsten in Friesland*. Groningen: Archeologisch Centrum Rijksuniversiteit Groningen.

Galliou, P. 1981. 'Western Gaul in the third century', in King, A. and Henig, M. (eds.), *The Roman West in the Third Century*. BAR International Series 109. Oxford: 259-286.

Garrard, T. F. 1982. 'Myth and metrology: the early trans-Saharan gold trade', *Journal of African History* 23: 443-461.

Garwood, A. 2004. 'Late Roman buildings at Bishop's House, Great Chesterford: excavations 1999', *Essex Archaeology and History* 35: 1-25.

Gentry, A. Ivens, J. and McClean, H. 1977. 'Excavations at Lincoln Road, London borough of Enfield, November 1974-March 1976', *Transactions of the London and Middlesex Archaeological Society* 28: 101-189.

Gerharz, R. R. von. 1987. 'Fibeln aus Afrika', *Saalburg Jaarbuch* 43: 77-107.

Gerrard, J. 2008. 'Feeding the Army from Dorset: Pottery, Salt and the Roman State', in Stallibrass, S. and Thomas, R. (eds.), *Feeding the Roman Army: the Archaeology of Production and Supply in NW Europe*. Oxford: Oxbow: 116-127.

Gerrard, J. 2009. 'The Draper's Gardens hoard: a preliminary account', *Britannia* 40: 163-183.

Gerrets, D. A. 1999. 'Conclusions', in Besteman, J. C. *et al.* (eds.), *The Excavations at Wijnaldum: Reports on Frisia in Roman and Medieval times*. Volume 1. Rotterdam: A.A. Balkema: 331-342.

Gil, E. Filloy, I and Iriarte, A. 2000. 'Late Roman equipment from the city of Iruña/Veleia (Álava, Spain)', *Journal of Roman Military Equipment Studies* 11: 25-35.

Gillam, J. 1984. 'A note on the numeri Brittonum', in Miket, R. and Burgess, C. (eds.), *Between and Beyond the Walls*. Edinburgh: John Donald: 287-294.

Gilliam, J. F. 1961. 'The Plague under Marcus Aurelius', *The American Journal of Philology* 82.3 (July 1961): 225–251.

Glasbergen, W. 1944. '*Terra sigillata* uit de province Groningen', *Jaarverslag*: 317-368.

Glasbergen, W. 1972. *De Romeinse Castella te Valkenburg Z.H.* Cingula 1. Amsterdam.

Glüsing, P. 1989. 'Die Germanen im Spannungsfeld der römischen Okkupation', in Trier, B. (ed.), *2000 Jahre Römer in Westfalen*. Mainz: 70-80.

Godłowski, K. 1984. '"Superiores Barbari" und die Markomannenkriege im Lichte archäologischer Qullen', *Slovenská Archeológia* XXXII 2: 327-346.

Godłowski, K. 1985. *Der römische Handel in die Germania libera aufgrund der archäologischen Quellen. Untersuchungen zu Handel und Verkehr derv or- und frühgeschlichen Zeit in Mittel- und Nordeuropa. Teil I. Abhandlungen der Akademie der Wissenschaften in Göttingen*. Göttingen.

Going, C. J. 1992. 'Economic 'Long Waves' in the Roman Period? A Reconnaissance of the Romano-British Ceramic Evidence', *Oxford Journal of Archaeology* 11 (1): 93-117.

Going, C. J. and Hunn, J. R. 1999. *Excavations at Boxfield Farm, Chells, Stevenage, Hertfordshire*. Hertford: Hertfordshire Archaeological Trust.

Gorin-Rosen, Y. 2000. 'The ancient glass industry in Israel: summary of the finds and new discoveries', in Nenna, M. D. (ed.), *La Route de Verre: ateliers primaires et secondaires du second millénaire av. J.-C. au Moyen Age*. Lyon: Maison de l'Orient Méditerranéen-Jean Pouilloux: 49-63.

Gosden, C. 1985. 'Gifts and kin in Early Iron Age Europe', *Man* 20: 475-493.

Grane, T. 2003. 'Roman sources for the geography and ethnography of Germania', in Jørgensen, L. *et al.* (eds.), *The Spoils of Victory: the North in the Shadow of the Roman Empire*. Copenhagen: Nationalmuseet: 126-147.

Grane, T. 2007. *The Roman Empire and Southern Scandinavia- a Northern Connection! A Re-evaluation of Military-Political Relations Between the Roman Empire and the Barbaricum in the First Three Centuries AD with a Special Emphasis on Southern Scandinavia*. Unpublished PhD thesis. University of Copenhagen.

Green, C. M. 1980. 'The Roman pottery', in Jones, D. M. *Excavations at Billingsgate Buildings 'Triangle', Lower Thames Street 1974*. London: London and Middlesex Archaeological Society: 39-79.

Green, C. M. 1986. In Miller, L. Schofield, J. and Rhodes, M. *The Roman Quay at St Magnus House, London*. London: London and Middlesex Archaeological Society.

Green, H. J. M. 1975. 'Roman Godmanchester', in Rodwell, W. and Rowley, R. (eds.), *The Small Towns of Roman Britain*. BAR 15. Oxford: 183-210.

Greenberg, J. 2003. 'Plagued by doubt: reconsidering the impact of a mortality crisis in the 2nd c. A.D', *Journal of Roman Archaeology* 16: 413-425.

Greene, K. 1978. 'Roman trade between Britain and the Rhine provinces: the evidence of pottery to c AD 250', in du Plat Taylor, J. and Cleere, H. (eds.), *Roman Shipping and Trade: Britain and the Rhine Provinces*. CBA London: Council for British Archaeology: 52-58.

Greene, K. T. 1979. *The Pre-Flavian Fine Wares*. Report on the excavations at Usk, 1965-1976, 1. Cardiff: University of Wales Press (for) the Board of Celtic Studies of the University of Wales.

Greene, K. 1986. *The Archaeology of the Roman Economy*. London: Batsford.

Gregarek, H. 1997. 'Der Hildesheimer Silberfund', in von Prittwitz Und Gaffron, H.-H. and Mielsch, H. (eds.), *Das Haus lacht vor Silber. Die Prunkplatte von Bizerta und das römische Tafelgeschirr*. Cologne: 91-98.

Gregory, C. A. 1982. *Gifts and Commodities*. London: Academic Press.

Gregory, C. A. 2000. *Savage Money: The Anthropology and Politics of Commodity exchange*. London: Routledge.

Gregory, R. A. 2007. *Roman Manchester: the University of Manchester's Excavations within the Vicus 2001-5*. Oxford: Oxbow.

Gregory, T. 1996. *A Romano-British Farmyard at Weeting, Norfolk*. Dereham.

Grew, F. O. Hassall, M. W. C. and Tomlin, R. S. O. 1981. 'Roman Britain in 1980', *Britannia* 12: 313-396.

Grimaldi, D. A. 1996. *Amber: Window to the Past*. New York: Harry. N. Abrams, Inc. in association with the American Museum of Natural History.

Grimm, O. 2001. 'Norwegian boathouses from the Late Roman and Migration Periods. An analysis of their military function', in Storgaard, B. (ed.), *Military Aspects of the Aristocracy in Barbaricum in the Roman and Early Migration Periods*. Copenhagen: 55-66.

Groenenwoudt, B. J. and van Nie, M. 1995. 'Assessing the scale and organisation of Germanic iron production at Heeten, the Netherlands', *Journal of European Archaeology* 3.2: 187-215.

Groenman-van Waateringe, W. 1986. 'The Horrea of Valkenburg Z.H', in Unz, C. *et al.* (eds.), *Studien zu den Militärgrenzen Roms III. 13. Internationaler Limeskongress, Aalen 1983*. Stuttgart: 159-167.

Groenman-van Waateringe, W. 1989. 'Food for soldiers, food for thought', in Barrett, J. C. *et al.* (eds.), *Barbarians and Romans in North-West Europe: from the Later Republic to Late Antiquity*. BAR International Series 471. Oxford: 96-107.

Groot, M. 2008. 'Surplus production of animal products for the Roman army in a rural settlement in the Dutch River Area', in Stallibrass, S. and Thomas, R. (eds.), *Feeding the Roman Army: the Archaeology of Production and Supply in NW Europe*. Oxford: Oxbow: 83-98.

Gruat, P. 1993. 'A propos de deux marques consulaires peintes sur amphores vinaires Italiques de type Dressel 1 trouvées à Rodez (Aveyron)', *Aquitania* 11: 236-242.

Gruel, K. and Haselgrove, C. 2007. 'British potins abroad: a new find from central France and the Iron Age in southeast England', in Gosden, C. Hamerow, H. de Jersey, P. and Lock, G. (eds.), *Communities and Connections: Essays in Honour of Barry Cunliffe*. Oxford: Oxbow: 241-262.

Gruen, E. S. 1996. 'The expansion of the Empire under Augustus' in Bowman, A. K. Champlin, E. and Lintott, A. (eds.), *The Cambridge Ancient History. Volume 10. The Augustan Empire, 43 B.C.-A.D. 69*. Cambridge: Cambridge University Press: 147-197.

Guest, P. and Popovitch, L. 2000. 'Plenty of Bricks but Where's the Mortar? Ancient Coin Hoards from France (reviews X. Loriot, D. Nony and H. Huvelin (eds.), *Corpus des trésors monétaires antiques de la France. Tome VII. Auvergne; Tome VIII/1. Picardie: Somme; Tome VII/2. Picardie/ Aisne et Oise; Tome IX. Ile-de-France*)', *Britannia* 31: 451-4

Guillaumet, J-P. and Schönfelder, M. 2001. 'Un manche de miroir de type britannique provenant de Compiègne; un nouveau témoignage des contacts à travers la Manche'. *Antiquités Nationales* 33: 125-128.

Guštin, M. 1996. 'Die Kelten von der Adria und ihre Nachbarn. Zu der Bernsteinfrage des West- und Zentralbalkans in der Jüngeren Eisenzeit' in Woźniak, Z. (ed.), *Kontakte längs der Bernsteinstraße (Zwischen Caput Adriae und den Ostseegebieten in der Zeit um Christi Geburt*. Kraków: 15-21.

Haalebos, J. K. 1986. *Fibulae uit Maurik.* (= *Oudheidkundige Mededelingen uit het Rijksmuseum van Oudheden te Leiden*, Supplement 65). Leiden: Rijksmuseum van Oudheden.

Haarnagel, W. 1979. *Die Grabung Feddersen Wierde. Methode, Hausbau, Siedlungs und Wirtschaftsformen, sowie Sozialstruktur. Feddersen Wierde. Die Ergebnisse der Ausgrabung der vorgeschichtlichen Wurt Feddersen Wierde bei Bremerhaven in den Jahren 1955 bis 1963*. Bd. II. Wiesbaden: Steiner.

Haley, E. W. 2003. *Baetica Felix. People and Prosperity in Southern Spain from Caesar to Septimius Severus*. Austin: University of Texas Press.

Hamilton, S. 2007. 'Cultural choices in the 'British Eastern Channel Area' in the Late Pre-Roman Iron Age', in Haselgrove, C. and Moore, T. (eds.), *The Later Iron Age in Britain and Beyond*. Oxford: Oxbow: 81-106.

Hachmann, R. 1990. 'Gundestrup-Studien: Untersuchungen zu den spätkeltischen Grundlagen der frühgermanischen Kunst', *Bericht der Römisch-Germanischen Kommission* 71: 565-903.

Hagberg, U.E. 1967. *The Archaeology of Skedemosse II. The Votive Deposits in the Skedemosse Fen and their Relation to the Iron-Age Settlement on Öland, Sweden*. Stockholm: Almqvist and Wiskell.

Hamilton-Dyer, S. 2008. *Suburban Life in Roman Durnovaria* 6. Environmental fishbone from selected contexts. Additional specialist report.

Harding, D. W. and Dixon, T. N. 2000. *Dun Bharabhat, Cnip: an Iron Age Settlement in West Lewis*. Volume 1. Calanais Research Series No. 2. Edinburgh.

Harris, W. V. 1993. 'Between archaic and modern: some current problems in the history of the Roman economy', in Harris, W. V. (ed.), *The Inscribed Economy Production and Distribution in the Roman Empire in the Light of Instrumentum Domesticum*. Journal of Roman Archaeology Supplement 6. Ann Arbor: 11-29.

Harris, W. V. 2006. 'A revisionist view of Roman money', *Journal of Roman Studies* 96: 1-24.

Harris, W. V. 2008. *The Monetary Systems of the Greeks and Romans*. Oxford: Oxford University Press.

Hartley, B. R. and Williams, D. F. 1988. In Potter, T. W. and Trow, S. D. 'Puckeridge-Braughing, Herts: The Ermine Street excavations, 1971-1972', *Hertfordshire Archaeology* 10: 1-191.

Hartz, S. and Segschneider, M. 2006. 'Helgolands-Agaten', *Skalk* Nr. 4 (August 2006): 9-11.

Haselgrove, C. 1977. *Supplementary Gazeteer of Find-spots of Celtic Coins in Britain, 1977*. London: Institute of Archaeology.

Haselgrove, C. 1982. 'Wealth, prestige and power: the dynamics of late Iron Age political centralization in south-east England', in Renfrew, A. C. and Shennan, S. (eds.), *Ranking, Resource and Exchange*. Cambridge: Cambridge University Press: 79-88.

Haselgrove, C. 1984a. ''Romanization' before the conquest: Gaulish precedents and British consequences', in Blagg, T. F. C. and King, A. (eds.), *Military and Civilian in Roman Britain*. BAR 136. Oxford: 5-63.

Haselgrove, C. 1984b. 'Warfare and its aftermath as reflected in the precious metal coinage of Belgic Gaul', *Oxford Journal of Archaeology* 3, 1: 81-105.

Haselgrove, C. 1987a. *Iron Age Coinage in South-East England: The Archaeological Context*. BAR British Series 174. Oxford.

Haselgrove, C. 1992. 'Iron Age coinage and archaeology', in Mays, M. (ed.), *Celtic Coinage in Britain and Beyond; the Eleventh Oxford Symposium on Coinage and Monetary History*. BAR British Series 222. Oxford: BAR Publishing: 123-137.

Haselgrove, C. 1993. 'The development of British Iron-Age coinage', *The Numismatic Chronicle* 153: 31-63.

Haselgrove, C. 1995. 'Late Iron Age Society in Britain and north-west Europe: structural transformation or superficial change?', in Arnold, B. and Gibson, D. B. (eds.), *Celtic Chiefdom, Celtic State*. Cambridge: Cambridge University Press: 81-87.

Haselgrove, C. 1996a. 'Roman impact on rural settlement and society in southern Picardy', in Roymans, N. (ed.), *From the Sword to the Plough. Three Studies on the Earliest Romanisation of Northern Gaul*. Amsterdam: Amsterdam University Press: 127-187.

Haselgrove, C. 1996b. 'Iron Age Coinage: recent work', in Champion, T. C. and Collis, J. R. (ed.), *The Iron Age in Britain and Ireland: Recent Trends*. Sheffield: JR Collis publications: 67-85.

Haselgrove, C. 1999. 'The development of Iron Age coinage in Belgic Gaul', *The Numismatic Chronicle* 159: 111-168.

Haselgrove, C. 2000. 'Archaeological dating of Iron Age coinage in northern France', in Kluge, B. and Weisser, B. (ed.), *XII. Internationaler Numismatischer Kongress, Berlin 1997*. Berlin: Staatliche Museen zu Berlin: 409-417.

Haselgrove, C. 2006a. 'The impact of the Roman conquest on indigenous coinages', in De Jersey, P. (ed.), *Celtic Coinage: New Discoveries, New Discussion*. BAR International Series 1532. Oxford: BAR Publishing: 97-115.

Haselgrove, C. 2006b. 'Early potin coinage in Britain: an update', in De Jersey, P. (ed.), *Celtic Coinage: New Discoveries, New Discussion*. BAR International Series 1532. Oxford: BAR Publishing: 17-27.

Hassall, M. 1970. 'Batavians and the Roman conquest of Britain', *Britannia* 1: 131-136.

Hassall, M. 1977. 'The historical background and military units of the Saxon Shore', in Johnston, D. E. (ed.), *The Saxon Shore*. CBA Research Report 18: 7-10.

Hassall, M. 1978. 'Epigraphic evidence for Roman trade', in du Plat Taylor, J. and Cleere, H. (eds.), *Roman Shipping and Trade: Britain and the Rhine Provinces*. London: Council for British Archaeology: 41-48.

Hassall, M. 2000. 'The Army', in Bowman, A. K. Garnsey, P. Rathbone, D. (eds.), *Cambridge Ancient History. Volume 11. The High Empire A.D. 70-192*. Cambridge: Cambridge University Press: 320-343.

Hassall, M. and Rhodes, J. 1974. 'Excavations at the new Market Hall, Gloucester, 1966-7', *Transactions of the Bristol and Gloucester Archaeological Society* xciii: 15-100.

Hattatt, R. 1987. *Brooches of Antiquity: a Third Selection of Brooches from the Author's Collection*. Oxford: Oxbow.

Hatton, R. and Wall, W. 2006. 'A late Roman cemetery at Durobrivae, Chesterton', *Proceedings of the Cambridge Antiquarian Society* 95: 5-23.

Haverfield, F. J. 1905. 'Romano-British Derbyshire', in Page, W. (ed.), *Victoria County History of Derbyshire* Vol. 1. London: 191-263.

Hawkes, C. F. C. 1931. 'Hill forts', *Antiquity* 5: 60-97.

Hawkes, C. F. C. 1959. 'The ABC of the British Iron Age', *Antiquity* 33: 170-182.

Hawkes, C. F. C. 1968. 'New thoughts on the Belgae', *Antiquity* 42: 6-16.

Hawkes, C. F. C. 1984. 'Ictis disentangled, and the British tin trade', *Oxford Journal of Archaeology* 3 (2): 211-233.

Hawkes, C. F. C. and Crummy, P. 1995. *Camulodunum 2*. Colchester Archaeological Report 11. Colchester.

Hawkes, C. F. C. and Dunning, G. C. 1931. 'The Belgae of Gaul and Britain', *Archaeological Journal* 87 (1930): 150-335.

Hawkes, C. F. C. and Hull, M. R. 1947. *Camulodunum. First Report on the Excavations at Colchester 1930-1939*. Reports of the Research Committee of the Society of Antiquaries of London. No.XIV. Oxford.

Hawkes, S. C. and Dunning, G. C. 1961. 'Soldiers and Settlers in Britain, Forth to Fifth Century - With a Catalogue of Animal-Ornamented Buckles and Related Belt-Fittings', *Medieval Archaeology* 5: 1-70.

Haywood, J. 1999. *Dark Age Naval Power: a Reassessment of Frankish and Anglo-Saxon Activity* (second edition). London: Routledge.

Heald, A. and Jackson, A. 2001. 'Towards a new understanding of Iron Age Caithness',

Proceedings of the Society of Antiquaries of Scotland 131: 129-147.

Hedeager, L. 1978. 'A quantitative analysis of Roman imports in Europe north of the Limes (0-400 AD), and the question of Roman-Germanic exchange', in Kristiansen, K. and Paluden-Müller, C. (eds.), *New Directions in Scandinavian Archaeology*. Copenhagen: National Museum of Denmark: 191-216.

Hedeager, L. 1987. 'Empire, frontier and the barbarian hinterland: Rome and northern Europe from AD 1-400', in Rowlands, M. Larsen, M. and Kristiansen, K. (eds.), *Centre and Periphery in the Ancient World*. Cambridge: Cambridge University Press: 125-140.

Hedeager, L. 1992a. *Iron Age Societies: From Tribe to State in Northern Europe, 500 BC to AD 700*. Oxford: Blackwell.

Hedeager, L. 1992b. 'Kingdoms, ethnicity and material culture: Denmark in a European perspective', in M. Carver (ed.), *The Age of Sutton Hoo*. Woodbridge, Suffolk: Boydell: 279-300.

Heidinga, A. 1999. 'The Frisian achievement in the first millennium AD', *Anglo-Saxon Studies in Archaeology and History* 10: 11-16.

Helbaek, H. 1964. 'The Isca grain, A Roman plant introduction into Britain', *New Phytologist* 63: 158-164.

Hencken, T. C. 1939. 'The excavation of the Iron Age camp on Bredon Hill, Gloucestershire, 1935-1937', *The Archaeological Journal* XCV: 1-111.

Henderikx, P. A. 1986. 'The lower delta of the Rhine and the Maas: landscape and habitation from the Roman period to c. 1000', *Berichten Rijksdienst Oudheidkundig Bodemonderzoek* 36: 445-599.

Henig, M. 1972. 'The origin of some ancient British coin types', *Britannia* 3: 209-223.

Henig, M. 1984. 'Amber amulets (from Dorchester and Colchester)', *Britannia* 15: 244-246.

Henig, M. 1993. *Roman Sculpture from the Cotswold Region, with Devon and Cornwall. Corpus Signorum Imperii Romani*. Great Britain, Volume I, Fascicule 7. Oxford.

Henry, F. 1933. 'Émailleurs d'occident', *Préhistoire* 2: 65-143.

Hesnard, A. 1990. 'Les Amphores', in (eds) Duval, A. Morel, J. P. and Roman, Y. *Gaule interne et Gaule Méditerranéenne aux IIe et Ier siècle savant J.-C.: confrontations chronologiques*. Revue Archéologique de Narbonnaise Supplément 21. Paris: 47-54.

Hessing, W. A. M. 1995. 'Het Nederlandse kustgebied', in (eds.), Bechert, T. and Williams, W. J. H. *De Romeinse rijksgrens tussen Moezel en Noordzeekust*. Utrecht: 89-102.

Hettner, F. 1901. *Festschrift zur Feier des Hundertjährigen Bestehens der Gesellschaft für nützliche Forschungen in Trier. Drei Tempelbezirke im Trevererlände*. Trier: Kommissionsverlag der Fr. Lintz'schen Buchhandlung, Friedr. Val. Lintz.

Hiddink, H. A. 1999. *Germaanse samenlevingen tussen Rijn en Weser, 1ste eeuw voor-4de eeuw na Chr.* Amsterdam: Akademisch Proefschrift, Universiteit van Amsterdam.

Hill, J. D. 1995. 'The Pre-Roman Iron Age in Britain and Ireland (ca. 800 B.C. to A.D. 100): An overview', *Journal of World Prehistory* 9(1) (March 1995): 47-98.

Hill, J. D. 1997. 'The end of one kind of body and the beginning of another kind of body'? Toilet instruments and 'Romanization' in southern England during the first century AD', in Gwilt, A., and Haselgrove, C. (eds.), *Reconstructing Iron Age Societies. New Approaches to the British Iron Age*. Oxford: Oxbow: 96–107.

Hill, J. D. 2007. 'The dynamics of social change in Later Iron Age eastern and south-eastern England c.300 BC-AD 43', in Haselgrove, C. and Moore, T. (eds.), *The Later Iron Age in Britain and Beyond*. Oxford: Oxbow: 16-40.

Hill, J. D. Score, V. and Leins, I. 2006. 'Community, Politics and Sacrifice: The East Leicestershire hoard', *British Archaeology* 89 (July/Aug 2006): 34-9.

Hills, C. M. 1999. 'Spong Hill and the Adventeus Saxonum', in Karkov, C. E. Wickham-Crowley, K. M. and Young, B. K. (eds.), *Spaces of the Living and the Dead*. Oxford: Oxbow: 15-26.

Hinchliffe, J. and Green, C. S. 1985. *Excavations at Brancaster, 1974 and 1977*. Dereham.

Historisches Museum der Pfalz Speyer (ed.), 2007. *Geraubt und im Rhein versunken. Der Barbarenschatz* (second edition). Stuttgart: Theiss.

Hitchner, B. 2009. 'Coinage and metal supply', in Wilson, A. I. and Bowman, A. K. (eds.), *Quantifying the Roman Economy: Methods and Problems*, Oxford Studies in the Roman Economy 1. Oxford: Oxford University Press: 281-286.

Höckmann, O. 1993. 'Late Roman Rhine vessels from Mainz, Germany', *International Journal of Nautical Archaeology* 22: 125-135.

Hodges, R. 1982. *Dark Age Economics: the Origins of Towns and Trade AD 600-1000*. London: Duckworth.

Hodges, R. 2000. *Towns and Trade in the Age of Charlemagne*. London: Duckworth.

Hodgkinson, J. S. 1999. 'Romano-British iron production in the Sussex and Kent Weald: a review of current data', *Journal of the Historical Metallurgy Society* 33.2: 68-72.

Holbrook, N. 2001. 'Coastal trade around the southwest peninsula of Britain in the later Roman period: a summary of the evidence', *Proceedings of the Devon Archaeological Society* 59: 149-158.

Holbrook, N. and Bidwell, P. T. 1991. *Roman Finds from Exeter*. Exeter: Exeter City Council and the University of Exeter.

Holder, P. 1982. *The Roman Army in Britain*. London: B. T. Batsford.

Hollevoet, Y. 2004. 'Le site militaire d'Oudenburg et la Bretagne insulaire Durant l'Antiquité tardive; quelques elements inédits', in Vermeulen, F. Sas, K. and Dhaeze, W. (eds.), *Archaeology in Confrontation. Aspects of Roman Military Presence in the Northwest. Studies in Honour of Prof. Em. Hugo Thoen*. Gent: Academia Press: 335-342.

Holman, D. 2005. 'Iron Age coinage and settlement in East Kent', *Britannia* 36: 1-54.

Hong, S. Candelone, J. P. Patterson, C. C. and Boutron, C. F. 1996. 'History of ancient copper smelting pollution during Roman and medieval times recorded in Greenland ice', *Science* 272: 246-9.

Hope, V. M. 1997. 'Words and pictures: the interpretation of Romano-British tombstones', *Britannia* 28: 245-258.

Hopkins, K. 1980. 'Taxes and trade in the Roman Empire (200 BC- AD 400)', *The Journal of Roman Studies* 70: 101-125.

Horden, P. and Purcell, N. 2000. *The Corrupting Sea: a Study of Mediterranean History*. Oxford: Blackwell.

Horden, P. and Purcell, N. 2006. 'The Mediterranean and "the new thalassology"', *The American Historical Review* 111, 3.

Horn, H. G. 1987. *Die Römer in Nordrhein-Westfalen*. Stuttgart: Konrad Theiss Verlag.

Horsnæs, H. W. 2003. 'The coins in the bogs', in Jorgensen, L. *et al.* (eds.), *The Spoils of Victory: the North in the Shadow of the Roman Empire*. Copenhagen: Nationalmuseet: 330-340.

Horsnæs, H. W. 2008. 'Roman coins and their contexts in Denmark', in Bursche, A. Ciołek, R. and Wolters, R. (eds.), *Roman Coins Outside the Empire. Ways and Phases, Contexts and Functions. Proceedings of the ESF/SCH Exploratory Workshop Radziwill Palace, Nieborow (Poland), 3-6 September 2005*. Wetteren: Moneta: 135-145.

Hörter, F. Michels, F. X. Röder, J. 1951. 'Die Geschichte der Basalt Lava industrie von Mayen und Niedermendig. Part I: Vor und Frühgeschichte', *Jahrbuch für Geschichte und Kultur des Mittelrheins und seiner Nachbergebiete* 2-3 (1950-1): 1-32.

Howe, M. D. Perrin, J. R. and Mackreth, D. F. 1980. *Roman Pottery from the Nene Valley: a Guide*. Peterborough: Peterborough City Museum and Art Gallery.

Howgego, C. 1992. 'The supply and use of money in the Roman world 200 BC- AD 300', *The Journal of Roman Studies* 82: 1-31.

Howgego, C. 1994. 'Coin circulation and the integration of the Roman economy', *Journal of Roman Archaeology* 7: 5-21.

Huggett, J. W. 1988. 'Imported early Anglo-Saxon grave goods', *Medieval Archaeology* 32: 63-96.

Huisman, K. 1995. 'De Drususgrachten: een nieuwe hypothese', *Westerheem* 44: 188-194.

Humphrey, R. 2002. 'A Roman agricultural landscape at the Old Golf Course site, Mill Hill, Braintree', *Essex Archaeology and History* 33: 103-122.

Hunold, A. 2001. 'Mayen', in *Reallexikon der Germanischen Altertumskunde Von Johannes Hoops* Vol. 19 (*Luchs-Metrum*). Berlin/New York: Walter De Gruyter: 470-473.

Hunter, F. 1998. 390-391, in Main, L. 'Excavation of a timber round-house and broch at the Fairy Knowe, Buchlyvie, Stirlingshire, 1975-8' *Proceedings of the Society of Antiquaries of Scotland* 128: 293-417.

Hunter, F. 2007. 'Silver for the barbarians: Interpreting denarii hoards in North Britain and beyond', in Hingley, R. and Willis, S. (eds.), *Roman Finds: Context and Theory*. Oxford: Oxbow: 214-224.

Hutcheson, N. 2007. 'An archaeological investigation of Later Iron Age Norfolk: analysing hoarding patterns across the landscape', in Haselgrove, C. and Moore, T. (eds.), *The Later Iron Age in Britain and Beyond*. Oxford: Oxbow: 358-370.

Ilkjær, J. 1990. *Illerup Ådal 1-2. Die Lanzen und speere*. Højberg: Jysk Arkæologisk Selskab.

Ilkjær, J. 2002. *Illerup Ådal: Archaeology as a Magic Mirror*. Aarhus: Moesgård Museum.

Ilkjær, J. 2003. 'Danish war booty sacrifices', in Jorgensen, L. *et al.* (eds.), *The Spoils of Victory: the North in the Shadow of the Roman Empire*. Copenhagen: Nationalmuseet: 44-65.

Immerzeel, M. 1990. 'Profession: *negotiator allecarius*. Fabrication et commerce de sauce de poissons dans le nord-ouest de l'Empire romain', *Oudheidkundige Mededelingen uit het Rijksmuseum van Oudheden te Leiden* 70: 183-192.

Ireland, S. 1986. *Roman Britain: a Sourcebook*. London: Croom Helm.

Jackson, C. M. Cool, H. E. M. and Wagner, E. C. W. 1998. 'The manufacture of glass in Roman York', *Journal of Glass Studies* 40: 55-61.

Jackson, R. P. J. and Potter, T. W. 1996. *Excavations at Stonea Cambridgeshire 1980-85*. London: British Museum.

James, S. 1984. 'Britain and the late Roman army', in Blagg, T. F. C. and King, A. C. (eds.), *Military and Civilian in Roman Britain*. BAR British Series 136. Oxford: 161-186.

James, S. 1988. 'The military fabricae: state arms factories of the Later Roman Empire' in Coulston, J. C. (ed.), *Military Equipment and the Identity of Roman Soldiers. Proceedings of the Fourth Roman Military Equipment Conference*. BAR International Series 394. Oxford: 257-331.

Jensen, J. 2003. *Danmarks Oldtid. Ældre Jernalder 500 f.Kr.-400 e.Kr*. Copenhagen.

Jobey, I. 1979. 'Housesteads ware- a Frisian tradition on Hadrian's Wall', *Archaeologica Aeliana* 7: 127-143.

Johns, C. 1996. *The Jewellery of Roman Britain*. London: UCL Press.

Johns, C. 1997. *The Snettisham Roman Jewellers Hoard*. British Museum Press.

Johns, C. and Potter, T. W. 1983. *The Thetford Treasure*. London.

Johnson, S. 1976. *The Roman Forts of the Saxon Shore*. London.

Johnson, S. 1983a. *Late Roman Fortifications*. London: Batsford.

Johnson, S. 1983b. *Burgh Castle Excavations by Charles Green 1958-61*. East Anglian Archaeology Report 20. Dereham: Norfolk Archaeological Unit.

Johnston, D. E. 1977. *The Saxon Shore*. London.

Jones, A. H. M. 1964. *The Later Roman Empire 284-602*. Oxford: Blackwell.

Jones, A. K. G. 1988. 'Fish bones from excavations in the cemetery of St Mary Bishophill Junior', in O'Connor, T. P. *Bones from the General Accident Site, Tanner Row*. Archaeology of York 15/2. London: 26-130.

Jones, G. B. D. 1979. 'The Roman evidence', in Crawford, H. (ed.), *Subterranean Britain: Aspects of Underground Archaeology*. London: John Baker: 85-99.

Jones, G. B. D. 1980. 'The Roman mines at Riotinto', *Journal of Roman Studies* 70: 146-165.

Jones, G. B. D. and Mattingly, D. 1990. *An Atlas of Roman Britain*. Oxford: Oxbow.

Jones, J. E. 2009. *The Maritime and Riverine Landscape of the West of Roman Britain: Water Transport on the Atlantic Coasts and Rivers of Britannia*. BAR British Series 493. Oxford: BAR Publishing.

Jones, M. J. 2004. 'Cities and urban life', in Todd, M. (ed.), *A Companion to Roman Britain*. Oxford: Blackwell: 162-192.

Jongman, W. 2009. 'Archaeology, demography, and Roman Economic Growth', in Wilson, A. I. and Bowman, A. K. (eds.), *Quantifying the Roman Economy: Methods and Problems*, Oxford Studies in the Roman Economy 1. Oxford: Oxford University Press: 115-126.

Jöns, H. 1997. *Frühe Eisengewinnung in Joldelund, Kreis Nordfriesland. Ein Beitrag zur Siedlungs- und Technikgeschichte Schleswig-Holsteins 1. Einführung, Naturraum, Prospektionsmethoden und archäologische Untersuchungen*. Bonn.

Jöns, H. 1999. 'Iron production in Northern Germany during the Iron Age', in Fabech, C. and Ringtved, J. (eds.), *Settlement and Landscape: Proceedings of a Conference in Århus, Denmark, May 4-7 1998*. Moesgård: Jutland Archaeological Society: 249-260.

Jope, E. M. 2000. *Early Celtic art in the British Isles*. Oxford: Clarendon Press.

Jørgensen, L. 2003. 'The spoils of victory- the north in the shadow of the Roman Empire', in Jorgensen, L. *et al.* (eds.), *The Spoils of Victory: the North in the Shadow of the Roman Empire*. Copenhagen: Nationalmuseet: 12-17.

Jørgensen, L. Storgaard, B and Gebauer Thomsen, L. (eds.), 2003. *The Spoils of Victory: the North in the Shadow of the Roman Empire*. Copenhagen: Nationalmuseet.

Jung, C. Odiot, T. Berger, J.-F. and Seris, D. 2001. 'La viticulture antique dans le Tricastin (moyenne vallée du Rhône)', in Brun, J.-P. and Laubenheimer, F. (eds.), 'La viticulture en Gaule', in *Gallia* 58: 113-128.

Kaul, F. 2003. 'The Hjortspring find- The oldest of the large Nordic war booty sacrifices', in Jorgensen, L. *et al.* (ed.), *The Spoils of Victory: the North in the Shadow of the Roman Empire*. Copenhagen: Nationalmuseet: 212-223.

Kaul, F. 2004. 'Social and religious perceptions of the ship in Bronze Age Northern Europe', in Clark (ed.), *The Dover Bronze Age Boat in Context: Society and Water Transport in Prehistoric Europe*. Oxford: Oxbow: 122-137.

Keay, S. J. 2001. In Anderson, A. S. Wacher, J. S. and Fitzpatrick, A. P. *The Romano-British 'Small-town' at Wanborough, Wiltshire: Excavations 1966-77*. London: Society for the Promotion of Roman Studies.

Keay, S. J. and Carreras, C. 1996. In Jackson, R. and Potter, T. W. *Excavations at Stonea, Cambridgeshire, 1980-85*. London: British Museum.

Keay, S. J. and Williams, D. 2005. Roman amphorae: a digital resource. University of Southampton, 2005. http://ads.ahds.ac.uk/catalogue/resources.html?amphora2005

Kehne, P. 2003. 'Vermarktung contra Wissenschaft: Kalkriese und der Versuch zur Vereinnahmung der Varusschlacht', *Die Kunde* 54: 93-112.

Keller, E. 1971. *Das spätrömischen Grabfunde in Südbayern*. Münchner Beiträge zur Vor- und Frühgeschichte 14. Munich: C. H. Beck.

Kemmers, F. 2005. 'Not at random: Evidence for a regionalized coin supply?', *TRAC 2004: Proceedings of the Fourteenth Annual Theoretical Roman Archaeology Conference*. Oxford: Oxbow: 39-49.

Kennett, D. 1969. 'Late Roman bronze vessel hoards in Britain', *Jahrbuch des römisch-germanischen Zentralsmuseum, Mainz*, 16: 123-148.

Kenrick, P. 1993. 'Italian *Terra Sigillata*: a Sophisticated Roman Industry', *Oxford Journal of Archaeology* 12 (2): 235-242.

Kent, J. P. C. 1978. 'The origins and development of Celtic gold coinage in Britain', in *Actes du Colloque International d'Archéologie*. Rouen: 313-324.

Kent, J. P. C. 1981. 'The origins of coinage in Britain', in Cunliffe, B. W. (ed.), *Coinage and Society in Britain and Gaul*. London: CBA Research Report 38: 40-42.

Kenyon, K. M. 1948. *Excavations at the Jewry Wall Site, Leicester*. Oxford: Oxford University Press.

King, A. 2004. 'Rural settlement in Southern Britain: a regional survey', in Todd, M. (ed.), *A Companion to Roman Britain*. Oxford: Blackwell: 349-370.

King, D. 1987. 'Petrology, dating and distribution of querns and millstones. The results of research in Bedfordshire, Buckinghamshire, Hertfordshire and Middlesex', *University of London Institute of Archaeology Bulletin* 23: 65-126.

Kossack, G. Behre, K. E. and Schmid, P. (eds.), 1984. *Archäologische und naturwissenschaftliche Untersuchungen an Siedlungen in Deutschen Küstengebiet. Band 1. Ländliche Siedlungen.* Weinheim: Acta humaniora.

Koster, A. 1997. *Description of the Collections in the Provincial Museum G. M. Kam at Nijmegen. XIII. The Bronze Vessels 2. Acquisitions 1954-1996 (Including Vessels of Pewter and Iron.* Gelderland.

Kramer, E. 2001. 'Romeinse bronzen emmer opgevist' in Bos, J. and de Langen, G. (eds.), 'Archeologische kroniek van Friesland over 2000', *De Vrije Fries* 81: 150-151.

Kristiansen, K. and Larsson, T. B. 2005. *The Rise of Bronze Age Society.* Cambridge: Cambridge University Press.

Kromann, A. 1989. 'Recent Roman coin finds from Denmark', in Carradice, I. A. (ed.), *Proceedings of the 10th International Congress of Numismatics, London 1986.* Wetteren: 263-274.

Kromann, A. 1995. 'Die römischen Münzfunde aus Seeland', in Lund Hansen, U. *Himlingøje, Seeland, Europa: Ein Gräberfeld der jüngeren römischen Kaiserzeit auf Seeland, seine Bedeutung und internationalen Beziehungen.* Copenhagen: Det Kgl. Nordiske Oldskriftselskab: 347-363.

Krugman, P. and Wells, R. 2006. *Economics.* New York: Worth.

Kuhnen, H.-P. 1992. 'Die Krise des 3. Jahrhunderts in Südwestdeutschland: Not, Gewalt und Hoffnung', in Kuhnen, H.-P. (ed.), *Gestürmt – Geräumt – Vergessen. Der Limesfall und das Ende der Römerherrschaft in Südwestdeutschland.* Stuttgart: 31-53.

Kunow, J. 1983. *Der Romische import in der Germania Libera bis den Markomannenkriegen: Studien zu Bronze und glasgefessen.* Neumünster: K. Wachholtz.

Künzl, E. 1993. *Die Alamannenbeute aus dem Rhein bei Neupotz. Plünderungsgut aus dem römischen Gallien.* Mainz.

Künzl, E. 1995. 'Großformatig Emailobjekte der römischen Kaiserzeit', in Mols, S. T. A. M. Gerhartl-Witteveen, A. M. Kars, H. Koster, A. Peters, W. J. Th. and Willems, W. J. H. (eds.), *Acta of the 12th International Congress on Ancient Bronzes, Nijmegen 1992.* Amersfoort: 39-49.

Künzl, E. 2008. 'Enamelled bronzes from Roman Britain: Celtic art and tourist knick-knacks', *Current Archaeology* 222: 22-27.

La Baume, P. 1968. 'Römische Bernsteinarbeiten in Köln', in Claus, M. Haarnagel, W. and Raddatz, K. (eds.), *Studien zur europäischen Vor- und Frühgeschichte, gewidmet Herbert Jankuhn.* Neumünster: 108-114.

Lambert, J. B. Beck, C. W. and Frye, J. S. 1988. 'Analysis of European amber by carbon-13 nuclear magnetic resonance spectroscopy', in *Archaeometry* 30: 248-263.

Lamprecht, H. 1906. *Der grosse römische Friedhof in Regensburg.* Verhandlingen des historischen Vereines von Oberpfalz und Regensburg.

Laubenheimer, F. 1985. *La production des amphores en Gaule Narbonnaise.* Centre de Rechereches d'Histoire Ancienne 66. Paris.

Laubenheimer, F. 2003. 'Amphorae and vineyards from Burgundy to the Seine', in Plouviez, J. (ed.), *Journal of Roman Pottery Studies 10. Amphorae in Britain and the Western Empire*: 32-44.

Laux, F. 1995. 'Metallene Urnen und römisches Tafelgeschirr', in Busch, R. (ed.), *Rom an der Niederelbe.* Hamburg: 81-95.

Lavender, N. J. 1997. 'Middle Iron Age and Romano-British settlement at Great Dumnow: excavations at Buildings Farm 1993', *Essex Archaeology and History* 28: 47-92.

Laycock, S. 2008. *Britannia: the Failed State.* Stroud: Tempus.

Laycock, S. 2009. 'Buckles, belts and borders', *Current Archaeology* 234: 12-19.

Layton, R. 1997. *An Introduction to Theory in Anthropology.* Cambridge: Cambridge University Press.

Leahy, K. 2007. *Interrupting the Pots: the Excavation of Cleatham Anglo-Saxon Cemetery.* York: Council for British Archaeology.

Leman-Delerive, G. Bonte, J. and Kruta, V. 1986. 'Une plaque émaillée celtique découverte à Paillart (Oise)', *Gallia* 44: 29-53.

Lendering, J. 2000. *De randen van de aarde. De Romeinen tussen Schelde en Eems.* Amsterdam.

Lennartz, K. 1969. *Zwischeneuropa in der geographischen Vorstellungen und der Kriegführung der Römer in der Zeit von Caesar bis Marcus Aurelius.* Bonn.

Lentacker, A. Ervynck, A. and Van Neer, W. 2004. 'The symbolic meaning of the cock. The animal remains from the mithraeum at Tienen', in Martens, M. De Boe, G. *Roman Mithraism: the Evidence of Small Finds.* Archeologie in Vlaanderen Monografie 5. Zellik and Tienen: Institute for the Archaeological Heritage of the Flemish Community: 7-80.

Lerat, L. 1957. *Catalogue des collections archéologiques de Montbéliard. Les fibulas gallo-romaines de Mandeure.* Monbéliard. Annales littéraires. Archéologie 16.4 Paris: Les Belles lettres.

Leveau, P. 2007. 'The western provinces', in Scheidel, W. Morris, I. and Saller, R. P. (ed.), *The Cambridge Economic History of the Greco-Roman World.* Cambridge: Cambridge University Press: 651-670.

Lewit, T. 1991. *Agricultural Productivity in the Roman Economy A.D. 200-400.* BAR International Series 568. Oxford: BAR Publishing.

Lewit, T. 2005. *Villas, Farms and the Late Roman Rural Economy (Third to Fifth Centuries AD)*. BAR International Series 568 (second edition). Oxford: BAR Publishing.

L'Hour, M. 1987. 'Un site sous-marin sur la côte de l'Armorique; l'épave antique de Ploumanac'h', *Revue Archaeologique de l'Ouest* IV: 113-131.

Lind, L. 1988. *Romerska denarer funna I Sverige*. Stockholm: Förlaget Rubicon.

Lind, L. 1991. 'Was Northern Europe an India to the ancient Roman?', in Jha, A. K. (ed.), *Coinage, Trade and Economy*. Anjaneri: 168-177.

Lista, M. 2007. 'L'ambra dei Romani in Plinio: dal moralismo alla *devotio*', in Nava, M. L. and Salerno, A. (eds.), *Trasparenze Dall'Antico Ambre*. Milan: Electa: 254-287.

Littman, R. J. and Littman, M. L. 1973. 'Galen and the Antonine Plague', *The American Journal of Philology* 94: 243-253.

Liversidge, J. 1973. *Britain in the Roman Empire*. London: Cardinal.

Lloyd Morgan, G. 1981. *The Mirrors, Including a Description of the Roman Mirrors found in the Netherlands, in other Dutch Museums*. Nijmegen: Ministry of Culture, Recreation and Social Welfare

Lo Cascio, E. (ed.), 2000. *Mercati permanenti e mercati periodici nel mondo romano: atti degli Incontri capresi di storia dell'economia antica, Capri 13-15 ottobre 1997*. Bari: Edipuglia.

Lo Cascio, E. 2007. 'The early Roman Empire: the state and the economy', in Scheidel, W. Morris, I. and Saller, R. P. (eds.), *The Cambridge Economic History of the Greco-Roman World*. Cambridge: Cambridge University Press: 619-647.

Lo Cascio, E. (ed.), 2010. *L'impatto della "peste antonina"*. Bari: Edipuglia.

Locker, A. 1990. 'The mammal, bird and fish bones', in Neal, D. S. Wardle, A. and Hunn, J. *Excavation of the Iron Age, Roman and Medieval Settlement at Gorhambury, St Albans*. London: 205-212.

Locker, A. 2003. In Germany, M. *Excavations at Great Holts Farm, Boreham, Essex, 1992-1994*. East Anglian Archaeology 105. Chelmsford: Essex City Council.

Long, A. J. Innes, J. B. Kirby, J. R. Lloyd, J. R. Rutherford, M. M. Shennan, I. and Tooley, M. J. 1998. 'Holocene sea-level change and coastal evolution in the Humber Estuary, eastern England; as assessment of rapid coastal change', *Holocene* 8.2: 229-247.

Loridant, F. 1999. 'Artisanat en milieu urbain: l'exemple des villes et des agglomerations secondaires du nord de la Gaule Belgique', in Polfer, M. (ed.), *Artisanat et productions artisanales en milieu rural dans les provinces du nord-ouest de l'Empire romain*. Monographies Instrumentum 9. Montagnac: Éditions Monique Mergoil: 185-193.

Loughton, M. E. 2003. 'The distribution of Republican amphorae in France', *Oxford Journal of Archaeology* 22 (2): 177-207.

Loughton, M. E. 2009. 'Getting smashed: the deposition of amphorae and the drinking of wine in Gaul during the Late Iron Age', *Oxford Journal of Archaeology* 28 (1): 77-110.

Louwe Kooijmans, L. P. 1980. 'Archaeology and coastal change in the Netherlands', in Thompson, F. H. (ed.), *Archaeology and Coastal Change*. London: 106-133.

Loveluck, C. and Tys, D. 2006. 'Coastal societies, exchange and identity along the Channel and southern North Sea shores of Europe, AD 600-1000', *Journal of Maritime Archaeology* 1: 140-169.

Lund, J. 2003. 'Woe to the vanquished!', in Jørgensen, L. *et al.* (eds.), *The Spoils of Victory: the North in the Shadow of the Roman Empire*. Copenhagen: Nationalmuseet: 166-171.

Lund Hansen, U. 1976. 'Das Gräberfeld bei Harpelev, Seeland', *Acta Archaeologica* 47: 91-158.

Lund Hansen, U. 1987. *Römischer Import im Norden: Warenaustausch zwischen dem Römischen Reich und dem freien Germanien während der Kaiserzeit unter besonderer Berücksichtigung Nordeuropas*. Copenhagen: Det Kongelige Nordiske oldskriftselskab, 1987.

Lund Hansen, U. 1995. *Himlingøje, Seeland, Europa: Ein Gräberfeld der jüngeren römischen Kaiserzeit auf Seeland, seine Bedeutung und internationalen Beziehungen*. Copenhagen: Det Kgl. Nordiske Oldskriftselskab.

Lund Hansen, U. 2001. 'Gold rings- symbols of sex and rank', *KVHAA konferenser* 51. Stockholm: 157-188.

Lund Hansen, U. 2003a. 'Rezension, Michael Erdrich: Rom und die Barbaren', *Prähistorisches Zeitschrift* 78: 236-242.

Lund Hansen, U. 2003b. '150 years of weapon-offering finds- research and interpretations', in Jorgensen, L. *et al.* (eds.), *The Spoils of Victory: the North in the Shadow of the Roman Empire*. Copenhagen: Nationalmuseet: 84-89.

Luttwak, E. N. 1976. *The Grand Strategy of the Roman Empire, from the First Century A.D. to the Third*. Baltimore and London: John Hopkins University Press.

Lyne, M. (Forthcoming). *Report on the Bestwall Kilns, Wareham, Dorset*.

Lyne, M A B, and Jefferies, R S, 1979. *The Alice Holt/Farnham Roman Pottery Industry*. London: Council for British Archaeology.

MacGregor, A. and Bolick, E. 1993. *A Summary Catalogue of the Anglo-Saxon Collections: (Non-Ferrous Metals)*. Oxford: Ashmolean Museum in association with BAR Publishing.

Mack, R. P. 1975. *The Coinage of Ancient Britain*. London.

MacKie, E. W. 1974. *Dun Mor Vaul: An Iron Age Broch on Tiree*. Glasgow: University of Glasgow Press.

MacKie, E. W. 2000. 'Excavations at Dun Ardtreck, Skye in 1964 and 1965', *Proceedings of the Society of Antiquaries of Scotland* 130: 301-411.

Mackintosh, M. 1995. *The Divine Rider in the Art of the Western Roman Empire*. BAR International Series 607. Oxford.

MacMullen, R. 'The epigraphic habit', *American Journal of Philology* 103(3): 234-246.

Major, H. (Forthcoming). Report on Elms Farm, Heybridge, Essex.

Makaske, B. Maas, G. J. and van Smeerdijk, D. G. 2008. 'The age and origin of the Gelderse IJssel', *Netherlands Journal of Geosciences* 87-4: 323-337.

Maloney, C. 1990. *The Upper Walbrook in the Roman Period*. The Archaeology of Roman London Volume 1. London: Council for British Archaeology.

Mangartz, F. 1998. *Die antiken Steinbru□che der Hohen Buche bei Andernach: Topographie, Technologie und Chronologie*. Mainz: Verlag des Römisch-Germanischen Zentralmuseums.

Mangartz, F. 2008. 'Römischer Basaltlava-Abbau zwischen Eifel und Rhein', *Vulkanpark-Forschungen* 7. Mainz.

Mankiw, G. N. 2007. *Macroeconomics* (sixth edition). New York: Worth.

Manley, J. 2002. *AD 43: the Roman Invasion of Britain; a Reassessment*. Stroud: Tempus.

Manley, J. and Rudkin, D. 2005. *Facing the Palace. Excavations in front of the Roman Palace at Fishbourne*. Lewes.

Mann, J. C. 1977. '*Duces* and *Comites* in the 4th Century', in Johnston, D. E. (ed.), *The Saxon Shore*. London: Council for British Archaeology: 11-15.

Mann, J. C. 1983. *Legionary Recruitment and Veteran Settlement during the Principate*. London: Institute of Archaeology.

Manning, W. H. 1985a. *Catalogue of the Romano-British Iron Tools, Fittings and Weapons in the British Museum*. London: British Museum.

Manning, W. H. 1985b. 'The iron objects', in Pitts, L. F. and St Joseph, J. K. *Inchtuthil: the Roman Legionary Fortress Excavations, 1952-65*. London: Society for the Promotion of Roman Studies: 289-299.

Manning, W. H. Price, J. and Webster, J. 1995. *Usk: The Roman Small Finds*. Cardiff: University of Wales Press.

Margary, I. D. 1973. *Roman Roads in Britain* (third edition). London: John Baker.

Mariën, M. E. 1961. *La Période de La Tène en Belgique: Le Groupe de la Haine*. Brussels: Musées Royaux d'art et d'histoire.

Mariën, M. E. 1980. *Belgica Antiqua: L'empreinte de Rome*. Anvers: Fonds Mercator S.A.

Markey, M. Wilkes, E. and Darvill, T. 2002. 'Poole Harbour. An Iron Age Port', *Current Archaeology* 181 (September 2002): 7-11.

Marlière, E. 2001. 'Le Tonneau en Gaule Romaine', in Brun, J.-P. and Laubenheimer, F. (eds.), 'La viticulture en Gaule', in *Gallia* 58: 180-260.

Marlière, E. 2002. *L'outre et le tonneau dans l'Occident romain*. Monographies Instrumentum 22. Montagnac: Éditions Monique Mergoil.

Marsden, P. 1987. *The Roman Forum Site in London*. London: Museum of London.

Marsden, P. 1994. *Ships of the Port of London, First to Eleventh Centuries AD*. London: English Heritage.

Marsden, P. 2004. 'Reconstructing the Dover boat', in Clark, P. (ed.), *The Dover Bronze Age Boat in Context: Society and Water Transport in Prehistoric Europe*. Oxford: Oxbow: 17-19.

Marsh, G. 1981. 'London's samian supply and its relationship to the development of the Gallic samian industry', in Anderson, A. C. and Anderson, A. S. (eds.), *Roman Pottery Research in Britain and North-West Europe*. BAR International Series 123 (i). Oxford: 173-238.

Martin-Kilcher, S. 1987. *Die römischen Amphoren aus Augst und Kaiseraugst: Ein Beitrag zur römischen Handels- und Kulturgeschichte 1: Die südspanischen Ölamphoren (Gruppe 1)*. Forschungen in Augst 7/1. Augst.

Martin-Kilcher, S. 2003. 'Fish-sauce amphorae from the Iberian peninsula: the forms and observations on trade with the north-west provinces', in Plouviez, J. (ed.), *Journal of Roman Pottery Studies 10: Amphorae in Britain and the Western Empire*: 69-83.

Marzano, A. 2007. *Roman Villas in Central Italy: A Social and Economic History*. Leiden: Brill.

Mason, D. J. 2001. *Roman Chester: City of the Eagles*. Stroud: Tempus.

Mason, D. J. 2003. *Roman Britain and the Roman Navy*. Stroud: Tempus.

Masson, M. A. 2005. 'Trade and exchange', in Maschner, H. D. G. and Chippindale, C. (eds.), *Handbook of Archaeological Methods*. Volume 1. Altamira: Rowman: 1138-1178.

Mattingly, D. J. (ed.), 2003. *The Archaeology of Fazzan*. London: Society for Libyan Studies.

Mattingly, D. J. 2006. *An Imperial possession: Britain in the Roman Empire*. London: Penguin.

Mattingly, D. J. & Salmon, J. (eds.), 2001. *Economies beyond Agriculture in the Classical World*. London: Routledge.

Mauss, M. 1954. *The Gift: Forms and Functions of Exchange in Archaic Societies*. London: Cohen and West.

Maxfield, V. A. 1989. *The Saxon Shore: a Handbook*. Exeter.

May, T. 1922. *The Roman Fort of Templeborough near Rotherham*. Rotherham: Henry Garnett and Co.

May, T. 1930. *Catalogue of the Roman Pottery in the Colchester and Essex Museum*. Cambridge: Cambridge University Press.

McCarthy, M. R. 1990. *A Roman, Anglian and Medieval site at Blackfriars Street, Carlisle: excavations 1977-9*. Stroud: Cumberland and Westmorland Antiquarian and Archaeological Society.

McCarthy, M. R. 2000. *Roman and Medieval Carlisle: The Southern Lanes*. Carlisle: Carlisle Archaeology Limited.

McCarthy, M. R. Padley, T. G. and Henig, M. 1982. 'Excavations and finds from the Lanes, Carlisle', *Britannia* 13: 79-89.

McCarthy, M. R. Padley, T. G. and Henig, M. 1983. 'An amber knife-handle from Carlisle', *Britannia* 14: 267-269.

McGrail, S. 1981. *The Brigg 'Raft' and her Prehistoric environment.* BAR British Series 89. Oxford.

McGrail, S. 1990. 'Boats and boatmanship in the late prehistoric southern North Sea and Channel region', in McGrail, S. (ed.), *Maritime Celts, Frisians and Saxons: Papers presented to a Conference at Oxford in November 1988.* London: Council for British Archaeology: 32-48.

McGrail, S. 2001. *Boats of the World: from the Stone Age to Medieval Times.* Oxford: Oxford University Press.

McGrail, S. 2004. 'North-west European seagoing boats before AD 400' in Clark, P. (ed.), *The Dover Bronze Age Boat in Context: Society and Water Transport in Prehistoric Europe.* Oxford: Oxbow: 51-66.

McIlwain, A. 1980. 'Quernstones', in Jones, D. M. *Excavations at Billingsgate Buildings 1974.* London: London and Middlesex Archaeology Society: 132.

McIsaac, W. Schwab, I. and Sheldon, H. 1979. 'Excavations at Old Ford, 1972-1975', *Transactions of the London and Middlesex Archaeological Society* 30: 39-96.

McLean, L. and Richardson, A. 2007. 'Early Anglo Saxon brooches in southern England: the contribution of the Portable Antiquities Scheme', Online article: http://www.finds.org.uk/documents/conf07/mclean.pdf

McPeake, J. C. and Moore, C. N. 1978. 'A bronze skillet-handle from Chester and other vessels from the British Isles', *Britannia* 9: 331-334.

Medlycott, M. 2000. 'Prehistoric, Roman and post-medieval material from Harlow: investigations at Church Langley 1989-1994', *Essex Archaeology and History* 31: 33-93.

Megaw, J. V. S. 1963. 'A British bronze bowl of the Belgic Age from Poland', *Antiquaries Journal* 43: 27-37.

Megaw, J. V. S. and Simpson, D. D. A. (ed.), 1979. *Introduction to British Prehistory.* Leicester: Leicester University Press.

Megaw, R. and Megaw, J. V. S. 2001a. *Celtic Art: from its Beginnings to the Book of Kells.* London: Thames and Hudson.

Megaw, R and Megaw, J. V. S. 2001b. 'D'anciens Bretons à l'étranger? Notes sur deux bronzes émaillès du Ier siècle après J.-C', *Revue du Nord.* 343: 51-58.

Merideth, C. 1998. *An Archaeometallurgical Survey for Ancient Tin Mines and Smelting Sites in Spain and Portugal. Mid-Central Western Iberian Geographical Region 1990-1995.* BAR International Series 714. Oxford: BAR Publishing.

Mertens, J. 1977 'Oudenburg and the northern sector of the continental *Litus Saxonicum*', in Johnston, D. E. (ed.), *The Saxon Shore.* London: Council for British Archaeology: 51-62.

Middleton, P. S. 1979. 'Army supply in Roman Gaul: An hypothesis for Roman Britain', in Burnham, B. C. and Johnson, H. B. (eds.), *Invasion and Response: the Case of Roman Britain.* BAR British Series 73. Oxford: 81-98.

Mildenberger, G. 1989. 'Elbgermanen', *Reallexikon der Germanischen Altertumskunde Von Johannes Hoops* Vol. 7. Berlin/New York: Walter De Gruyter: 107-113.

Miller, L. Schofield, J. and Rhodes, M. 1986. *The Roman Quay at St Magnus House, London.* London: London and Middlesex Archaeological Society.

Miller, S. N. 1922. *The Roman Fort at Balmuildy (Summerston, near Glasgow) on the Antonine Wall.* Glasgow: Printed for the Archaeological Society by Maclehose, Jackson and Co.

Millet, M. 1990. *The Romanization of Britain.* Cambridge: Cambridge University Press.

Millett, M. and McGrail, S. 1987. 'The archaeology of the Hasholme logboat', *The Archaeological Journal* 144: 69-155.

Millett, M. and Wilmott, T. 2003. 'Rethinking Richborough', in Wilson, P. (ed.), *The Archaeology of Roman Towns.* Oxford: Oxbow: 184-194.

Mills, P. S. 1984. 'Excavations at Roman Road/Parnell Road, Old Ford, London E3', *Transactions of the London and Middlesex Archaeological Society* 35: 3-191.

Milne, G. 1985. *The Port of Roman London.* London: B. T. Batsford.

Milne, G. and Wardle, A. 1993. 'Early Roman development at Leadenhall Court', *Transactions of the London and Middlesex Archaeological Society* 44: 23-169.

Mises, L. von. 1981. *The Theory of Money and Credit* (trans. Batson, H. E.) Indianapolis, IN: Liberty Fund, Inc.

Moltke, E. 1985. *Runes and their Origin. Denmark and Elsewhere.* Copenhagen: Nationalmuseet.

Mommsen, T. 1895. *C. Iulii Solini. Collectanea Rerum Memorabilium.* Berolini.

Monaghan, J, 1987. *Upchurch and Thameside Roman Pottery: a Ceramic Typology for Northern Kent, First to Third Centuries A.D.* BAR British Series 173. Oxford.

Monaghan, J. 1993. *Roman Pottery from the Fortress, 9 Blake Street.* London: Council for British Archaeology, for the York Archaeological Trust.

Monaghan, J. 1997. *Roman Pottery from York.* York: Council for British Archaeology, for the York Archaeological Trust.

Moore, C. N. 1973. 'Two examples of late Celtic and early Roman metalwork from south Lincolnshire', *Britannia* 4: 153-159.

Moore, C. N. 1978. 'An enamelled skillet handle from Brough-on-Fosse and the distribution of similar vessels', *Britannia* 9: 319-327.

Morris, F. M. 2009. *North Sea and Channel Connectivity during the Late Iron Age and Roman Period (175/150 BC-AD 409)*. Unpublished D. Phil. thesis. University of Oxford.

Morris, M. N. and Wainwright, A. 1995. 'Iron Age and Romano-British Settlement, Agriculture and Industry in the Upper Bulbourne Valley, Hertfordshire: an Interim Interpretation', in Holgate, R. (ed.), *Chiltern Archaeology: Recent Work*. Dunstable: 68-75.

Mould, Q. 2004. 'The metal vessels', in Cool, H. E. M. *The Roman Cemetery at Brougham, Cumbria*. London: Society for the Promotion of Roman Studies: 373-379.

Müller, R. 2000. 'Jastorf-Kultur' *Reallexikon der Germanischen Altertumskunde* Vol. 16. Berlin/New York: Walter De Gruyter: 43-55.

Müller-Wille, M. 1999. 'Settlement and non-agrarian production from the high mountain region to the shoreline: An introduction', in Fabech, C. and Ringtved, J. (eds.), *Settlement and Landscape: Proceedings of a Conference in Århus, Denmark, May 4-7 1998*. Moesgård: Jutland Archaeological Society: 205-211.

Musson, C. R. Britnell, W. J. Northover, J. P. and Salter C. (eds.), 1992. 'Excavations and metal-working at Llwyn Bryn-dinas hillfort, Llangedwyn, Clwyd', *Proceedings of the Prehistoric Society* 58: 265–83.

Myhre, B. 1985. 'Boat houses as indicators of political organization', *Norwegian Archaeological Review* 18: 36-60.

Myres, J. N. L. 1956. *Roman Britain and the English Settlements*. Oxford: Clarendon Press.

Myres, J. N. L. 1969. *Anglo Saxon Pottery and the Settlement of England*. Oxford.

Myres, J. N. L. 1977. *A Corpus of Anglo-Saxon pottery of the Pagan Period*. Cambridge: Cambridge University Press.

Myres, J. N. L. and Green, B. 1973. *The Anglo-Saxon Cemeteries of Caistor-by-Norwich and Markshall, Norfolk*. London: Society of Antiquaries.

Nash, D. 1987. *Coinage in the Celtic World*. London: Seaby.

Naylor, J. 2008. 'Sceattas and trade in Early Anglo-Saxon England' *The UK Detector Net* (UKDN). Issue 11 (July 2008). http://www.scribd.com/doc/13967189/UKDN-WORD-Issue-11-

Neal, D. S., Wardle, A. and Hunn, J. 1990 *Excavation of the Iron Age, Roman and Medieval Settlement at Gorhambury, St. Albans*. London: Historic Buildings and Monuments Commission Report Number 14.

Nenna, M.-D. Vichy, M. and Picon, M. 1997. 'L'atelier de verrier de Lyon, du Ier siècle ap.J.-C. et l'origine des verres "romains"', *Revue d'Archèomètrie* 21: 81-87.

Newman, J. 1992. 'The Late Roman and Anglo-Saxon settlement pattern in the Sandlings of Suffolk', in Carver, M. (ed.). *The Age of Sutton Hoo: the Seventh Century in North-western Europe*. Woodbridge: Boydell and Brewer: 25-38.

Niblett, R. 1985. *Sheepen: An Early Roman Industrial Site at Camulodunum*. London: Council for British Archaeology.

Niblett, R. 2001. *Verulamium*. Stroud: Tempus.

Niblett, R. 2007. 'The native elite and their funerary practices from the first century BC to Nero', in Todd, M. (ed.), *A Companion to Roman Britain*. Oxford: Blackwell: 30-41.

Nicolet, C. 1991. *Space, Geography, and Politics in the Early Roman Empire*. Ann Arbor: University of Michigan Press.

Nielsen, S. 1989. 'Roman *denarii* and Iron-Age Denmark', in Clarke, H. and Schia, E. (eds.), *Coins and Archaeology*. BAR International Series 556. Oxford: 29-36.

Nieto, X. 1997. 'Le commerce de cabotage et de distribution', in Pomey, P. (ed.), *La Navigation dans L'Antiquité*. Paris.

Nixon, C. E. V. and Rodgers, B. S. 1994. *In Praise of Later Roman Emperors: the Panegyrici Latini: Introduction, Translation, and Historical Commentary, with the Latin Text of R. A. B. Mynors*. Berkeley: University of California Press.

Nørgård Jørgensen, A. 2003. 'Fortifications and the control of land and sea traffic in the pre-Roman and Roman Iron Age', in Jørgensen *et al.* (eds.), *The Spoils of Victory: the North in the Shadow of the Roman Empire*. Copenhagen: Nationalmuseet: 194-209.

Northover, J. P. 1982. 'The metallurgy of the Wilburton hoards', *Oxford Journal of Archaeology* 1: 69-109.

Northover, J. P. 1988. 'Copper, tin, silver and gold in the Iron Age', in Slater, E. A. and Tate, J. O. (eds.), *Science and Archaeology, Glasgow 1987: Proceedings of a Conference on the Application of Scientific Techniques to Archaeology, Glasgow, September 1987*. Oxford: B.A.R (British Series) 196: 223-234.

Northover, J. P. 1991. 'Metallurgical analyses', in Cunliffe, B. W. and Poole, C. *Danebury: an Iron Age Hillfort in Hampshire. Vol. 5. The Excavations 1979-1988: the Finds*. London: Council for British Archaeology: 407-412.

Northover, J. P. 1992. 'Materials issues in the Celtic coinage', in Mays, M. (ed.), *Celtic Coinage in Britain and Beyond; the Eleventh Oxford Symposium on Coinage and Monetary History*. BAR British Series 222. Oxford: BAR Publishing: 235-299.

Northover, J. P. 1994. 'Bronze, silver and gold in Iron Age Wessex', in Fitzpatrick, A. P. and Morris, E. (eds.), *The Iron Age in Wessex: Recent work*. Salisbury: Association Française D'Etude de L'Age du Fer/Trust for Wessex Archaeology: 19-22.

Northover, J. P. 1995. 'The technology of metalwork: bronze and gold', in Green, M. J. (ed.), *The Celtic World*. London: Routledge: 285-309.

Notte, L. 1989. 'Les Seaux de Hemmoor en France et en Europe', *Amphorae* 58, Decembre 1989.

Nouwen, R. 2004. 'Roman politics and local history: Augustus and his military policy in the Low Countries', in Vermeulen, F. Sas, K. and Dhaeze, W. (eds.), *Archaeology in Confrontation. Aspects of Roman Military Presence in the Northwest. Studies in Honour of Prof. Em. Hugo Thoen*. Gent: Academia Press: 17-30.

O'Connor, B. 1980. *Cross-Channel relations in the later Bronze Age*. BAR International Series 91. Oxford.

Ortisi, S. 2002. *Ro□mische Kleinfunde aus Burgho□fe. Band 2. Die früh- und mittelkaiserzeitlichen Fibeln*. Rahden: Leidorf.

Ottaway, P. 1993. *Roman York*. London: B. T. Batsford/English Heritage.

Oxé, A. Comfort, H. and Kenrick, P. 2000. *CORPUS VASORUM ARRETINORUM. A Catalogue of the Signatures, Shapes and Chronology of Italian Sigillata* (second edition (revised by Philip Kenrick)). Bonn: Dr. Rudolf Habelt GMBH.

Painter, K. S. 1977a. *The Mildenhall Treasure*. London.

Painter, K. S. 1977b. *The Water Newton Early Christian Silver*. London.

Panella, C. and Tchernia, A. 2002. 'Agricultural products transported in amphorae', in Scheidel, W. and von Reden, S. (eds.), *The Ancient Economy*. Edinburgh: Edinburgh University Press: 173-189.

Parker, A. J. 1990. 'The wines of Roman Italy', *Journal of Roman Archaeology* 3: 325-331.

Parker, A. J. 1992. *Ancient Shipwrecks of the Mediterranean and the Roman Provinces*. BAR International Series 580. Oxford: BAR Publishing.

Palk, N. 1992. *Metal Horse Harness of the British and Irish Iron Ages*. Unpublished D.Phil thesis. University of Oxford.

Parkhouse, J. 1997. 'The distribution and exchange of Mayen lava querns in Early Medieval North Western Europe', in De Boe, G. and Verhaeghe, F. (eds.), *Exchange and Trade in Medieval Europe. Papers of the Medieval Europe Brugge 1997 Conference. Volume 3*. Zellik: 97-106.

Parleviet, D. 2002. 'De Brittenburg voorgoed verloren', *Westerheem* 51/3.

Partridge, C. 1981. *Skeleton Green. A Late Iron Age Romano-British Site*. London: Society for the Promotion of Roman Studies.

Pasquinucci, M. 1978. 'Il commercio dell'ambra nel mondo Romano', in *Ambra oro del Nord: Venezia, Palazzo Ducale, 30 giugno-1 ottobre 1978*. Venezia: Alfieri: 92-96.

Pauli-Jensen, X. Jørgensen, L. and Lund Hansen, U. 2003. 'The Germanic army- warriors, soldiers and officers', in Jørgensen, L. *et al*. (eds.), *The Spoils of Victory: the North in the Shadow of the Roman Empire*. Copenhagen: Nationalmuseet: 310-329.

Peacock, D. P. S. 1972. *Coll. De L'École française de Rome* XXXII: 261-278.

Peacock, D. P. S. 1977. 'Bricks and tiles of the Classis Britannica: Petrology and origin', *Britannia* 8: 235-248.

Peacock, D. P. S. 1980. 'The Roman millstone trade: A petrological sketch', *World Archaeology* 12, 1: 43-53.

Peacock, D. P. S. and Williams, D. F. 1986. *Amphorae in the Roman Economy*. London.

Pearson, A. F. 2002. *The Roman Shore Forts: Coastal Defences of Southern Britain*. Stroud: Tempus.

Pearson, A. F. 2005. 'Barbarian piracy and the Saxon Shore: a reappraisal', *Oxford Journal of Archaeology* 24 (1): 73-88.

Pearson. A. F. 2006. 'Piracy in late Roman Britain: a perspective from the Viking age', *Britannia* 37: 337-353.

Peddie, J. 1997. *Conquest: the Roman Invasion of Britain*. Stroud: Sutton.

Penhallurick, R. D. 1986. *Tin in Antiquity*. London: Institute of Metals.

Perring, D. 1991. *Roman London*. London: Seaby.

Peška, J. 2008. 'The Royal tomb of Mušov', in Aillagon, J.-J. (ed.), *Rome and the Barbarians: the Birth of a new World*. Milan: Skira; New York: Rizzoli: 106-109.

Petit, J. D. and Mangin, M. 1994. *Les agglomérations secondaires: la Gaule belgique, les Germanies et l'occident romain: actes du colloque de Bliesbruck-Reinheim/Bitche (Moselle) 21, 22, 23 et 24 octobre 1992*. Paris: Editions Errance.

Philp, B. 1981. *The Excavation of the Roman Forts of the Classis Britannica at Dover 1970-1977*. Gloucester: Alan Sutton.

Philp, B. 2005. *Excavation of the Roman Fort at Reculver, Kent*. Dover: Kent Archaeological Rescue Unit.

Piggott, S. 1949. *British Prehistory*. Oxford: Oxford University Press.

Pirenne, H. 1939. *Mohammed and Charlemagne*. London.

Plahter, U. Astrup, E. and Straume, E. 1995. 'Norwegian rosette-brooches of the 3rd century AD: their construction, materials and technique' in *Journal of Historical Metallurgy* 29/1: 12-24.

Pobjoy, M. 2000. 'Building inscriptions in Republican Italy: euergetism, resonsibility and civic virtue', in Cooley, A. (ed.), *The Epigraphic Landscape of Roman Italy*. Bulletin of the Institute of Classical Studies, Supplement 73. London: 77-92.

Polanyi, K. 1944. *The Great Transformation*. Boston: Beacon Press.

Polanyi, K. 1957. 'The economy as instituted process', in Polanyi, K. Arensberg, C. M. and Pearson, H. W. (eds.), *Trade and Market in the Early Empires*. New York: The Free Press: 243-270.

Polfer, M. 2000. 'Eisenproduktion und Eisenverarbeitung in Nordgallien und dem Rheinland während der römischen Kaiserzeit', in Feugère, M. Guštin, M. (eds.), *Iron, blacksmiths and tools. Ancient European Crafts: Acts of the Instrumentum Conference at Podsreda (Slovenia) in April 1999.* Monographies Instrumentum 12. Montagnac: Éditions Monique Mergoil: 67-77.

Ponisch, M. 1970. *Recherches archéologiques a Tangier et dans sa région.* Paris.

Ponisch, M. 1975. 'Pérennité des relations dans le circuit de Détroit de Gibraltar', in Temporini, H. and Hasse, W. (eds.), *Aufstieg und Niedergang der römischen Welt* 2.3: 655-684.

Potter, T. W. 1979. *Romans in North-west England: Excavations at the Forts of Ravenglass, Watercrook and Bowness on Solway.* Cumberland and Westmorland Antiquarian and Archaeological Society.

Powell, W. R. (ed). 1963. *Victoria County History of Essex volume III.* London.

Price, J. 1978. 'Trade in glass', in du Plat Taylor, J. and Cleere, H. (eds.), *Roman Shipping and Trade: Britain and the Rhine Provinces.* London: Council for British Archaeology: 70-78.

Price, J. 1995. 'Glass vessels', in Manning, W. H. Price, J. and Webster, J. *Usk: the Roman Small Finds.* Cardiff: University of Wales Press: 139-191.

Price, J. 2000. 'Roman glass production in western Europe', in Nenna, M. D. (ed.), *La Route de Verre: ateliers primaires et secondaires du second millénaire av. J.-C. au Moyen Age.* Lyon: Maison de l'Orient Méditerranéen-Jean Pouilloux: 123-124.

Price, J. 2002. 'Broken bottles and quartz-sand: glass production in Yorkshire and the north in the Roman period', in Wilson, P, and Price, J. (eds.), *Aspects of Industry in Roman Yorkshire and the North.* Oxford: Oxbow: 81-93.

Pritchard, F. A. 1986. 'Ornamental stonework from Roman London', *Britannia* 17: 169-189.

Pröttel, P. 1988. 'Zur Chronologie der Zwiebelknopffibeln', *Jahrbuch des Römisch-Germanischen Zentralmuseum Mainz* 35: 347-372.

Pryor, J. H. 1988. *Geography, Technology, and War: Studies in the Maritime History of the Mediterranean, 649-1571.* Cambridge.

Quillfeldt, I. von. and Roggenbuck, P. 1985. *Westerwanna II.* Die Urnenfriedhöfe in Niedersachsen 14. Hildesheim.

Radic, I. and Jurisic, M. 1993. 'Das antike Schiffswrack von Miljet, Kroatien', *Germania* 71: 113-138.

Rald, U. 1994. 'The Roman swords from Danish bog finds'. *Journal of Roman Military Equipment Studies* 5: 227-241.

Randsborg, K. 1991. *The First Millennium A.D. in Europe and the Mediterranean: an Archaeological Essay.* Cambridge: Cambridge University Press.

Rasmussen, K. L. Rahbek, U. and Voss, O. 2006. 'Radiocarbon dating of the iron production in slag-pit furnaces in Jutland', *Journal of Danish Archaeology* 14: 127-138.

Rausing, G. 1987. 'Barbarian mercenaries or Roman citizens?', *Fornvännen* 82: 126-131.

Rausing, G. 1992. 'On the origin of runes', *Fornvännen* 87: 200-204.

Rayner, L. and Seeley, F. 2002. 'The Roman pottery', in Drummond-Murray, J. and Thompson, P. *Settlement in Roman Southwark.* London: Museum of London: 162-212.

Reece, R. 1984. 'Mints, markets and the military', in Blagg, T. F. C. and King, A. C. (eds.), *Military and Civilian in Roman Britain: Cultural Relationships in a Frontier Province.* BAR British Series 136. Oxford: 143-160.

Reece, R. 1991. *Roman Coins from 140 Sites in Britain.* Cirencester: Cotswold Studies.

Reece, R. 1995. 'Site-finds in Roman Britain', *Britannia* 26: 179-206.

Reece, R. 2002. *The Coinage of Roman Britain.* Stroud: Tempus.

Reece, R. 2008. 'Roman silver goes abroad', in Bursche, A. Ciołek, R. and Wolters, R. (eds.), *Roman Coins Outside the Empire. Ways and Phases, Contexts and Functions. Proceedings of the ESF/SCH Exploratory Workshop Radziwill Palace, Nieborow (Poland), 3-6 September 2005.* Wetteren: Moneta: 59-88.

Reid, C. 1884. 'On Norfolk amber', *Transactions of the Norfolk and Norwich Naturalists' Society.* 3: 601-3.

Remesal-Rodríguez, J. 1986. *La Annona Militaris Y La Exportación De Aceite Bético A Germania.* Madrid: Universidad Complutense.

Remesal-Rodríguez, J. 1997. *Heeresversorgung und die wirtschaftlichen Beziehungen zwischen der Baetica und Germanien.* Stuttgart: Konrad Theiss Verlag.

Remesal-Rodríguez, J. 2002. 'Baetica and Germania. Notes on the concept of 'provincial interdependence' in the Roman Empire', in Erdkamp, P. (ed.), *The Roman Army and the Economy.* Amsterdam: Gieben.

Renfrew, C. 1973. *Before Civilization: the Radiocarbon Revolution and Prehistoric Europe.* London: Cape.

Rey-Vodoz, V. 1986. 'Les fibulas gallo-romaines de Martigny', *Annuaire de la Soc. Suisse de Préhistoire et d'Archéologie* 69: 149-198.

Rey-Vodoz, V. 1998. 'Les fibules', in Rey-Vodoz, V. *Beiträge zum römischen Oberwinterthur, Vitudurum 8: Ausgrabungen im Unteren Bu□hl: les fibules, keramische Sondergruppen: Bleiglasierte Keramik, Terrakotten, Lampen.* Zürich und Egg: 11-62 (with Planche).

Rhodes, M. 1986. In Miller, L. Schofield, J. and Rhodes, M. *The Roman Quay at St Magnus House, London.* London: London and Middlesex Archaeological Society.

Rhodes, M. 1989. 'Roman pottery lost en route from the kiln site to the user - a gazetteer', *Journal of Roman Pottery Studies* 2: 44-58.

Richardson, B. 1986. 'The pottery' In Miller, L. Schofield, J. and Rhodes, M. *The Roman Quay at St Magnus House, London*. London: London and Middlesex Archaeological Society 1986: 164-168.

Richardson, B. and Tyers, P. A. 1984. 'North Gaulish pottery in Britain', *Britannia* 15: 133-141.

Richmond, I. A. 1963. *Roman Britain* (second edition). The Pelican History of England. Harmondsworth: Penguin Books.

Rieck, F. 2003. 'The ships from Nydam bog', in Jørgensen *et al.* (eds.), 2003. *The Spoils of Victory: the North in the Shadow of the Roman Empire*. Copenhagen: Nationalmuseet: 296-309.

Riederer, J. 2002. 'The use of standardised copper alloys in Roman metal technology', in *I bronzi antichi: produzione e tecnologia. Atti del XV Congresso Internazionale sui Bronzi Antichi*. Monographies Instrumentum 21. Montagnac: Éditions Monique Mergoil: 284-291.

Riese, A. 1898. 'Römischer Fibeln aus Heddernheim', *Mitteilungen über römischen Funde in Heddernheim* 2, 3.

Rigold, S. E. 1969. 'The Roman haven at Dover', *Archaeological Journal* 126: 78-100.

Riha, E. 1979. *Die römischen Fibeln aus Augst und Kaiseraugst*. Forschungen in Augst 3. Augst.

Rippon, S. 1997. *The Severn Estuary: Landscape Evolution and Wetland Reclamation*. London: Leicester University Press.

Rippon, S. 2000. *The Transformation of Coastal Wetlands. Exploitation and Management of Marshland Landscapes in North West Europe during the Roman and Medieval Periods*. Oxford: Oxford University Press.

Rippon, S. 2008. 'Coastal Trade in Roman Britain: the Investigation of Crandon Bridge, Somerset, a Romano-British Trans-shipment Port beside the Severn Estuary', *Britannia* 39: 85-144.

Ritterling, E. 1913. 'Das frührömische Lager bei Hofheim im Taunus' *Annalen des Vereins für Nassauische Altertumskunde und Geschichtsforschung* 40.

Rives, J. B. 1999. *Germania / Tacitus; Translated with Introduction and Commentary by J. B. Rives*. Clarendon Ancient History Series. Oxford: Clarendon.

Rivet, A. L. F. 1969. 'Social and economic aspects', in Rivet, A. L. F. (ed.), *The Roman Villa in Britain*. London: Routledge and Keegan Paul: 173-216.

Rivet, A. L. F. and Smith, C. 1979. *The Place-names of Roman Britain*. London.

Roberts, O. 2004. 'Round the headland or over the horizon? An examination of evidence for British prehistoric efforts to construct a seaworthy boat', in Clark, P. (ed.), *The Dover Bronze Age Boat in Context: Society and Water Transport in Prehistoric Europe*. Oxford: Oxbow: 35-50.

Roberts, W. I. 1982. *Romano Saxon Pottery*. BAR British Series 106. Oxford.

Robertson, A. S. 2000. *An Inventory of Romano-British Coin Hoards*. London: Royal Numismatic Society.

Robertson, A. S. Scott, M. and Keppie, L. 1975. *Bar Hill: a Roman Fort and its Finds*. BAR 16. Oxford.

Rodwell, W. J. 1976. 'Coinage, oppida and the rise of Belgic power in south-eastern Britain', in Cunliffe, B. W. and Rowley, T. (eds.), *Oppida: the Beginnings of Urbanism in Barbarian Europe*. BAR Supplementary Series 11. Oxford: 181-367.

Rodwell, W. J. 1987. In Going, C. J. *The Mansio and other Sites in the South-eastern Sector of Caesaromagus: the Roman Pottery*. London: Chelmsford Archaeological Trust and Council for British Archaeology.

Rogeret, I. 1997. *La Seine-Maritime. Carte Archéologique de la Gaule* 76. Paris.

Rogers, A. 2005. 'Metalworking and late Roman power: a study of towns in later Roman Britain', *TRAC 2004: Proceedings of the Fourteenth Annual Theoretical Roman Archaeology Conference*. Oxford: Oxbow: 27-38.

Roskams, S. 1991. 'London – new understanding of the Roman city', in Jones, R. F. J. (ed.), *Roman Britain: Recent Trends*. Sheffield: J. R. Collis: 67-68.

Rostovtseff, M. 1923. 'Commodus-Hercules in Britain', *Journal of Roman Studies* 13: 91-109.

Rostovtzeff, M. I. 1926. *The Social and Economic History of the Roman Empire*. Oxford: Clarendon Press.

Rothenberg, B. Garcia Palomero, F. Bachmann, H. G. and Goethe, J. W. 1989. 'The Rio Tinto enigma', in Domergue, C. (ed.), *Mineria y metalurgia en las antiguas civilizaciones Mediterraneas y Europas*. Vol. 1. Madrid: 57-70.

Rowsome, P. (ed). (Forthcoming). *Excavations at No 1, Poultry*, London: Council for British Archaeology/English Heritage.

Roxan, M. 1981. 'The Distribution of Roman Military Diplomas', *Epigraphische Studien* 12: 265-286.

Roymans, N. 1990. *Tribal Societies in Northern Gaul: an Anthropological Perspective*. Amsterdam: Cingula.

Roymans, N. 1996. 'The sword or the plough. Regional dynamics in the romanisation of Belgic Gaul and the Rhineland area', in Roymans, N. (ed.), *From the Sword to the Plough. Three Studies on the Earliest Romanisation of Northern Gaul*. Amsterdam: Amsterdam University Press: 9-126.

Roymans, N. 2004. *Ethnic Identity and Imperial Power: the Batavians in the Early Roman Empire*. Amsterdam: Amsterdam University Press.

Rudd, C. 2006. 'The Belgae and Regni', in De Jersey, P. (ed.), *Celtic Coinage: New Discoveries, New Discussion*. BAR International Series 1532. Oxford: BAR Publishing: 145-181.

Rudd, C. Cottam, E. De Jersey, P. and Sills, J. Forthcoming. *Ancient British Coins*.

Rule, M and Monaghan, J. 1993. *A Gallo-Roman Trading Vessel from Guernsey, the Excavation and Recovery of a Third Century Shipwreck*. Guernsey.

Rupprecht, G. 1982. *Die Mainzer Römerschiffe: Berichte uber Endeckung, Ausgrabung und Bergung*. Mainz.

Saddington, D. 1990. 'The origin and nature of the German and British fleets', *Britannia* 21: 223-232.

Saddington, D. 2007. '*Classes*. The evolution of the Roman Imperial fleets', in Erdkamp, P. (ed.), *A Companion to the Roman Army*. Oxford: Blackwell: 201-217.

Salskov Roberts, H. 2002. 'A bronze statuette with hook-like hands found in Denmark', in *I bronzi antichi: produzione e tecnologia. Atti del XV Congresso Internazionale sui Bronzi Antichi*. Monographies Instrumentum 21. Montagnac: Éditions Monique Mergoil: 456-461.

Salway, P. 1993. *A History of Roman Britain*. Oxford: Oxford University Press.

Samuels, J. and Buckland, P. C. 1978. 'A Romano-British settlement at Sandtoft, South Humberside', *The Yorkshire Archaeological Journal* 50: 65-75.

Santa-Olalla, 1933-5. 'Bronce ingles de la Tene hallado en Játiba (Valenia)', *Annuario de prehistoria Madrilena* 4-6 (1933-35): 203-204.

Sas, K. 2004. '"Military" bracelets in Oudenburg: troop movements, origins and relations in the Litus Saxonicum in the 4th century AD', in Vermeulen, F. Sas, K. and Dhaeze, W. (eds.), *Archaeology in Confrontation. Aspects of Roman Military Presence in the Northwest. Studies in Honour of Prof. Em. Hugo Thoen*. Gent: Academia Press: 343-378.

Sauer, E. 2002. 'The Roman invasion of Britain (AD 43) in Imperial perspective: a response to Frere and Fulford', *Oxford Journal of Archaeology* 21 (4): 333-363.

Schäfer, K. 2000. 'Andernach - Drehscheibe des antiken Steinhandels', in Bockius, R. (ed.), *Steinbruch and Bergwerk: Denkmäler römischer Technikgeschichte zwischen Eifel und Rhein. Kataloghandbuch zu den Ausstellungen in den Museen von Mayen und Andernach. Vulkanpark-Forschungen* 2. Mainz: 83-109.

Scheers, S. 1972. 'Coinage and currency of the Belgic tribes during the Gallic War', *British Numismatic Journal* 41: 1-6.

Scheers, S. 1977. *Traité de numismatique celtique II: la Gaule belgique*. Annales littéraires de l'Université de Besançon 195. Paris: Les Belles Lettres.

Scheidel, W. 2002. 'A model of demographic and economic change in Roman Egypt after the Antonine plague', *Journal of Roman Archaeology* 15: 97-114.

Scheidel, W. 2009. 'In search of Roman economic growth', *Journal of Roman Archaeology* 22. 46-70.

Scheidel, W. Forthcoming. 'Coin quality, coin quantity, and coin value in early China and the Roman world', *Journal of the Oriental Society of Australia* (forthcoming).

Scheidel, W. Morris, I. and Saller, R. P. (eds.), 2007. *The Cambridge Economic History of the Greco-Roman World*. Cambridge: Cambridge University Press.

Schlüter, W. 1999a. 'The Battle of the Teutoburg Forest: archaeological research at Kalkriese near Osnabrück', in Creighton, J. D. and Wilson, R. J. A. (eds.), *Roman Germany: Studies in Cultural Interaction*. Portsmouth, R. I: Journal of Roman Archaeology: 125-159.

Schlüter, W. 1999b. 'Zum Stand der archäologischen Erforschung der Kalkrieser-Niewedder Senke', in Schlüter, W. and Wiegels, R. (eds.), *Rom, Germanien und die Ausgrabungen von Kalkriese*. Bramsche: 13-60.

Schmid, P. 1965. 'Die Keramik des 1. bis 3. Jahrhunderts n. Chr', *Probleme der Küstenforschung gebiet der südlichen Nordsee* 8: 9-72.

Schmid, P. 1981. 'Chauken: Archäologisches', in *Reallexikon der Germanischen Altertumskunde von Johannes Hoops* Vol. 4. Berlin/New York: Walter De Gruyter: 398-413.

Schmid, P. and Schuster, J. 1999. 'Dating the early layers of the wurt-settlement Feddersen Wierde', in Sarfatij, H. Verwers, W. J. H. and Woltering, P. J. (eds.), *In Discussion with the Past*. Zwolle: 97-106.

Schönberger, H. 1969. 'The Roman frontier in Germany: An archaeological survey', *Journal of Roman Studies* 59, no.1/2: 144-197.

Schönberger, H. 1985. 'Die römischen Truppenlager der frühen und mittleren Kaiserzeit zwischen Nordsee und Inn', *Bericht der Römisch-Germanischen Kommission* 66: 321-497.

Schrüfer-Kolb, I. 2004. *Roman Iron Production in Britain: Technological and Socio-economic Landscape Development along the Jurassic Ridge*. BAR British Series 380. Oxford: BAR Publishing.

Sealey, P. R. 1985. *Amphoras from the 1970 Excavations at Colchester Sheepen*. BAR British Series 142. Oxford.

Sealey, P. R. 2004. *The Boudican Revolt against Rome* (second edition). Princes Risborough, Buckinghamshire: Shire.

Sealey, P. R. 2007. *A Late Iron Age Warrior Burial from Kelvedon, Essex*. East Anglian Archaeology Report 118. Colchester.

Sealey, P. 2009. 'New light on the wine trade with Julio-Claudian Britain', *Britannia* 40: 1-40.

Seillier, C. 2004. 'La *castrum* et le port de *Gesoriacum* (Boulogne-sur-Mer), base de la *Classis Britannica* (IIe-IIIe siècles)', in Vermeulen, F. Sas, K. and Dhaeze, W. (eds.), *Archaeology in Confrontation. Aspects of Roman Military Presence in the Northwest. Studies in Honour of Prof. Em. Hugo Thoen*. Gent: Academia Press: 201-211.

Serneels, V. and Mangin, M. 1996. 'Sidérurgie ancienne (âge du fer-moyen âge): les zones productives principales entre le Rhin, les Alpes et les Pyrénées', *Revue archéologique de l'Est*: 193-198.

Service, E. R. 1971. *Primitive Social Organisation: an Evolutionary Perspective* (second edition). New York: Random House.

Shaffrey, R. 2003. 'The rotary querns from the Society of Antiquaries', excavations at Silchester 1890-1909'. *Britannia* 34: 143-174.

Sharples, N. 2007. 'Building communities and creating identities in the first millennium BC', in Haselgrove, C. and Pope, R. (eds.), *The Earlier Iron Age in Britain and the Near Continent*. Oxford: Oxbow: 174-184.

Sheldon, H. 1981. 'London and South East Britain', in King, A. and Henig, M. (eds.), *The Roman West in the Third Century*. BAR International Series 109. Oxford: 363-382.

Sheridan, A. 2007. 'Green treasures from the magic mountains', *British Archaeology* 96 (September/October 2007).

Sidrys, R. V. 2001. 'Roman imports among the west balts: commerce or "beads for the natives"', in Butrimas, A. (ed.), *Baltic Amber*. Vilnius: Publishing Office of Vilnius Academy of Fine Arts: 157-169.

Sills, J. 2003. *Gaulish and Early British Coinage*. London: Spink.

Sills, J. 2005. 'Identifying Gallic war uniface staters', in *Chris Rudd. List* 83 (September 2005).

Sills, J. 2006. 'Identifying 'boat type' quarter staters', *Chris Rudd. List 90* (November 2006): 2-5.

Simmons, B. B. 1980. 'Iron Age and Roman coasts around the Wash', in Thompson, F. H. (ed.), *Archaeology and Coastal Change*. London: Society of Antiquaries: 56-73.

Simmonds, A. Márquez-Grant, N. and Loe, L. 2008. *Life and Death in a Roman City: Excavation of a Roman Cemetery with a Mass Grave at 120-122 London Road, Gloucester*. Oxford: Oxford Archaeology.

Slim, H. Trousset, P. Paskoff, R. and Oueslati, A. 2004. *Le littoral de la Tunisie. Etude géoarchéologique et historique*. Paris.

Small, A. 1967. 'Excavations at Underhoull, Unst, Shetland', *Proceedings of the Society of Antiquaries of Scotland* 98: 225-248.

Smart, C. Rippon, S. Claughton, P. Forthcoming. 'Excavations at Calstock Roman Fort', *Britannia*.

Smekalova, T. and Voss, O. 2003. 'Field Procedures for Magnetic Investigations of Iron-Smelting Sites with Slag Pits', in Nørbach, L. C. (ed.), *Prehistoric and Medieval Direct Iron Smelting in Scandinavia and Europe: Aspects of Technology and Society: Proceedings of the Sandgjerg Conference, 16th to 20th September 1999, Comité pour la Sidurgie ancienne, L'UISPP*. Aarhus; Oxford: Aarhus University Press: 223-226.

Sommer, M. 1984. *Die Gürtel und Gürtelbeschläge des 4. und 5. Jahrhunderts im römischen Reich.* Bonner Hefte zur Vorgeschichte 22. Bonn.

Southern, P. 1989. 'The numeri of the Roman Imperial army', *Britannia* 20: 89-140.

Southern, P. 2001. *The Roman Empire from Severus to Constantine*. London: Routledge.

Southern, P. 2004. 'The army in Late Roman Britain', in Todd, M. (ed.), *A Companion to Roman Britain.* Oxford: Blackwell: 393-408.

Southern, P. and Dixon, K. 1996. *The Late Roman Army*. London.

Sparey Green, C. 1987. *Excavations at Poundbury, Dorchester, Dorset 1966-1982. Volume I: The Settlements*. Dorchester: Dorset Natural History and Archaeological Society.

Spaul, J. 2000. *COHORS 2: the Evidence for and a Short History of the Auxiliary Infantry Units of the Imperial Roman Army*. BAR International Series 841. Oxford: BAR Publishing.

Speidel, M. 1973. 'The Pay of the Auxilia' *Journal of Roman Studies* 63: 141-147.

Spitaels, P. 1969. *De Provinciaal-Romeinse Emailfibula*. Unpublished PhD thesis. University of Gent.

Spratling, M. 1972. *Southern British Decorated Bronzes of the Late Pre-Roman Iron Age*. Unpublished PhD thesis. University of London.

Stahl, M. 1989. 'Zwischen Abgrenzung und Integration: Die Verträge der Kaiser Mark Aurel und Commodus mit den Völkern jenseits der Donau', *Chiron* 19: 289-317.

Starr, C. G. 1960. *The Roman Imperial Navy 31 BC- AD 324* (second edition). Cambridge: W. Heffer.

Stary, P. F. 1995. 'Italic and Etruscan imports in the Baltic Sea area and in the British Isles during the pre-Roman Iron Age: Analogies, differences and backgrounds', in Swaddling, J. Walker, S. and Roberts, P. R. (eds.), *Italy in Europe: Economic Relations 700 BC- AD 50*. London: British Museum: 93-106.

Stead, I. M. 1967. 'A La Tene III burial at Welwyn Garden City', *Archaeologia* 101: 1-62.

Stead, I. M. 1979. *The Arras Culture*. York.

Stead, I. M. 1980. *Rudston Roman Villa*. Yorkshire Archaeological Society.

Stead, I. M. 1991. *Iron Age Cemeteries in East Yorkshire: Excavations at Burton Fleming, Rudston, Garton-on-the-Wolds and Kirkburn*. London: English Heritage in association with British Museum Press.

Stern, E. M. 2008. 'Glass production', in Oleson, J. P. (ed.), *The Oxford Handbook of Engineering and Technology in the Classical World*. Oxford: Oxford University Press: 520-547.

Stewart, N. 2002. *The Technology and Control of Mining in Roman Britain*. Unpublished D.Phil thesis. University of Oxford.

Stoklund, M. 2003. 'The first runes- the literary language of the Germani'. In Jørgensen *et al.* (eds.), *The Spoils of Victory: the North in the Shadow of the Roman Empire*. Copenhagen: Nationalmuseet: 172-179.

Storgaard, B. 1994. 'The Årslev grave and the relations between Funen and the continent at the end of the Late Roman period', in Nielsen, P. O. Randsborg, K. and Thrane, H. (eds.), *The Archaeology of Gudme and Lundeborg: Papers presented at a Conference at Svendborg, October 1991*. Copenhagen: Akademisk forlag, Universitetsforlaget i København, 1994: 160-168.

Storgaard, B. 2001. 'Himlingøje- barbarian Empire or Roman implantation?', in Storgaard, B. (ed.), *Military Aspects of the Aristocracy in Barbaricum in the Roman and Early Migration Periods. Papers from an International Research Seminar at the Danish National Museum, Copenhagen, 10-11 December 1999*. Copenhagen: The National Museum: 95-111.

Storgaard, B. 2003. 'Cosmopolitan aristocrats', in Jørgensen *et al.* (eds.), 2003. *The Spoils of Victory: the North in the Shadow of the Roman Empire*. Copenhagen: Nationalmuseet: 106- 125.

Strahl, E. 2006. 'Roman legionnaires and Germanic settlers at Bentumersiel', http://www.nihk.de/index.php?id=2234

Straker, V. 1984. 'First and second century carbonised cereal grain from Roman London', in van Zeist, W. and Casparie, W. A. (eds.), *Plants and Ancient Man: Studies in Palaeoethnobotany*. Rotterdam: Balkema: 323-329.

Strathern, M. 1988. *The Gender of the Gift: Problems with Women and Problems with Society in Melanesia*. Berkeley: University of California Press.

Strobel, K. 1999. 'Pseudophänomene der römischen Militär- und Provinzgeschichte am Beispiel des Falles desobergermanisch-raetischen Limes. Neue Ansätze zu einer Geschichte der Jahrzehnte nach 253 n. Chr. An Rhein und oberer Donau', in Gudea, N. (ed.), *Roman Frontier Studies 1997. Proceedings of the XVIIth International Congress of Roman Frontier Studies*. Zalău: 9-33.

Strong, D. 1968. 'The Monument', in Cunliffe, B. W. *Fifth Report on the Excavations of the Roman Fort at Richborough, Kent*. Oxford: 40-73.

Strong, D. E. 1979. *Greek and Roman Silver Plate*. London/New York: Methuen.

Stuart, J. 1865. 'Notices of a group of artificial islands in the loch of Dowalton, Wigtonshire, and of other artificial islands or "crannogs" throughout Scotland. *Proceedings of the Society of Antiquaries of Scotland* 6: 114-177.

Stuart, P and Bogaers, J. E. 2001. *Nehalennia. Römische steindenkmäler aus der Oosterschelde bei Colijnsplaat (I. Textband; II. Tafelband)*. Leiden: Rijksmuseum van oudheden.

Stylegar, F. A. and Grimm, O. 2005. 'Boat-houses in the North Atlantic', *International Journal of Nautical Archaeology* 34.2: 253-268.

Swain, H. and Williams, T. 'The population of Roman London', in Clark, J. et al. (eds.), *Londinium and Beyond: Essays on Roman London and its hinterland for Harvey Sheldon*. York: Council for British Archaeology: 33-40.

Swan, V. G. 2002. 'The Roman pottery of Yorkshire in its wider historical context', in Wilson, P. and Price, J. (eds.), *Aspects of Industry in Roman Yorkshire and the North*. Oxford: Oxbow: 35-79.

Swift, E. 2000a. *Regionality in Dress Accessories in the Late Roman West*, Monographies Instrumentum 11. Montagnac: Éditions Monique Mergoil.

Swift, E. 2000b. *The End of the Western Roman Empire: An Archaeological Investigation*. Stroud: Tempus.

Swift, E. 2003. 'Transformations in meaning: amber and glass beads across the Roman frontier' in Carr, G. Swift, E. and Weekes, J. (eds.), *TRAC 2002. Proceedings of the Twelfth Annual Theoretical Roman Archaeology Conference. Canterbury 2002*. Oxford: Oxbow.

Symonds, R. P. 2000 Samian ware and the port of Roman London, paper presented at the second International ROCT Conference: The Economy of Roman Pottery: Approaching Production Mechanisms and Exchange Patterns, the Catholic University of Leuven, Belgium, May 2000.

Symonds, R. P. 2003. 'Romano-British amphorae', in Plouviez, J. (ed.), *Journal of Roman Pottery Studies 10. Amphorae in Britain and the Western Empire*: 50-59.

Symonds, R. P. and Wade, S. M. 1999. *Roman Pottery from Excavations in Colchester, 1971- 1986*. Colchester Archaeological Report 10. Colchester.

Taayke, E. 1997. 'Die einheimische Keramik der nördlichen Niederlande, 600 v.Chr. bis 300 n.Chr. Teil V: Übersicht und Schlußfolgerungen', *Berichten van de Rijksdienst voor het Oudheidkundig Bodemonderzoek*. (1996-7): 163-208.

Taayke, E. 1999. 'The smell of higher nectar', in Sarfatij, H. Verwers, W. J. H. and Woltering, P. J. (eds.), *In Discussion with the Past*. Zwolle: 195-203.

Taylor, J. 2001. 'The Isle of Portland: an Iron Age port of trade', *Oxford Journal of Archaeology* 20(2): 187-205.

Taylor, J. 2007. *An Atlas of Roman Rural Settlement in England*. London: Council for British Archaeology.

Taylor, T. 1992. 'The Gundestrup Cauldron', *Scientific American* (March 1992): 66-71.

Tchernia, A. 1986. *Le vin de Italie Romaine. Essai d'histoire économique d'après les amphores*. Rome: Collection de l'école Française de Rome.

Teegan, W. R. 1997a. 'Das provinzialrömische Emailgefäß aus dem Vehner Moor. I Fundgeschichte und kulturgeschichtliche Auswertung', *Archäologische Mitteilungen aus Nordwestdeutschland* 20: 89-107.

Teegan, W. R. 1997b. 'Das provinzialrömische Emailgefäß aus dem Vehner Moor. II. Technologische Untersuchungen', *Archäologische Mitteilungen aus Nordwestdeutschland* 20: 109-114.

Teigelake, U. 2006. 'Inland water transport in the Pre-Roman Iron Age in northern Germany and its role in intra- and intercultural communication', in Blue, L. Hocker, F. and Englert, A. (eds.), *Connected by the Sea. Proceedings of the Tenth International Symposium on Boat and Ship Archaeology. Roskilde 2003*. Oxford: Oxbow: 152-156.

Temin, P. 2001. 'A market economy in the early Roman Empire', *The Journal of Roman Studies* 91: 169-181.

Tempelmann-Maczynska, M. 1985. *Perlen in Mitteleuropäischen Barbaricum*. Römisches-Germanische Forschungen Band 43. Mainz: Philipp Von Zabern.

Theune, C. 2004. *Germanen und Romanen in der Alamannia. Ergänzungsbände zum Reallexikon der Germanischen Altertumskunde* 45. Berlin.

Thoen, H. 1978. *De Belgische kustvlakte in de Romeinse tijd*. Brussels.

Thoen, H. 1981. 'The third-century Roman occupation in Belgium: the evidence of the coastal plain', in King, A. and Henig, M. (eds.), *The Roman West in the Third Century*. BAR International Series 109. Oxford: 245-257.

Thomas, R. 2008. 'Supply-chain networks and the Roman invasion of Britain: a case study from Alchester, Oxfordshire', in Stallibrass, S. and Thomas, R. (eds.), *Feeding the Roman Army: the Archaeology of Production and Supply in NW Europe*. Oxford: Oxbow: 31-51.

Thomas, R. and Stallibrass, S. 2008. 'For starters: producing and supplying food to the army in the Roman north-west provinces', in Stallibrass, S. and Thomas, R. (eds.), *Feeding the Roman Army: the Archaeology of Production and Supply in NW Europe*. Oxford: Oxbow: 1-17.

Thomas, S. 1966. 'Die provinzialrömischen Scheibenfibeln der römischen Kaiserzeit im freien Germanien', *Berliner Jahrbuch für Vor- und Frühgeschichte* 6. Berlin.

Thompson, E. A. 1977. 'Britain, A.D 406-410', *Britannia* 8: 303-318.

Thomsen, R. 1952. 'Ancient British coins found in Denmark', *Numismatic chronicle* ser.6, Vol. 12: 126-128.

Thorndeycraft, V. R. Pirrie, D. and Brown, A. G. 2004. 'Alluvial records of medieval and prehistoric tin mining on Dartmoor, southwest England', *Geoarchaeology* 19 (3): 219-236.

Timberlake, S. and Kidd, A. D. 2005. 'The archaeological excavation of a Roman mine shaft and gallery ('Pot shaft') at Engine vein, Alderley Edge', in Timberlake, S. and Prag, A. J. N. W. *The Archaeology of Alderley Edge: Survey, Excavation and Experiment in an Ancient Mining Landscape*. BAR British Series 396. Oxford: 79-97.

Timby, J. and Rigby, V. 2007. 'Gallo-Belgic pottery database: internet edition'. http://www.ox.ac.uk

Todd, M. 1996. 'Ancient mining on Mendip, Somerset: a preliminary report on recent work', in Newman, P. (ed.), *The Archaeology of Mining and Metallurgy in South-West Britain*. Matlock: 47-51.

Todd, M. 1998. 'The Germanic peoples', in Cameron, A. Garnsey, P. (eds.), *The Cambridge Ancient History. Volume 13. The Late Empire, A.D. 337-425*. Cambridge: Cambridge University Press: 461-486.

Todd, M. 2004. 'The Claudian conquest and its consequences', in Todd, M. (ed.), *A Companion to Roman Britain*. Oxford: Blackwell: 42-59.

Tomalin, D. 2006. 'Coastal villas, maritime villas; a perspective from Southern Britain', *Journal of Maritime Archaeology* 1: 29-84.

Tomlin, R. S. O. and Hassall, M. W. C. 2003. 'Inscriptions', *Britannia* 34: 361-382.

Tomber, R. 2008. *Indo-Roman Trade: from Pots to Pepper*. London: Duckworth.

Tomber, R. and Dore, J. 1998. *The National Roman Fabric Reference Collection: a Handbook*. London: Museum of London.

Toomey, W. 2003. 'Coins', in Germany, M. *Excavations at Great Holts Farm, Boreham, Essex, 1992-94*. East Anglian Archaeology 105. Chelmsford: Essex County Council: 68-73.

Trakadas, A. 2005. 'The archaeological evidence for fish processing in the western Mediterranean', in Bekker-Nielsen, T. (ed.), *Ancient Fishing and Fish Processing in the Black Sea Region*. Aarhus: Aarhus University Press: 47-82.

Trimpe Burger, J. A. 1973. 'The islands of Zeeland and south Holland in Roman times', *Berichten van de Rijksdienst voor het Oudheidkundig Bodemonderzok* 23: 135-148.

Trott, K. and Tomalin, D. 2003. 'The maritime role of the island of Vectis in the British pre-Roman Iron Age', *International Journal of Nautical Archaeology* 32 (2): 158-181.

Tuffreau-Libre, M. Mossmann-Bouquillon, A. Symonds, R. P. 1995. 'La Ceramique dite Black-Burnished dans le Nord dae la France', in Rivet. L. (ed.), *Actes du Congres de Rouen 25-28 Mai 1995, SFECAG*. Marseille: 91-112.

Tyers, P. 1996a. 'Roman amphoras in Britain', *Internet Archaeology* 1.

Tyers, P. 1996b. *Roman Pottery in Britain*. London: Batsford.

Tyers, P. Forthcoming. *Atlas of Roman pottery in Britain*. Oxford: Oxbow.

Tykot, R. H. 2004. 'Trade and exchange', in Bogucki, P. and Crabtree, P. J. (eds.), *Ancient Europe 8000 BC-AD 1000. Encyclopedia of the Barbarian World. Volume 1*. New York; London: 65-71.

Tylecote, R. F. 1986. *The Prehistory of Metallurgy in the British Isles*. London: The Institute of Metals.

Tyler, S. 1990. 'A supporting arm brooch from Springfield', *Essex Archaeology and History* 21: 144-146.

Tyler, S. 1995. 'A supporting-arm brooch from Henham', *Essex Archaeology and History* 26: 270-271.

Ulbert, G. 1977. 'Die Römischen Funde von Bentumersiel', *Probleme der Küstenforschung im südlichen Nordseegebiet* 12: 33-65.

Upex, S. G. 2008. *The Romans in the East of England. Settlement and Landscape in the Lower Nene Valley*. Stroud: Tempus.

Van Arsdell, R. D. 1989. *Celtic Coinage of Britain*. London: Spink.

Van Arsdell, R. D. 1992. 'Money supply and credit in Iron Age Britain', in Mays, M. (ed.), *Celtic Coinage in Britain and Beyond; the Eleventh Oxford Symposium on Coinage and Monetary History*. BAR British Series 222. Oxford: BAR Publishing: 139-150.

Van Buchem, H. J. H. 1941. *De Fibulae van Nijmegen*. Nijmegen: Centrale Drukkerij N.V.

Van de Noort, R. 2003. 'Ancient seascapes: The social context of seafaring in the Bronze Age', *World Archaeology* 35, 3: 404-15.

Van de Noort, R. 2004a. 'The Humber, its sewn-plank boats, their contexts and the significance of it all', in Clark, P. (ed.), *The Dover Bronze Age Boat in Context: Society and Water Transport in Prehistoric Europe*. Oxford: Oxbow: 90-98.

Van de Noort, R. 2004b. *The Humber Wetlands. The Archaeology of a Dynamic Landscape*. Bollington: Windgather.

Vanderhoeven, A. Martens, M. Ervynck, A. Cooremans, B. and Van Neer, W. 2001. 'Interdisziplinäre Untersuchungen im römischen vicus von Tienen (Belgien). Die integration von ökologischen und archäologischen Daten', in Frey, M. and Hanel, N. *Archäologie- Naturwissenschaften- Umwelt. Beiträge der Arbeitsgemeinschaft "römische Archäologie" auf dem 3. Deutschen Archäologenkongress in Heidelberg 25.5-30.5. 1999. BAR International Series 929*. Oxford: 13-31.

Van der Linden, E. (Forthcoming). Texel, Den Burg, pottery report.

Vander Linden, M. 2007. 'What linked the Bell Beakers in third millennium BC Europe?', *Antiquity* 81. No. 312: 343-352.

Van Der Roost, J. 1988. 'Die Römischen Fibeln von de Horden', *Berichten Rijksdienst Oudheidkundig Bodemonderzoek* 38: 141-202.

Van der Veen, M. 2008. 'Food as embodied material culture: diversity and change in plant food consumption in Roman Britain', *Journal of Roman Archaeology* 21: 83-109.

Van der Vin, J. P. A. 1996. 'Roman coins in the Dutch province of Friesland', in King, C. E. and Wigg, D. G. (eds.), *Coin Finds and Coin Use in the Roman World*. Berlin: Mann Verlag: 357-371.

Van der Vin, J. P. A. 1999. 'Roman coins from Wijnaldum', in Besteman, J. C. *et al.* (eds.), *The Excavations at Wijnaldum: Reports on Frisia in Roman and Medieval Times*. Volume 1. Rotterdam: A.A. Balkema: 185-189.

Van der Vin, J. P. A. 2002. 'Coin use in and around military camps on the lower-Rhine: Nijmegen-Kops plateau', in Blois, L. de. and Rich, J. (eds.), *The Transformation of Economic Life under the Roman Empire*. Amsterdam: J. C. Gieben: 160-171.

Van Dockum, S. G. 1995. 'Het rivierengebied', in Bechert, T. and Williams, W. J. H. (eds.), *De Romeinse rijksgrens tussen Moezel en Noordzeekust*. Utrecht: 77-88.

Van Doorselaer, A. 1973. 'In het vaarwater van Nehalennia', in Van Es, W. A. Hubrecht, A. V. M. and Stuart, P. (eds.), *Archeologie en Historie. Opgedragen aan H. Brunsting bij zijn zeventigste verjaardag*. Bussum: 275-280.

Van Enckevort, H. 2004. 'The Roman military complex in Nijmegen (NL)', in Vermeulen, F. Sas, K. and Dhaeze, W. (eds.), *Archaeology in Confrontation. Aspects of Roman Military Presence in the Northwest. Studies in Honour of Prof. Em. Hugo Thoen*. Gent: Academia Press: 103-124.

Van Es, W. A. 1967. 'Wijster: A native village beyond the Imperial frontier 150-425 AD', *Palaeohistoria* 11.

Vang Petersen, P. 1994. 'Excavations at sites of treasure trove finds at Gudme', in Nielsen, P. O. Randsborg, K. and Thrane, H. (eds.), *The Archaeology of Gudme and Lundeborg: Papers Presented at a Conference at Svendborg, October 1991*. Copenhagen: Akademisk forlag, Universitetsforlaget i København: 30-40.

Van Heeringen, R. M. 1985. *Archäologisches Korrespondenzblatt* 15: 371-83.

Vanhoutte, S. Dhaeze, W. and De Clercq, W. 2009. 'Pottery consumption at the Roman fort in Oudenburg, Northern Gaul', *The Journal of Roman Pottery Studies* 14.

Van Neer, W. and Lentacker, A. 1994. 'New archaeozoological evidence for the consumption of locally-produced fish sauce in the northern provinces of the Roman Empire', *Archaeofauna* 3: 53-62.

Van Neer, W. Hamilton-Dyer, S. Cappers, R. Desender, K. and Ervynck, A. 2005. 'New evidence from a Roman context in Belgium for fish sauce locally produced in northern Gaul', *Archaeofauna* 14: 171-182.

Van Ossel, P. 1992. *Etablissements ruraux de l'Antiquité tardive dans le nord de la Gaule*. Supplément à Gallia 51. Paris.

Verboven, K. S. 2007. 'Good for business. The Roman army and the emergence of a 'business class' in the northwestern provinces of the Roman Empire (1st century BCE- 3rd century CE', in Blois, L. de. and Cascio, E. (eds.), *The Impact of the Roman Army (200 BC- AD 476). Economic, Social, Political, Religious and Cultural Aspects. Impact of Empire Volume 6*. Boston: Brill: 295-313.

Verlinde, A. D. and Erdrich, M. 1998. 'Eine germanische Siedlung der späten Kaiserzeit mit umwehrter Anlage und umfangreicher Eisenindustrie in Heeten, Provinz Overijssel, Niederlande', *Germania* 76: 693-719.

Volkers, T. B. 1991. '*Terra sigillata* aus Friesischen Wurten', *Germania* 69: 176-186.

Volkers, T. B. 1999. 'The *terra sigillata* from Winsum-Tjitsma in regional perspective', in Besteman, J. C. *et al.* (eds.), *The Excavations at Wijnaldum: Reports on Frisia in Roman and Medieval Times*. Volume 1. Rotterdam: A.A. Balkema: 151-156.

Vollgraff, C. W. 1917. 'Eene Romeinsche koopacte uit Tolsum', *De Vrije Fries 25*: 71-101.

Vons, P. and Bosman, A. 1988. 'Inheemse boeren bezochten de verlaten Romeinse versterkingen Velsen I en II', *Westerheem* 37: 1-16.

Von Schnurbein, S. 2003. 'Augustus in Germania and his new "town" at Waldgirmes east of the Rhine', *Journal of Roman Archaeology* 16 (1): 93-107.

Von Uslar, R. 1938. *Westgermanische Bodenfunde des ersten bis dritten Jahrhunderts nach Christus aus Mittel- und West-Deutschland.* Berlin: W. de Gruyter.

Vos, P. C. 1999. 'The Subatlantic evolution of the coastal area around the Wijnaldum-Tjitsma terp', in Besteman, J. C. *et al.* (eds.), *The Excavations at Wijnaldum: Reports on Frisia in Roman and Medieval Times*. Volume 1. Rotterdam: A.A. Balkema: 33-72.

Vos, P. C. and Van Heeringen, R. M. 1997. 'Holocene geology and occupation history of the Province of Zeeland, SW Netherlands', *Mededelingen Nederlands Institut voor Toegepaste Geowetenschappen TNO* 59: 5-109.

Voss, H. U. 1998. *Corpus der römischen Funde im europäischen Barbaricum. Deutschland Band 3: Bundesland Mecklenburg Vorpommern.* Bonn: Dr. Rudolf Habelt GMBH.

Voss, O. 2003. 'The archaeology of iron smelting in Denmark', in *Archaeometallurgy in Europe*: Volume 1. International conference: 24-25-26 September 2003, Milan, Italy: proceedings. Milan: Associazione italiana metallurgia: 497-505.

Voss, O. and Smekalova, T. 2003. 'Using of magnetic prospecting for investigation of Roman Age iron smelting sites with slag blocks in Denmark', in *Archaeometallurgy in Europe*: Volume 1. International conference: 24-25-26 September 2003, Milan, Italy: proceedings. Milan: Associazione italiana metallurgia: 53-62.

Vouga, P. 1923. *La Tène.* Leipzig.

Walke, N. 1965. *Das römische Donaukastell Straubing-Sorviodurum.* Limesforschungen 3. Berlin: Mann.

Walker, D. R. 1988. 'The Roman coins', in Cunliffe, B. W. (ed.), *The Temple of Sulis Minerva at Bath. Vol. 2. Finds from the Sacred Spring.* Oxford: 281-339.

Walker, S. 1981. 'The burden of Roman grandeur: aspects of public building in the cities of Asia Minor and Achaea', in King, A. C. and Henig, M. (eds.), *The Roman West in the Third Century: Contributions from Archaeology and History.* Vol. 1. BAR International Series 109: Oxford: 189-197.

Wallace, C. and Turner-Walker, C. 1998. In Clarke, C. P. *Excavations to the South of Chignall Roman Villa, Essex, 1977-81.* Chelmsford: Archaeology Section, Essex County Council.

Wallerstein, I. 1974. *The Modern World System.* New York: Academic Press.

Walsh, M. 2002. 'Pudding Pan: a case study on the enhancement of the Romano-British maritime record', in (eds.), Georgiadis, M. and Muskett, G. M. *The Seas of Antiquity. Proceedings of the Liverpool Interdisciplinary Symposium in Antiquity. 20 May 2000.* Liverpool: Publications of the Humanities Graduate University of Liverpool: 76-87.

Walters, B. 1992. *The Forest of Dean Iron Industry: 1st to 4th centuries AD.* Unpublished M.Phil thesis. Milton Keynes: The Open University.

Walters, B. 1999. *The Forest of Dean Iron Industry: 1st to 4th centuries A.D.* Lydney: Dean Archaeological Group.

Ward-Perkins, B. 2005. *The Fall of Rome and the End of Civilization.* Oxford: Oxford University Press.

Warner, R. B. 1967. 'The Carnanton tin ingot', *Cornish Archaeology.* 6: 29-31.

Waterbolk, H. J. and Waterbolk, H. T. 1991. 'Amber on the coast of the Netherlands', in Nenquin, J. A. E. and Thoen, H. (eds.), *Liber amicorum Jacques A. E. Nenquin.* Gent: Universiteit Gent, Seminarie voor Archeologie: 201-209.

Watt, M. 2003. 'Weapon graves and regional groupings of weapon types and burial customs in Denmark, 100 BC-400 AD', in Jørgensen, L. *et al.* (eds.), *The Spoils of Victory: the North in the Shadow of the Roman Empire.* Copenhagen: Nationalmuseet: 180-193.

Webster, G. (Chadderton, J. (ed.)). 2002. *The Legionary Fortress at Wroxeter, Excavations by Graham Webster, 1955-85.* London: English Heritage.

Weder, M. 1997-8. *Münzen und Münzstätten der Gallisch-Römischen Kaiser.* Teil I SNR 76, 1997 and Teil II, SNR 77, 1998.

Welch, P. D. 1991. *Moundville's Economy.* Tuscaloosa: The University of Alabama Press.

Wells, C. M. 1972. *The German Policy of Augustus.* Oxford.

Wells, C. M. 1978. 'Review', Luttwak, E. N. The Grand Strategy of the Roman Empire: From the First Century A.D. to the Third. *The American Journal of Philology* 99 (4) (Winter 1978): 527-529.

Wells, C. M. 1999. 'The German policy of Augustus: 25 years on', in Gudea, N. (ed.), *Roman Frontier Studies: Proceedings of the XVIIth International Congress of Roman Frontier Studies.* Zalău: The County Council of Saălaj, The County Museum of History and Art Zalău: "Porolissum": 3-7.

Wells, P. S. 1994. 'Interactions between Denmark and Central Europe in the Late Prehistoric Iron Age: the prelude to Gudme and Lundeborg', in Nielsen, P. O. Randsborg, K. and Thrane, H. (eds.), *The Archaeology of Gudme and Lundeborg: Papers Presented at a Conference at Svendborg, October 1991.* Copenhagen: Akademisk forlag, Universitetsforlaget i København: 151-159.

Wells, P. S. 1996. 'Production within and beyond Imperial boundaries: goods, exchange, and power in Roman Europe', *Journal of World Systems Research* 2, No. 13. Electronic Journal, URL (accessed May 2010): http://jwsr.ucr.edu/archive/vol2/v2_nd.php

Wells, P. S. 2001. *Beyond Celts, Germans and Scythians. Archaeology and Identity in Iron Age Europe.* London: Duckworth.

Werner, J. 1936. 'Zur Herkunft und Zeitstellung der Hemmoorer Eimer und der Eimer mit gewellten Kanneluren', *Bonner Jahrbuch* 140-141: 395-410.

Werner, J. 1938. 'Die römischen Bronzegeschirrdepots des 3. Jahrhunderts und die mittel-deutsche Skellettgräbergruppe', in Sprockhoff, E. (ed.), *Marburger Studien*. Darmstadt: 259-267.

Werner, J. 1973. Bemerkungen zur mitteldeutschen Skelettgräbergruppe Hassleben-Leuna. Zur Herkunft der "ingentia auxilia germanorum" des gallischen Sonderreiches in den Jahren 259-274 n.Chr', in Beuman, H. (ed.), *Festschrift für Walter Schlesinger 1*. Mitteldeutsche Forschungen 74/1. Cologne; Vienna: 1-30.

Wheeler, R. E. M. 1932. *Report on the Excavation of the Prehistoric, Roman and Post-Roman Site in Lydney Park, Gloucestershire*. Oxford: Oxford University Press.

Wheeler, R. E. M. 1954. *Rome Beyond the Imperial Frontiers*. London: G. Bell and Sons.

Wheeler, R. E. M. and Wheeler, T. V. 1936. *Verulamium: a Belgic and Two Roman Cities*. Oxford.

White, D. A. 1961. *Litus Saxonicum: the British Saxon Shore in Scholarship and History*. Wisconsin.

Whittaker, C. R. 1983. 'Late Roman trade and traders', in Garnsey, P. Hopkins, K. and Whittaker, C. R. (eds.), *Trade in the Ancient Economy*. London: 163-180.

Whittaker, C. R. 1994. *Frontiers of the Roman Empire: a Social and Economic Study*. Baltimore.

Whittaker, C. R. 2004. 'Where are Roman frontiers now? An Introduction', in Whittaker, C. R. *Rome and its Frontiers: the Dynamics of Empire*. London: Routledge: 1-27.

Whittick, G. C. 1982. 'The earliest Roman lead-mining on Mendip and in North Wales: a reappraisal', *Britannia* 13: 113-123.

Wickenden, N. P. 1986. 'Prehistoric settlement and the Romano-British 'small town' at Heybridge, Essex', *Essex Archaeology and History* 17: 7-68.

Wickenden, N. P. 1992. *The Temple and other Sites in the North-eastern Sector of Caesaromagus*. Chelmsford.

Wickham, C. 2005. *Framing the Early Middle Ages. Europe and the Mediterranean 400-800*. Oxford: Oxford University Press.

Wightman, E. M. 1981. 'The fate of Gallo-Roman villages in the third century', in King, A. C. and Henig, M. (eds.), *The Roman West in the Third Century*. BAR International Series 109. Oxford: 237-243.

Wightman, E. M. 1985. *Gallia Belgica*. London: Batsford.

Wilbers-Rost, S. 2003a. 'Der Hinterhalt gegen Varus. Zu Konstruktion und Funktion der Germanischen Wallanlage auf dem Oberesch in Kalkriese', *Die Kunde* 54: 123-142.

Wilbers-Rost, S. 2003b. 'Die Befunde auf dem Oberesch in Kalkriese und die Varusschlacht', *Archäologie in Niedersachsen* 6: 30-36.

Wild, J. P. 1976. 'Loanwords and Roman expansion in north-west Europe', *World Archaeology* 8.1: 57-64.

Wild, J. P. 1978. 'Cross-Channel trade and the textile industry', in du Plat Taylor, J. and Cleere, H. (eds.), *Roman Shipping and Trade: Britain and the Rhine Provinces*. London: Council for British Archaeology: 79-82.

Wilkes, J. 2000. 'The Danube provinces', in Bowman, A. K. Garnsey, P. Rathbone, D. (eds.), *Cambridge Ancient History. Volume 11. The High Empire A.D. 70-192*. Cambridge: Cambridge University Press: 577-603.

Wilkes, J. 2005. 'Provinces and frontiers', in Bowman, A. K. Garnsey, P. and Cameron, A. (eds.), *The Cambridge Ancient History. Volume 12. The Crisis of Empire, A.D. 193-337*. Cambridge: Cambridge University Press: 212-268.

Willems, W. J. H. 1981. 'Romans and Batavians: A regional study in the Dutch eastern river area I', *Berichten Rijksdienst Oudheidkundig Bodemonderzoek* 31: 7-217.

Willems, W. J. H. 1984. 'Romans and Batavians: A regional study in the Dutch eastern river area II', *Berichten Rijksdienst Oudheidkundig Bodemonderzoek* 34: 39-331.

Willers, H. W. 1901. *Die römischen Bronzeeimer von Hemmoor*. Hannover.

Willers, H. 1907. *Neue Untersuchungen über die römische Bronzeindustrie von Capua und von Niedergermanien, besonders auf die Funde aus Deutschland und dem Norden hin*. Hannover; Leipzig.

Williams, D. F. 1986. 'Report on the amphorae', in Foster, J. *The Lexden Tumulus: a Re-appraisal of an Iron Age Burial from Colchester, Essex*. BAR British Series 156. Oxford: 124-132.

Williams, D. F. 1989. 'Amphorae', in Stead, I. M. and Rigby, V. *Verulamium: the King Harry Lane site*. London: English Heritage: 115-116.

Williams, D. F. 1990. In Perrin, J. R. *Roman Pottery from the Colonia 2: General Accident and Rougier Street*. London: Published for the York Archaeological Trust by the Council for British Archaeology.

Williams, D. F. 1999. In Niblett, R. *The Excavation of a Ceremonial Site at Folly Lane, Verulamium*. London: Society for the Promotion of Roman Studies.

Williams, D. F. 2003. 'Cretan wine in Roman Britain', in Plouviez, J. (ed.), *Journal of Roman Pottery Studies 10. Amphorae in Britain and the Western Empire*: 26-31.

Williams, D. F. 2004. In Dalwood, H. and Edwards, R. *Excavations at Deansway, Worcester 1988-89: Romano-British Small Town to Late Medieval City*. York: Council for British Archaeology.

Williams, D. F. and Carreras, C. 1995. 'North African amphorae in Britain: a re-appraisal', *Britannia* 26: 231-252.

Williams, D. F. and Dannell, G. B. 1978. 'Petrological analysis of Arretine and early samian: a preliminary report', in Arthur, P. R. and Marsh, G. D. (eds.), *Early Fine Wares in Roman Britain.* BAR British Series 57. Oxford: 5-13.

Williams, D. F. and Peacock, D. P. S. 1979. In Partridge, C. 'Excavations at Puckeridge and Braughing 1975-79', *Hertfordshire Archaeology* 7: 28-132.

Williams, D. F. and Peacock, D. P. S. 1983. 'The importation of olive-oil into Roman Britain', in Blazquez, J. M. and Remesal, J. (eds.), *Produccion Y Comercio Del Aceite En La Antiguedad, II Congresso.* Madrid: 263-80.

Williams, J. Burnett, A. La Niece, S. and Cowell, M. 2007. 'A new Gallo-Belgic coin die from Hampshire', in Gosden, C. Hamerow, H. de Jersey, P. and Lock, G. (eds.), *Communities and Connections: Essays in Honour of Barry Cunliffe.* Oxford: Oxbow: 357-366.

Williams, S. 1997. *Diocletian and the Roman Recovery.* New York: Routledge.

Williamson, T. 2005. *Sandlands. The Suffolk Coast and Heaths.* Bollington: Windgather.

Williams-Thorpe, O. and Thorpe, R. S. 2007. 'The provenance of donkey mills from Roman Britain', *Archaeometry* 30, 2: 275-289.

Willis, S. 1998a. In Main, L. 'Excavation of a timber round-house and broch at the Fairy Knowe, Buchlyvie, Stirlingshire, 1975-8', *Proceedings of the Society of Antiquaries of Scotland* 128: 293-417.

Willis, S. 1998b. 'Samian pottery in Britain: exploring its distribution and archaeological potential', *The Archaeological Journal* 155: 82-133.

Willis, S. 2002. 'A date with the past: Late Bronze Age and Iron Age pottery and chronology', in Woodward, A. and Hill, J. D. (eds.), *Prehistoric Britain: the Ceramic Basis.* Oxford: Oxbow: 4-21.

Willis, S. 2003. 'The character of Lyon ware distribution (with particular attention to the evidence from the Midlands and the North of Britain', in Plouviez, J. (ed.), *Journal of Roman Pottery Studies 10. Amphorae in Britain and the Western Empire*: 125-138.

Willis, S. 2005. 'Samian Pottery, a Resource for the Study of Roman Britain and Beyond: the Results of the English Heritage Funded Samian Project. An E-Monograph', *Internet Archaeology* 17.

Willis, S. 2007. 'Sea, coast, estuary, land and culture in Iron Age Britain', in Haselgrove, C. and Moore, T. (eds.), *The Later Iron Age in Britain and Beyond.* Oxford: Oxbow: 107-129.

Wilmott, T. 1982. 'Excavations at Queen Street and Roman wells in London', *Transactions of the London and Middlesex Archaeological Society* 33: 1-78.

Wilmott, T. (ed.), 2009. *Hadrian's Wall. Archaeological Research by English Heritage 1976-2000.* Swindon: English Heritage.

Wilson, A. I. 2002. 'Machines, power and the ancient economy', *The Journal of Roman Studies* 92: 1-32.

Wilson, A. I. 2006. 'Fishy business: Roman exploitation of marine resources', *Journal of Roman Archaeology* 19.2: 525-537.

Wilson, A. I. 2007. 'The metal supply of the Roman Empire', in Papi, E. (ed.), *Supplying Rome and the Empire: the Proceedings of an International Seminar held at Siena-Certosa di Pontignano on May 2-4, 2004, on Rome, the Provinces, Production and Distribution.* Journal of Roman Archaeology supplementary series 69. Portsmouth, R.I: Journal of Roman Archaeology: 109-125.

Wilson, A. I. 2009a. 'Economy and trade', in Bispham, E. (ed.), *Roman Europe: 1000 BC – AD 400.* Short Oxford History of Europe. Volume 2. Oxford: Oxford University Press: 170-202.

Wilson, A. I. 2009b. 'Approaches to quantifying Roman trade', in Bowman, A. K. and Wilson, A. I. (eds.), *Quantifying the Roman Economy: Methods and Problems,* Oxford Studies in the Roman Economy 1.Oxford: Oxford University Press: 213-49.

Wilson, A. I. 2009c. 'Indicators for Roman economic growth: a response to Walter Scheidel', *Journal of Roman Archaeology* 22: 71-82.

Wolagiewicz, R. 1970. 'Der Zufluss römischer Importe in das Gebiet nördlich der mittleren Donau in der älteren Kaiserzeit', *Zeitschrift für Archäologie* 4: 222-249.

Wollschläger, B. 1992. 'Ein Eisenverhüttungsplatz der spätrömischen Kaiserzeit und frühen Völkerwanderungszeit bei Göhlen, Kr. Ludwigslust', *Ausgrabungen und Funde* 37. Berlin: 151-155.

Woltering, P. J. 1979. 'Occupation history of Texel, II. The archaeological survey: Preliminary report', *Berichten Rijksdienst Oudheidkundig Bodemonderzoek* 29: 7-113.

Wood, I. 1990. 'The Channel from the 4th to the 7th centuries AD', in McGrail, S. (ed.), *Maritime Celts, Frisians and Saxons: Papers Presented to a Conference at Oxford in November 1988.* London: Council for British Archaeology: 93-97.

Woolf, G. 1993a. 'Rethinking the oppida', *Oxford Journal of Archaeology* 12 (2): 223-234.

Woolf, G. 1993b. 'The social significance of trade in Late Iron Age Europe', in Scarre, C. and Healey, F. (eds.), *Trade and Exchange in Prehistoric Europe.* Oxford: 211-18.

Woolf, G. 1998. *Becoming Roman: The Origins of Provincial Civilization in Gaul.* Cambridge: Cambridge University Press.

Worrell, S. 2007. 'Detecting the Later Iron Age: a view from the Portable Antiquities Scheme', in Haselgrove, C. and Moore, T. (eds.), *The Later Iron Age in Britain and Beyond.* Oxford: Oxbow: 371-388.

Worsaae, J. J. A. 1865. *Om Slesvigs eller Sønderjyllands oldtidsminder.* København.

Wright, M. E. 2002. 'Querns and millstones', in Wilson, P. R. *Cataractonium: Roman Catterick and its Hinterland. Excavations and Research, 1958-1997. Part II.* York: Council for British Archaeology: 267-285.

Young, C. J. 1977. *The Roman Pottery Industry of the Oxford Region*. BAR 43. Oxford.

Yule, B. 2005. *A Prestigious Roman Building Complex on the Southwark Waterfront. Excavations at Winchester Palace, London, 1983-90*. London: Museum of London.

Zadoks-Josephus Jitta, A. N. Peters, W. J. T. and van Es, W. A. 1967. *Roman Bronze Statuettes from the Netherlands*, I. Groningen.

Zanker, P. 1988. *The Power of Images in the Age of Augustus*. Ann Arbor: University of Michigan Press.

Zienkiewicz, J. D. 1986. *The Legionary Fortress Baths at Caerleon. II. The Finds*. Cardiff: National Museum of Wales.

Zimmer-Linnfeld, K. 1960. *Westerwanna I*. Hamburg: Hamburgisches Museum für Völkerkunde und vorgeschichte.

Zimmermann, W. H. 1969. 'Ein keltisches Bronzegerät aus dem Weserkies bei Dörverden, Kreis Verden (Aller)', *Neue Ausgrabungen und Forschungen in Niedersachsen* 4: 123-30.

Zimmermann, W. H. 1978. 'Economy of the Roman Iron Age settlement at Flögeln, Kr. Cuxhaven, Lower Saxony. Husbandry, cattle farming and manufacturing', in Cunliffe, B. and Rowley, T. (eds.), *Lowland Iron Age Communities in Europe*. BAR International Series (supplementary) 48. Oxford: 147-165.

www.ingramcontent.com/pod-product-compliance
Lightning Source LLC
LaVergne TN
LVHW071205210926
848482LV00015B/729
* 9 7 8 1 4 0 7 3 0 6 9 9 5 *